MANAGERIAL
ACCOUNTING
FOR THE
HOSPITALITY
SERVICE INDUSTRIES

MANAGERIAL ACCOUNTING FOR THE HOSPITALITY SERVICE INDUSTRIES

CLIFFORD T. FAY, JR., C.P.A.

RICHARD C. RHOADS, C.P.A.

ROBERT L. ROSENBLATT, C.P.A.

PARTNERS IN THE FIRM OF HARRIS, KERR, FORSTER AND COMPANY
CERTIFIED PUBLIC ACCOUNTANTS

WM. C. BROWN COMPANY PUBLISHERS
Dubuque, Iowa

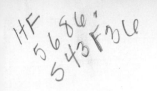

Contents

Definition and General Introduction, 1; Need for Better Managerial Systems, 4; Basic Consumer Rationale, 5; Ownership or Control Factors, 6; Hospitality Service Industries versus Product Industries, 7; *Marketing*, 7; *Cost Structure*, 8; *Financial Structure*, 9; Hospitality Service Categories, 9; *Development*, 10; *Specifics*, 11; *The Lodging Industry Complex*, 11; *The Food Service Industry*, 13; *Transportation Complexes*, 16; *Recreation and Leisure Services*, 16; *Health Care Service Complexes*, 17; *Educational Support Services*, 18; Problems of the Hospitality Service Industries, 18; *Financial Resources*, 18; *Operations*, 19; *Human Resources*, 20; Summary, 20; Discussion Questions, 21.

The Accounting System, 22; *Statements and Reports*, 22; *Considering the Needs of Users*, 25; *The Five Users of Financial Statements and Their Primary Concerns*, 25; *Guidelines to Usefulness*, 28; Management Accounting, 29; *Management Accounting Techniques*, 29; *Important Concepts*, 30; *Decision-Making Implications*, 31; Summary, 32; Discussion Questions, 32.

The Business Entity, 34; The Fundamental Equation, 36; Going-Concern Concept, 37; Money as a Unit of Measure, 38; Cost, 39; Recognition at Time of Exchange, 40; Matching Revenue and Expense, 41; Accrual Accounting, 42; Depreciation, 43; End-of-

Period Adjustments, 46; Cash Basis Accounting, 47; Disclosure, 49; Accounting Conventions, 50; *Objectivity*, 50; *Consistency*, 50; *Conservatism*, 51; *Materiality*, 52; Summary, 53; Discussion Questions, 54.

Types of Financial Statements, 55; External Users of Financial Statements, 56; *Stockholders and Absentee Owners*, 56; *Creditors*, 56; *Government Agencies*, 57; *The General Public*, 58; Internal Use of Financial Statements, 58; Uniform System of Accounts, 59; *Development of the Uniform Systems*, 59; *Contributions to Management and Accounting*, 60; The Income Statement, 60; *Basic Structure of the Income Statement*, 64; *Similarities in Income Statement Structures*, 69; The Balance Sheet, 70; *Composition of the Balance Sheet: Current Assets*, 73; *Composition of the Balance Sheet: Noncurrent Assets*, 73; *Composition of the Balance Sheet: Fixed Assets*, 77; *Composition of the Balance Sheet: Liabilities*, 80; *Composition of the Balance Sheet: Stockholders' Equity*, 81; *Composition of the Balance Sheet: Members' Equity*, 84; *Uniform Systems: A Final Note*, 84; Summary, 85; Discussion Questions, 86; Problems, 86-92.

The Accounting Dilemma, 94; Performance Comparisons, 94; *Selecting an Index*, 95; *Applying the Index Numbers*, 97; *Historical Dollar Reports*, 99; *Developing Adjusted Operating Data*, 99; *Data for Special Decisions*, 105; *Developing Adjusted Depreciation Data*, 106; Summary, 111; Discussion Questions, 111; Problems, 111-114.

Why Ratio Analysis, 115; The Mathematics of Ratio Analysis, 116; Ratio Analysis, 116; Liquidity Ratios, 117; Solvency and Leverage Ratios, 125; Activity Ratios, 127; Profitability and Rate-of-Return Ratios, 131; *The Profitability of the Owners' Investment in the Business*, 131; *The Profitability of Assets*, 132; *The Profitability of Business Operations*, 133; Operating Ratios, 134; An Analysis of Sales, 135; An Analysis of the Control of Costs, 138; The Limitations of Ratio Analysis, 142; Summary,

List of Exhibits

Foreword

The advance of technology has created changes in the way of life enjoyed by all people.

The technology of transportation has continued from the time of the horse and the invention of the wheel through to motor-driven vehicles. Transportation is the means by which human beings implement their innate desire to travel—to communicate with other people—and to satisfy the most desirable of all characteristics—curiosity.

Transportation has enabled the development of commerce over increasing geographic areas, and indeed across the oceans of our planet. Always following in the path of transportation is the accommodation industry—inns, hosteleries, hotels, motels, and motor hotels. In the past few decades other service industries have also developed providing the full service needed to gratify the desires of the traveller—restaurants, entertainment, golf courses, sightseeing facilities—entire tourist plants.

Today we stand at the threshold of a new era—an era of world tourism and commercial travel—an era which will witness finally an integration of the efforts of each segment of the service industries to provide the total plant needed for the transportation, housing, and entertainment of the travellers of the world.

This integrated industry will gross more dollars and employ more people throughout the world than any other industry.

Regrettably, the various segments of the industry have not applied professional management techniques comparable to the gross dollar volume achieved—a situation due in large part to the various parts of the service industries being comprised of a vast number of smaller businesses operated without the desire or the ability to harness progress in management techniques and thereby reap the maximum financial results.

The last two decades, however, have witnessed the first steps in the development of public corporations, investment in the service industries—the major airlines, the hotel and motel companies, to mention a few. This increasing accumulation of proprietorship and management is leading to an escalation of the necessity of and desire for the creation of professional management and particularly the tools to be utilized by management.

It is my pleasure to endorse *Managerial Accounting for the Hospitality Service Industries*, a work directed toward emphasizing the techniques of management control.

The authors express a lifetime of experience in the field of management and accounting techniques in the hotel, restaurant, and service industries.

Managerial Accounting for the Hospitality Service Industries deserves to find a place in the libraries of our industry, in colleges, and in the hands of those men charged with the control and direction of the industry in the years ahead.

The application of the principles of *Managerial Accounting for the Hospitality Service Industries* is a necessary step in the escalation of the quality of management and its tools if the great faith in the industry is to be justified and the benefits available are indeed to be reaped in the years ahead. The benefits will not be achieved by the ill-informed.

Roger Manfred
President and Chief Executive Officer
Travelodge International, Inc.

Preface

At some time in the middle fifties America moved from an industrial economy to a service-oriented economy. It is estimated that the service industries today comprise 60 percent of the nation's total employment force. Unfortunately, this sudden and dramatic economic change of emphasis has outdistanced relevant literature of practical application for management. To compound the problems posed by this "knowledge lag" the *hospitality* service industries—that portion of the service industries providing food, lodging and transportation to the public—have experienced accelerated growth and subsequent specialization replete with unique needs of their own.

This text, therefore, has been designed to apply practical accounting techniques to these hospitality service industries. Emphasis lies in the needs of management and the application of accounting concepts and techniques to managerial decision-making. It is hoped that this book will be an invaluable aid for those employed in or considering a career in the hospitality service industries, whether in accounting or in management positions.

Due to the rapid acceleration and growth of the hospitality service industries, there remains an unfortunately large number of persons in all levels of management who have not been exposed to the uses of accounting data for managerial decisions. It is, however, expected that management development courses and seminars will be presented with increasing frequency as larger business entities enter the field and as government and others realize the importance of sound management in areas such as health care, education, penal institutions, etc. Selected chapters herein could be most useful in such programs for all levels of management.

An increasing number of universities now offer degrees in the field of business management particular to the hospitality service industries. This text could easily be incorporated in one semester or in two quarter courses in these college programs. Its flexibility would avail itself for use either as the only accounting course in a management program or as a managerial course after completion of one or more introductory accounting courses. Such multiple usage would encourage communication between managers and accountants; they would, as a result, each be better prepared to function in their respective roles.

Finally, it is hoped that this work will be of service to the many junior colleges that have the task of educating the millions who will be employed in the future by the hospitality service industries. The design of the text would allow the omission or extension of several chapters without a loss of understanding the conceptual foundation of the whole.

This is a pioneer effort, and the authors recognize it as such. It is hoped that in the future more and better applications will evolve as the service industries continue to grow, particularly in that segment called "the hospitality service industries."

Many have contributed to this effort; the contribution of Merrick W. Leckey has been particularly valuable. Chapter twenty-three, Electronic Data Processing, is the work of G. Peter Buchband. Raymond J. Ball contributed in the areas of quantitive and statistical analysis.

Dean Robert L. Bloomstrom of Michigan State's School of Hotel, Restaurant and Institutional Management and Dean Robert A. Beck of Cornell's School of Hotel Administration and their staffs have been most helpful in every way during the classroom exposure process. Many of the staff of Harris, Kerr, Forster & Company have contributed including James E. Burr, Peter M. Mela, Scott Carter, Michael Patrick, Peter Kline, Robert Spindell and Brian Murcott. Finally, we are most grateful to all of our partners who have contributed in so many ways.

Clifford T. Fay, Jr.
Richard C. Rhoads
Robert L. Rosenblatt

Special Acknowledgment

Professor Donald L. Madden, Associate Professor of Accounting at the University of Kentucky, should receive a special acknowledgment for his work as a contributing editor. Professor Madden's contribution in the areas of price level accounting, cost accounting and responsibility accounting together with his assistance in the development of problem material is appreciated.

MANAGERIAL
ACCOUNTING
FOR THE
HOSPITALITY
SERVICE INDUSTRIES

CHAPTER 1

Introduction to the Hospitality Service Industries

DEFINITION AND GENERAL INTRODUCTION

Hospitality service industries is a modern-day expression concocted as an all-inclusive term, embracing almost every phase of rendering customer services except that of major retail merchandising and, even here, this type of customer service, to a degree, is not uncommon. By dictionary definition, the word "hospital" indicates a place of hospitality for those in need of shelter and maintenance. (For example, Greenwich Hospital in London is a home for retired seamen.) The main thrust of the hospitality service industries is that of rendering *services*. As such, it is included in the broad classification of *service industries* which render services of almost any description to the consumer for a price or fee, usually for a profit, but sometimes on a nonprofit basis. Voluntary hospitals and similar institutions fall in the latter category.

America's present service-oriented economy is firmly built upon past economic strength, developed in other areas of business and industry. During the first eighty years of its national existence, the United States prospered in an economy based on agriculture and export. In the early nineteenth century, the agricultural and industrial revolutions broadened that original economy. Then the steam engine, the carding machine, the spinning jenny, and the power loom precipitated the emergence of the commercial textile industry in England, and farmers in the southern United States felt the industry's impact when they attempted to provide an adequate supply of cotton for export to England's mills. At this time it took one man ten hours to seed a pound of lint from three pounds of raw cotton. Soon, however, Eli Whitney invented the water-driven cotton gin, (shortly before 1800), and 300 to 1,000 pounds of clean cotton could be produced daily by one man operating such a machine. As a result, the cotton industry blossomed in the South, together with related industries.

The opening in 1790 of the first American cotton yarn mill in Pawtucket, Rhode Island, introduced the first mass production techniques. Crude as they may have been, they were, nevertheless, a beginning and a forerunner of the great things yet to come. In 1831, Cyrus McCormick invented the grain reaper—a machine that cut as much grain in a day as six laborers could cut with hand scythes. Other agricultural improvements soon made it possible to mechanize food production, resulting in more and more food produced through the efforts of fewer and fewer men. Thus, many farm workers were released from the drudgery of the fields and migrated to the cities, where they were employed in the newly organized manufacturing industries. Manufacturing brought on new prosperity for the country, and factories sprung up everywhere. Urbanization developed and, when the city lights beckoned, many farm lights were darkened forever across the land.

The national economy was further accelerated by the Civil War. Later, as postwar demands required greater production and better distribution methods of consumer goods, America entered a new and significant phase of industrial development. During World War I, industry was obliged to further refine and sharpen its techniques of mass production, communications, and distribution to meet the demands of a devastating war in Europe and the then affluent public in the United States. One of the offsprings of this frantic period was the development of the mass advertising industry. These processes were all brought to their zenith during World War II—or at least, such was the general thinking at that time.

In 1945, when World War II ended, our national economic goals were of necessity shifted abruptly. A demand for civilian goods, which had been unsatisfied through the war years, could be suppressed no longer. A flood of civilian purchasing power gushed forth from savings accounts, war bonds, and mustering-out pay. Almost without interruption, American industry turned 180°, from full military emphasis to production of consumer goods. Factories literally closed down the war on one production line and opened the peacetime economy on another line just a few feet away.

In just four years, this flood of consumer demand was mostly met and, in fact, was, for all practical purposes, dangerously stemmed. So, by 1950, the present concept of marketing—the conscious attempt to anticipate the consumer's needs and desires and to provide him with a wide range of choice based on his particular interests—already had been introduced and was beginning to be practiced by alert companies. It appeared as though balance had been restored in the country's economy.

The economy, now consumer-oriented, accelerated through the fifties and sixties, soaking up and stimulating consumer debt for automobiles, homes, and other possessions. And for the first time in our history, a nation of prosperous and mobile people demanded more and better services. A mass market arose and America's third economic era—the era of the service industries—had begun. Exhibit 1.1 illustrates the growth in expenditures for services relative to durable and nondurable goods.

EXHIBIT 1.1
Personal Consumption Expenditures in the United States

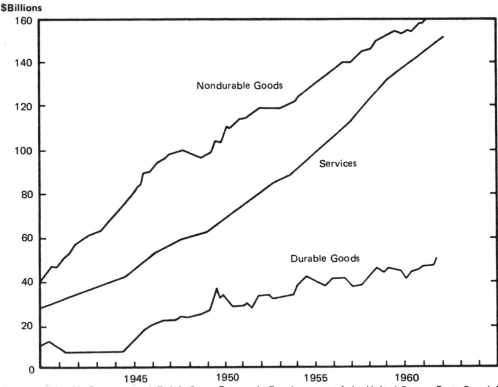

Source: John M. Peterson and Ralph Gray, Economic Development of the United States, Parts 3 and 4, 1966, 1967, p. 225. (Box 242, Fayetteville, Arkansas 72701).

One of the most promising and volatile sectors of the service industries is the group called *hospitality service industries.* In this area of business activity, earnings result from furnishing a great variety of services, including food, beverages, lodging, entertainment, sports activities, medical services, and many other hospitality services at a time and in a place, manner, choice, and price combination reasonable and acceptable to the customers being served.

Generally, hospitality services are concentrated on the voluntary consumer. An entire complex of services, particularly lodging, food, recreation, and entertainment services, has been formed to anticipate and provide a balanced program for those who travel. In 1968, United States residents spent approximately thirty-seven billion dollars on travel expenditures, of which 60 percent, or twenty-two billion dollars, was for vacation and pleasure travel.[1]

---

1. Estimated by *Travel Market Yearbook* (New York: Market Handbooks, Inc., 1969), p. 18.

However, hospitality service industries also include those services directed to involuntary consumers, particularly those in educational and health care institutions. These institutionalized services generally are not operated for the purpose of profit generation. Yet, the food and lodging phase of their operation contributes a modified form of profit that is represented by the excess revenue over cost of services provided (for example, services which generate funds to amortize dormitory or hospital construction bonds or even provide reserves for future contingencies).

Today's modern business executive thinks nothing of covering the country by jet airplane, either company or regular commercial, planning conferences with local management in cities widely separated by hundreds of miles. As he crosses the nation, he finds a broad range of hospitality services, all keyed to meet his needs while he is away from home.

The typical American man, too, can take his family on a vacation away from home with a wide choice of routes and destinations. In the family station wagon, armed with map, trailer, boat, and the perennial credit cards, he can travel across the country on a network of federally-funded, limited-access highways. Each day he can have his automobile serviced and drive to the day's recreation and an evening's rest at a motel or hotel of his choice. Without additional cost, he can make advance reservations with another member of the lodging chain or membership network. Through modern credit card systems, he can assemble his own "life support" services day by day, with a minimum cash expenditure, during the entire period away from home.

NEED FOR BETTER MANAGERIAL SYSTEMS

Although growth in the hospitality service industries has been phenomenal, development has lagged in managerial methods, marketing, and control within the executive structure of the industries.

There is a desperate need to take a broader look at the industry in action; but, unfortunately, there is a lack of meaningful data from which to project the industry's shape, thrust, and dimension. For example, the owner, manager, or executive of a hospitality service business may realize that he needs a better understanding of the industry in general and improved managerial accounting practices in particular. But, when he attempts to find meaningful information in his field, he meets a barrier. At the present time, there simply is not sufficient comparative operating data available for the various types of hospitality services nor is information available on particular hospitality service businesses in comparison to others with different operating requirements. This lack of information frequently is damaging in matters affecting fiscal policy decisions and creates an obstacle to organizing efficient and profitable operations. Furthermore, executives and loan officials are now beginning to require more sophisticated levels of managerial accounting systems than have been typically found in the industry.

BASIC CONSUMER RATIONALE

"Why does the service exist?"

Each type of hospitality service organization should be so clearly defined and planned that it fills an identified need in the economy, with full economic value accruing in return for its economic costs. In addition, it must produce a margin of excess value which can be reinvested in the system for subsequent upgrading and modernization, and leave an excess or profit for the efforts expended and capital invested.

"To whom is the service furnished?"

For a hospitality service to be truly successful, its functional niche and its preplanned "consumer rationale" for patronage must be clear and distinct to all concerned. It cannot be presented as an abstract idea with no really practical application.

The importance of relating to the ultimate consumer cannot be overestimated. In any type of hospitality service business, the managers must identify and study every type of consumer who is a potential user of the service. This must necessarily be a continuing activity, and must be monitored and evaluated by management regularly in order to ascertain current trends, and then such trends must be translated into income-producing results. In today's highly competitive economy, even the previously successful local entrepreneur in a restaurant, hotel, motel, or travel agency is forced by the sheer amount of capital at risk to begin to sharpen his focus on the customers he should be seeking and serving.

"How is the service performed?"

Generally, hospitality industry executives have begun to modernize and update their internal "manufacturing" or operating procedures. They are now planning their business from the point of customer contact or "point of purchase." Thus, there should be only as much on-premises "manufacturing" as is absolutely essential to meet the customers' needs and expectations. By focusing more clearly on the link between where the service system meets the customer and "the promise delivered," executives practice excellent consumer-oriented, market-oriented service industry management, in tune with their markets and customer demands.

OWNERSHIP OR CONTROL FACTORS

In every hospitality service organization, the exact nature, purpose, and "culture" of its ownership or control has great influence on its management methods and basic goals.

There are five major types of ultimate control centers in the hospitality service industries:

1. *Private entrepreneur interests (owner-operator).* This category includes single individuals, family or affinity groups, and private investor syndicates. The latter may operate as proprietorships, general or limited agreement partnerships, Sub-Chapter S Corporations, closely held private corporations, or some other combination of restricted corporate ownership and control.

2. *Absentee ownership with paid professional management.* This type of control is often closely related to the aforementioned type, except that absentee ownership is distinguished by the fact that the source of controlling capital and equity typically is not active in the daily operation and management of the business itself.

3. *Publicly owned companies.* With the continued growth and profitability of the hospitality service organizations as controlled under points numbered one and two, the company may "go public." Stock is sold on an unrestricted basis to the general public, generally under the jurisdiction of the Federal Securities and Exchange Commission, as well as the various state securities commissions and state laws.

The types of hospitality services which fall into this category virtually run the full gamut of related business and industry and include, in many instances, operations which in themselves appear to have no relationship to the basic industry. The publicly owned company may own and operate only one unit or it may have multi-unit operations spread over wide geographical areas. Its operations may include, among others, lodging; food service and food retailing; entertainment; food marketing, processing and distribution; transportation; financial services and others.

The forms such companies take vary widely. Many of these business or industry complexes may be franchised. There are joint ventures, management service companies operating under contracts, and other types of control groups designed to meet particular situations.

4. *Nonprofit organizations.* (These organizations are not engaged in so-called profit-making endeavors, although, frequently, their operations do result in an excess of income over costs.) In this category are included educational organizations and foundations; charitable foundations, religious organizations and denominations; voluntary hospitals; other organizations operating under these types of

charitable, educational, or social service charters; and clubs and fraternal organizations.

5. *Civilian tax-related organizations and complexes.* This category includes hospitality services offered by federal, state, county, municipal, or other governmental bodies and organizations. Some examples of these services are hospitals; schools and colleges; food and other services offered to employees; food, lodging, and other services offered to visitors; and other types of hospitality services provided as citizen services.

Often, these hospitality services are leased to and operated by concessionaires who obtain the concession through negotiation or competitive bidding procedure.

HOSPITALITY SERVICE INDUSTRIES VERSUS PRODUCT INDUSTRIES

There are several basic economic differences between a product or manufacturing enterprise and a hospitality service company. These fundamental differences might be summarized in the following areas:

Marketing (product-sales-pricing-competition)
Cost Structure
Financial Structure

MARKETING

The basic difference between a product manufacturing company and a hospitality service company is readily recognizable. The manufacturing company produces a tangible product that the customer sees and buys, whereas in the hospitality service company, the product is an intangible in the form of services rendered. In many segments of the hospitality service industries, there may be some products involved, such as food and beverage, as part of the service. In the case of the food service industry, this product is a substantial portion of the company's reason for being in business. However, in almost all cases, the product (food or beverage) is consumed by the customer/guest on the premises; and in a major portion of the food service industry, the food is not the reason for the customer patronizing the particular food service outlet.

As part of the fundamental marketing differences, it must be recognized that the user of the hospitality service industries' facilities must come to the servicer's place of business, whereas the product manufacturing company can schedule its production, store it for any length of time and distribute it throughout the country or all over the world through established distribution channels. In addition, because customers come to the product manufacturer with a predetermined need for that product, the product manufacturing company needs only to motivate its customers to buy its product brand, rather than that of competitors. The motivations of the customers for the hospitality service industries are varied and, in some cases, subtle. In any event, it is likely that the customer is motivated to come to the hospitality service companies' facilities because of some reason other than advertising or other forms of demand creation. For instance, the customer usually is a guest at a hotel or motel because of his need to travel either for business, education, or pleasure. Although an airline passenger may enjoy meals served en route, his primary motivation is that of transportation from one place to another. The customer of the hospital or the school dormitory is there for obvious reasons and none of these reasons is the demand or desire to use the hospital or school lodging and feeding facilities.

Finally, the established firms in the product sector of our economy tend to establish price patterns within their industry. These prices are based on a wealth of economic data and statistics both within and without the firm. Because the customer must come to the hospitality service industries' location, the marketing area of a given hospitality service enterprise is restricted and the typical hospitality service outlet has a limited capacity for expanding output and sales. The hospitality enterprise will be catering to the public taste, and there may be many individual hospitality service facilities of all types from which the customer can select. Because of this proliferation of hundreds and thousands of hospitality service outlets of all types and price ranges, the pricing structure tends to be more flexible and, in some cases, without the necessary financial and economic information needed to establish a sound pricing structure.

COST STRUCTURE

The hospitality service industries have a high labor cost percentage to the sales price and indeed, in some cases, the entire sales price is for service or labor. The labor cost in the industry has always been based on a low hourly wage rate as many of the job classifications do not require skilled or professional workers. However, this hourly labor cost for hotel restaurant workers, hospital employees, etc. has been increasing over the last two decades through increased minimum wages and unionization. In contrast, the product manufacturing company has a major portion of its cost structure in materials and distribution costs although historically, the product industries have always had a higher average hourly wage and unionization.

Within the comparative cost structure differences, it must be recognized that the product industries can and do have a high degree of mass production and automation. In addition, there is some economic knowledge in the product industries regarding the optimum size of an enterprise. This is not the case in the hospitality service industries, for there are no resources being devoted to answer the question of what is the most effective and efficient size of a hospital, hotel, restaurant, etc. Considerable time and resources are being devoted to the application of automation and mass production to the hospitality service industries, but to date limited progress has been made and, indeed, in view of the fundamental economics of the hospitality service enterprise, it is difficult to visualize any substantial use of the principles of automation, assembly line techniques, and mass production. So far, the rendering of services is an area in which machines have been unable to replace human labor to any appreciable extent.

FINANCIAL STRUCTURE

Hospitality service industries have the major amount of their resources invested in a fixed physical facility which houses space being held for sale and in which the services are rendered. These physical facilities usually are financed by long-term mortgages or other forms of borrowed money. Therefore, the typical hospitality service industry enterprise will have a limited amount of owner's investment when compared with lender's investment, including funds payable to vendors. The relatively large total cost involved in a single-purpose plant must be earned and repaid over a relatively long life; and, because of their specialized nature, assets will probably have limited value upon liquidation and bankruptcy. In contrast, if a product manufacturing company has to be liquidated, a larger portion of its assets will be liquid and salable, and even the smaller percentage devoted to plant investment may have more salability or realization in the event of "hard times."

HOSPITALITY SERVICE CATEGORIES

Although standard industrial classification categories and related data have become well accepted economic analysis tools, no standard system yet exists for classifying and categorizing the hospitality service industries. Neither the federal government nor any business, education, or trade association has developed a uniform classification and analysis system. The Department of Commerce uses its own figures and nomenclature; the Internal Revenue Service keeps records and data on only those hospitality service industries which file an annual federal tax return; and the Department of Agriculture uses still another set of criteria. The various trade associations and professional schools serving the hospitality service industries have similar problems of identification, classification, description, and comparison.

Within this text, the hospitality service industries are classified in six categories:

1. Lodging
2. Food service
3. Transportation
4. Recreation and leisure services
5. Health care
6. Educational support services

The common revenue production for all categories in the hospitality service industries is the sale of space or food or both. Except for a large segment of the food service category, the sale of food and/or beverage is a secondary adjunct or auxiliary to the primary revenue producer—the sale of space (guest rooms, hospital beds, airline seats, educational classrooms, club facilities, etc.).

The categories listed are broad and there should be no attempt to classify a specific hospitality service property neatly into one and only one category. There is an obvious overlap in that all categories are part of the food service industry; but more important is the full recognition of the vast growth of the last two decades in all sectors of the hospitality service industries, so that today there are many different gradations and types of properties within each category. For example, resorts have been included under recreation and leisure services whereas many famous resort areas are now occupied the entire year with groups of conventioneers or persons attending an educational seminar. Hence, the resort could be classified with equal logic as part of the lodging industry division or the educational services division and finally as a food service industry. Similar examples can be found throughout the entire field of the six listed categories or divisions.

DEVELOPMENT

In fundamental substance and in some rudimentary form, all of the categories of the hospitality service industries have been in existence for thousands of years, but recognition of their present-day form and substance would probably date back several hundred years to the days of the Elizabethan inn, London clubs, and stagecoach travel. Their full emergence has occurred within the last half-century and development has accelerated over the last two decades. The developmental periods of the last century would include:

. . .Prior to 1930, the rise and development of the industrial sector and the concentration of wealth, resulting in the development of the hospitality service industries' facilities for a relatively small percentage of the total population.

. . .1930-1946, the interruption of all new investment in the hospitality service industries resulting from the depression and World War II.

. . .1947 to date, the full development of the industrial section and the rise of the technical/scientific sector together with ever-expanding numbers of families with substantial discretionary income, resulting in major expansion in all areas of the hospitality service industries.

During the latter developmental period, in the early 1960's, a new phenomenon arose in the hospitality service industries. Large established companies from outside the industry began to buy hospitality service organizations. By diversifying their interests, these publicly owned corporations have been better able to follow the profit opportunities of a mobile, increasingly affluent American population in a service-oriented economy. Concurrently, financially oriented companies began to move from only providing investment capital for hospitality service businesses into more closely linked relationships with the direct-to-consumer service businesses. Now it is a common practice for lending institutions to not only require interest and amortization payments over a specified period of years, but also to participate in profit in order to have an inflation hedge for the future. It can be expected that many more hospitality service businesses probably will either be affiliated with or belong to and be controlled and directed by some type of centralized ownership and management group.

SPECIFICS

The various categories or divisions of the hospitality service industries, while similar in many respects, have features which make each of them distinct. Because of their distinctiveness, each respective growth pattern does not exactly parallel the general developmental periods of the hospitality service industries. Following is a brief description and history of each of the six categories of the hospitality service industries.

The Lodging Industry Complex

Included in this category are hotels, motels, motor hotels, tourist homes, rooming houses, and, to some degree, mobile homes, boatels, and health care accommodations.

The development of the lodging industry complex closely follows the three basic historical periods defined for the hospitality service industries in general. In the first historical period, the major hotels were built for travelling businessmen or the wealthy affluent traveler. Hotel construction consisted primarily of the small-town hotel and the full-service city or grand hotel. Most of these structures were built next to or near the railroad stations which were the primary source of guest patronage. This trend included the development of the grand resorts in the mountains, near seashores, spas, and other vacation areas. Some of this construction was done directly by the railroads and, in some cases, the ownership of the grand hotels still remains with railroads.

This era was eventually culminated by a huge building boom in the 1920's, and included the construction of many of the giant hotels still in operation today, such as the Waldorf-Astoria, Conrad Hilton, St. Francis, and others. In many cases, the useful life of these hotels has been extended by substantial funds expended to provide for the changing nature of their clientele from the more affluent travelers travelling by railroads to businessmen, conventioneers and large groups of people on tours using airplanes, busses or private automobiles.

Little construction of additional hotel rooms occurred during the thirties and forties, as many of the properties built in the preceding era were in bankruptcy or financial difficulties throughout the thirties and investment funds were not available until after the high-occupancy years of the second World War and subsequent years of the forties. The significant movement in the lodging industry complex during this period was the introduction of the tourist court as automobile and highway development began to accelerate.

Out of the highway development trend in the early fifties came the beginning of the motel segment of the lodging complex. The motel development period was fully under way by the latter fifties and continued to accelerate through the sixties. The result of this acceleration has been the grand motel, or motor hotel, having all of the facilities and services of a hotel. This development was enhanced by the multi-billion dollar federal interstate highway program, as well as by the vast expansion of air travel, so that now the motel is located in the suburban area at an interstate interchange or near the airport or, in some cases, near a golf course or other resort-type recreational facility. Although some minor new hotel properties were begun in the latter forties and early fifties, the replacement of older hotel facilities in the cities did not begin until the middle fifties and has continued to date; today there are many hotel rooms which have been built since 1955. This trend of building new downtown hotels has been benefited by the ever-expanding numbers of people attending conventions, meetings, exhibits, etc.

In the motel sector of the lodging complex, the roadside tourist court of the 1930's, with its frame cottages and on-premise ownership and management, has been superseded by a third generation descendant, the chain motor hotel and the large motel. For all practical purposes, the initial era of "Mom and Pop" financing and management is over. In view of soaring land costs in or near major regional or local area population centers, the motor hotel complex requires more than just an available husband and wife management team. Too much investment is at stake to hope to fill the house each night with those people who might pass by and seek a night's lodging. Today, in order to insure reasonable financial success, membership in an effective national marketing and referral network is very important.

Exhibit 1.2 indicates the growth in available and occupied rooms for hotels and motels.

The Food Service Industry

Operating separately or in conjunction with other hospitality service industry categories are two types of food service: table service (in which food is brought to the customer), and fast food service (in which food may or may not be brought to the customer). Included in the first type are luxury table service, regular table service, special on-premise group service (such as banquet service and buffet self-service), special off-premise group or individual service (catering), and tray service (as in hospitals, where tray service is provided for patients and on the airlines, where in-flight tray service is provided for airline passengers).

Fast food service includes coffee shop service (at counters, tables, and/or booths); cafeteria or buffeteria service featuring line pick-up by customer; snack bar carry-out service (primarily stand-up or take-away); drive-in or walk-up service, with or without seating; vending service (automatic dispensing from a machine); and regular off-premise delivery service.

The food service industry has expanded considerably since 1930. Food was served in the grand style of the large luxury hotels prior to 1930 as resorts or hotels vied for the services of the best chefs. Of course, there was also the small-town hotel, the diner or coffee shop, for those who needed to eat away from home. And finally, there has always been the institutional food service of the hospital, prison, army, etc. Exhibit 1.3 indicates the magnitude of the food service industry in 1969.

The 1930's saw the beginning of the fast food segment of the food service industry with the development of the low-priced hamburger chain and the acceleration of the cafeteria. The 1940's gave the impetus to mass feeding and the beginning of the airline food service as we know it today. The major developments in the food service industry have occurred in the last two decades and would include the following broad divisions:

1. *The specialty restaurant:* includes the major suburban restaurant or steak house as well as the Polynesian restaurant and extends to the smaller pizza parlor or fried chicken restaurant.

2. *The fast food franchise:* includes the development of a national image for a particular type of food or food service so that the customer can receive uniform

EXHIBIT 1.2

The Increase in Available Rooms and the Trend in Occupancy for Hotels and Motels 1939-1969

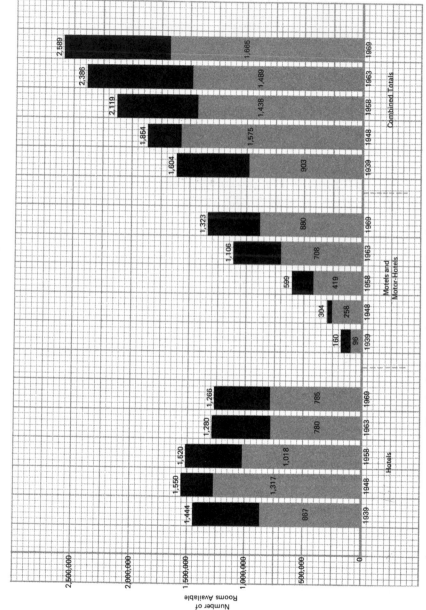

Showing in thousands, average number of rooms available and occupied per day

Source: Trends in Hotel-Motel Business—1970, Harris, Kerr, Forster & Company, Figure 3, Page 3.

14

EXHIBIT 1.3
Estimated Food Service Market - 1969

Type of Establishment	Number of Establishments	Food Sales Volume at Retail (Millions)
Restaurants and Other Commercial Eating Places		
Separate Restaurants	208,500	$ 17,950
Others	110,600	3,320
Hotels/Motels with Food Service	17,100	2,080
Hospitals, Nursing Homes and Other Health/Welfare Facilities	14,750	2,790
Colleges and Universities	2,650	2,100
School Systems with Food Service	77,000 (Schools)	3,140
Commercial/Industrial Employee Services	5,300	1,170
Clubs (Including Military Clubs)	6,000	480
Military Services	N.A.	3,170
Other	20,800	1,030
TOTAL	462,700	37,230

N.A. - Not Available

Source: Food Service Industry, 1969 (Baltimore, Maryland: Alex Brown & Sons, Inc., 1969), p. 3, table 2.

portions and quality throughout the country. Beginning with the hamburger stand and ice cream parlor, fast food franchises now include almost any type of food or restaurant service, including chicken, roast beef, hot dogs, fish 'n chips, and many others. This trend has resulted in a proliferation of many thousands of smaller chain-identified food outlets located in every community throughout the country.

3. *Contract or industrial feeding:* includes the renting of the food facility in a new office building to a recognized food operator as well as the many thousands of contracts let to run the food operation in industrial plants, schools and universities, hospitals, and governmental institutions.

Transportation Complexes

Included in transportation complexes are those services offered by airlines, railroads, motorcoach lines, rent-a-car operations, cruise ship lines, point-to-point passenger ships, and other transportation service organizations. The last includes air taxi and/or charter service, private limousine livery service, chartered yacht service (with or without crew), and any combination of these facilities.

The history and development of the transportation complexes segment of the hospitality service industries is well known. However, as with the other segments of the hospitality service industries, it must be emphasized that the true explosion occurred in only the last two decades or so, when the rapid development of air travel and high-speed highway networks vastly extended travel movements of millions of people. In addition, many transportation services are available today on a rental basis at prices that permit many more people to use them.

Recreation and Leisure Services

This category includes social, city, and country clubs with full facilities as well as city or suburban clubs with limited facilities. Also included are vacation resorts (either limited or with full facilities); summer and/or winter camps for youth, adult, or family groups; and participative and spectator sport complexes with services. (Military and defense installations also operate hospitality services; for example, officers' clubs, noncommissioned officers' clubs, enlisted men's clubs, and post exchanges.)

The recreation and leisure services segment of the hospitality service industries has been developed over the past fifty years in the same pattern as the lodging industry complexes. The vacation resort that existed prior to 1930 was the grand resort for the relatively few, as was the city and country club. Similarly, the thirties and forties brought no new facilities and, indeed, the 1930's brought many closings or reorganizations for the city and country clubs. In the last two decades, resorts and clubs have expanded in every direction, so that now there is a club or resort available at almost any income level. The city and country club expansion has included the development of many new private golf clubs, downtown luncheon clubs, and sports clubs, such as those for tennis, swimming, hunting, and sailing. The expansion of clubs has overlapped into the commercial area of the food service and lodging complex segments in the form of the Playboy Club, Gaslight Club, and other commercial membership-fee groups. In addition, the club concept has overlapped into such things as the condominium in recreation areas and club ownership of vacation resorts.

The expansion of the vacation resorts has generally included the following:

1. *The geographical vacation area:* vacation facility expansion in this cat-
egory would include historical vacation areas such as Arizona, California, and
Florida in the winter and the summer resorts in the northern areas such as New
England, the Pocono's, upstate New York, and the north woods of Michigan,
Wisconsin, and Minnesota. The advent of jet air transportation greatly stimulated
the expansion of winter resort areas to include the Caribbean, Mexico, and
Hawaii. The extensive development of ski resort facilities has been superimposed
upon this pattern as the popularity of skiing, snow-mobiling, and other winter
sports increased.

2. *The suburban resort-type property:* caters to the weekend vacationer and
the business meeting or convention guest. The suburban resort-type hotel and
motel generally include swimming, golf, theatre, and other forms of resort facilities.

3. *The national park and/or camping facilities:* with the federal interstate
highway system and other forms of faster and better travel, more people have
been able to travel farther, so there has been an expansion in this subdivision of
the recreation and leisure services. This division applies to state parks, campsites,
trailer parks, national parks, monuments, battlefields, and all historical tourist
attractions.

Health Care Service Complexes

Any operation in which the customers, patrons, or patients typically spend a
full daily living cycle within the complex is included in this category. Among such
services are the full-service general hospitals, specialized hospitals or sanitariums,
nursing or geriatric homes, and convalescent centers.

The health care service portion of the hospitality service industries has had its
growth as a result of two or three basic underlying factors. One is the fact that
medical care has improved spectacularly over the past twenty or thirty years,
including miracle drugs as well as organ transplants or other advanced medical
care that did not exist a half a century ago. The second factor, of equal importance in the vast development of total health care service, is the continued expansion of health and hospitalization insurance, including Medicare and Medicaid, so
that now almost all of the typical hospital's charges are billed to an insurance
company or the government. Finally, as an outgrowth of the above two factors,
there are increased numbers of the aged in the population, resulting in the expansion of care facilities for them including nursing homes and geriatric centers.

The expansion is now largely complete and health care is one massive "system" which affects all citizens. The daily patient cost in a hospital is rising rapidly
and is predicted to continue. The high cost of health care services has affected

medical and hospital insurance premiums, both group and personal, since these insurance organizations must pay to the provider the full cost of operating beds and fees for required services. Obviously, the effectiveness of the hospital system must be upgraded and costs reduced so that people can afford the amount, type, quality, and frequency of live-in health care services they need.

Segmentation by services and needs are two alternative methods of using health care resources more efficiently. A modern convalescent care system, including convalescent centers and long-term geriatric care centers, is one solution.

Educational Support Services

Herein are included food and lodging facilities for elementary schools, secondary schools, junior colleges, post-high school educational schools (vocational schools, etc.), residential preparatory schools, and colleges and universities. This category can be divided as to those which offer full board and lodging, those offering room only, and those offering food service only, either on a contract basis for the school term, or on an individual-purchase basis.

The educational complex at the beginning of the century was restricted to the Eastern preparatory school and the private college or university, where the lodging and food facilities were part of the educational complex, although the state universities did have some housing and food facilities in rooming or boarding houses near the college campus. In the past two decades, this has been changed in that today all colleges and universities have some form of such facilities under their direct ownership or control. The major impetus to this growth has been favorable federal financing aid in the form of low interest loans and guarantees of loans on dormitories and physical feeding facilities.

PROBLEMS OF THE HOSPITALITY SERVICE INDUSTRIES

With all the diversity of business and operational requirements facing this broad range of hospitality service industries, there also are common problems. To improve the managerial accounting processes of the hospitality service industries, certain common "clusters" of problems will be identified, and brief comments submitted on some of the causative factors.

FINANCIAL RESOURCES

Perhaps no other group of industries has such acute problems of start-up capital and growth capital. Traditionally, financial undertakings in the hospitality services have presented high levels of risk.

The hospitality service industries are just now beginning to exchange, first, experience and information to aid in developing sound growth plans and, second, better operating and cost data on how to develop management and capital to implement these growth plans. The techniques of simulation, including mathematical modeling, offer great promise in helping to plan and develop or upgrade hospitality service businesses.

New and larger ownership or control centers buying into the hospitality service industries may tend to bring their own financial resource base and leverage into the field. The tendency for Americans to devote a greater share of their increasing disposable income to the good life should attract even more sources of outside investment capital. In time, these outside control centers may force a changeover to their own traditional financing and financial performance goals.

OPERATIONS

In a hospitality service business, operations correspond to production in a manufacturing business. The total repetitive cycle of activity performed for each customer generates the output and revenues which support the business.

At present, the operational system of most types of hospitality service businesses tends to suffer from:

1. Low productivity, by whatever measure of input used (labor hours, labor dollars, dollars of sales per employee, etc.).

2. Low profitability per dollar of sales. (However, certain types of hospitality service businesses produce high returns on investment and, in certain cases, produce high rates of profit after taxes.)

3. Lack of effective total management information systems. Included are lack of fiscal controls, plus lack of current, historical, or projective data on labor utilization, materials consumption, breakdowns of sales dollar contributions by product or service provided, and other important quantitative data for better control and forecasting. Generally, operators in the field have only a limited knowledge of the "systems concept" (that is, a master system with individualized sub-systems). Consequently, they are unable to apply more advanced techniques to improve the total effectiveness of the basic operation.

4. A tendency toward a management philosophy of "Every unit a maximum profit unit," with little planned reinvestment of today's profits toward making tomorrow's operation better. Typically, this problem is compounded by day-to-day management; reacting to today's problems and crises, but not devoting time, attention, and resources to resolving their causes and planning for the future.

HUMAN RESOURCES

In the hospitality service industries, employees' physical activities and personal involvement contribute greatly to the ultimate success or failure of the enterprise. But too often, service employees lack basic skills, motivation, stability, and other important job qualities. High turnover rates in many positions indicate a symptomatic problem that has developed over the years.

Many types of hospitality service industries traditionally have drawn employees from the bottom of the labor market "barrel." Social status of many jobs has ranked low. At the same time, management attitudes have been out of touch with reality, to the point where pay scales and working conditions have not attracted potential employees with adequate training experience and aptitudes for the particular jobs.

The repetitive nature of many jobs leads to a dulling of customer-consciousness, little sense of pride in performance, and other morale-deadening aspects. The hospitality service industries appear to have had no system of identifiable, attainable "career ladders" leading to better positions and incomes.

Until very recently, there has been a chronic lack of job-related, people-related training programs which would enable the employee to develop his skills beyond the entry job-level. Furthermore, instead of investing in manpower development programs, management has tended to use someone else's training investment when hiring employees for better positions.

Lack of adequate fringe benefit programs—paid hospitalization, vacations, profit-sharing programs—has, historically, further complicated employee recruiting and retention, although in recent years with heavy unionization among employees, some of these deficiencies are being corrected.

SUMMARY

With the introduction of America's third economic era—the era of the service industries—and the subsequent growth in the service industries, has come the growth and diversification of the hospitality service industries. From their initial presence as inns, the hospitality service industries have expanded into such seemingly unrelated activities as institutional feeding and recreation activities for the leisure-conscious public. Among the trends which have materially affected the direction of the hospitality service industries have been

—the expansion of the motel-motor hotel concept until today over half of the room nights sold are in motels and motor hotels.

—the substantial growth in the market for group meetings and activities, including conventions, business meetings, social gatherings and group travel.

—the growing emphasis on better health and welfare which has resulted in an ever increasing demand for institutional feeding, including hospitals, health care centers, schools, colleges and universities.

—the growth in air and highway travel requiring the provision of food and lodging enroute and at the destination.

—the development of the chain franchise food and lodging systems, which have encouraged travel and eating away from home.

—the quest of people for expanded horizons and new adventures in travel, culture and recreation.

Though the hospitality service industries have traditionally been operated as social institutions with the manager there to greet all guests and patrons, in recent years the emphasis has shifted to the scientific management of these operations, not in order to minimize the personal touch but to maximize the operating efficiency.

Today the future of the hospitality service industries is as bright as any segment of the economy. But this potential can only be fully realized if management keeps abreast and utilizes current management tools and techniques.

Discussion Questions

1. How does the development of the service industries relate to the economic history of the United States?
2. What are the types of ultimate control centers existing in the hospitality service industries?
3. How is the financial structure of a hospitality service industry liable to differ from that of a manufacturing concern?
4. What are the six categories of the hospitality service industries and how do they overlap?

CHAPTER 2

An Introduction
to Management Accounting

Managers are responsible for directing the operations of a business organization. To accomplish this, the manager must utilize a variety of tools and resources. Perhaps the most significant of these resources is the accounting system, which generates all financial data. Since many operating decisions are based upon accounting information, it is important to obtain a thorough understanding of the financial and accounting reporting and control systems.

THE ACCOUNTING SYSTEM

The accounting system is designed to provide a logical framework for the accumulation of all financial data in such a way as to present both the financial position of the firm and the results of its operations. Because this data directly influences the decision-making process, managers must be familiar with the operations and procedures by which such information is developed.

Accounting has been described as a process directed to the recording, summarizing, and interpreting of financial data. In most of the hospitality service industries, recording and summarizing are accomplished through the use of uniform systems of accounts. These uniform accounts offer a formal structure within which financial data are accumulated and organized for the reporting of financial position and operating results.

As illustrated in Exhibit 2.1, the recording and summarization steps are generally referred to as "bookkeeping," and the interpretation function is more often associated with accounting. It is through this interpretation process that significant meanings are attached to the general financial data. In other words, data alone offer relatively little value to the operating manager. It is only through interpretation that the information becomes truly useful.

STATEMENTS AND REPORTS

The accounting process results in the presentation of financial data to a variety of users who are interested in the firm's performance.

EXHIBIT 2.1

The Flow of Bookkeeping and Accounting Functions

THE BOOKKEEPER PREPARES

The Books of Original Entry:

1. General Journal

2. Cash Receipts Journal

3. Cash Disbursements Journal

4. Sales Journal

5. Purchases Journal

AND

Posts the Books of Original Entry to the General Ledger

THE ACCOUNTANT PREPARES

The Financial Statements from the General Ledger

AND

Interprets the Financial Statements for Managerial Decisions

EXHIBIT 2.2

The Sample Motel
Balance Sheet
December 31, 19XX

Assets

Current Assets			
Cash on Hand and in Banks		$ 16,000	
Accounts Receivable	$ 18,000		
Less: Allowance for Uncollectible Accounts	1,000	17,000	
Inventories			
Food	$ 4,000		
Beverage	7,000	11,000	
Prepaid Expenses		15,000	
Total Current Assets			$ 59,000
Fixed Assets			
Land		$ 75,000	
Building	$900,000		
Less: Accumulated Depreciation—Building	600,000	300,000	
Furniture and Fixtures	$400,000		
Less: Accumulated Depreciation —			
Furniture and Fixtures	200,000	200,000	
Total Fixed Assets			575,000
Investments			1,000
Other Assets			
Liquor License		$ 15,000	
Organization Expense		5,000	
Total Other Assets			20,000
Total Assets			$655,000

Liabilities and Stockholders' Equity

Current Liabilities			
Accounts Payable			
Trade		$ 18,000	
Accrued Expenses and Taxes			
Salaries, Wages and Vacation Pay		16,000	
Workmen's Compensation Insurance		500	
Taxes		28,500	
Current Portion of Long-Term Note		26,000	
Total Current Liabilities			$ 89,000
Notes Payable		$476,000	
Less: Current Portion Shown as Current Liability Above		26,000	
Total Long-Term Liabilities			450,000
Stockholders' Equity			
Common Stock			
Authorized 5,000 Shares, $100 Par Value			
Issued and Outstanding, 1,000 Shares		$100,000	
Retained Earnings (Deficit)			
Balance January 1, 19XX	$ (4,000)		
Add: Net Income for Year Ended			
December 31, 19XX (Exhibit B)	20,000	16,000	
Total Stockholders' Equity			116,000
Total Liabilities and Stockholders' Equity			$655,000

Formal financial statements and informal management reports are generated for these purposes on a regular basis. These statements and reports are the primary means of communicating financial and operating data to the user. To be fully effective, the data must be tailored to the needs of each of these interested users.

The formal statements prepared are the balance sheet, the income statement, and the funds statement. The balance sheet (Exhibit 2.2) reports the firm's financial position at a specific point in time. Assets, liabilities, and owner's equities are listed and combined to indicate the firm's status at the end of the accounting period.

The income statement (Exhibit 2.3) is a financial summary of the results of the firm's operations for the period ended at the specified date. The net income is the amount by which the firm's revenues exceeded expenses incurred during the period; this income becomes particularly meaningful when it is considered with other factors. For example, net income can be compared to either the firm's total asset base or to its owner's equity position. By means of such comparison, the statement user is given a measure of return on investment and equity.

The funds statement (or the statement of sources and uses of funds) for the Sample Motel is illustrated in Exhibit 2.4. Such a statement is a summary of the sources of funds available to an organization over the accounting period and the uses to which the funds were put. By means of the funds statement, it is possible to follow the changes in the composition of the balance sheet from one period to the next.

Management reports are usually internally-oriented. They reflect measures of financial performance that are useful in making operating decisions. Examples of management reports are sales growth analyses (occupancy trends), gross margin (departmental profit), and other measures of asset growth (facilities expansion). These reports, in general, provide operating managers with an index of their progress during a specified period. Analyses and interpretation of these data are similarly the basis for decisions by other readers of the reports.

CONSIDERING THE NEEDS OF USERS

The users of financial statements are perhaps best classified in terms of their specific needs. Generally, five groups of users are identified: owners (and potential owners), creditors, managers, governmental agencies, and the general public.

THE FIVE USERS OF FINANCIAL STATEMENTS AND THEIR PRIMARY CONCERNS

1. Owner—How can I make more profit?
2. Creditor—Should I make the loan?

EXHIBIT 2.3

The Sample Motel
Statement of Income
For the Year Ended—December 31, 19XX

Departmental Revenue	
Rooms	$310,000
Food	260,000
Beverage	95,000
Telephone	9,000
Total Departmental Revenue	$674,000
Departmental Expenses	
Rooms	$126,000
Food	240,000
Beverage	64,000
Telephone	10,000
Total Departmental Expenses	$440,000
Departmental Profit from Operations	
Rooms	$184,000
Food	20,000
Beverage	31,000
Telephone	(1,000)
Total Departmental Profit	$234,000
Other Income	10,000
Total Gross Profit from Operations	$244,000
Deductions from Income	
Administrative and General	$ 64,000
Advertising and Sales Promotion	18,000
Heat, Light and Power	19,000
Repairs and Maintenance	28,000
Total Deductions from Income	$129,000
House Profit	$115,000
Capital Expenses	95,000
Net Income	$ 20,000

EXHIBIT 2.4
The Sample Motel
Source and Application of Funds
For Period Ended—December 31, 19XX

Source of Funds	
Operations	
Net Income (Exhibit 2.3)	$ 20,000
Add: Item Not Requiring the	
Use of Funds—Depreciation	60,000
Proceeds from Bank Loan	15,000
Total Sources of Funds	$ 95,000
Application of Funds	
Acquisition of Fixed Assets	$ 51,000
Repayment of Bank Loan	17,500
Repayment of Stockholder's Loan	25,000
Total Application of Funds	$ 93,500
Increase in Working Capital	$ 1,500

3. Manager—Is my performance up to expectations?

4. Governmental Agencies—Is the tax reported correctly?

5. General Public—Will it continue to benefit our community?

Owners and potential owners or investors are concerned with making decisions in managing their investments. In making investment decisions, the individual is concerned with historical performance to indicate probable financial performance in future periods of time. Therefore, decisions must be based on financial statements. It is imperative, then, that owners or potential owners understand thoroughly the fundamentals of financial statement preparation and presentation. Furthermore, since the supply of funds on the market may be limited, the owner is also concerned with presenting a favorable picture of his firm's performance. The decision-making needs of owners and potential investors are thus satisfied primarily by financial statements.

Creditors, as a group, need to make decisions regarding the selling of goods on credit or the loaning of monies to the firm. Analyses and interpretations of financial statements are the primary sources of information for making credit decisions. Unless the creditors are able to effectively evaluate the firm's ability to pay, they may be unwilling to make sales on credit or loan monies. Consequently, creditors' needs for relevant and meaningful information represent a significant demand on the accounting system.

Managers, responsible for making operating decisions, are the internal users of financial data. Their data needs relate to evaluating performance throughout the operation and developing plans for future activities. These phases of management are focal points toward which the accounting system output is directed. Both financial statements and management reports are prepared in an effort to satisfy recurring needs of performance evaluation and future projections. Ideally, data included in these statements and reports are useful and, consequently, are a means of increasing profits throughout the organization.

Governmental agencies are concerned in general with the need to generate revenues. Taxes paid by firms are the most significant source of revenue through which governmental operations are conducted. Financial statements serve these agencies in their efforts to collect the taxes owed by firms throughout the country.

The community is concerned, for several reasons, with the success and status of firms located within and adjacent to it. Many community residents are employed by these firms, and additional numbers will be employed by businesses that look to the employees and firms as customers. Residents and businesses alike will look to the firm as the supplier of desired goods and services. Nowhere is this more true than with the hospitality service industries. The general public looks to this segment of the economy for meals away from home, lodging for their friends, relatives, and business associates, entertainment and recreation, and health accommodations. The presence of these services is vital to the general public and to the community's continued well-being.

Although different user groups are obviously affected by and interested in financial data, managerial accounting is directed primarily to the internal management group. Our attention is, therefore, directed primarily to the needs of managers because it is they who must make the planning and control decisions.

GUIDELINES TO USEFULNESS

It is worthwhile to consider two guidelines with respect to the usefulness of financial information to the various user groups. These guidelines are understandability and timeliness. The data should be presented in such a manner that it can be easily understood by those who must use it in decision-making. All the information should be assembled with the user in mind. Naturally, the user should have knowledge as to the procedural composition of the accounting system, the constraints under which it operates, and in general, the complications involved in developing accurate financial information. This knowledge, coupled with a familiarity of general accounting concepts and techniques, should provide users with a basis for analyzing, interpreting, and evaluating the information.

The second guideline of timeliness is equally important. Unless financial data are provided at the times when decisions must be made, their value to the user is limited. In other words, if proper data are unavailable when needed, the probability of making valid, optimal decisions declines significantly. Furthermore, delaying decisions can undermine the action to be taken and the objective may not be accomplished if the decision is not made at the appropriate time.

MANAGEMENT ACCOUNTING

All hospitality service industries managers must rely on the accounting system for information to guide their decision-making activities. The concept of "management accounting" has been developed to satisfy this need more effectively. As a foundation for considering this concept, the following definition is offered.

Management accounting is the application of the appropriate techniques and concepts in processing the historical and projected data of an entity to assist management in establishing plans for reasonable economic objectives and in the making of rational decisions with a view toward achieving these objectives.[1]

This definition presents managerial accounting as a "tool of management." It is in this context that the entire discipline of accounting is considered in this book.

MANAGEMENT ACCOUNTING TECHNIQUES

Data generated from the accounting system must be analyzed and interpreted to add meaning to the information provided for decision-making purposes. A variety of techniques is available for use in effecting appropriate analyses. The following is a selection of techniques which are seemingly most appropriate for managerial planning and control decisions in the hospitality service industries. In addition, certain concepts are described to provide an introduction to the overall operation of the accounting system in a firm.

Financial statement analysis (discussed in chapters six and seven) revolves around a set of procedures designed to establish meaningful financial relationships. These relationships, or *ratios* as they are called, can be used as a reference point in guiding managerial action. Their interpretation affords management a basis for making decisions regarding control (i.e., reactions to deviations from plan) and planning (i.e., the implementation of these reactions to deviations into the projected future operations of the firm).

---

1. *A Statement of Basic Accounting Theory* (American Accounting Association, 1966), pp. 39-40.

Cost-volume-profit analysis (see chapter eleven) is a technique for analyzing financial relationships within the income statement. The effects of changes in the operating cost structure, whether volume related or otherwise, are evaluated in terms of corresponding changes in profit. Information developed can then be considered as plans for the future are formulated.

Cost accounting (chapter twelve) is a set of techniques directed to matching costs with functions and services performed by employees. Cost accounting assigns costs to related activities and to revenues generated, whereby the resulting profitability of specific activities is determined. Although cost accounting was developed to fulfill the need of the industrial economy, ways in which the techniques may be modified for application in the hospitality service industries are presented. Through the available methodology, useful cost information can be developed for operating managers.

Profit planning, or budgeting (chapters seventeen and eighteen) provides a set of techniques devoted to formalizing the managerial planning process. Budgets are used in formulating operating and financial objectives. They offer managers guidelines for use in selecting appropriate alternative courses of action. Budgets are also a control device in that they offer predetermined standards against which actual performance can be evaluated. Deviations between planned and actual performance give managers a basis for taking necessary actions.

Working capital and cash flow analysis (chapters nineteen and twenty) are techniques similarly devoted to improving information made available to managers. These tools are particularly useful in developing formal financial plans. Furthermore, they assist the manager in determining whether the firm's operations are likely to yield sufficient cash flow to satisfy expected cash and working capital requirements.

IMPORTANT CONCEPTS

Various concepts underlying managerial accounting are vitally important to successful management. They are:

Management Information Systems
Electronic Data Processing
Internal Control
Uniform Systems of Accounts
Responsibility Accounting

The concept of total *management information systems* is developed in chapter eight. These systems are the framework within which all information is developed, the accounting system being an integral part of the total management information system.

Electronic data processing (chapter twenty-three) is a second concept, but it too operates within the total management information system. Electronic data processing (EDP) provides managers with a means of rapidly generating the various kinds of quantitative information that are essential to decision-making activities.

The concept of *internal control* (chapter nine) is important for effective management. A system of checks and balances is developed in order to improve the accuracy and reliability of information, thereby improving the validity of decisions based on the information.

Uniform systems of accounts (chapter four) represents another concept that is particularly relevant to the hospitality service industries. The primary value of uniform systems is that of affording managers a more thorough basis for understanding and interpreting financial data. Uniform systems represent a foundation for responsibility accounting.

Responsibility accounting (chapter sixteen) is a concept whereby accounting data are accumulated and analyzed to monitor assigned tasks in the organizational structure of the firm. For example, managers are assigned responsibilities to achieve specific goals, the accomplishment of which requires that specialized data be provided to facilitate their decisions. The accounting system must relate specific data to decisions that are to be made, and to the responsibilities assigned. The uniform system of accounts and responsibility accounting operate cooperatively to facilitate management's attempts to accomplish objectives.

Decision-Making Implications

The accounting system has value in its capacity to generate useful information for decision-making purposes. The decisions are either control- or planning-oriented. Control decisions relate to managers' activities to control costs and revenues incurred in accomplishing planned activities. Planning decisions relate to evaluating and selecting courses of action consistent with attaining specific organizational objectives.

As an example of a control decision, let us assume that a manager responsible for the cost of meat receives the following information. Meat was to have been purchased at one dollar per pound. But the purchasing department has been paying a dollar and twenty-five cents per pound during a recent three-week period. The difference of twenty-five cents per pound was reflected as an unfavorable cost variation and brought to management's attention through a periodic cost control report. Further investigation revealed that actual usage of this meat exceeded planned quantities by nearly ten pounds. Therefore, the variances between planned and actual cost were caused both by prices paid and quantities used. The control report brought these unfavorable situations to management's attention, and corrective action was promptly taken. Profits would have been reduced further if this situation had been allowed to continue.

Another example of a control decision involves that of controlling overhead costs. Maintenance costs were found to have exceeded budgeted costs by nearly $2,000 during one monthly period. Upon analysis, it was learned that $1,250 of this total was uncontrollable because the heating plant had broken down and significant amounts of repair time were required. On the other hand, approximately $750 of this $2,000 variation was caused by improper scheduling. The latter was a controllable variation and was called to the attention of the manager who responded immediately, and the unnecessary cost was eliminated.

Planning decisions can be similarly illustrated. For example, a manager was responsible for menu prices under a policy of a balanced price structure. Certain prices had to be adjusted to bring them more into line with the others. In any planning decision the manager must select from various alternative courses of action, and in this case, each price represents an alternative. The manager must judge the propriety of each price relative to the clientele and relative to all other items on the menu.

SUMMARY

Accounting is a "tool of management," important because it generates information, which, if properly interpreted, is invaluable to owners and managers throughout the hospitality service industries. The real value of accounting information can be obtained only if managers thoroughly understand both the system through which the data flows, and the analytical and interpretative techniques which are applicable. Only then can accounting information be meaningful and useful and, thus, lead to significant profit improvements.

Discussion Questions

1. What is the difference between the bookkeeping and the accounting function?
2. What are the formal financial statements generated by an accounting system and what does each present?
3. What is management accounting?
4. How do the guidelines of timeliness and understandability of financial information affect decision-making?
5. Compare and contrast planning and control decisions.

CHAPTER 3

Review of Accounting

To account for a firm's or an organization's resources and the activity resulting from its operation, a means of recording this activity is needed. An orderly system of procedures, known as accounting, has evolved to fulfill this need.

Accounting may be called "the language of business." As with any language, accounting achieves its highest purpose only when its terms and structure are universally understood and agreed upon. Without this common understanding, financial statements and accounting reports have meaning only to those who develop them or others to whom their particular basis of generation or structure have been explained.

To further understanding of accounting information and to eliminate ambiguity, accounting has evolved specific terminology. This standardization of terminology has resulted from common usage and formal effort by such groups as the American Institute of Certified Public Accountants.

The basic financial statements are the most familiar output of the accounting system. Underlying the financial statement is a body of generally accepted principles or rules of accounting which serve as a standard for all accountants and others who rely upon accounting information. These principles provide the conceptual framework within which financial statements and other accounting reports are constructed.

Taken as a whole, these principles make up a logical and consistent body of accounting theory and practices with which to guide accountants who are responsible for recording and analyzing accounting information, and to aid users in the interpretation and application of this information. Without common agreement on accounting principles, a chaotic condition would exist in which each accountant followed his own unique ideas for developing and presenting financial data. Under these circumstances, anyone not having complete knowledge of how the data were generated would find them of little value.

The system through which accounting practices are applied and by which the resources, debts, revenues, and expenses of an entity are recorded and controlled is referred to as the *accounting system*. This system includes the books of accounts, forms, procedures and controls[1] through which the system operates.

The formal accounting structure has evolved to the point where it is universally understood; it is a system upon which managers, owners, creditors, governmental agencies and other users may rely. However, neither the accountants who prepare, nor the managements who use accounting information believe that accounting in its present state is perfect. Changes in the economy, the nature of business, the specifics of individual types of businesses, and the differing needs of accounting information users, indicate the need for changes in the accounting system; in response to changing needs, various accounting practices are created, revised, or abandoned.

Years ago, accounting was structured by the most widely used and accepted terminology and practices. When the need for change existed, and that change came to be generally accepted by the business community, the change became part of the system. Today the structure for change is formalized. In the United States, several national accounting organizations exist to consider the usefulness of accounting. Perhaps the most widely known of these is the American Institute of Certified Public Accountants (A.I.C.P.A.), representing certified public accountants throughout the United States. Within this group, the Accounting Principles Board exists to consider and recommend changes in accounting principles. This formal structure for revising accounting principles is primarily guided by the needs of all persons who are involved in the accounting process or rely upon information emanating from it. In this chapter we will review the principles, practices, and terminology underlying the accounting records and reports which measure and evaluate a business enterprise's performance and current status. In addition, we will review the accounting conventions which serve as guidelines in applying these principles and practices.

THE BUSINESS ENTITY

Any business must be kept separate and distinct from the personal accounts of those who supply its assets. Without this distinction it would be impossible to determine the organization's true performance and current status. For example, an independent restaurant operator who makes personal and family purchases from funds available in the cash register, without recording their withdrawal, not only violates good business procedures but destroys the integrity of the business as distinct from the owner's personal affairs. Under these circumstances, it is

---

1. Eric L. Kohler, *A Dictionary for Accountants*, 2nd. ed. (Englewood Cliffs, N.J.: Prentice-Hall, Inc., 1957), p. 424.

EXHIBIT 3.1

Selected Basic Accounting Principles and Practices

THE BUSINESS ENTITY

THE FUNDAMENTAL EQUATION

GOING-CONCERN CONCEPT

MONEY AS A UNIT OF MEASURE

COST

RECOGNITION AT TIME OF EXCHANGE

MATCHING REVENUE AND EXPENSE

ACCRUAL ACCOUNTING

DEPRECIATION

END-OF-PERIOD ADJUSTMENTS

CASH BASIS ACCOUNTING

DISCLOSURE

    ALTERNATIVE METHODS OF ACCOUNTING
    CONTINGENT LIABILITIES
    SUBSEQUENT EVENTS

---

impossible to correctly determine the actual expenses and profit of the restaurant because the funds withdrawn are never accounted for within the business.

Since profit-oriented activity is carried on by various economic and/or legal entities, operating results must be summarized in terms of these distinct entities.

The treatment of a business as a separate entity is, in accounting terms, the *business entity concept*. Without this concept, an accountant would have no means of correctly establishing whether particular transactions pertain to the business.

A business is an economic unit, and its legal status does not alter the business entity concept. A corporation is a legal entity as well as a business entity. Thus, for both legal and accounting purposes it is separate and apart from its owners and its shareholders; the business as a distinct entity is clearly indicated. In contrast, a partnership, while not separate and distinct from its owners for legal purposes, is also considered a business entity apart from the individual partners. Similarly, a single proprietorship is not separate from its owner for legal purposes, but for accounting purposes only those resources which are set aside for the business and those debts which are directly related to it are properly included in the accounts of that business.

THE FUNDAMENTAL EQUATION

The resources, debts and ownership interests of a firm or organization are referred to in accounting terminology as the assets, liabilities and capital respectively. The assets are the resources of the firm. They are defined as any physical object, right, or other economic resource owned by the firm, which has a monetary value and which can be reasonably expected to contribute to the future activities of the firm. Thus, assets are things of value which the business has the right to use or control for its own benefit.

Liabilities are amounts owed by the business (debtor) to any other party (creditor), payable in money, goods, or services. As protection for the creditors, liabilities represent priority rights of these creditors to the overall assets of the business.

Capital is the amount invested in the enterprise, by its owners or stockholders, be it a proprietorship, partnership, or corporation, plus the retention of income, which is reinvested in the firm. Thus, capital represents the rights of owners or stockholders to the assets of the business. The right of the owners is residual or secondary, and can be satisfied only after creditors' claims upon the assets are provided for.

The most familiar form of accounting for assets, liabilities and capital, is known as *double-entry accounting*. This is most clearly expressed in terms of the equation: assets equal liabilities plus capital. For accounting books to be in balance, each increase in assets must be accompanied by a corresponding decrease in another asset or increase in liabilities and/or capital, which will leave the equation once again in balance. The terms *debit* and *credit* relate directly to this equation.

Debit is an *increase* in an asset or a *decrease* in liability or capital. Credit is a *decrease* in an asset or an *increase* in liability or capital.

The fundamental accounting equation (assets equal liabilities plus capital) is most clearly reflected in the balance sheet. The balance sheet is a summary of the accounting formula for a given firm. In a later chapter, we will examine the balance sheet and its structure with regard to the accounting equation.

GOING-CONCERN CONCEPT

A basic assumption made in accounting is that a business will continue to operate for an indefinite period of time. That is, liquidation of the firm is not reasonably anticipated at any specific time in the future. This is not to imply that a given firm will exist permanently but simply that the business will continue to exist long enough to effectively make use of its assets and to meet all contractual commitments.

The purpose of the going-concern concept is to permit the firm's resources to be valued at a cost representing future benefits which could be reasonably expected to accrue to the firm, rather than at a cash price that would be received through immediate sale. Thus, it permits recording of cost for assets which may have little, if any, relation to realizable value in the market place.

An example of an asset which holds little or no value at liquidation but which benefits the firm in its future operation as a going concern is stationery imprinted with the firm's name. This stationery has no value to anyone except the firm for which it was made. Likewise, its value to the firm is evident in the fact that if the imprinted stationery did not exist, the firm would have to purchase such stationery. Another example of assets that hold little liquidation value is that of the expenses originally incurred in organizing the business, which are carried as an asset. Liquidation of the firm would indicate that all organization expense benefits have been realized, and future value for organization expenses cease to exist.

Assets should be recorded at cost rather than current market value because future benefits to be received from assets can be objectively related only to the original cost. For instance, if a dishwasher was purchased for $30,000 three years ago, the fact that it is resalable today for $25,000 is of no consequence to the firm unless it sells the dishwasher, because future depreciation provisions for the dishwasher are based solely on its original purchase price. Similarly, the fact that the depreciated value of a dishwasher is $15,000 and the current market value $10,000 is of no consequence if the firm's intention is to use the dishwasher for its entire economic operating life rather than to sell it immediately.

Because of the going-concern concept, the balance sheet of a business does not show the realizable value of the assets which it owns, but rather the cost of expected future benefits to be received by the firm as a result of owning these assets. To those who use accounting information, this concept emphasizes the income-generating aspects of assets, rather than the potential gain or loss that might be incurred through their sale. This, in turn, permits the accountant to allocate the cost of assets to the accounting periods during which benefits will be received, rather than having to determine their present market values.

MONEY AS A UNIT OF MEASURE

All business transactions are recorded for accounting purposes in terms of the dollar amounts involved. The underlying reason is, simply, that money is the only common factor in all business transactions, and its use as a unit of measurement lends uniformity to financial data. How else could one compare the benefits to the firm resulting, for example, from the sale of fifteen motel rooms and forty meals?

When we refer to money as a uniform unit of measure, we ignore all decreases (and increases) in the purchasing power of the dollar. Rather, the assumption is made that today's dollar is of the same value as it was ten years ago; this is called the *stable dollar assumption.*

During the period 1950-1970, the purchasing power of the dollar declined approximately 50 percent. Thus, vacant land purchased in 1950 for $100,000 is worth $200,000 in 1970, other things being equal. This $100,000 increase is not caused by a change in the real value of the land, but rather is solely the result of a change in price levels, a change in the purchasing power of the dollar. Because the 1970 dollar is only worth half of the 1950 dollar, to retain comparable purchasing power in 1970, the 1950 land price would have to be double, although the real land value remained unchanged. Nevertheless, the "money as a unit of measure" concept requires that the land be recorded at $100,000 if it was purchased in 1950, and at $200,000 if purchased in 1970. Furthermore, under the going-concern concept, the fact that the land purchased in 1950 is presently worth $200,000 is ignored in preparing a current balance sheet. The present land value would be significant only at the time of its actual sale, when its present worth is realized.

Because of the significant changes in the purchasing power of the dollar, the stable dollar assumption is being challenged. Critics contend that the balance sheet assembles dollars of different values and sizes. Assets which are normally valued in current dollars, such as cash, accounts receivable and marketable securities, are being added to long-lived assets, such as land, buildings, furniture and fixtures which are valued at previously existing dollar values. Similarly, the income statement matches dollars of different purchasing power and therefore does not, in an economic sense, accurately measure income. Expense charges based upon purchases made in earlier periods, and thus old dollars, are being matched with sales stated at current dollar values. Critics thus maintain that the comparison of balance sheets from different periods have lost their validity as changes in price levels have not been recognized.

Critics of the money concept have advocated "common dollar statements." Such statements are adjusted for price level changes using a specific year as a base. Each dollar shown represents the same amount of purchasing power. Thus, statements would offer more accurate data relating to the firm's economic position and progress. Most accountants, however, still favor the stable dollar assumption. They contend that during most periods, changes in the purchasing power of the dollar are so gradual that they do not destroy the usefulness of financial statements and that accounting must be based on objective evidence that can be easily verified. Price levels vary throughout the nation and the world, and for different kinds of goods and services purchased and sold; adjustments would also necessarily vary. Moreover, accountants differ as to which price level adjustments are appropriate; therefore, not all accounting statements would be prepared in a uniform manner, and comparability would be lost.

Yet, accountants recognize that under certain circumstances, financial statements based on the money concept do not fairly present the financial condition or results of a business operation during a period of fluctuating dollar values. For this reason, a current accounting technique involves including supplemental financial statements which are adjusted for price level changes, not necessarily on a uniform basis but at least attempting to isolate the effect of price level changes. This trend has been evident recently in the financial statements of publicly owned companies. With continued inflationary pressures, this approach probably will become generally accepted. But until a uniform, consistent basis is available to adjust financial statements for changes in the price level, those who use financial statements must remember that these statements are assembled under the stable dollar assumption and, therefore, dollars of varying purchasing power have been combined.

COST

The recording of any transaction or the valuation of any asset involves selecting a basis for determining dollar amounts. In any given instance, the available basis might include:

1. Current market value
2. Expected future market value or value at the time of expiration or sale
3. Cost at the time of acquisition

As previously indicated, the accounting process seeks to provide a consistent, standard basis for recording and presenting events and conditions. As we can see in the listed bases, cost is the only completely objective and verifiable basis. So that accounting may provide consistent and objective information, cost has been accepted as the only basis for recording transactions.

Cost is the amount, measured in money, of cash expended or other property transferred, capital stock issued, services performed, or liability incurred in consideration of goods or services received or to be received.[2]

Arguments in support of the cost concept, as opposed to recording assets or expenses at some appraised value, include the following.

1. Cost is objective, and can be easily verified, whereas the use of appraised values introduces opinion and subjectivity.

2. Profit is determined by matching costs against related revenues. The recovery of this cost, not appraised value, measures the amount that should be considered as profit.

3. The cost of appraisals for every event would be very high in relation to usefulness of the information obtained.

Although costs are recorded in contrast to appraised values, accepted accounting principles dictate that cost will not always be appropriate for valuing assets. Rather, conservatism in conjunction with the cost concept provides for downward adjusting of assets, to recognize declines in utility or exchange value. It does not, however, permit upward adjusting of assets to recognize increases in utility or exchange value. Hence, while the cost concept prohibits recording transactions at appraised values, it does permit adjustments in cost when the value of assets have declined.

Normally, this downward adjustment, referred to as *the lower of cost or market*, is applied only to those assets which are expected to be converted to cash in the foreseeable future, such as inventories, receivables and marketable securities. In contrast, building, furniture and fixtures accounts are stated at cost less accumulated depreciation to record an estimated reduction in their remaining usefulness. The net value is not adjusted for reductions in market value, since on a going-concern basis buildings, furniture and fixtures are not intended to be sold.

RECOGNITION AT TIME OF EXCHANGE

While it is well understood that sales, or the generation of revenue (revenue being defined as "the inflow of assets resulting from the operational activities of

2. "Cost, Expense and Loss," *Accounting Terminology Bulletin*, No. 4 (American Institute of Certified Public Accountants, July, 1957), p. 41.

the firm"[3]) are the source of potential profits for the profit-oriented firm and a (if not the) primary means of support for the nonprofit organization, consideration needs to be given to the point in time at which a sale is recorded.

The basic principle of the timing of revenue recognition is that a sale is considered as having occurred when there is an exchange of assets. For example, when a restaurant patron receives the meal which he or she has ordered, there is an exchange of assets. This exchange involves the delivery to the patron of the meal which the patron has the right to consume, for which the restaurant receives an implied promise to pay. Thus, the restaurant has traded a prepared meal for a receivable and a sale has occurred.

This same rule of revenue recognition at the time of exchange may be applied to other transactions in the hospitality service industries. Sales, or the generation of revenue, occur in the following circumstances:

a. A guest checks into a motel and receives the key to a room which he is told he may occupy for some period of time.
b. A club member is served a meal in the club dining room.
c. An in-flight food company delivers a load of food to a waiting airliner.
d. A plant employee puts a quarter in a vending machine and receives a sandwich.

MATCHING REVENUE AND EXPENSE

We have considered the point in time in which income or loss is earned (incurred) and realized. Since profits are stated accurately only if they reflect timely recorded revenue less the expense associated with generating that revenue, all applicable expenses should be deducted from sales to determine the profit of any given transaction. This relating of revenue with expenses is referred to as the *matching concept.*

A restaurant owner may purchase food in one accounting period and sell it in the following period. If the matching concept is not employed, the cost of the sale would appear in the accounting period prior to the period in which the sales are recorded. Costs would thereby be overstated in the first period and profit would be overstated in the succeeding period. Obviously, financial statements which do not properly match revenues and expenses are of limited value.

If costs are to be incurred in the future which relate to revenues in a current period, the matching concept indicates that the current period's income statement

---

3. Eldon S. Hendrikson, *Accounting Theory*, rev. ed. (Homewood, Ill.: Richard D. Irwin, Inc., 1970), p. 160.

should reflect the anticipated future costs resulting from the current sale. This applies, for example, when goods or services are sold under guarantee, since it may be reasonably expected that future expenses will be incurred because of the guarantee terms. Since it is not possible to determine the exact costs which may result from the guarantee, the best alternative is to estimate these future guarantee costs based on past experience.

The matching concept is the basis for accrual accounting, which will be considered next. The accrual basis of accounting provides us with the tools necessary to defer and accrue revenues and expenses to achieve the proper matching of earned revenues and applicable expired costs.

ACCRUAL ACCOUNTING

The basis for proper and acceptable accounting is to match expenses with their associated revenues. Accrual accounting provides a consistent method to accomplish this goal. The objective of accrual basis accounting is to report revenues in the period in which they are considered to have been earned, regardless of when they are collected, and to report related expenses in the same period.

The accrual basis of accounting is a method of accounting whereby revenues and expenses are identified with specific periods of time and are recorded as incurred without regard to the date of receipt or payment.

In order for the income statement to clearly reflect the operating results of an organization, it is necessary that all revenues earned during the period be included in the determination of income. Similarly, all expenses incurred during the period that were associated with the revenue earned should be charged against the revenue to determine the profit. Thus, in cases where sales have occurred which should be allocated to two or more time periods, it is necessary that the accounting records reflect this allocation of revenue. And, where expenses are incurred which should be allocated to two or more time periods, it is necessary that the accounting records reflect this allocation of expense.

An example of a circumstance where sales are allocable to two periods might be where a guest at a resort that ends its fiscal year on December 31 arrives on December 28 and departs on January 4. Although the settlement of his account for the charges incurred would normally not take place until January 4, the revenues resulting from his presence at the resort from December 28 through and including December 31 should be credited to the sales of the period ended December 31.

Continuing with this example, if the resort receives a week's supply of various foodstuffs on December 28, for which it pays cash at the time of delivery, a portion of the expense resulting from this purchase should be charged against each of the accounting periods. Those items used through December 31 should be charged against that period, and those not used until the following year, beginning January 1, should be treated as expenses of that year.

The inclusion of revenue in the period in which it was earned without regard to the time of payment has been previously considered in this chapter as the recognition of revenue at the time of exchange. The principle of allocating expenses to the period in which the associated revenue was earned is referred to in accounting as "matching," in reference to matching related revenues and expenses. Accrual basis accounting is the means by which these principles are followed.

DEPRECIATION

Depreciation is a systematic and rational means by which the costs associated with the acquisition and installation of an asset are allocated over the estimated useful life of that asset.

The most common depreciation method is *straight-line depreciation.* Using this method, the costs of an asset are uniformly distributed over the expected useful life of that asset. For example, a car is purchased for $3,500, and at the end of its three-year useful life it can be sold for $500. Since its estimated useful life is three years, under the straight-line method the $3,000 depreciation basis ($3,500 less $500 salvage value) is allocated at the rate of $1,000 per year ($3,000 divided by three years). After the first year, the automobile will be shown in the accounts as having a net book value of $2,500 ($3,500 purchase price, minus $1,000, the depreciation for one year). Thus, at the end of the third year, it will have depreciated to its salvage value of $500.

The straight-line depreciation method is based on the assumption that the utility of the asset depreciates in the same amount each year of its estimated useful life.

Because long-lived assets frequently decline in productive value fastest during the earlier portions of their useful lives, depreciation methods are in use that increase the rate of depreciation in earlier years and in subsequent years continually decrease the rate of depreciation. These methods are referred to as *accelerated depreciation methods;* that is, they are methods which accelerate the rate of depreciation in earlier years.

One accelerated depreciation method is the *sum-of-the-years-digits* method. Using the automobile example, the depreciation formula is calculated in the following manner:

1. Total the *sum-of-the-years-digits* of the estimated useful life of the automobile. In this case, with a three-year useful life, the total is six (3 + 2 + 1 = 6).

EXHIBIT 3.2

Straight-Line Depreciation Illustrated

$$D = \frac{C - S}{L}$$

D = Depreciation Expense

C = Cost of Asset

S = Estimated Salvage Value

L = Useful Life of Asset

$$D = \frac{3500 - 500}{3} = 1000$$

Year	Depreciable Cost	Depreciation Expense	Net Book Value
1	3500	1000	2500
2	2500	1000	1500
3	1500	1000	500

This number serves as the denominator of the yearly depreciation factor. The formula is $S = N \left(\frac{N + 1}{2} \right)$ when S = sum and N = number of years of useful life.

2. Determine the numerator, which is the year in the life of the asset. For example, with a three-year life, the numerator for the first year is three; for the second year, two; and for the third year, one.

3. Combine the denominator, or the sum of the years' digits, with the numerator appropriate for the year, which produces the yearly depreciation factor. For the first year's depreciation on the automobile, the factor is 3/6. For the second year, the factor is 2/6; and for the third year, 1/6. That is:

	Year	Depreciation Factor
	1	3/6
	2	2/6
	3	1/6
Total	6	6/6

4. Determine the cost subject to depreciation which is the purchase price less the salvage value ($3,500 minus $500 = $3,000).

5. Apply the depreciation factor for the year to this cost. For the first year, depreciation is $1,500 (3/6 of $3,000). For the second year, the depreciation is $1,000 (2/6 of $3,000); and for the third year, $500 (1/6 of $3,000).

Year	Depreciable Cost	Depreciation Factor	Depreciation Expense	Net Book Value
1	3000	3/6	1500	2000
2	3000	2/6	1000	1000
3	3000	1/6	500	500

Under the straight-line method for the automobile, the first year's depreciation was $1,000, whereas, using the sum-of-the-years-digits method, the first year's depreciation was $1,500. Over the life of the asset, the total depreciation is the same in both cases, $3,000. The sum-of-the-years-digits method records larger depreciation during the earlier years of asset life and smaller depreciation during the later years, while the straight-line method applies uniform depreciation throughout the asset life.

A second accelerated method is the *double-declining-balance* method of depreciation. This method uses a rate of depreciation which is twice the straight-line rate, and thus is referred to as *double-declining*. Again using the example of the automobile with a three-year life, the straight-line rate would be 33 1/3% annual depreciation on the purchase price. Under the double-declining-balance method, the first year's depreciation would be 66 2/3% of the cost subject to depreciation. For the second year, the 66 2/3% rate would be applied to the reduced book value of the asset, as it would similarly be applied the following year. Exhibit 3.3 illustrates this comparison.

The double-declining or other accelerated depreciation methods are the most realistic assignment of costs in many segments of the hospitality service industries. In all segments of the hospitality service industries, the risk of earlier obsolescence from changing technology and changing public taste is high, so that the economic flow of income from the usual hospitality service industries asset is higher in the earlier years of life and lower in the later years. The accelerated methods of depreciation recognize this declining economic utility of the hospitality asset and matches larger depreciation costs against the early, most productive years of the asset.

EXHIBIT 3.3

Double-Declining-Balance Depreciation

Straight-Line Depreciation Rate = 100/3 – 33 1/3%

Double-Declining - 2 x 33 1/3% = 66 2/3%

Year	Depreciable Cost	Depreciation Expense	Net Book Value
1	3500.00	66 2/3% x 3500.00 = 2333.31	1166.69
2	1166.69	66 2/3% x 1166.69 = 777.72	388.97
3	388.97	66 2/3% x 388.97 = 259.29	129.68

In addition to the straight-line and accelerated methods of depreciation, there are other methods, which utilize the units of production and service hours.

Units-of-production method: Using this method an estimate is made of the number of units of output which a depreciable asset will produce over the useful life. The depreciation for a year is then calculated, employing a factor which uses as its numerator the output for that year and as its denominator the total expected output. This factor applied to the depreciable cost (purchase price less estimated salvage value) is that year's depreciation.

Service-hours method: Similar to the units-of-production method, the service-hours method substitutes hours for units. Thus estimated useful life in hours becomes the denominator and yearly hours of service becomes the numerator.

Although utilization of the units of production and service hours is limited in the hospitality service industries, its potential applications include laundry equipment, golf carts, equipment of common carriers (airplanes, buses and rental cars) hotel-motel airport limousines, and certain resort facilities.

END-OF-PERIOD ADJUSTMENTS

Buildings, furniture and fixtures are not the only assets, or unexpired costs, which are paid in one accounting period and used over future accounting periods. For instance, if we purchase a three-year insurance policy and prepay the premium for the three-year period, we have an asset whose benefit extends beyond a one-year accounting period. At the time of purchase, the total amount of the three-year premium for the insurance policy will be shown as an asset of the firm.

Assuming that the policy was purchased on the first day of the fiscal year, one-third of the cost of that policy must be transferred from an asset to a cost of that year. At the beginning of the next fiscal year the balance sheet would show an asset (prepaid insurance) of two-thirds of the original purchase price, because two of the three years had yet to be used. Other expenses which may be prepaid include interest, rent, taxes, licenses, and supplies.

Just as adjustments are made to reduce assets for which some portion of their cost has expired, we must also recognize costs incurred for which we may not have paid. For instance, if employees are paid on Friday and the end of the reporting period falls on Wednesday, two-fifths of that week's wage expense belongs in the following period. If this division were not made, the entire week's wages would be reflected in the following period's expenses when the wages were paid. Under accrual accounting, we will make an adjusting entry or accrual to record three-fifths of that week's wages as an expense of the last period, and as a current liability.

There are also income items for which adjustments must be made to correctly recognize the income of the respective accounting periods. For example, if idle cash is invested in a six-month certificate of deposit, and this certificate is purchased three months prior to the end of the period, the interest on the certificate will be received three months into the following period. If an adjustment is not made to reflect the three months' earnings during the first period, then the earnings would be entirely reflected in the income of the second period in which the interest was received. Likewise, suppose that money is borrowed for six months, three months prior to the end of the period. Under the terms of the loan, interest is payable when the loan principle is due and unless an adjustment is made the first period will not reflect its portion of the interest expense, since the cash payment will not be made until three months into the second period. In both of these examples, the accrual basis of accounting requires an adjustment or accrual to allocate the correct interest income or expense to the appropriate periods.

Accrual accounting also includes the deferral or postponement of the recognition of revenue already collected until it is earned. An example of a revenue deferral is rental income received, but not yet earned. Such an amount is a liability, and represents unearned income received.

CASH BASIS ACCOUNTING

In direct contrast to accrual basis accounting is cash basis accounting. Using the cash basis method, just as the name might imply, revenue is recognized at the time of the receipt of cash and expenses are charged against the accounting period in which the payment is made. No effort is made to match expenses with related revenues.

The fundamental difference between cash and accrual basis accounting is a matter of timing. While cash basis accounting is not consistent with generally accepted accounting principles, and does not reflect the most realistic income statement, it is easy to use by those unfamiliar with accrual basis accounting methods. Thus, it is frequently employed by smaller hospitality service businesses. However, since it does not relate revenues and expenses, it is difficult to prepare accurate, meaningful reports to assist management in controlling costs and analyzing business performance.

There are several exceptions to strict adherence to cash basis accounting. Of primary importance to the hospitality service industries is the treatment of the cost of fixed assets whose value is reduced through operating activities. If the cost of fixed assets were to be charged against the period in which the asset was purchased, a substantial distortion of income would result. To overcome this, a hybrid system is frequently employed in which most accounting is on a cash basis except where such treatment would result in material distortions. Buildings and furniture and fixtures would be depreciated over their useful lives just as in accrual basis accounting.

For some segments of the hospitality service industries, inventories of merchandise are employed in the generation of revenue. Specifically, food and/or beverage operations maintain inventories of food and beverages. For these operations the calculation of beginning and ending inventories is a necessary part of operating expense determination and, therefore, the maintenance of accounting records on the accrual basis is necessary.

Reference to inventories of merchandise should not be confused with inventories of operating supplies. In a case where inventories consist of operating supplies, such as hotel supplies, the potential effect upon the determination of profit is usually minimal and, hence, does not necessitate the use of beginning and ending inventory calculations if the use of cash basis accounting is preferred.

Although the implication of previous pages may have been that the choice of accounting methods is entirely at the discretion of management or ownership, the Internal Revenue Service has placed restrictions upon the method employed in the calculation of Federal income taxes. The general rule applied by the I.R.S. is that the method employed for tax purposes "clearly reflect income." Thus, for food and beverage operations the use of accrual basis accounting for calculating income tax is required because of the presence of merchandise inventories. Where the presence of long-lived assets, such as buildings and furniture and fixtures, could distort income if expended at the time of payment, the I.R.S. requires the depreciation of these assets over their useful lives, although if no other conditions exist requiring the accrual method, cash basis accounting may be employed for reporting other activities.

DISCLOSURE

Disclosure is an accounting principle which is important to external users of accounting information. Disclosure means that all financial statements, along with the accompanying footnotes, should provide full information of all pertinent facts to those who use financial statements. The key to this statement rests in the determination of pertinent facts. Guidelines are set forth by the American Institute of Certified Public Accountants and the Securities and Exchange Commission as to the circumstances under which disclosure is required, but the matter is still very much subject to individual interpretation. What may be considered pertinent by one accountant may be considered irrelevant by another. The following specific areas of disclosures are usually required as a minimum.

In instances where there is at least one alternative method of accounting treatment and/or presentation of a particular transaction, the method employed should be disclosed since it may be important to those who must interpret financial statements (for example, inventory and depreciation methods).

A second area of required disclosure is contingent liabilities, such as pending lawsuits against the company, or the possibility that additional income tax is payable for past years. The estimated effect on the income statement and balance sheet of these contingencies should be disclosed in footnotes to the financial statements.

Another area of specifically required disclosures relates to events subsequent to the date of the financial statements. It is required that events occurring after the date of the financial statement be disclosed at the time of preparation (if they are known to those who prepare the statement), if those events would materially affect the firm's financial position and future profits. Examples include a fire which destroys a major portion of the business, or the settlement of pending litigation.

The need for ample disclosure is particularly important because financial and investment decisions are made on the basis of information presented in financial statements. Thus, appropriate disclosures should be made, as additional information may aid those who use accounting data to make financial and investment decisions.

ACCOUNTING CONVENTIONS

The accounting principles, practice and terminology which were reviewed are fundamental to accounting and actually prescribe the accounting process. Accounting is additionally modified by several widely accepted accounting conventions. The four most important of these are objectivity, consistency, conservatism, and materiality.

OBJECTIVITY

Objectivity, or freedom from bias, is particularly important in reporting financial data. This is even more so in the case of managerial accounting, as will be explored in a later chapter, because the preparer of the financial or other report has the opportunity to influence management decisions. Objective, verifiable evidence should be used as the basis for recording transactions and preparing financial statements. Accountants believe sound financial data is significant to decision-making and they view objectivity as one of the principal guidelines underlying the preparation of financial statements. It is an essential characteristic in determining the appropriate dollar amounts for reporting particular transactions. Objectivity in reporting is imperative to maintain the confidence of the many people who use financial information.

CONSISTENCY

It is immediately apparent that data cannot be compared accurately if this data has not been developed under the same rules. Thus, consistency is a particularly important convention for generating useful accounting information. For accounting information to be most useful, the accounting principles and practices adopted by a business should be consistent from period to period, so that financial data will be comparable and will have continuity. Without consistent accounting, trends indicated by supposedly comparable financial statements might well be incorrectly interpreted. For example, a change in the method of depreciation from the sum-of-the-years-digits method in one period to the straight-line method in the next period could materially affect the comparability of the profits being reported.

Where current accounting practices are found to be inappropriate for conditions in a particular company, a change may be warranted. Under the accounting principle of disclosure, it is necessary to disclose the nature and impact of these changes in accounting on the balance sheet and income statement. With this full information, users of the financial statements are aware of these changes and are able to adjust the accounting data to provide valid comparability.

Users of financial statements have a right to assume that a company's accounting practices are employed consistently unless otherwise informed. The American Institute of Certified Public Accountants has determined that all CPA's issuing independent auditor's opinions on the fairness of financial statements must report that the statements were prepared "in conformity with generally accepted accounting principles applied on a basis consistent with that of the preceding year." Where such is not the case, they are obligated to report in their opinion and in the footnotes to the financial statements the nature of the change and its effect on the comparability of the financial statements.

CONSERVATISM

The convention of conservatism refers to the moderation that should be applied in recording transactions and assigning values where there is a reasonable question or doubt about the value amount. In these circumstances, conservatism requires the procedure that yields recognition of smaller earnings or the recording of the lesser amount of asset value.

The convention of conservatism, however, definitely does not justify deliberate understatement of accounts. "It is rather a quality of judgment to be exercised in evaluating uncertainties and risks present in a business entity to assure that reasonable provisions are made for potential losses in the realization of recorded assets and in the settlement of actual and contingent liabilities."[4] If there is reasonable uncertainty as to whether revenue has been realized, the accountant will treat it as though it has not been realized. Conversely, if there is reasonable certainty that an expense or loss has been incurred, he will record the expense of loss as having been incurred.

Current accounting theory is not in complete agreement with the basic reasoning underlying the convention of conservatism. Some argue that logic and reason, not conservatism, should govern the matching of costs and revenue, the valuation of assets, and the determination of liabilities. Further, they contend that conservatism is inherently inconsistent in that it supports the writedown of the valuation of an asset and not its writeup in light of basically identical objectives and verifiable evidence.

Because of this controversy, accounting currently relies on objectivity, consistency, disclosure and materiality, and turns to conservatism when these conventions do not shed sufficient light on the problem.

---

4. "Inventory of Generally Accepted Accounting Principles for Business Enterprises," *Accounting Research Study*, No. 7 (American Institute of Certified Public Accountants, 1965), p. 35.

MATERIALITY

Absolute accuracy is neither practical nor economically feasible in presenting accounting information. In applying generally accepted accounting principles to the recording of business transactions and events, accountants must consider the relative dollar importance on the financial condition or operating performance of the business entity. To this extent, accountants have a degree of latitude in determining the recording treatment of particular events and facts. Generally, the size and nature of an item which affects the financial statement must be considered in relation to other items to determine its materiality. Thus, the accountant must exercise careful judgment in determining materiality if precise criteria are not available. For example, the erroneous exclusion from a balance sheet of a $2,000 loan to an officer when total accounts receivable amount to $100,000 and total assets amount to $2,000,000 would most likely be an immaterial error. However, if the officer's loan were $20,000 or if there were a specific stipulation in the organization's bylaws that officers were not to borrow money from the company, then the error would be considered material. If the error is considered material because of the $20,000 amount, the reason for its being considered material is probably because of its relationship to the $100,000 of accounts receivable rather than its relationship to the total assets.

Materiality also applies in the initial recording of transactions. For instance, where fixed assets totaled $2,000,000, the mistaken recording of $20 in a fixed asset account would not be considered a material error, because in its relation to the total fixed assets, a charge of $20 would not be expected to effect any decision that would result from relying on the dollar amount of fixed assets.

The selected four accounting conventions are summarized in Exhibit 3.4.

EXHIBIT 3.4

Summary of Accounting Conventions

OBJECTIVITY	—	Freedom from Bias in Reporting.
CONSISTENCY	—	Provides Comparability to Financial Statements.
CONSERVATISM	—	Prohibits Anticipating Income—and Requires Recording All Known Losses and Liabilities.
MATERIALITY	—	Relative Importance Dictates Degree of Required Accuracy.

SUMMARY

Accounting is structured by an underlying set of principles and conventions. It is this framework, which is generally accepted by all users of accounting information, which allows accounting to be universally understood.

Accounting records are maintained for specific units so that financial performance and status may be accumulated and reported for particular business entities. The records are most frequently kept and assembled using double-entry bookkeeping, which equate assets with liabilities and owners' equity (the fundamental equation).

The valuation of assets and resulting owners' equity on the books of an entity are the result of recording the acquisition of all assets at cost, the fair market value of the assets given up to carry out the acquisition. This valuation at cost assumes that the cost will be recaptured after some future period. Thus, the going-concern concept is required to employ the use of costs in valuing assets. The recording of all assets, liabilities and owners' equity is in monetary units because they are the only available common unit of measure.

Accrual basis accounting is the only method of accounting that is consistent with generally accepted accounting principles. Under this method revenues are recognized at the time of an exchange of assets, and costs are matched with their associated revenues regardless of the period of payment. Because the actual outlay for an asset may occur in only one fiscal period but the benefits from it may be received over several periods, methods are available to allocate such costs. *The most common method is that of depreciation.*

In contrast to accrual accounting is cash basis accounting. Under this method revenue is recognized when the cash is received and expenses recognized when payment is made.

In order to make financial statements as informative as possible, disclosure is required of all facts believed to be important to the users of financial statements.

Certain conventions have become accepted by accountants as guidelines in the preparation and presentation of accounting information. *Objectivity* requires that the recording of all transactions be done on an unbiased objective basis, with verifiable evidence in support of each transaction. *Consistency* requires that in order for financial statements to be comparable from period to period, transactions must be recorded in a consistent manner. *Conservatism* dictates that when the treatment of a particular transaction is uncertain it should be recorded to minimize earnings or asset value. And *materiality* recognizes that it is neither practical nor feasible to have accounting and financial statements 100 percent accurate and that therefore, only significant or material amounts are considered.

Discussion Questions

1. How has our formal accounting structure reached the point of universal understanding?
2. What is the purpose of an individual using the business entity concept for his business rather than running all transactions through his personal account?
3. How does the going-concern concept effect the financial statements?
4. What are the basic principles underlying the cost concept?
5. What is the matching process, and how does it become the basis of accrual accounting?
6. What is meant by adequate disclosure? What are the minimum disclosure requirements?
7. Why would an auditor state that in his opinion the accounting principles in the financial statements were "applied on a basis consistent with that of the preceding year"?
8. Why would a creditor want to know if the financial statements were presented conservatively?
9. Discuss the elements of the accounting equation.

CHAPTER 4

Financial Statements and Uniform Systems

TYPES OF FINANCIAL STATEMENTS

In the previous chapter we examined the fundamentals and concepts of financial accounting. It is the purpose of this chapter to examine the primary output of a financial accounting system, that is, the financial statements. Financial statements will be considered from several different aspects, including the specific needs of the hospitality service industries as to the type and organization of financial information required to monitor the business's operations and make sound decisions which will contribute to its future success.

The primary financial statements generated by a financial accounting system are the income statement or statement of profit and loss, the balance sheet or statement of financial condition, and the funds flow statement or statement of sources and application of funds. Additionally, other financial statements include the statement of changes in owner's equity and the cash flow statement.

The *income statement* is the financial report that sets forth the net income or profit of an organization. Additionally, it provides information about the revenues (sales) and expenses (costs) that resulted in the net income.

The *balance sheet* is the financial report that indicates what resources the firm has available to it, how much money it owes, and the value, as carried on the books of the enterprise, of the owners' investment. As mentioned earlier, the balance sheet is the complete presentation of the assets equal liabilities plus equity formula for an entity.

The *funds flow statement* supplies information about the sources of funds received by the enterprise and how funds were used.

Financial statements provide the communication link between the business entity's activities and decision-makers. The primary emphasis and concern of this book is that of supplying managers of hospitality service businesses with the necessary tools to make effective operational decisions. There are, of course, other decision-makers and interested persons who are concerned with the information presented in financial statements—the external users.

EXTERNAL USERS OF FINANCIAL STATEMENTS

External users of financial statements include stockholders, absentee owners (owners who are not actively engaged in the business), creditors, potential creditors, government agencies, and the general public. Each of these groups is seeking particular types of information; thus, their needs are different. The common element of these diverse interests is that all of their needs should be satisfied to the fullest possible extent by the financial statements.

STOCKHOLDERS AND ABSENTEE OWNERS

One would not invest in a business venture and then not monitor its performance. An owner is vitally concerned with its success and, in order to maximize benefits, there are certain decisions that must be made at appropriate times. Thus, an external user of financial statements is also a decision-maker.

The types of decisions which are made involve such basic alternatives as whether to buy or sell one's interest in the company. This is the principal decision available to stockholders of companies, in that most stockholders of large companies don't have sufficient ownership to influence its operation. However, as a substantial stockholder, or as an owner of a business not directly involved in its daily operations, there are additional decisions to be made. Such decisions as changes in management, changes in products or services, and changes in methods of operation are all decisions that owners must make. These decisions, of course, normally arise only when there is some dissatisfaction with the progress of the business.

For the owner of a business, primary concern is with the present and future profitability of the enterprise. Therefore, there is certain key financial information that is of particular interest. The income statement is the primary source of information since it presents information about the sales, expenses and profitability of the business. The balance sheet is the next most important source of information because it shows the financial condition of the business.

CREDITORS

Creditors, particularly short-term creditors, are very interested in the balance sheet because it enables them to analyze the potential for loan repayment or payment of account.

In the past, creditors and potential creditors, both long- and short-term, were almost exclusively interested in the balance sheet. They felt that a strong balance sheet provided the best indication of security for loans. Today, creditors realize that (particularly in the case of long-term loans) the ability of a business to generate profit is more significant to the future repayment of loans than the strength of the balance sheet. This is not to say that the current financial condition of a company is not considered in making loans, but rather that in the overall evaluation, profitability is the index of a company's repayment potential.

Particular characteristics that creditors and potential creditors examine in financial statements are the profitability, cash flow, liquidity, net working capital, debt-equity ratio and, in some cases, the prospective market value of the firm's assets. Briefly, let us consider each of these factors. We know that profitability is a major concern to creditors because a profit-oriented business not making a profit has little or no future. Cash flow, out of which loan payments can be made, is an indication of the company's ability to repay loans. The debt-to-equity ratio is significant in that it indicates the protection afforded creditors by the owner's investment. The market value of the firm's assets is of concern since the values carried in the financial statements may not necessarily reflect the current fair market value. Net working capital represents the excess of current assets over current liabilities, or those current assets which are not committed to current liabilities. Liquidity, of greatest importance to the short-term creditor, refers to the ease with which assets can be converted to cash for possible payment of loans.

Creditors seek this information to enable them to make informed decisions, such as whether to make a loan or extend credit, the size of the loan or credit limit, the interest rate and terms including required security and, of course, the decision to call a loan.

GOVERNMENT AGENCIES

Government agencies comprise a third classification of external users who are vitally interested in the condition and performance of a business. Included in this category are the public taxing agencies, such as the Internal Revenue Service and various state and local tax agencies. In addition, regulatory agencies such as the Interstate Commerce Commission, which deals with the regulation of interstate land transportation; the Civil Aeronautics Board, which regulates air line routes, service, and rates; the Federal Communications Commission, which regulates broadcasting; and the Federal Trade Commission, which regulates various business practices, are all becoming more active in the business sector. Also, the Justice Department and the Securities and Exchange Commission are ever watchful for restraint of trade practices and inaccurate or insufficient investor information.

An agency which has become very observant of the hospitality service industries is the Labor Department. Its concern is primarily with the enforcement of the Federal wage and hour laws and the equal employment opportunities laws.

Government agencies are interested in information provided by financial statements, such as return on investment in the case of the C.A.B., methods of accounting and full disclosure in the case of the S.E.C., and a wide range of other types of information.

The types of decisions with which the various government agencies are involved include imposing fines and possible imprisonment in the case of noncompliance with required actions, the restriction of particular methods of operation or practices, enforcing compliance with particular laws or regulations, and issuance or withdrawal of particular licenses or authorities under which an enterprise operates.

THE GENERAL PUBLIC

The general public is one of the most important users of financial statements. Labor unions are becoming increasingly interested in the financial statements of business entities. To a large extent, and particularly in times of highly profitable operations, labor unions base their wage and fringe benefit demands on the company's profitability as reported in its financial statements. Residents of an area may have an interest in the information presented in a local business's financial statements, since they are interested in its stability, success and future growth, and the effect these factors may have upon the economy of the area.

INTERNAL USE OF FINANCIAL STATEMENTS

Financial statements are the most important reports available to management because they present in a concise manner the operating results and the financial position of the entity.

Financial statements provide several types of necessary and basic information to management. They detail the operating results in terms of revenues, expenses and profit realized during a particular period of time. They provide a means of analyzing and controlling the various revenue and expense items, and reflect the entity's financial position in terms of assets and liabilities. Also, they indicate to management the resources available and the obligations to be met.

Financial statements can be classified as *flow*, or dynamic, statements and *point-in-time*, or static, statements. An income statement presents the operating results of an entity for a particular period of time, referred to as the *accounting* or *fiscal period*. In contrast, the balance sheet presents the financial position of the entity as of a specific time. A flow statement is one which reports activity for a specified period while a point-in-time statement presents the conditions as of some specific time. Thus, an income statement is a flow statement detailing financial operating activity between the beginning and the end of an accounting period; a balance sheet is a point-in-time statement presenting the financial condition as of the end of the accounting period. The statement of source and application of funds and the cash flow statement also are flow statements.

In the remainder of this chapter, we will examine the organization and content of financial statements specifically developed for some of the hospitality service industries.

UNIFORM SYSTEM OF ACCOUNTS

A uniform system of accounts provides for the uniform classification, organization and presentation of revenue, expense, asset, liability and equity items for a particular type of hospitality service business. The system includes a standardized format for reporting the performance of the operation—the income statement; and the financial condition of the organization—the balance sheet. Through the use of a uniform system, each revenue, expense, asset, liability or equity item is consistently classified making the exact nature of any account, category or classification readily understandable to those familiar with the uniform system for the particular hospitality service entity. Thus, the exact composition of all accounts is standardized, as are the account names and the organization of the specific accounts in the financial statements. In summary, then, a uniform system of accounts provides a method by which accounts may be classified and presented by all similar types of operating entities regardless of size, type or ownership.

DEVELOPMENT OF THE UNIFORM SYSTEMS

In 1925, the Hotel Association of New York City appointed a committee of hotel accountants to design a system for classifying, organizing, and presenting financial data, so that uniformity in the classification of revenues, expenses, assets, liabilities and equities for hotels might be attained and to provide comparable financial statements. The system designed has since been adopted by the American Hotel and Motel Association and has come to be known as the "Uniform System of Accounts for Hotels." It is widely used throughout the hotel industry, and has served as the basis for formulating other uniform systems in the hospitality service industries. Other systems include the "Uniform System of Accounts for Restaurants" sponsored by the National Restaurant Association, the "Uniform System of Accounts for Clubs" sponsored by the Club Managers Association of America, and the "Uniform System of Accounts for Motels, Motor Hotels and Small Hotels" sponsored by the American Hotel and Motel Association.

CONTRIBUTIONS TO MANAGEMENT AND ACCOUNTING

The importance of the uniform systems in the hospitality service industries is illustrated best by their contributions to the management and accounting processes.

For management, uniform systems facilitate comparability. Comparisons may be made with past performance, with other similar operations, or with data compiled on groups of similar operations.

Comparability also can be expanded to include the common language or communication aspects of uniform systems. With a uniform system, particular terms are understood to mean the same thing to all those who are familiar with the system. Thus, when two managers from different hotels refer to their respective house profits, a term common to the hotel business, each knows precisely what the other is referring to in terms of the revenues and expenses which are included in that term. Similarly the term *operating ratio* (the percentage of operating expenses to revenue) has precise meaning to the managers of common carriers.

An additional benefit of using the appropriate uniform system is the ability of interested groups and associations to compile meaningful industry-wide operating results and statistics. Without a uniform system, the data would not be comparable and, therefore, would be of little value.

A second feature is that the structure of the financial statements in the uniform system can significantly affect management's interpretation and use of them. This contribution primarily refers to the income statement—the single most important management report that an operating manager receives. Revenue and expense items are in an order and grouping that is most meaningful to management in terms of responsibility and control. The uniform system presents the format considered best suited by experts within the industry to serve the needs of the particular hospitality service operation.

The use of uniform systems also benefits the company's accounting function. Because such a system exists for a particular industry, the need to set up an individual accounting system at the commencement of business is alleviated. Even more important is the fact that it is a convenient and efficient method to provide for the accounting function, since each uniform system has been designed to meet unusual classification problems. Such a system is invaluable.

THE INCOME STATEMENT

The income statement is management's primary report. It shows the kind and amount of revenues, the kind and amount of expenses and the resulting net profit (or loss) over a specific period of time; it presents the net increase (or decrease) in resources as the result of operations. This increase (or decrease) occurs because resources received for the sale of goods or services (revenues) exceed or are exceeded by resources expended (expenses) in realizing the revenue.

The origin of the traditional form of the income statement is linked with the presentation of income and expense items for manufacturing firms. In its simplest form it appears as follows:

Sales	$ xxx
Less: Cost of Goods Sold	xxx
Gross Profit	$ xx
Less: Operating Expenses	xx
Net Income	$ xx

Using this format, an income statement for a manufacturing firm is shown in Exhibit 4.1.

For managers in the hospitality service industries the traditional or manufacturing firm type of income statement is not useful as a management tool because the direct product cost is less distinct from overhead costs. For this reason, a more useful format for the income statement was designed for the hospitality service industries, one which not only sets forth the revenues, expenses and profit, but does so by grouping and organizing these items to provide maximum usefulness for the hospitality industry manager.

To provide the maximum managerial informational content in the income statement, three basic criteria should be considered in its organization: responsibility, controllability and allocability. Responsibility refers to grouping revenue and expense items so that the performance of the individual responsible for that particular segment of the operation can be measured and judged. Controllability refers to the extent to which costs can be controlled. In the income statement, the classification of costs is determined by the level at which this control occurs. Allocability refers to meaningfully allocating costs as closely as possible to the related sale.

Since these three criteria may present a conflict in determining the placement of particular costs within the income statement it frequently is necessary to give greater weight to one or the other of the criteria in making this determination. For example, a specific portion of depreciation may be allocable to a restaurant, thereby indicating it should be deducted directly from restaurant revenues; however, this expense is not controllable by, or the responsibility of, the restaurant manager, thus suggesting that it should be deducted at a later point in the statement. To minimize this conflict, the hotel, motel, club and restaurant categories of the hospitality service industries have adopted a modified form, the contribution approach income statement, which is basically constructed as follows:

EXHIBIT 4.1

Sample Manufacturing Firm
Comparative Statement of Income

	Year Ended	
	Dec. 31, 19x(A)	Dec. 31, 19x(B)
Sales	$2,622,425	$2,163,293
Cost of Goods Sold		
Material	$1,276,297	$1,043,345
Direct Labor	626,560	556,003
Manufacturing Expense	166,895	144,700
Total Cost of Goods Sold	$2,069,752	$1,744,048
Gross Profit	$ 552,673	$ 419,245
Administrative, General and Selling Expenses		
Officers' Salaries	$ 72,930	$ 68,930
Administrative	82,264	54,981
Salesmen's Commissions	146,050	145,242
Advertising and Dues	35,370	27,523
Travel and Business Promotion	34,972	34,372
Depreciation	5,749	5,416
General Expense	2,129	851
Health and Life Insurance	9,066	7,821
Interest and Bank Charges	14,598	6,825
Legal, Audit and Collection Fees	11,491	7,358
Office Supplies	13,177	13,377
Bad Debts	3,222	4,174
Taxes and Licenses	10,189	9,126
Telephone	13,120	11,529
Donations	733	867
Administrative Service Charges	(13,952)	(66,830)
Total Administrative, General and Selling Expenses	$ 441,108	$ 331,562
Operating Profit	$ 111,565	$ 87,683
Other Income (Deductions)	1,983	(12,503)
Profit Before Income Taxes	$ 113,548	$ 75,180
Federal and State Income Taxes	48,546	33,717
Net Income	$ 65,002	$ 41,463

Sales	$ _____
Less: Direct Expenses	_____
Contribution Margin	$ _____
Less: Indirect Expenses	_____
Net Income	$ _____

This format focuses upon the contribution margin, from which indirect expenses are substracted in determining net profit.

The organizational format of the hospitality service industries' income statement places greatest emphasis on responsibility and controllability, separating the statement into essentially three levels. The first of these is profit from operated departments, that is, departmental revenues less direct departmental expenses. For example, the income statement for a hotel will show room department revenue less direct expenses (such as wages of front desk clerks and maids and laundry); food department revenue less the food cost, preparation cost and service cost; and beverage department sales less the cost of beverage sales and labor.

Profit from operated departments is controllable by, and the responsibility of, the individual department heads. Within each department are lesser responsibility centers which are reported by means of a supporting schedule setting forth the revenue and expense items for that department. This schedule is the primary managerial report for department heads.

The second level of the income statement consists of the overhead expenses which are controllable by the manager. In the hospitality service industries they are referred to as deductions from income and can be thought of as controllable unallocable expenses. These include administrative and general expenses, advertising and promotion, heat, light and power, and repairs and maintenance. These expenses are not allocable to individual operating departments but are controllable by the manager and are his responsibility.

The net result of these first two levels of responsibility is gross operating profit (in a hotel-motor hotel), profit before rent or occupation costs (in a restaurant), or income available for fixed charges (in a club). This is the level of profit generation for which operating managers are held responsible, since the manager has control over revenues realized and costs incurred to this level. Expenses appearing below this level are normally beyond his direct control and are not the operating manager's responsibility.

The third and last level in the income statement is that of noncontrollable expenses, or nonoperating expenses. These include rent, municipal taxes, insurance, interest, depreciation and amortization. These expenses are either totally noncontrollable, or are controlled by those responsible for the overall capital investment and financing (owners or top management).

Basic Structure of the Income Statement

The basic structure of the uniform systems for the hospitality service industries' income statements is shown in the following illustration.

Departmental Revenues (Sales)	$ xxxx
Less: Departmental Expenses	
(Direct Expenses)	xxx
Gross Operating Income	
(Contribution Margin)	$ xxxx
Less: Deductions from Income	
(Controllable Unallocable Expenses)	xxx
Gross Operating Profit	$ xx
Less: Rent, Taxes, Insurance Interest,	
Depreciation (Noncontrollable Expenses)	xx
Net Operating Profit	$ xx

From this organization of revenue and expense, observe that the profitability depends on the amount by which the profit contribution of the operated departments exceeds the controllable and noncontrollable expenses. Similarly, the profit contributions of each operated department depends on the amount by which departmental revenues exceed departmental expenses.

The conclusion, in terms of managerial operating emphasis, is to maximize gross operating income. This differs from maximizing revenues or minimizing expenses. It emphasizes, rather, attaining an optimum combination of revenues and expenses—one which provides the greatest total departmental profit (gross operating income). The hospitality service industries' uniform systems are designed to encourage and facilitate this managerial approach. A uniform system income statement for hotels is shown in Exhibit 4.2.

In the following material, opposite each caption in the statement of income, (Exhibit 4.2), is a reference to a supporting schedule. These schedules present detailed information regarding the composition of each of those captions. Exhibit 4.3 shows Schedule B-1, the detail for the rooms department.

Schedule B-1 provides an analysis of the revenue and expense which determines the rooms department profit. The revenue and expense listed are only those directly allocable to the rooms department.

Supporting schedules (B-2 to B-12), for each of the other departments, operated similar in format to that for the rooms department, are a part of the uniform system income statement for hotels.

EXHIBIT 4.2

The Hotel
Statement of Income
(Short Form)

		Current Period
Departmental Profit (Loss)		
Rooms	Schedule B-1	$
Food	B-2	
Beverages	B-2	
Telephone	B-3	
Barber Shop	B-4	
Beauty Shop	B-5	
Checkrooms and Washrooms	B-6	
Cigar and Newsstand	B-7	
Fountain and Gift Shop	B-8	
Garage, Parking Lot	B-9	
Guest Laundry	B-10	
Swimming Pool, Cabanas, Baths	B-11	
Valet	B-12	
Profit from Operated Departments		$
Other Income	B-13	
Gross Operating Income		$
Deductions from Income		
Administrative and General Expenses	B-14	$
Advertising and Sales Promotion	B-15	
Heat, Light and Power	B-16	
Repairs and Maintenance	B-17	
Total Deductions from Income		$
House Profit		$
Store Rentals	B-18	
Gross Operating Profit		$
Rent, Municipal Taxes and Insurance	B-19	
Profit Before Interest and Depreciation		$
Interest	B-19	
Profit Before Depreciation		$
Depreciation	B-19	
Net Operating Profit (Loss)		$
Other Additions and Deductions	B-20	
Net Income (Loss)—Before Income Taxes		$

EXHIBIT 4.3

The Hotel
Rooms Department
Schedule B-1

	Current Period
Gross Sales	
Guest Rooms	$
Public Room Rentals (Nonbanquet)	
Total Gross Sales	$
Allowances	
Net Sales	$
Departmental Expenses	
Salaries and Wages	$
Vacation and Holiday Pay	
Employees' Meals	
Payroll Taxes and Employee Benefits	
Total Payroll and Related Expenses	$
Other Expenses	
China and Glassware	$
Cleaning Supplies	
Commissions	
Contract Cleaning	
Decorations	
Dry Cleaning	
Garage and Parking	
Guests' Supplies	
Kitchenette Expense	
Laundry	
Linen	
Linen Rental	
Miscellaneous	
Printing and Stationery	
Reservation Expense	
Uniforms	
Total Other Expenses	$
Total Expenses	$
Departmental Profit (Loss)	$

Deductions from Income

The deductions from income include four groupings of expenses: administrative and general expenses; advertising and sales promotion; heat, light and power, and repairs and maintenance. Following are explanations of the expenses that are included in each of these captions in accordance with the uniform systems for the hospitality service industries.

Administrative and General Expenses. This caption includes the salaries and wages of all administrative personnel not directly associated with a particular department, including accounting personnel, data processing personnel, credit office employees and other unallocable salary expenses, plus the fringe benefits associated with their employment. Additionally, other expenses included in this category are outside accountant's fees, credit and collection charges, commission on credit charges, various operating expenses associated with functions which are unallocable to individual departments, franchise fees, legal expenses and management contract fees.

Advertising and Sales Promotion. Included herein are all expenses associated with advertising, such as the salaries of the sales manager and representatives, public relations manager, and associated secretarial and clerical staffs, plus the fringe benefits resulting from their employment. Also included are advertising expenses, such as newspaper, magazine, radio and televison fees. Promotional expenses include civic and community projects, house publications, literature distributed to guests, etc.

Heat, Light and Power. Included herein are wages and fringe benefits of engineers, boilermen, refrigeration mechanics and others directly involved in providing heat, electricity and air conditioning. Purchased fuel, electric current and related supplies are other expenses classified as heat, light and power.

Repairs and Maintenance. This caption includes the salaries, wages and fringe benefits of the repairs and maintenance personnel. Also included are the various supplies required for repairs and maintenance, service contracts, and repairs by outside firms.

Basic Structure: Long Form Income Statement

In addition to the short form statement of income, (Exhibit 4.2), the uniform system of accounts for hotels provides a more detailed format—the long form statement of income. This format presents the totals of the departmental revenues and expenses on the income statement. This long form statement of income is illustrated in Exhibit 4.4.

EXHIBIT 4.4

**The Hotel
Income Statement
(Long Form)**

Operated Departments		Net Sales	Cost of Sales	Current Period Payroll and Related Expenses	Other Expenses	Profit (Loss)
Rooms	Schedule B-1	$	$	$	$	$
Food	B-2					
Beverages	B-2					
Telephone	B-3					
Barber Shop	B-4					
Beauty Parlor	B-5					
Checkrooms and Washrooms	B-6					
Cigar and Newsstand	B-7					
Fountain and Gift Shop	B-8					
Garage, Parking Lot	B-9					
Guest Laundry	B-10					
Swimming Pool, Cabanas, Baths	B-11					
Valet	B-12					
Total Operated Departments		$	$	$	$	$
Other Income	B-13					$
Gross Operating Income						
Deductions from Income						
Administrative and General Expenses	B-14					
Advertising and Sales Promotion	B-15					
Heat, Light and Power	B-16					
Repairs and Maintenance	B-17					
Total Deductions from Income				$	$	
Total House Revenue; Expense and Profit	B-18	$	$	$	$	$
Store Rentals						
Gross Operating Profit	B-19					
Rent, Municipal Taxes and Insurance						
Profit Before Interest and Depreciation	B-19					
Interest						
Profit Before Depreciation	B-19					
Depreciation						
Net Operating Profit (or Loss)	B-20					
Other Additions and Deductions						$
Net Income (Loss) Before Income Taxes						

Similarities in Income Statement Structures

The first uniform system in the hospitality service industries was the uniform system of accounts for hotels. It has been the model and guiding influence for the uniform systems for restaurants, for clubs and for motor hotels.

A few moments of comparing the income statements of the four uniform systems should make apparent the similar structure of each. Differences exist only to provide for the distinct aspects of the four types of operations. As an aid in paralleling the systems, Exhibit 4.5 traces the comparable items through each of the income statements. The chart form, from left to right, shows the departmental food and beverage statement for a hotel; the comparable statement for a club; the income statement for a restaurant, for a hotel and for a city club.

This chart makes it apparent that the uniform systems for restaurants and clubs are actually a combination of the food and beverage schedule and the income statement for hotels. Tracing various items between the three uniform systems reveals this immediately. Thus, the upper portion of the restaurant income statement includes those items which are found in the hotel food and beverage schedule; the lower portion includes those items which are found in the hotel income statement. For purposes of income statement organization, a restaurant can be thought of as a hotel with only one major operating department. And since that department, food and beverage, represents the substance of the operation, its related revenue and expense items are presented in the income statement rather than in supporting schedules. Hence, down to the controllable expense item of music and entertainment, it is similar to the food and beverage schedule for hotels. Beginning with advertising and promotion, the remainder of the statement contains captions which are common to all operations.

Uniform System for Clubs. In the case of the uniform system for clubs, the income statement is structured to relate expenses and operating revenues to the primary source of revenue—member dues. Other than this, and other than those items unique to specific clubs, the organization of the statement is identical to the hotel system.

Because the activities, and thus the revenue and expense items, of city clubs are similar to those of hotels, the income statement for city clubs was selected for the previous illustration. A country club income statement additionally reflects sports activities, primarily golf. Therefore, a grouping of accounts entitled "golf and other sports income" would be included in the statement.

In Exhibit 4.6 income statements are presented for both a country club and city club, and similar items are traced between the two statements. The only material difference between the two statements is the insertion of the sports categories.

Uniform System for Motels, Motor Hotels and Small Hotels. The uniform system for motels, motor hotels and small hotels has two statements of income: one for motels with restaurant operations and one for motels which do not have a restaurant or have leased out their restaurant facilities. For motels and motor hotels with food operations the income statement is similar to the income statement for hotels. The statement for motels without food operations differs, the format being as illustrated in Exhibit 4.7.

THE BALANCE SHEET

The income statement is *the* primary report to management, but the balance sheet is also important for its managerial information content. The balance sheet presents the composition of the assets of an entity and the claims on these assets by creditors and owners in the form of liabilities and equity. It is actually a comprehensive and exhaustive presentation of the accounting formula, assets equal liabilities plus equity. Stated another way, the asset side of the balance sheet sets forth the type and quantity of the particular resources of the firm as of the date of the balance sheet. The liability and equity side of the balance sheet sets forth the source of the funds used to acquire and hold these resources.

Assets are the economic resources of a firm. They exist in the form of tangible property such as buildings and land, and in intangible forms such as leaseholds and copyrights.

Funds used to acquire these assets may come from one of two sources: loans which carry with them an obligation for repayment, and investments by the owners. These are respectively referred to as *debt*, and *equity;* the sources of debt and equity are referred to as *creditors* and *owners*.

For the protection of the creditors the assets of a firm are first made available to the creditors to satisfy their loans in the event that the firm is unable to meet its obligations. The amount by which the assets on the firm's books exceed the liabilities represents the owners' equity or net worth. This is not to say, however, that in the event of the firm's liquidation the owners would receive the dollar amount carried as owners' equity. Instead, the owners would receive the residual after the obligations to creditors are satisfied. Thus, in terms of security of capital, the owner or shareholders' interest is secondary to the creditors' interest. The less secure position occupied by owners, as well as the lack of a contractual obligation for the repayment of investment, is offset by other features of their ownership including control and the potential for a greater return on their investment.

The uniform system balance sheet for hotels is shown in Exhibit 4.8. It differs from other balance sheets only with respect to specific assets and account titles.

Composition of the Balance Sheet: Current Assets

The first group of assets to be examined are current assets, those assets of the organization which will be converted into cash within a relatively short period, usually less than one year.

Cash. In most hospitality service industry operations, cash is of three types: cash on hand in the form of working cash (in cash registers and other such locations as may be required for making change); undeposited cash receipts; and cash in the bank in the form of savings and checking account balances.

Accounts Receivable. Accounts receivable in the hospitality service industries represent obligations owed to the organization from sales made on credit. The amount of accounts receivable is primarily dependent on the credit policies of a business, and thus, credit management is a particularly significant aspect of the hospitality service industries management.

Allowance for Doubtful Accounts. Since it is unlikely that all accounts receivable will be ultimately collected, and to be consistent with the accounting principle which provides for the matching of expense with related revenue, it is necessary to estimate the amount of receivables which will not be collected. The bases upon which bad debts may be estimated includes the operation's past experience, the experience of similar operations, and industry averages.

Inventories. Although inventories normally represent a sizable portion of the assets of most businesses, in the hospitality service industries they are generally insignificant in relation to the total assets of the business. Inventories in the hospitality service industries usually consist of food, beverages and supplies.

Prepaid Expenses. This account represents the portion of licenses, local taxes, insurance, rental of telephone facilities, and other such expenses which have been paid but have not been fully absorbed. That is, additional benefits will be realized after the date of the balance sheet.

Composition of the Balance Sheet: Noncurrent Assets

Noncurrent assets represent amounts which are expected to benefit future periods beyond one year.

Cash Surrender Value of Life Insurance. This account represents an asset in the form of the amount which an insurance company will pay the insured if a life insurance policy is cancelled. It represents the amount by which insurance premiums may exceed the actual insurance cost and is refundable upon cancellation or surrender of the policy.

EXHIBIT 4.6

Country Club
Statement of Income and Expense
(Short Form)

	Schedule Number	Amounts	Percentages
Membership Dues and Guest Privileges	B-1	$	100.00%
Golf and Other Sports: Income or (Loss)			
Golf Operations	B-2	$	%
Swimming Pool	B-3		
Tennis	B-4		
Minor Sports	B-5		
Net Cost of Sports Activities		$	%
Dues Available for Clubhouse Operation and Fixed Charges		$	%
Clubhouse Operating Income or (Loss)			
Food	B-6	$	%
Beverages	B-6		
Cigar Stand	B-7		
Locker Rooms	B-8		
Rooms	B-9		
Bowling	B-10		
Minor Departments	B-11		
Other Income	B-12		
Total		$	%
Deduct: Undistributed Operating Expenses			
Clubrooms Expense	B-13	$	%
Entertainment	B-14		
Administrative and General	B-15		
Payroll Taxes and Employee Benefits	B-15a		
Heat, Light and Power	B-16		
Repairs and Maintenance: Clubhouse	B-17		
Grounds Maintenance	B-18		
Total		$	%
Net Cost of Clubhouse Operation		$	%
Dues Available for Fixed Charges		$	%
Rent, Taxes, and Insurance	B-19		
Dues Available or (Loss) Before Interest and Depreciation		$	%
Interest	B-19		
Dues Available or (Loss) Before Depreciation		$	%
Depreciation and Amortization	B-19		
Net Operating Income or (Loss)		$	%
Other Additions and Deductions			
Net Income or (Loss) — To Members' Equity		$	%

EXHIBIT 4.6

City Club
Statement of Income and Expense
(Short Form)

	Schedule Number	Amounts	Percentages
Membership Dues and Guest Privileges	B-1	$	100.0%
Clubhouse Operating Income or (Loss)			
Rooms	B-2	$	%
Food	B-3		
Beverages	B-3		
Cigar Stand	B-4		
Telephone	B-5		
Valet	B-6		
Baths and Swimming Pool	B-7		
Gymnasium and Athletics	B-8		
Barber Shop	B-9		
Billiards	B-10		
Cardroom	B-11		
Bowling	B-12		
Garage	B-13		
Other Income	B-14		
Total		$	%
Deduct: Undistributed Operating Expenses			
Clubrooms Expense	B-15	$	%
Entertainment	B-16		
Secretary's Office	B-17		
Administrative and General	B-18		
Payroll Taxes and Employee Benefits	B-18a		
Heat, Light and Power	B-19		
Repairs and Maintenance	B-20		
Total		$	%
Clubhouse Net (Loss)			
Dues Available for Fixed Charges		$	%
Add Store Rentals	B-21		
Income Available for Fixed Charges		$	%
Rent, Taxes, and Insurance	B-22		
Income or (Loss) Before Interest and Depreciation		$	%
Interest	B-22		
Income or (Loss) Before Depreciation		$	%
Depreciation and Amortization	B-22		
Net Operating Income or (Loss)		$	%
Other Additions and Deductions			
Net Income or (Loss) — To Members' Equity		$	%

EXHIBIT 4.7

Motels and Motor Hotels without Food Operation
or with Limited Food Operation
Statement of Revenue and Expenses

	Current Period
Revenue	
Room Sales	$
Food Sales	
Restaurant Lease Income	
Telephone Income	
Gas Station, Garage, Parking	
Other Income	
Total Revenue	$
Operating Expenses	
Payroll	$
Payroll Taxes and Employee Benefits	
Total Payroll and Related Expenses	$
Rooms	
Cleaning Supplies and Expenses	$
Commissions	
Guest Supplies	
Laundry	
Linen	
Miscellaneous	
Uniforms	
Total Rooms Expense	$
Cost of Food and Other Items Purchased for Resale	
Cost of Food Purchased and Incidental Expenses	$
Cost of Gas, Oil, Auto Supplies Purchased	
Other Merchandise Purchased for Resale	
Total Cost of Food and Other Items	$
Heat, Light and Power	
Electricity	$
Fuel	
Miscellaneous	
Water	
Total Heat, Light and Power	$
Repairs and Maintenance	$
Swimming Pool Expense	$
General Expenses	
Accounting and Legal Expense	$
Advertising and Sales Promotion	
Insurance	
Miscellaneous	
Printing, Stationery and Postage	
Telephone and Telegrams	
Trade Association Dues and Subscriptions	
Travel Expense	
Total General Expenses	$
Total Operating Expenses	$
House Profit	$
Rentals from Stores	
Gross Operating Profit	$
Deduct: Financial Charges	
Net Profit (Loss) Before Income Taxes	$

Composition of the Balance Sheet: Fixed Assets

Fixed assets (buildings, furniture and fixtures) are those assets of a relatively permanent nature which are used in operating the business and which are not intended for sale. Such assets would include land; buildings; leaseholds and leasehold improvements; furniture and equipment; and linen, china, glassware, silver and uniforms. If depreciable (such as buildings, leasehold improvements, and furniture and equipment), the fixed assets are shown at their purchase price (cost) less the accumulated depreciation to date.

Leasehold and Leasehold Improvements. In the case of a purchased lease or where substantial costs have been paid out to obtain a lease, costs are applicable to future years' rental and are called *leasehold costs.* It is necessary to allocate the leasehold costs over the applicable years of the lease.

During times of rising property values, such as has been experienced generally over recent years, the leasehold may actually represent an asset to the firm beyond the amount of the book value, where the lessor (the party leasing the asset) has the right to sublease. This practice allows him the potential to receive a greater annual sublease payment than the annual lease payment.

It is not unusual in the hospitality service industries to have buildings constructed upon leased land or substantial improvements made to leased buildings. This is referred to as a *leasehold improvement* and its cost should be amortized over the life of the improvement or the remaining period of the lease, whichever is shorter. Even though an option may exist to renew the lease and the leasehold improvement has a useful life in excess of the remaining life of the present lease, there is no assurance that the renewal will be exercised; thus, the leasehold improvement should be amortized over the remaining period of the present lease. For example, if a building having a useful life of thirty years is built on leased land with a twenty-five-year lease with the option to renew for an additional twenty-five years, the building should be amortized over the twenty-five-year period of the initial lease.

Linen, China, Glassware, Silver and Uniforms. This account represents the approximate value of these items and is determined by actual physical inventory basing the values on the original cost, age and conditions of the items. Generally, operating inventories not in use are carried at cost and in-use items are carried at some precentage of cost with replacements expensed.

Deferred Expenses. Deferred expenses represent expenditures made whose benefits will be realized over an extended future period. In this category we find such items as organization and financing expenses, and pre-opening expenses.

EXHIBIT 4.8

Hotel
Balance Sheet
December 31, 19XX

Assets

Current Assets
  Cash on Hand $
  Cash in Bank   _____ $
  Notes Receivable $
  Accounts Receivable
  Accrued Interest Receivable
    Total Receivables $ _____
    Less: Allowance for Doubtful Accounts
  Marketable Securities $ _____
  Deposits on Purchases
  Inventories of Merchandise
  Inventories of Supplies
  Prepaid Expenses
    Insurance
    Taxes
    Rental of Telephone Facilities
    Other Prepaid Expenses   _____
  Other Current Assets
    Total Current Assets $ _____
Deposits on Long-term Leases, Cash and Securities
Due from Officers and Employees
Due from Affiliated Companies
Funds in Hands of Trustees
Deposits with Public Utility Corporations
Cash Surrender Value of Life Insurance
Investments
Fixed Assets
  Land $
  Buildings $
    Less: Accumulated Depreciation   _____
  Leasehold and Leasehold Improvements $
    Less: Accumulated Amortization   _____
  Furniture and Equipment $
    Less: Accumulated Depreciation   _____
  Linen, China, Glassware, Silver and Uniforms   _____
Deferred Expenses
  Organization and Financing Expenses $
  Pre-opening Expenses
  Discount and Expense on Long-term Debt
  Rental Agent's Commissions
  Alterations for Tenants
  Advertising
  Other Deferred Expenses   _____
Trade Advertising Contracts

Other Assets

Total Assets $ _____

EXHIBIT 4.8

(continued)

Liabilities and Stockholders' Equity

Current Liabilities $
  Notes Payable
  Accounts Payable, Trade
  Taxes Payable and Accrued
  Income Taxes, Federal and State
  Dividends Payable
  Accrued Expenses $
    Salaries and Wages
    Interest on Long-term Debt
    Interest, Other
    Other Accrued Expenses ————
  Deposits on Banquets and Room Reservations
  Credit Balances in Accounts Receivable
  Unearned Income
  Long-term Debt Due within One Year
  Other Current Liabilities ————
    Total Current Liabilities $
Due to Affiliated and Associated Companies
Deposits on Long-term Leases
Trade Advertising Due-Bills Outstanding
Long-term Debt (Less Portion Due within One Year,
  Shown under Current Liabilities)
    Bonds and Mortgages $
    Debentures
    Notes ————
    Total Liabilities $
Deferred Credits
  Excess of Estimated Monthly Expense Over Actual Purchases
    Repairs and Maintenance $
    Linen, China, Glassware, Silver and Uniforms
    Other ————
*Stockholders' Equity
  Capital Stock
    Authorized Shares, Par Value
      $———— each $
    Issued ———— Shares
      Less: Treasury Stock ———— Shares ————
    Outstanding ———— Shares
  Retained Earnings (or Less Deficit) ————
    Total Stockholders' Equity
Total Liabilities and Stockholders' Equity $————

(If Partnership or Proprietorship)
  *Partners' Equity (or Owners' Equity if Individual)
    A $
    B ————

Total Partners' Equity $————

Organization and finance expenses are the expenses initially incurred in organizing an enterprise, and the expenses incurred in connection with long-term debt financing. Pre-opening expenses are all of the costs incurred prior to opening the hotel, including payroll and advertising costs.

Composition of the Balance Sheet: Liabilities

Current Liabilities. Current liabilities represent liabilities which must be paid within one year.

Accounts Payable: Trade. This account represents amounts owing to purveyors from whom merchandise equipment or other goods and services connected with the operation of the property have been purchased.

Taxes Payable and Accrued. This includes all taxes collected from or accrued for employees in the form of social security, unemployment, and income taxes; from guests in the form of sales and room taxes; and other accrued taxes such as personal property and real estate taxes.

Accrued Expenses. Consistent with the matching theory, all expenses incurred during the period which have not been paid or are not included in other liability accounts should be shown here. This includes accrued salaries, wages and interest. Other accrued items which might appear in this category include vacation pay, utilities, telephone expense, and rent.

Deposits on Banquets and Room Reservations. If deposits have been collected for future dates the unearned income is shown in this category.

Long-term Debt Due within One Year. This account includes that portion of long-term obligations which must be paid within one year and thus represent a current liability. In the uniform system of accounts for clubs, this account is titled "Amortization of Principal Due Within One Year."

Trade Advertising Due Bills Outstanding. Due bills result from agreements between various advertising media and a hotel, motor hotel, or restaurant, to furnish rooms and service in exchange for advertising. Thus, as the advertising is furnished, the due bills become liabilities of the property which must be honored under specified terms upon presentation. Although the practice is much less common today than in the past, the basic philosophy was considered sound in that it exchanged rooms that would have gone unoccupied for advertising opportunities that would have gone unrealized.

Long-term Debt. This account represents the portion of long-term obligations that are due beyond one year, in contrast to that portion due within one year, which is included under current liabilities. The long-term debt account includes such debt instruments as bonds, mortgages, and notes payable.

Composition of the Balance Sheet: Stockholders' Equity

This section of the balance sheet represents that portion of the business which is the ownership interest. For profit-oriented enterprises, the ownership may be in one of three forms.

1. Proprietorship: an unincorporated business owned by a single individual.
2. Partnership: an unincorporated business owned by two or more people.
3. Corporation: a business incorporated under the laws of a state with ownership held by the stockholders of the corporation.

In the case of a nonprofit incorporated club, the members are actually owners of the club and thus, in many respects, are similar to stockholders in a profit-oriented corporation.

The balance sheet in Exhibit 4.8 shows the equity section as it appears in the case of a corporation, and is supplemented with the format used in the case of a proprietorship or partnership (see final items in left-hand column).

In an incorporated business, the ownership in the business is represented by shares of stock in the corporation. Each share of stock represents a fraction of ownership of the corporation.

Capital Stock

Stock in a corporation may be essentially of two basic types: common stock and preferred stock.

The stock of a corporation having only one class of stock is referred to as *common stock*. The basic rights that ordinarily accompany ownership of shares of common stock in a corporation include:

1. The right to vote for directors, and thereby have representation in management of the business; and the right to vote in circumstances requiring the approval of the majority of the stockholders (including the amendment of the bylaws of the corporation, the sale or purchase of a substantial portion of the corporation, or the purchase of another corporation).

2. The right to share in the profits of the corporation by receiving dividends as declared by the board of directors, at their discretion.

3. The right to share residually in the distribution of assets in the event of liquidation; that is, prior to any distribution of assets to common stockholders, all creditors must be paid in full to the extent of the available assets.

4. The right to subscribe to additional shares of stock in the event that the corporation issues additional stock. Referred to as *preemptive rights*, this allows a stockholder to maintain his original percentage of ownership in the company in

the case of additional stock issuance, should he so desire. This fourth right does not always exist, however, because some corporate charters do not provide for preemptive rights for shareholders.

Preferred Stock

Where a second class of stock exists, it is normally referred to as *preferred stock*, or stock having preferential rights over other classes of stock. Generally speaking, preferred stockholders share in the corporation's profits prior to common stockholders (but only to a limited degree); they share in the liquidation of a corporation prior to common stockholders; and they may have preemptive and voting rights in the corporation.

The equity section of a balance sheet for a corporation is composed of two types or classifications of equity: contributed capital, and retained earnings. Contributed capital consists of the investment by shareholders. Retained earnings do not necessarily represent cash available for distribution because the earnings retained may have been invested in various types of assets (such as buildings, investments, and accounts receivable).

By law, the charter of each corporation must specify the maximum number of shares of each class of stock that may be issued by that particular corporation. This maximum number of shares is referred to as *authorized shares;* in no case may the number of shares which have been issued exceed the number of shares which have been authorized for that class of stock. When a corporation is initially chartered, the authorized number of shares is established by the incorporators, and only by amendment to the charter may this authorization be increased.

The number of shares which have been sold to the stockholders is referred to as the number of *shares issued.* However, the number of *shares outstanding* refers to the shares presently held by stockholders, as the corporation itself may repurchase and hold some shares. Thus, 100 percent ownership of the corporation lies with the total outstanding shares.

Those shares which have been reacquired by the corporation and have not been cancelled are referred to as *treasury stock.* Treasury stock consists of a corporation's own stock which has been issued, fully paid, but reacquired by the corporation, and not formally cancelled. Treasury stock may be held indefinitely by the corporation or may be resold, in which case it would then again become outstanding stock. Treasury stock carries no voting rights, no preemptive rights, and no rights to share in the corporation's assets in the event of liquidation. Treasury stock may be acquired by a corporation by purchasing the stock from shareholders, by having the stock donated to the corporation, or by accepting the stock in settlement of a debt owed to the corporation.

Exhibit 4.9 is an example of a stockholders' equity section of a balance sheet, and shows the existence of common stock and preferred stock, the number of shares of stock authorized and issued, and the number of shares of treasury stock held by the corporation.

EXHIBIT 4.9

Stockholders' Equity Section of a Balance Sheet

Stockholders' Equity
   Capital Stock

Preferred Stock—7% Cumulative, $40 Par Value; Authorized and Issued, 400 Shares	$ 16,000	
Common Stock—No Par Value; Stated Value $5; Authorized and Issued, 1,000 Shares, of which 50 Shares are Held in the Treasury	5,000	
		$ 21,000
Paid-in Capital in Excess of Par or Stated Value		17,000
Retained Earnings		44,000
Total		$ 82,000
Deduct: Cost of Common Stock Held in the Treasury		1,000
Stockholders' Equity		$ 81,000

In this corporation there have been some 400 shares of 7 percent cumulative preferred stock authorized and issued, with all of these 400 shares outstanding, since the treasury holds no preferred stock. The cumulative feature means that if the corporation in any given year is not able or does not wish to pay the 7 percent dividend, or $2.80 ($40 par value × 7 percent) per share of preferred stock, no dividends in future years may be paid to common stockholders until not only the current preferred dividends are paid, but all unpaid past years' dividends also are paid in full. The preferred stock paid-in capital is $16,000 ($40 par value × 400 shares).

Common stock outstanding is 950 shares: 1,000 shares authorized and issued, less 50 shares held in the treasury. Common stock paid-in capital is $5,000 ($5.00 stated value × 1,000 shares). Thus, paid-in capital in total is $21,000; this investment will normally remain in the corporation throughout its existence.

Capital in excess of par or stated value represents the value of assets received for stock in excess of the stock's par or stated value. For example, if a preferred stock with a $40 par value were sold for $45 per share, the $40 is capital and the remaining $5.00 is capital in excess of par. Similarly if a common stock with a $5.00 stated value is sold for $20, $5.00 is capital and $15 is capital in excess of stated value.

Composition of the Balance Sheet: Members' Equity

Exhibit 4.10 shows the members' equity section of a balance sheet for a city or country club; it is quite similar to the equity section of a corporation balance sheet. Just as in the corporation balance sheet, it is composed of the members' investment (contributed capital, in the case of a profit-oriented corporation) and retained earnings.

EXHIBIT 4.10

Club
Members' Equity Portion of the Balance Sheet

Members' Equity			
Members' Investment			
Capital Stock or Certificates	$ 90,000		
Initiation Fees	40,000		
Contributions	10,000		
		$140,000	
Retained Earnings or (Deficit)			
Balance Beginning of Year		$330,000	
Net Income or (Loss)—Year			
to Date—Exhibit B		30,000	
Total		$360,000	
Total Members' Equity			$500,000

Members' investments are received in three forms: the purchase of capital stock or certificates by members; initiation fees received; and contributions received. These, in total, represent the capital contributions of the members. The retained earnings or deficits represent the accumulation of net income or loss over the life of the club. Frequently, the retained earnings in total are negative, due to net losses which, over the life of the club, have exceeded income. Thus, in such a situation, the total of the members' equity is less than the total of the members' capital contributions.

UNIFORM SYSTEMS: A FINAL NOTE

Each of the uniform systems for the hospitality service industries referred to in this chapter is published in book form by the respective sponsoring association. As an aid to implementing and using each system and in facilitating the operation of the particular segment of the hospitality service industry, the books contain substantial additional information. For example, in the *Uniform System of Accounts for Hotels*, supplementary formats are provided for classifying and developing an overall schedule of salaries and wages for a hotel, with department-by-department breakdowns and guides for the proper classification of various positions.

Included in the *Uniform System of Accounts for Restaurants* are examples of the make-up of income statements and balance sheets for representative types of restaurant operations. Additionally, a system of "Recordkeeping for the Small Restaurant" is provided. Appendixes to the uniform systems for restaurants include a section on food cost control, beverage cost control, and a summarization of the Fair Labor Standards Act (otherwise known as the federal wage and hour law), containing the portions of this law that apply to the restaurant business.

The *Uniform System of Accounts for Clubs* includes, in addition to a schedule for the distribution and control of payroll costs, appendixes on "Comparative Forms of Operating Statements," the generation of "Operating Statistics for Clubs," and a "Simplified Food and Beverage Cost Control System for Clubs."

Additionally, an important aid to implementing and using the various hospitality service industry uniform systems is the *Expense and Payroll Dictionary* for each. In these various dictionaries, practically every expense item that will be encountered in the operation of a hotel, motor hotel, restaurant, or club is alphabetically listed and classified by major category and subclassification. For example, in the "Expense and Payroll Dictionary for Clubs," the expense item of fire insurance is indicated as belonging in the category of fixed charges, and under the subclassification, "insurance-building and contents." In the payroll section of the *Expense and Payroll Dictionary* for hotels, it is indicated that the entry "mail clerks" belongs in "rooms department" under the subclassification of "front office."

SUMMARY

The primary financial statements generated by an accounting system are the income statement, balance sheet and source and application of funds statement. Management is the internal user of these financial statements, and generally relies heavily upon them. The external users include stockholders and absentee owners, creditors, governmental agencies and the general public.

To facilitate accounting, to provide uniformity and comparability, and to maximize the effectiveness of the financial statements in presenting their information, uniform systems of accounts have been developed in the hospitality service industries for hotels, motels, motor hotels and small hotels, nursing homes, hospitals, restaurants, and clubs.

Because the income statement is most significantly effected by the information requirements of the hospitality service industries, the traditional form of a manufacturing income statement is not used. Rather, the income statement is based upon the contribution approach, whereby expenses are deducted in the order of their direct association with revenues. This results in an income statement in which departmental expenses are first deducted, followed by deductions from income, and finally, uncontrollable expenses, in order to arrive at net operating profit.

Discussion Questions

1. Why has there been a change of interest from the balance sheet to the income statement by creditors and potential creditors?
2. How does the standardization of accounts facilitate the managerial function?
3. How do grouping and detail of the income statement define the control responsibility?
4. What is the basis for the organization of the income statement?
5. What is a uniform system of accounts?
6. What are the major external groups of financial statement users and how do their information needs differ?
7. From the organization of the hospitality service industries' income statement, where should department heads place their emphasis? How is this done?
8. How is the uniform system income statement for restaurants derived from that for hotels?
9. What is the *Expense and Payroll Dictionary?*
10. What are pre-opening expenses?

Problem 1

Using the uniform system of accounts for restaurants, prepare an income statement in good form, using the following information.

Food Revenues	$180,000
Beverage Revenues	100,000
Food Purchases	6,000
Beverage Purchases	26,000
Beginning Foods Inventory	5,000
Beginning Beverage Inventory	4,000
Ending Foods Inventory	5,000
Ending Beverage Inventory	5,000
Reservation Expense	4,000
Office Salaries Expense	26,000

Problem 1 (continued)

Advertising Expense	30,000
Insurance Expense	5,000
Interest Expense	5,000
Depreciation: Building	36,000
Depreciation: Furniture	26,000
Miscellaneous General Expense	20,000

Problem 2

Prepare a classified balance sheet as of December 31, 1971 from the following information provided by the Jackson Hotel, using the appropriate uniform system.

Cash	$16,500
Retained Earnings	66,700
Accounts Payable	6,600
Prepaid Rental of Computer Facilities	1,000
Wages and Salaries Payable	3,400
Accumulated Depreciation: Buildings	14,400
Food and Beverage Inventory	18,500
Tableware and Linens	1,900
Stationery and Office Supplies	300
Capital Stock	50,400
U.S. Government Bonds	10,000
Allowance for Uncollectible Accounts	500
Building	62,900
Accounts Receivable	22,500
Furniture and Fixtures	17,700
Land	25,000
Advance Deposits on Rooms	500
Income Tax Payable	9,500
Bank Loan	13,000
Accumulated Depreciation: Furniture and Fixtures	6,400
Mortgage Payable	28,000
Notes Receivable	3,300
Accrued Interest Payable	900
Unexpired Insurance	700
Accumulated Depreciation: Tableware and Linens	700
Investment in Land (Future Building Site)	20,700

Problem 3

The Mercury Hotel operates with annual accounting periods that end each December 31. While the hotel's accountant was in the midst of the preparation of the financial statements for the year ended December 31, 1971, he was suddenly hospitalized. You have been asked to complete his work.

The accountant had completed most of the required adjustment of entries for the period and the bookkeeper has provided you with the following trial balance of accounts which reflects the completed adjustments.

THE MERCURY HOTEL
TRIAL BALANCE, DECEMBER 31, 1971

	Debit	Credit
Cash on Hand	$ 2,500	
Cash in Bank	111,900	
Accounts Receivable	129,150	
Inventories	27,200	
Prepaid Expenses	33,300	
Investments	33,100	
Land	178,300	
Land Improvements	5,500	
Buildings—at cost	2,151,100	
Furniture and Equipment—at cost	562,000	
Accumulated Depreciation on Fixed Assets		$1,243,900
Franchise Fee	26,800	
Accounts Payable		87,200
Payroll Taxes Payable		900
Accrued Expenses		21,126
Long-term Debt		878,200
Common Stock		450,000
Capital Surplus		150,000
Retained Earnings		326,000
Room Sales: transient		863,800
: permanent		62,400
Rooms Payroll Expense	198,200	
Employee Meals	3,600	
Payroll Taxes and Benefits	12,300	
Uniforms	400	
Laundry	31,100	
Linen	21,200	
China and Glass	1,100	
Cleaning Supplies	8,600	
Subtotal	$3,537,350	$4,083,526

Problem 3 (continued)

	Debit	Credit
Rooms: Dry Cleaning	$ 600	
Contract Cleaning	1,700	
Guest Supplies	6,700	
Printing and Stationery	1,900	
Decorations	500	
Paper Supplies	1,000	
Miscellaneous	4,200	
Food Sales		$ 734,600
Cost of Food Sold	313,100	
Food: Payroll	299,300	
Employees' Meals	12,600	
Payroll Taxes and Benefits	9,400	
Uniforms	100	
Laundry	11,800	
Linen	2,000	
Kitchen Fuel	3,500	
China and Glass	5,100	
Utensils	3,900	
Cleaning Supplies	6,300	
Contract Cleaning	800	
Paper Supplies	4,000	
Menus	3,300	
Banquet Expenses	1,100	
Miscellaneous	2,100	
Beverage Sales		200,500
Cost of Beverages Sold	64,000	
Beverage: Payroll	37,800	
Employees' Meals	1,300	
Payroll Taxes and Benefits	1,800	
Uniforms	600	
China and Glass	1,500	
Cleaning Supplies	2,300	
Contract Cleaning	700	
Paper Supplies	400	
Beverage Lists	300	
Banquet Expenses	200	
Bar Expenses	900	
Licenses	2,200	
Miscellaneous	500	
Newsstand: Sales		32,100
Cost of Sales	28,500	
Payroll and Related Expenses	600	
Other Expenses	400	
Telephone: Sales		31,500
Cost of Sales	42,500	
Payroll and Related Expenses	14,000	
Other Expenses	1,000	
Other Income		24,150
Subtotal—Page 2	$896,500	$1,022,850

Problem 3 (continued)

		Debit	Credit
Administrative and General:	Payroll	$ 116,900	
	Other Expenses	101,400	
Advertising and Promotion :	Payroll	300	
	Other Expenses	44,500	
Heat, Light and Power:	Payroll	22,000	
	Other Expenses	74,300	
Repairs and Maintenance:	Payroll	11,300	
	Other Expenses	42,100	
Store Rentals			$ 18,000
State and Municipal Taxes		96,500	
Fire Insurance		3,500	
Interest Expenses		8,326	
Depreciation Expense		134,400	
Provision for Federal Income Taxes		35,000	
Subtotal —This Page		$ 690,526	$ 18,000
Subtotal—Page Two		896,500	1,022,850
Subtotal—Page One		3,537,350	4,083,526
Grand Total		$5,124,376	$5,124,376

Additional Information

The following items had not been considered by the accountant before his illness.

(a) On June 1, 1970, the hotel purchased a three-year fire insurance policy for $1,800. The remaining portion of this policy, after the appropriate adjustment on December 31, 1970, is included in prepaid expenses.

An additional *two-year* fire insurance policy was purchased on August 31, 1971 for $1,800. The total cost of the policy was charged to fire insurance expense at the time of purchase.

(b) The true value of the land owned by the hotel was appraised at $225,000 by two members of the National Association of Real Estate Appraisers. Their consulting fee of $300 was not recorded and has not been paid although the hotel has been billed.

(c) The long-term debt is composed of 7 percent mortgage bonds. The annual interest expense for 1971 is payable on January 15, 1972 and bonds worth $69,500 will mature and be paid during 1972.

(d) The annual depreciation of the furniture in the lobby of the hotel has not been recorded. This furniture was purchased on July 1, 1970 at a cost of $12,000. It has an estimated life of five years with no salvage value. The sum-of-the-years-digits method has been chosen for the calculation of depreciation.

Problem 3 (continued)

(e) On December 20, 1971, the board of directors declared a dividend of $1.00 per share of outstanding common stock to be paid on January 10, 1972, to stockholders of record on December 30. These events have not been recorded in the hotel's accounting records.

(f) Investments include twenty ATT $1,000 bonds. The stated annual interest rate on the bonds is 6 percent. The annual interest for 1971 has not been received as of December 31, 1971.

(g) In the food department, wages earned but unpaid as of December 31, 1971 totaled $1,200. Payroll taxes and benefits are estimated at 7 percent of the food department's payroll. (All other payroll adjustments have been made.)

(h) Customer deposits on banquets which are scheduled for January 1972 have been included in food sales in the amount of $450.

(i) Guest room furniture which had been fully depreciated was sold to an employee on account for $150. No entry was made to record this transaction.

(j) Based on a careful investigation of the accounts receivable and on past experience, the accountant estimated that $3,200 of the present accounts would be uncollectable. Management wants to use the reserve method to write off bad debts.

Required

1. After considering the additional information, describe *briefly* how and why (or why not) each item must be accounted.

2. In accordance with the uniform system of accounts for hotels, prepare the following financial statements for the Mercury Hotel for the year ended December 31, 1971.

   a. Balance sheet (Exhibit A)
   b. Income statement (Exhibit B—long form)
   c. Schedule B-1, Rooms
   d. Schedule B-2, Food and Beverages

Emphasis should be placed on proper classifications and form.

Problem 4

Prepare an income statement for the M & M Restaurant from the following information using the correct uniform system form.

Sales:	Food	$48,684.00
	Beverage	28,470.00
Rent and Depreciation		$ 8,700.00
Other Income		16,872.41
Cost of Sales:	Food	70%
	Beverage	60%
Expenses:	Payroll	$15,642.00
	Bonus and Vacation Pay	1,876.52
	Employees' Meals	367.00
	Employee Benefits	872.67
	Advertising and Sales Promotion	670.31
	Utilities	658.00
	Administrative and General	9,673.42
	Repairs and Maintenance	976.44

CHAPTER 5

The Impact of
Price Level Changes

The purchasing power of a dollar has declined consistently since World War II. Consequently, today's dollar commands less than half as many goods and services as it did in 1941. The effects of inflation are felt at every level of the economy and the breadth of problems it creates becomes more significant every year. Inflation is an integral part of the economic environment in which firms must operate; the upward spiral of prices presents problems to all firms and their managers. However, because of the unique nature of hospitality service industries, inflationary trends are, perhaps, even more significant than in other industries.

The manager of a hospitality service business must base many of his decisions on both formal financial statements and informal management reports. If his conclusions and decisions are to be valid, the data he uses should include some recognition of inflation. One method to use in providing for inflation is to adjust the financial statements and reports for price level changes.

In this chapter, the needs of operating managers will be considered. Although external users (such as stockholders, creditors, and other outsiders who are interested in the firm's activities) are not considered directly in this chapter, the material is equally relevant for them. However, their information needs are somewhat different, since they generally relate to the firm as a whole rather than to its specific operating units.

The following questions emphasize the importance of recognizing changing price levels:

Do those who read financial statements truly realize the implications inherent in a failure to adjust for price level changes? If so, how do they react to the need for additional information? If not, how can they possibly make valid and reliable judgments based on data compiled by conventional accounting methods?

Are accountants doing all they can to insure that information is really meaningful to the decision-maker? Is the information understandable? Is it possible to modify conventional accounting information by using more modern methods?

THE ACCOUNTING DILEMMA

Since the price level phenomenon is an economic reality and should thus be considered explicitly in developing financial information, why are conventional (unadjusted) statements still prepared?

Conventional accounting measurements are based on the assumption that the dollar represents a stable unit of measure. This "stable dollar" assumption has served for many years as a relatively unyielding standard for developing financial statements and reports. Recently, however, this standard has been subjected to substantial criticism. Financial statements and management reports based on the stable dollar assumption are severely limited in their capacity to reveal the effects of inflation. When using conventional statements, each reader must consider whether inflation has occurred to the extent that unadjusted data are unreliable as a basis for their decision-making.

Consider briefly some management areas which are affected by inflationary pressures.

Performance Comparisons. Managers use comparative data as a basis for evaluating the firm's progress. Unadjusted data may lead to erroneous conclusions.

Pricing Decisions. Price schedules should be adjusted whenever necessary to coincide with price level changes, for if prices are not adjusted upwards in times of rising costs, a "profit squeeze" will result.

Renovation and Replacement Decisions. Significant investments in facilities and relatively high obsolescence rates prevail throughout the hospitality service industries. Thus, renovation and replacement decisions are extremely important. Depreciation treatment in conventional accounting methods does not necessarily fulfill current decision-making requirements.

PERFORMANCE COMPARISONS

Managers at every level are concerned with attaining goals that have been established for their areas of responsibility. These goals vary, depending on the kind of operation involved.

Let us assume that the management of a medium-sized listed corporation in the lodging and feeding industry is working toward attaining a 20 percent improvement in sales each year. Exhibit 5.1 shows sales produced from 1965 to 1969.

In a conventional approach to this analysis, each year's sales are compared to sales in the base year, 1965. Using 1965 as 100 percent, it appears that sales have increased approximately 20 percent per year (that is, $600 = 120 percent of $500; $700 = 140 percent of $500; etc).

EXHIBIT 5.1

Management Report
Sales Growth Analysis

Year	Sales*
1965	$500
1966	600
1967	700
1968	800
1969	900

*Historical data (unadjusted for price level changes).

These data would be more meaningful, however, if they were adjusted to reflect the "real growth" in sales. This can be done most effectively by adjusting each sales figure for relevant price level changes.

SELECTING AN INDEX

The first step in developing price level adjusted data is to select an appropriate index. The index should relate directly to the data being analyzed. For example, if revenues are generated from foods and beverage operations, a specialized index is the most appropriate; but if a variety of goods and services are provided for customers, a more generalized index can be applied. It is extremely important to select the index which appears to be most meaningful for the circumstances. Only then can a manager develop valid data for evaluating his progress toward chosen goals.

Three widely accepted general indexes are available for use in the price level adjustment process. These are the Consumer Price Index (CPI), the Wholesale Price Index (WPI), and the Gross National Product Implicit Price Deflator (GNP). Exhibit 5.2 summarizes the changes in these various indexes for the nine-year period, 1960-1968. The base year period, 1957-1959, is shown as 100 percent and changes in prices are computed as a percentage (for example, 101.2 is equal to 101.2 percent). Thus, it is easy to interpret the extent of price change during this time period.

EXHIBIT 5.2

Price Indexes

Year	Consumer Price Index	Wholesale Price Index	GNP Deflator
1957-1959	100.0	100.0	100.0
1960	103.1	100.7	103.3
1961	104.2	100.3	104.6
1962	105.4	100.6	105.7
1963	106.7	100.3	107.1
1964	108.1	100.5	108.9
1965	109.9	102.5	110.9
1966	113.1	105.9	113.9
1967	116.3	106.1	117.4
1968	121.2	108.7	121.8

The Consumer Price Index (CPI) measures average changes in retail prices of the "market basket" of goods and services generally purchased by an average consumer. Data are accumulated from selected communities and on selected products. These data are summarized and the index is developed to indicate the changes in price levels throughout the United States.

The Wholesale Price Index (WPI) measures average changes in prices on commodities sold in primary markets throughout the country. These commodities generally are sold in wholesale lots. Consequently, this index probably has less value to managers in the hospitality service industries.

The GNP (Gross National Product) Implicit Price Deflator is the most comprehensive available index. It is used by the Federal Government to value the nation's production during various time periods. In effect, the GNP deflator measures the value relationships of all goods and services produced in the nation's economy; that is, it compares output in the current year to that produced in the base year.

The GNP deflator is used in the following illustration because the subject motel offers a full range of hospitality services. However, the choice of index numbers rests with the manager. He is most familiar with the nature of his operations, the goods and services produced, and the specific environment in which he must earn profits. In the final analysis, these factors must guide the entire adjustment process.

APPLYING THE INDEX NUMBERS

The calculation of the price level adjustment for sales is shown in Exhibit 5.3.

EXHIBIT 5.3

Price Level Adjustment of Sales

Year	Sales*	Multiplier**	Adjusted Sales	Adjusted Increases	Calculation	"Real" Cumulative Growth Rate
1964	$500	122/109	$560	—		
1965	600	122/111	660	$100	100÷560	18%
1966	700	122/114	750	190	190÷560	34
1967	800	122/117	840	280	280÷560	50
1968	900	122/122	900	340	340÷560	60

*Historical data (unadjusted for price level changes), Exhibit 5.1.
**GNP Deflator Series, Exhibit 5.2.

Historical (unadjusted) sales volume data have been adjusted by applying the percentage change (base year to current year). Thus, the $500 sales revenues generated in 1964 are equivalent to $560 in terms of 1969 dollars.[1] This process is continued until all prior year sales data have been restated.

Note than an annual index number is applied in the adjustment process. Monthly and/or quarterly data might just as easily be used. In developing a proper index number, therefore, the time period must be defined. If a year is used as a basis for evaluation, monthly data may be averaged—either as a simple average (all monthly indexes added and divided by twelve) or as a weighted average (assigning weights to months according to their importance in sales activity, etc.). The illustration in Exhibit 5.3 is based on the assumption that all months are equally important with respect to volume. The resulting average is then applied to each year's total sales as a multiplier.

---

1. Looking at the 1964 data, it is seen that the multiplier is 122/109. This is the same as saying that prices have increased by approximately 12 percent (122 ÷ 109 = 112 percent) during the 1964-1968 time period. Thus, if we are to compare dollars of equal purchasing power, this change in prices (12 percent) must be taken into consideration.

The significance of this data is obvious in an evaluation of the firm's rate of growth. The unadjusted data indicate that the firm's sales have grown 80 percent during the five-year period. Thus, the management would appear to be meeting the sales growth goal. But the *true* growth after considering price level changes is only 60 percent over the five-year period.

These differences in data are portrayed even more vividly in Exhibit 5.4.

EXHIBIT 5.4

**Management Report
Sales Growth Analysis (Rate)**

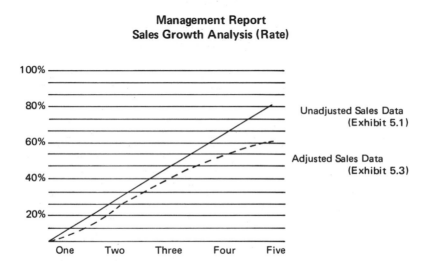

The gap between the lines represents the differences that exist between unadjusted data (historical dollars) and those which have been adjusted for price level changes. This type of information will undoubtedly help management to evaluate the firm's progress. Because the data is more valid, decisions should be improved substantially.

Other data can be analyzed similarly to accommodate the comparison of operations. For example, data for net income before tax could be developed through the same procedures. Graphic comparison (as shown) might then be useful to management when examining the firm's progress in attaining specified objectives. In general, this approach should provide a foundation for evaluating the significance of price level changes. By adjusting the data on which decisions are based, the probability of selecting proper alternatives should be improved.

HISTORICAL DOLLAR REPORTS

Operating managers frequently conduct analysis using historical dollar reports. In Exhibit 5.5, food and beverage departmental profits (before other departmental expenses) for a three-year period are presented.

EXHIBIT 5.5

Management Report
Gross Profits
Food and Beverage Operations
(Historical Dollars)

	Food			Beverages		
	1966	1967	1968	1966	1967	1968
Sales	$ 80	$ 90	$100	$ 32	$36	$ 40
Cost of Goods Sold						
Food Costs	$ 30	$ 33	$ 36			
Preparation, Services and Other Direct Labor	28	31	34			
Beverage Costs				$ 10	$ 12	$ 15
Total	$ 58	$ 64	$ 70	$ 10	$ 12	$ 15
Departmental Profit (Before Other Departmental Expenses)	$ 22	$ 26	$ 30	$ 22	$ 24	$ 25

In the illustration, the firm shows moderate increases in gross profit during the three-year period. When evaluating these data, however, the manager must note explicitly that prices have changed—perhaps significantly—during this period. Adjustment procedures should be applied in order to make the data comparable.

DEVELOPING ADJUSTED OPERATING DATA

Generally, adjusted data provide a more valid foundation for making pricing decisions. Therefore, numerous price indexes are available for use by hospitality service managers. In Exhibits 5.6, 5.7 and 5.8, three types of indexes are illustrated to indicate the kinds of data that are available for adjustment purposes. Every analyst must develop his own approach since each environment is unique.

EXHIBIT 5.6

Food Indexes

Month and Year	Restaurant Meals	Meats, Poultry and Fish
1966		
January	120.5	112.9
February	121.0	115.7
March	121.5	116.9
April	121.0	115.6
May	122.5	113.9
June	123.1	114.2
July	123.9	114.3
August	124.4	114.5
September	125.0	114.8
October	125.5	113.8
November	126.2	111.8
December	126.8	110.9
Annual Average	122.	114.
1967		
January	127.3	110.3
February	127.7	110.7
March	128.0	110.0
April	128.6	109.0
May	129.0	108.5
June	129.4	111.6
July	130.0	112.3
August	130.6	113.1
September	131.1	113.4
October	131.6	112.3
November	132.3	111.4
December	132.7	111.2
Annual Average	128.	111.
1968		
January	140.4	111.6
February	140.8	112.0
March	141.3	113.1
April	134.6	112.7
May	135.3	113.0
June	136.0	113.2
July	136.7	114.0
August	137.5	115.3
September	138.3	115.5
October	139.1	115.4
November	139.6	114.6
December	141.6	114.4
Annual Average	137.	114.

Source: Monthly Labor Review, U.S. Department of Labor, Bureau of Labor Statistics (Washington, D.C.: U.S. Government Printing Office, 1966-1968).

EXHIBIT 5.7

Beverages Index

Year	Beer[1]	Whiskey[2]	Wine[3]	Combined Index[4]
1964	100.6	104.9	99.9	102
1965	102.3	105.3	100.4	103
1966	105.5	105.9	100.9	104
1967	108.9	108.9	102.1	107
1968	114.9	108.7	106.0	110
1968 (by quarters)				
First quarter	112.9	108.4	105.8	109
Second quarter	114.3	108.7	105.9	110
Third quarter	115.9	108.8	106.2	110
Fourth quarter	119.3	109.0	107.1	112

Source: Survey of Current Business, U.S. Department of Commerce, Office of Business Economics, Vol. 44-48, 1964-1968 (Washington, D.C.: U.S. Government Printing Office).

1. Away from home.
2. Blended spirits and straight bourbon.
3. Dessert and table wine.
4. Index is developed by multiplying each of the individual indexes by 1/3.
    Thus, 110 (year 1968) is derived as follows:

$$[1/3 (114.9) + 1/3 (108.7) + 1/3 (106.0)]$$

(Base: 1957-59 = 100)

EXHIBIT 5.8

Wage Index

Year	Average Hourly Earnings*
1964	$1.26
1965	1.36
1966	1.43
1967	1.55
1968	1.65

1968 (by months)	
January	1.61
February	1.62
March	1.63
April	1.62
May	1.65
June	1.64
July	1.61
August	1.63
September	1.67
October	1.68
November	1.70
December	1.74

Source: Monthly Labor Review, U.S. Department of Labor, Bureau of Labor Statistics (Washington, D.C.: U.S. Government Printing Office, 1966-1968).

*Money payments only; tips not included.

Each specific factor in the profitability illustration (Exhibit 5.5) can be adjusted by applying specific price indexes. The financial data are thus translated into terms of current dollars, thereby giving the manager a basis for evaluating real performance during the period.

When considering the various index data presented in Exhibits 5.6, 5.7, and 5.8, remember that the base period 1957-1959 is defined as 100 percent. Successive years are then reflected as a percentage of this base year index number. Note, however, that each element in the departmental gross profit is adjusted by applying the same basic method (see Exhibit 5.9).

EXHIBIT 5.9

Application of Specific Indexes

A. Food Sales

Year	Sales Dollars	Exhibit 5.6 Multiplier	Adjusted Sales Dollars
1966	$80	137/122	$ 90
1967	90	137/128	96
1968	100	137/137	100

B. Beverage Operations

Year	Gross Profits	Exhibit 5.7 Multiplier	Adjusted Gross Profits
1966	$ 22	110/104	$ 23
1967	24	110/107	25
1968	25	110/110	25

C. Food Purchases

Year	Purchase Costs	Exhibit 5.6 Multiplier	Adjusted Purchase Costs
1966	$ 30	114/114	$ 30
1967	33	114/111	34
1968	36	114/114	36

D. Food Preparation, Service and Other Labor

Year	Labor Costs	Exhibit 5.8 Multiplier	Adjusted Labor Costs
1966	$ 28	165/143	$ 32
1967	31	165/155	33
1968	34	165/165	34

The restaurant meals index (Exhibit 5.6) is used to adjust food sales data because it is assumed that no specific item dominates food revenue. However, if one item is significant, the manager might consider using a more specific index (for example, note the treatment of food purchases).

Both beverage revenues and costs are adjusted by applying a general beverage index (Exhibit 5.7). Once again, it is assumed that the various types of beverages are equally important, so the combined index is used.

Food purchases are handled differently. In the illustration, these purchases are primarily meats, poultry, and fish; other items purchased comprise only a small portion of total costs incurred, so the combined meat, poultry and fish index from Exhibit 5.6 is applied.

The remaining cost element, food preparation and other labor, is adjusted by applying a specific wage index (Exhibit 5.8). Other more specialized data might be developed if the manager so desires.

After each element is adjusted, a more refined statement of departmental profit can be prepared (see Exhibit 5.10). These adjusted data provide the manager with a meaningful indicator of progress. By using these data in the decision-making process, the manager can substantially increase his ability to select the best alternatives and make proper evaluations.

EXHIBIT 5.10

Management Report
Price Level
Adjusted Gross Profits
Food and Beverage Operations

	Food			Beverages*		
	1966	1967	1968	1966	1967	1968
Sales	$ 90	$ 96	$100	$ 34	$ 37	$ 40
Cost of Goods Sold						
Food Costs	$ 30	$ 34	$ 36			
Preparation, Service and Other Labor	32	33	34			
Beverage Costs				$ 11	$ 12	$ 15
Total	$ 62	$ 67	$ 70	$ 11	$ 12	$ 15
Departmental Profit (Before Other Departmental Expenses)	$ 28	$ 29	$ 30	$ 23	$ 25	$ 25

*Exhibit 5.9 reflects only adjusted gross profit information. The same multiplier has been applied herein to sales and beverage costs.

DATA FOR SPECIAL DECISIONS

Price level adjustments can be similarly extended to other more specialized decision areas. Consider, for example, the replacement and/or renovation of facilities. A decision to invest funds in any major project calls for the responsible decision-maker to evaluate expected cash inflows and outflows. If analysis reveals an insufficient net cash inflow from a project, ownership will be reluctant to allocate necessary funds.

The concept of depreciation is particularly important in the hospitality service industries, since large investments in plant facilities are required in most cases. Depreciation accounting allocates an asset's initial cost over its estimated useful life. In recording this allocation in each fiscal period, accountants have adhered strictly to the cost principle. Since this practice does not give any effect to changing price levels it warrants specific attention.

In the cost method, the firm's resources are recorded and carried at the dollar amounts for which they were purchased. Consequently, a building purchased for $250,000 fifteen years ago is still reflected in the accounts at this price (less accumulated depreciation). Assuming that its useful life had been estimated at thirty years, only 50 percent of the original cost would therefore be reflected on the balance sheet as the book value (see Exhibit 5.11). Furthermore, successive income statements over the past fifteen years have reflected a depreciation charge of approximately $8,300 per year.

EXHIBIT 5.11

Financial Statements
(Selected Data)

Balance Sheet (12/31/xx)	
Building	$250,000
Less: Accumulated Depreciation	125,000
Book Value	$125,000
Income Statement (19xx)	
Operating Revenues	$ xxxxx
Less: Operating Expenses	xxxxx
Depreciation Charge	8,300
Net Income	$ xxxxx

It is apparent that this data has little relevance to the firm's current economic status. The situation is even more complex if costly renovations have been made over the years.

What can the manager do to improve these data? Unless adjustments are effected, both the firm's financial position and the results of its operations are distorted.

DEVELOPING ADJUSTED DEPRECIATION DATA

The process for adjusting depreciation cost differs only slightly from that presented in previous illustrations. A construction cost index (see Exhibit 5.12) for a recent five-year period (1964-1968) is used as the basis for considering the effects of price level changes.

An annualized index is computed in which not all months are weighted equally.

EXHIBIT 5.12

Construction Cost Index

Month	1964	1965	1966	1967	1968
January	111	113	118	123	127
February	111	114	118	123	128
March	111	114	118	123	128
April	111	114	119	123	129
May	112	114	120	124	130
June	112	116	121	126	132
July	112	116	122	128	132
August	113	117	122	129	133
September	113	116	122	129	134
October	113	117	122	130	135
November	113	117	123	129	135
December	113	117	123	129	135
Annual Weighted Average	112	116	122	128	132

(Base: 1957-59 = 100)

Source: Survey of Current Business, U.S. Department of Commerce, Office of Business Economics, Vol. 44-48, pp. 5-9, 5-10, 1964-1968 (Washington, D.C.: U.S. Government Printing Office).

In considering the importance of depreciation adjustments, let us assume that an operating manager is responsible for a $1,438,000 facility (original cost plus additions). Exhibit 5.13 shows the facility's operating results for a five-year period. Net income after tax is the prime criterion for evaluating managerial performance. Outsiders (potential investors, etc.) are also interested in the firm's earnings-per-share performance during the period.

EXHIBIT 5.13

Summary of Net Profits
(Unadjusted for Price Level Changes)

	Year				
	1964 (000)	1965 (000)	1966 (000)	1967 (000)	1968 (000)
Net Income Before Depreciation and Taxes	$ 200	$ 225	$ 250	$ 275	$ 300
Depreciation Charges (Schedule Below)	40	44	46	48	60
Net Income Before Tax	$ 160	$ 181	$ 204	$ 227	$ 240
Income Taxes (50%)	80	91	102	113	120
Net Income After Tax	$ 80	$ 90	$ 102	$ 114	$ 120
Earnings per Share*	$ 1.60	$ 1.82	$ 2.04	$ 2.28	$ 2.40

*50,000 shares of common stock outstanding.

Depreciation Schedule

	Year				
	1964 (000)	1965 (000)	1966 (000)	1967 (000)	1968 (000)
Capital Expenditure	$1,000	$ 96	$ 46	$ 44	$ 252
$1,000 (25 year life)**	$ 40	$ 40	$ 40	$ 40	$ 40
$ 96 (24 year life)		4	4	4	4
$ 46 (23 year life)			2	2	2
$ 44 (22 year life)				2	2
$ 252 (21 year life)					12
Annual Depreciation Charge	$ 40	$ 44	$ 46	$ 48	$ 60

**Depreciated using straight-line method. Original expenditure of $1,000,000 has an estimated useful life of twenty-five years. Subsequent expenditures (not expected to extend original useful life) are depreciated over the remaining useful life of the original expenditure.

The data in Exhibit 5.13 are not yet adjusted to reflect the effects of price level changes. Before we proceed, however, let us consider a basic question: "Why bother with price level adjustments in this situation—or in any other, for that matter?" Consider again the nature of depreciation. It is the allocation of expenditures from previous years. Furthermore, the annual charge is but a portion of the dollars spent at the time of purchase. If these dollars remain unadjusted, dollar charges deriving from a transaction in a previous period are matched with current-year operating revenues. Dollars of different purchasing power are thus combined as if they were completely comparable.

This inconsistency may be eliminated by using the current year as a numerator. All dollars from previous years are thus translated, first into terms of each individual year (Exhibit 5.14) and then into current-year dollars (Exhibit 5.15). Dollars of revenue, however, are already reflected in terms of each year's current dollars.[2] They need only to be adjusted into terms of current (1968) dollars (Exhibit 5.15).

EXHIBIT 5.14

Depreciation Charges
Adjusted to Year Indicated

Year	Unadjusted Depreciation Charge	Construction Cost Index Multiplier	Adjusted to Year Indicated	Total Adjusted Depreciation
1964	$ 40,000	112/112	$ 40,000	$ 40,000
1965	40,000	116/112	41,400	
	4,000	116/116	4,000	45,400
1966	40,000	122/112	$ 43,600	
	4,000	122/116	4,200	
	2,000	122/122	2,000	49,800
1967	40,000	128/112	$ 45,700	
	4,000	128/116	4,400	
	2,000	128/122	2,100	
	2,000	128/128	2,000	54,200
1968	40,000	132/112	$ 47,100	
	4,000	132/116	4,600	
	2,000	132/122	2,200	
	2,000	132/128	2,100	
	12,000	132/132	12,000	68,000

2. Recall that depreciation is, in part, a reflection of costs from a previous year. After it has been adjusted to each respective year, therefore, the reflected dollars can be adjusted directly to current dollars.

EXHIBIT 5.15

Adjusted Cumulative Income and Depreciation Data

A. Cumulative Income Data (000)

Year	Historical Income Dollars	Multiplier*	Adjusted Income Data
1964	$ 200	122/109	$ 223
1965	225	122/111	247
1966	250	122/114	268
1967	275	122/117	287
1968	300	122/122	300
Totals	$ 1,250		$ 1,325

B. Cumulative Depreciation Data

Year	Adjusted Depreciation Charges**	Multiplier***	Depreciation (1968 Dollars)
1964	$ 40,000	132/112	$ 47,100
1965	45,400	132/116	51,700
1966	49,800	132/122	53,900
1967	54,200	132/128	55,900
1968	68,000	132/132	68,000
Totals	$257,400		$276,600

*GNP Implicit Price Deflator Series (Exhibit 5.2).
**From Exhibit 5.14.
***From Construction Index (Exhibit 5.12).

with only the five-year period illustrated in Exhibit 5.16. These effects are compounded when considering the total useful life of an asset with a high risk of obsolescence, such as a motel facility. If unadjusted data are used for decision-making purposes, management decisions probably will differ significantly from those which occur when using adjusted price level information (since resulting earnings data are obviously changed). Outsiders, too, are undoubtedly affected by the impact on earnings per share.

EXHIBIT 5.16

A Summary of Net Income
(Adjusted for Price Level Changes)

	Year				
	1964 (000)	1965 (000)	1966 (000)	1967 (000)	1968 (000)
Income Before Depreciation and Taxes	$ 200	$ 225	$ 250	$ 275	$ 300
Depreciation Charges	40	45	50	54	68
Income Before Tax	$ 160	$ 180	$ 200	$ 221	$ 232
Income Taxes (50%)	80	90	100	111	116
Income After Tax	$ 80	$ 90	$ 100	$ 110	$ 116
Earnings per Share*	$ 1.60	$ 1.80	$ 2.00	$ 2.20	$ 2.32

EXHIBIT 5.17

A Comparison of Net Income
(1964-1968)

	Cumulative Totals	
	Unadjusted (000)	Adjusted (000)
Income Before Depreciation and Taxes	$ 1,250	$ 1,325
Depreciation Charges	238	277
Income Before Tax	$ 1,012	$ 1,048
Income Taxes (50%)	506	524
Net Income After Tax	$ 506	$ 524
Average Annual Earnings per Share *	$ 2.02	$ 2.10

*50,000 shares of common stock outstanding.

SUMMARY

Because the purchasing power of the dollar has been consistently declining since World War II due to price increases (inflation), financial statements and other management reports consist of dollars of varying purchasing power. Thus, the comparison of these statements between periods may lead to erroneous conclusions.

In order to eliminate the effect of price level changes upon the interpretation of financial statements adjustments may be carried out to restate all dollars in values of the same purchasing power. To do this, indexes are selected which allow the conversion to a given base year for each item to be restated.

Since the adjustment process is dependent upon the index employed, the validity of the price level adjusted number is only as good as the index selected. Broad indexes such as the consumer price index are valuable for mixed accounts; narrow indexes are available for specific accounts.

Nowhere today is consideration of rising prices (and thus costs) more important than in making and periodically revaluating pricing decisions. Price level adjustments provide management with a means of evaluating the impact of price level changes. Data are substantially more valid when modified by this method. These applications serve to improve the kinds and quality of decisions made by managers in the hospitality service industries.

Discussion Questions

1. What is meant by the term "inflation"?
2. What are the reasons for incorporating price level changes into accounting data?
3. Discuss some of the more significant management problems which can arise because of inflationary pressures.
4. Discuss the importance of choosing an appropriate index.
5. What three indexes are available for use in the price level adjustment process? How do these differ?
6. What are historical dollar reports?
7. Why should depreciation be adjusted?
8. How is the depreciation charge adjusted?

Problem 1

The following data have been taken from the income statements of the Happiness Motor Inn, located in Happytown, U.S.A. Using indexes provided in the chapter, prepare a set or price level adjusted financial statements for presentation to Mr. Happy, the owner and manager of the facility. Include a few paragraphs of explanation regarding the significance of these adjusted data as a part of the formal presentation. This will require the selection of a base period and indexes from those given in the chapter. An explanation should be made concerning the selection of a base period and the indexes.

	1966	1967	1968
Food Sales (000 omitted)	$200	$300	$400
Beverage Sales	100	150	200
Combined Sales	$300	$450	$600
Food Costs	$ 60	$ 90	$110
Beverage Costs	30	40	50
	$ 90	$130	$160
Combined Gross Profit	$210	$320	$440
Wages	$ 40	$ 60	$ 80
Depreciation*	20	20	20
Total	$ 60	$ 80	$100
Net Income Before Other Expenses	$150	$240	$340

*The facilities were constructed during 1966.

Problem 2

Progressive Hotels, Inc. has hired you as a consultant to perform analyses of their operations. As a specific part of your report, you have been asked to consider the effects of price level changes in two specific areas. First, you are to consider the cumulative (1965-69) effects of changes in wage costs on gross operating income. Second, you are to consider the cumulative (1965-69) effects of using historical dollar depreciation data (as opposed to price level adjusted information) on the firm's net income before tax position. The following data have been compiled for your use. (For purposes of analysis and evaluation, assume that data other than wages and depreciation need no additional price level adjustments.)

	1965	1966	1967	1968	1969
Gross Profit on Combined Sales	$600	$660	$700	$740	$800
Wages	300	320	350	360	390
Gross Operating Income	$300	$340	$350	$380	$410
Net Profit Before Depreciation and Taxes	$200	$220	$240	$280	$300
Depreciation	50	50	60	60	60
Net Profit Before Tax	$150	$170	$180	$220	$240

Problem 2 (continued)

The building and other facilities cost $2,100,000 during 1965. Salvage value is estimated to be $100,000 and the property is depreciated (straight-line basis) over forty years. A $400,000 addition was completed during 1967 (estimated salvage value, $20,000 with a thirty-eight-year life). In addition, two indexes are provided for use in your analysis.

Year	Wage Index	Construction Cost Index
1965	136	115
1966	143	121
1967	155	126
1968	165	132
1969	174	138

Problem 3

You are working as a trainee for a large hospitality industry organization, and a department head approaches you with the comment: "I have been reading much about inflation in our economy and its effects on business profits. In fact, I am seriously concerned with our own performance during the past three years. Would you restructure these operating summaries, giving full consideration to the effects of price level changes on our gross profit position?"

The following data are provided for your analysis (000 omitted).

	1967	1968	1969		1967	1968	1969
Food Revenues	$180	$200	$240	Beverage Revenues	$100	$110	$120
Food Cost	65	65	80	Beverage Cost	30	30	40
Gross Profit	$115	$135	$160	Gross Profit	$ 70	$ 80	$ 80

After some research, you have decided that the following general indexes (containing hypothetical data) are the best available for use in this project. If the results are revealing, of course, additional refinements will undoubtedly be requested by the department head.

Year	Restaurant Meals	Food Costs	Beverages
1965	117	112	103
1966	122	114	104
1967	128	111	107
1968	137	114	110
1969	142	116	113

Problem 4

Mr. X is willing to invest $250,000 in a motor hotel venture. He has been advised that one useful criterion for evaluating investments is the firm's "real" growth rate in sales. Since two properties are available for purchase in the area, he has asked that the following sales data be analyzed to provide this information. He will commit himself to the purchase only if the firm's revenues have increased by 50 percent in "real" terms during the period from 1965 to 1969.

Year	Firm A Sales	Firm B Sales
1965	$420,000	$350,000
1966	460,000	400,000
1967	520,000	450,000
1968	590,000	520,000
1969	640,000	580,000

Using the following price level index, compute the "real" growth trend for each of these firms. The GNP deflator series, a general index of the economy, reflects the following changes in price levels:

1965	109
1966	111
1967	114
1968	118
1969	122

CHAPTER 6

The Tools of Analytical Analysis—Ratio Analysis

The manager of a hospitality service firm has a constant need for information which can be used to evaluate the performance and condition of the business and to assist in making decisions regarding the future operation of the firm. The manager has available to him a large volume of quantitative material regarding the historical operation of the business. From this data he must draw the information upon which to base his decisions.

The financial statements of a business are one of the most valuable sources of information. Unfortunately, the informational content of financial statements and other quantitative reports is obscured by the great amount of detail required to satisfy the needs of the various users of this material. However, proper synthesis of financial data can provide valuable interpretive information. Answers cannot be derived from simply scanning the financial statements. The necessary analysis will include mathematical computations and comparisons which may be combined with managerial knowledge and interpretation so that information can be used effectively.

WHY RATIO ANALYSIS

Most financial information is presented in report form as a collection of totals or balances of accounts or other relevant data. The meaning or significance of a single account total or balance, if examined individually, is not readily apparent. For example, the dollar amount of food cost yields no more information than the total dollars spent on the food sold during the period. This expense is dependent upon many factors, including the volume of business, product mix and quality standards. Unless the food cost is related to food sales, little can be determined about its significance to the profitability of the enterprise.

There are significant relationships between the various accounts found on the financial statements and other financial reports. The first stage of the analytic process is in understanding and locating the meaningful relationships between accounts. These relationships can usually be expressed as ratios which facilitate analysis and comparability. Thus, a working knowledge of ratio analysis is an important part of effective total analysis of financial and operating statements.

The calculation of ratios is nothing more than a mechanical function and should be recognized as such. Unless the calculation is accompanied by interpretation through comparative techniques, the effort expended is wasted. In this chapter, concentration will be on the location of significant relationships between various financial accounts and the development of ratios to express these relationships. Comparative techniques and other analytical procedures will be discussed in chapter seven.

THE MATHEMATICS OF RATIO ANALYSIS

A ratio is a mathematical expression of the relationship between two items. As an illustration of the various ways to express a ratio, consider the following example.

Assume there is a significant relationship between two items, X and Y. The numerical value of X is 10 and the value of Y is 50. The relationship between X and Y might be expressed in any of the following ways:

(1) *As a common ratio.* The ratio between X and Y is 10 to 50, or in reduced form, 1 to 5 (1:5). The ratio between Y and X is 50 to 10, or 5 to 1 (5:1).

(2) *As a percentage.* X can be expressed as a percentage of Y by dividing X by Y. Since $X/Y = 10/50 = .20$, X is 20 percent of Y. Or Y is 500 percent of X, since $Y/X = 50/10 = 5.00$.

(3) *As a turnover.* Some relationships are best expressed as a turnover, or the number of times X must be "turned over" to yield the value of Y. This is calculated by simply dividing Y by X. In this example, $Y/X = 5$; X must be turned over 5 times to yield the value of Y.

(4) *On a per-unit basis.* If X is in dollars and Y is in units (guests, rooms, seats, etc.) the relationship would be expressed in dollars per unit. Therefore, X per unit of Y would be $X/Y = \$10/50 = \$.20$ per unit.

The method used to express a ratio or a relationship between two items will depend greatly upon the nature of the data being analyzed. Generally the method chosen is that which best lends itself to comparison and interpretation.

RATIO ANALYSIS

Ratio analysis has developed to include the needs of all users of financial information. A logical approach to analysis is to group the ratios by the type of information desired. Any specific user may employ one or a combination of the following groups in their analysis:

> Liquidity ratios
> Solvency and leverage ratios
> Activity ratios
> Profitability and rate of return ratios
> Operating ratios

Many of the ratios which will be discussed are common to any type of business. However, because of the peculiarities of the hospitality service industries, the interpretation of the ratios will be different from their meaning in the manufacturing or trade business. In addition, there are specific hospitality service industries' ratios to be considered.

A discussion of ratio analysis is more effective when examples are used to illustrate the location of pertinent data, the calculation of ratios and the resulting interpretations. The concept of ratio analysis will be developed around the financial information which will be supplied for a hypothetical hotel. The hotel example has been chosen because the transient hotel offers most of the services which are currently offered in the hospitality service industries, including the sale of space (rooms), and the sale of food and beverage. Many of the ratios used for the analysis of hotels are applicable for analysis of most segments of the hospitality service industries.

The Hotel Major is a hypothetical hotel containing 400 rooms, located in the Middle Atlantic States. Exhibits 6.1, 6.2 and 6.3 provide the necessary financial statements and statistics for a thorough ratio analysis of the Hotel Major. Exhibit 6.1a shows a comparison of the Hotel Major operating data with industry averages.

LIQUIDITY RATIOS

Liquidity ratios assist in the analysis of a firm's ability to meet short-term obligations as they become due. It is possible for a business to be profitable and yet have insufficient cash to pay its bills. It is essential that management maintain sufficient liquidity in the business. Whether the Hotel Major will be able to meet its obligations currently cannot be answered without additional analysis, including extensive cash flow analysis, as discussed in chapter twenty-two. However, the use of carefully selected liquidity ratios can provide an indication of liquidity.

The *current ratio* is probably the most commonly used liquidity ratio. This ratio expresses the relationship between the total current assets and the total

EXHIBIT 6.1a

The Hotel Major
Statement of Income
For the Year Ended December 31, 19xx

	Net Sales	Cost of Sales	Payroll and Related Expenses	Other Expenses	Profit or (Loss)
Operated Departments					
Rooms	$1,314,000	$ —	$262,800	$157,700	$ 893,500
Food	1,050,000	400,000	410,000	139,000	101,000
Beverage	350,000	105,000	70,000	21,500	153,500
Telephone	50,000	58,500	27,400	3,500	(39,400)
Other Operated Departments	30,000	18,500	6,300	2,200	3,000
Total	$2,794,000	$582,000	$776,500	$323,900	$1,111,600
Other Income	44,800				44,800
Gross Income					$1,156,400
Deductions from Income					
Administrative and General			$131,600	$105,800	
Advertising and Promotion			30,800	42,500	
Heat, Light and Power			15,700	65,000	
Repairs and Maintenance			64,700	62,300	
Total Deductions			$242,800	$275,600	518,400
Total House Revenue, Expense and Profit	$2,838,800	$582,000	$1,019,300	$599,500	$ 638,000
Store Rentals					39,400
Gross Operating Profit					$ 677,400
Municipal Taxes and Insurance					20,200
Profit Before Real Estate Taxes and Other Capital Expenses					$ 657,200
Real Estate Taxes					148,000
Profit Before Other Capital Expenses*					$ 509,200
Interest Expense					70,600
Profit Before Depreciation and Income Taxes					$ 438,600
Depreciation Expense					184,700
Profit Before Income Taxes					$ 253,900
Income Taxes (State and Federal)					119,000
Net Profit—to Retained Earnings					$ 134,900

*Profit before deducting rent, interest, depreciation, amortization and income taxes.

EXHIBIT 6.1b

The Hotel Major and Industry Averages
for the Year Ended December 31, 19XX

	The Hotel Major	Industry Averages**
Total Sales and Income		
Rooms	46.7%	54.0%
Food (Including Sundry Income)	37.3	29.5
Beverages (Including Sundry Income)	12.5	12.0
Telephone	1.8	2.8
Other Departmental Profits	.1	.7
Other Income	1.6	1.0
Total	100.0%	100.0%
Cost of Goods Sold and Departmental Wages and Expenses		
Rooms	15.0%	15.3%
Food and Beverages	40.7	35.8
Telephone	3.2	3.6
Total	58.9%	54.7%
Gross Operating Income	41.1%	45.3%
Deductions from Income		
Administrative and General Expenses	8.4%	9.2%
Advertising and Sales Promotion	2.6	3.2
Heat, Light and Power	2.9	4.3
Repairs and Maintenance	4.5	4.9
Total	18.4%	21.6%
House Profit	22.7%	23.7%
Store Rentals	1.4	1.2
Gross Operating Profit	24.1%	24.9%
Fire Insurance and Franchise Taxes	.7	.6
Profit Before Real Estate Taxes and Other Capital Expenses	23.4%	24.3%
Real Estate Taxes	5.3	4.5
Profit Before Other Capital Expenses*	18.1%	19.8%
Percentage of Occupancy	80.0%	66.6%
Average Rate Per Room Per Day	$11.25	$17.05
Average Daily Room Rate Per Guest	$ 9.56	$13.28
Number of Guests Per Occupied Room	1.18	1.28
Times Real Estate Taxes Earned	4.4	5.4
Average Size Rooms	400	355

*Profit before deducting rent, interest, depreciation, amortization and income taxes.
**Trends in the Hotel-Motel Industry, 1970. Harris, Kerr, Forster & Company (250 to 500 Rooms).

EXHIBIT 6.1b (cont.)

The Hotel Major and Industry Averages
for the Year Ended December 31, 19XX

	The Hotel Major	Industry Averages**
Ratios to Room Sales		
Food Sales (Including Sundry Income)	79.9%	54.7%
Beverage Sales (Including Sundry Income)	26.6	22.2
Combined Food and Beverage Sales	106.5%	76.9%
Cost Per Available Room Per Year		
Rooms Department Expenses	$ 1,051	$ 1,191
Telephone—Net Cost	99	62
Administrative and General Expenses	594	710
Advertising and Sales Promotion	183	247
Heat, Light and Power	202	335
Repairs and Maintenance	318	380
Fire Insurance and Franchise Taxes and Signs	51	46
Real Estate Taxes	370	352
Subtotal	$ 2,868	$ 3,323
Deduct:		
Food and Beverage Profit	$ 636	$ 442
Store Rentals	99	96
Other Profits and Income	120	136
Subtotal of Deductions	$ 855	$ 674
Net Operating Cost Per Available Room	$ 2,013	$ 2,649
Average Rental Per Available Room (Including Public Room Rentals)	3,286	4,187
Profit Per Available Room Per Year		
After Real Estate Taxes but Before Other Capital Expenses	$ 1,273	$ 1,538
Ratios to Room Sales		
Rooms Department Wages and Expenses	32.0%	28.4%
Telephone—Net Cost	3.0	1.5
Administrative and General Expenses	18.1	17.0
Advertising and Sales Promotion	5.6	5.9
Heat, Light and Power	6.1	8.0
Repairs and Maintenance	9.7	9.1
Fire Insurance and Franchise Taxes	1.5	1.1
Real Estate Taxes	11.3	8.4
Subtotal	87.3%	79.4%
Deduct:		
Food and Beverage Profit	19.4%	10.6%
Store Rentals	3.0	2.3
Other Profits and Income	3.6	3.2
Subtotal of Deductions	26.0%	16.1%
Net Operating Cost	61.3%	63.3%
Profit After Real Estate Taxes But Before Other Capital Expenses*	38.7%	36.7%

*Profit before deducting rent, interest, depreciation, amortization and income taxes.
**Trends in the Hotel-Motel Industry, 1970. Harris, Kerr, Forster & Company (250 to 500 Rooms).

EXHIBIT 6.2

The Hotel Major
Comparative Balance Sheet
As of December 31, 197(B) and 197(A)

Assets

	Current Year	Prior Year
Current Assets		
Cash on Hand	$ 18,000	$ 20,000
Cash in Bank	136,000	128,300
Accounts Receivable	164,300	158,500
Marketable Securities	34,800	27,200
Inventories		
Food	16,700	15,300
Beverage	20,300	21,500
Supplies	9,400	8,300
Prepaid Expenses	35,200	33,700
Total Current Assets	$ 435,300	$ 412,800
Fixed Assets		
Land	$ 400,000	$ 400,000
Building and Improvements	$3,215,000	$3,015,000
Less: Accumulated Depreciation	1,285,000	1,157,000
	$1,930,000	$1,858,000
	$ 880,000	$ 860,000
Furniture and Equipment		
Less: Accumulated Depreciation	587,000	530,700
	$ 293,000	$ 329,300
Total Fixed Assets	$2,623,000	$2,587,300
Total Assets	$3,058,300	$3,000,100

Liabilities and Stockholders' Equity

	Current Year	Prior Year
Current Liabilities		
Accounts Payable	$ 87,400	$ 88,700
Taxes Payable	12,500	11,300
Accrued Expenses	141,300	137,200
Current Portion of Long-Term Debt	86,200	71,400
Total Current Liabilities	$ 327,400	$ 308,600
Long-Term Debt	$1,176,100	$1,192,700
Less: Current Portion	86,200	71,400
Total Long-Term Debt	$1,089,900	$1,121,300
Total Liabilities	$1,417,300	$1,429,900
Stockholders' Equity		
Preferred Stock—5%	$ 83,000	$ 114,300
Common Stock, Par Value		
$10 Per Share, 50,000 Authorized, 41,130 Shares Issued	411,300	411,300
Capital Surplus	246,800	246,800
Retained Earnings	899,900	797,800
Total Stockholders' Equity	$1,641,000	$1,570,200
Total Liabilities and Stockholders' Equity	$3,058,300	$3,000,100

EXHIBIT 6.3

Miscellaneous Data

Number of Rooms in Hotel	400
Number of Rooms Sold in 1970	116,800
Number of Room Guests in 1970	137,400
Number of Food Covers in 1970	560,000

current liabilities of the business. The current ratio is calculated for the Hotel Major as follows:

$$\text{Current Ratio} = \frac{\text{Current Assets}}{\text{Current Liabilities}} = \frac{\$435,300}{\$327,400} = 1.3 \ : \ 1$$

This means that the Hotel Major has $1.34 of current assets for every dollar of current liabilities.

At best, this is a rough measure of bill-paying capabilities in the hospitality service industries, since it ignores the composition of assets and liabilities and the revolving cycle of the current accounts. The implication is one of liquidation wherein all current assets will be converted to cash to pay current obligations in the event of liquidation. Obviously, this is not possible in the hospitality service business since inventories are perishable foods, beverages and supplies of little value except in the continuation of the business.

The current ratio concept was originally developed as a measure of liquidity for mercantile and manufacturing firms, where inventories are held for sale and might represent as much as 50 percent of total current assets. As a result, a current ratio of 2:1 has traditionally been recognized as a rule-of-thumb minimum ratio. This "thumb rule" is not applicable, however, to the hospitality service industries, where the major products sold are not accounted for as inventories. Instead, the value of guest rooms, hospital beds, golf rounds, airplane seats, etc., are accounted for as noncurrent assets. In the hospitality service industries, inventories are supplementary to the major salable item and seldom exceed one-half percent of total assets. Consequently, a current ratio of approximately 1:1 is generally considered to be reasonable in the hospitality service industries.

However, creditors may consider a high current ratio as full assurance that they will receive payment for their goods and services. This is a concern to hospitality service industries' management, as they must guard against an excess build-up of cash or inventories. This excess is better utilized as revenue-producing assets.

The acid test ratio, sometimes referred to as the *quick ratio*, is a variation of the current ratio developed for mercantile and manufacturing business as a measure of liquidity. The quick ratio is another comparison of current assets and liabilities. However, it is a more accurate measure of the firm's bill-paying capabilities since it matches the current liabilities against cash and assets quickly converted to cash (liquid assets). These liquid assets are cash, accounts and notes receivable, and marketable securities held as temporary investments. The acid test ratio is calculated for the Hotel Major as follows:

$$\text{Acid Test Ratio} = \frac{\text{Cash} + \text{Accounts Receivable} + \text{Marketable Securities}}{\text{Current Liabilities}}$$

$$= \frac{\$154,600 + \$164,300 + \$34,800}{\$327,400} = 1.08 : 1$$

The Hotel Major has $1.08 of liquid assets for every dollar in current liabilities.

A quick ratio of 1 to 1 or of somewhat less than 1 to 1 is an acceptable ratio for most companies in the hospitality service industries.

The current liquidity of a business is closely related to the composition of the current assets. All divisions of the hospitality service industries, including hospitals, clubs, hotels, large restaurants and airlines have an increasing amount of charge sales. In these divisions, accounts receivable typically represent the greatest portion of current assets. For this reason, it is advisable to investigate certain aspects of these accounts as they relate to the liquidity of the hospitality firm.

Accounts receivable as a percentage of total revenue represents the portion of revenues which have not been converted to cash and thus are not available for payment of current obligations. Although it is less likely to occur in the hospitality service industries than in the product industries, the ending balance of accounts receivable could be distorted by an unusually large collection of charge sales. For this reason, the average of accounts receivable at the beginning and end of the year is used in the calculation. This ratio is calculated for the Hotel Major as follows:

$$\text{Accounts Receivable to Total Revenue} = \frac{\text{Average Accounts Receivable}}{\text{Total Revenues}}$$

$$= \frac{\$\ 161,400}{\$2,838,800} = 5.7\%$$

Note that this does not mean that charge sales represent 5.7 percent of total revenue. It means that over the year, about 5 to 6 percent of the total annual revenue has been in the form of uncollected accounts. In the hospitality service industries, this percentage will normally be between zero, for drive-ins and other fast food operations with no charge sales, to 10 percent or more for clubs where all sales are made on account. The percentage for the Hotel Major is typical for a 400-room transient hotel.

The accounts receivable turnover and the collection period for accounts receivable are two ratios which express the rapidity of the conversion of accounts receivable into cash. The turnover ratio is calculated for the Hotel Major below. It is simply the reciprocal of percentage of accounts receivable to total revenue.

$$\text{Accounts Receivable Turnover} = \frac{\text{Total Revenue}}{\text{Average Accounts Receivable}}$$

$$= \frac{\$2,838,800}{\$161,400} = 17.5 \text{ times}$$

This means that the average amount of accounts receivable is converted to cash 17.5 times a year. The turnover rate has more meaning when it is used to calculate the average collection period for accounts receivable.

$$\text{Average Collection Period} = \frac{365 \text{ Days}}{\text{Turnover}} = \frac{365}{17.5} = 21 \text{ Days}$$

Thus, the average account receivable at the Hotel Major is collected after twenty-one days.

The preceding calculations are rough estimates since the actual turnover and collection period are accurately estimated only by using charge sales as the numerator in the turnover equation rather than total revenue.

These ratios provide one indication of the effectiveness of the hotel's credit policies and the adherence to these policies. An unusually long collection period would indicate lax credit policies. An operation with an excessive collection period will experience a relatively high percentage of uncollectible accounts. But, credit is now expected by the guest and failure to recognize this practice may cause loss of business.

A general average for these ratios in a hotel or motel is a turnover rate of twelve times per year and an average collection period of thirty days. However, this is not an absolute norm which is applicable to all situations, since this ratio will be affected by the hotel's credit policies as well as the percentage of cash to charge volume. In addition to the ratios, management should analyze the individual delinquent accounts through the use of an aged trial balance (a periodic listing of all uncollected guest accounts by month in which the charge was made).

The collection period may be considerably less than thirty days in the hotel/motel segment of the hospitality service industries. The reason for this is that some cash sales continue in almost all properties and furthermore, there are some credit cards that provide for daily collection. These factors tend to increase the turnover ratio and decrease the collection period.

SOLVENCY AND LEVERAGE RATIOS

Solvency is the ability of a business to meet its debt obligations when they are due, including principal and interest on long-term borrowings.

There are two basic sources of money to finance a business. The owners may supply substantially all of the necessary funds or a combination of owner's investment and debt financing may be used. The risk of insolvency of a business is dependent on the amounts of monies contributed by lenders and by owners. Leverage refers to the amount of long-term debt used to finance the assets of the firm as compared to the amount of owners' equity. The following discussion will focus on the use of ratios to measure solvency and leverage.

The basic solvency ratio is the relationship of the firm's total assets to total liabilities. The solvency ratio for the Hotel Major is calculated as follows.

$$\text{Solvency Ratio} = \frac{\text{Total Assets}}{\text{Total Liabilities}} = \frac{\$3,058,300}{\$1,417,300} = 2.14 : 1$$

This means that if operations were not profitable and the hospitality facility was forced into bankruptcy, there would be $2.14 of book assets for every dollar of liabilities. Thus, long-term creditors have some reasonable assurance of being paid something in the event of liquidation and sale of the facility's assets. All debts would be covered if the assets were sold for less than half of their book values.

This ratio is a measure of solvency at a given point in time since it ignores the future inflow of funds from the continuing operation of the property. In effect, it simply provides some guesstimate of the firm's ability to pay debts upon liquidation.

Leverage ratios are used to express the relationship between the amount of debt and equity monies used to finance the assets of the firm.

The percentage of total debt to total assets ratio expresses the proportion of the total assets which were financed through the use of debt. This ratio is calculated for the Hotel Major as follows:

$$\text{Debt to Total Assets} = \frac{\text{Total Liabilities}}{\text{Total Assets}} = \frac{\$1,417,300}{\$3,058,300} = 46.7\%$$

Thus, 46.7 percent of the hotel's book assets are currently financed through borrowing. This debt includes both current liabilities which are non-interest bearing or "free debts" and long-term debts which have a stated interest rate. Since 70 to 90 percent of the total assets of a hotel or other hospitality service business are fixed assets, they have been highly leveraged, with total debt representing as much as 60 percent of total assets (and in some cases a greater percentage). However, with the explosion of the hospitality service industries in the last two decades, there has been a trend toward increased financial leverage and a ratio of up to 90 percent debt to total assets is not uncommon.

Another method used to express this same leverage factor is to relate total debt to total owners' equity. This relationship is expressed with the *debt-equity ratio* which shows total debt as a percentage of the owners' equity in the business. For the Hotel Major:

$$\text{Debt-Equity Ratio} = \frac{\text{Total Liabilities}}{\text{Total Equity}} = \frac{\$1,417,300}{\$1,641,000} = 86.4\%$$

This ratio expresses the creditors' financing of the hotel relative to the financing by the owners. At this time the hotel's creditors have invested 86¢ in loans for every $1.00 of the owners' investment.

Because of the expanding use of leases, joint ventures, management contracts and other financing techniques, leverage ratios must be carefully evaluated before conclusions can be drawn. If the cost of borrowed funds in any form is less than the earnings which can be generated from their use, it is advantageous to employ leverage.

Creditors see the debt-equity ratio as an indicator of the risk involved in extending credit to the firm and the cost of debt (interest rate) will be closely related to this risk factor, as will be all terms and conditions of the loan. At times it may be difficult for a highly-leveraged firm to find a source of borrowed funds, at even the highest of interest rates.

The greatest factor in the use of debt financing is the cost of debt, relative to the net-after-tax earnings which can be generated after paying tax-deductible interest for its use. Since the market value of equity shares is related to the earnings per share, the impact of debt financing on after-tax earnings will be a major consideration. If a highly-leveraged firm incurs a loss in the future, or a series of losses, the firm will not have sufficient funds to meet the fixed costs of "servicing the debt." This can only lead to a forced bankruptcy where the owners stand to lose their investment.

All of these factors must be considered in the evaluation of the debt-equity relationship. One estimate of the risk involved with leverage is the firm's past ability to meet interest payments. *The number of times interest earned* ratio is one such measure. Since interest is an ordinary and necessary expense of doing business, it is paid out of earnings before income taxes. For this reason, the number of times interest is earned is calculated by dividing net profit by the interest expense after all expenses except interest and income taxes. Since the usual format for the income statement does not provide this figure, the ratio is usually calculated as follows:

$$\text{Number of Times Interest Earned} = \frac{\text{Net profit before income taxes} + \text{interest expense}}{\text{interest expense}}$$

$$= \frac{\$253,900 + \$70,600}{\$70,600} = 4.6 \text{ times}$$

After all other expenses, the Hotel Major's earnings were sufficient to meet the annual interest charge 4.6 times. This ratio indicates the margin of safety or the amount which profits could decline and still meet interest obligations.

In the present financing structure of certain segments of the hospitality service industries (motels, hotels, restaurants, etc.), leases are a prevalent form of financing and the times interest is earned must be interpreted with a complete analysis of the rent commitments.

ACTIVITY RATIOS

Activity ratios are intended to show how effectively the assets of the business are being utilized. These ratios may assist in measuring the effectiveness of controls over the amount invested in certain assets. They are usually expressed as turnovers or percentages.

Inventory turnover ratios are designed to relate the size of inventories to the sales volume of the business. This relationship shows the number of times that the inventory is turned, that is, used up and replenished, during the year. Inventory turnovers are calculated by dividing the total cost of goods sold by the average inventory for the period.

Generally, inventories do not represent a significant portion of total current assets in the hospitality services industries and in almost all cases they are an insignificant portion of the total assets. Regardless of this factor, it is important to control the size and the turnover rate of inventories. In the hospitality service industries, inventories held for sale to the guests are primarily food and beverages, although as part of the complete hospitality facility there may be gift shops, drug counters, a pro shop or other retail inventories. Since the two primary products of food and beverages are inventoried separately, turnover rates for each inventory should be calculated.

The food inventory turnover can be high because of the perishability of the food products held in inventory. This ratio is calculated as follows for the Hotel Major:

$$\text{Food Inventory Turnover} = \frac{\text{total cost of food sold}}{\text{average food inventory}}$$

$$= \frac{\$400,000}{\$\ 16,000} = 25 \text{ times per year}$$

The Hotel Major turns its food inventory over twenty-five times per year or approximately every fifteen days (365 days divided by 25 times). With the exception of some remote resort locations, most food operations should have food supplied by purveyors daily or at least weekly. Proper purchasing techniques combined with accurate sales forecasting should result in a higher turnover rate. In some types of hospitality operations such as a fast food hamburger outlet, the annual turnover rate could be two to three hundred, or almost daily.

A low food inventory turnover when combined with a food cost higher than budgeted may be an indication of poor sales forecasting and purchasing policies and waste through spoilage and leftovers. However, a high turnover could indicate that the inventory is too small and that the operation continually runs out of menu items which can lead to lost business through dissatisfied guests.

The inventory turnover ratios in the hospitality service industries will have no relation to the usual commercial or manufacturing turnovers, since the time cycle from raw materials to finished product does not exist and there are no distribution pipelines involved in the hospitality service business. For the product company, the inventory time cycle could be many months from the purchase of raw materials to production to shipment to warehouse and finally to retail shelf and sale.

The beverage inventory turnover is calculated for the Hotel Major as follows:

$$\text{Beverage Inventory Turnover} = \frac{\text{total cost of beverages sold}}{\text{average beverage inventory}}$$

$$= \frac{\$105,000}{\$\ 20,900} = 5 \text{ times per year}$$

The hotel's beverage inventory is turned over five times annually, or approximately every seventy days. Note that this does not mean that there is a seventy-day supply of every item in stock. There will be some items which move very slowly and the supply on hand will last six months or more while other items may be sold within a week.

Although perishability is not an important factor in the storage of most beverage inventories, the turnover rate is very important because a slow-moving inventory represents cash which is not available for other uses in the business and this costs money either in the form of lost interest income or, in the event of a shortage of cash, through the cost of borrowing money.

The turnover of beverage inventories is largely dependent on the type or "class" of the operation and the resulting selection of wine, spirits and beer which is sold. Obviously, one would expect a lower turnover in a club or continental restaurant where a large selection of wines and spirits is offered. In these types of operations many brands must be stocked and there are always some items which do not sell quickly. Because of this, these operations will maintain a larger inventory of approximately thirty- to ninety-days supply or a lower turnover of between four and twelve times annually.

The most important "product" in all categories of the hospitality service industries is an intangible and is not included in inventories. This is true of hotels, motels, hospitals, golf clubs, resorts and common carriers where revenues are earned primarily through the sale of space. Although this intangible product of space is not held in inventory, it is probably the most perishable product in existence, for once the day ends, the space for that day can never be sold. Since this "product" is provided in the form of fixed assets and all categories of the hospitality service industries require an extraordinary large investment in fixed assets, it is important to evaluate the utilization of these assets.

The fixed asset turnover expresses the relationship between the dollar book investment in fixed assets and the annual revenue which is generated through their continuous sale in the form of space. This ratio can be useful in evaluating the utilization of assets to generate sales revenue in relation to other firms.

$$\text{Fixed Asset Turnover} = \frac{\text{total revenues (including store rentals in hotels)}}{\text{total fixed assets}}$$

$$= \frac{\$2,878,200}{\$2,623,000} = 1.1 \text{ times}$$

Except for the fast food segment of food services, the fixed asset turnover in the hospitality service industries is quite low in comparison to other industries. This is a result of the tremendous investment which is required to purchase the space that is sold over many years and the fact that there is no way of increasing output at times of maximum demand. Although the turnover rate can be informative, there are other ratios which are more valuable in the evaluation of the utilization of fixed assets in the hospitality service industries.

The percentage of occupancy is of importance to all categories of the hospitality service industries because it measures the use of facilities, where revenue is generated through the sale of space. This ratio refers to the percentage of the available rooms or beds which were sold in hotels, motels, resorts, hospitals, dormitories, nursing homes, or the percentage of available seats which are sold on common carriers. This percentage of occupancy in table service restaurants is measured at each meal period and is expressed in the number of persons served per seat. For example, a 200-seat restaurant serving an average of 400 luncheons has an occupancy of two; this is referred to as "two turns." This reflects the actual utilization of occupancy of fixed assets and is often calculated for a month or a year on an average basis.

Dining room turnovers (occupancy) will vary greatly between different types of operations. Continental dining rooms and restaurants will normally have a low turnover rate, for their guests usually enjoy a leisurely meal. This type of operation compensates for a low turnover by charging higher prices which yield a greater margin of profit per cover (customer). Coffee shops, cafeterias and other fast food operations will normally have a high turnover, and will have relatively low menu prices with a lower dollar of profit margin per cover.

The annual average occupancy percentage for the Hotel Major is calculated as follows:

$$\text{Annual Occupancy Percentage} = \frac{\text{Total rooms sold}}{\text{Available rooms}} = \frac{116,800}{400 \text{ rooms} \times 365 \text{ days}}$$

$$= \frac{116,800}{146,000} = 80\%$$

An annual occupancy rate of 80 percent is above average for the hotel and motel division of hospitality service industries. Currently, annual occupancy rates range from a low of 60 to an attainable high of 90 percent. There are many variables which influence occupancy rates in all divisions of the hospitality service industries, including location, rate structure, management, seasonal factors, advertising, and the general state of the economy. Over the past twenty years, there has been a downward trend in hotel occupancy rates, but this trend has been offset by the increasing occupancy in new motels.

As with any average calculation, the annual occupancy rate of a hotel can be misleading. Occupancy rates will fluctuate greatly from day to day or from month to month. The annual average occupancy rate may hide the fact that the hotel operates with a very high rate on most days of the week and a severe slump on specific days, or that December occupancy is less than half of August. If those periods where occupancy is low can be isolated, promotional techniques may be employed to increase the utilization of assets, which, if successful, would increase the overall average occupancy. Occupancy percentages are calculated daily because of the "perishability" of the product. Managerial action to improve occupancy cannot be done on a historical basis.

The percentage of double or multiple occupancy is another valuable measure of the utilization of assets in the transient hotel/motel business. This ratio is the proportion of the rooms sold which were occupied by more than one person and is expressed as an average number of guests per room. This ratio is an important indication of profitable use of the transient hotel/motel assets because room rates increase with an increased number of occupants.

$$\text{Double Occupancy Percentage} = \frac{\text{number of room guests}}{\text{number of rooms sold}}$$

$$= \frac{137,400}{116,800} = 1.2$$

PROFITABILITY AND RATE-OF-RETURN RATIOS

Although there is a large portion of the hospitality service industries which is not for profit, the primary motive behind most firms is the generation of maximum profits. A simple glance at the annual income statement of a firm will indicate whether a profit was earned and if so, the dollar amount of profit. However, there can be a significant difference between annual profits and *profitability*. Profit is an absolute term which is expressed as a monetary amount whereas profitability is a relative measure of profits as they relate to other factors. Profitability expresses the ability to generate profits from the available resources and the adequacy of profits in relation of revenues, assets and the owners' investment in the business. Profitability cannot be evaluated without studying some of these significant relationships.

THE PROFITABILITY OF THE OWNERS' INVESTMENT IN THE BUSINESS

The return-on-owners'-equity ratio measures the adequacy of the profits from operations in providing a return on the total owners' investment in the business. This ratio expresses the percentage relationships between the net profit after all expenses including income taxes are deducted, and the average stockholders' equity in the business.

$$\text{Return on Owners' Equity} = \frac{\text{net profit after income taxes}}{\text{average stockholders' equity}}$$

$$= \frac{\$\ 134{,}900}{\$1{,}605{,}600} = 8.4\%$$

The stockholders of the Hotel Major earned a return of 8.4 percent on their total cumulative equity investment in the business. If the ratio is considered by itself, it simply informs the owners that they earned a return on their investment and the rate of that return. If the full value of this ratio is to be derived, the owners must compare this rate with the other investment opportunities which are available.

In publicly owned corporations, individuals acquire an ownership interest by purchasing shares of stock at the current market price. The return on owners' investment may be calculated by dividing the market price paid per share by the annual earnings per share (net profit after taxes divided by the number of shares outstanding). This measure may reflect a more accurate rate of return on investment for those outside the firm since the market value represents the price paid for their equity investment in the business.

THE PROFITABILITY OF ASSETS

The nature of the hospitality service industries requires a major investment in assets for operations. It is imperative that this investment be used effectively to generate earnings sufficient to cover the costs of financing and to provide an adequate return to the owners.

The rate-of-return-on-assets ratio expresses the relationship between profits and the book value of the total assets of the firm. This ratio is calculated for the Hotel Major as follows:

$$\text{Return on Assets} = \frac{\text{profit before interest and income taxes}}{\text{total average assets}}$$

$$= \frac{\$\ 324{,}500}{\$3{,}029{,}200} = 10.7\%$$

The Hotel Major's assets are being used to earn an annual return of 10.7 percent on their average annual book value. Note that this return is based on profit before the interest cost of borrowed funds and income taxes. Interest expense is omitted because it is a variable which is a function of how much debt financing is used in a given firm. Its inclusion would distort the ratio so that it could not measure the true earning ability of the assets. The resulting ratio provides a measure by which the earning capability of assets can be compared with the interest rate for debt capital used in financing the assets. It is the first analysis step in the decisions regarding the purchase of assets and the use of debt financing. Obviously, the rate of return on assets should be greater than the interest rate on borrowed funds if debt financing is to be used.

A second means of financing assets is through the sale of equity interests. For example, capital for a proposed addition of two hundred rooms to the Hotel Major may be raised through the sale of additional shares of 5 percent preferred stock. This would result in a fixed cost of capital in the form of the 5 percent dividends, and this 5 percent return to the investor must be paid out of profits after income taxes. Therefore, the return-on-assets ratio would not provide a reliable tool to determine the advisability of additional financing through the sale of 5 percent preferred shares. Thus, the ratio is modified as follows:

$$\text{Net Return on Assets} = \frac{\text{net profit after income taxes}}{\text{total average assets}}$$

$$= \frac{\$\ \ 134,900}{\$3,029,200} = 4.4\%$$

This rate of return should now be compared with the fixed dividend obligations on the proposed preferred stock to be issued. The present fixed expenditures for dividend payments on the Hotel Major's 5 percent preferred stock are greater than the after-tax return on those assets which were financed with the present preferred stock. Either the after-tax return has declined since the sale of the stock or a poor decision was made to finance with 5 percent preferred stock. Therefore, unless the additional investment in new rooms is expected to earn a higher return than the past average, some other method of financing should be used.

Although these ratios are used by owners and managers to measure their rate of return and to assist in financing decisions, it is obvious that they can also be used by outsiders to evaluate the firm's financial management.

THE PROFITABILITY OF BUSINESS OPERATIONS

Profitability refers to the ability to generate profits and the efficiency of the business. The key relationship for this measurement is that between profits and dollar sales volume. The profit margin is the most common measure of operating profitability. This ratio expresses the relationship between net profit after income taxes and total revenues.

$$\text{Profit Margin} = \frac{\text{net profit after income taxes}}{\text{total revenue (including store rentals in hotels)}}$$

$$= \frac{134,900}{2,878,200} = 4.69\%$$

This ratio is a rough measure of overall operating and financial efficiency. It is computed after all costs including income taxes, occupation costs and financing charges, which are not always controllable but must be included in the measurement of overall profitability of the business. The profit margin is significant since it presents the record of annual performance expressed as a rate of net return on sales. A high profit margin on sales does not insure a high return on investment, nor does a low profit margin necessarily result in an inadequate return on equity. This is dependent on sales volume and investment. The important variable is the volume of sales needed in either case to produce an adequate dollar profit.

A second measure of the managerial performance or operating efficiency of a business is the *ratio of gross operating profit to total revenue*. Gross operating profit is defined as profits after all operating expenses, but before all occupancy and financing costs. Occupancy costs include rent, municipal taxes, real estate taxes, fire insurance depreciation and financing costs which are reflected in the interest expense. Income taxes are also excluded since the above exclusions have a direct affect on the actual tax liability.

$$\text{Operating Efficiency Ratio} = \frac{\text{gross operating profit}}{\text{total revenue}}$$
$$\text{(Gross Operating Profit Ratio)}$$

$$= \frac{\$\ 677,400}{\$2,878,200} = 23.53\%$$

The aforementioned occupancy expenses are excluded for two reasons. Operating management usually has very little control over these expenses, and with the exception of municipal taxes, real estate taxes and fire insurance, these expenses are not comparable between operations. To be a meaningful measure of operating efficiency, there must be comparability between different operations.

Based on the Hotel Major's size and room rate, its gross operating profit is about average (Exhibit 6.1a).

OPERATING RATIOS

The successful operation of a business will involve the generation of revenues and the control of expenses. Operating ratios are designed to relate the success of the business in these two basic areas.

Although the ratios presented in this section are directed toward an analysis of the Hotel Major, they are generally applicable to most segments of the hospitality service industries. The reasoning employed in the evaluation of these ratios is applicable to the hospitality service industries divisions except for certain not-for-profit institutions. The conclusions drawn are valid only for the Hotel Major and they cannot serve as rules of thumb for the industry. The establishment of such industry reference points is not possible except in the broadest terms because of the vast diversity in the types of operations in all segments of the hospitality service industries.

AN ANALYSIS OF SALES

The ability to generate sales is the most important aspect of any business. It is even more important in the hospitality service industries because the inventory for sale cannot be held over for sale tomorrow or next week. The human efforts and the financial commitment involved in the operation of a hospitality business are wasted unless the daily revenue which is generated is sufficient to cover the expenses incurred and provide an adequate profit. Effective management will analyze the present level and sources of sales and consider the potential for increased revenues.

The first factor to consider is the present composition of total revenue. This is accomplished by simply calculating the ratios of departmental sales to total revenue. The departmental sales percentages indicate the relative contribution to total revenues from each department's revenue-producing facilities. The composition of total revenue will be influenced by both the volume of business and the price structure within each department.

The ratios of departmental sales to total revenues for the Hotel Major are as follows:

Type of Revenue	Amount	Percent of Total
Rooms	$1,314,000	46.3%
Food	1,050,000	36.9
Beverage	350,000	12.3
Telephone	50,000	1.8
Other Departments	30,000	1.1
Other Income	44,800	1.6
Total Revenue	$2,838,800	100.0%

It is very difficult to see the significance of these relationships unless some basis of comparison is applied. The breakdown should be compared to previous periods and to industry averages (see Exhibit 6.1a). By doing so, management can evaluate both internal progress or change and the hotels' comparative position in the industry. This discussion will focus on the current status of the hotel's operations.

When the hotel's sales are compared to other hotels of a similar nature, in Exhibit 6.1b on pages 119 and 120, it is noted that room sales represent a smaller proportion of total sales than the industry average. Conversely, food sales represent a significantly greater portion than the average. There are many explanations which could account for these variations. For example, the hotel may have a very large local restaurant trade which contributes a greater percentage of total revenue than the average hotel. This explanation would have a favorable impact on the operations. However, the variation could also derive from inadequate revenue in the rooms department. In any event, the real explanation cannot be determined without further investigation.

Some general guidelines in the proper use of ratios can assist in the evaluation of the degree to which sales reach their maximum potential levels. However, a thorough market analysis would be required to actually determine maximum levels.

An important factor in the amount of total revenue mix is the price structure in the various departments. The price structure within the hospitality service industries and within a single operation generally consists of a range of prices for various items.

In the general evaluation of revenue, it is advisable to calculate the amount of an average sale. *Average room rate*, or its equivalent, is an important ratio for all divisions of the hospitality service industries including hospitals, dormitories, resorts, and others. This ratio represents the average receipt for each unit sold. It is calculated as follows for the Hotel Major.

$$\text{Average Room Rate Per Day} = \frac{\text{Total room sales}}{\text{Number of rooms sold}}$$

$$= \frac{\$1,314,000}{116,800} = \$11.25$$

A comparison with industry averages indicates that the hotel's average room rate and consequently its rate structure is lower than comparable properties. This would have a direct effect on the room department's contribution to total revenue. Since the percentage of total rooms revenue is low in spite of a high occupancy rate (as discussed in the section on activity ratios), the implication is that room sales are not reaching their potential level because room rates are too low.

The average restaurant check is also a measurement of the generation of sales dollars. This ratio represents the average sales value of food and beverages per food cover (customer).

$$\text{Average Restaurant Check} = \frac{\text{Total food and beverage sales}}{\text{Number of food covers}}$$

$$= \frac{\$1,400,000}{560,000} = \$2.50$$

This ratio can be refined by splitting it into the average food check and the average beverage check. It can then be refined further by calculating the ratios for each dining area and by meal periods. However, the one ratio is sufficient as a general guideline, and can be compared with restaurant industry averages.

The average restaurant check in the Hotel Major is lower than the industry average. This may be a reflection of the price structure in the dining areas or it could result from the type of restaurant sales. The average check could be low as a result of the majority of sales being generated in the coffee shop, where menu prices are generally lower than those in the dining room.

Other measures of the potential level of sales in the restaurant department include the *ratio of food sales to room sales* and the *ratio of beverage sales to food sales*. The volume of restaurant business is often related to the occupancy in the hotel since some percentage of room guests should eat in the restaurant. If the ratio of food sales to room sales is high, it may indicate that the hotel is maximizing its advantage of having a captured audience. When this ratio is low, it may indicate poor restaurant facilities and a definite lack of internal promotion. The ratio of beverage sales to food sales may be an indicator of the hotel's promotional efforts to sell beverages to its food customers.

There are other breakdowns of sales which are informative in the management of a restaurant. These would include the following:

Sales per seat
Sales per employee
Sales per menu item
Sales by meal
Sales by day of the week
Sales per food outlet (dining rooms)

There are many additional possibilities. Management should utilize those ratios which will produce the most valuable and useful information regarding sales.

AN ANALYSIS OF THE CONTROL OF COSTS

The control of costs is the primary responsibility of management after the maximization of profitable sales. Sufficient revenues at the proper per-unit price open only the first door towards profits. Profitability will greatly depend on managerial effectiveness in the control of operating expenses. The measurement of the effectiveness of cost controls can only be accomplished by relating costs to the revenues which they generate. The raw dollar amount of an expense is meaningless unless comparisons are made.

The cost of sales in the hospitality service industries represents the cost of food and beverage, goods and services which are sold. This does not include the cost of the labor that is needed to prepare and serve the food and beverages. There is no cost of goods sold in the rooms department of a hotel or in the sale of seats on a common carrier. The sale of a room is actually the sale of an intangible—the use of that room—hence there is no tangible product or goods to cost. The most important costs of goods sold in the hospitality service industries are the *costs of food and beverages.*

The cost-of-food percentage expresses the relationship between the dollars expended to purchase the food which was sold and the dollars received through its sales.

$$\text{Food Cost Percentage} = \frac{\text{cost of food sold}}{\text{food sales}}$$

$$= \frac{\$\ \ 400,000}{\$1,050,000} = 38.1\%$$

Since there are many different types of food outlets varying from the fast food franchise to the suburban night club restaurants, it must be recognized that there is no "right" food cost percentage. This ratio depends upon too many variables to establish such a rule. However, it is worthwhile to compare this percentage with the available hotel industry averages; the comparison shows that the food cost for the Hotel Major is higher than the average for similar hotels.

The menu prices are the greatest factor in the determination of this ratio. It was previously noted that the average check in the Hotel Major was quite low. The food which goes into a product will cost the same whether it sells for $4 or $5 a portion (assuming a standard portion and quality and no waste or pilferage loss). Therefore, low menu prices may be the factor causing a high cost relationship. However, the possibility of a lack of proper control procedures also exists, such as poor purchasing, over-production, or waste through spoilage. Combined, these factors would indicate that management might review its menu prices, purchasing procedures, and food controls.

The cost-of-beverages-sold percentage is the equivalent to the food cost percentage in the sale of alcoholic beverages.

$$\text{Beverage Cost Percentage} = \frac{\text{cost of beverage sold}}{\text{total beverage sales}}$$

$$= \frac{\$105,000}{\$350,000} = 30\%$$

The beverage cost percentage for the Hotel Major is also higher than the selected industry average. In addition to the general factors discussed in relation to the food cost percentage, food and beverage cost percentages can be influenced by the composition or mix of the sales. An operation which sells a large proportion of beer will often have a higher beverage cost since the markup on beer is usually lower than that on liquor. Continuous review of the beverage cost percentage is important because alcoholic beverages are expensive and a percentage point increase may represent many dollars.

The calculation of the other cost-of-goods-sold percentages for the hospitality service industries is suggested for a complete analysis. This discussion is limited to food and beverages since they are common to all divisions of the hospitality service industries. Other inventories are supplementary and held for direct sale to the guest similar to all retail operations.

In recent years, the control of the cost of labor and related expenses has emerged as the greatest single problem facing management in the hospitality service industries. Currently, payroll costs exceed 20 percent of sales in most rooms departments and are over 40 percent of sales in many food and beverage operations. For this reason, ratios which express meaningful payroll relationships are becoming more important in the management of hospitality businesses.

Except as a reference point, the ratio of total payroll and related expenses to total revenue is of limited significance. This ratio will indicate the relative proficiency of management in the control of total payroll costs. However, as a managerial tool, this is too broad a measure to be of direct use. The ratio of payroll and related expenses to total revenue for the Hotel Major is 35.9 percent, and is lower than the percentage found in the industry average for hotels of its type. A more complete analysis of payroll costs would also include the following ratios.

Departmental payroll percentages relate the cost of labor to the sales in each department. An unusually high percentage in one department can be offset in the above ratio of total costs by a low ratio in another department.

Departmental payroll percentages by time periods represent a refined version of the above ratios. This is accomplished by comparing the payroll costs during the week, day or time of day with the sales of the same time period. These ratios may provide an indication of the effectiveness of manpower scheduling procedures.

The ratio of payroll-related expenses to cash payrolls is indicative of the fringe benefits which are offered by the business. These expenses represent over 15 percent of cash payrolls in most hospitality industry operations.

Since payroll represents such a significant portion of the sales dollar in the hospitality service industries, it would be advisable to develop some measures of labor productivity in the industry. One such measure is the ratio of the number of guests to the number of employees. This can be broken down by specific areas of the operation to provide a more effective measure. For example, this ratio could be employed in the restaurant department as:

1. The number of covers served to the number of service employees.
2. The number of covers served to the number of preparation employees.
3. The number of covers served to the number of dishwashing employees.

In those areas where customers are served directly by specific employees, the ratio can be refined to measure the number of customers served by specific job classifications (waiters, cashiers, desk clerks, etc.). One additional measure is the dollar sales which can be attributed to specific employees. This would reflect the performance of key personnel in terms of the generation of revenues.

Under the various uniform systems of accounts for the hospitality service industries, the other departmental expenses include the remaining departmental expenses (after cost of sales, payroll and related expenses) which can be directly attributed to the operation of specific departments. Other expenses in the rooms department include laundry, linen, china and glass and cleaning supplies. Other expenses in the restaurant department include those mentioned for rooms, and entertainment, kitchen fuel, licenses and others shown in the chart of accounts in chapter four. An analysis of these expenses must include the ratio of each departmental expense to that department's revenue. The resulting ratios might then be compared to past results and industry averages. Any significant variations represent potential control problems which should be investigated.

The dollar amount of most operating expenses will vary to some degree with the volume of sales. A higher sales volume will lead to higher operating expenses, so that the percentage relationship between operating expenses and revenues will frequently remain fairly stable with changes in volume. For this reason, the ratios to sales provide meaningful relationships which can be employed in comparative analyses.

The remaining expenses in the hospitality service industries are those that are not directly assignable to producing departments and are sometimes referred to as *overhead expenses.* In the uniform system of accounts for hotels, they are referred to as *deductions from income.* The cost of management, accounting, advertising, heat, light and power, and repairs and maintenance are generally considered as non-assignable overhead expenses. These expenses will vary with the volume of sales, although certain types will not vary immediately. Therefore, the percentage relationship between overhead expenses and revenues must be analyzed as to the nature of each cost so that comparison between time periods or between different operations can be useful. In addition, other relative measures should be employed which will be meaningful in a comparative analysis.

The greatest factor which influences the raw dollar amount of overhead expense is the size of the operation. In hotels and motels the size of the operation can be adequately measured by the number of available rooms or occupied rooms, and in restaurants, the number of seats or covers served may be employed. The ratios of individual overhead expenses to the number of available rooms provide a meaningful measure which can be used for comparative analyses. These ratios are calculated by dividing the dollar amount of specific overhead expenses by the number of available rooms or occupied rooms in the hotel. The results of the ratios are expressed as a dollar amount per room. This is illustrated for the Hotel Major as follows:

Deductions From Income	Total Amount	Amount Per Available Room
Administrative and General	$237,400	$594
Advertising and Promotion	73,300	183
Heat, Light and Power	80,700	202
Repairs and Maintenance	127,000	318

When overhead expenses are exprssed in this form, comparisons with industry averages are possible, and significant deviations from the industry average should be investigated.

The capital costs of providing the facilities needed for operations have been omitted from the example expenses. These costs of occupation and financing are seldom comparable between operations. If the property is owned, occupation costs will include real estate taxes, fire insurance on building and contents, and depreciation on fixed assets, whereas if the property is under lease, there will be rent and selected other costs. The extent of these expenses will vary significantly between properties depending on the nature of the lease contract, the method of depreciation used, etc. Also, the wide variety of available financing techniques result in the non-comparability of these expenses.

Except for local taxes and insurance, no realistic comparisons of occupancy costs can be made between operations. These expenses must be evaluated on an individual basis in relation to the profitability of the specific operation.

THE LIMITATIONS OF RATIO ANALYSIS

Ratio analysis should be recognized as an effective tool for the evaluation of financial stability, operating results, managerial effectiveness and as a managerial aid in decision-making. However, the users of ratio analysis must be aware of the limitations and pitfalls of this tool.

Ratios must be recognized for what they are: the mathematical comparison of two figures expressing the relationships between them. For example, the ratio of food cost to land would have no meaning because there is no significant relationship between them. Thus, if ratios are going to be at all meaningful, they must be used to express significant relationships. In addition, the relationship must be understood by the user of the ratio, and the results of the ratios must be carefully evaluated in light of all the known facts.

Even when caution is exercised in the application of ratios, the resulting information is far from conclusive. Since ratios are mathematical comparisons between two figures, the result of the ratio can be manipulated and any abnormality or error in the value of one or both of the figures will result in a misleading ratio, as shown in the following example of a current ratio.

Let us assume that a hotel has total current assets of $100,000 and current liabilities of $60,000 at the end of the year. The current ratio would be 1.7 : 1 ($100,000/$60,000). If management had paid $40,000 of current liabilities just before the end of the period, total current assets would have equaled $60,000 and current liabilities would have totaled $20,000. This simple maneuver would have increased the current ratio from 1.7 : 1 to 3 : 1 ($60,000/$20,000). This manipulation is called "window dressing," and it will usually have an adverse affect on another ratio. Therefore, it is always advisable to use groups of ratios for the evaluation of any particular aspect of the firm.

Ratios are a means of comparing two figures in an attempt to derive some useful information about the status of the business. Very little can be determined about the significance of ratio results unless some further comparisons are made. Ratio results should be compared to the past performance of the business, to the prescribed objectives of management and to the results of other businesses within the same industry.

The need for comparison is sometimes obstructed by the lack of comparability in the reporting of financial data. Consistency in accounting procedures, as between operations being compared and as between periods, is a prerequisite to the comparability of ratios and other financial data. The creation of a uniform systems of accounts for most all segments of the hospitality service industries has contributed greatly to the consistency of financial data within the industry. However, variations in the valuation of assets, the determination of depreciation methods and other such "judgment factors" in accounting can make comparisons difficult not only with industry data but even between years within the same company.

Another factor which can influence the validity of ratios is the timing of the financial transactions of the business. This was previously illustrated in the discussion of the manipulation of the current ratio. It is important to remember that financial statements are static representations of a dynamic process.

Some of the ratios become more accurate if the use of averages is incorporated into the ratio. This was made apparent in the calculation of accounts receivable and inventory turnovers. In a thorough analysis of financial data, it is frequently necessary to use average data, since in many cases averages will provide a more accurate evaluation of a firm. However, it is imperative that the shortcomings of averages are understood. As a tool, the use of averages is dependent upon the material; while in some cases it may be valuable, in others it may seriously distort the data. Chapter seven, pages 153 to 157, presents additional discussion of averages (arithmetic means).

In spite of the many limitations to ratio analysis, it can be a very valuable tool. Ratios should be calculated with care and the analyst should use the results in conjunction with all other sources of information before making a definite decision as to the meaning of the ratio.

SUMMARY

Ratio analysis is the single most powerful analytical tool available to managers. Many operating statistics may be brought into meaningful context only through the application of ratio analysis.

Managerial reports, to be used most effectively in the decision-making process, must be thoroughly examined and expanded to optimize their potential for interpretation. While financial statements are designed to communicate pertinent data efficiently, no attempt is made therein to present the relationships between various accounts. The first step to be undertaken in analysis, therefore, is that of understanding and locating meaningful relationships contained within managerial reports. Such relationships can usually be expressed as ratios.

The nature of the data being analyzed and the user to whom the information is directed are important determinants of the relationships studied and the formulas used. As with financial statements, it should be remembered that the ratio in itself is of little value; the accompanying interpretation of comparative techniques and additional analytical procedures define the perspective in which this information is viewed and is of value to the user.

The various types of ratios are commonly grouped with regard to the type of information desired. Following is a compilation of all formulas presented in the chapter.

LIQUIDITY RATIOS

$$\text{Current Ratio} = \frac{\text{Current Assets}}{\text{Current Liabilities}}$$

$$\text{Acid Test Ratio} = \frac{\text{Cash + Accounts Receivable + Marketable Securities}}{\text{Current Liabilities}}$$

$$\text{Accounts Receivable to Total Revenue} = \frac{\text{Average Accounts Receivable}}{\text{Total Revenues}}$$

$$\text{Accounts Receivable Turnover} = \frac{\text{Total Revenue or Total Credit Sales}}{\text{Average Accounts Receivable}}$$

$$\text{Average Collection Period} = \frac{365 \text{ Days}}{\text{Accounts Receivable Turnover}}$$

SOLVENCY AND LEVERAGE RATIOS

$$\text{Solvency Ratio} = \frac{\text{Total Assets}}{\text{Total Liabilities}}$$

$$\text{Debt-to-Total-Assets Ratio} = \frac{\text{Total Liabilities}}{\text{Total Assets}}$$

$$\text{Debt-Equity Ratio} = \frac{\text{Total Debt}}{\text{Total Equity}}$$

$$\text{Number of Times Interest Earned Ratio} = \frac{\text{Net Profit Before Income Taxes and Interest Expense}}{\text{Interest Expense}}$$

ACTIVITY RATIOS

$$\text{Food Inventory Turnover} = \frac{\text{Total Cost of Food Sold}}{\text{Average Food Inventory}}$$

$$\text{Beverage Inventory Turnover} = \frac{\text{Total Cost of Beverage Sold}}{\text{Average Beverage Inventory}}$$

$$\text{Fixed Asset Turnover} = \frac{\text{Total Revenues (Including Store Rentals in Hotels)}}{\text{Total Fixed Assets}}$$

$$\text{Occupancy Percentage} = \frac{\text{Total Rooms Sold}}{\text{Available Rooms}}$$

$$\text{Double Occupancy Percentage} = \frac{\text{Number of Room Guests}}{\text{Number of Rooms Sold}}$$

PROFITABILITY AND RATE OF RETURN RATIOS

$$\text{Return on Owners' Equity} = \frac{\text{Net Profit After Income Taxes}}{\text{Average Stockholders' Equity}}$$

$$\text{Return on Assets} = \frac{\text{Net Profit Before Interest and Income Taxes}}{\text{Total Average Assets}}$$

$$\text{Net Return on Assets} = \frac{\text{Net Profit After Taxes}}{\text{Total Average Assets}}$$

$$\text{Profit Margin} = \frac{\text{Net Profit After Income Taxes}}{\text{Total Revenue (Including Store Rentals in Hotels)}}$$

$$\text{Operating Efficiency Ratio} = \frac{\text{Gross Operating Profit}}{\text{Total Revenue}}$$

OPERATING RATIOS

$$\text{Average Room Rate Per Day} = \frac{\text{Total Room Sales}}{\text{Number of Rooms Sold}}$$

$$\text{Average Restaurant Check} = \frac{\text{Total Food Sales}}{\text{Number of Food Covers Sold}}$$

$$\text{Food Cost Percentage} = \frac{\text{Cost of Food Sold}}{\text{Food Sales}}$$

$$\text{Beverage Cost Percentage} = \frac{\text{Cost of Beverage Sold}}{\text{Total Beverage Sales}}$$

Discussion Questions

1. What are the four forms in which a ratio may be presented?

2. What do liquidity ratios mean as compared to solvency ratios?
3. What is the difference between the current ratio and the acid test ratio?
4. What does the number of times interest is earned mean to a creditor?
5. What effect does the multiple occupancy factor have on average room rates?
6. What is the difference between profit and profitability?
7. How is a restaurant's revenue affected by turnover (turns)?
8. What would be some useful ratios for monitoring employee productivity?

Problem 1

The data shown were taken from the financial records of the Clark Hotel at the close of the current year.

Accounts and Notes Payable	$ 52,300
Accrued Liabilities	30,700
Beverage Inventory, Beginning	10,000
Beverage Inventory, Ending	12,000
Cash	32,000
Facility Cost (Building and Equipment)	136,000
Food Inventories, Beginning	12,300
Food Inventories, Ending	16,900
Marketable Securities	31,000
Operating Expenses	221,000
Prepaid Expenses	7,500
Income Taxes Payable	19,000
Purchases, Foods	241,600
Purchases, Beverages	110,000
Receivables, Beginning	85,400
Receivables, Ending	70,600
Capital and Retained Earnings, Ending	204,000
Revenue from Food Sales	300,000
Revenue from Beverage Sales	226,000

On the basis of this information (assuming a tax rate of 50 percent), compute the following:

1. Current ratio.
2. Quick ratio.
3. Inventory turnovers for food and beverages.
4. Turnover of accounts receivable (and number of days credit sales are outstanding).
5. Returns on sales and assets.

Problem 2

The year-end statements of Drake Catering Company follow.

Drake Catering Company
Income Statement for Year Ended December 31, 1970

Sales		$365,000
Cost of Goods Sold		
Food and Beverage Inventory 1/1/70	$ 29,400	
Purchases	241,200	
Available for Sale	270,600	
Food and Beverage Inventory, 12/12/70	30,600	
Cost of Goods Sold		240,000
Gross Profit on Sales		125,000
Operating Expenses		106,200
Operating Income		18,800
Interest Expense		3,000
Income Before Income Taxes		15,800
Income Taxes		3,300
Net Income		$ 12,500

Drake Catering Company
Balance Sheet December 31, 1970

Cash	$ 6,500	Accounts Payable	$ 20,000
Accounts Receivable (Net)	22,500	Mortgage Payable	50,000
Food Inventory	30,600	Owners' Investment	100,000
Prepaid Expenses	400	Retained Earnings	30,000
Fixed Assets Net	140,000		
Total Assets	$200,000	Total Liabilities	$200,000

Calculate the following:

1. Current ratio.
2. Acid test ratio.
3. Days' sales uncollected.
4. Food inventory turnover.
5. Return on stockholders' equity.
6. Return on total assets employed.

Problem 3

The condensed statements of Thompson Restaurant are given. The restaurant operates approximately three hundred days per year.

Thompson Corporation
Comparative Balance Sheet
December 31, 1969 and 1970

	1970	1969
Cash	$ 6,000	$ 8,000
Accounts Receivable, (Net)	16,000	14,000
Foods Inventory	32,000	28,000
Building and Furniture (Net)	186,000	180,000
Total Assets	$240,000	$230,000
Current Liabilities	$ 20,000	$ 15,000
Mortgage Payable	80,000	85,000
Common Stock ($10 par value)	100,000	100,000
Retained Earnings	40,000	30,000
Total Equities	$240,000	$230,000

Thompson Corporation
Comparative Income Statement
Years Ended December 31, 1969 and 1970

	1970	1969
Revenues	$200,000	$180,000
Cost of Goods Sold	120,000	109,000
Gross Profit on Sales	80,000	71,000
Operating Expenses	49,000	45,000
Operating Income	31,000	26,000
Interest Expense	5,000	5,500
Income Before Income Taxes	26,000	20,500
Income Taxes	6,000	5,500
Net Income	$ 20,000	$ 15,000

Calculate the following:

1. Current ratios for 1970 and 1969.
2. Acid test ratios for 1970 and 1969.
3. Days' sales uncollected for 1970 and 1969.
4. Food inventory turnover for 1970.
5. Earnings per share for 1970 and 1969.
6. Return on total assets for 1970 and 1969.
7. Return on stockholders' equity for 1970 and 1969.

Problem 4

John Anderson, a partner in a "meats purveying" venture (Anderson and Bench), has decided to reduce the amount of time he spends on the firm's business. Anderson has offered to sell half of his partnership interest to Cook as of the end of Year 2 at book value; also, if Cook should decide to join the firm he would pay Anderson personally for one-half of his capital interest. Cook would receive a salary of $10,000 a year and half of Anderson's 60 percent share of the residual profits.

Anderson and Bench now pay themselves salaries of $15,000 and $10,000 respectively. These salaries are paid in cash and are treated as expense on partnership income statements, since the partners believe their shares commensurate with the value of their personal services to the firm. Anderson has agreed to cut his salary to $7,500 if Cook joins the firm, since he plans to devote only part of his time to the business in the future.

The following financial data of the firm of Anderson and Bench for the past two years have been given to Cook for his consideration.

Anderson and Bench
Comparative Balance Sheets
as of December 31

Assets	Year 2	Year 1*
Cash	$ 18,500	$ 25,200
Receivables	98,000	84,600
Less Allowance for Uncollectibles	(500)	(800)
Inventories (Meats)	84,000	60,000
Total Current Assets	$200,000	$169,000
Land	30,000	30,000
Buildings	350,000	350,000
Allowance for Depreciation: Building	(84,000	(70,000)
Furniture and Fixtures	180,000	120,000
Allowance for Depreciation: Furniture and Fixtures	(62,000	(48,000)
Total Assets	$614,000	$551,000
Liabilities and Partners' Equity		
Notes Payable	$ 50,000	$ -
Accounts Payable	51,400	60,000
Accrued Liabilities	36,000	42,000
Total Current Liabilities	$137,400	$102,000
Mortgage Payable Due December 31, Year 10	180,000	180,000
Anderson, Original Capital	80,000	80,000
Anderson, Reinvested Earnings	114,360	96,000
Bench, Original Capital	50,000	50,000
Bench, Reinvested Capital	52,240	43,000
Total Liabilities and Partners' Equity	$614,000	$551,000

*At beginning of Year 1 inventory was $60,000 and accounts receivable (net) was $74,000.

Problem 4 (continued)

Anderson and Bench
Statement of Partners' Reinvested Earnings

	Anderson		Bench	
	Year 2	Year 1	Year 2	Year 1
Reinvested Earnings	$ 96,000	$ 75,600	$ 43,000	$ 34,400
Net Income (after salaries)	18,360	20,400	12,240	13,600
	114,360	96,000	55,240	48,000
Drawings			3,000	5,000
Reinvested Earnings	$114,360	$ 96,000	$ 52,240	$ 43,000

Anderson and Bench
Comparative Income Statements

	Year 2	Year 1
Combined (Food and Beverage) Revenues	$540,000	$600,000
Cost of Goods Sold	334,800	402,000
Combined (Food and Beverage) Gross Profit	205,200	198,000
Operating Expenses:		
Sales Force	27,000	28,000
Advertising and Promotion	37,800	30,000
Occupancy	21,600	25,200
Buying	10,800	6,600
Administrative	40,100	38,400
Interest	12,300	10,800
Total Expenses	149,600	139,000
Net Income	55,600	59,000
Salaries to Partners	25,000	25,000
Net Income (Return on Investment)	$ 30,600	$ 34,000

Cook has brought this statement to you for analysis and advice.

Required

1. As part of your analyses, compute the following ratios for both Year 1 and Year 2.

   Current ratio.
   Quick ratio.
   Inventory turnover.
   Receivable turnover.
   Debt-equity ratio.
   Rate of gross profit on sales.
   Rate of net profit on sales.
   Times interest charges earned.

Problem 4 (continued)

Rate of return on total assets.

Rate of return on invested capital (partner's average capital).

2. Write a report to Cook pointing up any financial weakness of the firm that you may find. Compute the possible rate of return that he might expect to earn if the earnings during Year 3 were equal to the average of earnings during Years 1 and 2.

CHAPTER 7

Tools for Comparison and Analysis

The objective evaluation of quantitative material requires the use of comparisons. Analysis involves the manipulation of data to make it more meaningful, as in ratio analysis. However, unless there is some standard with which quantitative material can be compared, the value of analysis may be lost.

The comparative analysis of quantitative material involves several factors. Comparable data must be selected which will offer some standard by which management can measure the effectiveness of the current (or actual) status of business operations and financial structure. And, when the comparative data has been selected, objective techniques must be employed to isolate and evaluate the differences which exist between the operation being analyzed and the comparative data.

MAJOR TYPES OF COMPARISONS

The value of quantitative operating information is very limited in the absence of some means of comparison to determine its significance. An individual hospitality service firm may use both internal and external data for comparative measures. The major sources of comparative data are:

Internal	*External*
Budgeted Performance	Similar Operations
Past Performance	Industry Performance

Budget comparisons assume the existence of realistic budgets, which are periodically updated. Continual comparison of actual with budgeted costs will provide an excellent basis for the evaluation of the operation's performance and the effectiveness of revenue and expense controls. The significance of this comparison will be dependent upon management's ability to provide sound and effective operating budgets.

Current operating performance is often compared to past performance; such a comparison is an indication of the change or growth of an operation. Change or growth is either a decrease (negative growth) or an increase (positive growth). An evaluation of this growth can be useful to management in the planning process.

Another measure of operating performance for the individual hospitality service unit is that of comparisons with similar operations. Comparative data is used by the management of multi-unit operations to evaluate individual units within a chain and by all managements to compare unit operating results with other similar establishments in an area. However, if an establishment is not a unit within a chain, the availability of specific reliable data from other operations may be limited.

There are many industry surveys and studies available for the various categories or divisions of the hospitality service industries. These studies are published as often as once a month, and report current operating statistics and economic trends. Also, special governmental or educational studies are published periodically with statistical information for comparison. In most cases, there is some attempt to make the statistics and trends more useful for comparison by dividing the total population into reporting categories, such as all motels in a geographical location or all those with over two hundred and fifty rooms, etc. Because the operating costs and other statistics cannot be identified for individual hospitality service units, industry information available for comparison will be in the form of averages or other measurements of group data.

ARITHMETIC MEAN AND MEDIAN

The arithmetic mean, which is commonly known as an average, is the most frequently used method of describing the typical value of groups of quantitative data in the published studies of hospitality service industries. Means or averages are calculated by dividing the total of a group of data by the number of items in the group. The mean provides nothing more than a measure of the central tendency of the group.

A less-frequently used measure of the central tendency or typical value in a group of data is the median. The median value is the value of the middle item in the group; half of the items have higher values and half of the items have lower values. When there is an odd number of items the median value is found by listing the items in the group in ascending or descending order and selecting the middle item. When there is an even number of items in the group, the mean (average) of the two middle items is the median.

The following illustrates how an extreme value can distort the arithmetic mean.

	30
	75
	80
	85
	90
Total	360

The median is 80 since it is the middle item in the group. The average is 75 (360 divided by 5 observations).

The median of this group is probably more typical of the expected value of the items since it ignores the extreme value of the first item. Exhibits 7.1 and 7.2 illustrate the advantages and disadvantages of both means and medians in describing the typical value in a group of data.

Exhibit 7.1 presents daily food sales on Thursdays for seven successive weeks. The data is presented in tables, and both the mean and the median have been calculated. While the calculated mean and median are close in value, the median better tends to show what the central tendency has been over the seven-week period, since on six of the seven Thursdays, sales have been over $550. Thursday's sales of week two represent a single extreme item which has affected the value of the average so that it may not represent the most typical value of Thursday sales. In the case where there is a small percentage of unusually high or low values in a group, the median will be more representative of the typical value because it is not affected by extreme values within the group. Where both extreme high and low values similar in frequency and extremity exist in industry statistics, the advantage of the median is lost as the highs and lows tend to offset each other in the calculation of both the median and the average. Therefore, the advantage of the median exists when extreme values favor one end of the range of data.

When there are no extreme values in a distribution of items, the mean is usually a more reliable measure of the typical value. Such an example is illustrated in Exhibit 7.2, which represents Thursday food sales over another seven-week period. In this case, sales were low on the first three Thursdays, while sales in the last four weeks were much higher.

These examples illustrate that the choice between the use of the average or the median is largely dependent upon the composition of the data which is being evaluated. It is important to understand these factors since both methods are used to present data for the hospitality service industries. Because most people are more familiar with averages, the arithmetic mean is generally more widely used in various industry-published statistical information.

CHANGES AND VARIATIONS

The basic purpose of comparative analysis is to isolate and evaluate any differences between the compared items. These differences are denoted as changes

EXHIBIT 7.1

The Advantage of the Median

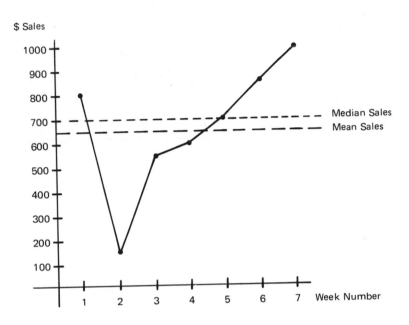

Mean (Average) Thursday Food Sales

Week	Thursday Sales
1	$ 800
2	150
3	550
4	600
5	700
6	850
7	950
Total	$ 4600

$$\text{Mean Sales} = \frac{\$4600}{7} = \$657$$

Median Thursday Food Sales

Week	Thursday Sales
2	$ 150
3	550
4	600
5	700
1	800
6	850
7	950
Total	$ 4600

Since the middle term of the distribution is $700, it is the *median* sales.

EXHIBIT 7.2

The Advantage of the Mean

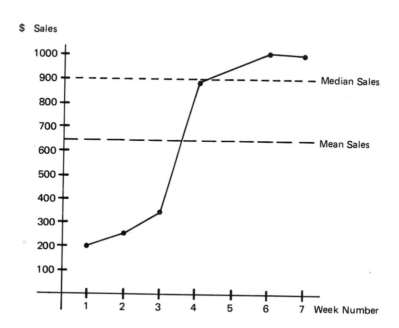

Mean (Average) Thursday Food Sales

Week	Thursday Sales
1	$ 200
2	250
3	350
4	900
5	950
6	1000
7	1000
Total	$ 4650

$$\text{Mean Sales} = \frac{\$4650}{7} = \$664$$

Median Thursday Food Sales

Week	Thursday Sales
1	$ 200
2	250
3	350
4	900
5	950
6	1000
7	1000
Total	$ 4650

Since the middle term of the distribution is $900, it is the *median* sales.

when comparing data between time periods and as variations when comparing current operating data with budgeted performance, other operations, or industry performance.

Changes and variations can be isolated only when the items being compared are in comparable units. Dollar amounts must be compared with dollar units, percentages with percentages, and other quantitative units with similar units.

When comparisons are made to other operations or to industry averages, favorable or unfavorable variations must be taken for what they are, comparisons of different operations. Because each hospitality service unit is unique, identical performance would not be realistic. Industry averages represent a composite of many circumstances and no single unit may be actually experiencing the average.

COMMON-SIZE STATEMENTS

The comparison of financial and operating statements between two hospitality service units or with industry averages can be limited by significant differences in size. Where there is a significant difference in size it is of limited value to compare the absolute dollar amounts of expenses and profit. However, the relative importance of each amount is readily comparable. Thus, if all amounts are expressed as a percentage of a common factor on each statement, meaningful comparisons are possible. This is done by expressing income statement accounts as a percentage of total revenue and balance sheet accounts as a percentage of total assets. Financial statements which are expressed in percentage terms are known as *common-size statements*. The need for common-size statements and their value in comparative analysis is illustrated in Exhibit 7.3.

The Multiple Restaurant Corporation owns and operates two restaurants in different metropolitan areas. The annual income statements for the two operations are presented in Exhibit 7.3. Unit I is a coffee shop operation with three hundred seats located in a shopping center. Unit II is a table service specialty restaurant with five hundred seats, banquet space, and a cocktail lounge. The obvious differences in size are reflected by the dollars in the unit income statements. The total sales in Unit II were twice that of Unit I, and the profit before rent and occupation costs exceeded that of Unit I by 75 percent, or $110,000.

As a result of the substantial differences in volume, the comparison of dollar expenses and profit gives no indication of the relative operating efficiency of the two units. In addition, there is no way of comparing the expense amounts resulting from the difference in the physical size of the two units, such as the larger dollar utilities expense, or repairs and maintenance expenses.

The comparison of two units of different size and volume can be facilitated by the construction of common-size statements. The dollar statements are

EXHIBIT 7.3

Multiple Restaurant Corporation
Unit Income Statements
for Year Ended December 31, 19XX

	Unit I	Unit II
Sales		
Food	$1,094,800	$1,481,900
Beverage	113,980	964,600
Total Sales	1,208,780	2,446,500
Cost of Sales		
Food	392,034	555,800
Beverage	34,437	270,600
Total Cost of Sales	426,471	826,400
Gross Profit	782,309	1,620,100
Other Income	9,642	19,200
Total Income	791,951	1,639,300
Controllable Expenses		
Payroll	415,295	851,300
Employee Benefits	47,478	143,200
Direct Operating Expenses	74,643	151,900
Advertising and Promotion	25,806	74,500
Utilities	28,556	53,300
Administrative and General	41,108	85,800
Repairs and Maintenance	12,664	21,700
Total Controllable Expenses	645,550	1,381,700
Profit Before Rent and Occupation Costs	$ 146,401	$ 257,600

converted to common-size statements by expressing all classifications as a percentage of total sales. Common-size income statements for Unit I and Unit II are presented in Exhibit 7.4.

In these common-size statements, the sum of the percentage costs of food and beverage sales do not equal the total cost of sales. This results from the modification of the base for the calculation of the food and beverage cost percentages. Since the cost of food sales is directly related to food sales and the cost of beverages to beverage sales, it is more meaningful to express these costs as a percentage of their respective sales. With the exception of these cost categories, all classifications, including total cost of sales, are expressed as a percentage of total sales.

EXHIBIT 7.4

Multiple Restaurant Corporation
Common-Size Unit Income Statements
for Year Ended December 31

	Unit I	Unit II
Sales		
Food	90.6%	60.6%
Beverage	9.4	39.4
Total Sales	100.0	100.0
Cost of Sales		
Food	35.8	37.5
Beverage	30.2	28.0
Total Cost of Sales	35.3	33.8
Gross Profit	64.7	66.2
Other Income	.8	.8
Total Income	65.5	67.0
Controllable Expenses		
Payroll	34.3	34.8
Employee Benefits	3.9	5.9
Direct Operating Expenses	6.2	6.2
Advertising and Promotion	2.1	3.0
Utilities	2.4	2.2
Administrative and General	3.4	3.5
Repairs and Maintenance	1.1	.9
Total Controllable Expenses	53.4	56.5
Profit Before Rent and		
Occupation Costs	12.1%	10.5%

A comparison of the percentages for the cost of sales sections of the income statements can be indicative of the effectiveness of controlling these costs and of the possible impact on profits of the mix between total food and beverage sales. The lower food cost percentage in Unit I implies that this operation has a higher menu price ratio to cost or better control over the cost of food. The opposite is true in the beverage department, as Unit II has a lower cost relationship. The lower total cost of sales percentage in Unit II results from the higher proportion of lower cost beverage sales. Thus, as a result of the sales mix and lower beverage cost, Unit II generated a proportionately higher gross profit on sales. In spite of a lower gross profit percentage, Unit I has attained a greater percentage profit before rent and occupation costs by maintaining a smaller percentage of total controllable expenses where the greatest differential is in the employee benefits expense.

Although common-size statements have been illustrated with the income statement, common-size balance sheets can also be a valuable comparative tool. Dollar balance sheets are converted to common-size by expressing all asset classifications as a percentage of total assets and all liability and equity classifications as a percentage of total liabilities and equities. Common-size balance sheets can be used to compare the financial structure of different operations, but they are more useful in evaluating changes in the proportionate amounts of balance sheet accounts between periods.

Common-size statements are needed to make valuable comparisons of operating performance between an individual hospitality service operation and the industry performance. Much of the industry data is presented in the common-size format and an individual operation must convert its statements to common-size before any comparison is possible.

Degree of Changes and Variations

The general significance of comparisons can frequently be determined by simple observation of the compared items. The discussion of the common-size food costs for the Multiple Restaurant Corporation exemplified this type of evaluation. The variation between food costs of the two units revealed that Unit I's food cost percentage was less than that in Unit II, and some general conclusions were drawn from that comparison. However, the significance of differences cannot be determined without calculating the degree of changes and variations. The degree of change or variation can be expressed as the absolute difference between items, or as the percentage relationship between the difference and one of the compared items.

When calculating the degree of change or variation, it is necessary to select one of the items as the base of the comparison. The other item is then compared to the base and the difference shown as a change or variation from the base.

Absolute Change or Variation

Although there are no standards for the selection of a base, some general guidelines can be given for the comparative analysis of financial statements. The earliest period is usually selected as the base of the calculation of changes between periods. In comparisons between current (or actual) data and budgeted or industry data, the latter is usually employed as the base. After a base has been selected, the absolute change or variation is calculated by subtracting the base from the other item.

The direction of the differences is denoted with symbols: a plus sign (+) indicating an item is larger than or has increased from the base, and a minus sign (-) denoting that an item is smaller than or has decreased from the base.

The calculation of selected absolute variations for the Multiple Restaurant Corporation are presented in Exhibit 7.5. Three types of quantitative data are presented: absolute dollar amounts, absolute non-dollar amounts, and percentage relationships. The data provided for Unit I has been arbitrarily selected as the base for the comparisons in this case.

EXHIBIT 7.5

Absolute Variations Illustrated

Item	(Base) Unit I	Unit II	Absolute Variation
Number of Seats	300	500	+200 seats
Other Income	$9,642	$19,200	+$9,558
Percentage Beverage Cost	30.2%	28.0%	-2.2% points

In comparisons which involve absolute amounts (dollars, seats, covers, etc.), the absolute variation is expressed in the same units. Hence, the number of seats in Unit II exceeds the capacity of Unit I by 200 seats, and other income in Unit II was $9,558 greater than in Unit I. In comparisons of percentage relationships, the absolute variation is expressed in percentage points. In the previous example, it would be incorrect to show the variation as -2.2 percent, because this would indicate a percentage relationship between the two cost percentages. Unit II's beverage cost percentage was 2.2 percentage points lower than that of Unit I.

The major limitation in the use of absolute variations is that the significance of the variation relative to the base is not reflected. For example, an absolute variation of 200 seats can have varied significance. If Unit I had only 50 seats and Unit II had 250 seats, the 200-seat variation would have considerable importance. However, if Unit I had 1,000 seats and Unit II had 1,200 seats, the difference has less significance.

Relative Changes and Variations

The aforementioned limitation can be removed by the calculation of the relative difference between the compared items. Relative changes and variations represent the absolute difference as a percentage of the base used for the comparison. This measure indicates the significance of absolute changes and variations as they relate to the compared items.

EXHIBIT 7.6

Relative Variations Illustrated

Item	(Base) Unit I	Unit II	Absolute Variation	Relative Variations
Number of Seats	300	500	+200 seats	+67%
Other Income	$9,642	$19,200	+$9,558	+99%
Percentage Beverage Cost	30.2%	28.0%	-2.2% points	-7.3%

Exhibit 7.6 illustrates the relative (percentage) variations for the same data that was presented in Exhibit 7.5. This calculation provides a means of evaluating the significance of the absolute variations between the compared items. For instance, it is more meaningful to consider the differential in seating capacities as Unit II having 67 percent more seats than Unit I. When stated in this manner, the variation in seating capacity is significant whether Unit I has 50 or 1,000 seats. The relative variation in other income shows that Unit II's income exceeds that of Unit I by 99 percent. Thus, without consideration of the dollar amounts involved, the relative variation shows that the other income of Unit II is about twice as much as that of Unit I.

The relative variation can be confusing when comparing percentage relationships as in the comparison of percentage beverage costs. For this reason, considerable emphasis is placed on the expression of the absolute difference in percentage points. The absolute difference of -2.2 percentage points represents 7.3 percent of the base (Unit I's beverage costs percentage). Thus, Unit II's beverage cost percentage is 7.3 percent less than that of Unit I.

There are also limitations on the significance of relative change or variation. The calculation of relative differences involves the use of mathematical ratios. Consequently, the resulting percentages are largely dependent upon the size of the base. If the base of the comparison is small, a small absolute difference can result in a very large percentage change or variation. In contrast, very large dollar differences will be shown as very small variations if the base is very large. The relative variation of 99 percent in other income exemplifies this limitation. This expression of the variation in other income implies a very significant differential between the two units. However, the absolute dollar variation of $9,558 is not material when considered in relation to the dollar revenue of the units.

Thus, when absolute variations are employed in the evaluation of comparisons of operating data and to express the differences, the significance of the differences may not be apparent. This may be compensated for by using the relative variance. However, it must be recognized that exclusive use of relative changes and variations can also be misleading. Therefore, consideration of both factors is necessary for effective evaluation of comparisons.

TREND ANALYSIS

Trend analysis is the technique of reviewing historical observations in search of a pattern which may be employed to project a path or trend into the future. It is used frequently in the hospitality service industries to forecast future revenues and levels of activity. Using trend analysis, past experience is projected into the future, making adjustments for known or expected changing conditions.

Trend analysis is a particular type of comparison, a comparison of results over several periods of time, and changes or variations may be noted in either absolute amounts or percentage changes (growth rates) using a selected base. The use of both absolute differences and growth rates is important in the search for trend patterns, for if the absolute difference does not result in a distinguishable pattern of change, the percentage rate may disclose such a pattern. This twofold analysis is illustrated in Exhibit 7.7, which sets forth the annual beverage revenue of a new cocktail lounge. In absolute changes the revenue is increasing substantially and each year's increase is greater than that of the year previous. Using the percentage change, the pattern is that of revenues increasing about 25 percent annually.

EXHIBIT 7.7

Four-Year Annual Beverage Revenue

Year	Revenue	Absolute Change	Percentage Change
1	$ 50,000		
2	63,000	+$13,000	+26%
3	79,000	+ 16,000	+25
4	100,000	+ 21,000	+27

Trend analysis is readily applicable in the planning and control responsibilities of management. As a planning tool, trend extension is valuable for projecting

future activity levels. As a control tool, trend analysis provides a means of anticipating the occurrence of an unacceptable operating result before its occurrence,
thus providing the opportunity to take corrective action before the loss occurrence. For example, the manager of a city club had established a policy of a food
cost percentage of no more than 40 percent, with an optimum food cost of 38
percent. For the past six months, weekly food costs had varied between 37.8 and
38.2 percent. However, in the current four-week period, food costs had been
increasing at approximately 2/10 of one percent each week and were now at 39.0
percent. With this information presented in a form that readily disclosed the
trend, the manager could determine the cause for this increasing cost and take
corrective action; if this trend continues for the next six weeks, food costs would
be in excess of his policy limit and substantially greater than the established
optimum.

Without the simple application of trend extension, this observation and alert
would not be possible. With the use of trend analysis, the manager is able to
detect trends and take the appropriate action before the unacceptable performance actually occurs and thus is able to keep the costs within predetermined
acceptable limits.

Trend analysis can neither provide complete answers for planning future
needs and levels of activity nor can it anticipate unsatisfactory results, since it is
based upon an assumption that the conditions which resulted in past performance
will continue, or that changing conditions are known and measurable. This
assumption is necessary to utilize trend analysis effectively. If all the pertinent
conditions are known to the analyzer, any expected changes in those conditions
can be forecast and their effect upon operating results estimated. The success of
trend analysis is entirely dependent upon the isolation and knowledge of the
pertinent conditions, the anticipation of their change, and the estimation of the
effect the changes will have on the data trends.

Charts are one of the most frequently used means of trend analysis. Patterns
that may not be apparent by studying the figures frequently become clear when
charted. For example, Exhibit 7.8 presents data for a country club experiencing
membership problems. In studying the figures, it may be clear that the current
trend is down even though there are three years in which increases were experienced. Looking at the chart, it is immediately apparent that the downward trend
is severe and that if it continues for several more years, the club will no longer
exist.

Going back to the city club food cost trend referred to above, it may be seen
that maintenance of a food cost chart would greatly facilitate the monitoring of
this cost for control purposes. Exhibit 7.9 illustrates the chart of these food costs.
Again, using a chart for presenting the data, the trend of the food cost percentage
is apparent.

EXHIBIT 7.8

Membership Trend

Year	Total Members	Absolute Change
1	250	
2	200	−50
3	225	+25
4	150	−75
5	200	+50
6	225	+25
7	125	−100
8	75	−50

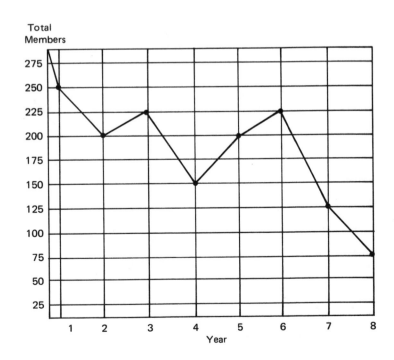

EXHIBIT 7.9

City Club
Food Cost Percent

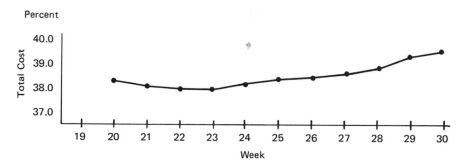

In seeking answers from trend patterns, determinations must be made as to how far back data should be considered and the weight to be given to observations that appear to differ substantially from some overall trend pattern. (See, for example, Exhibit 7.10.)

EXHIBIT 7.10

Trend Analysis
Period 8 to 20

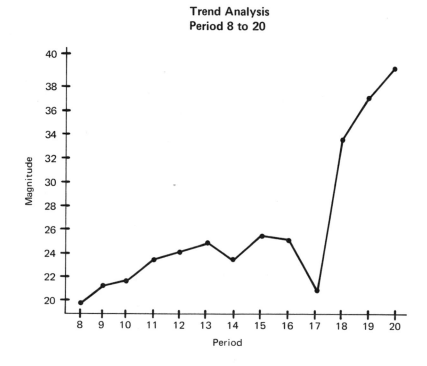

If only the last three periods are considered, the trend is apparent. Similarly, if the last five periods are used but period seventeen is eliminated (because it is contrary to the trend), the same trend is disclosed. But, if period seventeen should be included, or all periods back to period eight, a somewhat different trend is suggested.

In a circumstance such as this, it may be possible to determine the underlying conditions that caused such results. Thus, if the condition that caused the period seventeen results can be isolated, a determination may be made as to the likelihood of it recurring and a weighting may be determined to be given to the results of period seventeen.

COMPARATIVE RATES OF RETURN—FINANCIAL LEVERAGE

In the profit segment of the hospitality service industries, the most important measure of success is the annual return on the owner's investment. In the smaller, closely held hospitality firm, the return is the annual earnings after taxes equated to the total owner's investment; in the publicly owned company, it is the annual earnings per share equated to the quoted market price.

Analysis and comparison of these relationships are fundamental to the overall evaluation of the total progress of the firm. Comparisons of these rates of return are made between periods and between firms within the profit sector of the hospitality service industries, and with various other investment opportunities available in the market place, including common stock ownership in an industrial or other commercial enterprise.

In analyzing and evaluating the comparative rates of return between two hospitality service entities, the underlying financial structure of each must be recognized because one company may have borrowed more capital than the other. The company that borrows maximum amounts is using the technique of trading on the equity or financial leverage.

Whenever the earnings derived from the use of borrowed funds yield a greater rate of return than the interest charged for the use of the borrowed capital, the excess yield accrues to the owners of the business and increases the rate of return on their invested capital. This fundamental leverage concept must be considered in all analysis and comparisons of the various rates of return on equity capital.

The benefits and the hazards of the use of leverage can be illustrated through the use of a hypothetical comparison. The Restful Restaurants and the Risky Restaurants are two corporations which were organized to own and operate fast food restaurants. They both own an equal number of restaurants and they earn equal profits from operations (net earnings before interest and income taxes). The only difference between the two organizations is the means of financing used.

Exhibit 7.11 presents condensed balance sheets for the two companies. Total assets are the same for both organizations, as are the current assets, fixed assets and current liabilities. However, the source of monies to finance these assets

EXHIBIT 7.11

**Restful Restaurants
and
Risky Restaurants
Condensed Balance Sheets
December 31, 19XX**

Assets	Restful Restaurants	Risky Restaurants
Current Assets	$ 300,000	$ 300,000
Fixed Assets	2,000,000	2,000,000
Total Assets	$2,300,000	$2,300,000
Liabilities and Stockholders' Equity		
Current Liabilities	$ 300,000	$ 300,000
Long-term Debt @ 8%	-	1,000,000
Stockholders' Equity	2,000,000	1,000,000
Total	$2,300,000	$2,300,000
Shares of Common Stock Outstanding	100,000	50,000

differs markedly. All of the Restful Restaurants' fixed assets have been financed through the sale of 100,000 shares of common stock at $20.00 a share. The Risky Restaurants have employed financial leverage by financing $1,000,000 worth of assets with long-term debts at 8 percent interest, and the remaining $1,000,000 through the sale of 50,000 shares of common stock at the identical price of $20.00 per share.

This single difference in the financial structure between the two organizations will result in an additional annual fixed interest expense of $80,000 for the Risky Restaurants. This additional expense will have a significant impact on the annual profits. At equal volumes, the annual dollar profits for the Risky Restaurants will always be less than annual profits for the Restful Restaurants. However, this does not mean that the rate of return on the owners' investment will always be lower for the Risky Restaurants because the owner's investment in the Risky Restaurants is only half of that in the Restful Restaurants. Thus, a smaller annual dollar profit for Risky may result in a higher rate of return on the owners' investment.

The impact of financial leverage on the rate of return is illustrated in Exhibit 7.12 with four graduated levels of annual income for the high-leverage company (Risky) and the no-leverage company (Restful).

EXHIBIT 7.12

Restful Restaurants
and
Risky Restaurants
Graduated Income Statements
for Year Ended December 31, 19XX

	Restful Restaurants				Risky Restaurants			
	Case #1	Case #2	Case #3	Case #4	Case #1	Case #2	Case #3	Case #4
Earnings Before Interest and Income Taxes	$0	$100,000	$160,000	$300,000	$ 0	$100,000	$160,000	$300,000
Less: Interest	0	-	-	-	80,000	80,000	80,000	80,000
Earnings Before Income Taxes	$0	$100,000	$160,000	$300,000	$(80,000)	$ 20,000	$ 80,000	$220,000
Income Taxes—Estimated	0	48,000	76,800	144,000	-	9,600	38,400	105,600
Net Income	$0	$ 52,000	$ 83,200	$156,000	$(80,000)	$ 10,400	$ 41,600	$114,400
Net Income (Loss) Per Share	$0	$ .52	$ .83	$ 1.56	$ (1.60)	$ .20	$ .83	$ 2.29
Return on Stockholders' Equity	0%	2.6%	4.2%	7.8%	(8.0%)	1.0%	4.2%	11.4%

169

Case 1

Case #1 represents the volume of sales at which net profit before interest charges and income taxes equals zero. Restful Restaurants break even at this level (total revenues equal total expenses) since there are no interest charges. If there is no profit, there is a zero rate of return on owners' investment; the owners neither make nor lose any money. However, at this same level of profit, Risky Restaurants incur a fixed interest charge of $80,000, resulting in a net loss of the same amount. This represents a negative return on the owners' investment, and the owners' investment would be involuntarily reduced by the $80,000. Thus, net profit before interest and taxes must be $80,000 before the Risky Restaurants can break even.

Case 2

If net earnings before interest and taxes (NEBIT) reach $100,000, both companies will earn a positive rate of return for their investors. However, investors in the Restful company would earn a greater rate of return at this profit level.

Case 3

This case shows the profit level at which there is no difference between equity and debt financing. When NEBIT reach $160,000, both companies earn a return of 4.2 percent on their owners' investment. When annual profits are in excess of this profit level, the use of debt financing becomes advantageous. The rate of return will be greater for the Risky owners than for the Restful owners at any level of NEBIT above $160,000.

Case 4

With NEBIT at $300,000, the use of financial leverage benefits Risky Restaurant owners. At this profit level, the owners of the Restful Restaurants earn a rate of 7.8 percent on their invested capital. Although the Risky Restaurants will generate $41,600 less in total dollar profits, the return on their smaller owners' investment is 11.4 percent. Thus, leverage has benefited the Risky owners by yielding a return on invested capital which is nearly 50 percent greater than in the Restful company which has been financed totally through equity capital.

The impact of leverage on earnings per share (EPS) is shown graphically in Exhibit 7.13. This presentation makes it possible to visualize the paths of earnings per share for the two companies as net income before interest and income taxes increases. The intersection of the two EPS curves, when net earnings before interest and taxes equals $160,000, is the point at which the application of

EXHIBIT 7.13

**A Graphic Representation
of the Impact of Leverage
on Earnings per Share**

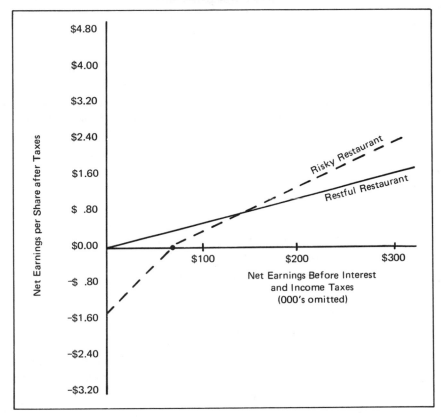

financial leverage will benefit the owners. Below this point, the graph shows earnings per share declining at a higher rate in the leveraged firm. However, as NEBIT grow larger than $160,000, net earnings per share increase at a much higher rate in the leveraged company.

The preceding discussion of leverage has been focused on a comparative analysis of two hypothetical companies which were identical except for the method used to finance their assets. This would seldom occur, but the effect of financial leverage on the comparison process must always be considered before a final conclusion is made. In addition, a single company which is evaluating the effect of two financing proposals for the expansion of the business will make the financial leverage analysis an integral part of their financing decisions.

SUMMARY

Quantitative information is valuable only where comparisons are made to disclose the significance of the information. These comparisons are most effective when made to budgeted performance but other internal and external comparisons may also be useful.

The mean and median are frequently employed techniques for describing the central tendency of a group of data. Where extreme values are present, the median may provide a better estimate of the central tendency than the mean.

Where differences occur as the result of making comparisons, they are referred to as *changes* when the comparison is made between time periods, and as *variations* when the comparison is for the same period of time such as comparisons with budgets, other operations, or industry performance. The use of common-size statements facilitates the comparison of different-sized operations. When comparing two items, one should be designated as the base. The other may then be compared to the base by determining the absolute or percentage difference.

Trend analysis is a frequently employed tool in the hospitality service industries. Through its application it is possible to forecast future activity levels and anticipate unacceptable operating results before their occurrence.

When profits increase the application of financial leverage provides a means for a profit-oriented operation to increase its potential return on owners' investment. However, when profits decline, the use of financial leverage increases the losses and the risk to owners.

Discussion Questions

1. What are the pertinent factors to consider when establishing a trend analysis?
2. What is trend analysis and how would it aid managerial decision-making?
3. How does relative variation differ from absolute variation?
4. What are the limitations involved in the use of the absolute and the relative variation?
5. How do common-size statements aid in the comparison of financial statements?

Problem 1

Express the following income statement in common-size percentages and tell whether the situation shown is favorable or unfavorable.

	1970	1969
Revenue	$100,000	$ 90,000
Cost of Goods Sold	67,500	60,390
Gross Profit	32,500	29,610
Operating Expenses	25,300	22,860
Net Income	$ 7,200	$ 6,750

Problem 2

Calculate trend percentages for the following items and tell whether the situation shown by the trends is favorable or unfavorable.

	1966	1967	1968	1969	1970
Combined Revenue	$150,000	$169,500	$178,500	$186,500	$195,000
Combined Inventories	30,000	36,000	39,600	42,600	46,200
Accounts Receivable	18,000	23,040	24,300	25,200	27,360

Problem 3

Condensed comparative financial statements for the Jones Restaurant appear below.

Jones Restaurant
Comparative Balance Sheet
as of October 30
(in Thousands of Dollars)

	Year 3	Year 2	Year 1
Assets			
Current Assets	$1,100	$1,000	$1,200
Furniture and Fixtures			
(Net of Accumulated Depreciation)	6,600	6,000	4,200
Intangible Assets (Net)	400	500	600
Total Assets	$8,100	$7,500	$6,000
Liabilities and Stockholders' Equity			
Current Liabilities	$ 450	$ 500	$ 600
Long-term Liabilities	900	1,000	1,200
Capital Stock ($25 par)	4,050	3,750	2,400
Capital in Excess of par Value	900	750	300
Retained Earnings	1,800	1,500	1,500
Total Liabilities and Stockholders' Equity	$8,100	$7,500	$6,000

Jones Restaurant
Comparative Income Statement
for Years Ended October 30
(in Thousands of Dollars)

	Year 3	Year 2	Year 1
Net Revenue (Food and Beverage)	$30,000	$25,000	$20,000
Cost of Goods Sold (Food and Beverage)	19,500	15,500	12,000
Gross Profit	10,500	9,500	8,000
Selling Expenses	6,000	5,100	4,000
Administrative Expenses	3,300	3,250	3,000
Interest Expense	90	75	80
Total Expense	9,390	8,425	7,080
Net Income Before Income Taxes	1,110	1,075	920
Provision for Income Taxes	510	500	420
Net Income	$ 600	$ 575	$ 500

Problem 3 (continued)
Required

1. Prepare common-size comparative balance sheets for the three-year period, expressing all assets as a percentage of total assets, etc.
2. Prepare the common-size comparative income statements for the three-year period, expressing all items as percentage components of net sales.
3. Comment on significant trends and relationships revealed by the analytical computations in (1) and (2).

Problem 4

Comparative balance sheets and income statements for the X Hotel Corporation are presented.

X Hotel Corporation
Comparative Balance Sheet
as of December 31
(in Thousands of Dollars)

	Year 2	Year 1	Increase or (Decrease)
Assets			
Current Assets	$2,340	$1,890	$450
Building and Fixtures (net)	1,025	840	185
Total Assets	$3,365	$2,730	$635
Liabilities and Stockholders' Equity			
Current Liabilities	$ 970	$ 900	$ 70
Long-term Liabilities	400	500	(100)
Total Liabilities	1,370	1,400	(30)
Capital Stock ($20 Par Value)	1,100	800	300
Capital in Excess of Par Value	340	100	240
Retained Earnings	555	430	125
Total Stockholders' Equity	1,995	1,330	665
Total Liabilities and Stockholders' Equity	$3,365	$2,730	$635

X Hotel Corporation
Details of Current Assets and Liabilities
as of December 31
(in Thousands of Dollars)

	Year 2	Year 1	Increase or (Decrease)
Current Assets			
Cash	$ 550	$ 440	$110
Receivables (net)	830	700	130
Food and Beverage Inventories	750	500	250
Prepaid Expenses	210	250	(40)
Total Current Assets	$2,340	$1,890	$450
Current Liabilities			
Accounts Payable	$ 590	$ 690	($100)
Accrued Expenses	380	210	170
Total Current Liabilities	$ 970	$ 900	$ 70

Problem 4 (continued)

X Hotel Corporation
Comparative Statement of Retained Earnings
for Years Ended December 31
(in Thousands of Dollars)

	Year 2	Year 1	Change
Balance Beginning of Year	$ 430	$ 365	$ 65
Net Income	200	105	95
Dividends	(75)	(40)	(35)
Balance End of Year	$ 555	$ 430	$125

X Hotel Corporation
Comparative Income Statement
for Years Ended December 31
(in Thousands of Dollars)

	Year 2	Year 1	Year 2	Year 1
Net Revenue	$2,600	$2,300	100.0%	100.0%
Cost of Goods Sold	1,600	1,500	61.5	65.2
Gross Profit	1,000	800	38.5	34.8
Operating Expenses	600	580	23.1	25.2
Net Operating Income	400	220	15.4	9.6
Interest Expense	20	25	.8	1.1
Net Income Before Income Taxes	380	195	14.6	8.5
Provision for Income Taxes	180	90	6.9	3.9
Net Income	$ 200	$ 105	7.7%	4.6%

Additional information: Additional shares of common stock were issued on July 15, year two. Of the dividends paid during year two, $55,000 was paid after the issue of the new shares.

At the beginning of year one, food and beverage inventories were $440,000 and net receivables were $620,000. Terms of payment are net thirty days.

The market value of the common stock was $20 per share at the end of year one and $40 per share at the end of year two.

Required

1. Make a comparative analysis of the current working capital position of the X Hotel Corporation for the two years. Compute whatever ratios you feel are useful and write a brief statement of your conclusions as to favorable and unfavorable trends, from the viewpoint of a prospective short-term creditor.

2. Prepare an analysis of the X Hotel Corporation from the viewpoint of a prospective long-term investor in the common stock. Compute any ratios you feel would be useful and write a brief statement of your conclusions.

CHAPTER 8

Management Information Systems

BASIC CONCEPTS OF MANAGEMENT INFORMATION SYSTEMS

In the terminology of business, "information systems," "total systems," "the systems approach" and "integrated systems" are all related to and often used synonymously with the term "management information system" (MIS). A management information system is the network for the generation and communication of pertinent and timely quantitative and qualitative information to all levels of management for planning, directing and controlling the operations of an organization.

In dealing with management information systems the following terms will be used:

Data: unorganized raw facts which become the basis from which information is developed. An example of data would be a group of restaurant checks for one day.

Information: organized data that is significant to management. An example of information would be the total dollar volume by meal period of restaurant sales for one day. This information would come from organizing and accumulating the data on the restaurant checks.

System: a framework of interconnected parts through which an activity is performed. An example of a system would be the way in which restaurant checks flow from the waitress to the cashier to the bookkeeper who organizes the data on the checks into information.

MIS—A COMMUNICATION SYSTEM

Underlying the aforementioned definitions is the concept that an MIS, in its broadest sense, is the communication system of the organization. Its total objective is to provide the means to collect, analyze, summarize, store and transmit data provided by the operating systems of a firm. The MIS should be designed to insure that management receives the information it needs to carry out its decision-making functions in planning, directing and controlling the activities of the organization.

As the communication system of an organization, the MIS must be designed to generate the kind of information that is required for that particular organization. Management information systems for the hospitality service industries will vary between each segment and between different firms within each segment.

All hospitality service firms are service-oriented and cost-control conscious, while only some are profit-oriented in their goals. For example, a cafeteria could be operated as a commercial venture to produce a return on the owners' investment, or as part of a school dormitory, a company cafeteria, or a military mess hall. The primary information requirements for the profit entity may differ from the information required to meet the service goals of the not-for-profit service firm. Accordingly, hospitality service industries managers should be concerned with both profit- and service-oriented information for their decision-making process.

Examples of profit-oriented information would be financial reports on earnings per share, income tax plans and projected returns on alternative investments. Service-oriented information deals with service units by hour and other reports as to the use of the firm's facilities to achieve guest satisfaction.

FORMAL AND INFORMAL ASPECTS OF A MANAGEMENT INFORMATION SYSTEM

A good MIS provides for both formal and informal transmission of information. The formal transmission of information involves the use of forms and reports at various levels of management on a predetermined time schedule. Data is collected as various events occur and are recorded. The record in turn is transmitted to a collection point where it is analyzed and a determination made as to its informational significance within the framework of the entire organization. If the data has a possibility of becoming pertinent information in making a decision, it is either transmitted to the decision-makers, included with other facts in another form or report, or filed as future reference for inclusion in a report.

Exhibit 8.1 is an example of the formal information flow. This exhibit illustrates how a guest's food order in a hotel restaurant becomes information for management at several levels in the organization.

The informal transmission of information includes oral communications and visual inspections or observations. An example of an informal information flow would be when a waitress fails to report to work for a banquet. The maitre d' might orally communicate this to the catering manager who would in turn have to take action. His action might be to transfer a waitress from the main dining room staff or to call in another waitress.

EXHIBIT 8.1

The Formal Information Flow
for the Cash Restaurant Sale

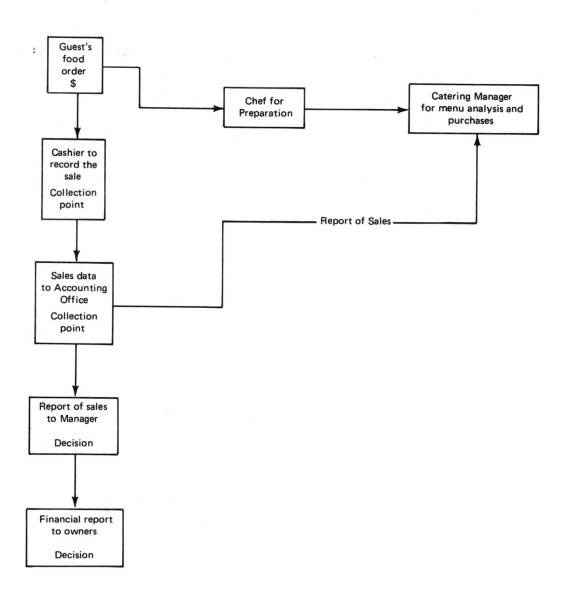

THE FLOW OF INFORMATION IN AN ORGANIZATION

In the hospitality service industries, as in most other industries, the logical flow of information would be through the formal lines of authority and responsibility established by the firm's organization chart. Exhibit 8.2 is an example of an organization chart from a typical unit in the lodging segment of the hospitality service industries.

EXHIBIT 8.2

**The ABC Motel
Organization Chart**

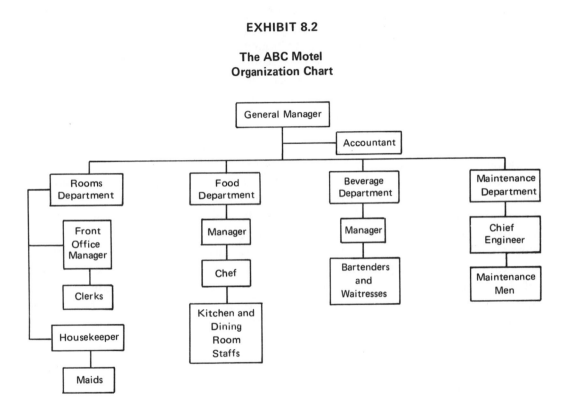

Information should flow up and down throughout the organization and horizontally at the upper levels of management. In the illustration, some information should flow horizontally among the department managers who report to the general manager. If information flows diagonally in the organization, the lines of authority and responsibility become hazy and confused.

MANAGEMENT INFORMATION SYSTEMS AND DECISION-MAKING

The information system forms the basis of management decisions and of management's continuing functions of coordinating and controlling the firm's operations. The most important decisions that management makes are those in the area of planning for the future.

THE PLANNING FUNCTION

The planning function can be segmented into strategic or long-range planning and short-range planning. The strategic or long-range planning activities are made by the firm's ownership and are basic policy decisions. These policy decisions must be made within the constraints of the firm's internal strengths and weaknesses. These internal factors include the financial resources, plant and equipment, managerial and operating manpower resources. In addition, strategic plans must be made within the constraints of the external environment. Forecasts should be made of the economic climate, the competition, the changing preferences of guests and the changing technology of the industry. All of these factors must be considered when a firm prepares its strategic or long-range planning.

Strategic planning establishes the goals and objectives which form the basis of all operational decisions. For example, the owners of a nursing home might decide to build a second home in another suburb. This is a strategic decision, and it is followed by the strategic or long-range plan. Planning will allocate resources, determine financing and the size and types of facilities for the proposed property. The time span of this planning phase will vary with the nature, size and location of the property. However, in all segments of the hospitality service industries, this would involve a major investment in a fixed plant. It may take from two to five years to carry out long-range plans. When the project is finished and operational, short-range planning is implemented. Short-range planning usually covers a period of one year or less.

THE DECISION-MAKING MODEL

The management information system must be designed to assist the planning process and it must also assist management in the step-by-step process of reaching decisions. For in order to reach any decision, the decision-maker goes through an evaluation process similar to the decision-making model shown in Exhibit 8.3.

Before any decisions can be made, the objectives of the firm must be known in order to give direction in the decision-making process. Relevant information should be formulated and alternative solutions detailed and examined. With all the alternatives fully explored and outlined, the decision-maker must rank the alternatives on the following scale.

EXHIBIT 8.3

A Decision-Making Model

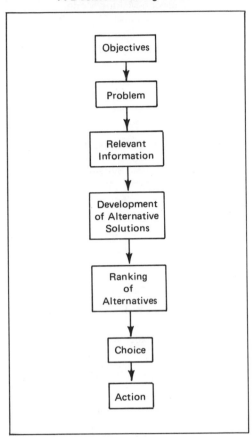

Certainty: accurate knowledge of the cost and benefit of each alternate.

Risk: accurate knowledge of the probable cost and benefit of each alternate.

Uncertainty: incomplete knowledge of the cost and benefit of each alternate.

Complete certainty is almost nonexistent in business decisions. Most business decisions are based on risk. On the other hand, there is no reasonable basis for choosing an alternative based on uncertainty. Business decisions are rarely made with complete and correct information, because of the cost and time involved in compiling competent and relevant information.

A mathematical approach called "operations research" can be used in decision-making. Operations research uses the concept of mathematical modeling. The steps taken in this decision-making approach are shown in Exhibit 8.4.

EXHIBIT 8.4

**Operations Research
Decision-Making Model**

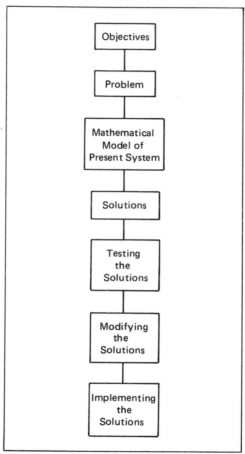

As with the traditional approach, the objectives must be determined and the problem defined. Then a mathematical model of the system under study is constructed. Next, solutions to the problems are devised and put into the mathematical model. Finally, the solution is tested and modified to obtain and implement the optimal choice.

Whether the traditional or operations research approach is followed, the decision-maker needs all the pertinent information available if he is to reach the best decision. A firm's MIS should be designed to generate and transmit this information to the decision-maker as quickly and simply as possible. The decision-maker should receive only relevant information and he should receive no more and no less information than he needs.

CRITERIA OF A SOUND MANAGEMENT INFORMATION SYSTEM

A properly designed management information system would have the following characteristics:

1. It should function through the lines of communication established by the firm's organization chart.
2. It should be clear and simple so that employees can understand the system and operate within its constraints.
3. It should report information on a timely basis.
4. It should provide the necessary information for good internal control, including the control reports to be used in evaluating performance.
5. It should generate reports for all levels of management and ownership.
6. It should be adaptable to changing requirements, as it is important to have a system that can be adapted quickly to produce more information or to function in a more sophisticated environment.

A properly designed management information system must produce information with the following characteristics:

1. *Usefulness and relevancy.* If the information is not going to provide a basis for evaluating performance or for future planning, then the MIS should not produce it.
2. *Significance.* The information should be important enough to influence the decisions of the user.
3. *Understandability.* The information should be stated simply and concisely, and, where possible, should be quantified in a format that allows it to be compared with similar information.
4. *Accuracy and reliability.* There should be adequate documentation to support the accuracy of the information. The degree of accuracy will depend upon the source of the information, which should be free from bias.
5. *Practicality and economy.* The value of the information should exceed the cost of producing it.

DESIGN AND MAINTENANCE OF THE MANAGEMENT INFORMATION SYSTEM

The designer of the MIS must use care and judgment to provide as many of the aforementioned sound characteristics as possible. Considerations of economy must not override efficiency. The least expensive method may be too slow and, therefore, the usefulness and relevancy criteria would not be satisfied.

All of the characteristics in the previous section should be considered in designing and maintaining the MIS, and the system design must consider both the formal and informal flow of information. The system should begin with a formal written manual describing job duties and responsibilities and the flow of data and information throughout the organization.

DATA COLLECTION POINTS

In most hospitality service industries firms, the central collection point for data is the accounting department. In some larger hotels, hospitals and schools with computers, the accounting department shares this responsibility with the data processing department. Depending on the size of the hospitality service firm, there could be many other collection points for data. For example, in a large resort there might be the front desk, several food and beverage outlets and many recreational departments. These secondary collection points eventually transfer most of their data to the accounting or data processing departments. They do, however, retain some data to be used in preparing reports that are part of the MIS.

The accounting department collects all data needed to perform its reporting and record-keeping functions. It receives data or information from each operating department on sales, costs, labor, expenses and credit and collections. This data is then analyzed, summarized, reported and stored in the records of the firm. These records are designed in conformity with the appropriate Uniform System of Accounts and include the firm's books of account for cash receipts, cash disbursements, purchases, sales, payroll, plant assets, accounts receivable and food, beverage and miscellaneous inventories.

The most important accounting department function is to analyze and disseminate information. Secondary information must be sorted out and only the pertinent information needed for decision-making forwarded to management and ownership. For example, the front office manager is not interested in food cost, but the food manager is interested in occupancy and projected occupancy for staff planning. The accountant who collects most information and supervises the MIS must be able to get the correct information in the hands of those who need it.

The accountant must analyze the information and provide appropriate comments in reports so that the information can be properly interpreted by the user. The manager must be able to use the reports he receives; they must contain the information he needs.

CHARACTERISTICS OF REPORTS

Reports should be designed so that they present information in the best possible way. All reports should be designed to include the following characteristics of good reporting:

1. *Clarity:* reports should be clear, concise and written in good style so that they are easy to read.
2. *Consistency:* reports should stay within the proper context. Meanings and terms should not change within the report.
3. *Adequacy:* the report should be complete in all respects.
4. *Timeliness:* information should be presented as soon after the event as possible.
5. *Responsibility-oriented:* the person receiving the report should receive only that information which is pertinent to his responsibility and duties.
6. *Exception-oriented:* the report should highlight areas where actual performance deviates from established standards. For example, if labor costs exceed the forecasted level, the report should bring this to the immediate attention of the reader.
7. *Comparability:* whenever information can be compared to other information, the report should contain such comparisons. This point is particularly important in the reporting of operations. For example, the monthly income statement should contain budgeted figures so that the reader can have a basis for comparison of performance.

REPORTING LEVELS

Management reports exist at all levels in an organization. While many reports are intended to be forwarded to individuals at more than one reporting level, it is common to find reports intended for a single individual. These reports should provide that individual with the information required to monitor the functions for which he has direct responsibility. Examples of this type of report are the food cost report for the chef and the beverage cost report for the beverage manager.

As the level of management for which reports are intended gets higher, the nature of the information contained in the reports changes. At the departmental level the information is rather specific and frequently in such terms as output per man hour and cost per unit of service. These reports provide information that allows the department head to immediately isolate deficiencies in his operation. At higher reporting levels, the information tends to be broader and more general in nature, so that at the chief executive level the information may be condensed to the financial statements, operating statistics, departmental performance, budgets and special study reports.

Since different operating executives at the same reporting level have different areas of responsibility, they generally have different information needs. The food and beverage manager does not need the housekeeping labor report, nor does the housekeeper need the food cost report. However, there are instances where several department heads may use the same information for different purposes. For example, a catering sales report is required by both the catering manager and the catering sales manager.

EXCEPTION REPORTING

Management is responsible for the performance of the total operation and must be in a position to take corrective action in the event of unsatisfactory performance. An efficient method of keeping management informed is through exception reporting. Exception reporting is a method by which management can keep informed about current deficiencies while, at the same time, diminishing the volume of information received. Exception reporting involves the development of standards for monitoring operating departments or areas in a firm. Usually the standards provide for an acceptable range of performance. Only data which deviates to an unacceptable level from these standards is reported to management. Thus, a manager will have information reported to him only about departments or areas where his attention is or may be required. It may then be assumed that all other areas are operating satisfactorily, that is, within the range of performance which has been established as acceptable.

Exception reporting is a useful tool in the design of all management reports in addition to those which are solely on an exception basis, for it isolates problem areas.

TIME PERIOD AND FREQUENCY OF REPORTS

Effective management consists of the ability to react to and correct deficiencies in operations at the earliest possible moment. As a result, the frequency of reports should be closely related to the ability of management to influence or control items included within particular reports. Some elements of operations, such as food and beverage costs and payroll costs, can be controlled readily and should be the subject of frequent reporting. Other items, such as interest expense, depreciation, and other overhead expenses are not readily controllable and less frequency in reporting them is required.

The time period of a report refers to that period over which the reported activity occurred. This is different from the frequency of a report. For example, dining room sales could be reported over the time period of the day, meal period, or hour, but the report might be transmitted to management daily. Often, the time period and frequency correspond, as would be the case if meals were reported on a daily basis.

The length of time between the end of the reporting period and the delivery of the report must be kept to a minimum. This time lapse should be related to the length of the reporting period in that the shorter the reporting period, the less time it should take to prepare the report and deliver it. For example, daily reports received early the next day maintain their value for prompt corrective action.

Without exception, reports should reach management early in the following reporting period. Management will then have the opportunity to affect the following period's results. Thus, daily reports should reach the recipient during the morning of the following day, while annual information is useful even if the time lapse is a few weeks after the end of the fiscal year.

TYPES OF INFORMATION

Some reports will be only quantitative; some will be only qualitative; and some will be both quantitative and qualitative. Most business reports are primarily quantitative and include both financial and statistical information.

Financial information involves the reporting of absolute dollar values, amounts which may be presented independently or in statement form. The most common financial reports are the income statement, balance sheet, source and application of funds statement, and supporting schedules.

Statistical information involves the presentation of quantitative data in other than absolute dollar amounts. Frequently the information is the analysis of financial data and includes various ratios, common-size statements, and average cost and average revenue items. Additional types of statistical information include units of activity and productivity.

Statistical and financial information together provide management with only quantitative information. However, management frequently needs information which must be presented qualitatively. Qualitative information is information which cannot be expressed numerically. This type of information, and the reports in which it is contained, range from a description of the weather on a daily operating report to a special report on employee morale. Many times qualitative information is in narrative form, as contrasted with a single word or a short phrase, and may involve interpretation of financial or statistical information.

Some of the basic reports that should be included in the MIS of hospitality service industries include the daily activity reports as well as departmental or unit operating and financial statements.

The following hospitality service industry reports are listed here to provide an example of the reporting framework of the management information system.

DAILY REPORTS

1. *Manager's daily report:* a summary of the previous day's sales, cash balance and accounts receivable balances, which allow the manager to quickly see what is happening to current business. This report should contain month-to-date information and comparative information of the previous year.

2. *Housekeeping report:* a detailed report of rooms serviced by the housekeeping department prepared by the housekeeper. This report would be used by the front desk and the accounting department to be sure all room charges have been recorded in the accounting records.

3. *Occupancy report:* a short report prepared by the front desk to be used as a basis for scheduling by the housekeeping department and the food and beverage departments. This report would contain information about current occupancy and expected occupancy based on reservations that have been made.

MONTHLY AND YEARLY REPORTS

1. *Budgets:* these reports would be prepared on a monthly basis for a minimum of one year into the future. All department heads and middle level managers would participate in the preparation of the budget. Past reports and information about the future expectations of occupancy would be used to forecast sales and costs and expenses. All current reports would be related to the budget, in that significant variances from the budget would be highlighted.

2. *The balance sheet:* this statement would be prepared by the accountant and used by owners and the management. It should be prepared in comparative form with that of the previous year.

3. *Statement of profit and loss:* a statement prepared by the accountant and used by owners and the management, it should include a comparison of the operating results of the previous period with the budget for the current period. Significant variances between budgets and/or previous periods should be highlighted for corrective action.

4. *Statement of source and application of funds:* this would be prepared by the accountant and used by owners as a basis for planning future major capital requirements and projects.

5. *Food and beverage cost reports and labor cost reports:* these reports would be prepared by the accountant for the manager and the applicable depart-

ment heads. Cost reports should present budgeted amounts, with significant variances highlighted for corrective action.

SUMMARY

A management information system is an organized method of providing owners and managers with the financial and operating information they need at the time that it is needed. It should supply the information needed to plan, coordinate and control the operations of the firm. The MIS should utilize standards and budgets to facilitate the use of exception reporting, wherever possible. The system should be all-inclusive and recognize the needs of all departments so that the requirements of each can be satisfied with a minimum of duplication.

One of the important functions of an MIS is to generate information for both strategic or long-range planning, and short-range planning. In evaluating alternatives in preparing plans, each alternative should be ranked on the basis of available information.

Information provided by an MIS should be useful and relevant, significant, understandable, reasonably accurate and reliable, and practical and economical.

Reports, the primary formal output of an MIS, should be clear, consistent, adequate, timely, responsibility-oriented, exception-based, and comparative.

Discussion Questions

1. What is a management information system?
2. Explain the difference between data and information.
3. How does informal communication supplement formal reports and forms?
4. What part does an organization chart play in the MIS?
5. What are the criteria for a sound management information system and why is each important?
6. How does exception reporting make more effective use of management?

Problem 1

On October 17, 19XX, Mr. Edwards sent a check for $48.00 to the Merry Hotel as a deposit for a room for three nights. November 30, Mr. Edwards arrived. The room rate is $24.00 per day. During his brief stay, his charges at the restaurant amounted to $51.60 while charges at the bar were $26.80. Show symbolically the flow of information from each of the departments to his guest folio at check-out time.

Problem 2

From the following information prepare a daily revenue report.

Beginning Balance	$42,972.00
Sales Tax	148.00
Guest Paid-outs	27.00
Telephone—Local	16.00
Complimentary Rooms	37.00
Vending Machines	8.00
Rooms	1,200.00
Beverage	470.00
Guest Laundry	18.00
Food	400.00
Telephone—Long Distance	24.00

Problem 3

You recently were brought in as president and chief executive officer of The Complex Resort Company. The company has experienced a prolonged downward trend in earnings and you were sought out by the Board of Directors because of your reputation for making real money-makers out of unsuccessful companies.

One of the first areas you look into is the company's organizational structure. Your investigation reveals the following information.

The organizational structure presently consists of nine operating and staff divisions and departments reporting directly to the president. They consist of the following:

Retail Division
Transportation Department
Hotel Division
Sales Department
Advertising Department
Summer Sports
Maintenance Department
Accounting Department
Personnel Department

To assist in analyzing the lines of authority and responsibility, you prepared a chart of the organization currently in effect as shown on page 193.

Problem 3 (continued)

The functions and responsibilities of each of the divisions and departments are as follows.

Retail Division

This division presently consists of a mixture of the retail sales operations of the company, that is, the gift shops, service stations, stands, vending machines, winter sports and stores and of support and administrative services—purchasing, warehousing and distributing.

Transportation Department

This department consists of the transportation system, which operates buses within the resort complex and between the resort and the airport, and the garage, which services and repairs visitors' motor vehicles.

Hotel Division

This division is responsible for the operation of all the overnight accommodations and restaurants throughout the resort.

Sales Department

This department has responsibility for all the sales efforts of the company and is responsible for recording and controlling reservations for overnight accommodations. In addition, it has direct authority over the functions of the sales offices in various cities in the country.

Advertising Department

This department directs all advertising and promotional activities.

Summer Sports

The manager of this department has the responsibility of providing and maintaining all the summer sports activities.

Maintenance Department

The maintenance department is responsible for the repair and maintenance of all buildings and equipment. It occasionally constructs new operating facilities. In addition, it prepares cost estimates of all major maintenance and construction projects whether they are to be contracted by outsiders or to be performed by the maintenance department.

Accounting Department

This department is responsible for all of the accounting and financial reporting functions. In addition, most insurance contracts are negotiated by this department.

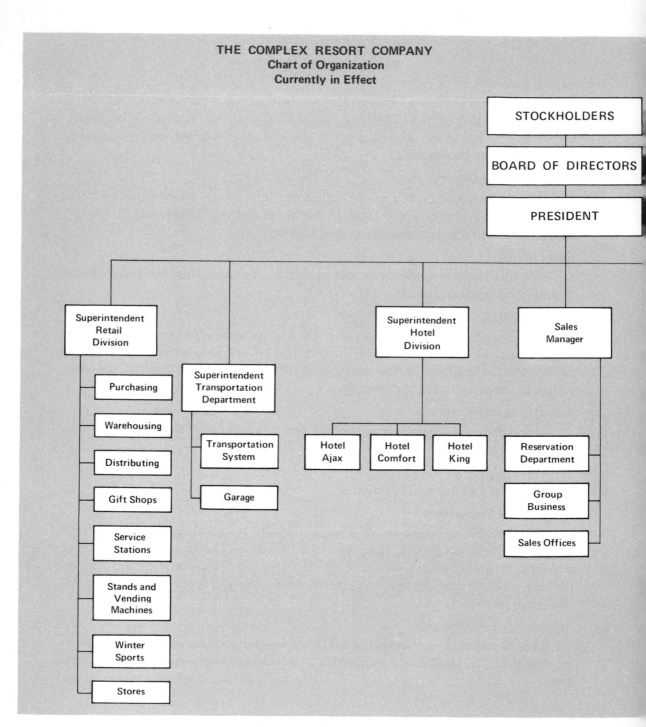

THE COMPLEX RESORT COMPANY
Chart of Organization
Currently in Effect

STOCKHOLDERS

BOARD OF DIRECTORS

PRESIDENT

Superintendent Retail Division

- Purchasing
- Warehousing
- Distributing
- Gift Shops
- Service Stations
- Stands and Vending Machines
- Winter Sports
- Stores

Superintendent Transportation Department

- Transportation System
- Garage

Superintendent Hotel Division

- Hotel Ajax
- Hotel Comfort
- Hotel King

Sales Manager

- Reservation Department
- Group Business
- Sales Offices

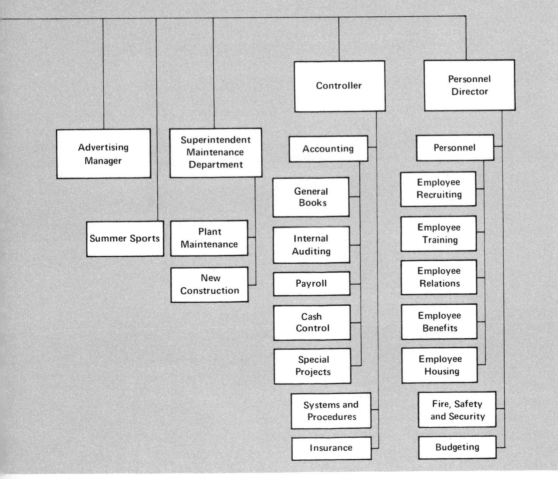

Problem 3 (continued)

Personnel Department

The personnel department is responsible for employee recruiting and training, employee relations and benefits and employee housing. In addition, it is responsible for the fire, safety and security functions of the company. Also, the budget committee is under the chairmanship of the director of personnel.

Required

1. Prepare a recommended chart of organization.
2. In order to gain the acceptance of the board of directors, explain the reasons for your recommended changes.

CHAPTER 9

Internal Control

The simplest business enterprise needs no records and controls. The single entrepreneur operating a business with no employees generally has the necessary information for planning and control available to him from his past experience and his general knowledge. This single entrepreneur's need for record-keeping and controls is restricted to the data used in reporting his business operation to government taxing authorities and other governmental units. However, there is a continuing trend toward increased scope and size of the individual business entity, including those in the hospitality service industries. Although a large portion of the hospitality service industries is conducted by the single unit enterprise (hospital, restaurant, medical clinic, country club, etc.), the trend to a larger business unit is apparent in franchise corporations, nursing home chains, fast food companies, hotel and motel chains, and large publicly held conglomerate companies. This expansion has increased to the point where the larger organization is widespread in the hospitality service industries. To control operations effectively, management must rely on dependable reports, analyses, and other data originating both within and outside of the organization.

Concurrent with the growth in size of the hospitality service industries entity, there is an increasing awareness of the need for various control techniques to measure performance at each level of responsibility within this larger business entity. Records and controls that were adequate for the single entrepreneur are not adequate to measure performance within the varying levels of the larger business entity, and to prevent and detect fraudulent conversions of assets.

Internal controls are all of the procedures and methods adopted by management to measure, evaluate, and assure proper performance and efficient operation. To this end, sound internal controls can be applied to all enterprises, profit or not-for-profit; the importance of sound controls to the hospitality service industries varies only in emphasis due to the nature of the assets devoted to the hospitality service enterprise activities.

BASIC REASONS FOR SOUND INTERNAL CONTROL

There are four basic objectives to be obtained by installing and enforcing a sound system of data accumulation, review, and reporting.

USEFUL AND TIMELY FINANCIAL AND OPERATING REPORTS

A sound system of internal control is devised to insure clear and proper rules for conduct and action, and to provide consistent and prompt reports. Prompt, accurate operating reports are needed to fully measure and evaluate daily operation, and to indicate the need for immediate corrective action wherever necessary. In addition, the data accumulation methods and procedures must provide for timely financial reports, including periodic interim income statements and balance sheets. Without accuracy and timeliness in issuing these periodic financial reports, there is no way for management to continuously measure the progress of the business entity against the previously determined and obtainable results.

CLERICAL ACCURACY AND ELIMINATION OF ERROR

A properly designed system of controls will provide for efficient paperwork flow and a data procedure that, through its functioning, will eliminate errors wherever possible. The elimination of errors at all levels of the data accumulation process is absolutely necessary for sound, efficient management. Without accurate accumulation of sales statistics, there can be no sound management decisions as to how and what to do to expand sales and the profitability of those sales. On the contrary, inaccuracies in accumulating the fundamental data, and the preparation of reports from this data, may lead to unsound conclusions and poor business decisions on the part of management.

ECONOMY OF OPERATIONS

To design, install, and enforce a sound system of record-keeping, procedures, and reports requires an intelligent review of what management needs to operate the business entity most efficiently. This intelligent review must precede the development of the proper system; later, it must be performed periodically in order to determine that the system is functioning properly and meets the primary needs as originally designed. This continuing review of the systems and procedures is a self-analysis process which, if performed properly, will provide better operating controls, more economical methods, and elimination of duplication.

PREVENTION AND DETECTION OF FRAUDULENT CONVERSION

A properly designed system of records and procedures, and the automatic review at varying levels which is inherent in the system tend to prevent fraudulent conversions of assets at all levels. No system will prevent fraud of all types, because the cost of such a system would far exceed the relative risks involved in the possibilities of fraudulent conversion. In addition, no system will prevent a fraudulent conversion which is a result of collusion between employees, or between employees and outsiders.

Even in those circumstances where the system, as designed, is not expected to disclose the existence of fraud, a soundly designed and properly maintained system will tend to reveal the areas of loss if a fraudulent conversion does occur. Good controls tend to readily disclose and report these fraudulent conversions. A soundly designed system of records and controls will continually reduce the loss of assets and, hence, lead to more efficient and profitable operations. The cost of installing a good system of internal control should never exceed the expected benefits.

The protection which a properly designed system of controls affords against human weaknesses is important in the hospitality service industries. The check and review which is built into a good system of controls reduces the possibility that errors or fraud will remain undetected for any continuous period of time, and enables management to place greater confidence in the reliability of data.

DEFINITION OF INTERNAL CONTROL

The American Institute of Certified Public Accountants has studied the relationship of good internal controls to sound reliable financial reporting as it affects the Certified Public Accountant's work in examining annual financial statements. In this study, the AICPA defines internal control as follows:

Internal control comprises the plan of organization and of the coordinate methods and measures adopted within a business to safeguard its assets, check the accuracy and reliability of its accounting data, promote operational efficiency, and encourage adherence to prescribed managerial policies.[1]

This definition goes beyond the checks and balances inherent in a well-designed system of paperwork flow within a business entity; that is, it goes beyond the concept of safeguarding assets by simply having cash registers, pre-numbered sales tickets, pre-numbered checks, and other techniques of paperwork control. The emphasis in this definition is on broader controls. As such, it includes such techniques and control devices as:

1. Budgetary controls and planning.
2. Predetermined standards and performance reports.

---

1. American Institute of Certified Public Accountants, *Internal Control Elements of a Coordinated System and its Importance to Management in the Independent Public Accounting* (New York, N.Y.: American Institute of Certified Public Accountants, 1949), p. 6.

3. Personnel policies (training, education, supervision, compensation, bonding, etc.).
4. Statistical analyses, including quality control.
5. All types of physical safeguards: proper layout, locks and keys, recording machines, storage safeguards.
6. Sales and production planning and forecasting.
7. A continuous evaluation and check of the accuracy of the reports through internal auditing and an independent certified public accountant.

The definition encompasses all of the methods and measures used by management to produce efficient operations. It includes such areas as company organization, policies, and procedures not previously associated with the record-keeping accounting cycle.

CHARACTERISTICS OF A PROPERLY COORDINATED SYSTEM OF CONTROL

What are the basic fundamental characteristics of a satisfactory system of internal control? What are the basic ways to recognize that all the elements are there to provide the protective and constructive values of a sound system? Several elements must be in a properly coordinated system; they include:

A plan of organization which provides appropriate segregation of functional responsibilities, a system of authorization and record procedures adequate to provide reasonable accounting control over assets, liabilities, revenues and expenses, sound practices to be followed in the performance of duties and functions of each of the organizational departments and a degree of quality of personnel commensurate with responsibilities.[2]

PLAN OF ORGANIZATION

The continuing increase in size and scope of the average hospitality service enterprise (including the present trend toward ownership of food service outlets by publicly owned conglomerate corporations and/or franchise companies) is such that ownership can no longer exercise any degree of personal supervision over the operations of the entity. Operations management must come through varying levels of employed organizational responsibility. Under these circumstances, the establishment of a suitable organizational structure is imperative. The organizational structure must vary with the size of the hospitality service industries enterprise, geographical locations, types of outlets, and other factors unique to the

---

2. American Institute of Certified Public Accountants, *ibid.* p. 4.

particular entity. Each entity must have a satisfactory plan of organization. This plan must be in writing, and should be clearly understandable by all those involved in the business operations. Simplicity of design is the first characteristic of a sound plan of organization.

A second criterion as to the adequacy of any plan of organization is the extent to which it provides for organizational independence between the operating, custodial, and accounting functions. This organizational divorcement of the operations, record-keeping, and custodianship functions is a basic protective mechanism to prevent fraudulent conversion and to assist in providing reliability and integrity in the records.

The basis for separation and independence of functions rests on the premise that no department should control the accounting records pertinent to its own operations. For example, the establishment of performance standards is an operations function; the recording of actual performance against these standards should not be under the control of operations but, rather, under the record-keeping function of accounting. Similarly, the cashier is a custodianship function and should have no authority over the record-keeping and recording of cash receipts and disbursements. In all cases, the checks and balances that result from the divorcing of operations, record-keeping, and custodianship provide for a sound automatic check. Hence, records and reporting will be more reliable.

The third criterion for a sound organization plan is that it should provide clean and clear lines of responsibility and should delineate clearly the major duties and responsibilities of each position and function.

SYSTEM OF AUTHORIZATION AND RECORD-KEEPING

No business can afford any more record-keeping than is absolutely necessary to provide a basis for a sound, efficient operation. Therefore, all records, procedures, forms, and systems must be designed to provide maximum integrity in the financial and operating report at a minimum cost to the business. Because the recording of all transactions will ultimately rest in a final ledger of accounts which will serve as the basis for meaningful and prompt financial reporting, it is imperative that the business enterprise begin its record-keeping with a sound and meaningful chart of accounts. This chart of accounts should be carefully prepared and should:

1. Facilitate the economic preparation of financial statements and reports.
2. Include those accounts which are needed to reflect adequately and accurately the assets and liabilities and revenues and expenses, sufficiently broken down to be useful to management in its control of operations.

3. Describe accurately and concisely what should be contained in each account.
4. Delineate as clearly as possible the boundary lines between capital assets, inventories, and expense items.
5. Provide for controlling accounts where necessary.[3]

The chart of accounts should clearly and concisely define the specific content of each account and give examples, so that similar transactions can be consistently handled. The formal structure of the accounts should not be complex beyond the reasonable needs of management and should provide no breakdown beyond that which is absolutely needed for effective use by management in business operations.

In addition to a sound chart of accounts, the paperwork system and forms should be designed to provide for efficient and automatic flow and cross-check wherever possible. Forms and procedures should be designed with copies provided only where they are useful, and with prenumbered control techniques used wherever possible. Each form should be challenged periodically to determine that it is still useful in the paperwork flow, and whether it might be eliminated or combined with other forms or reports currently being used in the operation.

The maintenance of a sound plan of organization and a system of authorization and record-keeping have often been referred to as the *strategic elements* of good internal control, whereas the following two elements—sound practices and personnel practices—have been referred to as the *tactical elements*.

SOUND PRACTICES

The finest written plan of organization, when combined with the finest system of authorization and record-keeping, would not provide a good system of internal control without sound practices to implement these elements in day-to-day business operations. Wherever possible, practices should be instituted to provide accurate records and reports. For example, time clocks are used to further verify the hours worked; bank accounts are reconciled monthly to assure the accuracy of the bookkeeping process; and labor hours as shown on the time summaries are balanced with the labor hours paid by the payroll department. These practices encourage integrity in reporting operating data and, hence, provide accurate records to be accumulated and reported to management periodically.

---

3. American Institute of Certified Public Accountants, *op. cit.*, p. 11.

PERSONNEL PRACTICES

The final element of a sound system of internal control is the effective selection and supervision of personnel. In order to provide accurate data to management, a major portion of the accuracy must be maintained by the people who originate, transfer, accumulate, and record this data. To assure maximum accuracy, the employees who are engaged in the data handling process must be properly trained and educated as to the duties they are to perform in the process, as well as the possibility for error in the accumulation process. Clear, accurate job descriptions and delineation of duties is required to assure this element of a sound system of controls. Continuous supervisory review is an essential part of the training and educational process. Finally, an adequate compensation and fringe benefit level must be maintained in order to attract employees who can and will function to provide a strong degree of integrity in the data accumulation and reporting process.

When the various elements of good internal control have been melded into a system, it is still necessary to provide for some form of continuous review and challenge of the entire system. Internal auditing, in the larger companies, is designed to meet this need. The internal auditing activities of most large companies include continuously reviewing and appraising the adequacy of the accounting and operating controls; continuously determining the degree of compliance with established policies and procedures; and continuously checking the reliability of reports, records, and other supporting data, as well as other checking to determine that assets are accounted for properly.

INTERNAL CONTROL IN SMALL BUSINESS

Although there is a current and seemingly continuing trend for the hospitality service industries to be part of a multi-unit corporate entity, there is still a major segment of the hospitality service industry that is operated by the owner-manager or is owned by a small group of owners with a single manager. Such small businesses are likely to continue because the hospitality service entity is in a different economic situation then the industrial product entity. The product entity has a tangible end product that is movable and salable beyond the immediate market area. This means that productive capacities can be expanded in a single location to service the entire country with the product or, indeed, to ship the product throughout the world. (For example, cameras are made by the Eastman Kodak Company in New York and are most assuredly shipped from there throughout the free world.) However, in the hospitality service industries, the size of the productive plant is limited by the restricted market area as well as the limitations on productive plant operations. For example, a lodging establishment in any city will be patronized by only those people who wish to stay in that city. Similarly, a food service operation cannot put on a second shift of chefs and waitresses to handle the extra demand beyond its peak physical capacity because this extra demand will not wait until "swing shift time" to eat.

These fundamental economics of the hospitality service industries cause each location in each market place to be a productive unit or productive outlet with its own individual maximum profit potentials. There are no mass production or automation techniques in the service industries to provide the extraordinary profits of mass marketing of a product. Therefore, the hospitality service industries will always have, either through franchise or direct ownership, a major portion of their economic value created by the single business location. This location may continue to be owned privately, and may be operated by management directly responsible to itself or to a single owner.

DEVELOPMENT OF INTERNAL CONTROLS FOR THE SMALL BUSINESS

To lay the groundwork for a better understanding of some of the concepts and applications of controls, and to show the nature of internal controls in practice, the following illustrations are given. They will illustrate the development of internal controls in relation to the size and complexity of the business entity.

Case 1

One man owns and operates a hamburger carry-out stand as a single entrepreneur. Other than the need for substantiation to pay the minimum allowable taxes, there would be no need for this business to have records. From the viewpoint of an outsider, no internal control could exist in this small, single entrepreneur business entity.

Case 2

The entrepreneur in Case 1 retires and hires a manager to run the business. The employed manager has complete authority and responsibility. The only aspect of control is the retired owner's general knowledge that he is getting an adequate or expected return on the investment he left under the employed manager's control. When the retired owner proceeds to sign checks, post general books, challenge operating results, prepare performance standards, make periodic measurements, and take other actions that he deems necessary to maximize the return, a degree of internal control has been established.

Case 3

The size of the business entity once again increases and there are fifteen to twenty hamburger outlets and six office employees as well as the retired absentee owner. Employee 1 is the general manager and directs all sales activities. Employee 2 makes all purchases. Employee 3, the general ledger bookkeeper, prepares payroll taxes and other tax returns. Employee 4, the subsidiary ledger clerk, also helps prepare the periodic payrolls. Employee 5 is the cashier, and Employee 6 is the office manager as well as the check signer. In this example, a simple system of internal control can be developed so that there is a sound disassociation of custodianship, operations, and record-keeping; the work of accumulating and recording data is thus subject to automatic check.

For example, in a purchase transaction, Employee 2 authorizes the purchase and places the actual purchase order; Employee 6 sees that the merchandise is received as ordered and processes it for payment; and Employee 3 records the receipt of this merchandise and the payment. Similarly, in the case of daily sales, several employees would be involved in recording. Additionally, the absentee retired owner still retains certain duties for himself and obtains copies of timely and accurate operating and financial reports for his review and challenge.

Even with only six employees, the possibility of collusion toward fraudulent conversion of assets has been minimized because several people, including the owner, are necessarily involved in a purchase, or a sale. In this example, it can be seen that increased size through multiple units (outlets) has resulted in increased opportunity for review and analysis of transactions, and an automatic cross-checking of the accuracy of recording of these transactions.

Another example of internal control would be a publicly held corporation which owns and operates 110 restaurants throughout the United States. Each restaurant represents a separate level of operating responsibility; each district or geographical territory is a second level of authorization and responsibility; and the home office is the final level of responsibility. Therefore, in the large corporate multi-unit operation, each unit is a profit responsibility center, and records and reports should measure and control each unit of profitability.

From the examples given, it can be seen that the smaller the business, the less certain the division of duties will be, and the fewer levels or opportunities for measurement and control will exist. However, because the service industries are unique in that each unit can only be so big, there will always be individual ownership with employees working at a single outlet operation. For example, at the present time there are many thousands of individually owned and operated restaurants, nursing homes, motels (both franchised and as part of referral organizations), resorts, dormitories, rooming houses, etc. This means that anyone associated with the hospitality service industries must be prepared to deal with specific controls that are available to the smaller business entity. These controls do exist; in many cases, they may be superior controls because owner-review is generally superior to employee-review. For example, the owner's review of payroll should be excellent because the owner would know his employees personally and would know those who worked and did not work during the particular period.

Some controls that can be effectively used in the smaller (as well as larger) hospitality service industries operations include:

1. The use of cash registers, pre-check machines, and other mechanical devices.
2. The use of the double-entry bookkeeping system and other proof or balancing techniques.
3. Preparation of timely and accurate financial statements for the owner's review and evaluation.
4. The use of periodic statistical reports and their comparison to current available operating statistics.
5. Use of standards and an informal budgetary planning and control system.
6. Approval and authorization by the owner of payroll exceptions, write-offs of bad accounts, invoices for payment, and owner-signing of checks, notes, etc.
7. Accounting for voided checks; use of pre-numbered checks and a check protector; use of petty cash and other separate accountable funds; bank reconciliations; and voiding of invoices on payment.
8. Maintenance of employee fidelity bonds on all employees; investigation of employees before hiring; adequate training and supervision; etc.

From this list, it can be seen that the adoption of sound controls for the smaller single-unit operator is not an economic impossibility. Although the cost of some of the above controls may exceed their apparent benefit, the controls can and should be in operation, wherever possible, for the single-unit operator.

HOSPITALITY SERVICE INDUSTRIES AND CASH CONTROL

Until a decade ago, the hospitality service industries were a cash business; indeed, currently a much greater percentage of service sales are made for cash when compared with the almost total credit sale of a product at the industrial, retail, or wholesale level. However, the past ten years this has changed with the adoption of the travel credit card, hospital insurance, bank credit cards, and other forms of credit, so that in a number of cases today a substantial majority of the hospitality service industries' sales dollars are made on credit.

Nonetheless, a definite need continues for more and better controls over cash and receivables in the hospitality service industries because of the nature and size of the individual sale. Generally speaking, the maximum sale is the amount that a specific individual, or an individual and his guest, can consume on a single visit to a hospitality establishment. Although there are many cases today of credit being granted directly to corporations for business meetings, salesmen visits, etc., the major portion of the sales dollar in the hospitality service industries is for sales to individuals, and generally averages less than one hundred dollars per customer. An industrial or product company can sell hundreds and thousands of dollars in products to a given customer; hence, its credit and collection policy is entirely different from that of the hospitality service industry company. In addition, the product company deals with a limited number of customers—generally, the same customers year in and year out, whereas the hospitality service entity may be dealing with many more customers who may or may not return to purchase more services over a long period of time. In these circumstances, it is imperative that the hospitality service industries recognize the need for both cash and credit controls which are germane and effective.

CASH RECEIPTS CONTROL

In a large segment of the food service category of the hospitality service industries, sales are made for cash, resulting in the need for strong cash control procedures. Included in this category are the vast array of food service outlets owned or franchised by publicly listed corporations or other forms of absentee ownership. For these restaurants, cafeterias, fast food outlets and others, a system must be designed to control cash from the point of sale to the bank account. Controls over cash receipts rising from cash sales include cash registers, customers' receipts, written orders on pre-numbered invoices, bank accounts, and cashier controls.

To provide the beginning of any control system, the amount and type of sale must be recorded at the time of the cash sale. Usually, this is done in the form of a cash register recording wherein the various keys on the register are coded to provide the necessary sales breakdown. In addition, the cash register should provide some sort of customer verification on the sale amount (such as a cash register receipt, a visual reading, or an automatic visual change computation). As part of the cash control, there should be no access to the cash register by anyone other than the cashier, and the cash register readings should be made daily or more frequently by management personnel.

In many cases, before the cash sale is recorded, an invoice is prepared in the form of a restaurant check. This may be prepared by the waiter or the counterman at the time of taking the order. The amount of the check is priced and extended, so that the restaurant check serves as the original recording of the sale.

These restaurant checks should be pre-numbered and controlled, from the time of order, through storage, issuance, and final use. This system of pre-numbered service invoices provides the basis for periodic review to determine that all sales have been accounted for.

The cash received through the cash register should be balanced at least daily; the cash over and short amounts should be recorded in the accounts, and daily deposits should be made to the bank accounts intact. Generally, it is advisable to have the bank account designed to facilitate the most efficient use of cash and to provide, wherever possible, an audit trail which will assist in a future audit or verification process. Bankers always are willing to cooperate with the business entity to provide the form of banking service which best facilitates the company's controls.

In addition to the daily cash received for over-the-counter sales, the hospitality service industries will have a greater number of cash funds on hand, primarily to give service of some kind to the guest. In addition to the normal petty cash funds that are on hand in all types of companies, there must be a sufficient number of change funds so that each cashier who is accountable for cash collections will have a change fund. The change funds are a fixed amount for which the individual is held responsible throughout the period of his employment on accountable cashier duties. These change funds, like the normal petty cash fund, stamp fund, freight fund, etc., are on the imprest system. The imprest system provides for charging responsibility for a given number of dollars to an individual, and holding that individual responsible to produce the dollars or the receipts for authorized disbursements, so that at all times the fund can be accounted for by adding the money on hand to the authorized disbursements to equal the total original amount assigned to the individual custodian.

In addition to cash sales, all categories of the hospitality service industries will have sales on credit. The originating documents for sales on account will be the various forms of pre-numbered invoices (charge tickets). These tickets represent all accumulated charges made by the guest, and generally will be recorded on the statement of account or bill to be rendered to the guest. In the hotel-motel industry, this pre-numbered statement of account is called a *folio;* while the guest is in the house, this document is located in the front office where all charges originating in the various departments throughout the hotel are accumulated and posted to the guest folio. When the guest checks out, he receives this statement of account. If he does not pay in cash, the folio serves as the basis for the invoice sent to him. In many cases, a copy of the folio is mailed to him immediately with a request for payment. All categories of the hospitality service industries follow this procedure of basic accumulation of charges on a folio or statement.

After the statement has been sent to the guest and the cash has been received in the mail, a separate pre-listing of these mail receipts should be made in triplicate by someone other than the cashier. The original sheet of this listing should go to the city ledger receivable clerk for posting to the account, a duplicate should go to the cashier to be combined with other cash to make the daily deposit, and the third copy should be used by management to periodically audit the mail receipts procedures.

After the mail receipts have been combined with the regular cash sales, the daily deposit ticket should be prepared in duplicate to provide a permanent record of the daily deposit. In addition, the bank should be instructed to notify the management immediately and make a charge-back to the bank account, if any checks are dishonored.

For sales on account, there must be soundly conceived and continually implemented credit and collection policies. These include the authority for granting credit as well as the proper authority for writing off uncollectible accounts.

CASH DISBURSEMENT CONTROLS

The systems and procedures for cash disbursement should be designed to provide good control over purchases, expenses, and payroll. The basic control device for proper disbursements for purchases and expenses is a system of authorization and approvals, used in conjunction with properly designed forms. The disbursement for purchases begins with the purchase order, and when goods are received, a receiving report should be prepared. When an invoice is received from the vendor, it should be matched with the purchase order and receiving report so that a disbursement voucher and a check can be prepared for payment. All of these forms should be pre-numbered, and should provide for automatic flow and checking within the organization. After the vendor's invoice has been processed, the final approval for disbursement can be in the form of the signatures on the check. The determination of these authorizations to sign checks and the control over signatures on the checks are important elements of control over cash disbursements.

Wherever expense disbursements involve the receipt of a product, the above procedures should be followed, and a receiving report should be issued to provide evidence that the item received was the item ordered. Wherever the expense involves a service, the receiving approval should be recorded directly on the invoice to provide the evidental authority for disbursement.

Because payroll cost is a major element of expense in the hospitality service industries, there is a continuous need for designing and implementing sound payroll control and procedures. The payroll cost controls begin with the hiring procedures and continue through the scheduling and pre-planning by departmental heads.

In addition, there should be a properly designed system of controls in accounting for payroll costs. This includes a separate payroll bank account operated on an imprest basis with controls over the signatures on this account. The bank account should not be reconciled by anyone taking part in accumulating or preparing the payroll. The processing or preparation of the payroll by the accounting department should be subject to a sound system of approvals, checking, and review, so as to provide an accurate distribution of these costs for management to compare with their pre-planned targets.

TYPES OF CASH FRAUDS AND/OR ERRORS

No system of controls can prevent all manipulations or errors. The cost of complete protection against fraud and error would far exceed the benefits. All employees who handle cash should be bonded, and all steps should be taken by management to install and enforce proper controls so employees will not be tempted to mishandle funds. Emphasis should not be on those controls that are designed primarily to prevent fraudulent conversions, but rather on those controls and procedures which assist management in maximizing profitable operations. However, management should have some knowledge of the techniques and methods used for fraudulent conversions of assets. The following types of fraud are listed briefly without full description of the manipulative process leading to the fraudulent conversion of the asset.

Fraud or error in the area of cash receipts includes the failure to record a sale, or the purposeful recording of a sale at less than the proper selling price. Further, cash receipts may be borrowed by an employee and this action covered by a delayed credit to the customer's account. This classic method of manipulation is referred to as "lapping," and it involves taking receipts from Customer A and, when the receipts from Customer B arrive, crediting these receipts to A's account and continuing the process by crediting Customer C's receipts to Customer B, and so forth. Finally, miscellaneous cash receipts (such as insurance refunds, equipment scrap value, sale of grease, quantity discounts, etc.) are always difficult to control because the basic documentary evidence is not always available to initiate and implement the necessary controls.

Fraudulent conversions in the area of cash disbursements for purchases and expenses include the payment of an invoice twice and the payment of a purchase in an amount exceeding the contracted purchase price. Further variations on this fraudulent disbursement include payments for merchandise not received or for quality below that ordered—all of which may be the result of an agreement between an employee and a vendor providing some form of kickback. In all these cases, the hospitality service firm does not receive the proper value for the cash paid. Improper accounting may be used to hide these fraudulent disbursements (as in the case where improper allowance vouchers are prepared, or where improper journal entries are made). The classic example of accounting manipulation to cover a fraudulent disbursement is the practice known as "kiting," whereby a check is drawn on Bank A without recording this check as a disbursement, and depositing this check in Bank B and recording the deposit. This results in an overstated combined cash account by an amount equal to the unrecorded check drawn.

Fraudulent conversions in payroll may be divided similarly into two types: payment for no services received, and accounting manipulations to cover fraud. Ghost payrolls, hours not worked, and improper payroll rates—all forms of payroll frauds—are generally classified as "payroll padding." Recording the wrong withholding amounts, incorrect journal entries, payroll bank account adjustments, and other accounting manipulations can be part of the fraud and may provide the means to prevent its disclosure. Payroll kickbacks may be classified in either of the two types of fraudulent payroll practices.

IMPLEMENTATION, REVIEW, AND SURVEILLANCE OF THE SYSTEM OF CONTROLS

Management must be responsible for designing and maintaining a sound system of controls. A well-designed system of controls is so important to the efficient conduct of the business that it is incumbent upon management to continually review and evaluate the control system. This continuous review and surveillance is necessary because controls may become obsolete with changing business conditions and circumstances. For example, a particular bank account may exist to handle the receipts of three restaurants. When one of these restaurants is replaced with a new outlet at a different location, review may indicate that a change in banking methods and locations would be more efficient.

From time to time, controls might break down from the lack of supervision and continuous review. This may happen when an employee fails to perform a particular technique or procedure one time and, because no one challenged the lack of this procedure, the employee continues to omit the procedure periodically. For example, a cashier required to make a daily deposit of each day's receipts intact was unusually busy and was unable to prepare the daily deposit. No supervisory controls were involved, so the cashier proceeded to change the procedure from a daily deposit to a deposit twice a week. This resulted in a loss of earnings on undeposited cash as well as the loss of the daily deposit intact as an audit trail.

Turnover of employees requires continuous training and instructions in order to maintain the system of controls. Promotions, transfers, and other personnel changes require continuous training and instruction as well as periodic reviews to determine that employees understand the system and have the ability to carry out the instructions.

There are many methods of periodic review and analysis of the systems and controls in effect within an organization. One method is the systems and procedures approach. This involves a narrative description of the control use of all forms, procedures, and methods. In a large business entity, the entire controls are described in a series of written communications to delineate policies and procedures. The written descriptive information about the systems and procedures is included in accounting and procedural manuals for all employees' education. Another method is to use checklists and questionnaires as guidelines in periodically reviewing the systems and controls. These questionnaires are designed so that the "yes" answer indicates good internal controls, whereas the "no" answer indicates a need for investigation. Each question is designed to determine if a particular control or procedure is in use. A typical questionnaire for cash control procedures at a motel is shown on Exhibit 9.1.

The questionnaire and other methods of review, however, are merely tools in the review process; the task of evaluating and interpreting any control or lack of control must be left to management. Not every good procedure or technical control can be used by every business entity, due to differences in size, employees, product, etc. A system of controls for a hospital will not necessarily resemble the systems and controls for a fast food service company; nor will the system of controls for one fast food service company necessarily be the same as those for another.

Although the typical outlet for a unit in the hospitality service industries may be small, some of the categories (hospitals, hotel/motel chains, colleges, and other institutions) have enough physical plant, sales volume, and employees to warrant the creation of a separate department to assist management in its continuous review and surveillance program. This department is called the *internal auditing department*, or the internal auditors. The separate internal auditing department or the internal auditor is also feasible in those categories of the hospitality service industries where there are many outlets under the ownership of a publicly listed company (such as nursing home chains, motel chains, fried chicken or hamburger chains, and all others operating under the franchise and company-owned-store concept).

EXHIBIT 9.1

Internal Control Questionnaire
for Motel Cash Controls

	Yes	No	Initials of Reviewer

Cash

Are procedures in effect to verify that departmental cashiers deposited their daily receipts in safe?

Is there a witness to the withdrawal of cashiers' monies from the safe?

Is list of checks prepared and checked to city ledger credits?
To miscellaneous income?

Are cash receipts deposited intact?

Are two signatures necessary on checks drawn?
Regular:
Payroll:

Are petty cash vouchers drawn in ink and cancelled?
Are they pre-numbered?
Are supporting vouchers attached?

Are receipts given for interchange of funds between general and other cashiers?

Does someone other than cashier reconcile bank accounts?

Are receipts on hand for all house banks?

Are guest advances approved and checked to cashier sheets daily?
Are vouchers signed by authorized individual?
Are telegram charges checked?

Are front office cash sheets or books maintained?

Is there a separate cash book for each cashier at the front office?

Is authority to cash checks restricted and controlled?

Is credit limit set at a reasonable level and maintained?

Are checks stamped on back to show exchange and on account?

Does accounting department add and prove cash sheets daily?

Are postings of receipts and disbursements test-checked to guest accounts?

Who controls number of times front office machine has been cleared?

Are COD's on guest accounts checked to receiving record?

Are returned checks charged to bank account?
Is copy of charge-back memo sent to authorized person to follow up?

Does front office disburse petty cash?
Do disbursement vouchers require approved signatures?

Is there a daily bank count report from each cashier?

Are check cashing fees controlled?

Does auditor or member of accounting office handle cash receipts?

Are house banks controlled when banks are not in use?

Are combinations to safes under proper control?

Does auditor confirm daily deposits to bank?

211

The Institute of Internal Auditors defines internal auditing as follows:

Internal auditing is an independent appraisal activity within an organization for the review of accounting, financial, and other operations as a basis for service to management. It is a managerial control, which functions by measuring and evaluating the effectiveness of other controls.[4]

The objective of the internal auditor is to assist management in its prime responsibility of safeguarding the assets and promoting efficient operations. In attaining this objective, the internal auditor must continuously review the adequacy of the accounting and operating controls and see that they are being followed within the organization. In addition, the internal auditor must review and evaluate the continuous adherence to management's policies, and appraise the quality and performance of the personnel in carrying out their assigned responsibilities.

No matter how small the particular hospitality service entity may be, the concept of internal auditing should be thoroughly considered and implemented in some form. Even in the smallest owner-operated food service outlet, the owner should be prepared to perform the necessary internal audit periodically. In this way he will obtain maximum profits and provide maximum service to the guest.

SUMMARY

The continuing trend toward increased scope and size of business entities puts a premium on the design and maintenance of effective internal controls. The objectives of sound internal controls are to promote the generation of useful and timely management reports, to maximize clerical accuracy and minimize error, to facilitate operating economy, and to provide prevention against and detection of fraudulent conversions of an organization's assets.

The characteristics of a sound system of internal controls include a plan of organization which provides segregation of functional responsibilities, an effective system of authorization and record-keeping, the implementation of sound practices in daily operations, and an effective program for the selection and supervision of personnel.

The extent of a particular internal control system will be dependent upon the size, nature, management, and ownership of the entity. In no case should the cost of the controls exceed the expected benefit. In the hospitality service industries the control over cash and payroll expenses is a particularly important aspect of internal control.

Discussion Questions

1. What are internal controls and in what enterprises would they be applicable?
2. What are the basic objectives for establishing sound internal control?

---

4. Institute of Internal Auditors, *Statement of Responsibilities of the Internal Auditor* (New York, N.Y.: Institute of Internal Auditors, 1957).

3. What are some of the broad control techniques and devices included in the A.I.C.P.A. definition of internal control?
4. Discuss briefly the elements of a properly coordinated system of control.
5. What are some of the controls that can be used in a smaller hospitality service business?
6. What are some specific procedures in controlling cash receipts?
7. What are some specific procedures in controlling cash disbursements?
8. What is the best method of periodic review and analysis of the present system?

Problem 1

The Assistant Auditor of Hill House, a medium-sized motor inn, was responsible for the inn's city ledger. Included among her other responsibilities was working the front desk in the capacity of the room clerk/cashier during the lunch hour.

Periodically, this employee would take a check received in payment of a city ledger account and, during her front desk shift, would put the check in the cash drawer and remove the same amount of cash, appropriating this money for her personal use. The credit to the city ledger account was not made on the same date that the check was received.

Required

1. Discuss the basic deficiency in internal control.
2. Assuming the above deficiency is corrected, briefly describe the proper cash receipts procedures in these circumstances.

Problem 2

Internal control over cash disbursement is very important since cash is such a liquid asset. To illustrate the importance of the cash disbursement function, some common forms of fraud in cash disbursements are presented.

1. Issuance of unrecorded checks.
2. Omission of outstanding checks from bank reconciliation.
3. Duplicate payment of vouchers.
4. Preparation and payment of false vouchers.
5. Understating and underfooting of purchase discounts.
6. Overstating the column totals for cash credits accompanied by understatement of cash received.
7. Writing checks.
8. Understatement of purchase returns and allowances accompanied by the theft of an equivalent amount of cash.

9. Forging checks and obtaining authorized signatures to blank checks.
10. Overstatement of petty cash disbursements.

What are some of the internal control measures that would prevent some of these manipulations and misappropriations of cash?

Problem 3

The Y Company has come to you with the following problem. It has three clerical employees who must perform the following functions:

1. Maintain general ledger.
2. Maintain accounts payable ledger.
3. Maintain accounts receivable ledger.
4. Prepare checks for signature.
5. Maintain disbursements journal.
6. Issue credits on returns and allowances.
7. Reconcile the bank account.
8. Handle and deposit cash receipts.

Assuming that there is no problem as to the ability of any of the employees, the company requests that you assign these functions to the three employees in such a manner as to achieve the highest degree of internal control. It may be assumed that these employees will perform no other accounting functions than the ones listed and that any accounting functions not listed will be performed by persons other than these three employees. With the exception of the nominal jobs of the bank reconciliation and the issuance of credits on returns and allowances, all functions require an equal amount of time.

Required

1. State how you would distribute the functions among the three employees.
2. List four possible unsatisfactory combinations of the listed functions.

CHAPTER 10

The Nature of Cost

Cost management is a major portion of the management process, and hence it is no accident that managerial accounting was referred to as "cost accounting" for many decades. A survey of 700 hotels and motels by Harris, Kerr, Forster & Company[1] revealed that in 1969, 77.7 percent of all revenue was expended upon costs, even without including depreciation, rent, interest and income taxes in this figure. Costs are involved, in one way or another, in all decisions which management makes. Consequently, much of this text is devoted to the specialized techniques of cost management which the accounting profession has adopted to assist managers.

The cost manager is faced with many different and specific types of decisions concerning costs. For example, he might have to decide whether to employ better, and more costly, personnel. He might have to decide whether to accept a request that his resort host a convention. Or he might have to decide whether the cost of remodeling his resort is too high. Since there are many types of decisions concerning costs, it is not surprising that there are many different techniques for dealing with costs, and many different ways of looking at costs.

A discussion of cost management techniques requires, among other things, an introduction to the terminology of these techniques. Each body of knowledge, and especially a technical knowledge such as cost management, must establish a language to deal with its specific problems. Cost management has some terminology and some techniques which must be introduced so that those who prepare and use cost management reports can "speak the language." There are many cost concepts to be learned, as there are many managerial uses to which the cost techniques may be put. The terminology exists only to support useful techniques for cost management. The purpose of this chapter is to provide an explanation of terms as they relate to the major concepts of cost management in the hospitality service industries.

---

1. Harris, Kerr, Forster & Company, *Trends in the Hotel-Motel Business* (Thirty-Fourth Annual Review, 1970), p. 7.

GENERAL NATURE OF COST

Before exploring some of the more specific types of costs, it is necessary to be aware of what a "cost " is.

COST DEFINED

A cost is the reduction in the value of an asset of an organization with the purpose of securing some benefit or gain. It is a deploying of the organization's resources, the purpose of which is to return more than is sacrificed. Some facets of this definition follow.

If there is no asset usage, then no cost arises. For example, a restaurant's purchase of linen or chinaware or fixtures does not deplete the restaurant's assets; it merely changes their form from cash to fixtures. The expenditures of an organization are not always concurrent with its consumption of assets, primarily because many assets must be purchased at one point in time, regardless of the fact that they provide services over a long period of time.

If an asset becomes wholly or partially depleted, then a cost is incurred to the extent of that depletion. Deterioration by usage or by breakage of linen or chinaware constitutes a cost in the period in which the deterioration occurs. A cost arises when the potential of an asset to give services in the future is reduced. It should be noted that the deterioration is in a sense deliberate: the purpose of cost incurrence is to gain revenue, say from food sales. The manager must accept that a certain proportion of assets will deteriorate with use.

Expenditures on labor, heating, or telephone give rise to the concurrent reduction in an asset (cash) without going through the intermediate stage of creating another asset (such as restaurant linen or chinaware). Such an expenditure results in the immediate incurrence of a cost because the expenditure occurs at the same time as the organization's assets are purposefully used.

An asset can be depleted without achieving any purpose. For example, fire can destroy linen or chinaware. It is useful to distinguish this type of non-purposeful reduction from the purposeful use of an organization's assets, because a manager is interested in knowing the effects of his decisions upon profitability and in knowing whether an outlay will be recurring. Accordingly, accountants usually refer to a non-deliberative asset depletion as a loss rather than a cost.

An asset exists to the extent that there is a potential to assist in some purpose, such as the earning of revenue from food sales. That is, an asset is a reservoir of unused ability to meet the purpose for which it is acquired. Fixtures in a restaurant are thus assets of the restaurant, at least to the extent that they are useful. An asset is converted into a cost as it is used for some purpose, and becomes a cost of the activity which has that purpose; a loss arises when the future service potential is completely depleted with no benefit to the organization, as in the case of destruction by fire.

COSTS AND PURPOSES

The definition of cost emphasizes its purposeful nature. *To the manager, costs can only be meaningfully interpreted in light of the purpose for which they are incurred.*

An organization exists for a purpose: to make a profit for its owners, to provide benefits to a group or community, or perhaps both. To produce a product or service, the organization must combine managerial skills, labor, and other resources. It cannot make a profit (an excess of inflows of assets over outflows) without an outflow of assets—without incurring costs, without depleting resources.

The importance of this point will be apparent throughout the book. An enlightened management does not place paramount importance on reducing costs, for that policy alone could lead to curtailing costs which are necessary to achieve desired objectives.

PREDETERMINED AND HISTORICAL COSTS

In managing cost incurrence, the profit-oriented manager is faced with two general classes of decisions:

1. Will a particular cost incurrence (outflow of assets) generate a profit? That is, should I decide to incur the cost?
2. Has a particular cost incurrence generated the sort of profit that I envisaged at the time of deciding to incur it? That is, was I justified in incurring the cost in the past?

The second question, which is asked in evaluating past actions so as to learn from experience, has two aspects. One might ask whether a particular cost has been of the magnitude that was anticipated at the time the decision was made to incur it; and if not, why not. The second aspect is whether a particular cost incurrence of a given magnitude resulted in the generation of more or less profit, or gains, than originally anticipated, and why.

The objective of making these kinds of inquiries is to make decisions. In the first case, the decision relates to the future. For example, a decision might be made as to how much to advertise. In the second case, the decision concerns the past but, once again, relates to future action. For example, a manager might discover that the cost of food per cover served has been higher than originally anticipated. He might trace it to higher prices from the supplier, in which case a new supplier might be sought. Or he might decide to rescind an earlier decision to advertise using a particular media because previous advertising did not bring sufficient results.

These two types of decisions are, respectively, *planning* and *controlling* decisions. Segregating decision-making into planning and controlling is somewhat arbitrary. However, the distinction is a highly useful one as the techniques for dealing with planned costs, as opposed to actual costs, are different.

PLANNING OF COSTS

A planned cost is generally referred to as a predetermined cost, in contrast to historical (or actual) cost.

The *budget* is the primary managerial mechanism for dealing with planned costs. Managerial plans are transferred into quantitative cost terms and are embodied in the budget. The budget can cover planned costs for only some resources or some departments, or it can cover planned costs for all of the organization's resources in all departments. The budget normally plays an important role in integrating and coordinating the planned cost-incurring activities of all departments.

Standard costing is a widely-used technique developed to assist in planning decisions. A standard cost is an expected average cost of producing a product or service, or part of a product or service. A standard cost is thus a planned unit cost, which may be different from what the actual cost will turn out to be; it is a predetermined cost. It is a *unit cost* in that the cost per unit of a product or service or part thereof, is determined rather than a total cost for a given period's total unit output.

One way to estimate a standard cost is to analyze the inputs required to produce the product or service. In this procedure, the cost of each required input at each stage in the production of the product or service is estimated; then, these costs are added together to determine the standard cost of the total product or service. Alternatively, the standard can be the average historical cost incurred for that particular product or service by the firm, or firms, in the industry. As an example of this latter technique, the Exemplary Holiday Resort wishes to plan its operations for 1970. Exhibit 10.1 shows the actual performance displayed during 1969 by an average resort hotel in the northeastern United States.[2] The figures are the average cost per day per guest which were experienced by a sample of year-round resort hotels.

----

2. Reported by Harris, Kerr, Forster & Company, *ibid.*, p. 30.

EXHIBIT 10.1

Exemplary Holiday Resort
Standard Unit Costs

Type of Cost	Cost per Guest-day	
Cost of goods sold and departmental wages and expenses		
Rooms	$ 4.30	
Food and beverages	10.22	
Telephone	.53	
Total		$15.05
Other costs		
Administrative and general	$ 2.51	
Advertising and sales promotion	1.38	
Heat, light and power	1.23	
Repairs and maintenance	2.59	
Total		7.71
Insurance and local taxes		.22
Total cost per guest-day*		$22.98

*Excluding real estate taxes, depreciation, rent, interest, amortizations, and income taxes.

In this example, the *unit of activity* is characterized as one guest-day. Not all guests and not all days are responsible for the same amount of cost; however, the average historical cost is a reasonable measure of the amount that would be expected to be added to costs to accommodate an average guest. A take-out hamburger franchise would define its unit of activity as, say, one cheeseburger; or if decisions were being made concerning the cost of producing french fries, it would estimate cost of one serving of fries.

If Exemplary Holiday Resort can be regarded as a typical resort hotel in the northeastern United States, then we can use the industry averages for planning. And if there is no reason to suspect that its costs in 1970 will differ from those in 1969, then the 1969 industry averages can be used. Thus, if Exemplary Holiday Resort expects to achieve a volume of 100,000 guest-days in 1970, the average historical costs can be converted into budget form, as presented in Exhibit 10.2. Any expected departures from the 1969 industry averages would, of course, be used to modify the budgeted figures—the budget being a quantitative expression of expected performance. The budgeted costs in Exhibit 10.2 could be estimated using the experience of past periods concerning average costs per individual guest-day.

It must be emphasized that the budget is a device which assists immensely in the management of costs, for it forces management to answer the question as to

EXHIBIT 10.2

Exemplary Holiday Resort
Budgeted Costs, 1970

Type of Cost		Total Cost
Cost of goods sold and departmental wages and expenses		
Rooms	$ 430,000	
Food and beverages	1,022,000	
Telephone	53,000	
Total		$1,505,000
Other costs		
Administrative and general	$ 251,000	
Advertising and sales promotion	138,000	
Heat, light and power	123,000	
Repairs and maintenance	259,000	
Total		771,000
Insurance and local taxes		22,000
Total cost*		$2,298,000
Budgeted level of activity (guest-days)		100,000

*Excluding real estate taxes, depreciation, rent, interest, amortizations, and income taxes.

whether a specifically quantified level of planned expenditure is justified in terms of the organization's purpose. Further, it assists in the coordination of the cost-incurring efforts of different managers. Standard costs can help in preparing budgets.

CONTROL DECISIONS

The question as to whether the incurrence of a given cost was entirely warranted, in terms of what it achieved, is a managerial and not an accounting judgment. Yet an accountant can apply his specialized techniques to draw a manager's attention to possible cases of unjustified cost incurrence. Basically, he can compare the actual amount of cost incurred (the historical cost) with the amount expected at the time of the original decision to incur it (the predetermined cost). Further, he can assist the manager in tracing the reasons why actual costs differed from those expected. The techniques for tracing these reasons are generally referred to as the *analysis of cost variances.* Differences from budget are referred to as *variances.*

Planning decisions involve estimating future costs. Control decisions involve subsequently determining actual costs and comparing them with expected, planned costs. For example, the Exemplary Holiday Resort found, at the end of 1970, that costs as shown in Exhibit 10.3 were incurred, as compared to the original budget levels which were presented in Exhibit 10.2.

EXHIBIT 10.3

Exemplary Holiday Resort
Performance Report, 1970

Type of Cost	Budgeted	Actual	Difference Amount	Percentage
Cost of goods sold and departmental wages and expenses				
Rooms	$ 430,000	$ 463,000	$ 33,000	+ 7.7%
Food and beverages	1,022,000	1,136,500	114,500	+11.2
Telephone	53,000	47,000	6,000	−11.3
Total	$1,505,000	$1,646,500	$141,500	+ 9.4
Other costs				
Administrative and general	$ 251,000	$ 247,800	$ 3,200	− 1.3
Advertising and sales promotion	138,000	161,600	23,600	+17.1
Heat, light and power	123,000	124,200	1,200	+ 1.0
Repairs and maintenance	259,000	227,200	31,800	− 12.3
Total	$ 771,000	$ 760,800	$ 10,200	− 1.3
Insurance and local taxes	$ 22,000	$ 25,000	$ 3,000	+13.6
Total cost*	$2,298,000	$2,432,300	$134,300	+ 5.8%
Level of activity (guest-days)	100,000	110,000	10,000	+10.0%

*Excluding real estate taxes, depreciation, rent, interest, amortizations, and income taxes.

On the basis of such an analysis of deviations from planned levels, a manager can investigate possible reasons for the results. It is obvious from the report on actual performance for 1970 that most of Exemplary Holiday Resort's costs were above budget. But the manager's important questions are not whether expectations in fact turned out to be accurate, but why this was so. The manager might investigate whether the advertising and sales promotion cost was increased deliberately over the budgeted level by 17.1 percent, and whether this led to the 10 percent over-budget volume. Then he might determine whether this increased volume in turn led to a sufficient increase in profit to justify the extra advertising cost. Perhaps the advertising cost rose because agencies raised their rates, and perhaps the increase in volume merely reflected a generally good year for the resort hotel industry. Or, the higher advertising expenditure could have been due to some poor decisions by the resort's promotion staff, in which case the manager would wish to correct the source of the errors.

Accounting information can only give the manager a clue as to where he should investigate suspected unsatisfactory performance. For example, in Exhibit 10.3, the resort accountant could have presented the comparison in terms of standard and actual unit costs, by comparing the standard and actual costs per average guest per average day. The Exemplary Holiday Resort volume turned out to be 10 percent over the budgeted level, whereas all costs differed from their budgeted levels by figures other than 10 percent. It appears, for example, that the unit cost for a room decreased as the volume increased, and that the costs of food and beverages rose (volume rose 10 percent, while total food and beverage costs rose 11.2 percent). Administration costs decreased only slightly with volume, and insurance costs were 13.6 percent above the expected. Thus, one of the important lessons of cost management is illustrated; that is, the way in which one reports costs is entirely dependent upon the information needs of the manager who is utilizing those reports.

COST REDUCTION VERSUS COST CONTROL

The essence of cost control lies in deciding whether the particular level of asset use was justified in terms of the benefits which accrued. It is always possible to cut costs by cutting quality of service or neglecting advertising; in the extreme form, one can minimize costs by going out of business completely. But the question is whether such actions would benefit the organization. There are many costs which must be maintained at a minimum level, to achieve a desired level of customer loyalty or service performance and, in general, to make desirable profits. Examples are advertising, cleaning, supervisory staff, and customer-service costs. Cutting these costs is not equivalent to controlling them. An example is shown in the repairs and maintenance cost of Exemplary Holiday Resort, which turned out to be 12.3 percent lower than planned. Were unexpected efficiencies found during 1970? Or did the unanticipated volume leave insufficient time to complete a full season's complement of preventive maintenance and needed repairs? Or was preventive maintenance minimized and repairs carried out only when necessary?

The accounting system's task in helping to control costs is to help determine whether the costs incurred did achieve the results required of the outlays.

RESPONSE OF COST TO VOLUME

Changes in volume must be considered in controlling costs. One of the most important distinctions in cost management is between those costs which are assumed to be responsive to changes in volume, and those which are assumed to be unresponsive to volume changes. If a decision involves a change in the volume of operations, then it is important to have information covering the effect of this change upon costs. This is *relevant* information for cost management.

An example of the usefulness of information concerning responsiveness to volume is shown in the performance report in Exhibit 10.3. Although Exemplary Holiday Resort's volume during 1970 was 10 percent above the budgeted level, some costs (such as administration and repairs and maintenance costs) either did not differ from their budgeted levels, or differed only slightly. In contrast, food and beverage costs rose more or less proportionately with volume. To decide whether a given level of actual cost incurrence is satisfactory, it is necessary to know which cost could reasonably be expected to change with volume.

MEASURING VOLUME

Volume is a rate per unit of time. The specific way in which that rate is measured depends upon one's purpose. Volume for the Exemplary Holiday Resort is the number of guest-days operated during a year. There is no reason for the resort's management to restrict itself to this particular index of volume. For a special analysis of the cost of serving food, the volume index might be the number of meals served, or the dollar value of meals served. The choice between volume measures depends entirely upon two factors: the usefulness of the resulting analysis under one measure versus the other; and the cost of preparing the respective analyses. Thus, if it is as easy to prepare a cost analysis using the number and dollar value of meals, then the choice depends upon that volume index which most closely reveals the true relation between cost and volume.

FIXED COSTS

Fixed costs are those which are assumed to be totally unresponsive to changes in volume. In Exhibit 10.3, it appears that administrative and general costs, heat, light, and power costs, and insurance and taxes were not responsive to the 10 percent increase in volume over the planned level.

The graphic relationship between fixed costs and volume is shown in Exhibit 10.4. The first graph depicts total fixed cost as a function of volume. The second depicts average fixed cost per unit of volume, also as a function of volume.

It can be seen that the total fixed cost is a constant amount (OA) regardless of the volume level. The average fixed cost per unit accordingly falls as volume increases.

VARIABLE COSTS

Variable costs are those costs which are assumed to be proportionately responsive to changes in volume. For example, in Exhibit 10.3, the resort's

EXHIBIT 10.4

Fixed Costs in Relation to Volume

Graph A
Total Fixed Cost as a Function of Volume

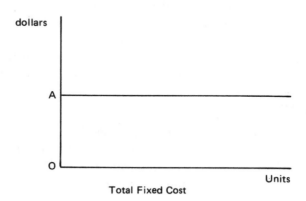

Total Fixed Cost

Graph B
Unit Fixed Cost as a Function of Volume

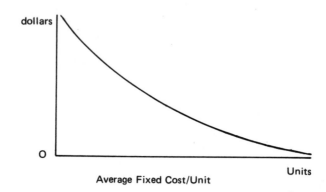

Average Fixed Cost/Unit

total cost of goods sold responded in an almost equal proportion to the 10 percent volume change.

Total and average variable costs are graphed in Exhibit 10.5. It can be seen that the total variable cost varies directly with the level of volume, and that the average variable costs remain constant.[3]

---

3. Thus, *average* fixed cost varies with volume, and *average* variable cost does not.

EXHIBIT 10.5

Variable Costs in Relation to Volume

Graph A
Total Variable Cost

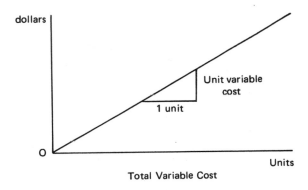

Total Variable Cost

Graph B
Unit Variable Cost

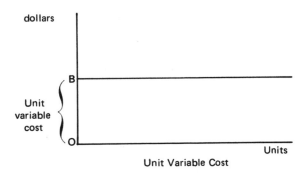

Unit Variable Cost

SEMIVARIABLE COSTS

Semivariable costs are those costs which are assumed to be composed of two elements, a portion which is independent of volume (a "fixed" portion), and a portion which varies proportionately with volume (a "variable" portion). Exhibit 10.6 graphs a semivariable cost in total and unit terms. The performance report, in Exhibit 10.3, indicates that telephone costs may be semivariable.

EXHIBIT 10.6

Semivariable Costs in Relation to Volume

Graph A
Total Semivariable Cost

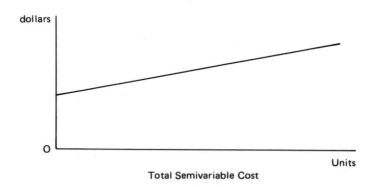

Total Semivariable Cost

Graph B
Unit Semivariable Cost

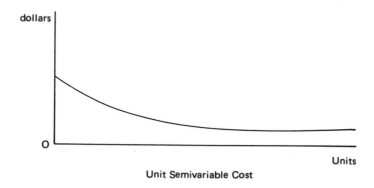

Unit Semivariable Cost

COSTS AND CAPACITY

Fixed costs are, generally, the costs of providing capacity. They are costs of operating, administering, and financing the organization's structure. In contrast, variable costs are costs of utilizing that capacity.

Large volume changes most probably require changes in capacity. There is no such thing as an absolutely fixed cost, because the cost of providing capacity is likely to be a function of the amount of capacity provided.

This emphasizes an important qualification to the definition of fixed, variable, and semivariable costs: the qualification that a cost can be treated as responding in a certain manner to volume changes over only a limited range of volume. This range is referred to as the *relevant range*. It is the range over which the fixed-variable dichotomy is assumed to hold. If Exemplary Holiday Resort were to plan to increase its volume in 1970 to twice that of 1969, it would be most unlikely that it could plan for an almost unchanged level of administrative, heating, or insurance cost, because it would require more buildings and more administrative staff. That is, it would move outside of the relevant range.

For example, a cost such as supervisory staff wages might appear to respond in relation to volume, as shown in Exhibit 10.7. For the purpose of decisions which affect volume over the whole range of volume, (OC), this cost could be treated as a variable cost without losing much precision; thus, OC is the relevant range. Alternatively, for decisions which hardly affect volume, say over the range AB, it could be treated as a fixed cost. In the latter case, AB is the relevant range. These costs are stepped costs and this particular cost behavior pattern is the step function.

VALIDITY OF DICHOTOMY

The distinction between the fixed and the variable components of costs is highly artificial. Only rarely will costs either be totally unresponsive to volume, respond perfectly proportionately to volume, or be decomposable exclusively into elements of either.

This dichotomy between fixed and variable costs is made solely for its usefulness, and not for its descriptive validity. That is, the decision-maker should be aware that, in dealing only in fixed, variable, and semivariable costs, his aim is to simplify the behavior of costs in order to make cost behavior understandable. While the assumptions of the fixed-variable model are not always applicable, they do enable management to make reasonable decisions without becoming lost in intricate cost-volume patterns.

Whether the assumptions of the fixed-variable model are thus justified depends on the usefulness of the resulting cost information. The assumptions are justified in two cases:

1. When workable alternatives are impossible because there is insufficient evidence as to the actual behavior of costs in response to volume; and

EXHIBIT 10.7

Treatment of Stepped Costs

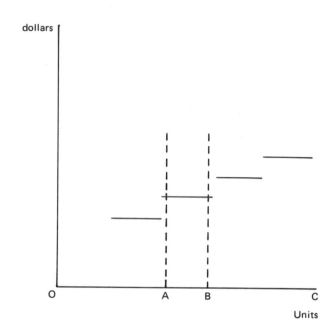

2. When it would be unnecessarily expensive to study the response in more detail (for example, when only a limited study is available for a decision, or where a finer study would be desirable but unrealistically expensive).

VARIATIONS IN FIXED COSTS

Fixed costs have been defined as costs which are fixed with respect to volume. However, fixed costs do vary. In some cases, their level is subject to managerial discretion. In others, they may vary due to factors beyond management control. The pertinent question here is whether *volume* is the reason for the variation in cost. The advertising and sales promotion and repairs and maintenance costs of Exhibit 10.3 illustrate this point.

ESTIMATING COST-VOLUME RESPONSES

It is one thing to define costs as either fixed, variable, or semivariable and it is another to classify costs into these categories. It is even more difficult to estimate the fixed and the variable components of a semivariable cost.

Many estimation procedures are available, such as the following:

1. Inspection of cost categories.
2. Managerial analysis of cost determinants.
3. Rudimentary analysis of past data on costs and volume.
4. Statistical analysis of past data on costs and volume.

Inspection of cost categories is simply a process of systematically checking the chart of accounts to decide whether the costs collected under each account are fixed, variable, or semivariable. For example, the costs listed in Exhibit 10.3 might be classified as follows:

> Rooms: *Variable* (with number of guest-days)
> Food and beverage: *Variable*
> Telephone: *Semivariable*
> Administrative and general: *Fixed*
> Advertising and sales promotion: *Fixed*
> Heat, light and power: *Fixed*
> Repairs and maintenance: *Fixed*
> Insurance and local taxes: *Fixed*

The next step is to estimate the level of the fixed cost per period and the amount of the variable cost per unit of volume. This may be done by inspecting actual past historical costs which have been collected under the particular cost classification.

A pitfall of this method is its tendency to lead to underestimating the amount of fixed costs. Under this method, it is easy to overlook the fixed component of a semivariable cost and to classify it as a variable cost. This in turn leads to overestimating the degree of response of costs to volume, and, hence, results in misleading cost information.

Managerial analysis of cost determinants is a process of analyzing the operations which must be performed in order to provide a product or service, and of estimating the cost of each of these operations. For example, Exemplary Holiday Resort might have estimated its telephone costs by estimating the basic monthly charge for the service, and adding to it the expected cost of the anticipated number of calls to be made per guest per day. This is the only feasible method of operation for a new business, unless it is prepared to accept past data from other firms in the industry.

Rudimentary analysis of past data can take many forms. For example, the resort's observed telephone costs over the years 1957-1970 are presented in Exhibit 10.8. A simple way to analyze these data would be to ignore changes in the underlying cost-volume relationship, such as changes in prices or changes in rental

EXHIBIT 10.8

Exemplary Holiday Resort
Telephone Cost in Relation to Volume

Year	Volume (Guest Telephone Calls)	Telephone Cost
1957	131,000	$ 56,000
1958	101,000	43,000
1959	104,000	43,000
1960	118,000	51,000
1961	120,000	49,000
1962	107,000	41,000
1963	92,000	34,000
1964	81,000	35,000
1965	115,000	51,000
1966	112,000	44,000
1967	134,000	51,000
1968	127,000	52,000
1969	129,000	49,000
1970	110,000	47,000

structures. The data could then be plotted on a scatter diagram and a relationship between cost and volume could be estimated visually. (See Exhibit 10.9.) Careful inspection leads to an estimation that these telephone costs are fully variable, at a rate of almost 40¢ per guest telephone call.

$$C = .40V$$

where C = total cost (in dollars)
and V = total volume (in guest telephone calls)

Statistical analysis of past data can also take many forms. Perhaps the most useful form is regression analysis, whereby one can obtain estimates of the fixed and variable components of cost which are both unbiased and accurate.[4] This analysis is charted in Exhibit 10.10.

The result of regression analysis is the equation for the line known as the "least-squares" line because the sum of the individual deviations between the observations and the line when squared and totaled is minimized. Regression analysis does not rely upon visual estimation and has other desirable qualities. Applied to the Holiday Resort data, it estimates telephone cost as a semivariable

---

4. The interested reader is referred to almost any applied statistics text, such as: John E. Freund, *Modern Elementary Statistics* (Englewood Cliffs, N.J.: Prentice-Hall, Inc., 1960). The method of least-squares, when applied carefully, gives rise to the best linear unbiased estimates of relationships between variables. Note that such problems as changing prices over time can be solved by multiple regression analysis.

EXHIBIT 10.9

Observed Cost-Volume Relationship, Estimated Visually

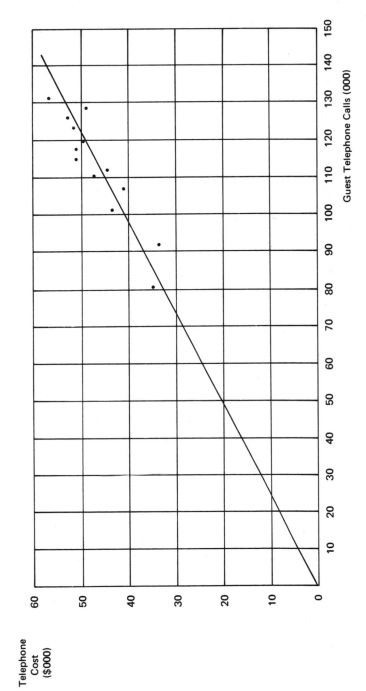

EXHIBIT 10.10

Observed Cost-Volume Relationship Estimated by Method of Least-Squares

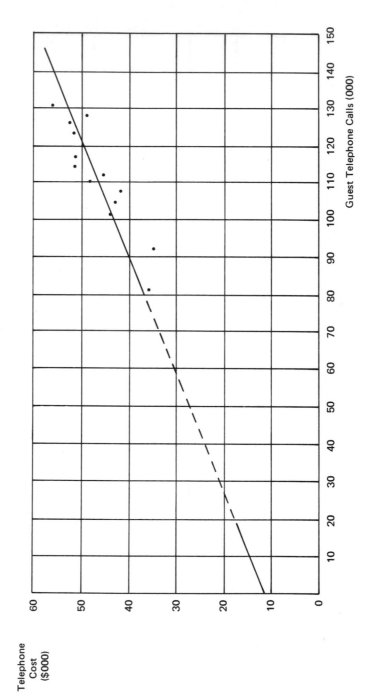

cost, with a fixed component of $11,320 per year and a variable component of 30¢ per guest day, the equation for the line is C = $11,320 + 0.30 V.

In Exhibit 10.10, the broken line indicates uncertainty of the cost-volume relationship outside of the relevant range. It is interesting to compare the regression analysis results with those of the less accurate visual analysis. Visual analysis overestimated the variable component of the cost.

DIFFERENTIAL COSTS

A decision inevitably involves a choice between alternatives. This fact might not be obvious, in that one of the alternatives might be to leave things as they are; but the basic point remains that if there are no alternatives, then there is no decision to be made. Because a decision involves choosing between alternatives, a decision-maker requires information concerning the differences between costs under those alternatives.

A *differential cost* is one which differs among alternative courses of action. A differential cost is termed an *incremental cost* if the decision will increase it, and a *decremental cost* if the decision will decrease it. Where a decision concerns only the level of volume, then (within the relevant range) differential cost equals variable cost. Where a decision concerns matters other than volume, or where volume is to be taken outside of the relevant range, differential cost can no longer be equated with variable cost.

For example, Exemplary Holiday Resort is considering an offer by an outside firm to process all of its laundry. Differential costs would include laundry employees' wages, laundry supplies, utilities, sale value of the resort's laundry equipment, and the outside firm's contract price. Not all of these are "variable" costs.

SUNK COSTS

A sunk cost is a cost which resulted from a past decision and cannot be affected by the decision under consideration. By definition, it cannot be a differential cost, because it cannot differ among alternative courses of action.

For example, Exemplary Holiday Resort's laundry equipment cost $150,000 in 1967 and has been depreciating at $15,000 per year for three years. Its current book value is therefore $105,000 (that is, the financial accounting records show the equipment's unexpired cost as an initial cost of $150,000, less accumulated depreciation of $45,000). In deciding whether to continue processing the laundry internally or to send it outside, the figure of $105,000 is not relevent. The decision cannot possibly affect either the $150,000 initial cost or the $45,000 depreciation. The $105,000 is a sunk cost. However, the resale value of the laundry equipment *is* a differential cost.

OPPORTUNITY COST

An opportunity cost is an important concept in decision-making. An opportunity cost is the expected value of an opportunity foregone; it is the cost of the sacrifice made when a course of action is undertaken. As such, it is seldom overtly measured by accountants, in spite of its importance. An opportunity cost is not an out-of-pocket cost, and therefore is never entered in the accounting records. It is the value of a benefit that could be obtained from an alternative that is rejected.

For example, the resort could sell its laundry equipment for $75,000, after paying for removal expenses. While the $105,000 sunk cost (depreciated original investment) is not alterable by any future decision and is therefore not a differential cost, the $75,000 is, however. One of the costs of operating the present equipment is the opportunity cost of not selling it, or the lost interest income on $75,000.

AVOIDABLE COSTS

An avoidable cost is a form of differential cost. The term "avoidable cost" is usually restricted to the case where management faces the alternatives of continuing or discontinuing operations. Some fixed costs are avoidable when volume is reduced to zero (which is obviously outside the relevant range within which they are fixed). If management is considering discontinuing operation of a hotel at a specific location, then it is important to know how many of its fixed costs are avoidable, that is, how many can be eliminated with the closing of the hotel. Those which are *unavoidable* are not differential costs insofar as the abandonment decision is concerned; they are, in essence, sunk costs.

DIRECT AND INDIRECT COSTS

The distinction between a direct cost and an indirect cost is difficult, primarily because of the origin of indirect costs. Indirect costs arise for two reasons. The first reason is real and the second is due to accounting measurement practices.

First, indirect costs arise whenever a cost is incurred jointly by two processes, products, departments, or segments. This type of indirect cost also is known as a *joint cost.* For example, a doorman, as part of his duties, might park the restaurant guests' cars. His salary is a cost which is joint with the operations of the hotel and the restaurant. This is an economic fact, and no amount of allocating his salary between the operations will provide useful information; the cost is joint, and cannot meaningfully be divided between the two operations. If the doorman ceases to park the restaurant guests' cars, then no part of this salary is saved (the opportunity cost of parking cars is therefore zero). If he ceases to keep door, then no part of his salary is saved (the opportunity cost of keeping door is therefore zero). But if he ceases both to park cars and keep door, then all of his salary is saved, and the opportunity cost of the two processes is not the sum of the opportunity costs of each, because the processes are joint.

Second, indirect costs also arise whenever it is convenient to treat a cost as if it were joint. For example, it is technically feasible to sift through a hotel's cancelled checks to determine which of the hotel's departments were responsible for requiring checks to be drawn. The cost of operating the checking account could thus be traced to each individual department. But the trivial size of the cost allocation and the amount of effort involved in tracing it to departments combine to make the tracing impractical. Hence, the cost of the checking account is treated as a joint cost. More accurately, it is generally known as an untraced or unallocated cost. Note that this is not a real effect, but a measurement effect.

OVERHEAD COST

An overhead cost is essentially an indirect cost and can arise for either of the two reasons given. Most industrial cost accounting systems, and in particular, the cost accounting systems of firms which produce to meet individual job orders, make great use of the distinction between overhead costs and materials and labor costs. Because the distinction is not nearly so important in the hospitality service industries, it is sufficient to use the terms "indirect cost" and "overhead cost" synonymously.

CONTROLLABLE COSTS

In an organization, an individual manager often may be evaluated on the basis of the profitability in the area over which he has authority and responsibility. The evaluation may affect compensation or promotion decisions. To effectively evaluate a decision-maker, it is necessary to investigate only those factors over which he has control. It would be a misleading evaluation if he were held responsible for factors beyond his control.

A controllable cost is a cost over which an individual exerts sufficient influence to hold him responsible for its amount. Controllability has three dimensions.

1. *Time.* All costs are controllable in the long-run, including such short-run uncontrollables as rental and leasing costs.
2. *Authority.* A cost which is controllable by one person might not be controllable by persons who are junior to him in the organization. A person's salary, for example, is only controllable at a higher level than his own.
3. *Environment.* Many factors are beyond the control of an entire organization. For example, a firm cannot control cost increases which are due to rises in prices during a period of inflation.

Responsibility accounting is a term which has arisen to describe a system of managerial accounting whereby the cost information which is reported to individuals is only for costs over which they have control. As one rises in the organizational hierarchy, his decisions become more and more general; one of the features of a responsibility accounting system is, therefore, that reports to higher levels of management contain cost information which is less detailed but which spans a wider area of control.

COST CENTERS

A cost center is a segment of an operation for which separate cost information is kept. If the costs of individual departments are collected, then these are cost centers.

Cost centers and areas of responsibility coincide in an effective accounting system. If cost information collection were itself costless, then a cost center would be a very small area. Because information cannot be collected without effort, cost centers tend to be departmental areas.

DISCRETIONARY COSTS

Discretionary costs are costs which do not necessarily have to be incurred within the short-run, and over which there is thus a wide range of short-run managerial discretion. Some examples are market research, advertising, and preventive maintenance costs. To neglect these costs in the long-run would be dangerous. Over the short-run, they can be referred to as "discretionary" (*managed* or *programmed*) costs.

Discretionary costs are fixed costs in relation to actual volume, in that there is no reason for volume changes to alter them. For example, there is nothing inherent in increased volume which causes advertising costs to rise, while this is not true for the cost of servicing rooms. However, discretionary costs could be variable costs in relation to planned volume. For example, the greater the size of a market, the greater is the optimal quantity of advertising; more customers means more maintenance in the long-run.

THE RELEVANT COSTS CONCEPT

An obvious, though easily and frequently forgotten, proposition of cost management and decision-making is that in making a decision concerning costs, a manager should consider *all* of the costs which are relevant to that decision and he need not consider any others. Relevant costs are those costs which will be affected by the particular decision under consideration.

This basic proposition underlies much of the discussion of costs in this chapter. It merely states that decision-makers require information which pertains to their decisions and that they require no more than this. One of the most important reasons why accounting uses the phrase, "relevant costs," is that it is easy to err by reporting *irrelevant* costs.

For example, the Exemplary Holiday Resort estimates that an expenditure of $15,000 on a promotion scheme, arranged in conjunction with an airline, will increase volume by 3,000 guest days over the coming season. Volume in subsequent years will remain unaffected. It is further estimated that revenue will be $27.34 per guest per day.[5]

Which of the costs in Exhibit 10.1 are relevant to this decision? It is tempting to use the total unit cost figure of $22.98, which would make the promotion scheme unprofitable.

Revenue: 3,000 days at $27.34		$82,020
Less Costs:		
Promotion Outlay	$15,000	
3,000 days at $22.98	68,940	
Total Costs		83,940
Loss		$ 1,920

However, some of these costs are not relevant to the decision. In particular, the unit cost of $22.98 includes an averaged portion of such fixed costs as administration and heating costs—costs which would not be increased if the scheme were undertaken. As discussed earlier, the only variable costs are the costs of rooms and food and beverage; the semivariable telephone cost has a variable component of 30¢ per guest telephone call. Taking into consideration only the relevant costs, the promotion scheme appears profitable.

---

5. Harris, Kerr, Forster & Company, *op. cit.*, p. 30.

Revenue: 3,000 days at $27.34 $82,020
Less Costs:
    Promotion Outlay $15,000
    Rooms: 3,000 at $4.30   12,900
    Food: 3,000 at $10.22   30,660
    Telephone: 3,000 at 30¢[6]   900
    Total Costs   59,460
Profit $22,560

If the average fixed costs per guest day were erroneously included, the manager probably would have made the wrong decision.

RELEVANT COSTS FOR DECISIONS

When a decision involves alternative courses of future action, costs are relevant if—and only if—they are future, expected, or differential under the various alternatives, one of which may be to continue the status quo.

RELEVANT COSTS FOR EVALUATING PAST DECISIONS

When actual costs are calculated to evaluate past decisions, they are relevant to that evaluation if—and only if—they are measured and collected upon exactly the same basis as the planned costs with which they are to be compared.

RELEVANT COSTS FOR EVALUATING SEGMENTS

When evaluating the performance of individual departments (e.g., a cafeteria), products (e.g., a specific food line), operations (e.g., dishwashing), or managers, costs are relevant if—and only if—their incurrence can be traced to that segment. In the case of evaluating a manager, he must exercise some control over a cost before it is relevant to his evaluation.

SUMMARY

Cost is defined as a reduction in the value of an asset with the purpose of securing some benefit or gain. Management is constantly faced with a wide variety of situations in which decisions should be based on cost factors, as prepared and submitted by the accounting department. These costs can only be meaningfully interpreted in light of the purpose for which they were incurred, and how well

---

6. It is assumed here that on the average each guest makes one telephone call each day at the resort.

they fulfilled these purposes. A business cannot hope to operate without an outflow of assets; the uses to which these assets are put is the responsibility of management.

One of the most important distinctions in cost management is between those costs which are assumed to be responsive to changes in volume, and those which are assumed to be totally unresponsive to changes in volume. *Fixed* costs are those costs which are assumed to be totally unresponsive to volume changes; *variable* costs are those which are assumed to be proportionately responsive to volume variables; and *semivariable* costs are those which are assumed to be composed of two elements, a portion of which is independent of volume, and a portion of which varies directly with volume. While it is recognized that such a categorization is highly artificial, the utility of simplification enables management to make reasonable decisions without becoming lost in intricate cost-volume patterns. This simplification makes cost behavior manageable and assists management in analyzing past cost performance (control) and in estimating future costs (planning).

In managing cost incurrence, two general classifications of costs are noted: historical and predetermined costs. While historical cost refers to the *actual* cost involved in a decision, predetermined costs refer to preplanned, expected costs. The historical cost may often differ, then, from the predetermined cost.

Managerial decisions require a choice between alternatives, even if one alternative involves maintaining the status quo. Because a decision involves choice, the difference in cost between each alternative is necessary for profitable decision-making. Such costs are referred to as *differential costs*. *Sunk* costs result from a past decision and cannot be affected by the decision under consideration. Opportunity costs are the costs of the unchosen alternatives. Other terms discussed include avoidable costs, direct and indirect costs, overhead costs, controllable costs, cost centers, and discretionary costs.

In making a decision regarding costs, management should consider all costs which are relevant; others need not be utilized.

Discussion Questions

1. What is the definition of cost?
2. Name some different techniques used in the planning of costs. Discuss each briefly.
3. What is the analysis of cost variances? What is a cost variance—how and why is it analyzed?
4. What are discretionary costs? Give some examples.

5. What are fixed costs? Variable costs?
6. What is meant by semivariable costs?
7. Name some estimating procedures to classify costs into fixed, variable, or semivariable.
8. What are differential costs? Sunk costs?
9. What is an opportunity cost?
10. Why do indirect costs arise?
11. What is a controllable cost? Discuss controllability.
12. What is responsibility accounting?
13. What criteria are used to determine costs that are relevant to managerial decisions?

Problem 1

The Bell Hotel has been having extensive trouble in the area of expense control. Listed are some of their key costs.

Salary to manager and department head	$12,000
Salary to full-time help	24,000
Salary to part-time help	6,000
Depreciation on building	10,000
Front office supplies	1,500
Accounting reports (computer expense)	2,640
Heat, light and power	3,600

The accounting reports (computer expense) are based on a fixed rate of $100 per month for a monthly balance sheet and income statement and $20 for each special report. These reports are as follows:

(1) Occupancy, by category of room (rate-type).
(2) Restaurant analysis revenues, by meal paid and menu item.
(3) Food inventory turnover, by type of food—meats, poultry, fish, fruits and vegetables, etc.
(4) City receivables, aged trial balance.
(5) Lounge, revenues analysis, beer, liquor, mixed drinks.
(6) Lounge, inventory turnover, beer, liquor, and wines.

The salary for full-time help is divided into 50 percent for rooms, 40 percent for restaurant and 10 percent for lounge. Salary for part-time help relates only to the restaurant.

Problem 1 (continued)

The management has asked you to study these costs and separate them into categories: controllable and uncontrollable costs; fixed and variable costs; and direct and indirect costs.

Problem 2

John R. Uris owns and operates the John R.U. Catering Company. He and two other members of his family do the preparation work in an area he has annexed to his home. He has one truck in which he makes all deliveries and occasionally earns extra money by making special deliveries for people. Last year his operating costs were:

Depreciation on the truck	$ 800
Licenses	60
Insurance	100
Repairs, oil, tires, etc.	200
Gasoline	400
Wages	7,500
Cost of food	12,000
Depreciation of building and equipment	300

Last year, on a rather full schedule, John drove the truck 13,000 miles catering various functions and making deliveries. His sales last year were $33,000. He estimates that he spent 2,500 hours of his time to generate this revenue. John knows that he should earn at least $3.00 per hour because that was what he was earning before he started the catering business and he knows that he could get the same wage again. He has decided that he must earn a 30 percent annual return on his investment in the truck, which cost $2,400, and the equipment and building which cost $3,000. All depreciation is presently taken using the straight-line method.

Just as John made a delivery to a country club 50 miles away from home, he was asked to deliver some food to another club which was twenty miles further away from home, on the same road. John estimates that it will take him two hours to make this extra delivery. The club has offered him $10.00 to make the delivery.

Problem 2 (continued)

Required

1. Identify and explain thoroughly the following cost concepts as they relate to this operation.

    Fixed costs
    Variable costs
    Out-of-pocket costs
    Sunk costs
    Opportunity costs

2. Indicate whether or not John should make the additional delivery and support your conclusion with calculations.

3. If John had depreciated his truck using the units of production method (miles driven), how would his decision regarding the delivery be effected? Support with calculations.

CHAPTER **11**

Cost-Volume-Profit Analysis

In the previous chapter we saw that predetermined costs are useful in making decisions concerning future courses of action. We also saw that the specific concept of cost, predetermined or otherwise, to be used in a specific type of decision depends on the nature of that decision. One specific concept of cost involved the assumption that costs behave in linear relation to volume; that is, that costs are either *fixed* (do not respond to volume changes), *variable* (respond proportionally to volume changes), or *semivariable* (combine elements of fixed and variable costs).

This assumption that costs behave linearly to volume is rich in implications and applications. A further assumption is that total revenues behave linearly with volume; that is, that unit selling price is independent of volume. From these assumptions a summary picture of the sources of profit variation for a firm can be derived.

Graphically, the picture is called a *cost-volume-profit graph.* Like all summary pictures, the cost-volume-profit analysis which is based upon the assumption of linearity has its limitations. In the previous chapter it was pointed out that assumptions are made only if the decisions which result are better than those based on alternative assumptions. Thus, while the cost-volume-profit analysis at first might seem to be a highly abstract manner of viewing a firm's profitability, this does not mean that it is not a useful manner of viewing the firm. Therefore, the limitations of the analysis shall be stated as well as the obvious areas in which cost-volume-profit analysis can be applied.

THE COST-VOLUME-PROFIT GRAPH

Continuing the example of the Exemplary Holiday Resort, the cost structure of the resort can be estimated as follows.

By an inspection of cost categories, the individual cost items of Exemplary Holiday Resort can be classified into fixed, variable, and semivariable costs (see chapter ten, page 229).

The *fixed costs* can be taken from chapter ten, Exhibit 10.2 as follows:

Administrative and general	$251,000
Advertising and sales promotion	138,000
Heat, light and power	123,000
Repairs and maintenance	259,000
Insurance and local taxes	22,000
Total fixed costs	$793,000

The *variable cost* per unit of output, which in Exemplary Holiday Resort's case is measured in guest-days, can be taken from chapter ten, Exhibit 10.1, as follows:

Rooms	$ 4.30
Food and beverage	10.22
Total variable cost	$14.52

The *semivariable cost*, which in Exemplary Holiday Resort's case is telephone cost only, can be broken down into fixed and variable components. Suppose that the technique which is used to do this is the regression analysis technique, as discussed in the previous chapter. Then, the telephone cost is estimated at $11,320 (fixed) plus 30¢ per guest telephone call (variable). It will again be assumed that on the average each guest makes one telephone call per day.

Thus, the total cost picture of Exemplary Holiday Resort is the sum of the fixed and semivariable annual dollars (793,000 + 11,320) plus the variable cost per day or $804,320 + $14.82 per guest-day.

For example, an annual volume of 100,000 guest-days, under the assumption of linearity, would give hotel costs of $2,286,320 (which is very close to the figure estimated in chapter ten, Exhibit 10.2).

This result is graphically illustrated in Exhibit 11.1.

From the individual costs, an aggregate cost-volume relationship is derived. The aggregate is, under the assumption of linearity, the sum of the parts. Because a portion of the parts are fixed costs and a portion are variable costs, the sum is a semivariable cost.

Finally, we add the assumption that sales price is independent of volume, and derive a graph showing the relation of total revenue to volume (Exhibit 11.2). A graph of total cost and total revenue superimposed on one another is the cost-volume-profit (CVP) graph (Exhibit 11.3).

The revenue in Exhibits 11.2 and 11.3 is $27.34 per guest-day. Hence, at a volume of 120,000 guest-days, revenue would be 120,000 × $27.34, or a total of $3,280,800. Note that total revenue behaves proportionally to volume and that total costs, after the initial fixed costs of $804,320, respond in a similar manner.

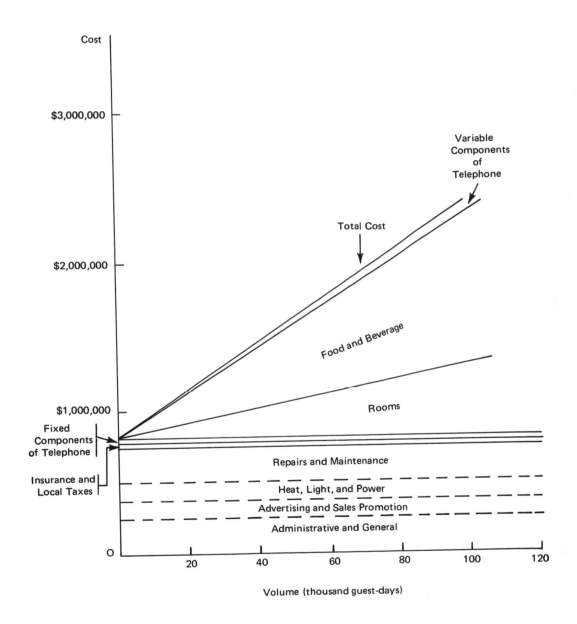

EXHIBIT 11.1

Total and Individual Costs

Cost

$3,000,000

Variable
Components
of
Telephone

Total Cost

$2,000,000

Food and Beverage

$1,000,000

Rooms

Fixed
Components
of Telephone

Insurance and
Local Taxes

Repairs and Maintenance

Heat, Light, and Power

Advertising and Sales Promotion

Administrative and General

O

20   40   60   80   100   120

Volume (thousand guest-days)

EXHIBIT 11.2

Total Revenue

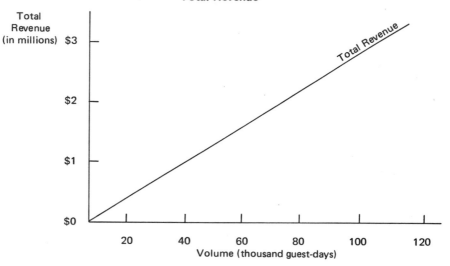

Total Revenue (in millions)

Volume (thousand guest-days)

EXHIBIT 11.3

Costs and Revenues Relative to Volume
(The Cost-Volume-Profit Graph)

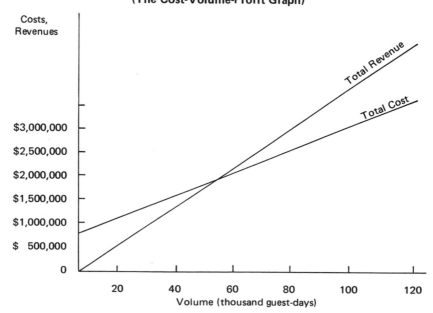

Costs, Revenues

Volume (thousand guest-days)

This behavior of costs and revenues follow under our assumption that costs and revenues are *linearly* related to volume.

This linear assumption is a realistic cost/revenue behavior assumption and it is used as a basis for useful decision-making tools in the area of cost and revenue controls.

USES OF CVP ANALYSIS: GRAPHIC FORM

The main advantage of the graphic form of cost-volume-profit analysis is that it gives management a simplified knowledge of their firm's cost, revenue, and profit structure. For example, a chart similar to Exhibit 11.4 can give a quick and easily comprehensible answer to such questions as:

—What will profit be at a given volume?
—What effect will a change in volume of a given magnitude have on profit?
—At what level of volume do we make zero profit; that is, when do we just break even?

COST-VOLUME-PROFIT ANALYSIS: ALGEBRAIC FORM

There are many uses of cost-volume-profit analysis, most of which require a more rigorous form of analysis than a graphic presentation. A simple algebraic equation can express the relationship of cost, volume, and profit under the assumption of linearity.

The following are some symbolic notations for the variables (such as profit) and the parameters (such as the variable cost per unit of volume) which were introduced earlier.

Notation:

X	=	Volume
X_{BE}	=	Volume at which total revenue equals total cost, and therefore at which profit is exactly equal to zero
S	=	Unit selling price
SX	=	Unit selling price times volume, or total revenue
F	=	Total fixed cost
V	=	Unit variable cost
VX	=	Unit variable cost times volume, or total variable cost
I	=	Income, or total revenue less total cost

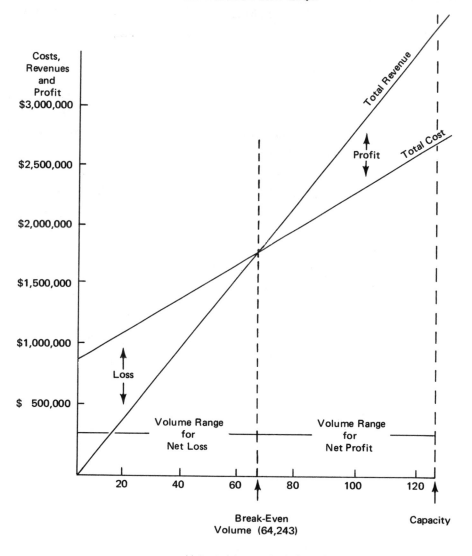

EXHIBIT 11.4

Cost-Volume-Profit Graph

Costs, Revenues and Profit

$3,000,000

$2,500,000

$2,000,000

$1,500,000

$1,000,000

$ 500,000

Total Revenue

Total Cost

Profit

Loss

Volume Range for Net Loss

Volume Range for Net Profit

20   40   60   80   100   120

Break-Even Volume (64,243)

Capacity

Volume (thousand guest-days)

BASIC EQUATION

Since the net income of the firm is the difference between its total revenue and its total cost, we may write:

Net income = Total revenue - total cost

= Total revenue - fixed cost - total variable cost

Alternatively, we may write:

$$I = SX - F - VX$$

This equation provides the basis of cost-volume-profit analysis. Its results show exactly the same thing (and no more) than the graphical analysis in Exhibit 11.4. The mathematical form, however, is easier to work with.

USE OF CVP ANALYSIS: ALGEBRAIC FORM

The advantage of making the assumptions which lead to the basic cost-volume-profit equation is that the equation conveys information. Specifically, there are five factors in the equation (I, S, X, V, and F); a knowledge of any four of them, when applied to the structural form of the equation, allows us to determine any fifth factor. For example, a knowledge of S, X, F, and V, together with the equation, gives us the value of I.

Desired profit level. Management has estimated the variable costs (V), the fixed costs (F), and the selling price (S) of a product. Further, management requires a profit figure of I for the period. What volume of sales (X) is necessary to reach this desired profit figure? The basic equation is:

$$I = SX - F - VX$$

Rearranged, this is:

$$I = X(S-V) - F$$

and

$$X = \frac{F + I}{S - V}$$

X is then the required volume level to produce a profit of I.

For example, if Exemplary Holiday Resort requires a net income of at least $100,000, it will need a volume of at least 72,230 guest-days. The calculations are:

$$X = \frac{F + I}{S - V}$$

$$= \frac{\$804,320 + \$100,000}{\$27.34 - \$14.82}$$

$$= \frac{\$904,320}{\$12.52}$$

$$= 72,230 \text{ guest-days}$$

At a volume of less than 72,230 guest days, Exemplary Holiday Resort will make less than $100,000 of net income. At a greater volume, net income will exceed $100,000.

If we define the *contribution margin per unit of volume (CM)* as the difference between selling price and variable cost per unit,

$$CM = S - V$$

then the equation for the volume required to reach a given level of profit can be stated as:

$$X = \frac{F + I}{CM}$$

An intuitive explanation is as follows: The product contribution margin (CM) is the difference between the extra *revenue* that a guest day generates (S) and the extra *cost* that a guest day generates (V). As one extra day is sold, net income is increased by S - V, or CM, since fixed costs are unchanged. Sufficient units (X) must be sold at a contribution per unit (CM) to absorb all total fixed costs (F) and provide the desired income (I). Total fixed costs (F) divided by the contribution per unit (CM) equals the number of units (X) to absorb all fixed costs, or break even. Income (I) divided by contribution margin per unit (CM) equals the additional number of units which must be sold to provide the desired income (I).

Break-even volume. The break-even volume or break-even point is defined as the determination of the level of volume at which profit is zero.

Since $I = X (S - V) - F$

and since $I = O$ at break-even volume

then $X_{BE} (S - V) = F$

and $X_{BE} = \frac{F}{S - V}$

or $X_{BE} = \frac{F}{CM}$

For example, Exemplary Holiday Resort will break even at a volume of 64,243 guest-days. This is calculated as:

$$X_{BE} = \frac{F}{S - V}$$

$$= \frac{\$804,320}{\$12.52}$$

$$= 64,243 \text{ guest-days}$$

Alternatively, we can calculate the volume in dollars rather than in units of volume. If we define CMR to be the *contribution margin ratio* (or the ratio of the contribution per unit to the selling price per unit), then:

$$CMR = \frac{S - V}{S}$$

$$= \frac{CMR}{S}$$

Since the break-even volume in dollars is the unit volume (X_{BE}) multiplied by the selling price (S):

$$O = SX_{BE} - F - VX$$

and $$SX_{BE} = S\frac{F}{CMR}$$

$$= \frac{F}{CMR}$$

In the case of Exemplary Holiday Resort:

$$CMR = \frac{\$12.52}{\$27.34} = 0.4579$$

and break-even sales are:

$$\frac{\$804,320}{0.4579} = \$1,756,407$$

which is the earlier unit result (64,243) times the unit price of $27.34.

Break-even analysis is only a special form of profit-volume analysis. The break-even point is not, of itself, an important concept because few managers will operate at a volume level which provides zero profit. On the other hand, knowledge of the break-even point is useful to managers of new hospitality service businesses which frequently incur initial losses.

Other unknowns. The previous two uses of CVP analysis have taken volume as an unknown factor, and have then solved for the volume which would be required to earn a certain level of profit. As noted initially, given *any* four factors one can solve for the fifth factor, using the basic CVP equation. For example, the management of Exemplary Holiday Resort wishes to know the selling price (S) which must be set in order to make a profit of $100,000 at a volume of 75,000 guest-days. As before, fixed costs are $804,320 and variable costs are $14.82 per unit.

Since $I = SX - F - VX$

then $SX = I + F + VX$ (total revenue = income + costs)

and $S = \dfrac{I + F + VX}{X}$

           $= V + \dfrac{I + F}{X}$

Substituting the numbers:

$$S = \$14.82 + \frac{\$100,000 + \$804,320}{75,000}$$

$$= \$14.82 + \$12.06$$

$$= \$26.88$$

Hence, at a price of $26.88 per unit and a volume of 75,000 guest-days, Exemplary Holiday Resort would make $100,000 profit.

Note that as calculated earlier, at a (higher) unit price of $27.34 and a (lower) volume of 72,230 guest-days, Exemplary Holiday Resort would make a profit of $100,000 also. Actually, we can use the framework of CVP analysis to calculate *all* of the combinations of selling price (S) and volume (X) which will produce a given level of income (I).

There are other examples which the reader can calculate. For example, it is possible to compute the amount of fixed costs (F) which can be incurred, if S, V, X, and I are given. An advertising scheme, for example, might be expected to yield a given volume (X), with selling price (S) and variable costs (V) constant. One could determine the amount of fixed costs (F), including advertising, which could be incurred without reducing income (I). The advertising scheme's profitability could then be determined by comparing the amount expected to be spent with the computed amount which could be spent without endangering profit.

Changes in factors. There is a fourth broad class of use of CVP analysis. So far, concentration has been on finding one factor, given the basic equation and the other four factors. The fourth class of use consists of finding the changes in income which would be caused by changes in one or more of the other four factors.

For example, if Exemplary Holiday Resort increased its price by $1.00 per guest-day, without affecting unit variable costs, total fixed costs, or volume, then (at a volume of 100,000 guest-days) profit would be increased by $100,000.

However, it is highly unlikely that Exemplary Holiday Resort could change one factor without causing changes in the other factors. In the example, it is unlikely that a price increase of $1.00 could be sustained without either spending more on advertising or sustaining a drop in sales volume. If $60,000 were spent on extra advertising, then the profit increase would be $40,000, provided that volume did not change. If the $1.00 price increase were coupled with an increase in advertising, and a drop in volume of 5,000 guest-days, then the change in profit would be more difficult to compute.

For example, if a $10,000 increase in advertising and a drop in volume of 5,000 guest-days would permit a $1.00 increase in the rate per guest-day, the effect on profit would be:

	Effect on Profit
Lost contribution margins (old sales): 5,000 at $12.52	- $62,600
Increase in advertising (approximately):	- 10,000
Extra contribution on 95,000 (lower) volume: 95,000 at $1.00	+ 95,000
Net effect on profit	+$22,400

Cost-volume-profit analysis can be used to demonstrate the effects of various changes on the firm's *profit structure.* Previous examples have examined the effects of changes on the *level* of profit. We shall now consider the effect of a change in costs upon the *range* of profits which the firm would earn at different volumes.

The total costs of Exemplary Holiday Resort at the break-even volume of 64,243 guest-days per year are estimated at approximately $1,750,000. More precisely, they are estimated to be $804,320 (fixed) plus $952,081 (variable). Exemplary Holiday Resort could alter their relative magnitudes at the break-even volume, by substituting capital for labor. For example, they could replace dishwashers, whose wages are a variable cost, with leased dishwashing machines, which would incur a primarily fixed leasing cost. If Exemplary Holiday Resort estimated that the savings in variable costs were 25¢ per guest day, and that the annual leasing charge is $16,000, then its break-even volume would essentially remain unchanged. Exhibit 11.5 illustrates this point. The total costs at the old break-even volume of 64,243 guest days are almost exactly the same as before; therefore, the new break-even volume is almost exactly the same. This is because the variable cost savings of 64,243 times 25¢ is almost exactly equal to the extra fixed costs of $16,000.

However, Exhibit 11.5 also illustrates an important change which has occurred in the cost and profit structure of Exemplary Holiday Resort. Because the contribution margin has been increased by 25¢ per unit, the sensitivity of the resort's income to changes in volume has been increased. Operations at a level above the break-even point now result in greater profit and operations at a level below the break-even point result in greater losses.

This trade-off of variable for fixed expenses is known as *operating leverage*. A firm with a high proportion of fixed costs is said to have a high operating leverage. This is exemplified by the Hospitality Service Industries operations in which a large proportion of costs are fixed.

A similar analysis could be conducted at any level of volume other than break-even volume. The technique is the same. Further, there is no reason why the total costs at any volume should remain unchanged, as they did in the previous example. There could be net cost savings on losses from substituting fixed for variable costs at a given volume. The example, however, was constructed to accentuate the effect of changing costs on not only the present volume, but on the whole range of volumes. That is, CVP analysis can be usefully employed to illustrate the effects of cost decisions upon the entire cost structure of the firm. As such, it is a useful planning device.

PROFIT-VOLUME GRAPHS

The cost-volume-profit graph shown in Exhibit 11.4 can be changed, without substantial modification, into a more simplified picture of the firm's profit structure, the profit-volume graph. The cost-volume-profit (CVP) graph revealed the assumed relationships between cost and volume, and revenue and volume. The vertical difference between the cost and revenue lines was the firm's profit (or, below the break-even point, its loss). The profit-volume (PV) graph simplifies the picture by omitting the cost and revenue lines; it merely plots the firm's profit or loss as a function of volume.

Continuing the example of the Exemplary Holiday Resort, Exhibit 11.6 illustrates the PV graph, equivalent of the CVP graph in Exhibit 11.4. At zero volume, the loss is equal to the fixed costs of $804,320. As before, the break-even volume is 64,243 guest-days.

EXHIBIT 11.5

Effect of Change in Cost Structure
or the Application of Operating Leverage

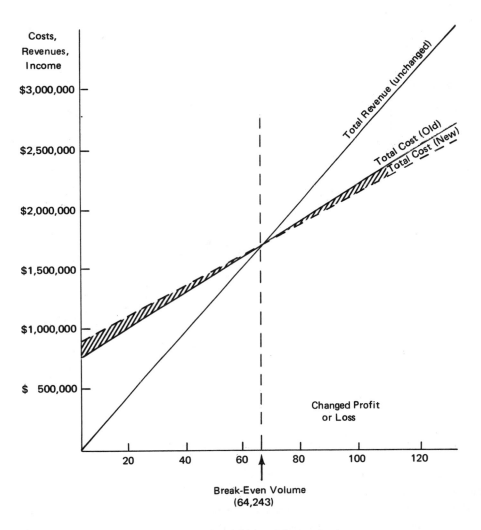

Costs, Revenues, Income

$3,000,000

$2,500,000

$2,000,000

$1,500,000

$1,000,000

$ 500,000

Total Revenue (unchanged)

Total Cost (Old)

Total Cost (New)

Changed Profit or Loss

20   40   60   80   100   120

Break-Even Volume
(64,243)

Volume (thousand guest-days)

 Changed Profit or Loss

255

EXHIBIT 11.6

Profit-Volume Graph

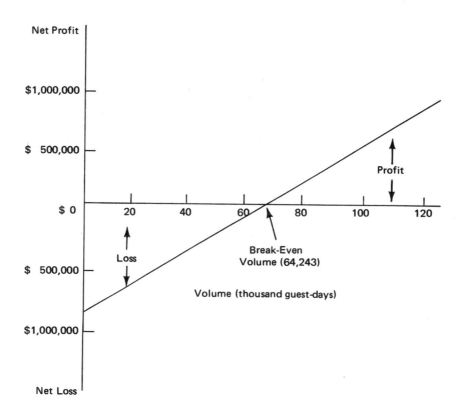

The PV graph is a handy tool for quick reference by top management. It has additional uses, however. It can be expanded to reveal the change in profit which would be expected to result from a change in another factor, such as a change in volume. While more than one change cannot be considered at once, the resulting graphical presentation is a convenient and easily understood way of summarizing the input of changes in factors, such as selling price upon profit. This extension of the PV graph is called a *star chart*. Such a chart is illustrated in Exhibit 11.7.

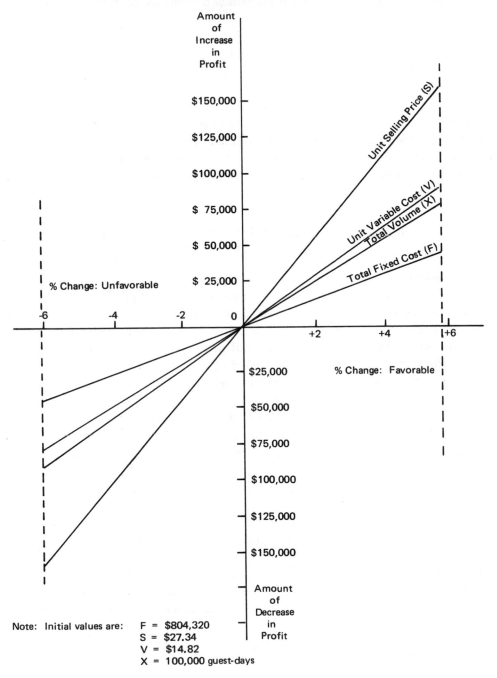

EXHIBIT 11.7

Star Chart
Changes in Profit as a Function of Changes in Other Factors

Amount
of
Increase
in
Profit

$150,000

$125,000

$100,000

$ 75,000

$ 50,000

$ 25,000

% Change: Unfavorable

-6   -4   -2   0   +2   +4   +6

Unit Selling Price (S)

Unit Variable Cost (V)
Total Volume (X)

Total Fixed Cost (F)

% Change: Favorable

$25,000

$50,000

$75,000

$100,000

$125,000

$150,000

Amount
of
Decrease
in
Profit

Note: Initial values are: F = $804,320
                                S = $27.34
                                V = $14.82
                                X = 100,000 guest-days

Reading from the star chart in Exhibit 11.7, the *amount* (not the percentage) change in profit which is due to each *individual* percentage change is as follows:

Factor Change	Profit Effect	Explanation
6% decrease in F:	+ $ 48,259	6% × $804,320
6% increase in S:	+ 164,040	6% × $27.34 × 100,000
6% decrease in V:	+ 88,920	6% × $14.82 × 100,000
6% increase in X:	+ 75,120	6% × $12.52 × 100,000

Since we have plotted the *amount* of the change in profit due to each individual factor change, and since we have assumed that costs and revenues respond linearly to volume changes, the star chart's relationships are linear.

The star chart is a handy expositional tool in that the effect of any individual change in price, cost, or volume can be readily established.

THE SEGMENT (OR DEPARTMENTAL) CONTRIBUTION INCOME STATEMENT

The distinction between fixed and variable costs is carried into the hospitality service industries' formal reporting system. For example, the income statements reorganize the segregation of fixed and variable costs, so that users can gain some knowledge of responses of costs (and, therefore, of profits) to volume.

Conventional reporting methods do not permit a decision-maker to identify costs as either fixed or variable, and hence do not convey as much information as possible. Instead, it is more usual to group costs by standard classifications rather than by their responsiveness to volume.

Exhibit 11.8 is adopted from Robert N. Anthony's *Management Accounting*.[1] It shows a conventional income statement for a restaurant, and an income statement following the uniform system of accounts for restaurants, which attempts to isolate factors which cause variations in profit. The segment contribution form requires that semivariable costs be segregated into fixed and variable elements, and that costs be segregated by segments (such as by food or beverage). Note that some costs (such as utilities, which are used by both the food and the beverage operation) cannot be broken down by segments because they are *joint costs*.

This particular example illustrates the additional information contained in the contribution form of reporting used in the uniform systems of accounts for the many categories of the hospitality service industries. In this example, the

---

1. Robert N. Anthony, *Management Accounting*, 4th ed. (Homewood, Ill.: Richard D. Irwin, Inc., 1970), p. 466.

EXHIBIT 11.8

Conventional Form of Income Statement

Sales		$6,700,000
Less: Costs		
Cost of Sales	$2,070,000	
Salaries and Wages	2,170,000	
Employee Benefits	281,000	
Uniforms	24,000	
China, Linen and Glassware	310,000	
Advertising and Promotion	160,000	
Utilities	134,000	
Administrative and General	301,000	
Music and Entertainment	68,000	
Rent or Occupation Costs	750,000	
Depreciation	40,000	
Other	401,000	
Total Costs		6,709,000
Restaurant Profit (Loss)		$ (9,000)

Segment Contribution Form of Income Statement

	Food	Beverage	Total
Sales	$4,900,000	$1,800,000	$6,700,000
Less: Variable Costs			
Cost of Sales	$1,590,000	$480,000	
Salaries and Wages	1,810,000	360,000	
Employee Benefits	210,000	71,000	
Uniforms	21,000	3,000	
China, Linen and Glassware	193,000	117,000	
Other Variable Costs	295,000	106,000	
Total Variable Costs	4,119,000	1,137,000	5,256,000
Contribution to Fixed Costs	$ 781,000	$ 663,000	$1,444,000
Less: Fixed Costs			
Advertising and Promotion			$ 160,000
Utilities			134,000
Administrative and General			301,000
Music and Entertainment			68,000
Rent or Occupation Cost			750,000
Depreciation			40,000
Total Fixed Costs			1,453,000
Restaurant Profit (Loss)			$ (9,000)

conventional form of income statement indicates a net loss for the business; furthermore, there is an absence of useful information. Yet the income statement which highlights the profit margin contribution of each segment reveals that it would not be a wise decision to shut down any part of the operation. The accounting figures show a total loss of $9,000; but the contribution figures show that this loss would not be avoided if one segment of the business were shut down.

LIMITS OF COST-VOLUME-PROFIT ANALYSIS

As is the case with all analytical tools, the tool of CVP analysis cannot be used for every job. Such tools should not be used when their limitations are too great for the purpose at hand. The decision-maker must decide whether to use CVP analysis for a given purpose; in this section and the next, some of the factors of which the decision-maker should be aware will be outlined.

THE LINEARITY ASSUMPTION

In an absolute sense, one cannot with confidence state that a cost is either fixed, variable, or semivariable, because no costs behave *perfectly* in proportion to volume. The question is whether, for a given purpose, their behavior is close enough to make the assumption of linearity. In this behavior assumption, the concept of the *relevant range* is applied to CVP analysis as in Exhibit 11.9.

If a firm typically experiences volumes within the banded limits, then the behavior of costs and revenues outside of those limits is irrelevant to its decision-making. Although the revenues and costs outside of the relevant range may not behave linearly, the important question is whether their behavior can be approximated by straight lines *within* the relevant decision-making range. For example, a firm with a cost-volume relationship similar to that of Exhibit 11.10 (A) could safely ignore the cost curvature for most purposes; but a firm with cost behavior similar to that of Exhibit 11.10 (B) probably should investigate alternative techniques. In the latter case, no linear approximation to the actual curve will be satisfactory over the relevant range indicated, and CVP techniques are not recommended.

MEASURE OF VOLUME

In the example of the Exemplary Holiday Resort, volume was consistently measured in terms of the number of guest-days. Although this may seem to be a natural way of measuring volume, it is not necessarily the best. One usually has a wide range of alternative volume measures; hence, it would be useful to establish a criterion for choice between alternative measures.

EXHIBIT 11.9

Relevant Range and Cost-Volume-Profit Analysis

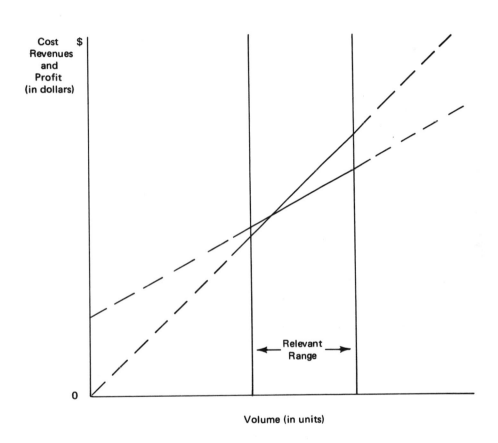

Note: If the break-even point falls outside of the "relevant range," then it is (for this entity at least) an irrelevant concept.

EXHIBIT 11.10

Alternative CVP Relationships

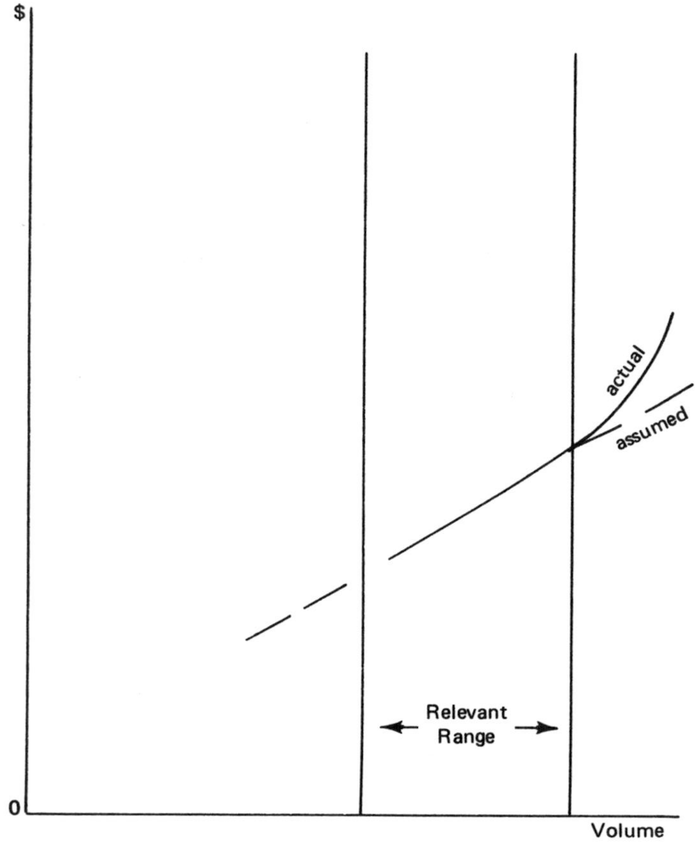

Case A: Acceptable behavior within the relevant range.

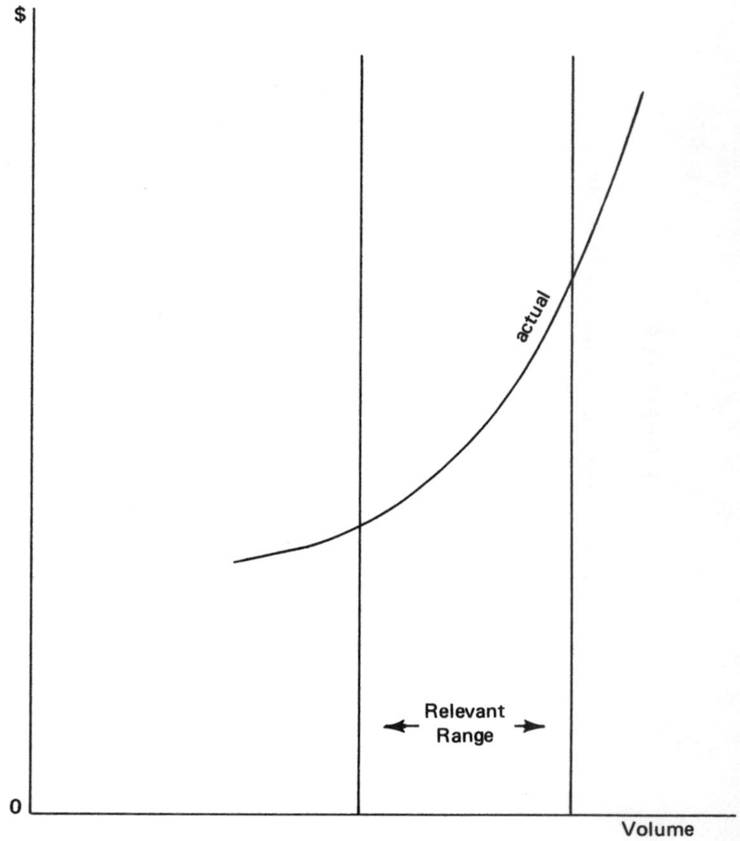

Case B: Unacceptable behavior over the relevant range.

The purpose of CVP analysis is to give a decision-maker information concerning effects of changes in one variable (such as volume) on another (such as profit). The essential question is, therefore, the ability of one variable to predict another. It follows, then, that the choice between alternative measures of volume should be based upon their respective abilities to predict other variables. If, in Exemplary Holiday Resort's case, the number of guest-days is less closely associated with costs and revenues than is the dollar volume of sales, then (other things being equal) the dollar value of sales should be used as a measure of volume. The reason is simple: estimated sales dollar changes in this case will better predict profit changes than will estimated changes in the number of guest-days.

This points out one of the limitations of CVP analysis; that is, CVP analysis does not give error-free decisions because the relationships between costs, revenues, and profits are not exact.

THE SALES-MIX PROBLEM

So far, we have assumed that firms produce only one product. In the example, Exemplary Holiday Resort's volume was measured in guest-days only. However, in the hospitality service industries, it is extremely unlikely that firms will have only one department. In the Exemplary Holiday Resort, for example, there are at least two separate products—rooms, and food and beverages.

One could break down the product, "food and beverages," into much more detail; for example, by the facility in which the food and beverage is served. This would not present a problem if either the sales mix of individual products remained stable, or if their respective contribution margin ratios were identical. But the departmental profit margins on foods, beverages, and rooms vary widely; so in Exemplary Holiday Resort's case, the latter condition is not likely to be met. Perhaps the proportions of each type of product's sale will be relatively stable over time, but this is not necessarily so.

The example in Exhibit 11.11 illustrates this problem. It is adopted from the National Association of Cost Accountants, Combined Research Series No. 16, 17, and 18.[2]

Exhibit 11.11 shows that both the expected profit for a period and the break-even sales volume depend upon the proportions in which each of four

---

2. National Association of Cost Accountants, *The Analysis of Cost-Volume-Profit Relationships* (Combined Research Series 16, 17, and 18, original printing 1949-1950), Exhibit 7, p. 72.

EXHIBIT 11.11
Two Examples of the Sales Mix

Case A	Rooms	Food	Beverage	Other	Total
Sales (Percentage of Total)	56.8%	29.1%	10.4%	3.7%	100.0%
Contribution Margin Ratio	73.0%	15.0%	30.0%	90.0%	52.0%*
Sales	$397,000	$204,000	$73,000	$26,000	$700,000
Contribution Margin	290,000	31,000	22,000	23,000	366,000
Less: Fixed Costs					175,000
Profit					$191,000

Break-Even Sales $\dfrac{\$175,000}{0.52}$ = $336,500

Case B	Rooms	Food	Beverage	Other	Total
Sales (Percentage of Total)	49.6%	31.8%	13.4%	5.2%	100.0%
Contribution Margin Ratio	73.0%	15.0%	30.0%	90.0%	49.0%*
Sales	$347,000	$223,000	$94,000	$36,000	$700,000
Contribution Margin	253,000	33,000	28,000	32,000	346,000
Less: Fixed Costs					175,000
Profit					$171,000

Break-Even Sales $\dfrac{\$175,000}{0.49}$ = $357,000

*Weighted Average

products are sold. Thus, with total sales remaining constant, as the proportion of items with lower contribution margins increases, profit declines (Case B).

The sales-mix problem is a special case of the more general problem of volume measurement. Since CVP analysis assumes a contribution margin which is independent of volume, and since the sales mix might be expected to vary with volume, the CVP technique is accordingly limited in applicability.

The sales-mix problem is a common one to most hospitality service industries managers because most deal with sales mixes with individual margins that vary widely from one to another, and with sales mixes that are susceptible to change. For example, the typical motor hotel has a sales mix consisting of at least room sales, food sales and beverage sales. The departmental profit margins in each of these revenue categories is very different with room departmental profit in a range of 65 to 80 percent, beverage departmental profit ranging from 20 to 45 percent, and food departmental profit of between 10 and 35 percent. Obviously, a change in the sales mix will substantially affect profit as a percentage of total revenue.

JOINTNESS

A final limitation of CVP analysis is its inability to consider the effects of jointness in costs or revenues; no analytical technique is capable of this. Joint costs, by their very nature, cannot meaningfully be considered individually as one cannot be changed without changing the other.

CVP analysis can be used to investigate a firm's cost, revenue, and profit structure, as it has been in the examples in this chapter. Further, when costs and revenues are not jointly incurred or earned by more than one segment of the firm, CVP analysis can be used on the costs, revenues, and profits of each segment. The analysis is exactly the same. For example, it is easy to conceive Exhibit 11.4 as applying to the profit structure of an individual product of Exemplary Holiday Resort (say, food), or to an individual operating division (say, motels), or to an individual unit of operation (say, a particular motel).

CVP analysis of sements breaks down when costs and revenues are joint, but, so do all such managerial techniques. In Exhibit 11.8, the fixed costs have not been assigned to food or beverage because most of them are incurred by both. If these fixed costs were to be changed, then the effect of the change on the firm's profit could be calculated, but the effect on each segment's profit could not be so calculated. The reason is that the change in fixed costs could not be assigned to either segment. The conclusion is that whenever costs and revenues are jointly incurred or earned, managerial decisions can be made only at a *total* level, and not for individual segments.

SUMMARY

This chapter has dealt with many examples of the application of cost-volume-profit analysis; there are many other applications left undescribed.

The main uses of cost-volume-profit analysis in practice are, briefly, as follows.

CVP analysis is frequently used as a device for conveying to top management a quick picture of the firm's profit structure. Graphical devices, such as the CVP graph, the PV graph, and the star chart, are particularly useful in this regard. Frequently, top management is not interested in long, detailed presentations on cost, revenue, and profit behavior, and is prepared to accept a rougher but quicker analysis.

CVP analysis is frequently used when a low degree of accuracy is required in a decision. Such an example is given in the preceding paragraph; that is, CVP is utilized when top management is prepared to leave detailed accuracy to subordinates, thus freeing themselves to concentrate on broader pictures of the firm. However, there are also many uses of CVP analysis at a lower level of management when a high degree of accuracy is not required. A frequent use of CVP analysis is as a screening device. Proposals for changing selling prices, costs, and volumes can be quickly classified into those which are obviously profitable, obviously unprofitable, and uncertain, purely on the basis of simple CVP analysis. Those which are uncertain can later be investigated in more detail; the purpose of this procedure is to save the cost of a detailed investigation into those projects which are obviously profitable or unprofitable. For these projects, a simple CVP analysis, with its assumptions of linearity in costs and revenues and of a constant sales mix, is sufficient.

Finally, CVP analysis is frequently used because there is not always an alternative. Such a situation could arise for two reasons. First, the assumptions of linear cost and revenue behavior and of a constant sales mix could be reasonable assumptions, in many cases. For example, the linear approximation to the cost behavior in Exhibit 11.10, Case A, is a very good approximation. Second, the assumptions of CVP analysis will be accepted in cases where there is no other information available to present an alternative method. Stated another way, it might not be worth the cost to attempt to isolate more detailed relationships.

The concept of operating leverage, the trade-off between fixed and variable costs in an organization's cost structure, is particularly important in the hospitality service industries because of the generally high proportion of fixed costs, and the inability to materially alter the fixed-to-variable cost relationshiips.

A useful expansion of the CVP graph is the star chart. Using a star chart, the approximate effect upon an outcome that would result from changes in a factor may be determined.

Discussion Questions

1. Why are graphical forms of CVP analysis useful in the management decision-making process?
2. What are the basic assumptions underlying the plotting of total revenue and total cost curves on the CVP graph?
3. What is the meaning of "contribution margin" per unit of output?
4. What is the contribution margin ratio?
5. Define the break-even point.
6. What are some of the limitations in CVP analysis?

Problem 1

The following data has been extracted from the annual financial statements of the Parsons Motor Hotel.

Total revenue	$500,000
Variable costs	175,000
Gross operating margin	$325,000
Fixed costs*	285,000
Net profit	$ 40,000

*Annual rent of $40,000 is included in fixed costs.

Required

1. If these relationships are assumed to remain constant, at what level of sales does the Parsons Motor Hotel break even?
2. If the owners of the hotel have invested $500,000 in the business, what level of sales is required to provide them with a 12 percent return on their investment?
3. In the renegotiation of their lease, management has been offered the following proposal. In lieu of the fixed annual rent of $40,000 per year, the landlord has offered to accept 10 percent of the hotel's annual *gross operating margin* as the annual rent on the property.
   a. If management accepts this proposal, what would be the break-even level of sales?
   b. Should management accept this proposal if they expect next year's total revenue to be $600,000?
   c. Should management accept this proposal if they expect next year's sales to be $700,000?
   d. If management's decision should change between case 2 and 3, isolate the level of sales at which this change in decision should take place.

Note: Show calculations in each of the above cases.

Problem 2

The Bell Hotel has been having extensive problems in the area of expense control. Their key expenses are listed.

Manager's salary	$12,000
Supervisor's salary (kitchen)	7,500
Wages to full-time help*	24,000
Wages to part-time help (restaurant only)	6,000
Depreciation on building	10,000
Front office supplies	1,500
Accounting reports (computer time)	2,640
Heat, light and power	3,600

*Wages for full-time help is divided into 30 percent for rooms, 50 percent for restaurant and 20 percent for cocktail lounge.

The accounting reports are based on a fixed rate of $100 per month for a monthly balance sheet and income statement and $20 each for various special reports which management can request.

You are to study these costs and classify them within one or more of the following categories:

> Controllable and uncontrollable costs
> Fixed and variable costs
> Direct and indirect costs

Problem 3

R.T. Cee, a liberal arts professor, has been offered an opportunity to invest in a small vending machine business involving thirty vending machines in various office buildings around the city.

To start the R.T.C. Vending Co., Cee must invest $15,000, of which $4,200 is for an inventory of merchandise for the machines and $10,800 for the total cost of the thirty vending machines. The machines have a service life of five years and no salvage value. The merchandise retails for $.10 per unit and will cost Cee $.045 per unit. The building owners are granted a rental commission of $.015 per unit sold in the machines. Cee can hire a man to service and maintain the machines for $400 per month and he anticipates that other expenses will amount to $140 per month. Depreciation on the machines will be computed on a straight-line basis.

The machine manufacturers report that similar vending machine routes have produced a sales volume ranging from 500 to 1,000 units per machine per month.

Problem 3 (continued)

Required

1. What level of monthly sales would be required to generate an annual return of 10 percent on Cee's investment?
2. Prepare a graph showing total revenue, fixed costs, and total costs for sales volumes from 0 to 1,000 units per machine per month.
3. Cee is considering offering the building owners a flat rental of $10 per machine in lieu of the sales commission. What effect would this change have on the sales volume required to generate the desired 10 percent rate of return?

CHAPTER 12

Cost Accounting

Cost accounting, as applicable in the hospitality service industries, is a set of concepts and techniques designed to facilitate the accumulation, analysis and utilization of historical and projected per unit cost data for use in management decision-making. The timely and accurate accumulation of cost data is of primary importance to the effectiveness of the management process because unit cost information may be the foundation for many decisions.

Cost accounting systems operate to provide data for managers who are responsible for making operating decisions. Some of these decisions are made routinely on a daily basis, while others are more complex and require specialized information. The nature of operations in a firm—or in one of its departments—often dictates the type of cost accounting system that should be available for use.

Cost accounting systems were originally developed for production cost control and inventory valuation in manufacturing firms. The basis for control is the establishment of unit costs for each item manufactured. The unit cost estimates have been prepared under one of the following basic concepts of cost.

Historical Costs. Under the assumption that past unit costs should continue into the future, historical costs have been used as control standards.

Estimated Costs. Realizing that historical costs may not be the best cost objective because of inefficiencies that may have existed in past performance and changing conditions, historical costs are adjusted based on estimates of improvable performance and future conditions.

Standard Costs. Because an estimate of the potential efficiencies may be unreliable, engineering and time and motion studies may be carried out to arrive at reasonably attainable standard costs. While the time and expense required for such studies may be substantial, the increased reliability and accuracy of the standards frequently justifies such expenditures for manufacturing concerns.

The first part of the cost accounting system then is the establishment of control standards. Of the three widely used alternative methods for providing control standards, the standard cost approach is the most effective.

For the valuation of inventory and for the generation of actual costs for comparison to the established control standards, the second part of the cost accounting system is the accumulation of actual unit costs. The cost system is just an extension of the traditional general accounting system, with two modifications. First, in a general accounting system costs are reported in the whole amount whereas a cost accounting system reports costs on a unit basis. And second, in a manufacturing cost accounting system manufacturing overhead cost, (that is, overhead directly associated with the production process, such as supervisors' salaries, production equipment, repairs and maintenance, utilities in the production area, and depreciation on the production facilities), is allocated to the units produced. Thus, if total direct manufacturing overhead costs were $100,000 and 200,000 units were produced, the cost per unit would include $0.50 of direct overhead costs.

The cost accounting system which accumulates and reports costs on a per unit basis can do so on a standard cost basis or on an actual cost basis. In an actual cost system the direct labor, direct materials and direct overhead are reported. In contrast, a standard cost system records the costs per unit as determined in the engineering studies used to arrive at the standard cost of the product. Any variations between the standard costs and the actual costs are then recorded in separate accounts and serve to point out to management that a variance from the established standards did occur.

The unit costs that are generated by the manufacturing cost accounting system are used for inventory valuation and control. Completed units of production remaining in inventory (finished goods) at the end of the fiscal period are valued at the actual cost determined under the cost accounting system. Partially completed units (work in process) are valued based on the accumulation of individual costs incurred thus far in their production plus a proportionate share of allocated manufacturing overhead.

Control comparisons vary according to whether the actual or standard cost accounting system is employed. As noted, if the standard cost accounting system is in use, any variances are immediately apparent by the existence of variance accounts. If the actual cost system is in use, unit costs must be compared to the budget or other predetermining standards to determine if any unfavorable variances occurred.

The costs under either the actual or standard cost accounting systems may be accumulated under one of several cost accumulation methods. These alternative methods exist because of the different nature of the manufacturing process and because of the varying information needs of management. The two primary methods for the accumulation of manufacturing costs are the job-order and process-cost systems.

Using either the job-order or the process-cost system, the basic objective is the same, the accumulation of unit costs. The difference between the two approaches is the result of the difference in the nature of the production process. Where many of the same items are produced on a regular basis involving one or more processes, a process manufacturing system exists. In contrast, where a few items are being manufactured generally to order and with little homogeneity, the manufacturing is done on an individual job basis, or job order.

Because of this difference in manufacturing, the accumulation of costs is most easily accomplished by using a system that is consistent with the manufacturing. Under the process-cost system costs are accumulated by individual process and the unit cost of each process is determined by dividing the total cost of that process by the number of units processed. Under the job-order system, costs are directly accumulated on a log for each particular job as it is manufactured.

COST ACCOUNTING FOR THE HOSPITALITY SERVICE INDUSTRIES

While managers in the hospitality service industries require unit cost information just as do manufacturing firm managers, the nature of activities in the hospitality service industries makes the traditional cost accounting systems unapplicable. Included in the differences that make the traditional cost accounting systems inappropriate for the hospitality service industries are:

1. The output of the hospitality service industries firm is primarily intangible; that is, services are the "product" rather than tangible goods.

2. Because the hospitality service industries' product is primarily intangible there is no production for inventories; instead, production is for immediate consumption. Even where a tangible product such as food or beverages is involved, the production remains for immediate consumption only; there are no finished goods for shipment or warehousing.

3. The price and/or volume of individual services rendered generally does not justify precise engineering studies to determine "standard costs." The cost of maintaining a sophisticated unit cost bookkeeping system is also generally unjustified.

The exception to the latter case may be in the large scale production of food for educational and institutional feeding, and airline in-flight feeding. However, even for these activities the "production runs" are generally only a few hours long and thus the practicality of an elaborate unit cost bookkeeping system is questionable.

An example of production in the hospitality service industries is that of a restaurant, wherein food and beverage production occurs immediately after a customer orders from a list of selections. Preparation time requires only a few minutes, and the entire production cycle may be consummated in less than one hour. Selections are varied, and frequently changing patterns of customer demand must be satisfied. A degree of consistency in the times available to perform functions is similarly lacking. Functions must be performed more rapidly in periods of heavy demand, and the quality of performance may well vary.

Taken together, these environmental constraints limit the utilization of the traditional methods for the management of costs in the hospitality service industries. Thus, the cost accounting needs of the hospitality service industries require a revised and less vigorous approach to providing unit cost information, both historical and projected, for the hospitality service industries manager.

PURPOSE OF COST ACCOUNTING IN THE HOSPITALITY SERVICE INDUSTRIES

As a result of the unique unit of output for the hospitality service industries the purpose of cost accounting will differ slightly, in that the need for inventory valuation of completed and partially completed products is not present. In the hospitality service industries the objectives of cost accounting are to:

1. Provide cost estimates to aid managers in developing formalized operating plans (budgets) for coming periods.
2. Generate historical cost data to assist managers in making control decisions.
3. Serve as the primary cost data for evaluating present pricing and as a basis for establishing future pricing.
4. Develop cost data required for specialized, nonrecurring decisions.

Each of these objectives relates to a particular kind of operating decision.

COST FOR PLANNING

In planning, managers attempt to evaluate and select those courses of action which will most likely generate acceptable profit or service levels. The planning process requires that a number of alternatives be evaluated and a study be made of the advantages and disadvantages associated with each alternative.

The planning process is complex and no attempt will be made here to delineate each of the steps taken by a manager as he develops plans for a firm, but three phases of planning are illustrated in a practical situation.

IDENTIFYING CRITICAL FACTORS

First, the manager must attempt to identify those factors which he considers important in attaining adequate profit levels. These factors may be either internal or external. People and physical resources (i.e., the facility, the furnishings, and all operating equipment, etc.) are internal factors that will have an influence on the attitudes and responsiveness of guests. The state of the economy and the competitive environment are external factors that will have an effect on the future demand for the firm's services and goods. After identifying these critical factors, general plans can be developed.

EVALUATING THE FACILITY'S CAPACITY

The second phase of planning is management's evaluation of the facility within the competitive environment. Management must capitalize on favorable features of their facility and formulate long-range plans based upon present and planned facilities. For example, the more closely the total decor of a restaurant is tailored to the tastes and needs of a particular clientele, the higher the probability that it will succeed. A night club environment is probably inappropriate for a small community, and a family-type setting would be equally inappropriate for a downtown, metropolitan club.

DEVELOPING PLANS OF ACTION

Third, the manager must develop a strategy—a plan of action which will allow the firm to achieve the best profit or service levels possible within a given environmental framework. Development of a strategy means that the manager attempts continuously to select the best of all available courses of action consistent with the long-range plans. Since there is a larger future uncertainty in the hospitality service industries, each of the proposed courses of action must be evaluated in terms of the manager's predictions of changes in the environment. Thus, all factors which may influence profits, including all possible changes in the facility, must be reexamined in this phase of the planning process.

Planning requires that managers look forward into the future in an attempt to influence factors in the environment that can assist in achieving objectives.

As an illustration of the need for cost data in the planning process, a firm is conducting an analysis and evaluation of departmental operating profits throughout the organization. The manager of food and beverage operations has been requested to reevaluate the department pricing structure. The department head in charge of food service is requested to estimate food service costs on a daily basis. In particular, the manager has asked for an indication of the number of dollars of daily payroll cost expected in the coming period (Exhibit 12.1).

EXHIBIT 12.1

Estimated Daily Food Service Costs
for Period Ending February 28, 19XX

A. *Analysis of Covers Served*

Meal Period	Average Daily Covers	Number Served/Hr.	Required Emp. Service Hours
Breakfast	100	12	8*
Luncheon	300	10	30
Dinner	150	6	25
			63/Day

B. *Waitress Costs—Daily*

Full-Time 6 x 8 hr.	48 x $1.75	$ 84
Part-Time 5 x 3 hr.	15 x 1.60	24
	63 hrs.	$108
Fringes (15% of Hourly Wage Total)		17
Daily Wage Cost		$125

*100 daily covers ÷ 12 served per hours = 8 1/3 employee service hours.

As a starting point, the historical record of the number of daily covers served would be reviewed. Since historical records are not necessarily the best indicators of the future, all predictions and expectations should be discussed thoroughly with others in the organization. If substantial changes in the volume of business are anticipated, plans should be adjusted.

Assuming, in this case, that history is a good indicator of future demand patterns, the next step is to determine the number of waitresses needed under the firm's level of service policy to serve the projected number of covers at each meal period. The underlying productivity assumptions guide this scheduling process— that is, each waitress can serve twelve covers at breakfast, ten covers at lunch, and six covers at dinner.

Dividing average daily covers by the number of covers served per hour will give the required employee service hours. A total of eight hours in waitress time is required to service the breakfast meal period. If this period includes three hours each day (7:00 A.M. to 10:00 A.M.), at least three waitresses must be available to satisfy anticipated demand. However, the hourly demand and the physical facilities must be considered before final scheduling can be accomplished.

A similar evaluation is required for the luncheon and dinner periods. Estimating the average covers each day, the number of covers served per hour of employee time, and the average hourly wage for waitresses, a department head is able to estimate the daily food service costs.

Part B of Exhibit 12.1 illustrates the computation of the daily food service costs. Six full-time employees and five part-time employees are used to satisfy the day's food service estimated requirements. At the rates of $1.75 per hour and $1.60 per hour respectively, the total direct wage costs for 63 service hours would be $108.00. Assuming that fringe benefits approximate 15 percent of hourly wages, an additional $17.00 must be built into the budget for total daily wage costs of $125.00.

When these data are subsequently incorporated into a comprehensive profit plan, the profitability prospects for the entire facility can be evaluated well before the fact. If the planned budget indicates that desired profits are not likely under predicted conditions, management may make adjustments. By planning for the future, management is given an opportunity to provide for those factors which will affect profitability.

COSTS FOR CONTROL

Control is best described in terms of a manager's efforts to remedy problems that caused variations between planned and actual operations. For example, a manager's reaction to a situation where costs differ significantly from those which are planned would be to judge whether or not the dollar amount involved in the variation warrants immediate attention and corrective action. If the variance is relatively small, the analysis may be postponed, but if the variation is large the manager must immediately determine the probable cause.

For example, a manager is confronted with a weekly food cost variance of $5.00 on a particular menu item. Actual cost of $5.00 greater than the planned cost level does not dictate that large sums of money be expended to correct the problem. Conversely, a variance of $500.00 would undoubtedly bring about a positive decision to immediately investigate.

Exhibit 12.2 illustrates a situation where actual costs are substantially greater than estimated costs for a one-week period.

It is assumed that each maid earns $90.00 per week and cleaning supplies are estimated at $.25 cents per occupied room. Occupancy averaged 64 percent—128 rooms of a 200-room motel—so the total cost of supplies for the week amounts to $224.00. An analysis of costs incurred in prior periods provides further that

EXHIBIT 12.2

Estimated Housekeeping Costs
(Room Cleaning Activities)
for Week Ending February 28, 19XX

	Planned	Actual	Variance
Maids' Wages (14 x $90)*	$ 1,260	$1,320	($ 60.00) U
Cleaning Supplies (128 x 7 $.25)	224	260	(36.00) U
Miscellaneous Expenses**	136	160	(24.00) U
Totals	$ 1,620	$1,740	($120.00) U
Housekeeping Cost per Room (896 Rooms Occupied)	$ 1.80	$ 1.94	$ 0.14 U

U = Unfavorable variance.

*Equivalent full-time maids.
**Miscellaneous expenses are estimated to be approximately 60 percent of the expenditure for cleaning supplies.

miscellaneous expenses should approximate 60 percent of expenditures for cleaning supplies, or $136.00. These estimates are reflected in the "planned costs" column of Exhibit 12.2.

After the planned costs have been evaluated by the department head at the beginning of the period, they become a part of his operational budget. These planned costs provide the department head with a foundation for making control decisions. He must understand thoroughly both the nature of costs included in the report and the basis upon which computations have been prepared. With this full understanding, planned costs serve as guidelines for the manager as he operates his department during the period.

Planned costs represent attainable targets for the operating manager. He achieves success to the extent that he attains the planned activity goals within the planned costs. When the targets are reasonably attainable, the manager is provided with a bona fide challenge, and planned costs will be a motivational device.

COMPARING ACTUAL TO PLANNED COSTS

The second column of Exhibit 12.2 represents a report of actual costs incurred. The cost accounting system has operated to accumulate costs incurred. Those costs incurred in direct support of the housekeeping function are assigned directly to the rooms department. In the example, the $1,740.00 reported is the total amount of costs incurred to accomplish the housekeeping function for the week ended February 28. As a result of the actual costs incurred, housekeeping costs per room were $0.14 higher than planned for a total unfavorable cost variance of $120.00.

COSTS FOR PRICING DECISIONS

The third purpose of the cost accounting system is to assist management in evaluating the pricing structure. Actual unit costs should be periodically compared to selling prices in order to adjust prices when necessary. Although pricing decisions are not accomplished without considering competition and other external factors, cost data is a significant part of the information upon which pricing decisions should be based.

Exhibit 12.3 illustrates a changing cost structure for breakfast menu item #3.

The costs of breakfast menu item #3 have increased substantially during the two-year period and they are expected to increase further. Menu item costs are presented on a per unit basis and are computed as a simple average—the food cost incurred for this menu item is divided by the number of times that the menu item was served. In the first year, the cost of juice served with this menu item was approximately $360.00. Analyses of sales slips indicated that menu item #3 was

EXHIBIT 12.3

Food Cost for Pricing Decisions
Breakfast Menu Item #3

	Year One	Year Two	Future Year Three (Estimated)
Sales Price	$1.40	$1.40	$1.50
Food Cost			
Juice	$ .03	$ .05	$ .07
Eggs	.08	.10	.12
Meat	.15	.17	.19
Toast	.02	.02	.02
Butter	.01	.01	.01
Coffee	.01	.01	.01
Total Food Cost	$ .30	$ .36	$ .42
Margin	$1.10	$1.04	$1.08
Margin Percentage	79%	74%	72%

served 12,000 times during year one; the simple average cost of juice served per meal was $.03 ($360.00 divided by 12,000).

However, it is important to recognize that changes in cost should cause reviews and changes in the pricing of menu items. If the average cost for each menu item sold cannot be developed with reasonable effort, some other form of estimating food costs must be used.

A failure to increase prices in this illustrated situation will cause the unit profit margin to be reduced. In the year one the menu item was sold for $1.40. Its total food cost was 30¢, and a margin of $1.10 resulted from each sale. With no price increase in the following year, an increase in food cost of 6¢ per unit results in a corresponding reduction in the margin of profit. And, even with a change in selling prices in the final year, the margin will drop by seven percentage points. If this margin decline were to extend throughout all menu items, the restaurant's profitability would be undermined. In this illustration, management is confronted with a definite need to increase prices as a result of increases in food cost.

Managers must be aware of these cost/price relationships. Since there is no set and accepted approach to evaluating cost/price relationships, there is a need for frequent management reevaluations of the pricing policies in the firm. The time spent in such evaluations will prove of value, because only in this way can the erosion of the firm's profits as a result of cost increases without price increases be prevented.

COST FOR SPECIAL DECISIONS

The fourth purpose of cost accounting is to provide the necessary information to assist managers in making specialized, nonrecurring decisions. These decisions may occur at infrequent intervals and at various points in the organization. There are no universally acceptable formulas for the development of relevant cost data for these decisions. Each decision is relatively specialized in nature. The manager is confronted each time with the need to identify and gather those bits of information which relate directly to the question at hand.

For example, the Valley Oaks Country Club members requested that an informal snack bar be constructed. The club's present restaurant facility is formal in decor, and all its dining facilities cater to those who choose to dine in a formal atmosphere. No dining facility was available for those members who were golfing, swimming, playing tennis, etc. Of primary concern was the possible effect of a proposed snack bar on the profitability of the dining room.

Data are presented (Exhibit 12.4) to summarize the average monthly results of operations in the restaurant facility during the preceding two-year period. The profitability of the food and beverage activity increased by $1,000 from the base

EXHIBIT 12.4

Costs for Special Decisions
Addition of Informal Snack Bar

Summary of Monthly Operating Profits

Average Monthly	Base Year	Year Two	Year Three*
Revenues	$12,000	$13,000	$14,000
Operating Costs	9,000	9,000	10,000
Profit	$ 3,000	$ 4,000	$ 4,000

Projected Monthly Profits with Addition
  of Snack Bar (Years Three to Five)

Average Monthly	Dining Area	Snack Bar	Total
Revenues	$13,000	$ 4,000	$17,000
Operating Costs	10,000	2,000	12,000
Profit	$ 3,000	$ 2,000	$ 5,000

*Estimated without addition of snack bar.

year to year two. An estimate made at the beginning of the third year indicates that there is no expectation of significant changes in profits during the immediate future. Monthly revenues are projected at $14,000, costs at $10,000, and a resulting profit of $4,000 for the next calendar year. At the time of the projection no significant changes in the club's operations were expected during the coming three-year period unless substantial changes in membership were experienced.

A committee of the board was appointed to evaluate the feasibility of constructing a snack bar. It was determined that the snack bar could be constructed at a cost of approximately $36,000. Since this facility is to be completed prior to the spring and summer season, the committee estimates that the snack bar should generate approximately $4,000 in monthly revenue. An estimated 50 percent cost factor is expected ($2,000), and an average monthly profit of $2,000 is projected. The project appears to be economically feasible as the $36,000 investment should generate $24,000 in profit on an annual basis. Thus, only approximately one and one-half years would be required to obtain repayment of all funds invested.

However, the projected monthly revenues for all food and beverage activities amount to $17,000 for the forthcoming year. With a projected monthly operating cost of $12,000, the monthly profits of $5,000 appear to be a reasonable estimate for coming periods. Therefore, an estimated increase of only $1,000 in monthly profits will result from the proposed snack bar. Some of the persons now using the present facilities will use the snack bar, but total profits are estimated to increase by the addition of the snack bar. The $1,000 net addition in monthly profits allows recovery of the snack bar investment in approximately three years ($36,000 ÷ 1,000 = 36 months or 3 years).

THE COST ACCOUNTING METHODOLOGY

Various kinds of cost data are required to facilitate different managerial decisions. The specialized activities in each department of the hospitality service industries firm dictate varying approaches to developing relevant cost information.

Costs flow through the organization as resources are obtained and goods and services are provided. Initially, a system of accounts is established to allow the uniform and consistent recording of transactions that occur most frequently. The various uniform systems of accounts for the hospitality service industries provide a basic structure within which to accomplish the cost accounting process.

Exhibit 12.5 reflects a very simple system of accounts with only five major expenditure accounts used. These accounts serve as the basis for recording the key transactions. However, these costs must be further segmented and analyzed before they can be used in the decision-making process. After the costs have been recorded in a particular account in the accounting system they must be assigned to specific operating areas.

Only three departments have been used in the illustration—rooms, food (restaurant), and beverage (lounge). The costs recorded initially in these account classifications are in turn assigned to the three operating departments.

For example, when food and beverages are issued from inventory, the requisitioning department should be identified on the form that is used to record the transfer. In this way the inventory costs can be traced directly to the appropriate department.

In the recording of wage costs, employee time should be assignable to a specific department. Other expenses should be identified to the extent possible with a particular operating department.

Certain costs will be indirect in nature and are not directly traceable to any service department in the organization. These costs should not be assigned to a department. They represent indirect overhead expenses that are to be covered by the contributions of each of the operating departments.

DEVELOPING COSTS ON A PER UNIT BASIS

After departmental expenses have been recorded and assigned according to established procedures, it is necessary to develop cost information through an additional step. There is a need to relate cost information to revenues generated. To fill this management need, costs are developed on a per unit basis.

The first step in developing a unit cost is to define the unit of output from each of the departments. The output unit of the rooms department is the rooms occupied by guests. In the food department, an effective unit of cost measurement is covers served, while for beverages, the output measure would be the number of drinks served. In Exhibit 12.5, unit costs are developed for occupied rooms ($6.00), covers served ($1.20), and drinks served ($.40).

The basic structure of a cost accounting system can be defined at any time. For example, it may be desirable for management to have information about the cost of higher priced rooms and suites versus the cost of lower priced rooms (studios, singles, etc.). In the food department, managers may be interested in the cost per meal served during specific meal periods on particular days. This added degree of precision in the cost accounting system will require additional time and

EXHIBIT 12.5

Operating Expense Summary
for the Month of August, 19XX

Expenses	Rooms	Restaurant	Lounge	Total
Foods		$10,000		$10,000
Beverages		1,000	$ 5,000	6,000
Wages	$20,000	11,000	9,000	40,000
Supplies	4,000	1,000	1,000	6,000
Other Expenses	6,000	1,000	1,000	8,000
Total Expenses	$30,000	$24,000	$16,000	$70,000
Occupied Rooms	5,000			
Covers Served		20,000		
Drinks Served			40,000	
Average Cost per Unit	$ 6.00	$ 1.20	$ .40	

cost. If the benefits that can be obtained exceed the additional costs that must be incurred, the cost accounting system should be expanded.

JOB-ORDER AND PROCESS-COST ACCOUNTING IN THE HOSPITALITY SERVICE INDUSTRIES

In Exhibit 12.5, the goods and services generated during the period comprise the denominator and a simple average cost is developed. This average cost per unit is the output of a process cost system.

The following examples show the possible use of process-cost systems in the hospitality service industries. First, there is mass meal preparation in a hospital, prison, school, etc. Management wants to determine the costs incurred in preparing the noon meal for 1,000 hospital patients. The food cost requisitions for the noon meal would be costed and assuming food costs of approximately $8,000, the food cost per patient would be 80¢.

A second example might occur in the airline industry. The preparation of meals for in-flight service requires a production system that closely parallels many manufacturing process-cost operations. Many thousands of the same meal might be prepared during a given shift. The basic process cost methodology is applicable only in situations where units of goods and services produced are homogeneous. If the units of output are similar and the production volumes relatively large the process-cost system is the most effective cost system available for accumulating costs of operations.

Job-order costs differ from process-cost systems as they are designed to develop costs for specific jobs or special orders. The job-cost system measures total costs assignable to a particular function (job) or a set of interrelated tasks. As an example, all tasks performed in serving a banquet would be considered as part of one job, and all related costs would be assigned to this job—the banquet. Costs can be accumulated for the menu items selected by the customers and for the number of waitresses assigned to accommodate the group. When these costs are estimated and combined with an overhead charge for the facilities, the manager is able to issue a bid on the banquet. A second example would be a business conference. Costs would be accumulated for each segment of the conference.

A DETERMINED COST SYSTEM

Some cost systems act as generators of average historical cost data. In these, past activities are analyzed and serve as the reference point for managers in their attempts to establish meaningful cost relationships. Past costs are related to prior period revenues, and resulting percentages serve as a basis for decisions. Consequently, historical data are extended to future periods and little or no consideration is given to changes in the environmental setting.

Standard costs represent studied estimates of what costs should be incurred in future periods. With such data, a manager can assume with reasonable certainty that his estimates of future revenue/cost relationships are valid. Decisions based on such precise data are more likely to result in success, but the dollar outlays required to develop and implement a total standard cost system may be prohibitive for most small and medium-sized firms in the hospitality service industries.

Historical cost data alone are not sufficient to meet the decision-making needs of hospitality service industries management. Furthermore, since it is expensive and hence doubtful that the degree of precision in standard costs is feasible in the hospitality service industries, some alternative approach to cost accounting for the hospitality service industries must be available. Such an approach should serve as a bridge between historical averages and engineered standards and provide a basic cost accounting methodology for the hospitality service industries.

THE DETERMINED COST CONCEPT

The determined cost concept provides the compromise between the precise standard cost systems which are used in many manufacturing industries (product) and the average historical cost systems used by many smaller business firms in all industries. *Determined cost* can be defined as a carefully calculated projection of the total amount of expenditures required to provide a product or service upon demand by a guest. Computations of determined costs are based on a careful investigation of the operating environment in which the good or service is to be provided, with each factor which influences either the amount or the behavior of the cost considered and evaluated.

Returning to the previous banquet example, these services are to be provided in approximately six months. When asked to provide such catering services, the manager's first inclination might be to use only historical costs in estimating prices. In other words, he would look primarily at costs incurred in catering similar activities in the past. However, he should not use these historical costs as the sole basis for making a bid in this situation. Suppose that the cost of a similar engagement in the prior year had been $600. The manager might assume that, since price levels have increased approximately 5 percent in the last year, a total cost of $630 would be adequate to cover services that will be offered. His price then might conceivably be based on this estimated cost which includes the normal percentage established as a required profit margin.

A determined cost is an estimate of the costs that should be incurred in providing goods and services in near future accounting periods. As a compromise between historical averages and engineered standards, it represents the estimate of those responsible for making decisions and those actively engaged in the interpretation of cost data. Determined costs, like standards, are indicators or guidelines as to costs that are anticipated in future periods.

DEVELOPMENT OF DETERMINED COSTS

Each of the factors that influenced past performance and corresponding costs must be carefully examined, since these or similar circumstances will probably exist in the future. Instead of assuming that historical performance will repeat in the future, the manager begins by analyzing, thoroughly, every area in which monetary expenditures were required in the past to provide goods and services.

In this approach each task or duty will be periodically reevaluated. The more repetitive the task, the less need for extensive reinvestigation of the costs. Nevertheless, by considering relevant factors and by making judgments about future conditions, the manager is giving consideration to changes in the environment and operating structure. He should then be able to develop a reasonably accurate indication of future costs. These are the determined costs of goods and services to be provided to customers in the expected operating environment.

Although determined costs are not as precise as standard costs, they serve the needs of managers of the hospitality service industries. Since they offer defined guidelines as a basis for making various decisions, determined costs are a practical alternative to precise standards. When combined with measures of revenues generated for goods and services sold during a period, they should afford management an indication of attainable future profit levels.

Determined costs offer managers a set of guidelines within which to make operating decisions. They represent targets that are reasonably attainable on a consistent basis.

Discussion Questions

1. Describe and discuss briefly the various phases of a cost accounting system.
2. How does a cost system aid in the planning process?
3. What are the steps to cost control?
4. Discuss the process-cost system as compared to the job-order cost system.
5. Select examples of management planning and control decisions and indicate how cost accounting data can assist in this regard.

6. What do standard costs represent?

7. What are the pertinent steps in the development of cost information?

8. Describe in your own words the meaning of the concept of determined cost. How does the concept differ from historical costs? Standard costs?

9. What are the general overhead accounts in the Uniform System of Accounts for Hotels?

10. In developing costs for decision-making, it is necessary to establish appropriate units of output as reference points. What would you recommend as a proper common denominator—unit of output—for each of the major departments in firms in the hospitality service industries? Describe briefly the reasons for your selection in each case.

Problem 1

You are the general manager of a brand-new facility and are interested at this early date (during the period of pre-opening training, etc.) in obtaining some ideas as to the potential profitability of your location. The experts have provided you with summaries of data (based on their recent feasibility study and rounded to the nearest $10,000 on an annual basis).

Rooms   200 rooms with an average room rate of $15.00.

Foods   365 days a year with the following covers served and approximate average guest check receipts per meal period.

	Maximum Daily Covers	Average Receipts
Breakfast	200	$1.25
Lunch	300	2.00
Dinner	200	4.00

Beverages   304 days per year (52 weeks × 6 days, holidays subtracted) for eight hours per day (5 P.M. to 1 A.M.). The lounge will generate a maximum of $100 in sales per operating hour. In addition, during the dinner hours (5 P.M. to 9 P.M.), a maximum of $50 per hour can be derived from the sale of beverage to food customers in the dining room.

During the first three years the following levels of activity are expected:

Rooms	65% of occupancy
Foods	72% of maximum covers served
Beverages	97% of maximum beverage sales

Problem 1 (continued)

Further, a projected statement of maximum gross operating profit is provided for the first three years' operations. (All percentages are based on total firm revenues.)

	Rooms	Food and Beverage	Total
Revenues	55%	45%	100%
Cost of Goods Sold		14%*	14%
Direct Department Expense	20%	20%*	40%
Gross Operating Income	35%	11%	46%
Overhead (Deductions from Income, etc.)			20
House Profit			26%

*It is assumed that food costs will approximate 33 1/3 percent of food revenues, and beverage costs 25 percent of beverages revenue, and direct operating expenses are divided evenly between food and beverages.

Required

1. Compute rooms, food and beverage earnings capacity for:
   A. Maximum
   B. Expected
2. Compute gross operating income:
   A. Maximum
   B. Expected
3. Allocate overhead (total deduction from income) by departments and determine the resulting departmental house profit using the sales dollar basis and the gross operating income dollar basis.
   A. Maximum Revenue
   B. Expected Revenue
4. Discuss the principles involved and how they should be applied in determining a proper allocation of overhead.

Problem 2

A team of consultants has recently completed an extensive analysis of your facility's operations for the most recent three-year period. In one section of the report they point to the following data as being of vital importance to your boss, the general manager.

Problem 2 (continued)

	19A	*19B*	*19C*
Cost per Occupied Room	$ 8.00	$ 8.50	$ 9.25
Cost per Cover Served	1.40	1.50	1.60
Cost per Operating Hour—			
Cocktail Lounge	$60.00	$65.00	$75.00

Your boss has verified the supporting detail and is satisfied with respect to its mathematical accuracy and the validity of the consultants' approach. Nevertheless, he remains somewhat bewildered as to the ways that the data can be used in making management decisions and you are called and asked to react to this information.

Required

1. Explain the nature of each of the measures and how you would have determined the cost had you been the consultant.
2. Would you request any refinements in the cost measures indicated? Why or why not, and be sure to specify the kinds of modifications you would desire.
3. Write a memo to your boss indicating specifically how these kinds of data can assist in making management decisions. Give examples of decisions to clarify your position.

Problem 3

As a trainee in a large hospitality service industries corporation, you are working as the assistant to the manager responsible for convention bookings. He has just finished a rather "heated" telephone conversation with an agent representing a large professional organization. Generally, nearly 1,000 organization members convene at this facility for three days each year.

In view of the fact that all costs are increasing, the corporation has decided to attempt to increase revenues approximately 10 percent across the board. Consequently, since the fee for the last two years' conventions had been $45,000 (up from $42,000 three years previously), your boss has proposed to the agent a charge of $50,000 for this year's convention.

After a flat refusal to accept the increase and an apparent threat to change sites, the manager assigns you the task of determining whether a profit can be earned with no change in price for this and other conventions.

Upon investigation, you learn that prices generally have been established in the past on a cost plus 50 percent basis. Obtaining appropriate cost data thus requires that you delve into the job-order cost accounting system to determine the cost of prior years' conventions for this group.

Problem 3 (continued)

The accountant in charge informs you that he suspects that the 50 percent margin had not consistently been applied in the past; thus, for learning purposes, he asks you to analyze the cost flows relative to this convention. Much to your surprise, you easily find the following document, but no further support is available.

Billing

ABC Convention   June, 1969

Rooms

1,000 Rooms at $15 $15,000

Meals

Breakfasts   2,400 at $1.00
Lunches   2,800 at 1.50
Dinners   2,850 at 4.00   18,000

Beverages

480 Bottles at $12.50   6,000

Other Incidental Costs   6,000

Total Billing (per Contract) $45,000

A memo is attached offering the following cost data.

Rooms Department
  Wages, 800 Hrs. at $2.50 $2,000
  Other Direct Expenses   3,000

                                                                    $ 5,000

Foods Department
  Foods Issued from Stores $6,000
  Preparation and Service Cost
    2,400 Hrs. at $2.50   6,000
                                                                     12,000
Beverages, 480 Bottles at $6.25   3,000

Other Costs   5,000

Total Costs Incurred $25,000

Required

1. After searching vainly for additional information, you are forced to abandon the effort. Instead, you chose to write a memo to your boss describing the inadequacies in the current job-order cost system. Prepare the memo,

Problem 3 (continued)

specifically indicating the supporting documentation that you expect to have available when confronted with the present decision situation.

2. Discuss the propriety of using a cost-plus-percentage pricing philosophy for this or any other area in the business. Is full cost really the best basis for pricing, or would some other measure serve adequately?

3. In your judgment, should the group be accepted again at a $45,000 contract price? Why or why not?

Problem 4

Acting as a management consultant, you are contacted by the proprietor of a restaurant in a small, junior-college community. He is quite concerned about the increasing costs—and declining profits—of his business and your expert assistance is requested.

An analysis of relevant historical data reveals the following relationships:

Meal period	Daily Covers Served	Average Receipt per Cover	Total Daily Revenues	
Breakfast	200	$ 1.25	$ 250	
Lunch	300	2.00	600	
Dinner	300	3.50	1,050	
Total Revenues			$1,900	100%
Related Food Costs			750	39
Gross Profit (Daily)			$1,150	61%
Wages and Other Direct Expenses			1,000	53
Profit Before Capital Charges and Taxes			$ 150	8%

During a most recent three-year period, food costs have increased by approximately 15 percent in total and wage costs are up at least 9 percent in total.* The facility was refurnished two years ago; in general, therefore, the entire cost structure has changed with very little fluctuation in menu prices.

Upon visiting the locality for a few days, it is your observation that this facility's breakfast and dinner prices are below those of competitors; some flexibility in this area is thus available.

---

*Food costs approximated $650 for the same volume three years ago.

Problem 4 (continued)

Required

1. Using a goal of 20 percent profit before capital changes and taxes, prepare a partial profit plan for the restaurant for the next three years. Incorporate price changes as required and round data to nearest $10.

   Establish revenue targets for each menu item, assuming that price changes are possible only for breakfast and dinner menu items.

   Establish desired cost percentage levels as a part of the plan.

2. Discuss briefly the specific changes in strategy that are seemingly necessitated by changes in the cost structure.

Problem 5

The following set of transactions has been extracted from the books of a middle-sized hotel operation. The organization is divided into three segments— rooms, food and beverage and other departments (leased shops, newsstand, etc.). Determine from this information the cost assignable to occupied rooms in this facility. The facility has 150 rooms and averages 67 percent occupancy with an average room rate of $14.50. Rooms revenues, on the average, comprise 53 percent of total revenues (food and beverages 42 percent; other departments 5 percent).

Inventory balances at beginning and end of the period were:

Foods	$30,000
Beverages	1,000
Supplies	1,000

Food and beverage purchases during the period were:

Foods	$90,000
Beverages	30,000

Total wages and other direct expenses during the period were $388,000.

Rooms	$152,000
Food and Beverage	216,000
Other Departments	20,000

Supplies purchased and used were $12,000. Rooms used 67 percent of all supplies with the remainder issued to food and beverage operations.

Overhead costs during the period were $230,000. These costs are allocated to departments on the basis of each department's proportionate share of profit before overhead costs.

Problem 6

You are the manager of a 200-room facility. Both food and beverage opera-tions (a restaurant and a lounge) are leased to other individuals at a flat fee plus a percentage of gross revenues. In evaluating your own area of operations—rooms and related guest services—the need for improved profits is becoming rather appar-ent. The following are data developed from your operation during the past year:

Average Occupancy Rate	70%
Average Room Rate	$10
Maids Wages	
Pay scale, 8 hrs. at $1.75* (Maids clean two rooms per hour)	
Other Payroll Expenses: Benefits and Employer Taxes $1.40 per day (10% of direct wage costs)	
Other Wages (Rooms Department)	$280 per day
Supplies and Other Direct Costs	$1.00 per occupied room**

*Part-time employees must be paid for one-half of a day at a minimum.
**For a normal month's operation, these operating costs approximate $4,200 for 4,200 occupied rooms.

As the manager, you have established a goal of earning a 67 percent depart-mental profit on the rooms operations.

Required

1. Using the given information, establish a budget for total daily operating costs for the rooms department (rounded to the nearest $10).
2. Determine the current level of departmental profit and recommend any changes in room rates that are required to attain the profit goal.
3. Discuss briefly ways in which these kinds of financial information may be used in controlling costs and overall operations in this department.

CHAPTER 13

Food and Beverage Control

Food and beverage sales are a rapidly growing segment of today's economy. Estimates by the National Restaurant Association indicate that the restaurant business (including institutions) in 1970 had sales of approximately $30 billion, and may reach $40 billion by 1975.[1] Combining the estimate of the food-away-from-home market with the estimated value of on-premises consumption of beverages ($6 billion)[2] results in a total of $36 billion, representing the food service division of the hospitality services industries. Surveys of operations in various phases of the service industries show that savings of as much as 5 percent of revenue can be obtained by reducing excess food and beverage costs. If we assume that 2 percent of food and beverage sales is the average excess cost throughout the industry, collective savings of over $700 million could be realized by strengthening food and beverage controls.

DEVELOPMENT OF FOOD AND BEVERAGE CONTROL

In the early years of the food-away-from-home industry costs were low, and in many instances, food was given away or sold at a nominal price to attract patrons who would purchase beverages. With little federal regulation and taxation, the cost of beverages sold was similarly low, and profits were at such high levels that controls rarely were considered necessary.

National prohibition brought a need for food controls. Restaurants found that profits had to be derived from the food operation if they were to remain in existence. At that time, few hotels viewed the food operation as a profit generator. However, it did present cost considerations which they desired to hold to a minimum.

---

1. *Washington Report*, published by the National Restaurant Association, August 18, 1969.
2. U.S. Department of Commerce, *Survey of Current Business*, November, 1970.

When prohibition was repealed, and alcoholic beverage sales were returned to the industry, new standards, taxes, and licensing brought increased costs. This resulted, of course, in greater concern on the part of operators to control these costs. Early controls were developed and installed to monitor food and beverage costs. Reflecting the low labor costs of the times, these controls generally required a great deal of clerical effort and were somewhat cumbersome. The controls were made after-the-fact; that is, they reported the activity for a particular day, week, or month, in order to compare the results to those in earlier similar periods. Management was provided with voluminous reports which analyzed the increases or decreases in cost by component parts. For example, food cost was broken down into beef, poultry, vegetable, butter costs; and beverage costs were described by type of spirit, beer, or wine. Fluctuations in a particular cost segment provided a signal to management that investigation was necessary.

Although the early concerns enabled operational management to monitor the operation, there were several disadvantages.

1. The system did not indicate a level at which costs were acceptable. Comparison with a previous period could be favorable, indicating no need for action, but there was no way to determine how efficient the operation actually had been in the previous period. Thus, management was able to take action to prevent profits from deteriorating, but was unable to determine the operation's potential profitability.

2. Early controls did not adequately account for fluctuations in market prices of raw foodstuffs.

3. With the early controls, management was unable to determine whether an increase in a particular commodity cost was due to inefficiencies in the operation, or to a change in sales pattern.

4. The system required an extensive clerical effort. Not only did this increase the possibility of error, but as labor costs increased, the cost/benefits of the control system became more marginal.

5. Frequently, because of the system's complexity, reports were delayed, thus limiting the effectiveness of management action.

In response to the deficiencies in available control systems and the changing times, a new system of food and beverage control was developed. The new system was designed to be dynamic rather than static. Scientific management standards were applied to the operation to determine true cost levels when standards were observed, and the profit potential of the operation under those costs. Because this system is based on advance planning and predetermined costs, it is referred to as the pre-cost, pre-control system.

PHILOSOPHY OF FOOD AND BEVERAGE CONTROL

To be effective, food and beverage controls must be considered a tool to assist the operating department manager. If long-term benefits are to be gained, the routines, procedures, and reports must be genuinely useful to him. The food and beverage control system is not a device to take decision-making power out of the manager's hands; rather, it is a tool to help him to make better cost-managing decisions.

The controls must be simple, they should not require undue clerical effort, and the results must be understandable to those who will be using them. The routines and procedures must not interfere with the operation to the point that customer service is impaired. The controls also must be flexible enough to permit an adjustment to changes in the operation.

Food and beverage controls must be structured so that timely reports may be issued. These reports must be designed to point out variances from established standards, so that investigation can begin immediately and corrective measures instituted before further excessive costs are incurred.

The control system must be appropriately designed for the individual food and beverage operation. Because there are identifiable costs incurred in maintaining controls, the savings in cost of food and beverage sold must be sufficient to warrant these costs. Thus, a small restaurant will operate with a few basic controls that can be maintained by the manager or bookkeeper, while a major hotel with extensive food and beverage facilities will have more elaborate controls maintained by a full-time staff. The small operation will prepare few formal worksheets or reports, while the larger operation will establish more elaborate control systems.

COST-DETERMINING FACTORS

Three basic factors determine the cost of goods to be sold: markets, policies, and operations.

Markets include the customer market and the supply market. The patron's characteristics, his area of residence, and his cultural and economic level, as well as existing competitive establishments, are considerations in establishing the quality level of foodstuffs and beverages to be served. The supply market, that is, the sources and availability of raw foodstuffs and beverages, affects the price that must be paid to obtain them.

Policies are determinations by top ownership and management as to how the operation is to be conducted. A policy statement that the operation will not run out of any menu item, or that it will purchase nothing but prime grade beef for all uses, may foster the public image of the facility; however, these policies also may result in higher than average costs.

Although new sources of patronage and alternative sources of supply can be found, and top ownership-management sometimes can be persuaded to change its policies, these two factors generally are relatively inflexible. It is the third factor, *operations*, that presents the greatest opportunity to increase profits, through the application of sound operating cost controls.

FOOD COST CONTROL

The food cost control system is designed to prevent or limit excessive costs at each point as the raw foodstuffs flow through the operation, from the time they are ordered, to their eventual service to the customer, and thereafter to the recording of sales and accounting for costs.

There are eight basic sequential steps in the flow of foodstuffs through the operation.

1. Purchasing
2. Receiving
3. Storing
4. Issuing
5. Pre-preparation and portioning
6. Preparation
7. Service
8. Sales

Convenience food products, which have been processed before arrival at the operation, flow through the system in a similar manner; however, the pre-preparation and processing stage, and some steps in the preparation stages, are eliminated. The basic principles of control are the same for these products as for raw foodstuffs; however, the task is simplified because in-house control of the steps that have already taken place is not necessary.

The food cost control system begins with the establishment of basic operating procedures for each of these eight points.

PURCHASING

Control over purchasing must insure that the foodstuffs purchased are for immediate needs, that the quality of the food is optimum for the intended use, and that the lowest available price in the market is paid for merchandise of the desired quality and form.

The first element of control is to establish detailed specifications. These can be drawn only after extensive study and testing, in which the processing losses, cooking losses, portioning losses, and potential utilization of by-products are considered. Specifications must be sufficiently detailed to insure that the operation describes the exact type of merchandise desired, merchandise which has been predetermined as capable of being put to the most economic use. For example, a complete meat specification will include the desired U.S. Department of Agriculture grade, cut, weight, degree of aging, the amount of fat covering permitted, special cutting instructions and desired dimensions.

The second element of control is the purchasing for immediate needs. An oversupply of stores not only ties up capital, but also increases the possibility of spoilage and pilferage. To guard against excessive quantities of foodstuffs being purchased, a special order sheet is used, indicating the quantity of merchandise on hand as well as the quantity to be ordered. The purchaser should then review the forecast of anticipated volume, noting the quantity of merchandise on hand, and investigating any orders that are considered excessive.

The third element of sound purchasing control is to obtain competitive bids. The purchaser must actively and aggressively test the market to obtain the merchandise as specified at the lowest price available. Usually it is good practice to get at least three competitive bids. All competing purveyors must be furnished with copies of the purchase specifications, to provide a common basis for bidding.

The fourth element of purchasing control is to establish a focus of authority. Because food purchasing is a repetitive process, it is not normally necessary to formalize each purchase with a purchase order. Nevertheless, it is necessary to vest the authority to purchase with a specific individual who is then held accountable for seeing that standard procedures are followed.

RECEIVING

Control over the receiving activity is maintained by installing standard procedures for receiving merchandise, by requiring formal acceptance or rejection of all delivered goods, and by spot-checks by management to determine whether standard procedures are followed.

Sound receiving procedures require that all foodstuffs be inspected at delivery. They should be weighed or counted, depending on the way in which the item is purchased, to determine that the quantity ordered is delivered and that this agrees with the quantity shown on the invoice. The quality, grade, etc., should be checked to see that it conforms to the specifications.

When all the receiving procedures have been carried out, formal acceptance should be signified by recording in writing what steps have been performed and who performed them. The receiving data then will be forwarded to the accounting department for appropriate action.

If it is necessary to reject all or part of a shipment because of variance from specifications, or if an error of weight or count is detected, the vendor should be formally notified via a "request for credit" or "notice of error" memorandum.

Management should schedule unannounced spot-checks at the receiving area to insure that established receiving procedures are followed. Because the person assigned to such inspections must have a knowledge of food quality, and an independent objectivity, this function may be performed by outsiders employed by management.

STORING

Control over merchandise in storage is established by assigning responsibility for the foodstuffs in storage, by effective physical security, and by sound material handling procedures.

Responsibility for merchandise in storage must be fixed. A particular individual should be made responsible for receiving goods destined for the storeroom, regardless of whether he receives them initially. This person should see that the storeroom is properly secured and that access is denied to unauthorized persons. In this regard, it is advisable to systematically replace locks in the storeroom to prevent loss from unauthorized duplicate keys.

Foodstuffs must be promptly put away in the proper place and held at the proper temperature. Frozen foods, for example, will deteriorate significantly if left out of the freezer for any substantial length of time. Butter or cheese will assume a distinctive off-flavor if stored near a basket of melons. Tomatoes will become undesirable if stored in the freezer. A health hazard will occur if storage areas are not protected against insects and vermin.

All incoming merchandise should be dated to permit rotation of stock, and all foodstuffs should be issued from the storeroom on a first-in, first-out basis; that is, previously ordered supplies should be used before more recently delivered goods. This practice will result in systematic turnover of inventory and minimize the risk of deterioration or spoilage.

Management should receive sufficient information to effectively evaluate the storeroom operation's efficiency. For example, a refrigerator temperature report indicating the thermometer reading on the various refrigerators at different times during the day is useful to determine whether the equipment is functioning properly and that the temperature is being checked so that there is minimum risk of spoilage. Physical inspection of the storeroom area will reveal any deficiencies in sanitation or proper storage practices. Formal reports of spoilage will reveal procedural lapses which, if left uncorrected, may result in further loss.

A reconciliation statement of the storeroom physical inventory should be prepared at the end of each month to determine the effectiveness of physical control and security. This is usually prepared on a dollar basis, as follows, rather than by individual item.

Opening Inventory: Physical	$ 20,000
Plus: Purchases for Storeroom	25,000
Total Food Available	$ 45,000
Less: Issues from Storeroom	25,000
Total Value of Food that Should be on Hand	$ 20,000
Closing Inventory: Physical	$ 19,800
Overage (Shortage)	$ (200)

When there is substantial movement of high-cost items through the storeroom (such as caviar or foie gras), it may be advisable to maintain a perpetual inventory control over the specific items. This is done on an item basis (such as number of pieces, pounds, or portions), using the same procedure as in the dollar value reconciliation.

ISSUING

Control of issuing has two important aspects. First, goods should not be removed from the storeroom without proper authorization. Second, only the quantity of foodstuffs required for preparation should be obtained. A requisition system usually is used to provide these control elements. The person requesting the merchandise will submit to the storekeeper a written list of items required. To facilitate preparation, the most frequently requested merchandise should be pre-printed on the requisition form, so that only the quantity required will have to be filled in. Because many preparation employees tend to overorder to avoid subsequent requests, the requisitions should be reviewed by the chef or other person in charge of production, and his signed approval obtained before the requisition is presented. With such a system, the storekeeper will first determine if the requisition is authorized. (A sample of approved signatures should be posted in the storeroom to facilitate this check.) The storekeeper will then fill the requisition, delivering only the items requested.

PRE-PREPARATION AND PORTIONING

Pre-preparation and portioning encompass the preliminary processing of foodstuffs before actual cooking or preparation begins. Trimming meat, cutting steaks, and peeling vegetables are examples. Lack of sufficient skill, carelessness, or failure to adhere to established standards can result in substantial excess costs in this area. If a butcher portions beef tenderloin into 9-ounce filet mignons instead of the 8-ounce filets specified by management, the cost of the portion served will be increased by over 10 percent; yet only the original menu price can be charged. Because control of preliminary processing is difficult and requires constant attention, and because labor costs are high, more and more operations are minimizing the processing activity that must be done on the premises, and are purchasing raw foodstuffs in a ready-to-use form. Pre-cut steaks, formed hamburger patties, peeled potatoes, and prepared cole slaw are a few examples of the pre-processed foods in wide use today.

Controls should be in effect whenever on-premise preparation and processing is carried out. Because of the high cost of meat, poultry, and fish, greatest attention should be placed on their processing. Standard trim instructions and portion sizes should be posted in the butcher shop. For example, a portion of a standard portion size chart might read:

Filet mignon	8 oz.
Junior filet	6 oz.
Strip steak (boneless)	14 oz.
Junior sirloin (boneless)	10 oz.

A portion scale should be positioned near the worktable so that the butcher can check his work periodically, and so management can spot-check portions for adherence to standards.

Butchering yield tests should be conducted to establish parameters of acceptable processing losses and to determine the actual cost of the primary items fabricated. The latter is accomplished by deducting the market value of the secondary items obtained from the total cost of the wholesale cut as received. An example of a butchering yield test appears in Exhibit 13.1.

PREPARATION

Control of preparation must be accomplished if the establishment is to serve a consistent product at an acceptable cost. If the method of preparation and ingredients are left to the individual cook, the appearance, taste, acceptability, and cost will vary each time the selection is served.

The production sheet is an important feature in the control of preparation. It is a summary of instructions to the cooks, indicating the quantity to be prepared and any special instructions that are necessary. It permits tight control of the amount produced and permits modification of the standard recipe, where appropriate, to work off any leftovers. A sample of part of a production sheet appears in Exhibit 13.2.

EXHIBIT 13.1

Butchering Yield Test
Basic Test Score

Date _____   File No. _____

Item Being Tested _____Tenderloin_____   Specification Code _____

Government Grade _____Prime_____   Avg. Wt. ____8 lb. 8 oz.____

No. Being Tested ____6____ Pieces Weighing ____51__ Lbs. _0____ Oz.

Total Cost $ _77.52_ at $ ____1.52____ per Lb.

Details	Weight Lbs. Oz.		% Weight	Market Value per Lb.	Total Value		Cost per Lb.	Cost Factor per Lb.*
Filet mignon	17	0	33.3%		$69	96	$4.12	2.7
Tenderloin tips	3	0	5.9	$1.30	3	90		
Hamburger meat	6	0	11.8	.61	3	66		
Fat	25	0	49.0					
	51	0	100.0%		77	52		

*The cost factor is utilized to provide a constant figure which then can be used with any market price to calculate the actual cost per pound of any item. The cost factor per pound is obtained by dividing the calculated cost per pound by the market price of the primal cost per pound. For example, if the price of prime tenderloin rose to $1.65, the cost per pound of the filets would be $1.65 x 2.7 or $4.46.

The use of standard recipes facilitates production of a product that is consistent in appearance and taste. In addition, it permits advance calculation of the cost per portion served. Recipes must be prepared by each establishment, giving consideration to the state of readiness of foodstuffs purchased, work load, physical equipment, the staff's culinary skills, and the tastes of customers. An example of a standard recipe is given in Exhibit 13.3.

Standard cooking and roasting procedures are necessary to consistently produce attractive and palatable food; but more important, to minimize weight loss

EXHIBIT 13.2

Production Worksheet

Date _____

Day _____

Item	Portion Size	Standard Recipe No. Special Instructions	Assigned to	Portions to be Prepared	Actual Portions Prepared	No. Left Over or Time Ran Out	Remarks
Beef stew	4 oz. beef 4 oz. vegetables	1214 Use #10 deckle meat to replace #10 of chuck	Jones	50	52	5	
Breast of Chicken Archiduc	8 oz.	4019 For private party, must be ready at 11:30 a.m.	Smith	30	30	2	2 no shows
London broil	5 oz. R.T.E.	1305 Use triangles instead of flanks	Jones	60	50	1:30	overportioned

EXHIBIT 13.3

Standard Recipe

No. _____

Date _____

Production _____ 10 gal. _____

Portions _____ 426 _____

Cost per Portion _____ $ .056 _____

Size Portions _____ 3 oz. _____

Item _____ Beaujolais Sauce _____

Comments

Quantity	Unit	Ingredients		Cost	Cost	Cost
3/4	#10 can	Beef Base	at $3.77	$2.83		
1	gal.	Burgundy Wine		1.63		
3	lb.	Flour	at .11	.33		
5	lb.	Butter	at .80	4.00		
20	lb.	Mushrooms	at .75	15.00		
9	gal.	Water		-		
		Total		$23.79		

Preparation and service:
   Slice mushrooms and saute in part of butter.
   Drain and make a roux.
   Add water to beef base. Thicken with roux.
   Add wine and mushrooms.

in cooking. For example, if a beef rib roast is cooked at 450° Fahrenheit, shrinkage is high; but if the same roast is cooked at 325° for a longer period, shrinkage is reduced. If meat is roasted too long, it becomes overdone, and loses customer appeal in addition to losing weight.

After standard recipes and portion sizes are established, cooking yield tests should be performed to determine the cost of the merchandise served, and to serve as a yardstick for measuring future production. An example of a cooking yield test is given in Exhibit 13.4.

EXHIBIT 13.4
Cooking Yield Test
Basic Test Score

Date _____   File No. _____

Item Being Tested ___Rib___   Specification Code _____

Government Grade ___Choice___   Avg. Wt. _37 lbs., 4 oz._

No. Being Tested _5_ Pieces Weighing _186_ Lbs. _8_ Oz.

Total Cost $ ___139.88___ at $ ___.75___ per Lb.

Details	Weight Lbs.	Oz.	% Weight	Market Value per Lb.	Total Value		Cost per Lb.		Cost Factor per Lb.
Ribs, ready to cook	110	0	59.0	—	118	08	1	07	1.43
Short ribs	9	0	4.8	.62	5	58			
Hamburger meat	23	8	12.6	.69	16	22			
Fat	21	8	11.5	—	—				
Bones	22	8	12.1	—	—				
	186	8	100.0		139	88			

Cooking Loss

Cooked* _____ Hours _____ Minutes at _____ Degrees

Weight after cooking	91	8							
Loss in cooking	18	8							
Loss in carving	32	8		Breakdown					
Salable meat	59	0			118	08	2	00	2.67

Tested By _____   Comments _____

At a cost of $2.00 per pound of salable meat, this results in a 10-ounce portion of roast beef costing
$1.35 to serve.

*Actual hours, minutes, and degrees to be inserted.

SERVICE

The purpose of controlling service is to prevent excessive cost and provide a standard of appearance for the food served to the customer. Standard portion sizes must be established for all items which are prepared as a unit and later divided into individual portions. This includes roasts, soups, stews, hash, salad mixtures, etc. A standard portion chart should be posted near the portioning area for convenient reference. Similar in form to the example shown in Exhibit 13.5, the standard portion size may be stated in ounces but frequently is stated in terms of the portioning tool used (such as #10 scoop, 6 oz. ladle, etc.).

Garniture is important in enhancing the appearance of food. An excessive garniture cost of 2¢ per portion may not seem significant, but if not brought under control, this would cost lost profits of nearly $1,500 a year in an operation serving 200 persons daily. To prevent such losses, standard garniture charts should be prepared. These are frequently incorporated into the standard portion size chart (see Exhibit 13.5).

SALES

Foodstuffs may be tightly controlled as they flow through the operation, but without control of sales, the operation still may not be profitable.

The first element of effective sales control is to insure that all foodstuffs served are charged. This can be accomplished by one of several systems, including:

1. A duplicate check system. The server writes the order on a guest check, simultaneously preparing a carbonized duplicate. The duplicate must be submitted to the preparation area to obtain food.

2. A pre-check system. The server writes the order on a guest check and registers the correct prices in a machine. The machine "throws" a tape which is presented to the preparation area to obtain food.

3. A checker. Traditionally used throughout the industry, the checker system generally is being phased out in favor of other systems. In this system, an employee who is positioned between the preparation area and the dining area inspects each outgoing item and verifies that it appears on the guest check.

The second element of sales control is to charge the proper prices, that is, those prices that management has determined will produce the desired profit. This can be accomplished by developing a standard price manual which lists every menu item to be served and its price. Menus should be checked against the standard price manual to verify that the correct price has been printed; the guest checks should be audited on a spot-check basis to determine that the established prices have been followed. Mechanical and electronic systems also are available, in

EXHIBIT 13.5

Standard Portion and Garniture Chart

Item	Portion Size	Accompanying Items	Served on/in	Garnish	Side Dish
Steak Sandwich	8 oz. ready to cook	1 slice toast 4 oz. french fried potatoes	10″ luncheon plate	3 slices tomato on lettuce leaf	—
Shrimp Creole	6 shrimp 6 oz. sauce	4 oz. rice	12 oz. casserole	Sprig of parsley	Cole slaw
Pot Roast	5 oz. ready to eat	3 oz. noodles 2 oz. gravy	10″ luncheon plate	Sprig of parsley	Tossed salad
Grilled Capon Leg	8 oz.	3 oz. whipped potatoes 2 oz. gravy	10″ luncheon plate	Sprig of parsley Spiced peach half	Vegetable of the day
Eggs Benedict	2 eggs	(2) 1 oz. slices Canadian bacon English muffin 2 oz. Hollendaise sauce	10″ luncheon plate	1/2 ripe olive	—
Seafood Salad	2 oz. crabmeat 4 shrimp	2 1/2 oz. mixed greens 4 egg wedges 4 tomato wedges	7-1/4″ salad bowl	1 radish rose 2 ripe olives 2 green olives	2 oz. dressing (choice) in gooseneck

which the prices can be preset, thus eliminating the need for a guest check price audit.

The third element of the sales control system is to insure that all checks are settled. This is accomplished by serially numbering all guest checks; by keeping reserve stocks of checks in locked storage; by issuing checks in numerical order to cashiers or supervisors, who then will reissue them to servers in limited quantities; and by sorting the used checks into numerical order to ascertain that none are missing.

It is also useful to mark each check with a time stamp or by other means when it is issued to the server, and again when the check is settled. This will identify a check that is held overlong by the server, and will limit the possibility for it to be presented to two different customers. (It also will reveal any "slow service" problems which may require investigation.)

The last element in sales control is to avoid allowances which diminish sales. This can be accomplished by establishing policies regarding circumstances under which allowances will be permitted, and by limiting the number of persons authorized to make them and the amount of the allowance that can be made. In addition, management should be given a formal report of each allowance, indicating in detail the reason for it having been granted.

THE PRE-COST, PRE-CONTROL SYSTEM

The foregoing system of procedures, reports, and management review is designed to minimize excessive costs as foodstuffs flow through the operation. As such, the focal point of the control effort is placed on insuring that standard procedures are followed. It can be determined that excess costs will occur if the standard procedures are not followed; however, at this point there is no accurate way of measuring the efficiency of the efforts and no possibility of determining the potential profitability of the operation. Thus, the next step is necessary—the installation of a system called the pre-cost, pre-control system.

The pre-cost, pre-control system is actually a method of operation rather than simply a means of control. It is based on intelligent planning to establish a realistic, attainable profit goal; executing the plan; and measuring performance against the established goal. In this system, sound principles of manufacturing control are adapted to the food service industry.

PRE-COSTING

Pre-costing is the predetermination of the cost of each item to be offered on the menu. To accurately accomplish this, controls over the food as it flows through the operation must be in effect. When standard methods of preparation and standard portion sizes are adhered to, the standard recipes, butchering yield tests, and cooking yield tests can be analyzed to calculate the cost of each portion sold.

Next, the cost of the accompanying items must be determined. This cost depends on the menu policy and may include a garniture only (a la carte menu); or it may include an appetizer, potato, vegetable, dessert, and beverage (table d'hote menu). The cost of gratis items (such as candies, relishes, rolls and butter, etc.) must also be included in the make-up cost.

After determining the portion cost and the make-up cost, the two can be added to obtain the total item cost. This can be conveniently done on a "cost of menu selection" form, such as appears in Exhibit 13.6.

After the total costs of each item on the menu have been calculated, the probable profitability of the menu can be determined. Sales history records are used as a base to forecast the anticipated number of sales for each item. The forecast is then extended by the calculated item costs to obtain the total potential cost, and by the menu selling prices to obtain the total potential sales. An allowance of 5 to 10 percent of calculated cost, depending on the complexity of the menu, is added to cover the cost of table condiments, cooking butter, and other fats and oils, which were not sufficiently costly to be included in the item cost calculations.

An example of the potential cost calculation appears in Exhibit 13.7.

The calculated food cost ratio represents the potentially "perfect" cost if there are no losses throughout the system. However, because some losses due to overproduction and waste are unavoidable, a tolerance factor must be added to arrive at the cost that can be anticipated in actual operation. Generally, from 1 to 3 percent is allowed, depending on the menu, complexity of the operation, general level of production staff ability, and the state of preparation of foodstuffs purchased. The calculated potential cost plus the tolerance factor becomes the food cost goal that should be reasonably attainable from the menu.

The goal, as initially calculated, may not be acceptable to the operator because it may provide insufficient profit. The selling prices, portion sizes, or individual menu items must then be revised until the food cost goal reaches the desired profit level.

In institutions and in operations such as airline feeding, no direct sales are derived from the service of food; thus it is not possible to determine a potential cost ratio. In these instances, the potential cost is expressed in terms of persons served. This may be referred to as cost per cover; however, it is often expressed in terms of a particular industry. For example, a hospital may determine the poten-

EXHIBIT 13.6

Cost of Menu Selection

Item: Steak Tartare			No.		
Menu selling price	$ 5	00	Date		
Total cost		99	Menu		
Cost per dollar sale	19	8%	Comments		
Selling price to realize % gross profit					
Difference					

Portion size	Description		Raw cost	Cost Factor	Cost to serve	
8 oz.	Chopped tenderloin		$ .75 lb.		$	37.5
1 slice	Rye bread		.40 lb.			01.7
1/2 each	Tomato	(6 x 7)	4.25/flt.			05.0
1/2 each	Egg, cooked		.60/doz.			02.5
1 tbsp.	Capers	pt.	1.50			06.3
1/4 cup	Onion, chopped		5.25/bag			04.4
1-1/2 oz.	Green beans, whole, canned (303 can)		.34/can			05.6
2 each	Anchovies	(2 oz. can)	.29/can			05.8
1 each	Egg, raw		.60/doz.			05.0
	Garniture					03.0
	Make-up cost					22.0
Total					$	98.8

EXHIBIT 13.7

Potential Cost of Food Sold Computation

Item	Primary Ingredient Unit of Purchase	Market Cost	Cost Factor	New Cost Price
Tomato juice	46 oz.	$ .46		
Hamburger platter	lb.	.64		
Steak sandwich	Strip, boneless, lb.	1.41	1.7	$2.40
Grilled cheese sandwich	Sliced, lb.	.80		
Tuna sandwich	7 oz. can	.40		
Bacon, lettuce and tomato sandwich	18-20 slices/lb.	.80		
Fried chicken	2 lb.	.40		
Franks and beans	6/lb.	.72		
Tenderloin tips	lb.	1.60		
French fried potatoes	lb.	.32		
Apple pie	indiv.	1.05		
Ice cream	gal.	2.40		
Coffee	lb.	.93		
Milk	qt.	.32		

Condiments and miscellaneous unproductive
   at 5% of cost

Total

RTC = Ready to Cook

EXHIBIT 13.7

(continued)

Portion Size	Portion Cost	Average Make-up Cost	Total Item Cost	Item Sales Price	Average Number Forecasted	Total Sales	Total Cost	Cost Ratio
4 oz.			$ .04	$ .20	3	$ .60	$ .12	20.0%
6 oz. RTC	$ .28	$ .13	.41	1.25	20	25.00	8.20	32.8
6 oz. RTC	.94	.13	1.07	2.50	7	17.50	7.49	42.8
3 oz.	.21	.04	.25	.55	23	12.65	5.75	45.5
3 1/2 oz.	.26	.04	.30	.75	16	12.00	4.80	40.0
2 strips 2 leaves 3 slices	.23	.04	.27	.95	14	13.30	3.78	28.4
1/2	.40	.29	.69	2.25	35	78.75	24.15	30.7
2 ea./4 oz.	.28	.22	.50	1.25	12	15.00	6.00	40.0
5 oz. RTC	.55	.29	.84	2.65	30	79.50	25.20	31.7
4 oz.			.08	.30	28	8.40	2.24	26.7
1/7			.15	.40	8	3.20	1.20	37.5
#12 scoop			.10	.35	10	3.50	1.00	35.0
5 oz.			.05	.15	60	9.00	3.00	33.3
8 oz.			.08	.20	20	4.00	1.60	40.0
						$282.40	$ 94.53	33.5%
							4.73	1.6
						$282.40	$ 99.26	35.1%

tial cost per patient day, while a resort hotel serving in the American plan (breakfast, luncheon, and dinner) may refer to the cost per guest day. Alternatively, a theoretical sales value of each item or meal may be established to permit the computation of a potential cost ratio.

PRE-CONTROL

Pre-control translates the menu sales forecast into a food production guide. This involves determining the number of portions to be prepared and the raw material required.

To establish a realistic food production guide, the initial step is to review past sales. The sales history is a record of the number of orders of each item sold during previous appearances on the menu. The simplest means of obtaining this data is to have the cashier tabulate (perhaps on an extra copy of the menu) the number of portions listed on each guest check.

After assembling sufficient item sales history, a popularity index is constructed. This is the ratio of each item sold to the base total, times one hundred. The base total is restricted to total entree sales; or, if the menu is elaborate, to the specials of the day only. A sample of a popularity index appears in Exhibit 13.8.

EXHIBIT 13.8

Popularity Index

	Portions Sold	Ratio to Total	Popularity Index
Fillet of Pike	18	12.9%	12.9
Eggs Benedict	9	6.4	6.4
Yankee Pot Roast	20	14.3	14.3
Creamed Turkey	52	37.1	37.1
Breaded Pork Chop	16	11.4	11.4
Braised Lamb Shank	25	17.9	17.9
Total	140	100.0%	100.0

The next step in pre-control is to forecast volume. Historic records again serve as a base, but adjustments must be made for anticipated factors which, when they occurred in the past, increased or decreased business or may do so in the future. Examples include a convention in a city, high occupancy in a hotel, or special events in the community. The completed volume forecast should estimate the total number of persons to be served at each meal period.

The popularity index is then applied to the volume forecast to obtain the forecast sales of each menu item. If, for example, the volume forecast indicated that 200 persons were anticipated, the popularity indices under Exhibit 13.8 would be utilized to calculate the number of portions to be prepared as follows:

Item	Popularity Index	x	Volume Forecast (00)	=	Portions to be Prepared
Fillet of Pike	12.9		2		25.8 = 26

Utilizing the standard portion sizes, the standard recipes, and the standard yields that have been determined for the operation, the production supervisor can determine the kind and amount of foodstuffs to be requisitioned. This is entered on the production worksheet as was shown in Exhibit 13.2.

ACCOUNTING PROCEDURES

Through the initial steps in the pre-cost, pre-control system, the operation has been targeted to a specific food cost goal which must be attained if the desired level of profit is to be achieved. Management now must take the pulse of the operation at appropriate intervals to determine if the goal is being attained, to investigate any variances, and to institute corrective action where required.

The most commonly available monitoring device is the monthly operating statement. Unless control of accounting procedures is in effect, however, the operating statement may not reflect the actual food cost ratio of the operation. This might lead management to erroneous conclusions. While the majority of accounting procedure controls are the same as those which apply to any accounting situation, there are three particular areas of concern in a food operation; they are revenue, purchases and inventories, and credits to cost.

In control of revenue, it is important that sales be recorded strictly according to the uniform system of accounts. Cover charge income, for example, should not be included in food sales, but should be recorded as other department income. If it were to be erroneously included in food sales, the cost of goods sold ratio would be artificially decreased.

Lack of control over inventory procedures is a major cause of incorrect inventory information. An accounting department representative should be present at the time of inventory; he should insist that stock is counted in the order in which it is stored, rather than skipping from place to place, to avoid the possibility of any stock being overlooked. The item prices and extensions also should be spot-checked to ascertain that the total reported value of the food inventory is correct.

In most food operations, credits to food cost arise. One of the most frequent is the cost of meals served without charge to employees. Too frequently the actual cost of employees' meals is not determined and an estimate is used. Often the estimate is based on amounts determined by state minimum wage law or other legislation. While the employer may be obligated to base his wage rates and applicable taxes on such amounts, he is not required to use them in determining the cost of food sold. The credit to cost for employee meals should reflect the actual cost of food consumed, as determined by consumption records. If these are not maintained, the actual meal cost per employee per meal should be calculated during a test period, and the average cost per meal multiplied by the number of employees entitled to meals in a subsequent period, to obtain a realistic estimate of the cost.

Another credit is food sold at cost to employees or others, referred to as "steward's sales." Because the income received from these sales normally is sufficient to cover only the merchandise cost, to include these items in revenue would reflect a food cost ratio of 100 percent, artificially inflating the overall food cost ratio. For this reason, the income received from steward's sales should be recorded as a reduction of the cost of goods sold, or a credit to cost.

MONITORING THE OPERATION AND FOLLOW-UP PROCEDURES

While the monthly operating statement is valuable in a small operation, it has limited usefulness in a large operation because it does not provide data soon enough to permit timely detection of variances. An interim monitoring tool is the weekly or daily food cost report based on issues. Although daily costs will fluctuate substantially due to advance preparation, the amount of food in production will tend to remain fairly constant over a period of time. Thus, the month-to-date data should be a reasonable indicator of the current food cost ratio.

The report of food cost based on issues is prepared by pricing and extending the requisitions, and adding the value of these issues from the storeroom to the cost of any merchandise (such as bread, rolls, and milk) that is delivered directly to the kitchen. Beverages used for cooking also are added, and credits to cost for employees' meals or other reasons are deducted. A sample of a weekly food cost summary based on issues appears in Exhibit 13.9.

The actual food cost may vary from the plan for a number of reasons. The forecast sales-mix may have been in error; or customer buying patterns may have changed, resulting in a different sales-mix. The market prices of foodstuffs may have risen or declined. A breakdown in the basic operating procedures may have occurred. The latter is probably one of the most common reasons for an excessive food cost. Nonadherence to standard recipes, overproduction, and over-portioning can quickly drain away profit dollars.

EXHIBIT 13.9

Food Cost Summary

| Date | Add | | Deduct | | Net Food Cost | | Food Sales | | Cost Ratio | |
	Direct Purchases	Storeroom Issues	Beverage to Food	Employee Meals Cost	Other Credits	Today	To Date	Today	To Date	Today	To Date
Jan. 1-7	$220	$2,529	$35	$175	—		$2,609		$6,852		38.1%

To pinpoint the reason for the variance, a potential cost calculation based on actual menu sales and current market prices should be performed in the same manner as in Exhibit 13.7. The period selected for this computation must be long enough to be representative. With a cycle menu, the entire cycle should be covered. With a limited menu, a period of three to five days should be adequate.

The new potential cost calculation will reveal changes that have occurred in the sales-mix or market prices. If these do not fully explain the variance, the problem can be attributed to a breakdown in basic operating procedures.

Because the calculation of potential costs requires a significant amount of time and effort, it is not necessary to recalculate it every time management wishes to take a reading on the operation. As long as the sales-mix remains relatively stable, the potential based on actual sales can be updated by the use of a market price index. Various methods can be used. The simplest is to convert the abstract of item sales into basic raw materials through the use of the yield tests and standard recipes. In doing this, it is not necessary to include all ingredients; a listing of the major items will be satisfactory, as the effect of the miscellaneous items would be small. The raw material quantity is multiplied by the base period purchase price and the products are extended to arrive at a base period cost. Current prices are inserted and the same process is carried out to arrive at a current cost. The difference between the two is divided by the base period cost to determine the percentage of increase or decrease which should have been reflected in the food cost ratio. A sample of the market price index appears in Exhibit 13.10.

In a large operation, it is desirable to apply the updated potential cost ratios to the actual sales on a weekly or semi-monthly basis, and compare the calculated food cost with the cost reported based on issues. If the percentage of difference between the actual cost and the calculated cost significantly exceeds the tolerance factor, further investigation is indicated.

An example of the food cost comparison appears in Exhibit 13.11.

CONVENIENCE AND SPECIAL FOOD CONTROLS

Frequently it is useful to establish special controls over items of high cost. These are established on a unit basis: piece, ounce, pound, or order. Items often controlled on this basis include steaks, prime ribs of beef, lobsters, shrimp, and caviar. The unit system is utilized to control convenience food items which are packaged by the portion. To establish a special control, an opening inventory is taken. Additional production or issues are added to arrive at total items available. A closing inventory is taken; the results are deducted from total available, to determine total consumed. This total then is reconciled with the abstract of sales.

EXHIBIT 13.10

Market Price Index

Item	Quantity Consumed	Base Period Prices	Base Period Cost	New Period Prices (Date)	New Period Cost
Eggs	5 doz.	$ .45	$ 2.25	$ .52	$ 2.60
Bacon	3 lb.	.92	2.76	.96	2.88
Sausage	1/2 lb.	.78	.39	.81	.41
Ham	1/2 lb.	1.08	.54	1.07	.53
Tomato Juice	2 cans	.33	.66	.33	.66
Orange Juice	1 gal.	1.16	1.16	1.20	1.20
Grapefruit	4 each	.12	.48	.18	.72
Bread	3 loaves	.28	.84	.29	.87
Sweet Rolls	1 1/2 doz.	.95	1.43	.97	1.46
Doughnuts	1/2 doz.	.75	.38	.79	.40
Coffee	2 lb.	.93	1.86	1.04	2.08
Half-and-Half	1 qt.	.58	.58	.59	.59
Butter	2 lb.	.84	1.68	.88	1.76
Total			$15.01		$16.16
Percentage Increase (Decrease)				7.7%	
Potential Cost Ratio			28.0%		30.1%

$$\frac{\text{Base Period Potential Cost Ratio (\%) x New Period Cost (\$)}}{\text{Base Period Cost (\$)}} = \begin{array}{l}\text{New Period}\\ \text{Potential}\\ \text{Cost Ratio}\end{array}$$

$$\frac{28.0\% \times \$16.16}{\$15.01} = 30.1\%$$

EXHIBIT 13.11

Food Cost Comparison

Outlet	Sales-to-Date	Potential Cost Ratio	Calculated Food Cost
Coffee Shop			
Breakfast	$ 4,000	28.0%	$1,120
Luncheon	3,200	32.5	1,040
Dinner	2,600	36.0	936
Total	$ 9,800		$3,096
Steak House			
Luncheon	$ 5,500	33.0	$1,815
Dinner	8,500	38.5	3,273
Total	$14,000		$5,088
Total Sales	$23,800		
Total Calculated Cost			$8,184
Actual Cost per Issues			8,779
Difference (Over) Under			$ (595)
Ratio of Difference to Sales			2.5%

Variances are investigated immediately to determine the reasons for the loss. A sample of a special control appears in Exhibit 13.12.

BEVERAGE COST CONTROL

Beverage cost is controlled in a manner similar to that of food cost; however, the system is somewhat less complex. The flow of goods through the operation must be controlled; the sale volume of the merchandise issued must be determined on a per-bottle basis; and the operation must be monitored to ascertain that the desired beverage cost ratio is being achieved.

Purchasing problems are minimized by federal regulations which insure uniformity of bottle fill, and set standards of identity for each type of spirit. In

EXHIBIT 13.12

Special Control

Date _____

Item	Opening Inventory	Issued/ Received	Total Available	Closing Inventory	Consumed	No. Sold per Checks	Over (Short)	Unit Value	Total Value	Remarks
Sirloin steak, 14 oz.	10	10	20	8	12	12	-	$ 7.95	-	
Minute steak, 10 oz.	15	20	35	20	15	13	(2)	$ 5.75	$11.50	1 returned — overcooked
Lobster tails 12 oz.	6	30	36	25	11	10	(1)	$ 6.95	$ 6.95	
Shrimp cocktail, 5 /order	20	18	38	16	22	19	(3)	$ 1.75	$ 5.25	

many states, the availability of certain brands and the use of certain bottle sizes is restricted. The purchasing decision ultimately depends on customer preferences and house policy.

ELEMENTS OF THE BEVERAGE CONTROL SYSTEM

The first step in beverage control is to establish standards to be used in the individual operation. The drink size and strength must first be established; will the principal ingredient be one ounce, 1 1/4 ounces, 1 1/2 ounces, or more?

Standard cocktail recipes must then be determined. These should include all ingredients, mixing instructions, and garnish. For example:

> Manhattan........... $1.00
> 1 3/4 oz. blended whiskey
>   3/4 oz. sweet vermouth
> Stir with cracked ice.
> Garnish with maraschino cherry.
> Serve in 4-oz. stemmed cocktail glass.

Standard recipes are a matter of management policy. Their establishment is necessary to provide the customer with a cocktail of uniform strength, quality, and taste; and to provide a uniform cost to the operation each time the item is served.

Standardization of glassware is the second step in beverage control. It is necessary, not only as a means of providing a drink that is standard in appearance each time it is served, but also to provide eye appeal to the customer. If a 3 1/2-ounce Manhattan is served in a 6-ounce cocktail glass, the customer may feel he has received short measure; but if the same cocktail is served in a 4 ounce glass, he will feel that a full portion has been served.

Standard glassware also is utilized as a portioning tool. The jiggers used at the bar should be of uniform size, which is that of the standard drink. Whether the measurement is taken to the brim, at the line, or above the line depends on management policy. Frequently, the specified jigger size has limited capacity above the line, to limit over-pouring. It is useful to incorporate the standard glassware instructions into the standard recipe.

The third step is to standardize prices. The selling price must be determined for each brand of spirit and each cocktail that is served. Often this is accomplished by grouping items and listing exceptions. The standard cocktail prices should be incorporated into the standard recipes. Standard drink prices should be listed for reference.

BASIC OPERATING PROCEDURES

The elements of beverage purchasing, receiving and storing, and control are similar to those of food. Issuing procedures, however, are distinctive and encompass three separate aspects. First is the establishment of bar par stocks. This is a listing of the brands and the number of bottles of each brand to be carried at the bar. Par stocks are utilized to minimize the value of inventory at the bar and to maintain the inventory at a constant level so that costs can be estimated on the basis of issues. They must be established individually for each operation, and are determined by the service policy, number of stations, and volume of business in the operation.

Issues to the bar are made on receipt of a signed requisition, and only in exchange for an empty bottle of like kind. The bottle should then be broken to prevent the possibility of reuse. The issues should be marked in a manner that will identify them as belonging to a particular bar to prevent the use of unauthorized spirits. This may be accomplished by means of a specially designed rubber stamp or gummed label.

At the end of the month, the effectiveness of the beverage storeroom should be reviewed by preparing a reconciliation statement in the same manner as outlined for the food storeroom.

DETERMINATION OF SALES VALUE

Control of sales is initially established by determining the sales value of each bottle sold. Three types of sales may result from the issue of a bottle of spirits.

1. The contents may be sold at the bar by the drink.
2. The contents may be used at the bar in preparing cocktails.
3. The contents may be sold as a unit (such as in hotel room service or in private parties).

The income derived from sales will vary, depending on the type of sale.

First to be considered is the sale of spirits by the drink, which represents the majority of consumption in most operations.

To calculate the sales value of a bottle when sold by the drink, the number of drinks obtainable per bottle must be determined. This is done by dividing the standard drink size into the bottle contents, after deducting an allowance of from one-half to one ounce for spillage and over-pouring. Thus, if the standard drink size is 1 1/4 ounces and a particular brand is issued by the quart, the number of drinks obtainable is 25 (32 oz. − 1 = 31 oz. ÷ 1.25 oz. = 24.8 = 25). If the standard price for the brand in question is $1.00 per drink, then the sales value of the bottle is 25 × $1.00, or $25.00.

When the bottle is used—at least in part—in preparing cocktails, some deviation from the standard price usually occurs. For example, a vodka highball may sell for the standard price of $1.00, but a Bloody Mary cocktail made with the same measure of vodka as the highball may sell for $1.10. A vodka martini may sell for the same price as the highball, or command the premium price of the Bloody Mary; yet more than the standard measure of vodka would be required to produce a martini of acceptable proof. Certain cordials, such as white creme de cacao and white creme de menthe, are rarely sold by the drink but are customarily combined with primary ingredients to produce a cocktail that may sell for more than the standard price of the base spirit. Obviously, some adjustments in the initial sales values are required. Adjustments can be accomplished in one of two ways.

Average method. In the average method, a record is kept as to the individual orders prepared during a selected test period. The cocktails and highballs are then analyzed by primary spirit. The sales value of a bottle is determined by relating the number of ounces used to the sales value of the drinks sold. For example, to establish the sales value for quarts of vodka, the procedure would be as follows:

Analysis of Sales for Test Period

Primary Spirit and Uses	Ounces per Drink	Number of Drinks Sold	Total Ounces Required	Price per Drink	Total Sales
Vodka, Domestic					
Vodka Martinis	2	50	100	$1.00	$50.00
Bloody Marys and Screwdrivers	1 1/4	20	25	1.10	22.00
Vodka Highballs	1 1/4	16	20	1.00	16.00
		86	145		$88.00

Sales Value per Ounce: $88.00 ÷ 145 oz. = $.606

Sales Value per Quart: 32 oz. – 1 oz. = 31 oz. x .606 = $18.79 = $18.80

Secondary ingredient method. This method utilizes the secondary ingredient issues to adjust the sales value. If six Bloody Marys are obtained from each can of tomato juice, and there is a 10¢ premium for this drink, the sales value of the can will be 60¢. If the pricing policy indicates that each one-half ounce of white creme de menthe used in a cocktail will add 25¢ to the selling price of the primary ingredient, the sales value of each quart will be $15.50 (32 oz.- 1 = 31 oz. X 1/2 oz. = 62 oz. X 25¢ = $15.50).

The issue of dry vermouth indicates that martinis are to be prepared. Because these will require more than the standard pour of vodka or gin (the primary ingredient), the sales value of these items must be reduced. This is accomplished by using the standard recipe.

Martini.................. $1.00

    2 oz. gin or vodka

1/2 oz. dry vermouth

Stir with cracked ice.

Garnish with olive or lemon twist, as requested.

Serve in 4-oz. stemmed cocktail glass.

    Vermouth is usually purchased in 30-ounce bottles. The number of drinks that can be obtained from one 30-ounce bottle is 58 (30 oz. - 1 = 29 oz. × 1/2 oz. = 58 oz.). To make 58 martinis will require 116 ounces (58 × 2 oz.) of gin or vodka, the primary ingredient. If the standard pour of gin or vodka is 1 1/4 ounces at the bar, this would be equivalent to 93 drinks if poured individually.

93 individual drinks of gin or vodka × $1.00 would produce revenue of:	$93.00
If sold as martinis, the revenue would be only 58 × $1.00, or:	58.00
Difference:	$35.00

    The difference, in this case $35.00, would be deducted from the sales value totals each time a bottle of dry vermouth is issued.

    The third possibility is that a bottle will not be dispensed at the bar, but will be sold as a unit. Examples are a bottle of wine sold in a restaurant, a bottle of liquor sold to a guest in his room, or a bottle of liquor sold to a table at a private function. Because the price that normally can be charged for this type of service is lower than the price when sold by the drink, the difference in sales volume must be recognized. This is accomplished by maintaining a record of sales by the bottle and deducting the difference. For example:

10 qt. Scotch issued at a unit sales value of:	$34.10	$341.00
2 qt. Scotch sold to room service guests, at a price per bottle of:	12.00	
Difference per bottle:	$22.10	
Credit for two bottles:		44.20
Total sales value:		$296.80

POTENTIAL SALES AND COST CALCULATION

After determining the sales values and adjustments, the potential profitability of the beverages issued can be established. The total sales value is obtained by multiplying the values for each brand by the number of bottles issued. The total cost is obtained by multiplying the cost per bottle by the number of bottles issued, and adding the cost of soft drinks, minerals, and food used for mixing. An example of a potential sales and cost calculation appears in Exhibit 13.13.

MONITORING THE OPERATION AND FOLLOW-UP

Monitoring the beverage operation, as in the food control system, consists of taking the pulse of the operation at appropriate intervals to determine whether the profit goals are being achieved. In a very large operation, this may be done daily. Frequently, it is done once a week. In a small operation, twice a month may be adequate. Because daily cost figures may fluctuate due to inventory levels at the bar, the period-to-date data should be used. The bar—not the sales outlet—is the unit of control, because one bar may serve several sales outlets. The actual sales should be compared to the potential sales for each bar during the period, and the difference noted. The actual and potential cost ratios then should be calculated. An example of the beverage summary appears in Exhibit 13.14.

Recall that a tolerance for spillage and over-pouring was allowed when the bottle sales values were established. Therefore, limited variation between actual sales and potential sales is acceptable. If the ratio over or short exceeds one-half of one percent, investigation is called for. This is carried out by first taking a "spot" inventory of the bar, to ascertain that par stocks have been observed. If the inventory is in order, the problem lies in a breakdown in basic operating procedures.

Note that the beverage cost ratio will fluctuate from month to month, depending on the proportion of bottle sales to the total, the drink sales-mix, and changes in the prices of purchased spirits. As the "sales value of potential" system reflects the income that should be derived which can be related to actual merchandise costs, the potential cost ratio is automatically adjusted for these fluctuations.

The use of the secondary ingredient method for adjusting sales values requires one further step. The intentional waste of vermouth would result in an excessive sales value credit, which would cause the potential to be understated. Therefore, the ratio of vermouth consumption should be verified on a spot-check basis by using the average method. Assuming that the ratio of gin use is identical to the example cited for vodka, and that gin and vodka are issued in quarts and ver-

EXHIBIT 13.13

Potential Sales and Cost of Beverages Consumed Computation

Item	Size	Number of Drinks per Bottle	Price per Drink	Sales Value per Bottle	Cost per Bottle	Issues	Total Sales Value	Total Cost	Cost %
Rum	Q	31	$1.00	$31.00	$4.25	1	$ 31.00	$4.25	13.7%
Gin, imported	Q	31	1.00	31.00	5.50	2	62.00	11.00	17.7
Canadian	F	25	1.10	27.50	5.25	2	55.00	10.50	19.1
Bourbon, bonded	F	25	1.10	27.50	5.50	2	55.00	11.00	20.0
Scotch	Q	31	1.10	34.10	6.50	5	170.50	32.50	19.1
Vodka	Q	31	1.00	31.00	4.25	3	93.00	12.75	13.7
Bourbon, 86 proof	Q	31	1.00	31.00	4.50	5	155.00	22.50	14.5
Gin, domestic	Q	31	1.00	31.00	4.00	6	186.00	24.00	12.9
Vermouth, dry	30 oz.	-	-	(58.00)	1.50	2	(116.00)	3.00	-
Creme de Cacao, white	F	-	-	N.V.	3.50	1	-	3.50	-
Beer	12 oz.	Ind.	.50	.50	.15	30	15.00	4.50	30.0
Soft Drinks and Minerals for Mixing	-	-	-	-	-	-	-	10.00	-
Food to Bar	-	-	-	-	-	-	-	20.00	-
Bottle Sales Adjustment: 2 at $15							(31.00)	-	-
Total							$675.50	$169.50	25.1%

Notes: 1. Standard drink size = 1 oz.
2. Martini formula: 2 oz. gin or vodka; 1/2 oz. dry vermouth; selling price, $1.00.
3. Two bottles of bourbon, 86 proof; issued to room service for sale at $16.00 per bottle.
4. N.V.—Not Valued.
5. Q = quarts, F = fifth.

EXHIBIT 13.14

Summary of Beverage Sales, Costs and Potentials

Month to Date _____

	Total Operation	Bar #1	Bar #2	Bar #3
Sales Actual	$23,000	$10,000	$ 8,400	$ 4,600
Potential	23,350	10,150	8,430	4,770
Actual Sales Over (Short)	(350)	(150)	(30)	(170)
Percent Over (Short)	(1.5%)	(1.5%)	(0.4%)	(3.7%)
Cost per Dollar Sale Actual	27.1%	27.5%	26.2%	27.8%
Potential	26.7%	27.1%	26.1%	26.8%

mouth in 30-ounce bottles, a minimum of 5 1/2 bottles of gin or vodka should be issued for each bottle of dry vermouth.

MECHANICAL CONTROLS

A number of mechanical controls are available on the market which can assist—or even take over—the task of controlling beverage costs. The simplest is a device which fits into the neck of the bottle of spirits to insure a uniform pour. More complex equipment integrates a dispenser with a counter and a locking device. At the upper end of sophistication, mechanical controls are linked with electronics to dispense a highball or cocktail at the press of a button, and simultaneously ring up the sale.

SUMMARY

Because food and beverage costs represent a major portion of the expenses associated with the hospitality service industries, effective controls are vital. The three basic factors determining food and beverage costs are markets, policies, and operations.

The control of food costs requires that control procedures be in effect at each step in the flow of food through the operation: purchasing, receiving, storing, issuing, pre-preparation and portioning, preparation, service, and sales.

The means of maintaining control over the complete food service sequence is the pre-cost, pre-control system in which food cost goals are established based upon standard quality recipes and portioning, and actual results are evaluated based upon the planned results.

Beverage cost control, similar to food cost control, is based upon the utilization of control procedures at each step in the flow of beverages from purchase to sale. The overall control systems involve the determination of potential retail sales based upon the beverages used and comparison of actual retail sales to the potential.

Discussion Questions

1. What is the purpose of the food cost control system?
2. What factors must be considered in attempting to control purchases?
3. Why is it unwise to buy an oversupply of foods, even though the "price may be right"?
4. How is control over receiving accomplished?
5. What are the two important aspects in the control of issuing items for use in operations?
6. What are the primary purposes of installing controls over food preparation?
7. What is the primary element in effective sales control?
8. What is the purpose of the pre-cost, pre-control system?

Problem 1

Last year, after operating the "Place to Eat" Restaurant for five years, James Morgan added a cocktail lounge to enhance his profits. However, after one year, he finds that the cocktail lounge has lost money and has detracted from his profits on food sales. Mr. Morgan is seriously considering the closing of the lounge because he incurred this loss. Based on the following financial statement, advise Mr. Morgan whether or not he should continue to operate the lounge. Show supporting comments and calculations.

	Restaurant	Lounge	Total
Revenue	$ 60,000	$ 28,000	$ 88,000
Cost of Goods Sold	24,000	9,800	33,800
Gross Operating Margin	$ 36,000	$ 18,200	$ 54,200
Direct Expenses	21,000	12,000	33,000
Indirect Expenses	7,000	7,000	14,000
Total Expenses	28,000	19,000	47,000
Net Income	$ 8,000	$ (800)	$ 7,200

Problem 2

The Davis Hotel has a total revenue of $1,500,000 from room rental, food and beverage service and other services. Room rental contributed 55 percent to total revenue, food services contributed 29 percent, beverage service contributed 12 percent and other services contributed 4 percent. Cost of foods sold is 33 1/3 percent and cost of beverages sold is 25 percent. Wage expense for rooms was 22 percent of total room's revenue, and other services had a wage expense of 33 percent. Other expenses in the rooms department were 6 percent; for foods they were 16 percent; for beverages 16 percent; and other department expenses were 17 percent of their respective revenues. The total gross operating income was 48 percent of total revenue.

Required

1. Compute the gross operating income for each department.
2. Deductions from income are as follows: heat, light and power, 4 percent of total revenue; repairs and maintenance, 5 percent of total revenue; administrative and general expense, 9 percent of total revenue; advertising and promotion expense, 4 percent of total revenue. Compute house profit.

Problem 3

Mr. E. Picure has invested $50,000 in a specialty restaurant which serves only three menu items: cornish game hen, sirloin steak, and Maine lobster. All items are sold as a complete dinner with a complimentary glass of wine. The menu prices and relevant costs for each item are shown. The restaurant has annual fixed costs of $90,000.

Item	Menu Price	Food Cost	Other Variable Costs
Cornish game hen	$6.25	$2.00	$1.75
Sirloin steak	6.50	2.48	1.75
Maine lobster	7.50	3.50	1.75

Required

1. If the total revenue is derived from a sales-mix between the three menu items as 20 percent game hens, 50 percent steaks, and 30 percent lobster, what level of total revenue would be required to generate a return of 20 percent on E. Picure's investment?

Problem 3 (continued)

2. If receipts from each menu item represented one-third of total revenue, what level of sales would be required to generate a return of 20 percent on the investment?

3. *Briefly* explain why there is a difference in the required revenues in cases (1) and (2).

CHAPTER 14

Payroll Control

In recent years salaries, wages, and fringe benefits have risen steadily. In the hospitality service industries this rise, which has out-paced increases in industrial wages, has been a result of greater unionization, Federal and state minimum wage legislation, and a realization on the part of operators that in order to attract and hold better employees more competitive wages are necessary.

It is not always possible or desirable to increase sales prices to meet rising payroll costs as well as increased operating expenses. Thus, there is a growing need for effective payroll control. The resulting payroll control systems are somewhat sophisticated in the larger establishments, and handled by the manager himself in the small operations.

Although unemployment has existed to varying degrees over the past years, there remains a tight labor market in the area of unskilled workers. In the hospitality service industries the major complement of employees fall into the unskilled or semi-skilled category.

This dependence on a separate labor market limits the flexibility that a facility would normally have in reducing staff during temporary or even extended periods of declining volume. In the past, an adequate supply of labor allowed the hospitality service industries manager to reduce his work force, knowing that replacement labor was readily available. The more current labor market removes this opportunity for payroll flexibility.

Today's manager faces a dilemma that is a direct outgrowth of our changing economy and also reflects the changing demands made upon the hospitality service industries. The practices of the past do not apply readily to current conditions; management must be prepared to meet change. Within this framework of change, the manager must increase the efficiency of his operating procedures and controls, with specific and direct emphasis on efficient labor utilization.

MANAGEMENT OBJECTIVES

It is essential for management to thoroughly understand the labor problem, and to maximize labor utilization within the framework of collective bargaining or other agreements. To attain the optimum use of labor requires a concerted effort and the use of specially designed programs that provide proper procedures for payroll control. Managers must create an awareness of the problem and a positive attitude that should permeate through several organizational levels. This attitude, along with various control procedures, will help to produce the maximum labor utilization.

THEORY OF CONTROL

In attempting to achieve sound payroll control, it is essential that any operation first be budgeted to produce a reasonable profit. In the budget preparation the projected performance of the integral departments will influence the entire unit's profit results. Therefore, it is necessary to estimate the departmental results required to obtain the profit objectives.

ELEMENTS OF THE CONTROL PROCESS

The elements of the control process first require that a determination be made of the reasonable minimum levels of activity either attained for existing properties or anticipated for new ventures, in order to provide a sound basis for analysis of the functions needed for the services offered. With this background data, the next step in the control process is to carry out job analysis and prepare job descriptions which should be simultaneously correlated with the proposed staffing.

Essential to the control of payroll costs, but frequently overlooked as part of the payroll control system, is effective supervision. This encompasses work planning, scheduling of shifts and breaks, and control of tardiness and absenteeism. It also encompasses training of employees in organized and efficient work methods.

JOB ANALYSIS

Job analysis is undertaken for two purposes. First, analysis may reveal inefficiencies or an opportunity for improving operations. Second, job analysis serves as the basis for formalizing job positions within the operational structure. In carrying out job analysis it is necessary to review all elements or duties performed by the employee under actual working conditions. The greatest accuracy is achieved when the various elements are time-studied. However, estimated time expenditures and direct observation can also produce workable data.

In analyzing employee productivity, reference should be made to the following guideline questions commonly utilized in time and motion studies.

Why is the job done?
Why is it done at this station?
Why is it done at this time?
Why is it done by this employee?

In analyzing the efficiency of specific tasks performed by the worker, the following questions should be answered.

Were all the steps used to complete the task necessary?
Were the steps completed in the proper order?
Was time lost between various "do" parts of the series of steps?

Job Descriptions

For effective labor control, it is necessary to prepare a job description for each category of employee, one which accurately describes the duties to be performed. Included in each job description should be: job title, department, purpose and responsibility, means for carrying out responsibility, and qualifications required to fill the position. On pages 333 and 334 are examples of typical job descriptions in a hotel.

In planning and preparing each job description, care should be taken that the duties of each employee's position actually reflect the job performance desired by management. It must not reflect what the employee would like his duties to be, or thinks they should be, or what a supervisor would like the duties to be.

In preparing job descriptions, the analyst often includes too much detail. The job description should clearly summarize the duties of the position it is intended to cover, but it is not absolutely essential to indicate that Clerk A on Monday processes Report A and on Tuesday Report B. It is sufficient to indicate that Clerk A is responsible for processing paperwork which includes mail, reports, statements, reservation requests, etc.

Labor-Saving Devices

Once the job or position analyses and the job descriptions are prepared, they should be reviewed in detail by management to determine whether they truly reflect the duties of the position and the work to be performed.

On a random or selective basis, the position should be observed under actual working conditions, to determine whether productivity can be improved by using labor-saving devices. A substitution of equipment (for example, an electric broom rather than a broom or carpet sweeper) often may mean that an employee can function more productively than what was previously possible. Examples of more

---

JOB TITLE _____ GENERAL MANAGER _____

Administrative and General   Manager's Office

JOB DESCRIPTION

SUMMARY: The General Manager, reporting to the Board of Directors, is directly
                      responsible for supervision of all operations and all employed personnel
                      of the hotel.

WORK PERFORMED: Carries out policies and directives as approved and communicated by
                      the Board of Directors.

                      Responsible for the business conduct of all functions of the hotel as
                      illustrated in the organization chart.

                      Responsible for the profit levels of all operating departments and in-
                      sures that all departments are complying with company policy with
                      respect to established quality and profit standards.

                      Effects the procurement of supplies, equipment, and services through
                      formal or informal contracts and insures that purchasing agents operate
                      in accordance with company regulations and policies.

                      Communicates with department heads through regularly held staff
                      meetings.

QUALIFICATIONS: Ten years of experience in hotel-restaurant operations, of which at least
                      five years was in a top-level supervisory capacity. College degree essen-
                      tial. Graduate of Hotel, Restaurant, and Institutional Management
                      school preferred.

---

efficient labor utilization in various departments which may result from job analysis include:

Repairs and maintenance: use of pocket page or other similar equipment for giving employees new job assignments, eliminating the unproductive time consumed by reporting back for each assignment.

Kitchen: use of pre-prepared vegetables and prefabricated cuts of meat to reduce employee preparation time.

Front office: use of various types of recording equipment for messages linking the front office with other departments, such as housekeeping, which results in the elimination of unproductive time carrying messages.

JOB TITLE ___ FOOD AND BEVERAGE COST ACCOUNTANT
AND STAFF PLANNER ___

Food and Beverage   General

JOB DESCRIPTION

SUMMARY: To supply the food (and beverage) manager with the information neces-
                      sary for planning and control of his department(s).

WORK PERFORMED: Acts in a staff capacity, without any direct authority, to provide assist-
                      ance and information to the department heads and to digest raw infor-
                      mation supplied by them and prepare timely reports for the food and
                      beverage manager.

                      Is responsible for accumulation of food requisitions and calculation of a
                      weekly food cost for each restaurant.

                      Accumulates food revenue and cover statistics, and issues a weekly
                      report.

                      Handles initial preparation of volume forecasts and distributes the
                      adopted forecasts to all concerned.

                      Is responsible for accumulation of weekly work schedules, analysis, and
                      recommendations for improved personnel utilization; reports actual re-
                      sults compared to planned results and the average output achieved per
                      employee.

                      Serves as a resource to the department heads for scheduling, budgeting,
                      and other information.

                      Conducts butchering and cooking yield tests, time studies or other
                      projects as directed by the food and beverage manager.

                      Suggests improved methods and procedures on products to department
                      heads, and makes appropriate recommendations to the food and bever-
                      age manager.

QUALIFICATIONS: This person should have a working knowledge of the food (and bever-
                      age) department and possess analytical ability.

Payroll preparation: use of outside service groups to process payrolls eliminates the need for a full payroll staff within the accounting department.

Administration: use of dictating equipment by management eliminates secretaries' time in taking dictation and allows the hiring of secretaries without shorthand capability.

Similar opportunities for more effective labor utilization exist in most operations. Through the use of job analysis, such opportunities may be realized.

Station or Position Layout

Job analysis may indicate that other areas may also be improved. Poor station locations or position layout may require an employee to do excessive walking or reaching, which not only reduces productivity but causes fatigue. It is management's direct responsibility to continually review all positions to determine if labor-saving equipment can be instituted which will justify its cost, and to see if methods are applicable and station layouts are efficient. Other characteristics of the position also must be periodically reviewed and improved where feasible.

Management must challenge every aspect of the position, placing specific emphasis on long-standing positions to determine whether they include functions that are now obsolete. The results achieved will be in direct proportion to the effort and imagination expended by the person or team performing the review of positions.

SCHEDULING OF MANPOWER

The primary objective of scheduling manpower is to provide the type and number of employees required to furnish service in accordance with policy standards and in conformance with the volume and pattern of business anticipated. Inadequate staffing would impair the proper functioning of service departments, while excessive staffing unnecessarily burdens the operation with increased payroll costs.

It should be recognized that demands for position coverage as determined by the physical installation as well as the basic operating policies will require a certain minimum staff regardless of volume levels.

Determination of the minimal staffing requirements is primarily based on the needed coverage for all services established. At the lower volume levels, some combination of employee tasks may be feasible for improved staff utilization when the physical configuration permits. For example, in coffee-shop type operations during periods of limited business activity, the short order cook may be delegated responsibility for salad and sandwich preparation where the two stations are adjacent. This basic staffing schedule then becomes the reference standard for planning additions and subsequent reductions to the labor force based on productivity standards.

With the hospitality service industries there are three distinct employee categories.

1. Employees whose work load is directly related to the number of guests served, such as maids, waiters, etc.
2. Employees whose job requirements are determined by assigned station, which may or may not have a relationship to the number of guests, such as cashiers, supervisors, timekeepers, etc.
3. Employees whose job requirements are determined by management policy, such as management executives, sales representatives, etc.

The task of scheduling these categories efficiently for the hospitality service industries is somewhat more difficult than in others in that it is concerned with a seven-day, and in some cases twenty-four-hour, operation. The various service departments must be staffed accordingly by employees who in many cases work a five-day, forty-hour week. It is apparent that relief or substitute employees are required to provide such coverage. Thorough consideration should be given to the utilization of part-time personnel as a means of achieving improved scheduling efficiency.

There are many variations of the work week and the number of hours worked per day. However, in this chapter our illustrations follow the five-day, forty-hour week, subject to arithmetical changes, where necessary.

Employee scheduling is generally the responsibility of a department head in a large operation, although usually it is delegated to a subordinate supervisor subject to the final approval of the department head. In a small operation the manager probably prepares or assists in the preparation of these schedules. Caution must be used that the schedule is not merely a duplicate of the previous schedule with little thought given to anticipated volume or a change in staffing. Emphasis should be placed on scheduling the staff to meet the work load patterns.

Stacked Scheduling

The term *stacked* or *shift scheduling* evolves from the configuration produced when employees in an area are all assigned the same starting and finishing time (as is shown in Exhibit 14.1). This is a common staffing practice which, when reviewed, might require revision.

In Exhibit 14.1, a staffing pattern is set up to cover dishwashing for three meal periods over sixteen hours, divided into two basic shifts. Meal service begins at 7:00 A.M. and concludes at 12:00 midnight, covering seventeen hours.

EXHIBIT 14.1

Stacked or Shift Scheduling

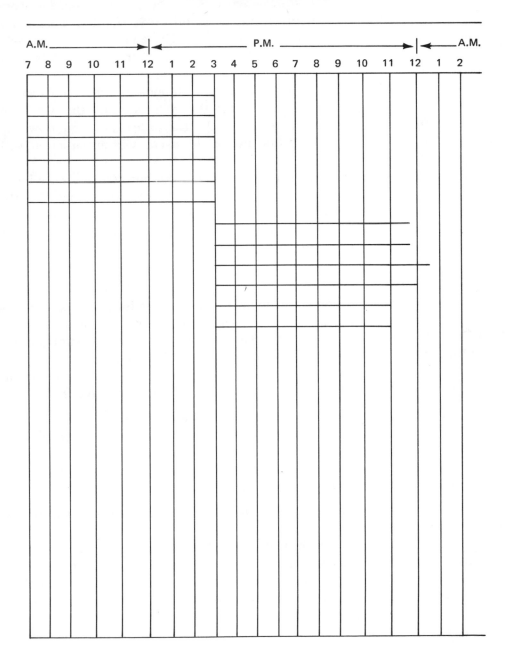

Six dishwashers begin at 7:00 A.M. (the commencement of breakfast service). Dishes in any substantial quantity will not arrive in the dishwashing area until 7:30 to 7:45 A.M. One or two dishwashers prepare the dish machine for operation. However, there are four other employees on duty. If other work is not provided, there is a potential loss daily of between 120 and 180 man-minutes or two to three man-hours of unproductive labor. A similar situation loss could occur at the beginning of the second shift.

Moving ahead to the close-down period of 12:00 midnight, this configuration shows that all employees go off duty at 11:00 P.M. This means that some employees' shifts must be extended to process the last dishes and close down the dishroom. Therefore, this configuration also produces an overtime situation, with resultant higher payroll costs.

In general, there are very few situations within the hospitality service industries that lend themselves to a rigid application of stacked scheduling. Unfortunately, the method has been traditionally used and remains in use in many operations. The same method of scheduling may be applied to any operative or non-operative department.

Staggered Scheduling

Often a staggered system of scheduling which provides for employees arriving at various starting times will enable a facility to achieve a greater degree of flexibility in scheduling manpower. The staggered scheduling configuration (shown in Exhibit 14.2) provides much better labor utilization.

Using the staggered configuration in place of the previous stacked schedule results in the processing of the same work load with one less employee by:

1. Reducing the idle time at the start of the stacked shifts.
2. Minimizing the loss of worker momentum inherent in the sharply defined shift change.
3. Recognizing the variation in the pattern and volume of business between the luncheon and dinner meal periods.

Additionally, the staggered scheduling eliminates the overtime expense by providing straight-time coverage for closing.

Replacement of stacked schedules with staggered hours frequently offers potential for reduction of the number of employees. However, any decision in this regard should be very closely scrutinized by management, since problems with shop stewards and unions may be encountered if the plan is not well thought out and completely organized. Emphasis should be placed on the *least number of employees* that can competently carry out any given work program. Management

EXHIBIT 14.2

Staggered Scheduling

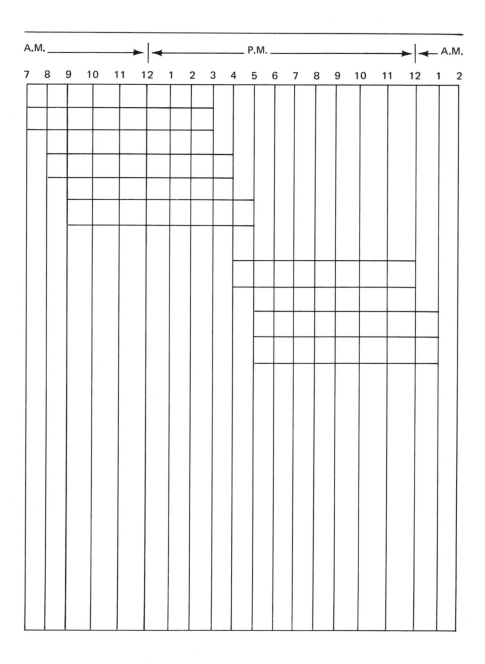

must avoid merely shifting personnel when fewer can do the same job. This principle applies to every department subjected to this type of study.

Scheduling of Days Off

Frequently the assignment of days off does not permit management the flexibility it should have in order to operate efficiently. Often days off are not changed to meet fluctuations of business activity with the result that premium time must be paid in order to maintain staffing service. Key personnel are found to be scheduled off on weekends when management supervision is also reduced. Thus, it is essential for management to maintain maximum flexibility in scheduling the days off of all personnel. With the utilization of forecast data in conjunction with the scheduling flexibility achieved through the use of the staggered schedule, management is able to provide straight-time coverage which parallels the volume of business activity.

In those departments in which the normal work load is reduced by limited volume experienced on certain days, it may be appropriate to schedule special tasks normally not recurring on a daily or weekly basis. For example, in the maintenance department, it would be desirable to utilize these periods for painting, equipment overhaul or replacement. This scheduling represents a minimum degree of inconvenience to guests and patrons as well as reducing the impact of interruption to regular work routines of other personnel.

Exhibit 14.3 represents a chart of standard man-hours, which can be effectively used in assigning the days off of employees. In this illustration, the repairs and maintenance department is staffed on a one-shift basis.

The same procedure for assigning days off can be followed in all other departments, and adjusted as necessary to meet changing conditions. Sufficient flexibility is avilable to the department in handling planned as well as unexpected work on the weekends which otherwise would have to be staffed on an overtime basis.

Bar charts can be used to plot employee scheduling assignments and volume; the chart can also pinpoint periods during which scheduled employees are available. Thus, potential idle time is identified and other duties may be assigned. A bar chart is presented as Exhibit 14.4.

Scheduling of Vacations

A paid vacation of two weeks is now common throughout the hospitality industry. Frequently, this is extended to a period of three weeks or longer for employees with several years of service. While vacation payroll is frequently reported as part of the regular payroll, it is more correctly a part of employee benefits.

EXHIBIT 14.3

Chart of Standard Man-Hours

Name or Job Title	Sun	Mon	Tues	Wed	Thurs	Fri	Sat	Total Hours
Chief Engineer	Off	Off	8:00 am 4:00 pm	S*	S	S	S	40
Secretary	Off	8:00 am 4:00 pm	S	S	S	S	Off	40
Project Coordinator	8:00 am 4:00 pm	S	S	S	S	Off	Off	40
Electrician	10:00 am 6:00 pm	S	S	S	Off	Off	10:00 am 6:00 pm	40
Carpenter	8:00 am 4:00 pm	Off	Off	8:00 am 4:00 pm	S	S	S	40
Plumber	Off	Off	10:00 am 6:00 pm	S	S	S	S	40
Painter	8:00 am 4:00 pm	S	Off	Off	8:00 am 4:00 pm	S	S	40
Utility Man	Off	10:00 am 6:00 pm	S	S	S	S	Off	40
Laborer - Driver	10:00 am 6:00 pm	S	S	Off	Off	10:00 am 6:00 pm	S	40
On Duty	5	6	7	7	7	7	6	
Off Duty	4	3	2	2	2	2	3	
Total Employees	9	9	9	9	9	9	9	360

*S = Same hours worked.

It is important that the hospitality industry manager devote adequate effort to the planning of vacations. If this is not done, additional costs are usually incurred in the form of overtime or training and wage costs for replacement workers. By planning vacations in advance, and moving away from the traditional practice of scheduling all vacations during the summer months, it is frequently possible to schedule vacations during periods of low volume so that replacement of the vacationing employee is not required. Similarly, this also results in fewer marginally productive employees on the staff during the low volume periods.

EXHIBIT 14.4

Waitress Utilization Bar Chart
Charles V Dining Room Department

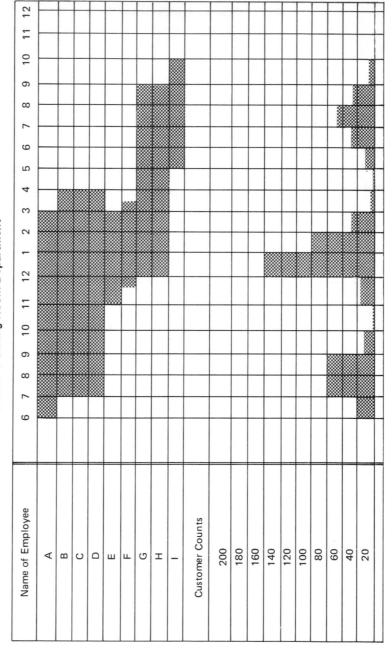

Effective scheduling of vacations can be accomplished by requesting each employee to submit his vacation preferences, with alternates, early in the year. A master vacation schedule is then prepared for each department, and eventually for the entire operation.

OTHER MEANS OF PAYROLL CONTROL

In most establishments, there are some departments which are not subject to procedures of manpower control because productivity cannot be measured in a direct relationship to unit volume, other than in a broad ratio of payroll percentage to total sales. While this ratio may produce a general guide, it is generally too broad to provide an accurate analysis of manpower utilization. As an alternative, the use of special control systems may be employed. For example, in the maintenance department a repair and work order system can provide management with a basis for detailed analysis of manpower utilization.

Required Information

If a repair and work order system is to be effective, it is necessary to accurately record all tasks performed by repair and maintenance personnel. This requires that the total time expenditure be shown on the repair or work order document. It is calculated from the time the maintenance man leaves the shop or dispatch point, until he returns after completing the repair. When the work is completed, the document is signed by the repairman and the department head in whose department the work was done, and is given to the chief engineer for review. All such labor on repair and work orders is recorded. It should include time spent performing other duties, such as preventive maintenance, groundskeeping, setting up equipment for functions, training time, and other forms of activity.

The time expended by departmental personnel for all categories of work, for any given period, is totaled and can be included in a "Manpower Utilization Report" as shown in Exhibit 14.5.

The weekly preparation and submission of a summary report enables management to identify the areas requiring greater control. Since supporting detail of repair orders and work orders are required to determine the total time expended in the various categories, these documents are subject to review and audit, if necessary. In reviewing the illustrated report (Exhibit 14.5), repair and work orders accounted for 64.3 percent of activity, while preventive maintenance accounted for roundly 20.0 percent. Manpower utilization at 72.1 percent of available hours produced 78 non-productive hours at a cost of $175.50. This equals the man-hours of two full-time employees, who could have been assigned to preventive maintenance functions (if maintenance was required). This is not to

EXHIBIT 14.5

Manpower Utilization Report
Summary of Repairs and Maintenance

	Week Ended _____	
	Hours	Percentage of Total
I. Work Accomplished		
Total Time Expended on Repair Orders	70	34.6%
Total Time Expended on Work Orders	60	29.7
Total Time Expended on Preventive Maintenance	40	19.9
Total Time Spent in Preparation for Major Activities	16	7.9
Other Activity (Explain in Attached Memo)	16	7.9
Total Hours	202	100.0%
II. Aggregate Man Hours Worked		
Supervisory	80	22.3%
Non-Supervisory	280	77.7
Total Hours	360	100.0%

III. Utilization of Manpower

$$\frac{\text{Total Work Accomplished in Hours}}{\text{Aggregate Non-Supervisory Man Hours}} = \frac{202}{280} = 72.1\%$$

Cost of Non-Utilized Man Hours

Average hourly wage $2.25 x 78 Non-Productive Hours = $175.50

say that there will never be idle time, but the objective is to keep it at the absolute minimum.

After much testing and reviewing, on the basis of these reports, management can determine the optimum effective utilization of manpower in any department and under varying conditions. Further, even after the acceptable range has been established, it cannot remain static. As shown in Exhibit 14.5, the 72.1 percent utilization may be raised to 85 percent or more by reduction of unnecessary personnel or improvement in scheduling.

IMPLEMENTATION OF FORECAST PROCEDURES

Forecasting is a means by which an organization reviews historical business trends and advance reservations or bookings, considers coming local or regional events that would affect business, and on the basis of the aforementioned, forecasts the business volumes that may be expected. When forecasting procedures are properly utilized, there is a greater degree of accuracy in planning for manpower requirements, since the forecast information is the nucleus for sound staff planning in all departments.

Payroll forecasting periods may vary, but generally cover a minimum of one to two weeks with ranges up to several months. The length of time the forecast encompasses can best be determined by the individual establishment based on its own historic trend records and anticipated business activity.

For whatever period selected, sufficient overlap should be included to provide continuity, updating of data, and sufficient time for re-scheduling and the notification of personnel of time changes.

THE FORECASTING TEAM

In a large establishment there is a forecast committee; in a smaller property, the manager and some, if not all, department heads participate in the forecast preparation. To achieve the most accurate results, the team should represent a broad cross-section of operating departments. For example, the team might meet on Wednesday to forecast the activity for the week beginning the following Sunday. Immediately after the forecast meeting, the initial report should be prepared and distributed. This data is essential to determine departmental staffing.

THE FORECAST DOCUMENT

The forecast should be expressed in terms of occupied rooms, number of guests expected, food and banquet or function covers, anticipated beverage sales, or other business units depending upon the particular service or hospitality category. Other information, such as the weather, special events and holidays, may be provided, as necessary. An illustration of a forecast document covering a seven-day period is given in Exhibit 14.6.

As the period progresses, the forecast must be revised, often on a daily basis, to permit affected department heads to make whatever last-minute schedule changes are necesary to align the skill covering with the anticipated work load. To facilitate such changes, one person should be assigned to coordinate and distribute change notifications to the other team members.

DETERMINING THE FORECAST'S ACCURACY

After being reviewed, changed as necessary, and updated, the forecast should be used by various departments to plan their manpower requirements for the specified period. The forecast will rarely be completely accurate; but to be effective, it must be reasonably close to actual. Therefore, the resulting actual sales or unit volume should be compared to the forecast figure, and the percentage of variation calculated. Variations of up to 15 percent in dollar or unit volume can be handled by the planned manpower complement. Higher percentage variations indicate that the forecasting method needs review and revision. This review should include analysis of both the information source used for input purposes and the method of making adjustments to the forecast.

Much effort must be directed to refining the forecast procedure. The manpower planning function should be the result of a concerted and well-defined management effort and should not be left to chance.

Exhibit 14.6 illustrates a sample forecast report for a small hotel for one week. Expansion can be provided with space for the actual figures at the end of the week, as well as the percentage variation from the forecast figures.

DETERMINATION OF PERFORMANCE STANDARDS

The forecast information, as developed and revised, is used as a guide for department heads in determining their manpower needs for any period. It is necessary to develop productivity standards or norms for those job classifications that may be directly measured against unit volume. There are no overall standards for the hospitality service industries. This is because the development of such standards requires a thorough analysis of the individual operation with regard to:

1. Pattern of business.
2. Physical layout of facilities.
3. Level of employee competence.
4. Level of supervisory competence.

EXHIBIT 14.6

Volume Forecast for the Period March 1, Through March 7, 19XX

	Sunday March 1	Monday March 2	Tuesday March 3	Wednesday March 4	Thursday March 5	Friday March 6	Saturday March 7	Weekly Total
Room Department								
Estimate of Occupied Rooms	100	125	140	150	150	110	100	875
Percentage of Occupancy	50.0%	62.0%	70.0%	75.0%	75.0%	55.0%	50.0%	62.0%
Guest Count	130	162	182	195	195	143	130	1,137
Food and Beverage Department								
Coffee Shop								
Breakfast	100	130	150	162	162	110	100	914
Lunch	50	85	90	100	80	75	50	530
Total Covers	150	215	240	262	242	185	150	1,444
Restaurant								
Lunch	45	80	85	90	90	125	85	600
Dinner	75	80	90	120	120	100	150	735
Total Covers	120	160	175	210	210	225	235	1,335
Function Rooms								
Breakfast	—	25	35	—	20	—	—	80
Lunch	—	50	65	50	100	50	—	315
Dinner	150	50	70	40	80	25	200	615
Total Covers	150	125	170	90	200	75	200	1,010
Grand Total Covers	420	500	585	562	652	485	585	3,789
Beverage Revenue Forecast								
Bar A	$ —	$ 300	$ 375	$ 425	$ 450	$ 400	$ 625	$2,575
Bar B	220	450	525	495	500	550	750	3,490
Total Beverage Forecast	$ 220	$ 750	$ 900	$ 920	$ 950	$ 950	$1,375	$6,065

5. Hours of operation.
6. Union contract provisions (if any).[1]

Productivity standards may be determined by several approaches. The management of each establishment, after thorough study, must make the final decision as to which method is preferred.

Position Analysis

Under this method, the duties performed in a position are observed directly. This review requires an analyst to spend considerable time observing the work elements performed before being able to determine a reasonable level of output or performance. The same position should be reviewed during various shift periods so that appropriate allowances may be made for high or low volume periods in a given day. Although this method of analysis is expensive in terms of the analyst's time, when properly conducted, it does produce the most accurate results.

Historic Analysis

Every hospitality service industries establishment should maintain reliable statistics that indicate the daily and cumulative volume of business. Often it is beneficial to have figures and data by seasonal periods, if they apply. For food and beverage reporting, statistics should be recorded on a per meal basis.

Usually, this information is found in a "Daily Report of Business" which reflects cumulative volume to date and, in most cases, indicates the volume for the same period in the preceding year. These reports are used to analyze volume to determine employee performance or productivity trends.

The comparisons should be established for several test periods and should represent activity during the various seasonal periods of business. Certain facilities may have relatively stable volume situations, while others may experience substantial fluctuations from day to day, week to week, or season to season. It is important that the test periods reflect these fluctuations so that the resulting conclusions regarding productivity will represent the actual average attainment and can be accepted as achievable norms.

Obviously, the historic analysis method cannot be used by a new facility. The position analysis approach would most logically be considered in this instance.

Exhibit 14.7 shows a format for the analysis of food covers and a work output analysis for a test period. The output is determined by the formula:

Volume in units ÷ number of employees = output per employee.

---

1. Even where there is no union contract, it is necessary, in most instances, to meet union pay rates, hours, and fringe benefits, in order to obtain competent personnel.

EXHIBIT 14.7

Analysis of Covers Served for Summer Five-Week Test Period*

	Sunday	Monday	Tuesday	Wednesday	Thursday	Friday	Saturday
Breakfast Covers Served							
Week of:							
July 11-17	112	233	286	257	295	273	236
July 18-24	117	258	309	287	283	245	180
July 25-31	141	263	301	302	306	252	224
August 1-7	108	243	311	315	303	257	213
August 8-14	120	235	282	271	313	269	209
Total for Test Period	598	1,232	1,489	1,432	1,500	1,296	1,062
Average for Test Period	120	246	298	286	300	259	212
Luncheon Covers Served							
Week of:							
July 11-17	247	262	264	291	318	285	259
July 18-24	261	277	325	303	293	285	253
July 25-31	328	253	254	285	286	245	272
August 1-7	276	314	314	326	299	272	231
August 8-14	302	231	280	297	290	251	244
Total for Test Period	1,414	1,337	1,437	1,502	1,486	1,338	1,259
Average for Test Period	283	267	287	300	297	268	252
Dinner Covers Served							
Week of:							
July 11-17	135	230	224	227	235	223	175
July 18-24	124	205	216	211	222	206	184
July 25-31	142	193	182	225	195	190	189
August 1-7	194	223	257	243	219	203	197
August 8-14	153	211	209	231	191	181	169
Total for Test Period	748	1,062	1,088	1,137	1,062	1,003	914
Average for Test Period	150	212	218	227	212	201	183
Supper Covers Served							
Week of:							
July 11-17	49	63	104	160	120	152	174
July 18-24	56	51	81	117	96	105	127
July 25-31	42	57	120	126	112	141	180
August 1-7	49	70	96	158	88	108	158
August 8-14	63	64	111	156	104	139	149
Total for Test Period	259	305	512	717	520	645	788
Average for Test Period	52	61	102	143	104	129	158

*If fluctuations from week to week are considerable, a longer test period should be used.

EXHIBIT 14.7 (continued)

Work-Productivity Analysis

	SUNDAY	MONDAY	TUESDAY	WEDNESDAY	THURSDAY	FRIDAY	SATURDAY
BREAKFAST							
Average Covers Served	120	246	298	286	300	259	212
Waiters on Duty	10	12	12	12	12	12	10
Average Covers per Waiter	12.0	20.5	24.8	23.8	25.0	21.6	21.2
LUNCH							
Average Covers Served	283	267	287	300	297	268	252
Waiters on Duty	10	12	12	12	12	12	10
Average Covers per Waiter	28.3	22.3	23.9	25.0	24.8	22.3	25.2
DINNER							
Average Covers Served	150	212	218	227	212	201	183
Waiters on Duty	11	14	14	14	14	14	14
Average Covers per Waiter	13.6	15.1	15.6	16.2	15.1	14.4	13.1
SUPPER							
Average Covers Served	52	61	102	143	104	129	158
Waiters on Duty	11	14	14	14	14	14	14
Average Covers per Waiter	4.7	4.4	7.3	10.2	7.4	9.2	11.3

Note: The foregoing are illustrative as to method only and are not to be considered as general standards.

If there are extremely sharp fluctuations in the volume, an effort should be made to determine the specific causes. It may be prudent to staff for the normal level of business and, depending on the availability of local labor, to obtain extra personnel when sharp rises in volume are forecast. If there are heavy fluctuations, it may be advisable to establish the work loads at 10 to 15 percent lower than the highest volume, rather than the average for the test period.

We will not attempt here to set forth standards for positions in any departments, since there can be wide variations from establishment to establishment, even though they may be contiguous and have many similar operating elements. Work standards are unique, and must be determined by management after individual study and inquiry.

DETERMINING MANPOWER REQUIREMENTS

After standards of performance are determined, the department heads should review the forecasted information for the stipulated period, to determine the numerical staffing required to properly service the anticipated volume.

Referring to Exhibit 14.7, note that aside from the breakfast meal on Sunday, there is a relatively even level of performance relating to the waiters' output (that is, covers served per waiter per meal). Here serving personnel are on duty over two meal-periods during a full shift (that is, breakfast and luncheon, or dinner and supper).

The work productivity analysis shows an average total of 1,741 breakfasts, 1,954 lunches, 1,403 dinners and 749 suppers for the five-week test period. For this same period, 80 waiters were scheduled for breakfast and lunch, 95 for dinner and supper. The output per waiter per meal-period as a result of the allocation was 21.8 meals per waiter for breakfast, 24.4 for lunch, 14.8 for dinner and 7.9 for supper. These varying levels of waiter productivity per meal-period are partially the result of scheduling waiters in eight-hour shifts rather than scheduling by meal-period and partially the result of a failure to schedule waiters according to the varying daily activity patterns.

Analyzing the historic data by daily meal-period average covers served per waiter, it appears that scheduling one waiter for each 23 covers forecast for breakfast, 24 covers for lunch, 15 covers for dinner, and 10 covers for supper is realistic. However, the 10 covers per waiter for supper is subject to question as, in the past, waiters may have been overstaffed at supper. Further analysis is probably required for supper staffing guides. Using this historical pattern to plan manpower requirements, the department head or manager has available a reasonable basis for employee scheduling.

The suggested scheduling by waiter meal-period productivity ratio does not provide for contingencies, such as absentees, unexpected volume surges or other unusual situations. In actual practice, the scheduling of manpower would make some provisions for contingencies and, in most operations, short-term adjustments can be made within the assigned manpower allocation.

The procedural method of assigning manpower for waiter coverage can be used equally well to determine the manpower requirements for other departments once a relationship has been established between the particular position and the level of activity.

Staff structure, however, cannot be based solely on an arithmetical calculation of work productivity. Other factors relative to the specific operation must be considered. The determination of performance standards, when approached by the position or historic analysis method, gives consideration to these other factors. The resulting performance standards will be reasonable and will represent the specific requirements of any given position in its working environment.

Hiring Employees

The hiring policies and procedures for the establishment should be well defined and controlled. In addition to the job descriptions and position analyses, all positions should have assigned numbers for easy identification, and for processing use in preparing payrolls and various personnel and related reports.

An employment requisition should be prepared for each open position and submitted through the established channels for approval. Where there is a payroll analyst, approval would be coordinated through his office, but he should not have superseding authority to hire or fire personnel.

The employment requisition should include pertinent information, such as shift hours, rate of pay, and a brief description of duties. The probable days off and the reason the position is open could also be included when this information is available, the latter being the usual justification for engaging a replacement. (However, sometimes a position is not filled as a means of reducing personnel through attrition.)

The employment requisitions, when approved, are forwarded to the personnel department for action. If the requisition is not approved, the requesting department head should be so informed, and further discussion or other courses of action should be explored.

The Hiring Process

After receiving a properly approved employment requisition, the personnel department is authorized to interview qualified and competent candidates for the position. The brief job description enables the personnel interviewer or screener to gain some insight as to what the prospective employee's duties would be. The department head will make the final determination to hire after interviewing the candidate.

When he has accepted the job, the candidate is processed by the personnel department, and the appropriate paperwork is prepared to place the employee on the payroll.

The personnel department should also provide suitable procedures for preparing data regarding salary and wage rates, to determine whether the current wage rates being paid are competitive. In addition, there should be procedures for preparing turnover reports, which should contain the reasons for turnover as well as the number of hirings and firings.

Exit Interviews

In any organization it is important to review the reasons for employee terminations and voluntary resignations. It is even more important to see what steps or actions can be taken by management to improve the situation. Aside from the real costs involved in advertising for screening, interviewing, processing employees, and training, excessive turnover has a damaging effect on service and employee morale.

On the employee's last day of work, an interview should be arranged between the employee and a management representative (usually from the personnel department or, in a small property, with the manager himself). It is desirable to use a prepared form which enables the interviewer to ask key questions. The object of the interview is to determine if there are underlying reasons for the termination of voluntary resignations which, if not corrected, could cause further expensive turnover.

Turnover Reporting

A report should be prepared at least monthly, if not more frequently, which reflects the turnover percentage for the period. The following formula should be used.

$$\frac{\text{Number of terminated employees}}{\text{Number of employees on the payroll}} \times 100 = \text{Turnover \%}$$

The report should be prepared and submitted for management review. Some of the frequent reasons for voluntary employee terminations, determined by the exit interview, can be incorporated into the report in a summary form. Thus, the report serves a dual purpose: it shows the number and turnover percentage for a given period, and it lists the chief reasons for employee terminations and voluntary resignations. This report should be broken down by departments and by job classifications.

CONTROLLING OVERTIME

One of management's major responsibilities is to effectively control overtime hours and the associated premium expense. This control should become a basic philosophy of an organization and should emanate from all managerial and supervisory levels. To achieve true control, overtime must be subjected to a management review for its approval or disapproval, preferably daily. There are numerous instances in the hospitality service industries where true overtime is essential but many operations incur overtime expenses substantially greater than necessary.

Control Procedure

Effective overtime control is based on a department head or supervisor recognizing early in a shift that overtime hours for particular employees will be necessary and requesting overtime approval. The request (see Exhibit 14.8) is prepared by the department head or supervisor and submitted for management approval.

Overtime requests should be prepared and submitted at a designated time for each shift on a daily basis. This daily submission of overtime requests exerts a degree of psychological control. If the reason for overtime is considered to be controllable, the person submitting the request must so indicate this reason daily. The review by the person approving overtime would reveal the repetitiveness of the reason, and would instigate some form of corrective action. A prompt approval or disapproval of overtime requests is required so that appropriate action can be taken to plan for proper service to the guests.

The properly authorized overtime request, after it has been returned to the department head, should be forwarded to the accounting department, which will use it later to check overtime hours appearing on a time card to determine whether the overtime hours were authorized.

This procedure, while not designed to eliminate all overtime, should materially reduce unnecessary overtime. In smaller operations, a simplified method of overtime control is more practical. Usually, the department head gives the explanation on an employee's time card, and management reviews the time cards each day before they are sent to the bookkeeping department or payroll clerk.

Where an operation has frequent occasion to engage "extra" employees (such as banquet waiters or waitresses, cooks, dishwashers, maids, etc.), a similar daily form should be prepared for approval of management *prior* to the particular function for which they are to be engaged.

EXHIBIT 14.8

Request for Overtime Authorization

Date _____ Department _____ Title _____

Reason for Overtime:

Explain in detail why overtime is necessary:

Number of employees to work overtime _____

Number of hours per employee   _____

Total hours requested   _____

Name and clock number of employees

1.   4.   7.

2.   5.   8.

3.   6.   9.

Will employees be supervised?   Yes _____   No _____

If yes, by whom? _____ Position _____

Requesting Department Head

Designated Management Official: Approved _____

                                           Total Hours Requested _____ Approved _____

                                           Disapproved _____

Comment:

TIMELY PAYROLL REPORTS

Payroll control procedures require a report of the results of manpower control and the efficiency of the system to management. Although the final monthly operating statement provides a summary of operations, it is not issued until after the end of the month. By that time, the results are historic, and corrective action is not only too late, but often is impossible to accomplish. Though corrective action can be formulated for the future, more timely response to an unsatisfactory situation is necessary.

The establishment of formal reporting procedures in both man-hours and dollars is an essential and integral element of payroll control. In its most refined and effective state, such controls enable management to review, determine the need for, and, where necessary, change procedures for hiring, approving overtime, scheduling, and other areas that directly affect the operation.

Manpower control and the frequency of reporting should generally correspond to the established payroll periods. At the end of the month, the manpower utilization and the performance of the various departments should be summarized. Where necessary and, if feasible, particularly in unusual situations, management should receive interim or daily reports. Through the use of properly prepared periodic payroll reports, management will be able to maintain effective control.

Preparing Manpower Summary Reports

The personnel assigned to prepare manpower reports varies with the size of the facility. In a large establishment a payroll controller or payroll analyst may coordinate the program, while in a small property it may be another duty of the manager, auditor, or payroll clerk.

In a large hospitality service firm, the payroll analyst usually reports to either the manager or some other designated executive. Obviously, the results reported and reasons for such results reflect the ability of supervisors to efficiently manage their departments. Because of this, the payroll analyst should be relatively independent; he should never be placed in the position where he is required to report on a person for whom he is working.

Once a system of forecasting is established and performance standards are determined, the resulting performance may be compared with budgeted performance, prior periods and, in some situations, other similar operations.

Method of Preparation

Using the forecast document, the employee performance standards, and the actual performance, the payroll analyst can prepare a summary of manpower utilization for the operating departments. Thus, if 1,050 rooms were occupied for a given period, and the maids' performance standard was established at 14.0 rooms per maid, 75 maid-days would be required. Reviewing the aggregate actual payroll hours, the analyst finds that 600 maid-hours were generated. Assuming that the standard shift is 8 hours, $\frac{600}{8}$ = 75 maid-days is the required number under the established performance standard. The department operated at standard with no variance in man-hours.

However, if the aggregate hours were 700, then $\frac{700}{8}$ or 87.5 maid-days were generated, and the resulting performance was 12.0 rooms per maid-day rather than the 14.0 per maid-day as established, or 12.5 days over the established standard. The payroll analyst should contact the department head to determine the reasons for such variation. If necessary, he will assist the department head in scheduling the department to produce established standards.

A similar approach is used to tabulate the manpower utilization for each department with an established performance standard. The results are shown on a "Summary of Manpower Comparisons" (Exhibit 14.9).

To increase the value of the summary report and make it more meaningful in terms of dollar reporting, the variations (either above or below standard) are equated to dollars. This is done by determining the average daily wage, and extending it by the number of man-day variations. Thus, in the example of maids, the 12.5 maid-day variation at an average of $12.80 per maid-day equals $160 in excess labor cost for the period. On the report, man-days and the equivalent dollar variations are carried forward, and shown in a cumulative variation column.

Distribution of Manpower Summary Reports

The completed report should first be reviewed by the manager and then the sections distributed to the appropriate department heads. Distribution should coincide, whenever possible, with weekly staff meetings so that manpower performance can be discussed.

DISCUSSIONS OF PERFORMANCE

The manager should discuss a department's performance with the person who is directly responsible for the overall operation of that department. Because of the close interrelationship of many departments, it may be advantageous to discuss one department's performance before a group. However, if performance is extremely poor when compared to the standard, it may be advisable for the manager to discuss the situation privately, with only the concerned persons present. This

EXHIBIT 14.9

Summary of Departmental Manpower Comparisons for Week Ended

Department	Average Number of Employees	Aggregate Hours Worked	Actual Equivalent Man-Days (Hours/8)	Established Standard Man-Days	Man Days Variance	Cumulative Variance to Date	Payroll Dollar Variance	Cumulative Variance to Date	Average Cost per Man-Day of Variance
Front Office	7	280	35	35	-	-	-	-	-
Housekeeping	24	960	120	110	10	10	$128	$128	$12.80
Front Service	10	400	50	50	-	-	-	-	-
Food Preparation	30	1,200	150	140	10	10	200	200	20.00
Steward	15	600	75	75	-	-	-	-	-
Food Storeroom	3	120	15	15	-	-	-	-	-
Food Service Dining Room	25	1,000	125	120	5	5	40	40	8.00
Totals	114	4,560	570	545	25	25	$368	$368	$14.72

discussion may reveal situations which make it difficult or unrealistic to adhere to the standard. The manager then must review the reasons for nonstandard performance and determine what type of corrective action is warranted. This could include reviewing performance standards or other factors incorporated in the manpower control program.

As with any system or control procedure, it is necessary periodically to modify procedures and adjust to changing business, competitive, or other conditions. The efficiency of operation gained through efficient manpower utilization more than offsets the time and effort involved in creating, maintaining, and adjusting the manpower control elements.

SUMMARY

With rising payroll costs has come the need for more effective payroll control.

The first step in effective payroll control is the preparation of job analyses and job descriptions. With staffing of positions, the next step is forecasting activity and scheduling to meet the forecast demand. The use of staggered rather than stacked scheduling generally provides better labor utilization. Bar charting is an effective means of evaluating scheduling and anticipating idle periods.

To the extent possible, productivity standards should be established and productivity should be monitored with weekly reports. Forecasting accuracy should also be evaluated by comparing forecasts with actual activity experienced.

Employee hiring should be on the basis of job descriptions and only where a vacancy exists. Employee turnover should be monitored to disclose excessive turnover.

A primary reason for excessive payroll costs in the hospitality service industries is unnecessary overtime. Therefore, overtime must be authorized prior to the time it is to be worked.

Discussion Questions

1. Discuss the objectives of management with respect to the payroll control area.
2. How does a job description help with the control process?
3. What is the purpose of job analysis?
4. What advantages can be gained by a formal management review of all job positions?
5. What is the prime objective of scheduling manpower?
6. Describe three employee categories of the hospitality service industries.

7. How does a weekly report on a summary of repair and maintenance activities aid in payroll control?
8. Describe the process of forecasting volume for labor scheduling.
9. How does forecasting aid in the payroll control process?
10. Why is it necessary to review the reasons for voluntary employee resignations?
11. Why is it sometimes difficult to set up control procedures based on previous performances?
12. What are two methods of establishing productivity standards?

Problem 1

The manager of the Hamilton Hotel thinks it would be good for the hotel to hire a maintenance man to be on call twenty-four hours a day. He knows a semi-retired man who would be ideally suited for the job. The manager is going to offer a "compensation package" to the maintenance man—a room in the hotel, three daily meals, and a salary of $300 a month. The manager estimates that room would normally cost $10 a day and meals $5 a day. The present maintenance man is retiring next month. His salary was $500 a month. The manager has asked you what you think of his proposed plan. Include in your discussion consideration of both opportunity cost and out-of-pocket cost.

Problem 2

How can budgets be used to maintain control over labor cost?

Problem 3

What division of duties among independent departments is desirable to achieve maximum internal control over payrolls?

CHAPTER 15

The Pricing Decision

All costs and expenses in the hospitality service industries may be stratified into three classifications:

Departmental Expenses (direct expenses)
Deductions from Income (controllable unallocable expenses)
Rent, Taxes, Insurance, Interest and Depreciation (noncontrollable capital expenses)

The subtraction of all direct expenses from the departmental revenues results in the departmental contribution margin (DCM). The sum of all the departmental contribution margins is the amount of income available to cover the remaining two expense categories, unallocable expenses and capital expenses. Any residual is profit. In all segments of the hospitality service industries it is necessary to have a pricing structure so that the DCM is in excess of all controllable unallocable expenses and noncontrollable capital expenses.

Total revenue equals the number of units of products or services sold multiplied by the selling price of these units. In this formula the first factor to be determined by management is the selling price. In the not-for-profit segments of the hospitality service industries, the selling prices do not have a material effect on the number of units sold. Many hospitals, schools, and clubs have a pricing structure based on a policy of charging to cover full and continued increasing costs of services, and there is sufficient demand for the services to support this pricing policy. In these not-for-profit segments of the hospitality service industries, there is minor direct competition so that price does not have the same significance to the number of units sold as in the profit sector of the hospitality service industries. Because pricing decisions are important to maximum profits in the competitive firms, this chapter will be devoted to the hospitality service industry firms in business for profit. These for-profit or competitive categories of the hospitality service industries must consider pricing dynamics: the determination of the full cost associated with a product or service; the elasticity of demand; the interrelationships of the various products and services offered for sale; and the effect of the sales-mix upon departmental contributions, margins and total profits.

INFORMAL PRICING METHODS

Pricing within the profit-orientated divisions of the hospitality service industries may be based upon one or more of the following five informal pricing methods:

> Intuition
> Competitive
> Trial and Error
> Follow-the-Leader
> Psychological

Intuition is a basic and easily employed pricing method as it establishes prices on some intuitive feeling for public demand for the service primarily in terms of "what the traffic will bear." Generally, little may be known about the expected volume that a particular price will generate, or the full cost of the service. Intuitive pricing can result in a failure to recover full costs plus a satisfactory profit margin.

Competitive pricing is a simple method of pricing that charges the same for a particular product or service as the competitor in the market area. This will be a satisfactory method for pricing if the product or service is completely comparable to that offered by competitive facilities charging the same price, and if this selling price will result in a satisfactory profit. This pricing method has been employed by the hospitality service industries in the pricing of rooms, food, and beverages.

Competitive pricing may not recognize that the product or service provided may be superior in the minds of customers and hence able to command a higher price without reducing volume to an unsatisfactory level. Similarly, the full cost of providing the good or service may not be the same as the full cost incurred by competitors. Unsatisfactory competitive pricing may result from insufficient research and knowledge of the relative merits of the competition's products or services.

The trial and error pricing method establishes prices for a test period while monitoring sales activity during that period. Price adjustments are then made up or down with continuous monitoring to estimate the optimum price to provide a maximum departmental contribution margin. This method is sensitive to consumer reaction and may have merit in selected circumstances. However, it assumes that consumer reaction will occur in a sufficiently short period of time to arrive at the proper price. And after the price has been determined, it assumes that market conditions and consumer tastes will remain constant for some reasonable period of time.

The follow-the-leader pricing method implies that there is a leader or dominant form whose price structure and price changes are followed by others in the market. This method is similar to competitive pricing except that the particular dominant firm establishes the price. The follow-the-leader method makes the same assumptions as competitive pricing, and has the same deficiencies.

Psychological pricing is a method of pricing where management sets the pricing structure based upon a conscious expectation of what the consumer expects to pay for the product or service offered. Psychological pricing is generally associated with goods that are unique or not widely available, and specialized services. This pricing method may be used in those segments of the hospitality service industries where style and exclusiveness have separated a portion of the total market, such as a famous gourmet restaurant, the newest resort, or a restricted membership club.

PERCENTAGE MARK-UP PRICING FOOD AND BEVERAGES

While pricing methods employed in the lodging and food service categories of the hospitality service industries have been influenced by some of the informal methods, lodging and food service pricing has also relied upon the gross margin percentage mark-up. This may be applied primarily to the pricing of food and beverages, and it relates the selling price to the prime food or beverage cost of each major item. For example, if the cost of a 16 oz. sirloin steak was $1.80, the price of a complete sirloin steak dinner might be $7.20. The price is arrived at by applying a multiple to the prime ingredient cost, or, stated another way, the menu price is established to result in a predetermined 25 percent prime ingredient cost. The multiple used would depend on the type of restaurant, for each type of restaurant has a different cost-profit structure. The same steak dinner could have a multiple of three or less in a steak house or a cafeteria where volume, labor, costs, and overhead vary from the restaurant cost structure used in this example of a four multiple.

The prime ingredient cost method is used frequently in the pricing of alcoholic beverages because the liquor cost is a large percentage, if not all, of the ingredient cost. If 1 1/2 ounces of bourbon are used in mixing a whiskey sour, and bourbon is purchased for $4.00 a fifth, whiskey sours might be priced at $1.25 based upon the following calculation:

Ounces in a Fifth   = 26
Drinks per Fifth
   (after allowance for spillage) = 16
$4.00/Fifth ÷ 16 Drinks/Fifth   = $0.25/Drink
Using a Target Prime Ingredient
   Cost of 20 percent   = $1.25 Drink Price

The prime ingredient cost method is likely to be used to establish the general price level for all drinks. Individual drink prices would then be determined by making adjustments to the general price level based upon cost differentials for the various ingredients.

Prime ingredient cost for pricing assumes that changes in the cost of other ingredients will parallel changes in the prime ingredient cost. To the extent that this is correct, the price or price changes derived by using either method would be the same. However, those using the prime ingredient cost method may find that the multiple they are using is unsatisfactory due to changes in the relationship of prime cost to other food cost. In order to more closely relate costs to prices the total cost of all items served can be used in pricing.

ROOMS PRICING IN THE LODGING DIVISION OF THE HOSPITALITY SERVICE INDUSTRIES

Some hotels and motels have relied upon informal competitive pricing methods in pricing rooms. This method of establishing prices involves the determination of the competitive properties' pricing and adjusting for differences in facilities. These differences might include the size and furnishings of rooms, the location of the property, and the level of services offered. Where no competitive facilities exist in the immediate area, prices might be based upon the prices in areas closest to their location, or on prices used by similar properties.

Tradition has also provided the hotel-motel industry with formulas to be used for the pricing of rooms. The simplest formula is that of one dollar of average room rate to be charged for each $1,000 of project cost. For example, if the total cost of a 100-room project was $1,500,000, the cost per room would be $15,000 and the price structure would be established to result in an average room rate of $15.00. This would require that the room rate structure take into account the expected sale of various types of rooms and the expected multiple occupancy factor so that an average room rate of $15.00 would result.

The $1.00 for $1,000 guideline was established many years ago and has not been revised to reflect current operating cost structures and financial terms. When this formula was first used it was based on the then-existing attainable average occupancy and operating costs, normal financing terms, and an acceptable rate of return after taxes. Within recent years these fundamentals underlying the guideline have changed substantially, so that today the utility of this pricing rule-of-thumb has been lost.

An alternative method for rooms pricing is the Hubbart Formula. Developed for the American Hotel and Motel Association, this method has been in limited use for many years. The approach taken by the Hubbart Formula is one of working from estimated unit sales, other department profits, operating costs and financial costs to arrive at an average room rate which would provide a predetermined profit. Exhibit 15.1 shows the application of the Hubbart Formula to compute an estimated average room rate for a 250-room motor-hotel with full facilities. With the estimation of the $20.00 required average room rate, a comprehensive room rate structure may be developed based upon noticeable differences in rooms and number of occupants.

The Hubbart Formula is an improvement over informal competitive and $1 per $1,000 pricing as it estimates the full costs associated with the room accommodations. However, the Hubbart Formula does have some basic deficiencies in that the contribution from the food and beverage department, and other profit generating departments, uses estimates. The expected level of occupancy and the desired rate of return are more basic estimates. Hence, the room price resulting from the application of the simple computations of the Hubbart Formula is germane to the validity and accuracy of the many estimates that go into the computation of the formula.

PRICING THEORY

The basic theory of pricing in the lodging and food service areas of the hospitality service industries should result in a price or combination of prices in which the departmental contribution margin is maximized. Each of the many departmental products or services should be priced so that the total of all revenues less the respective departmental costs is maximized. For a specific department this is graphically illustrated in Exhibit 15.2. In this exhibit the horizontal axis represents the quantity of units sold and the vertical axis represents the revenue in dollars per unit. The two factors superimposed on the chart are the estimated demand curve running down to the right and the departmental cost line parallel to the horizontal quantity axis. The demand curve reflects the sensitivity of volume to changes in prices. As the price is lowered the volume of units which would be sold increases (demand moves along the demand curve down to the

EXHIBIT 15.1

Hubbart Formula Average Room Rate Calculation

Investment	
Cost of Land, Building, Furniture and Fixtures	$3,900,000
Working Capital	100,000
Total Investment	**$4,000,000**
Financing of Investment	
Debt at 10% Interest	$3,250,000
Equity	750,000
Total Financing	**$4,000,000**
Projected Number of Rooms Occupied (75% Occupancy)	68,500
Desired Return on Equity at 15%	$ 110,000
Income Taxes at 50%	110,000
Required Profit Before Income Taxes	$ 220,000
Interest Expense ($3,250,000 at 10%)	325,000
Required Profit Before Interest and Taxes	$ 545,000
Estimated Depreciation, Municipal Taxes and Insurance	320,000
Required House Profit	**$ 865,000**
Budgeted Deductions from Income	
General and Administrative Expenses	$ 250,000
Advertising and Sales Promotion	100,000
Heat, Light and Power	90,000
Repairs and Maintenance	65,000
Total	$ 505,000
Required Gross Operating Income	**$1,370,000**
Estimated Departmental Profit Excluding Rooms	
Food and Beverage	$ 240,000
Other	30,000
	$ 270,000
Required Rooms Department Profit	$1,100,000
Estimated Rooms Department Expense	300,000
Required Rooms Department Revenue	$1,400,000
Required Average Room Rate ($1,400,000 ÷ 68,500)	$ 20.00

EXHIBIT 15.2
Pricing for Maximized Departmental Contribution Margin

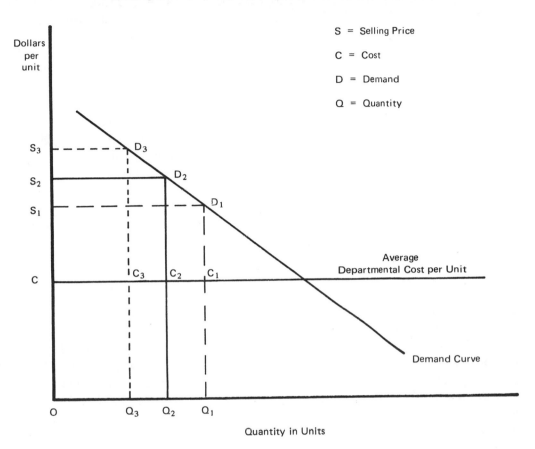

right), and as the price is raised the volume of units sold decreases (demand moves up to the left on the demand curve). In this exhibit the assumption is made that the departmental costs are completely variable so that each additional unit sold costs the same additional amount.

Total revenue in this graph is calculated by multiplying the quantity of units sold times the price per unit. Similarly, total cost is calculated by multiplying the quantity sold times the cost per unit. In this illustration three alternative prices are considered, S_1, S_2 and S_3. A price of S_1 results, according to the demand curve, in a quantity sold of Q_1, a price of S_2 represents a quantity sold of Q_2, and a price of S_3 represents a quantity sold of Q_3. Thus, the total revenue resulting from a price of S_2 would be S_2 times Q_2 or the rectangle OS_2 D_2 Q_2. The departmental cost associated with this volume level is represented by the rectangle $OC\ C_2\ Q_2$. The departmental contribution margin (DCM) is represented by the rectangle $CS_2\ D_2\ C_2$ which is the rectangle $OS_2\ D_2\ Q_2$ less the rectangle $OC\ C_2\ Q_2$.

To maximize the departmental contribution margin in this example, the area in the rectangle $CS_2\ D_2\ C_2$ must be at a maximum. When this is accomplished the price associated with the quantity level would be the optimum selling price under the assumed circumstances.

To illustrate this, the two alternative prices (S_1 and S_3) are shown on Exhibit 15.2 in addition to the price of S_2. The price S_1 results in a total revenue of $OS_1\ D_1\ Q_1$, a departmental cost of $OCC_1\ Q_1$, and a departmental contribution margin of $CS_1\ D_1\ C_1$. The price S_3 results in a total revenue of $OS_3\ D_3\ Q_3$, a total cost of $OCC_3\ Q_3$ and a departmental contribution margin of $CS_3\ D_3\ C_3$. Each departmental contribution margin (DCM) rectangle can be computed by multiplying the length times the width; the rectangle containing the greatest area is the optimum and indicates the appropriate price. In Exhibit 15.2 the rectangle $CS_2\ D_2\ C_2$ is the largest and price S_2 is the optimum price, given the existing demand curve and departmental costs.

Exhibit 15.2 uses a vertical axis with the scale in dollars per unit. Exhibit 15.3 illustrates the same conditions using a vertical axis scale stated in total dollars. In this exhibit the revenue is presented in terms of the total revenue which would result from various alternative prices. Though it is not possible from this exhibit to determine the price which resulted in a particular total revenue, it does provide total revenue immediately without the necessity of multiplying the quantity times the price as was necessary to determine revenue in Exhibit 15.2. Similarly, the departmental cost curve is an accumulation of the total direct cost, which would be associated with the various quantities sold. To determine the optimum price in this exhibit, one must determine the location on the total revenue at which the greatest departmental contribution margin is achieved. In this exhibit, the line R_2 represents the total revenue which would be realized from the sale of Q_2 units.

Line $Q_2\ C_2$ represents the departmental cost associated with that quantity level; thus, the line $C_2\ R_2$ must represent the departmental contribution margin. Alternative levels of operation are also shown in the quantities Q_1 and Q_3. For the quantity Q_1, total revenue is R_1, total direct expense is $Q_1\ C_1$ and departmental contribution margin is $C_1\ R_1$. For the quantity Q_3, the total revenue is represented by R_3, total departmental cost is represented by $Q_3\ C_3$ and the departmental contribution margin is $C_3\ R_3$. Because the departmental contribution margin $C_3\ R_3$ and the departmental contribution margin $C_1\ R_1$ are both less than the departmental contribution margin $C_2\ R_2$, the quantity Q_2 and the total

EXHIBIT 15.3
Pricing for Maximized Departmental Contribution Margin

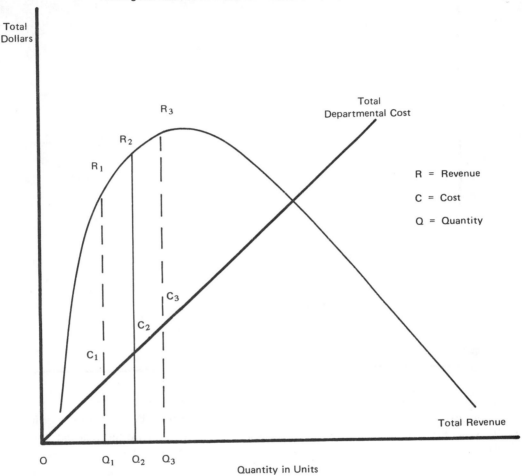

revenue R_2 are the optimum points for the firm, and the underlying selling price creating R_2 should be used.

Another method of determining the optimum price is marginal revenue-marginal cost analysis. Exhibit 15.4 illustrates this method. This exhibit plots the additional revenue resulting from the sale of each additional unit of product or service (marginal revenue) and the additional departmental cost of each additional unit of product or service (marginal departmental cost). Using this method the optimum operating level is the point at which marginal revenue equals marginal departmental cost, or the quantity Q_2, which is determined by the intersection of

EXHIBIT 15.4
Marginal Revenue—Marginal Cost Analysis

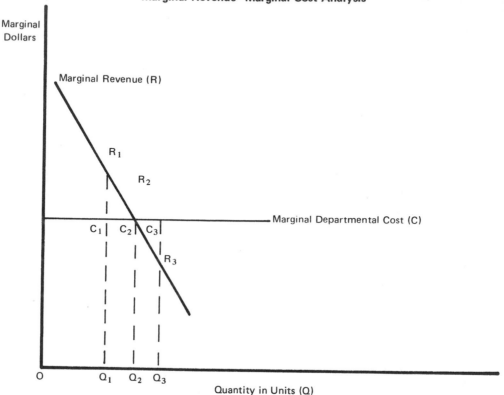

the marginal revenue curve and the marginal departmental cost curve at point R_2 and C_2. To operate at the quantity Q_3 would mean that additional units of activity $Q_3 - Q_2$ would result in marginal revenue $Q_3 R_3$. This revenue would be less than the marginal departmental cost $Q_3 C_3$, resulting in a net loss on each additional unit sold beyond quantity Q_2. To operate at quantity level Q_1 would mean that the opportunity for additional departmental contribution margin was being foregone. Here the marginal revenue $Q_1 R_1$ is greater than marginal departmental cost $Q_1 C_1$ and thus the additional quantity $Q_2 - Q_1$ would be desirable.

In Exhibit 15.2 the demand curve is assumed to be linear, as is the departmental cost curve. This assumption is made for simplicity in the presentation, although in some circumstances one or both of these curves may indeed be linear. However, a more likely circumstance is presented in Exhibit 15.5.

Here, neither the demand curve nor the departmental cost curves are linear, but the optimum pricing solution is the same, to maximize the area of the rectangle $CSDC_1$ with a total revenue of $OSDQ$ and departmental costs of $OCC_1 Q$.

EXHIBIT 15.5
Maximized Departmental Contribution Margin

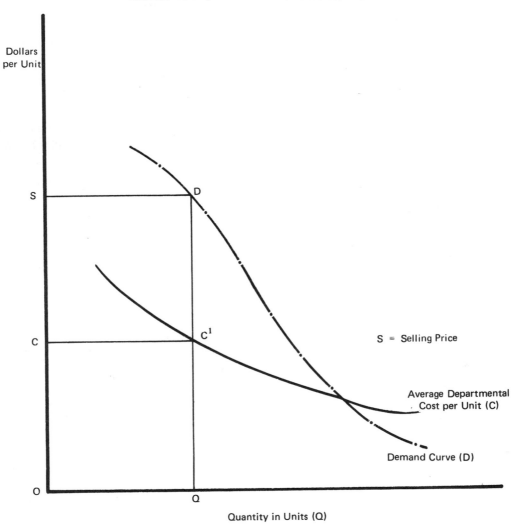

Quantity in Units (Q)

ELASTICITY OF DEMAND

The demand curves used in the preceding exhibits assumed that quantity sold is effected by the selling price: as the selling price decreases, the amount sold increases, and as the price increases, the amount sold decreases. This sensitivity of the quantity sold to price changes is referred to as the *elasticity of demand*. This is expressed by the formula:

$$\frac{\text{Percentage Change in Quantity}}{\text{Percentage Change in Price}} = \text{Elasticity of Demand}$$

If the result is greater than one, the demand is elastic, or sensitive to price change. An elastic demand is one in which a price change results in a more than proportionate quantity change. When the result of the formula is less than one, the demand is inelastic, or insensitive to price changes. An inelastic demand is one in which a price change would result in a less than proportionate change in quantity.

The degree of elasticity or inelasticity of demand is determined by the amount by which the result of the formula exceeds or is less than one. The degree of elasticity of demand is important information for price setting. If it is known that an item is inelastic (insensitive to price change), prices may be increased with relatively little effect upon the quantity sold, thus increasing total revenue and departmental contribution margins. Similarly, a reduction in the selling price would not be expected to have much effect upon the quantity and would only reduce total revenue and departmental contribution margins.

Inelastic price sensitivity is the result of one or both of two market conditions: the lack of competitive products or services and the desire or need for guests to obtain the product or service regardless of the price. The less competitive the conditions and/or the greater the desire or need, the greater the inelasticity.

Inelastic demand is not common in the lodging and food service areas because direct or indirect competition exists at some level for all firms. Some resorts or specific properties with unusual guest appeal may be operating in slightly inelastic price sensitivity circumstances but these situations are few in number.

Elastic demand sensitivity is the one in which most hospitality service industry firms operate. For example, in the fast food segment, which is highly competitive, price changes of only a few cents could have a substantial impact upon volume. In this situation the range in which prices may be varied is limited.

SALES-MIX

Many segments of the hospitality service industries have the pricing decision in more than one department. The best example of this is the relationship between rooms, food and beverage sales in a hotel, motor hotel or resort. None of the three individual departmental pricing structures should be determined independently of the others.

The objective in pricing where multiple departments exist is to arrive at a combination of prices which maximizes the sum total of all the departmental profits.

In the single department examples, the solution required an estimate of the demand curve for that particular departmental unit of output. While such an estimate may vary from the actual, the conscious estimation of it will in most circumstances provide better information for pricing decisions. Where many departmental units of output are available to the guest, not only must an estimate be made of each demand curve, but the interrelationships must be estimated. While the estimates of these interrelationships will in most instances be uncertain, the manager must be aware of the existence of these relationships in establishing the price structure.

The concept of pricing in the main departments of a hotel-motel is known as *integrated pricing* or *total business pricing*. It emphasizes the interrelationship of departmental sales and the need where this interrelationship exists to co-ordinate pricing. The outcome of such co-operated pricing is the sub-optimization of individual item or department pricing in the interest of optimizing total departmental profits. For example, a restaurant is reevaluating the general price levels in the cocktail lounge and the dining area. If priced independently, cocktail lounge prices might be set at a level which would maximize the cocktail lounge departmental contribution margin. However, analysis might reveal that the cocktail lounge DCM would be lower but the total DCM from both the dining area and the cocktail lounge higher if integrated pricing were employed. In order for this to be true a reduction in the cocktail lounge DCM must be exceeded by the dining area's increase in DCM with integrated pricing policies.

The means by which initial prices or changes in prices are arrived at should encompass all of the available pricing analyses techniques and methods. Throughout the pricing process, the basic truism must be recognized that total units sold times total selling price must exceed total costs if the operation is to be profitable. While in the short run management may be willing to violate this principle by setting prices in individual areas at less than maximum, in the long run it is inviolable. Without full knowledge of the total cost structure, management will not be able to properly implement the pricing decision which must be based on the market factors of the competitive conditions, consumer demand, departmental price relationships and elasticity.

SUMMARY

The pricing decision is an important management consideration because it effects total revenue in the "price times units equals revenue" equation, and also it may effect the units sold depending upon the elasticity of demand. Services are said to have elastic demand when a change in the selling price is more than offset by a change in the quantity sold, and inelastic demand when a change in the selling price results in a less than proportionate change in the quantity sold. A knowledge of the demand curve, and consequently the elasticity of demand, is important in making pricing decisions.

Historically the hospitality service industries have arrived at prices using some form of informal pricing such as the intuition, competitive, trial and error, follow-the-leader, and psychological methods. The pricing of food and beverages is improved through the use of percentage mark-up methods. However, future pricing methods in the hospitality service industries must give consideration to integrated pricing, understanding of the demand curve and the determination of the full cost of each unit of service. Pricing for the single service organization should optimize departmental profit, and for the multi-service or multi-department organization, should optimize total house profits.

Discussion Questions

1. What are five informal pricing methods normally used by the lodging and food service firms in business for profit? Explain each method.
2. Contrast competitive and follow-the-leader pricing.
3. In what types of operations has psychological pricing been thought to be appropriate?
4. What are the deficiencies of each of the five informal pricing methods?
5. Why is percentage mark-up pricing often used in determining the sales price of meals and beverages?
6. What is the underlying assumption for basic ingredient percentage mark-up pricing, and how is it eliminated by using total item cost?
7. Name three methods or formulas of establishing room rates.
8. Why is elasticity of demand important in establishing prices?
9. Why is the concept of integrated pricing or total business pricing important to multi-department hotels and motels?

Problem 1

You are the owner of a night club and are trying to maximize your departmental cost in the restaurant. To determine the maximum cost, the restaurant pricing theory should be used. When doing the problem, assume that departmental costs are variable so that each additional unit sold cost the same additional amount.

Average Departmental Cost per Cover Served = $2.00.

Problem 1 (continued)

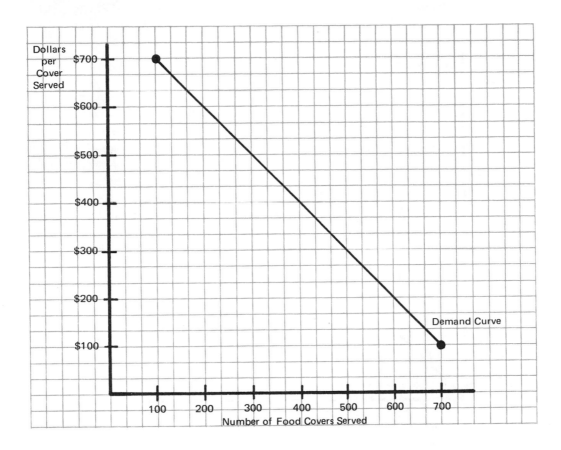

1. Determine total revenue for the restaurant at $4.00, $5.00 and $6.00 for meal cover served.
2. Determine the total cost of food served at $4.00, $5.00 and $6.00.
3. Determine which dollar amount per food cover served gives the restaurant the greater contribution margin.

Problem 2

1. What does line AB represent? (See page 376.)
2. What does line CD represent?
3. You are trying to decide the number of meals to serve at your restaurant. You are going to serve either 300, 400 or 550 meals. Which of these numbers of meals will give you the greatest contribution margin?

Problem 2 (continued)

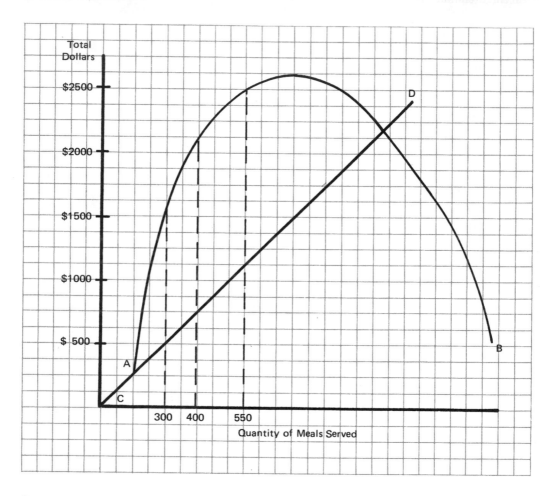

Problem 3

1. The marginal cost is $3.00. What is the break-even point where marginal revenue equals marginal cost?
2. What happens when you produce a quantity of goods that is to the right of where the marginal cost curve and the marginal revenue curve intersect?
3. What happens when you produce a quantity of goods that is to the left of the break-even point?

Problem 3 (continued)

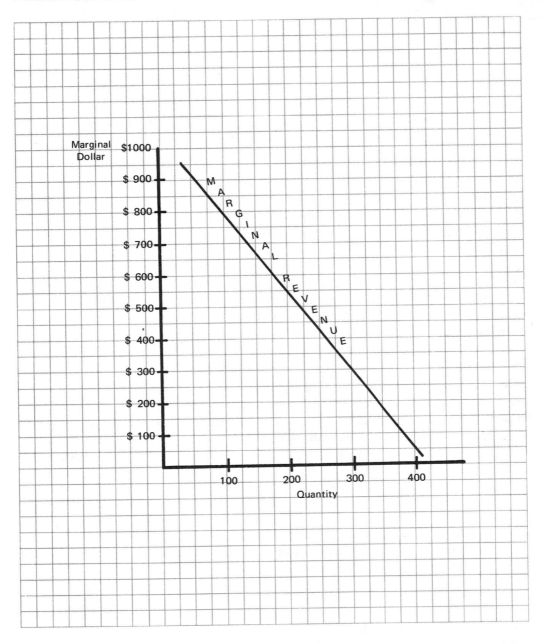

CHAPTER 16

Responsibility Accounting in the Hospitality Service Industries

A wide variety of personalized services and specialized functions are offered in the hospitality service industries. The dynamic nature of these activities has generally led to the development of organizations in which no single person directs every facet of the operation. Instead, numerous levels of limited supervision are established throughout the organization, and key persons are assigned specific responsibilities.

The concepts of planning and control, in turn, serve as the foundation upon which the accomplishment of such responsibilities rests. Based on the theory that particular individuals will assume responsibility for specific segments of a business operation, each manager must be given full authority to take necessary actions. In turn, he is held accountable for achieving desired results.

These elements are obviously closely interrelated; not so obvious, though, is the fact that their effective operation is dependent to a large extent on the availability of a complete reporting system. In general, reports are merely a means of communication within a firm. From a managerial viewpoint, however, these reports allow the monitoring of the actions of individuals as they strive to achieve objectives for which they are responsible.

Responsibility accounting, then, is the theory and the system through which:

1. Authority is given to specified personnel.
2. Each person in authority is held accountable for attaining planned objectives.
3. The actions of responsible individuals are monitored.
4. Relevant data are transmitted to those responsible for conceiving and executing the company's planning and control functions.

The hospitality service industries offer an excellent opportunity for studying the concept of responsibility accounting. Since organizations are normally organized in terms of departmental activities, only a limited number of people are responsible to any one superior. The success of most hospitality service industries organizations is thus closely associated with a superior's abilities to organize and administer employee activity. His continuous observation of employee activities is particularly vital because of the nature of services. If service is inadequate, customer dissatisfaction occurs immediately, and serious damage to the facility's reputation can occur if significant problems persist in an operating area.

These circumstances make the pinpointing of responsibility and the monitoring of employee activities especially important. The responsibility accounting system can therefore offer valuable assistance to the managerial process. Plans serve as guides to action, while controls limit deviations from predetermined courses of action. The system thus provides a framework within which decisions are made, and plans, controls, and actions are correlated.

The responsibility accounting system serves to facilitate management's efforts to attain specified organizational goals. Through the responsibility accounting network, each manager receives financial information that is specifically tailored to help him as he continuously makes decisions and takes actions. At the end of the accounting period (that is, after services have been provided to customers), actual financial results will be compared to those which were projected. Significant variations between planned and actual results will be analyzed, and corrective measures will be designed to be integrated into future plans. The circular process—planning for the coming period, control of ongoing activities, and planning for the long run—goes on.

A CONCEPTUAL FRAMEWORK FOR RESPONSIBILITY ACCOUNTING

Four fundamental concepts—authority, planning, control, and accountability—provide the basic structure for the responsibility accounting system. These fundamental elements are identified in Exhibit 16.1.

Authority. Authority provides the basis for the system. Managers must be given broad powers so that they are free to make all decisions considered necessary to provide quality services. This authority makes it possible to execute the organization's plans and controls.

Planning (Action). The manager's job is to select and accomplish those actions which most effectively satisfy the organization's aims. The best available course of action should be chosen only after thoroughly considering both the environment and the personnel influencing the firm's operations.

Control (Achievement). Control is the attempt to eliminate deviations between actual and planned results, thereby insuring that the firm meets its planned objectives. When achievements differ significantly from planned results, the responsible manager must take quick action to correct the cause of the deviation.

EXHIBIT 16.1

A Conceptual Framework
for Responsibility Accounting

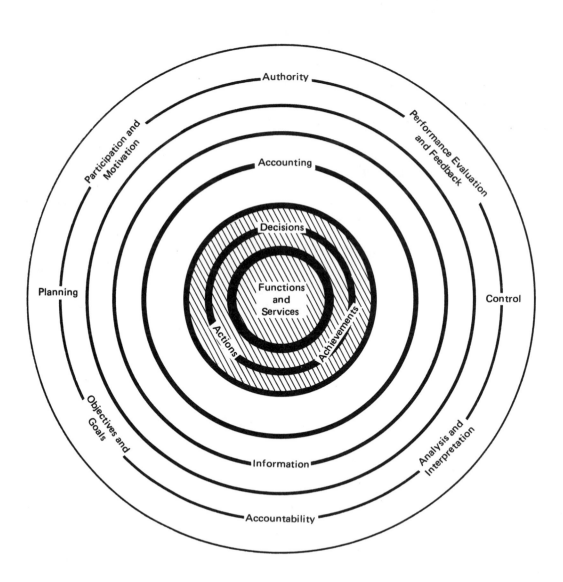

Accountability. Accountability insures that managers are held responsible for the results they have achieved. Although the manager is free to select and implement particular courses of action, such freedom obviously is not boundless. It is limited to some degree, in that the manager must account to his superiors for his achievements. If his results prove to be consistently unacceptable, his power (authority) to act freely probably will be restricted.

LINKS BETWEEN THE CONCEPTS

These fundamental concepts are not totally independent. Four additional elements provide a link between them. Each of these additional elements plays a significant role in the operation of an effective responsibility accounting system.

Participation and Motivation. Authority and accountability alone do not insure that operations will be performed effectively. Psychological studies reveal that employees often are influenced favorably by being allowed to participate in setting the goals toward which they will direct their efforts. These same personnel are also an excellent source of performance information.

Managers are primarily responsible for motivating employees to perform functions more efficiently. From a psychological standpoint, the firm's goals are intended to stimulate actions at all levels in the organization; managers have a responsibility to guide these actions in order to achieve planned results.

Objectives and Goals. Establishing reasonable objectives and goals is essential to the management process. They also provide a starting point when developing formal financial plans for the firm. In general, the accounting system provides information about the results of past operations; based on assumptions and quantitative projections, this process translates operational goals into a financial framework. Guidelines formulated in the planning and control process are thus projected in the form of financial statements. The end result of this process is a proforma or projected balance sheet and a proforma income statement. These provide a synthesis of management's objectives and goals in a financial perspective—a financial plan which can lead the firm to successful accomplishment of its objectives.

Analysis and Interpretation. After reports are prepared, the manager's emphasis again shifts. Now he must analyze the summarized data, considering thoroughly both the probable causes of events and the effects which they generate. Using this approach, he should be able to draw these data into a more meaningful context. These reports, analyses, and related interpretations comprise the basis for management action.

Performance Evaluation and Feedback. The management process culminates in performance evaluation. The quality of functions performed and services rendered throughout the organization are considered, and every responsible individual is held accountable for his actions. Accountability is thus effected by measuring and appraising the firm's progress toward attaining its objectives.

Management is responsible for providing "feedback" information to those who are taking actions. Using these data, managers and employees should be able to determine whether their achievements and performance levels are consistent with those planned.

DECISIONS, ACTIONS, AND ACHIEVEMENTS

The center of the framework represents the core of activity in any firm—its operations. Managers must continuously evaluate functions and services performed, and decisions must be made regarding the need to effect changes in the current system. Actions are taken which ideally will result in desired achievements. Although all such activities are not revenue-producing in nature, they undoubtedly comprise the essence of a firm's existence—the hub around which the wheel of operations revolves.

ACCOUNTING INFORMATION

The accounting system is concerned generally with accumulating financial data (accounting information) as transactions are completed. As services are provided to customers, monetary amounts are recorded. After being summarized in the proper accounts, the data are integrated into formal financial statements—the balance sheet and the income statement. It is easy to see why the management process is tied relatively closely to accounting activities. Plans are often expressed in terms of financial data, and controls are effected by comparing actual to planned financial results. Thus, accounting information is vital to achieving managerial effectiveness.

Managers rely more and more on financial data. Decision-making information must be obtained from every area in the organization, and, in turn, must be forwarded to all affected personnel. The accounting system must operate effectively at all times if the manager is to achieve desired results. It follows, further, that a manager must thoroughly understand the accounting operations to be able to use its output effectively in executing his responsibilities.

The accounting system operates to assign monetary values to actions taken (providing goods and/or services to customers) and results achieved (profits generated from operations or satisfactory services performed). The dollar effects of these operations are translated into terms of the firm's overall financial position.

Statements and reports are developed to convey these data to managers, thereby giving them an objective foundation on which to base decisions. Certain requirements must be satisfied, however, if these data are to be useful to operating managers.

INFORMATION STANDARDS

Because financial data are so vital to management effectiveness, standards should be established to guide their development and transmission. Four standards are proposed as general guidelines to assist in attaining this objective. These standards are understandability, reliability and accuracy, timeliness, and clarity in reporting format.

Understandability. Understandability dictates that the decision-making manager must be able to evaluate easily all data provided.

Further, data must relate closely to the daily decisions that are required in his position. The standard thus clearly recognizes the need for tailoring information to specific needs of individuals in the organization. Since facilitating the decision-making process is the underlying purpose of responsibility accounting, this standard is most significant. It is the fundamental principle around which all information-providing functions must revolve.

Reliability and accuracy. The reliability and accuracy standard is based on the principle that decisions made by managers can be no better than the information on which they are based. If inaccurate or unreliable data are used in making decisions, it is highly probable that actions taken will fail to accomplish planned results. The accounting system is designed to insure that data are reasonably accurate and reliable.

Timeliness. The timeliness standard is predicated on the assumption that the effective use of data requires timely transmission to points in the organization where actions are to be taken. Thus, information must be developed and transmitted to the responsible manager in time to prevent the reoccurence of unsatisfactory results. Since managers are often required to make almost instantaneous decisions regarding functions performed and services rendered, they would be severely handicapped if relevant data were not available at the proper times. Inefficiencies in the transmission system thus prove most damaging to the overall effectiveness of responsibility accounting in an organization.

Clarity in Reporting Format. The requirement of clarity in reporting format is closely related to the first standard, understandability. If data are not clearly presented, the manager may have difficulty in selecting those bits of information which are most relevant to the decisions he must make. It is important, therefore, to develop a relatively constant format for reporting purposes. In this way, key information can be extracted immediately. Exception reporting becomes a valuable technique here.

The importance of these standards will become much more apparent as we continue our discussions of responsibility accounting. It is recognized generally that success in managing firms in the hospitality service industries hinges to a large extent on the performance of planning and control functions. First, management is responsible for establishing meaningful goals in each operating area. These goals are complemented by a network of control procedures. When integrated properly, the system should insure that reasonable progress toward the attainment of stipulated objectives is being accomplished.

Responsibility accounting thus provides a framework within which goals and controls can be integrated into an operational setting. This system provides explicitly for the implementation of authority, action, achievement, and accountability in the management process. Successful and profitable organizations in the hospitality service industries generally rely on the effectiveness with which the responsibility accounting system operates from day to day.

RESPONSIBILITY CENTERS

A primary objective of the responsibility accounting system is to provide information for those making planning and control decisions. Ideally, the system focuses only on those elements which can be influenced directly by a manager's action. Thus, it is extremely important that the scope of each manager's authority and responsibility be defined rigorously before plans and controls are formally developed.

To establish a general foundation for these purposes organizations are segmented. The scope of a manager's authority is defined in terms of a "center" of activity in the organization for which he is ultimately responsible. This segment of the firm is termed a "responsibility center." Within this specialized center, one designated individual is held accountable for performance during a given period of time.

Responsibility centers may be classified generally into four distinct categories: investment centers, profit centers, revenue centers, and cost centers. The scope of managerial authority and responsibility declines as the number of controllable elements is reduced. For example, at the higher levels of management the executive's performance is measured in terms of his ability to earn the desired return on investments. Therefore, this responsible individual must have influence on the investment base as well as revenues and costs. In a profit center, the manager is evaluated only in terms of revenues and costs; thus, investments in assets are considered to fall beyond his scope of authority and accountability. The managers of revenue and cost centers restrict their attention to revenues generated or to costs incurred, whichever is the primary controllable factor. These classifications, although not perfect, offer a good definitional basis for studying the nature of a responsibility accounting system.

Investment Centers. Investment centers represent the broadest segment of a responsibility accounting system. These may be locations, or divisions, in a large volume operation. The responsible executive's performance is evaluated in terms of both the assets that are available for his use and the net income after tax that is generated by his utilization of these resources. An individual responsible for an investment center has authority to make decisions regarding the level of investment in his area of responsibility. He is accountable also for both revenues generated and costs incurred (net profit) in the process of providing goods and services to customers. As plans and controls are developed for guiding activities, attention must be devoted to each of these factors. All data provided must similarly be tailored to include each of these factors, since decisions are likely to be influenced significantly by these variables.

For example, consider a motor-hotel having a $1 million investment in facilities—land, building, furniture and fixtures. The manager is responsible primarily for generating net income through the use of these resources. Let's assume that his target is an after-tax return on investment of 10 percent, a net income of $100,000 on the present $1 million investment. The manager has authority to make decisions which have a direct influence on this return. He can decide to expand the size of the motel, thereby increasing the investment base; he has authority to adjust the price structure to increase revenues earned; and he can make decisions regarding the level of costs to be incurred at present or in the future. In these ways, the manager works to obtain the highest attainable return— net income on the investment in facilities—during each operating period.

Profit Centers. Profit centers are defined to include responsibility only for revenues earned and costs incurred in a particular segment of the organization. The manager in charge of a profit center is responsible for a more specific phase of operation: the profits generated from services rendered in the area over which he has control. Profits are defined for these purposes as the difference between revenues earned and direct costs that are traceable to and controllable in this segment of the organization.

The narrowing of authority stems from the fact that a manager in charge of a profit center is held neither responsible nor accountable for changes in the asset base. Although his decisions may influence, to some extent, the amounts of resources invested in a particular area of operation, he is primarily concerned with optimizing the profits that are generated from the activities over which he assumes responsibility. Thus, he must focus his primary attention on revenues and costs because his performance is judged on the profitability of his responsibility center.

In general the profit center manager has authority to make decisions regarding policies on revenue and cost matters. He can decide to change the price on a menu item—or all menu items if it is deemed necessary—and he is authorized similarly to manage costs. He may choose to increase or decrease expenditures in a particular cost category—the wage levels paid to a specialized group of employees, the cost incurred in preventative maintenance programs, or any of the other costs for which he is responsible. His performance, measured in terms of profits earned, is thus dependent almost wholly on his ability to effectively manage relevant revenue and cost factors.

Revenue and Cost Centers. Revenue and cost centers are even more narrow in scope than profit centers. The supervisor or department head responsible for activities at this level in the organization is evaluated in terms of his ability either to generate revenues or to achieve cost levels consistent with planned amounts. His authority is limited to decisions which relate to either of these two factors. He is judged on a more limited criterion than are the previous levels of management because his decision will affect only one of the specified categories.

A department head responsible for a revenue center might thus be concerned only with obtaining bookings or revenues for future periods. His performance is measured in terms of his ability to attain predetermined revenue goals. Let us assume, for example, that top management has determined that his facility must strive to attain a 25 percent increase in revenues during the next three years. The manager responsible for bookings might set his personal target at an increase of 7 percent in revenues each year.[1] His responsibility, therefore, is restricted to revenue-generating activities; he can make decisions affecting only future bookings, and is held accountable only for actions taken in satisfying this responsibility.

Similarly, a department head who is responsible for managing a cost center is restricted to those factors which have a direct effect on the cost structure in his specific operation. The department head in charge of food preparation, as an example, is authorized to manage any element in that specified activity. He is authorized to grant wage increases as long as they comply with overall management policy, and he similarly has authority to influence the number of employee hours worked in a particular period.

In general, it is important to note that the scope of responsibility becomes more limited as the focus shifts downward from level to level in the organization. The number of controllable factors decreases as authority limits become more

---

1. Seven percent compounded for three years equals approximately 25 percent.

restricted. Likewise, the degree to which the department head in a cost center is held accountable for actions differs significantly from a manager's responsibility for either investment or profit centers.

When considering the concepts involved in responsibility accounting, it is important also to keep in mind that managers are often evaluated in terms of their abilities to meet specified goals. Each manager strives to achieve targets that have been established for his own level of authority and accountability. If his scope of responsibility has been defined rigorously during the planning stage and specified goals are reasonably attainable, the manager should find the task of achieving the targets a bona fide challenge.

DEVELOPING A PRACTICAL RESPONSIBILITY ACCOUNTING SYSTEM

Responsibility accounting operates in conjunction with the firm's organizational structure. To illustrate these important relationships, an organization chart for Hospitality Services, Inc., is presented (Exhibit 16.2). In this hypothetical organization, each vice-president reports directly to the president. It will be noted that only subordinates to the vice-president of operations are identified specifically. Were the chart expanded more fully, each of the functional areas would be enlarged accordingly (for example, a treasurer and/or controller would be shown as reporting to the vice-president of accounting and finance).

Hospitality Services, Inc., consists of six operating locations. Each facility functions under the guidance of a general manager and his two principal subordinates—a lodging manager and a food and beverage manager. These managers, in turn, are responsible primarily for guiding the activities of department heads. Reporting to the lodging manager are department heads for the front desk, housekeeping, and the various functional service departments. The food and beverage manager, in turn, assumes responsibility for activities of department heads in food and beverage purchasing, food preparation, food service and beverage operations.

The organization chart serves also as a method of pinpointing the formal communication channels that exist within a firm. Data flowing along these lines facilitate decision-making at all levels in the organization, from the president to the department heads. Initially, goals are established at each level in the organization and plans are formulated to guide all operating activities. Managers are given authority to take all necessary actions, achievements are recorded, and each responsible individual is held accountable for the activities that have taken place within his operating area.

In practice, implementing a responsibility accounting system requires that each of the key concepts—authority, action achievement, and accountability—be combined into an integrated network. One approach to accomplishing such

EXHIBIT 16.2

The Operation of Responsibility Accounting
An Organizational Structure

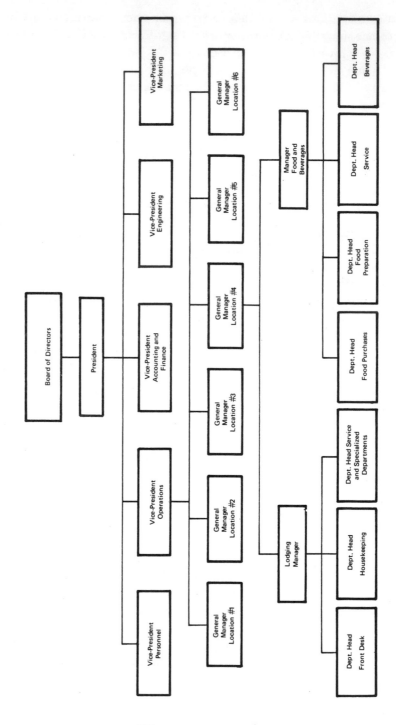

integration, for example, is to establish a set of performance evaluation criteria (Exhibit 16.3).

EXHIBIT 16.3

Performance Evaluation Criteria

President
  A. Total Profitability
  B. Return on Investment—Assets
  C. Return on Owner's Equity

Vice-President, Operations
  A. Return on Sales*
  B. Return on Assets Employed

General Manager
  A. Location "Controllable" Net Income**
  B. Return on Location Sales
  C. Return on Location Assets
  D. Revenue/Cost Relationships

Manager
  A. Contribution Margin***
  B. Payroll Costs and/or Food and Beverage Costs

Department Head
  A. Costs Incurred
  B. Productivity (Direct Payroll)/(Revenues Generated)

*Net income before tax divided by net sales.
**Sales revenue less direct location costs.
***Sales revenue less direct departmental costs.

In this exhibit, the scope of accountability narrows as the authority is reduced at each level. The president, since he has full authority to take any action that he deems desirable, is held accountable for the total profitability of the firm, the return on all of its assets, and the return to owners. A vice-president's authority is generally restricted to more specific activities (operations, personnel, accounting and finance, engineering, marketing, and others). He is held accountable for only a designated segment of the operations. In this illustration, the performance of the vice-president of operations is measured in terms of return on sales (that is, relationship of income before tax to net sales). Tax rates are thus considered to be uncontrollable in this vice-president's capacity.

The same narrowing process is accomplished at each succeeding responsibility level; the firm is segregated into responsibility centers. Performance at each succeeding level of mangement is evaluated by considering only those elements over which the executive in charge has control. Thus, the scope of the manager's authority and accountability dictates both the nature and the size of the responsibility center within which he operates.

AN ILLUSTRATED RESPONSIBILITY ACCOUNTING FRAMEWORK

The illustrations presented in Exhibits 16.4 through 16.9 represent a sample framework of financial data. These projected statements serve two purposes. First, the illustrations correlate the organization chart (Exhibit 16.2) with the specified performance evaluation criteria (Exhibit 16.3). Second, they illustrate the responsibility accounting system's ability to facilitate the planning and control process.

DEFINING TOP MANAGEMENT RESPONSIBILITIES

In any organization, the top level of management is generally responsible for activities in an investment center. Since these executives are vested with broad responsibilities, their scope of authority and accountability covers a larger span in the organization.

Proforma statements are presented as a starting point in considering top management's responsibilities. Both the balance sheet and the income statement contain data that are used to establish relevant guidelines and ratios for planning and controlling purposes at this level. For example, it might be assumed that in a future year the firm is interested in expanding its asset base. A corresponding increase in sales is expected, and relatively constant return ratios (returns on investment, sales, and assets) are similarly planned.

These general objectives are easily translated into numerical targets. For instance, the Hospitality Services, Inc., reflected $9,000,000 in assets on its balance sheet at the beginning of 1971. The firm's general objectives state that it should strive for at least a 10 percent annual increase in assets; thus, if $10,000,000 in assets are owned at December 31, 1971 (Exhibit 16.4), the target will have been exceeded.

In general, it is expected that the firm in 1971 will generate approximately $0.50 in sales for each dollar invested in assets. Using this guideline relationship, a $5,000,000 sales projection is an appropriate target (Exhibit 16.5).

Given this estimate of annual sales, the president is responsible further for achieving an adequate return. The owners of Hospitality Services, Inc., use the following returns as targets:

Return on Assets	3%
Return on Sales	6%
Return on Owner's Equity	5%

EXHIBIT 16.4

Hospitality Industries, Inc.
Proforma Balance Sheet
December 31, 1971

Current Assets			Current Liabilities		
Cash	$	600,000	Accounts Payable	$	300,000
Accounts Receivable		200,000	Notes Payable, Current		600,000
Inventory		200,000	Other Current Liabilities		100,000
Other Current Assets		200,000			
Total Current Assets	$	1,200,000	Total Current Liabilities	$	1,000,000
Fixed Assets			Long-term Liabilities		
Land	$	3,000,000	Mortgage Payable	$	3,000,000
Buildings		5,000,000			
Furniture and Fixtures		2,000,000	Owner's Equity		
	$	10,000,000	Capital Stock	$	5,000,000
Less: Accumulated			Retained Earnings		1,000,000
Depreciation		1,200,000	Total Owner's Equity	$	6,000,000
Total Fixed Assets	$	8,800,000	Total Liabilities		
Total Assets	$	10,000,000	and Owner's Equity	$	10,000,000

EXHIBIT 16.5

Hospitality Industries, Inc.
Proforma Income Statement
for the Year Ended December 31, 1971

Sales	$5,000,000
Cost of Sales	1,000,000
Gross Profit	$4,000,000
Direct Departmental Expense	1,500,000
Operating Income	$2,500,000
Indirect Expenses	800,000
Contribution to Fixed Costs	$1,700,000
Fixed Costs	1,100,000
Net Income Before Tax	$ 600,000
Income Taxes, Federal and State	300,000
Net Income After Tax	$ 300,000

Translated into terms of the pro forma financial statements, it will be noted that the specified target ratios are achieved (Exhibit 16.6). Net income after tax is $300,000, the amount required for achieving desired return levels. The president's authority to act and his accountability for results can be clearly perceived in this setting. The illustrations serve to portray responsibilities of the president as they are viewed in a responsibility accounting context.

EXHIBIT 16.6

Operational Goals
Responsibility Center—President/Total Firm
for the Year Ended December 31, 1971

I. Return on Assets $= \dfrac{\text{Net Income after Taxes}}{\text{Total Assets}} = \dfrac{\$300,000}{\$10,000,000^*} = 3\%$

II. Return on Sales $= \dfrac{\text{Net Income after Taxes}}{\text{Total Period Sales}} = \dfrac{\$300,000}{\$5,000,000} = 6\%$

III. Return on Owner's Equity $= \dfrac{\text{Net Income after Taxes}}{\text{Total Owner's Equity}} = \dfrac{\$300,000}{\$6,000,000} = 5\%$

*Total assets used in attaining the net income.

DEFINING OTHER MANAGEMENT RESPONSIBILITIES

As the scope of management responsibility decreases, the firm is segmented into smaller and more specialized operating areas. Referring to Exhibit 16.7, it will be noted that the vice-president of operations is concerned primarily, in this hypothetical situation, with net income before tax. This scope of responsibility is not quite as broad as that at the presidential level. The presumption is that the vice-president of operations has no control over major tax-planning decisions. Instead, he restricts his focus to matters relating directly to operating assets, revenues, and costs throughout the organization. Broader policy decisions are made by the president and other vice-presidents (marketing, finance, etc.).

The general manager at each location is concerned with still a more limited scope of responsibility. Although the net income before tax orientation is similar to that of the operations' vice-president, the unit manager uses a somewhat different reference point as his target. He is accountable only for the revenues and costs that occur at location #4. Also relevant is the fact that he is responsible for managing only those resources that are found in that one location (Exhibit 16.8).

When considered in terms of ratios, both the vice-president of operations and the general manager (location #4) are responsible for the return on assets and return on sales (Exhibit 16.9).

EXHIBIT 16.7

Hospitality Industries, Inc.
Proforma Income Statement
for the Year Ended December 31, 1971

	I	II	III	IV		V	
				Location #4		Location #4	
						Lodging Dept. Head	Food and Beverage Dept. Head
	President	Vice-President Operations	General Manager Location #4	Manager Lodging	Manager Food and Beverage	Rooms	Beverages
Sales	$5,000,000	$5,000,000	$1,000,000	$570,000	$430,000		
Cost of Sales	1,000,000	1,000,000	180,000	-	160,000		$ 80
Gross Profit	$4,000,000	$4,000,000	$ 820,000	$570,000	$270,000		
Direct Departmental Expenses	1,500,000	1,500,000	270,000	170,000	125,000	$100*	$ 20**
Gross Operating Income	$2,500,000	$2,500,000	$ 550,000	$400,000	$145,000	$100	$100
Deductions from Income	800,000	800,000	200,000				
Contribution to Fixed Costs	$1,700,000	$1,700,000	$ 350,000				
Fixed Costs	1,100,000	1,100,000	230,000				
Net Income Before Tax	$ 600,000	$ 600,000	$ 120,000				
Income Tax	300,000						
Net Income After Tax	$ 300,000						

Level of Responsibility

*Operating expenses (salaries $95 and supplies $5).

**Wages.

EXHIBIT 16.8

Hospitality Industries, Inc.
Balance Sheet
December 31, 1971

	Total Organization	Location #4
Current Assets		
Cash	$ 600,000	$ 100,000
Accounts Receivable	200,000	50,000
Inventory	250,000	50,000
Other Current Assets	200,000	
Total Current Assets	$ 1,200,000	$ 200,000
Fixed Assets		
Land	$ 2,000,000	$ 500,000
Buildings	5,000,000	1,200,000
Furniture and Fixtures	3,000,000	300,000
	$10,000,000	$2,000,000
Less: Accumulated Depreciation	(1,200,000)	(200,000)
Total Fixed Assets	$ 8,800,000	$1,800,000
Total Assets	$10,000,000	$2,000,000

		Total Organization	Location #4
Current Liabilities			
Accounts Payable		$ 300,000	$ 80,000
Notes Payable, Current		600,000	60,000
Other Current Liabilities		100,000	60,000
Total Current Liabilities		$ 1,000,000	$ 200,000
Long-term Liabilities			
Mortgage Payable		$ 3,000,000	$ 800,000
Owner's Equity			
Capital Stock	$5,000,000		
Retained Earnings	1,000,000		
Total Owner's Equity		$ 6,000,000	$1,000,000
Total Liabilities and Owner's Equity		$10,000,000	$2,000,000

EXHIBIT 16.9

Return on Assets and Return on Sales

	Vice-President Operations	General Manager Location #4
Return on Assets	$\dfrac{\$600,000}{\$10,000,000} = 6\%$	$\dfrac{\$120,000}{\$2,000,000} = 6\%$
Return on Sales	$\dfrac{\$600,000}{\$\ 5,000,000} = 12\%$	$\dfrac{\$120,000}{\$1,000,000} = 12\%$

It is particularly important to recognize that the scope of authority and accountability declines as we proceed downward in the organizational hierarchy. (Note the declines in assets and sales for which each executive is responsible.)

DEPARTMENTAL CONTRIBUTION MARGINS

The lodging and food and beverage department heads are oriented to an even narrower goal; their respective departmental contributions are lodging, $400,000; and food and beverage, $145,000. The elements included in determining the departmental contribution factor are controllable by the particular manager. These data reflect each of the division's relative contributions to the coverage of overall fixed costs throughout the organization.

The lowest level in the organization, the department head, is guided to a target that is still more limited in scope. This standard is based on the premise that department heads operate most effectively by restricting their attention to controlling only the planned costs in their segment of the operation. The department head in charge of rooms, etc., is depicted as being responsible for salaries ($95) and supplies ($5), while the beverage department head is concerned with the costs of beverages sold ($80) and the wages in this area ($20). The purpose is to restrict focus to those elements (in this example, direct departmental expenses) over which the department head can exert influence. Only in this way can the standards assume the meaningful stature that is so vital to the operation of the responsibility accounting system.

RANGES OF ACCEPTABLE PERFORMANCE LEVELS

In conjunction with the need to define a set of desired operating targets, it is worthwhile to consider one possible expansion. In principle, the modification recognizes the basic fact that many managers find it nearly impossible to predict exactly the level of performance they can expect in a specific hospitality service industry situation. Furthermore, most supervisory personnel readily admit that relatively few service employees can be expected to perform at a continuous level of excellence. For this reason, it has been suggested that the performance evaluation format explicitly recognize the various possible levels of output relative to a given standard.[2] Graphically, this is illustrated in Exhibit 16.10.

EXHIBIT 16.10
Standards Relative to Levels of Output

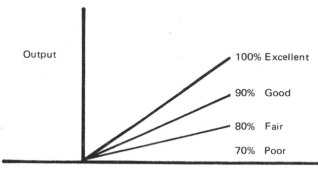

If a responsible manager (or any employee) consistently attains 100 percent of the desired standard during a stated period, his performance is evaluated as excellent. (Similarly, 90 percent of quota may be rated as good, etc.). The intrinsic value of this approach is that personnel performance evaluations are not based on an absolute scale.

SUMMARY

Responsibility accounting is the reporting structure whereby managers, department heads, and supervisors are periodically informed of the performance of their responsibility centers. Conceptually, responsibility accounting is much broader in that it guides the organizational structure of an organization and establishes the means by which the organization's objectives may be achieved. Planning ultimately is broken down to responsibility centers and control accomplished by responsibility centers.

The scope of the responsibility center differs with the management level, managers at higher levels having broader responsibilities. At the highest levels the responsibility centers are investment centers, at middle management levels the centers are profit centers, and at lower levels they are cost or revenue centers.

Individual managers may be evaluated on the basis of how close they were to achieving their goals.

2. Chester A. Sneider, "Setting Operating Goals and Measuring Achievements," *NAA Bulletin*, July, 1958, pp. 25-31.

Discussion Questions

1. What is responsibility accounting?
2. List and explain the four fundamental concepts which provide the basic structure for a responsibility accounting system.
3. What elements link the fundamental concepts into an effective system?
4. List and briefly explain the information standards.
5. Explain the term "responsibility center" and list the four categories or types of centers.
6. How is a responsibility accounting system implemented?
7. Explain the "narrowing" process of responsibility accounting.

Problem 1

SAM'S RESTAURANT, INC.
Balance Sheet Accounts
December 31, 1970

	Debits	Credits
Other Current Assets	$ 300,000	
Accounts Payable		$ 250,000
Notes Payable		700,000
Cash	400,000	
Land	2,500,000	
Accounts Receivable	150,000	
Buildings	5,000,000	
Other Current Liabilities		250,000
Mortgage Payable		2,000,000
Furniture and Fixtures	3,000,000	
Capital Stock		4,600,000
Retained Earnings		750,000
Inventory	200,000	
Accumulated Depreciation		3,000,000

SAM'S RESTAURANT, INC.
Income Statement
for Year Ended December 31, 1970

Sales	$6,000,000
Cost of Sales	1,500,000
Gross Profit	$4,500,000
Direct Departmental Expense	2,000,000
Operating Income	$2,500,000
Indirect Expenses	500,000
Contribution to Fixed Cost	$2,000,000
Fixed Cost	500,000
Net Income Before Tax	$1,500,000
Income Tax	750,000
Net Income After Tax	$ 750,000

Problem 1 (continued)

Required

1. Prepare a balance sheet in good form.
2. Compute the following:
   (a) Return on assets
   (b) Return on sales
   (c) Return on owner's equity

Problem 2

SAM'S LODGE

Balance Sheet
December 31, 1970

Assets

	Total Organization	Location #4
Current Assets		
Cash	$ 400,000	$ 100,000
Accounts Receivable	250,000	50,000
Inventory	200,000	75,000
Other Current Assets	300,000	200,000
Total Current Assets	$ 1,150,000	$ 425,000
Fixed Assets		
Land	$ 1,000,000	$ 500,000
Building	7,000,000	3,000,000
Furniture and Fixtures	3,000,000	1,500,000
	$11,000,000	$5,000,000
Less: Accumulated Depreciation	3,000,000	1,500,000
Total Fixed Assets	$ 8,000,000	$3,500,000
Total Assets	$ 9,150,000	$3,925,000

Liabilities and Owner's Equity

Current Liabilities		
Accounts Payable	$ 500,000	$ 300,000
Notes Payable, Current	200,000	100,000
Other Current Liabilities	400,000	200,000
Total Current Liabilities	$ 1,100,000	$ 600,000
Long-term Liabilities		
Mortgage Payable	$ 4,000,000	$1,500,000
Owner's Equity		
Capital Stock	$ 3,000,000	$1,500,000
Retained Earnings	1,050,000	325,000
Total Owner's Equity	$ 4,050,000	$1,825,000
Total Liabilities and Owner's Equity	$ 9,150,000	$3,925,000

Problem 2 (continued)

SAM'S LODGE
Proforma Income Statement
for Year Ended December 31, 1970

	Level of Responsibility						
	I	II	III	IV Location #4		V Location #4	
	President	Vice-President Operations	General Manager Location #4	Manager Lodging	Manager Food and Beverage	Lodging Dept. Head Rooms	Food and Beverage Dept. Head Beverages
Sales	$7,500,000	$7,500,000	$2,000,000	$1,200,000	$800,000		$ 400
Cost of Sales	2,000,000	2,000,000	500,000	300,000	200,000		
Gross Profit	$5,500,000	$5,500,000	$1,500,000	$ 900,000	$600,000		
Direct Departmental Expenses	1,000,000	1,000,000	400,000	250,000	150,000		100
Gross Operating Income	$4,500,000	$4,500,000	$1,100,000	$ 650,000	$450,000	$ 500	
Deductions from Income	2,500,000	2,500,000	600,000	350,000	250,000	$ 500	$ 500
Contribution to Fixed Costs	$2,000,000	$2,000,000	$ 500,000	$ 300,000	$200,000		
Fixed Costs	1,000,000	1,000,000	200,000				
Net Income before Tax	$1,000,000	$1,000,000	$ 300,000				
Income Tax	500,000						
Net Income after Tax	$ 500,000						

Problem 2 (continued)

Required

Compute the following ratios.

1. President
   (a) Return on investment—assets
   (b) Return on owner's equity
2. Vice-President
   (a) Return on sales
   (b) Return on assets employed
3. General Manager
   (a) Location "controllable" net income
   (b) Return on location sales
   (c) Return on location assets
4. Manager
   (a) Contribution margin

Problem 3

Required

Compute the following ratios.

1. Prepare for the total organization:
   (a) Return on investment assets
   (b) Return on owner's equity
   (c) Return on sales
2. Compute for each department:
   (a) Location "controllable" net income
   (b) Return on location sales
   (c) Return on location assets

Problem 3 (continued)

Western Resorts, Inc.
Balance Sheet
December 31, 1970

Assets	Total Organization	Department Number 1	Department Number 2	Department Number 3	Department Number 4	Department Number 5
Current Assets						
Cash	$ 1,000,000	$ 300,000	$ 175,000	$ 150,000	$ 200,000	$ 175,000
Accounts Receivable	500,000	150,000	100,000	75,000	125,000	50,000
Inventory	300,000	100,000	50,000	25,000	75,000	50,000
Other Current Assets	700,000	300,000	100,000	75,000	150,000	75,000
Total Current Assets	$ 2,500,000	$ 850,000	$ 425,000	$ 325,000	$ 550,000	$ 350,000
Fixed Assets						
Land	$ 2,000,000	$ 800,000	$ 300,000	$ 200,000	$ 400,000	$ 300,000
Buildings	4,000,000	1,500,000	750,000	500,000	750,000	500,000
Furniture and Fixtures	3,000,000	750,000	500,000	500,000	750,000	500,000
	$ 9,000,000	$3,050,000	$1,550,000	$1,200,000	$1,900,000	$1,300,000
Less: Accumulated Depreciation	1,500,000	500,000	200,000	200,000	300,000	300,000
Total Fixed Assets	$ 7,500,000	$2,550,000	$1,350,000	$1,000,000	$1,600,000	$1,000,000
Total Assets	$10,000,000	$3,400,000	$1,775,000	$1,325,000	$2,150,000	$1,350,000
Liabilities and Owner's Equity						
Current Liabilities						
Accounts Payable	$ 500,000	$ 125,000	$ 75,000	$ 100,000	$ 100,000	$ 100,000
Notes Payable, Current	300,000	100,000	50,000	25,000	50,000	75,000
Other Current Liabilities	300,000	75,000	100,000	50,000	25,000	50,000
Total Current Liabilities	$ 1,075,000	$ 300,000	$ 225,000	$ 175,000	$ 175,000	$ 200,000
Long-term Liabilities						
Mortgage Payable	$ 4,000,000	$1,000,000	900,000	300,000	$1,025,000	
Owner's Equity						
Capital Stock	$ 4,000,000	$1,000,000	$ 500,000	$ 750,000	$ 750,000	$1,000,000
Retained Earnings	900,000	300,000	150,000	100,000	200,000	150,000
Total Owner's Equity	$ 4,900,000	$1,300,000	$ 650,000	$ 850,000	$ 950,000	$1,150,000
Total Liabilities and Owner's Equity	$10,000,000	$3,400,000	$1,775,000	$1,325,000	$2,150,000	$1,350,000

Western Resorts, Inc.
Income Statement
for the Year Ended December 31, 1970

	Total Organization	Department Number 1	Department Number 2	Department Number 3	Department Number 4	Department Number 5
Sales	$7,000,000	$2,000,000	$1,250,000	$1,000,000	$1,500,000	$1,250,000
Cost of Sales	2,000,000	750,000	250,000	250,000	500,000	250,000
Gross Profit	$5,000,000	$1,250,000	$1,000,000	$ 750,000	$1,000,000	$1,000,000
Direct Departmental Expense	1,000,000	300,000	175,000	150,000	200,000	175,000
Gross Operating Income	$4,000,000	$ 950,000	$ 825,000	$ 600,000	$ 800,000	$ 825,000
Deductions from Income	1,500,000	400,000	350,000	200,000	300,000	250,000
Contribution to Fixed Cost	$2,500,000	$ 550,000	$ 475,000	$ 400,000	$ 500,000	$ 575,000
Fixed Cost	1,500,000	300,000	275,000	200,000	350,000	375,000
Net Income Before Tax	$1,000,000	$ 250,000	$ 200,000	$ 200,000	$ 150,000	$ 200,000
Income Tax	500,000	125,000	100,000	100,000	75,000	100,000
Net Income After Tax	$ 500,000	$ 125,000	$ 100,000	$ 100,000	$ 75,000	$ 100,000

CHAPTER 17

Budgeting—Profit Planning

Organizations with objectives need plans in order to accomplish their objectives with the minimum allocation of resources. This plan is referred to as a *budget* or *profit plan*, and the process of preparing it is referred to as *budgeting*.

Although budgeting is referred to as profit planning, it should be recognized that in budgeting for the non-profit organizations in the hospitality service industries, the techniques and approaches used are identical. But in the educational complex, social club, or hospital, the financial objective is something other than profit, such as a residual for capital replacements and future operations, or sufficient revenues to equal expenses, or a cash excess to liquidate a loan.

Formally defined, "A business budget (profit plan) is a management plan covering all phases of operations for a definite period in the future. It is a formal expression of the policies, plans, objectives and goals established by management for the concern as a whole and for each subdivision thereon."[1]

Simply stated, the purpose of a profit plan is to achieve the maximum benefit from the resources available to an organization over a particular span of time. The benefits associated with profit planning are:

1. It is the best means for analyzing alternative courses of action and investment opportunities, and forces management to examine alternatives prior to adopting particular courses of action.

2. It compels management to examine the facts regarding what is necessary to achieve particular profit levels.

3. It provides management with a standard for comparison which is necessary for control and thus presents a means whereby control can be accomplished.

4. It allows management the opportunity to anticipate and prepare for future conditions.

5. It requires management to periodically carry out a self-evaluation of the organization and its progress towards its financial objectives.

---

1. Glenn A. Welsch, *Budgeting: Profit Planning and Control* (Englewood Cliffs, N.J.: Prentice-Hall, Inc., 1964), p. 5.

6. It provides a communication channel whereby the organization's objectives are communicated to various operating levels.
7. It provides a strong motivation to managers who have participated in the budget to establish their own operating objectives and evaluation criteria.
8. It provides management with reasonable estimates of future expense levels to assist in the setting of prices.

ANALYSES OF ALTERNATIVES

The decision-making process is the selection of the optimum course of action from two or more alternatives. The decision to follow a particular course of action may be the result of intuition, familiarity with the situation, previous experience with the same or similar circumstances, analysis of the expected outcome associated with the various alternatives, and numerous other considerations which may effect a particular decision. Most frequently, decisions result from some combination of these approaches, but the analysis of the expected outcome of alternative decisions must weigh heavily if the best possible decision is to be made.

Profit planning is the means whereby alternative operating and capital investment decisions may be evaluated in terms of their short- and/or long-range impact upon the financial performance of an organization. This is accomplished by estimating the expected revenues that should result from alternatives and the impact that alternatives may have upon other revenue generation, the costs which would result directly or indirectly from alternative courses of action, and the overall impact of alternatives upon net profit after taxes, and the future of the organization.

As a result of profit planning, management is faced with examining their estimates of what the results will be of a particular course of action and thus is likely to devote adequate time and resources to arriving at optimum decisions.

EXAMINATION OF REQUIRED PERFORMANCE

As a result of the preparation and adoption of a profit plan, management is familiar with the composition of that plan. They know what revenues must be generated from what sources, and what expense level must be held in order to achieve the planned profitability. This is in contrast to circumstances in which management has only some intuitive feel or scratch paper figures indicating what levels of sales must take place and what expenses associated with those sales should be. This incomplete and informal planning is more frequently associated with smaller businesses and organizations. However, the size of an organization is not a valid criterion for questioning the design and implementation of a profit plan. While it is certainly true that there are smaller organizations which have succeeded and even thrived without formal profit planning, this can be explained by a superior goods or service, or other managerial skills which more than compensate for the lack of a profit-planning system. With the increase in the size of an organization the likelihood of needing a formal plan for successful operation increases.

STANDARDS FOR COMPARISON

All information is relative and management information is only valuable where some means of evaluation exists. This means of evaluation is a comparison. For example, the information that an organization had a $15,000 profit this month is only useful if some comparison is available. The comparison might be last month's profit, this month's profit one year ago, or this month's planned profit. While last month's or the same month last year's profitability is interesting and may offer some insight as to the acceptability of this month's profit, the most useful comparison in an economy in which conditions are changing constantly is to some projected level of profitability based upon expected operating conditions, levels of activity, and expenses. This comparison to budgeted amounts is summarized in a projected or proforma financial or operating statement. *Proforma* is a term applied to balance sheets or other statements which are based on tentative, projected, hypothetical figures. By providing a basis of comparison, unsatisfactory conditions are revealed, and the organization is prepared to act upon these conditions in order to maximize the use of resources.

PREPAREDNESS

Advanced preparation is an absolute in the operation of a successful organization. A profit plan provides management with information as to what must be provided in order to carry out the plan, and when these resources must be available. Similarly, a profit plan will reveal to management where particular courses of action will result in the need for resources beyond the organization's present ability to provide these resources.

Frequently, there is a time lag between the beginning of the effort to obtain required resources and the time that they are available to the organization. For instance, an additional chair lift is necessary in order for a ski area to realize the planned potential. The lift must be ordered many months prior to the time of the anticipated need as financing must be arranged and the installation and testing must take place prior to the arrival of winter. Other examples of resource needs which must be anticipated include skilled or hard-to-obtain labor, various physical improvements or additions, and seasonal cash.

PERIODIC SELF-EVALUATION

The existence and proper implementation of a profit-planning system forces management to evaluate its performance and progress. Throughout the preparation of a profit plan, past performance serves as a reference point for estimates and provides a check on projections. This forced introspection can be the major source of improvements where management has the ability to use this technique of self-evaluation.

PARTICIPATION

Top management can prepare profit plans without consulting with lower levels of management, but higher-level management is not familiar with daily departmental operations. Therefore, a realistic profit plan must have the cooperation of all supervisory levels. Even with the best management information system, top management will not have continuous exposure to daily operations. Hence, the preparation and review of profit plans must involve all levels of management. The ultimate result of this involvement is a more realistic profit plan and a feeling of teamwork and cooperation.

COMMUNICATION AND MOTIVATION

The participation of all department heads in the profit-planning process results in the communication of organizational objectives and expectations of top management. When all levels of management are involved in the planning process, they must become familiar with the past performance and future expectations of the organization. When all department heads know specifically what is expected of them, upon what basis they will be evaluated, and where the organization as a unit is headed, more satisfactory performance is likely to result. And where department heads and supervisors have participated in the preparation of profit plans and their analysis and advice has been considered in that preparation, they have much more incentive and motivation to achieve the planned revenues and expense goals.

These participation, communication and motivational values of the profit planning process are underestimated by some, with the result that much of the potential benefits of the planning process are lost. A management team with well understood and agreed upon objectives is sure to contribute to success.

PRICING

Realistic pricing requires complete estimates of the total costs associated with the provision of a good or service. The profit planning process results in the best estimate of these costs for the period under consideration and thus provides the means for pricing based upon projected costs. In times of rising costs, the use of historical costs will result in prices insufficient to absorb all costs and leave a satisfactory profit margin. The estimated costs developed in a profit plan eliminate the necessity of using historical costs.

PLANNING AND CONTROL IN BUDGETING

The budgeting (profit-planning) process involves two phases, the planning phase and the budgetary control phase. Planning is the process of formulating the operating plans to accomplish predetermined objectives. Profit planning is management's thinking through all stages of the plan before any actions are taken. In the planning phase, management establishes formal objectives, projects expected levels of activity based upon the determined pricing structure, estimates the levels of costs to be incurred, and compiles this information in the form of a comprehensive profit plan.

Budgetary control is differentiated from profit planning in that it occurs after the fact. Control begins with the comparison of actual performance to the expected performance as set forth in the profit plan. Any significant variations from estimated performance must be isolated and analyzed to determine what corrective action is indicated.

PLANNING HORIZONS

LONG-RANGE PLAN

The first of three planning horizons in the profit-planning process is the long-range or strategic plan. It provides in broad terms a strategic design for the future of the organization in sales, profit levels, assets, capital structure, and return on owner's investment. The long-range plan covers a time span of from three to five years, but in some instances is developed for planning horizons of ten years or longer.

Long-range planning begins with the determination of the overall objectives of the organization. This includes the overall purpose, the services to be provided, the particular resources necessary, financing, management, and the growth objectives. In arriving at these organizational objectives, both internal and external factors expected to exist over the time span of the plan must be taken into consideration. Internal factors include the existing and proposed operating facilities, the changing services to be offered, and the nature of the organization. External factors include the existing and projected economic conditions nationally and in the specific market areas, including population, competition, demand for the services offered, and growth patterns.

OPERATING PLAN

The second planning horizon is the operating plan. It sets forth the operating plans and objectives of the organization for the next one-year period. Within this annual time span the opportunity does not exist to make substantial changes in the facilities, services offered and organization. The operating plan's purpose is to control and to provide for short-term resource requirements.

The operating plan is the primary tool of management setting forth the operating objectives and the expected operating results throughout the various departments. It is on the basis of this plan that departmental and supervisory management will be evaluated. The operating plan begins with an annual sales forecast which serves as a basis for the proforma income statement; departmental profit objectives; budgets for administrative and general expense, advertising and promotion, heat, light and power, and repairs and maintenance; annual cash flow and funds flow projections; and the proforma year-end balance sheet. Together, these components of the operating plan serve as the guide posts and measuring sticks for the coming year.

ACHIEVEMENT PLAN

The third planning horizon and component of a profit plan is the achievement or monthly plan. This is the plan that sets forth for department heads and supervisors specifically what is expected of their individual responsibility centers over one-month periods. This achievement plan must be sufficiently comprehensive and detailed to indicate exactly the breakdown and timing of revenues projected and specific expense levels which are to be achieved. Achievement plans serve as the control tools of middle management to whom the department heads and supervisors are responsible, and as the operating guidelines and expectations for department heads and supervisors. Included in achievement plans are monthly departmental sales forecasts, departmental payroll budgets, departmental profit plans setting forth expected expenses, proforma income statements and projected cash flow estimates. It is the achievement plan that is the day-to-day operating tool of profit planning.

Exhibit 17.1 lists the components of a comprehensive profit plan, which cover all three planning horizons.

EXHIBIT 17.1
Structure of the Profit Plan

A. *Long-Range (Strategic) Plan*

Forecasted by years for three to five years into the future; revised and updated annually.

1. Proforma income statements.
2. Proforma balance sheets.
3. Capital expenditure budgets.
4. Source and application of funds projections.
5. Cash projections.

B. *Annual Profit (Operating) Plan*

Prepared for the forthcoming year.

1. Sales forecast.
2. Proforma departmental profit projections.
3. Administrative and general expense budget.
4. Advertising and promotion budget.
5. Heat, light and power budget.
6. Repairs and maintenance budget.
7. Proforma income statement, and balance sheet.
8. Capital expenditure budget.
9. Source and application of funds projections.
10. Cash projection.

C. *Achievement (Monthly) Plan*

Prepared for the forthcoming month.

1. Departmental sales forecasts.
2. Departmental payroll budgets.
3. Proforma departmental profit projections.
4. Proforma income statements.
5. Cash projections.

THE PROFIT-PLANNING PROCESS

The starting point for the preparation of the profit plan is the sales forecast, as it is to sales that all expenses must be geared. The accuracy of forecasting sales is important to the planning process; inaccuracy in this forecast can make the difference between a profitable and unprofitable year. Revenue forecasting begins with the forecast of unit sales. Unit sale forecasts are the guidelines for staffing and purchasing and when combined with expected selling prices will provide the dollar sales forecast.

The starting point for unit sales forecasting is historical unit sales. However, caution must be exercised to insure that historical sales levels are not used unadjusted for the expected activity level. Historical sales are more valuable as a forecasting tool when additional information regarding the breakdown of the sales and the conditions existing at that time are maintained and available. For example, in forecasting room night sales, the percentage of rooms which were reserved as compared to walk-in sales, the number of room nights sold to conventions and group meetings, and various activities taking place in the area which might affect room night sales, all should be taken into consideration. The number of weekends as compared to the number of week days in the period, and the history of daily room sales fluctuations are important considerations.

From this starting point of historical unit and total sales, adjustments must be made for expected economic conditions, changes in competitive conditions, advertising and promotion expenses, modifications of facilities, and changes in prices.

Frequently sales levels in the hospitality service industries are affected by the activity levels of other related goods and services. This is referred to as *derived demand*, as this demand is the result of or derived from other departmental activity levels. For example, in a lodging facility, food sales are affected by room sales and in a restaurant, beverage sales are affected by food sales. Other examples of derived demand include increased food and beverage sales at a country club resulting from a golf tournament and increased food sales at a university feeding complex as a result of a football game.

As with all forecasts and projections, the amount of detail provided in the forecast and taken into account in preparation is dependent on the time span of the forecast. For example, when forecasting for the coming month, daily forecasts may be required, but when forecasting for a year, monthly or quarterly forecasts may be sufficient. If a food forecast is for a one-week period, it would take into account each meal period, but for a one-month period these detailed estimates probably would not be necessary.

Exhibit 17.2 is a monthly departmental sales forecast for a hypothetical ski resort with a fiscal year ending May 31. Throughout the remainder of this chapter, other segments of the profit plan for Big Ski, Inc. will be used as exhibits.

Big Ski has five operating departments: rooms, food, beverage, mountain (the skiing activities), and ski school and rentals. January forecasted room sales have been computed by room-type, taking into account prior January room night sales by type, adjusting for the number of week days and weekends in the thirty-one-day period, where New Years falls in the week, reservations, the trend of sales in earlier months, and this season relative to previous seasons. Food sales have been estimated by covers per meal period in each of the three food service areas and the estimated food vending machine sales. Factors affecting food sales estimates include room sales and the projected number of non-lodging skiers for the period. Beverage sales have been projected for the three beverage outlets primarily on the basis of food sales and expected number of skiers. However, if entertainment were provided in the Cave Cocktail Lounge, the estimates would have to be

EXHIBIT 17.2

Big Ski, Inc.
Departmental Sales Forecasts
January 197X
31 Days

	Month			Year to Date		
	Budgeted	Actual	Variance $/%	Budgeted	Actual	Variance $/%
Rooms						
Type I	$ 32,000			$106,000		
Type II	36,000			127,000		
Type III	9,000			28,000		
Two-room Suites	2,000			6,000		
Total	$ 79,000			$267,000		
Food						
Big Ski Dining Room	$ 43,000			$147,000		
Schuss Snack Bar	27,000			62,000		
Yodeler Warming Hut	14,000			23,000		
Vending Machines	8,000			18,000		
Total	$ 92,000			$250,000		
Beverage						
Cave Cocktail Lounge	$ 27,000			$ 74,000		
Big Ski Dining Room	14,000			46,000		
Yodeler Warming Hut	4,000			7,000		
Total	$ 45,000			$127,000		
Mountain (Lift Tickets)						
Full Day	$ 64,000			$109,000		
Half-day	12,000			21,000		
Junior	8,000			14,000		
Total	$ 84,000			$144,000		
Ski School and Rentals						
Group Lessons	$ 10,000			$ 17,000		
Private Lessons	2,000			4,000		
Rentals	10,000			18,000		
Total	$ 22,000			$ 39,000		
Other	$ 1,000			$ 4,000		
Total Revenue	$323,000			$831,000		

revised for this impact. Lift ticket sales are projected on the historical sales pattern over the past several seasons and the earlier part of this season, and the past breakdown of ticket sales, all adjusted for expected changed conditions. Ski school and rental revenues are projected primarily in relation to lift ticket sales. The sales forecast provides for monthly and year-to-date budgeted sales, with columns provided for actual sales and the difference between the budgeted and actual.

SALES FORECAST

In preparing the annual sales forecast for the operating plan, two approaches may be taken. The first is to prepare monthly forecasts such as Exhibit 17.2 and total them to arrive at an annual forecast. The second is to forecast annual departmental revenues in total, taking into account historical sales levels, price changes, and making other such adjustments as are warranted by changes in economic and market conditions, and then dividing this annual estimate into monthly forecasts. The first method goes from the specific estimates to the general, and the second goes from the general estimates to the specific.

Where sale forecasts are done on a monthly basis prior to the beginning of the fiscal year, it is necessary to revise the monthly departmental sales forecast several weeks prior to the beginning of the monthly period in order to adjust for more current conditions. Where annual departmental sales are forecasted in total it is necessary to prepare monthly sales forecasts several weeks prior to each monthly operating period. The monthly sales forecast should be a cooperative effort between department heads and management. More realistic projections are obtained when the forecast is initially prepared by the appropriate department head, reviewed by the manager and differences resolved.

DEPARTMENTAL PAYROLL BUDGETS

A necessary element in effective payroll management and control is employee scheduling based upon accurate sales forecast. Employee scheduling involves weekly forecasts prepared three to five days in advance of the week to be scheduled. Staffing schedules are prepared by department heads based upon the monthly departmental sales forecast and modified by changing conditions subsequent to the time of the original monthly forecast.

Guiding the weekly payroll scheduling are the monthly departmental payroll budgets prepared on the basis of monthly departmental revenue forecasts. Therefore, day-to-day operating control of payroll is primarily accomplished through the use of daily or weekly scheduling from the current forecast of activity levels, and overall planning and control of payroll levels takes place on a monthly basis.

The departmental payroll budget (Exhibit 17.3) is prepared by relating the forecast unit activity level to the productivity standard established, taking into account the minimum staffing required to operate. Thus, to forecast the maid portion of the total housekeeping payroll expense, the expected number of room nights sold must be related to the number of rooms cleaned per day per maid. Added to the forecasted maid payroll expense would be the salary of others in housekeeping, including the housekeeper, housemen, and other cleaning personnel. This monthly departmental payroll budget must be considered as the framework within which the daily or weekly scheduling must be prepared for all departments.

Having estimated sales and prepared a budgeted payroll for the monthly achievement plan it is then necessary to estimate other departmental expenses for the month. Exhibit 17.4 presents the total rooms department profit plan for the month. This schedule combines the room sales as forecasted in the departmental sales forecast; the salaries and wages as budgeted in the departmental payroll budget; and other expenses estimated for the operation of the rooms department. Both departmental payroll and other expenses must be budgeted and standards determined after analysis of past historical relationships to sales (either unit or dollar sales), modified by changing conditions. For example, analysis reveals laundry expense per occupied room for the previous period was 20¢ and a known 10 percent price increase will result in a budget of approximately 22¢ per occupied room.

After the departmental profit plans are completed, the budgeting for deductions from income (controllable unallocated expenses) must be prepared. Each of these four unallocated expense categories (general and administrative expenses, advertising and sales promotion, heat, light and power, and repairs and maintenance) may be budgeted annually, seasonally, and monthly. The scope and content of budgeting for these expense categories is at the discretion of management. All must be budgeted by determining the fixed and variable proportions of each expense and relating this expense to projected levels of activity. Advertising and sales promotion may have a higher amount of discretionary estimates and would be budgeted with the knowledge of some overall sales promotion program.

Exhibit 17.5 is a monthly proforma income statement summarizing the departmental profit plans previously prepared as in the example given for the rooms departmental profit plan (Exhibit 17.4). Deductions from income have been budgeted and the only remaining expenses are noncontrollable or capital expenses. Their monthly amount may be estimated from the individual yearly estimated totals. These amounts are financial charges and are included in the budgetary process to complete the estimates for financial planning and not for operations budgeting.

EXHIBIT 17.3

Big Ski, Inc.
Departmental Payroll Budget
January 197X

31 Days

	Month			Year to Date			Monthly Productivity — (Dollar Sales/Dollar Payroll)		
	Budgeted	*Actual*	*Variance $/%*	*Budgeted*	*Actual*	*Variance $/%*	*Budgeted*	*Actual*	*Variance $/%*
Rooms									
Front Desk	$ 4,500			$ 15,800			$ 17.50		
Housekeeping	5,500			17,000			14.40		
Total	$ 10,000			$ 32,800			7.90		
Food									
Big Ski Dining Room									
Service	$ 6,000			$ 19,300			$ 9.50[1]		
Preparation	7,000			21,100			6.14		
Dishwashing	4,000			13,000			10.70		
Total Big Ski	$ 17,000			$ 53,400			3.30		
Schuss Snack Bar	7,000			16,000			3.90		
Yodeler Warming Hut	5,000			8,800			3.70		
Total	$ 29,000			$ 78,200			3.80		
Beverage									
Cave Cocktail Lounge	$ 9,000			$ 28,700			3.00		
Mountain									
Lifts and Grooming	$ 11,000			$ 28,600			7.65		
Snowmaking	9,000			19,300			9.35		
Total	$ 20,000			$ 47,900			4.20		
Ski School and Rentals									
Ski Instructors	$ 6,000			$ 10,000			2.00		
Rental Clerks	4,000			7,200			2.50		
Total	$ 10,000			$ 17,200			2.20		
Administrative and General	$ 12,000			$ 37,200			27.00[2]		
Repairs and Maintenance	$ 5,000			$ 40,000			65.00[2]		
Total Payroll	$ 95,000			$282,000			3.40		

1. Includes both food and beverage sales.
2. Ratio to total revenue.

EXHIBIT 17.4

Big Ski, Inc.
Rooms Department Profit Plan
January 197X

	Month			Percentage of Sales (Month)			Year to Date		
	Budgeted	Actual	Variance $/%	Budgeted	Actual	Variance $/%	Budgeted	Actual	Variance $/%
Room Sales (Exhibit 17.2)	$ 79,000			100.0%			$267,000		
Departmental Expenses									
Salaries and Wages (Exhibit 17.3)	$ 10,000			12.7%			$ 32,800		
Wage-Related Expenses	1,500			1.9			4,900		
Total Labor	$ 11,500			14.6%			$ 37,700		
Other Expenses									
Cleaning Supplies	700			.9			$ 2,200		
Guest Supplies	400			.5			1,200		
Laundry	1,800			2.3			5,600		
Linen	800			1.0			2,600		
Reservation Expense	400			.5			1,300		
Uniforms	600			.8			1,900		
Other	2,100			2.7			5,500		
Total Expenses	$ 18,300			23.2%			$ 38,000		
Departmental Profit (Loss)	$ 60,700			76.8%			$209,000		

EXHIBIT 17.5

Big Ski, Inc.
Proforma Income Statement
January 197X

	Month			Percentage of Sales (Month)			Year to Date		
	Budgeted	Actual	Variance $/%	Budgeted	Actual	Variance $/%	Budgeted	Actual	Variance $/%
Departmental Profit (Loss)									
Rooms (Exhibit 17.4)	$ 60,700			39.2%			$209,000		
Food	17,400			11.2			60,100		
Beverage	12,400			8.0			42,800		
Mountain (Lifts)	44,800			28.9			96,700		
Ski School and Rentals	17,900			11.5			38,200		
Other	1,800			1.2			9,800		
Gross Operating Income	$155,000			100.0%			$456,600		
Deductions from Income									
Administrative and General	$ 24,000			15.5%			$ 74,400		
Advertising and Sales Promotion	8,400			5.4			40,700		
Heat, Light and Power	13,000			8.4			43,800		
Repairs and Maintenance	12,000			7.7			69,000		
Total Deductions from Income	$ 57,400			37.0%			$227,900		
Gross Operating Income	$ 97,600			63.0%			$228,700		
Rent, Municipal Taxes and Insurance	4,800			3.1			$ 38,000		
Profit Before Interest and Depreciation	$ 92,800			59.9%			$190,700		
Interest	10,800			7.0			86,000		
Profit Before Depreciation	$ 82,000			52.9%			$104,700		
Depreciation and Expense Amortization	14,200			9.2			115,200		
Net Operating Profit (Loss)	$ 67,800			43.7%			$ (10,500)		

However, the financial plans are also an integral part of the profit-planning process, as operations may be the sole source of cash flow for current and long-range financing. There is a minimum need for short-term financial plans in the hospitality service industries as minimum dollars are devoted to current assets and current liabilities. This is not to say that the organization's current resources may be poorly managed, but rather that the planning and control associated with their management must be accomplished over longer periods of time.

Exhibit 17.6 presents quarterly proforma balance sheets for Big Ski, Inc. These balance sheets are the projected financial condition to result from the projected operating performance and other estimated changes in the firm's financial condition. The quarterly proforma balance sheets are a portion of the yearly operating plan rather than the monthly achievement plan. On a quarterly basis, proforma balance sheets are useful primarily for their presentation of cash and working capital positions.

LONG-RANGE PLAN DEVELOPMENT

The preparation of the long-range plan should accompany the development of operating and achievement plans. In the operating and achievement plans, the resources of the firm are managed and are alterable only within a limited range. The long-range plan can provide for major changes in the firm's resources.

The development of a long-range plan must be prefaced by the establishment of the organization's overall objectives and goals. For a profit-oriented organization, this will be presented in terms of return on owner's equity, debt-equity relationships, and growth patterns. For service-oriented organizations such as non-profit clubs and hospitals, the objectives will frequently be presented in both quantitative and qualitative terms. That is to say, objectives such as revenues equaling expenses may be coupled with some desired level of service to members or patients.

After the establishment of the organization's objectives, a determination must next be made of the expected conditions or environmental constraints within which the organization must function over the long range, and then the available courses of action be considered in the light of the objectives and environment. With the evaluation of alternatives and selection of the optimum courses of actions, the long-range plan may be assembled.[2]

Exhibit 17.7 presents the proforma income statements for the five-year long-range plans of Big Ski, Inc. It summarizes the expected revenues, expenses, and

---

2. Glenn A. Welsch, *Budgeting: Project Planning and Control*, 2nd ed. (Englewood Cliffs, N.J.: Prentice-Hall, Inc., 1970).

EXHIBIT 17.6

Big Ski, Inc.
Quarterly Proforma Balance Sheets
Fiscal Year Ended May 31, 197X

		Actual *May 31, 197(B)*
Assets		
Current Assets		
Cash		$ 36,000
Accounts Receivable		56,000
Inventory		7,000
Other Current Assets		90,000
Total Current Assets		$ 189,000
Fixed Assets		
Land		122,000
Buildings	$3,148,000	
Less: Accumulated Depreciation	394,000	2,754,000
Ski Equipment and Trails	$ 739,000	
Less: Accumulated Depreciation	82,000	657,000
Furniture and Fixtures	$ 811,000	
Less: Accumulated Depreciation	109,000	702,000
Total Fixed Assets		$4,235,000
Other Assets		$ 32,000
Total Assets		$4,456,000
Liabilities and Stockholders' Equity		
Current Liabilities		
Accounts Payable		$ 46,000
Accrued Expenses		4,000
Deposits on Room Reservations		1,000
Long-term Debt Due Within One Year		208,000
Total Current Liabilities		$ 259,000
Long-term Debt		
Mortgages		$1,832,000
Notes		453,000
Total Long-term Debt		$2,285,000
Total Liabilities		$2,544,000
Stockholders' Equity		
Common stock, $10 Par		$ 853,000
Paid-in-Capital in Excess of Par		1,169,000
Retained Earnings		(110,000)
Total Stockholders' Equity		$1,912,000
Total Liabilities and Stockholders' Equity		$4,456,000

EXHIBIT 17.6 (Continued)

Big Ski, Inc.
Quarterly Proforma Balance Sheets
Fiscal Year Ended May 31, 197X

	Projected						
	Aug. 31, 197(B)		**Nov. 30, 197(B)**		**Feb. 28, 197(C)**		**May 31, 197(C)**
	$ 46,000		$ 38,000		$ 23,000		$ 47,000
	24,000		19,000		83,000		62,000
	4,000		17,000		34,000		9,000
	75,000		94,000		47,000		29,000
	$ 149,000		$ 168,000		$ 187,000		$ 147,000
		122,000		122,000		122,000	122,000
$3,155,000		$3,158,000		$3,159,000		$3,159,000	
423,000	2,732,000	452,000	2,706,000	481,000	2,678,000	510,000	2,649,000
740,000		742,000		742,000		742,000	
88,000	652,000	94,000	648,000	100,000	642,000	106,000	636,000
$ 811,000		$ 811,000		$ 811,000		$ 811,000	
117,000	694,000	125,000	686,000	133,000	678,000	141,000	670,000
	$4,200,000		$4,162,000		$4,120,000		$4,077,000
	$ 30,000		$ 31,000		$ 31,000		$ 34,000
	$4,379,000		$4,361,000		$4,338,000		$4,258,000
	$ 26,000		$ 51,000		$ 83,000		$ 38,000
	3,000		5,000		9,000		5,000
	1,000		11,000		3,000		2,000
	206,000		205,000		203,000		201,000
	$ 236,000		$ 272,000		$ 298,000		$ 246,000
	$1,813,000		$1,793,000		$1,772,000		$1,750,000
	423,000		392,000		360,000		327,000
	$2,236,000		$2,185,000		$2,132,000		$2,077,000
	$2,472,000		$2,457,000		$2,430,000		$2,323,000
	$ 853,000		$ 853,000		$ 853,000		$ 853,000
	1,169,000		1,169,000		1,169,000		1,169,000
	(115,000)		(118,000)		(114,000)		(87,000)
	$1,907,000		$1,904,000		$1,908,000		$1,935,000
	$4,379,000		$4,361,000		$4,338,000		$4,258,000

EXHIBIT 17.7

Big Ski, Inc.
Five-Year Long Range Plan
Proforma Income Statements

Fiscal Year Ended May 31	Actual		Projected				
	197(A)	197(B)	197(C)	197(D)	197(E)	197(F)	197(G)
Revenues							
Rooms	$ 284,000	$ 296,000	$ 314,000	$ 332,000	$ 352,000	$ 400,000	$ 420,000
Food	322,000	332,000	365,000	402,000	443,000	530,000	570,000
Beverage	155,000	162,000	178,000	195,000	214,000	250,000	265,000
Mountain (Lifts)	255,000	270,000	305,000	355,000	410,000	460,000	500,000
Ski School and Rental	91,000	97,000	110,000	125,000	140,000	150,000	160,000
Other	16,000	18,000	20,000	23,000	26,000	30,000	35,000
Total Revenues	$1,123,000	$1,175,000	$1,292,000	$1,432,000	$1,585,000	$1,820,000	$1,950,000
Departmental Expenses							
Rooms	$ 66,000	$ 68,000	$ 72,000	$ 75,000	$ 79,000	$ 85,000	$ 88,000
Food	236,000	245,000	268,000	290,000	320,000	380,000	405,000
Beverage	96,000	101,000	110,000	121,000	133,000	153,000	162,000
Mountain (Lifts)	75,000	80,000	90,000	102,000	118,000	131,000	140,000
Ski School and Rental	19,000	22,000	25,000	28,000	31,000	33,000	35,000
Other	4,000	5,000	6,000	7,000	8,000	10,000	11,000
Total Departmental Expenses	$ 496,000	$ 521,000	$ 571,000	$ 623,000	$ 689,000	$ 792,000	$ 841,000
Gross Operating Income	$ 627,000	$ 654,000	$ 721,000	$ 809,000	$ 896,000	$1,028,000	$1,109,000
Deductions from Income							
Administrative and General	$ 104,000	$ 110,000	$ 120,000	$ 132,000	$ 145,000	$ 164,000	$ 175,000
Advertising and Sales Promotion	44,000	47,000	55,000	60,000	65,000	80,000	85,000
Heat, Light and Power	67,000	68,000	73,000	80,000	87,000	99,000	105,000
Repairs and Maintenance	81,000	84,000	92,000	96,000	104,000	116,000	130,000
Total Deductions from Income	$ 296,000	$ 309,000	$ 340,000	$ 368,000	$ 401,000	$ 459,000	$ 495,000
Gross Operating Profit	$ 331,000	$ 345,000	$ 381,000	$ 441,000	$ 495,000	$ 569,000	$ 614,000
Rent, Municipal Taxes and Insurance	52,000	54,000	57,000	60,000	63,000	70,000	74,000
Profit before Interest and Depreciation	$ 279,000	$ 291,000	$ 324,000	$ 381,000	$ 432,000	$ 499,000	$ 540,000
Interest	142,000	136,000	129,000	121,000	110,000	100,000	89,000
Profit before Depreciation	$ 137,000	$ 155,000	$ 195,000	$ 260,000	$ 322,000	$ 399,000	$ 451,000
Depreciation and Expense Amortization	167,000	170,000	172,000	171,000	172,000	190,000	189,000
Net Profit (Loss) before Income Taxes	$ (30,000)	$ (15,000)	$ 23,000	$ 89,000	$ 150,000	$ 209,000	$ 262,000
Income Taxes	-	-	-	1,000	66,000	94,000	119,000
Net Profit (Loss)	$ (30,000)	$ (15,000)	$ 23,000	$ 88,000	$ 84,000	$ 115,000	$ 143,000

resulting net profit after taxes over the coming five-year period as a result of a course of action which is consistent with the objectives of the organization and the resources to be employed. In this example additional room facilities will go into operation during the fourth fiscal year 197(F) and the proforma income statements show increases in room revenue from 197(E) to 197(F). To a lesser extent, similar increases are included in food and beverage revenues, as the present facilities are adequate to handle the estimated volume resulting from the guests occupying the new rooms.

The operating plan and achievement plan are based primarily on maximizing revenues and profits given the present resource mix. The long-range plan has no mix constraint. Thus, the planning alternatives are much greater in number, as are the potential sources of revenue and profit. The estimation of the revenues and expenses associated with the long-range alternatives selected are less detailed than in the achievement and operating plans.

The forthcoming year in the long-range plan is a current and accurate forecast. It should be identical to the operating plan proforma income statement. In the four years beyond, estimates become progressively less certain and more subject to change.

In order for the long-range plan to function it is necessary that it be updated and revised annually so that a current five-year plan always exists. This periodically updated plan is known as a *rolling or revolving budget*. This merely implies that as the current year is dropped, revisions are made to the remaining years, and a new fifth year is added. A similar approach may be taken with the operating plan so that a twelve-month forecast is always available.

SUMMARY

The profit plan or budget provides the framework for planning the organization's future courses of action, both long- and short-run, and for guiding the organization to the established objectives. If properly designed and implemented, it can be a motivational tool and a means of communication.

The profit-planning process includes three planning horizons, the long-range plan, the operating plan, and the achievement plan. Each has a different scope and purpose in the overall planning and control of an organization.

The success of any organization is highly dependent upon its ability to anticipate and provide for the future. An effective profit plan is vital to the success of an organization, daily, annually, and over the longer run.

Discussion Questions

1. Define a budget.
2. What are the benefits associated with profit planning?
3. Explain the two phases involved in the total budgeting process.
4. Describe and compare the:
    (a) Long-range plans
    (b) Operating plans
    (c) Achievement plans
5. How does forecasting relate to the profit-planning process?
6. List the components of a profit plan, covering all three planning horizons.
7. Explain the importance of proforma balance sheets.

Problem 1

The Rusty Restaurant Corporation operates a restaurant in suburbia. The restaurant's facilities include a 100-seat dining room, a 50-seat cocktail lounge and a 50-seat banquet room.

In recent years, the Rusty Restaurant has been very profitable and has provided an excellent return on the owners' investment. However, recently management has become concerned over a dwindling cash balance. You have been called in to analyze the situation.

An analysis of recent financial statements shows the following.

Regarding Revenues

Regular food revenues average $6.00 per food cover.
Beverage revenues average $2.00 per food cover.
Banquet revenues average $5.00 per banquet cover.
Other income averages 2 percent of food revenues.

Regarding Expenses

The cost of goods sold ratios are:
    Regular food cost = 35 percent of food revenue.
    Beverage cost = 25 percent of beverage revenue.
    Banquet cost = 30 percent of banquet revenue.
    Cost of other income = 50 percent of other income.

Direct operating expenses total $12,400 per month when volume is at 4,000 regular food covers per month. However, if volume increases, direct operating expenses increase by $2,500 for each additional 500 regular food covers.

Indirect operating expenses are fixed at $5,500 per month.

Fixed overhead expenses include:

Interest on long-term debts totaling $250 per month and payable monthly.

Rent of $1,200 per month, due and payable every month.

Insurance premiums totaling $3,600 annually are payable in four equal installments (in January, April, July and October of each year).

Depreciation on fixed assets totaling $750 per month (including amortization of leasehold improvements).

Schedule of Anticipated Receipts

As of December 31, accounts receivable include $25,000 in regular food and beverage accounts and $5,000 in banquet accounts. The collection of these accounts is expected to be $18,000 of regular food and beverage accounts and $3,000 of the banquet accounts to be collected in January, 1971; the remainder will be collected in February, 1971.

Based on past experience, the collection of revenues is normally as follows (shown as a percentage of sales).

Type of Revenue:	Collected during the		
	Current Month	*Second Month*	*Third Month*
Regular Food and Beverage Sales	40%	30%	30%
Banquet Sales	20%	50%	30%
Other Income	100%		

Schedule of Payment of Expenses

As of December 31, 1970, accounts payable (trade) totaled $13,800 and accrued expenses totaled $5,250 (including $3,000 in direct operating expenses and $2,250 in indirect operating expenses). All of these liabilities are payable in January, 1971.

Based on past experience, the payment of expenses is as follows (shown as a percentage of the expense).

Type of Expense:	Paid during the	
	Current Month	*Second Month*
Cost of Goods Sold	20%	80%
Direct Operating Expenses	80%	20%
Indirect Operating Expenses	50%	50%

Problem 1 (continued)

Fixed overhead expenses are payable monthly except for the payment of insurance premiums as previously mentioned.

Additional Information

Principal payments on the current portion of long-term debt, totaling $300 per month, are payable monthly.

Dividends on common stock of $2.50 per share are payable in February, 1971. In addition, the board of directors have declared another dividend of $2.50 per share, which will be payable in August, 1971.

The actual balance sheet as of 12/31/70 and the projected balance sheet as of 3/31/71 are shown.

Business activity for the months of January, February and March of 1971 has been forecasted as follows:

	January	*February*	*March*
Number of Food Covers (reg.)	4000	4500	5000
Number of Banquet Covers	800	900	1000

Required

Based on the figures and relationships as given, develop:

1. A cash budget for the months of January, February and March of 1971. In the event of a cash deficit in any month, assume that the restaurant can get a one-month note at an annual interest rate of 6 percent to cover the deficit. If such a situation does occur, round the amount of the deficit *up* to the nearest thousand dollars and borrow the money from the bank. Remember that the loan plus interest must be repaid in the following month.
2. A proforma income statement for the period January 1 to March 31, 1971.
3. A proforma statement of sources and applications of funds (working capital) for the period January 1 to March 31, 1971.

The Rusty Restaurant
Balance Sheet

	12/31/70 Actual	3/31/71 Expected
Assets		
Current		
Cash	2700	2370
Accounts Receivable		
Regular	25000	34800
Banquet	5000	5350
Inventories	10300	10300
Total Current Assets	43000	52820
Fixed		
China, Glass and Silver	10000	10000
Leasehold Improvements	35000	35000
Less: Amortization Reserve	6000	6250
	39000	28050
Furniture and Fixtures	60000	60000
Less: Accumulated Depreciation	12000	13500
	48000	46500
Total Fixed Assets	87000	84750
Total Assets	130000	137570
Liabilities and Stockholders' Equity		
Current Liabilities		
Trade Accounts Payable	13800	11840
Dividends Payable	5000	5000
Accrued Expenses	5250	6230
Current Portion of Long-Term Debt	3600	2700
Total Current Liabilities	27650	25770
Long-Term Debt	37850	37850
Total Liabilities	65500	63620
Stockholders' Equity		
Common Stock $10 par	20000	20000
Capital Surplus	30000	30000
Retained Earnings	14500	23950
Total Stockholders' Equity	64500	73950
Total Liabilities and Equity	130000	137570

Problem 2

As the new manager of the Lakeside Development Company, you have been requested to prepare a cash operating budget (profit plan) and cash projection for the coming calendar year 197X.

Your research revealed the following information.

1. The company is in its first full year of operation.
2. The company's operation consists of:

   Lodging—50 unit motel.
   Day-use facilities—picnicking, sightseeing, hiking, etc. for which a $1.00 entrance fee is charged.
   Boat launching facilities.
   Camping.
   Harbor Master—sales of gas, oil and boating accessories.
   Concessions—food and beverage facilities.
   Miscellaneous—other concessions.

3. Cash in bank at the beginning of the year amounted to $124,000.
4. The company has a $200,000 note payable due the bank in equal annual installments over a four-year period beginning in the coming year.
5. The company has a $75,000 demand note payable due to a stockholder. The stockholder has requested payment in equal annual installments commencing in the coming year.
6. The company owes vendors for equipment which was purchased under various contracts that are due in monthly installments of $2,916.67.
7. The operation is highly seasonal; therefore, certain of the facilities are closed during the period October 1 to May 31.
8. Monthly revenues, net of cost of sales where applicable for last year, were as follows.

	Jan.-May	June	July	August	Sept.-Dec.	Total
Lodging	$ -	$ 516	$ 3,847	$ 9,553	$ 3,079	$16,995
Day-use Facilities	2,900	3,565	4,835	3,264	2,035	16,599
Boat Launchings	1,000	1,076	627	1,953	1,731	6,387
Camping	400	490	1,448	2,150	474	4,962
Harbor Master	2,400	2,776	4,320	5,525	3,832	18,853
Concessions	-	-	2,170	2,356	1,197	5,723
Miscellaneous	-	658	310	1,464	-	2,432
Totals	$ 6,700	$ 9,081	$17,557	$26,265	$12,348	$71,951

Problem 2 (continued)

9. Staffing and their monthly compensation is as follows. Seasonal employees are indicated by the number of months they work.

Manager		$1,000
Chief of Maintenance		600
Maintenance Assistant #1		400
Maintenance Assistant #2,	4 mos. @	250
Landscape Gardener		400
Landscape Helper		200
Marina Operator		400
Gatehouse Keeper		400
Motel Manager		350
Motel Maids	4 mos. @	600
	4 mos. @	300
Secretary		200
Accountant		350
Allowance for Summer Help —		
(Six college students for		
lifeguard, babysitters,		
park cleanup,		
gatehouse, etc.)	3 mos. @	225

10. Operating expenses, excluding salaries, are expected to increase over actual expenses experienced last year based on a projected 50 percent increase in revenue. Annual expenses are therefore projected as follows:

Insurance		$15,000
Advertising		35,000
Office Supplies, Printing		
and Postage		2,500
Travel		3,300
Utilities		
Electricity	$ 6,000	
Telephone	3,600	
Propane Gas	3,600	
		13,200
Taxes and Licenses		
Property		15,000
Payroll		3,000
Sanitation		4,000
Laundry		3,000
Legal and Accounting		5,000
Interest Expense		36,000
Repairs and Maintenance		15,000
Contingency (10 percent of all		
other expenses)		15,000

11. The company acquired for cash ten boats at a cost of $3,400 each in December. The cost of these boats is expected to be recovered ratably over the next two years from rental revenue.

Problem 2 (continued)

Required

1. Prepare an estimated cash operating budget for the next year ending December 31.
2. Prepare a schedule (supporting the cash budget) detailing budgeted annual cash operating expenditures.
3. Prepare a schedule (supporting the cash budget) detailing budgeted revenue based on possible increases of 10, 20, 50 and 100 percent over actual revenues of last year. (After deliberation with your board of directors, it is agreed the projected revenue for use in the estimated cash budget should be based on a 50 percent growth plus rentals from the newly acquired boats.)

Problem 3

The owners of the Seasonal Resort Hotel Company have requested that you prepare a budget for the approaching new fiscal year.

Information available indicates:

1. Based on current economic trends operating conditions for the coming year should be similar to those most recently experienced.
2. The hotel has 119 rooms, the average daily rate per occupied room has been $18.50, and annual occupancy has averaged 42 percent.
3. The rooms department expenses and profit has experienced the following percentage relationships to room sales.

	Percent
Room Sales	100.0%
Departmental Expenses	
Salaries and Wages	23.1%
Related Payroll Costs	
Including Employees'	
Meals and Payroll Taxes	5.9
Laundry	4.4
Linen, China and Glassware	1.2
Other Expenses	4.5
Total Departmental Expenses	39.1%
Departmental Profit	60.9%

4. The food and beverage facilities, in addition to being used by hotel guests, enjoy an exceptionally large volume of business from non-guests

Problem 3 (continued)

visiting the resort-oriented area. Therefore, food sales average 31.4 percent of total hotel sales and income and beverage sales average 30.5 percent of total hotel sales and income.

The food and beverage departmental costs and expenses and profit have been as follows:

	Percent
Food Sales	100.0%
Cost of Food Sold	
Cost of Food Consumed	36.0%
Less: Credit for	
Employees' Meals	4.0
Cost of Food Sold	32.0%
Gross Food Profit	68.0%
Beverage Sales	100.0%
Cost of Beverages Sold	28.5
Gross Beverage Profit	71.5%
Total Food and Beverage Sales	100.0%
Cost of Food and Beverages Sold	30.3
Gross Food and Beverage Profit	69.7%
Departmental Expenses	
Salaries and Wages	28.0%
Related Payroll Costs	
Including Employees'	
Meals and Payroll Taxes	6.5
Music and Entertainment	3.5
Laundry	1.4
Linen, China, Glassware	
and Silver	2.0
Other Expenses	4.0
Total Departmental	
Expenses	45.4%
Departmental Profit	24.3%

5. Telephone income has consistently been $6,000 annually and telephone departmental costs have been $2,000 larger.

6. Deductions from income during the last fiscal year were the following percentages of total hotel sales and income.

Administrative	9.0%
Advertising	3.4
Heat, Light, and Power	2.1
Repairs and Maintenance	5.5
Total	20.0%

7. Store rentals are based on fixed amounts in the leases which total $36,000 annually.
8. Property taxes, based on current assessments and rates, will be $40,000 annually while fire insurance premiums will be $20,000 annually.
9. Interest is due at 8 percent annually on a $200,000 term loan.
10. Depreciation is computed on a straight-line twenty-year composite life on the $1,500,000 investment in building and equipment.
11. Income taxes are to be computed at a rate of 50 percent.

Required

1. Prepare an operating budget for the coming fiscal year in the format of the uniform system of accounts for hotels showing dollar amounts and percentages.
2. Complete a rooms department schedule of sales and expenses and departmental profit showing dollar amounts and percentage to total room sales.
3. Present a food and beverage departmental schedule of sales and expenses and departmental profit showing dollar amounts and percentage to the related food and beverage or total food and beverage sales.
4. Prepare a written report to accompany your budget (including the schedules), explaining to the owners the source of your budget figures.

CHAPTER 18

Budgeting Control

Maximum operating performance is achieved with profit planning and operations control. In profit planning, the planned objectives are set forth, detailed actions to obtain this objective laid out, and the resources necessary to realize the objective assembled. Periodic monitoring and evaluating of the actual performance is budgetary control. Budgetary profit planning and budgetary control are equally important to attain maximum operating performance of a profit plan.

THE CONCEPT OF BUDGETARY CONTROL

Operations controls may be exercised only where a comparison is made. Performance can only be determined to be satisfactory or unsatisfactory relative to a predetermined standard. This budgetary control process consists of three steps:

1. Comparison of actual operating results with planned results to disclose significant variations.
2. Detailed analyses to determine the problem and its probable cause.
3. Prompt action to correct the problem.

Comparison of actual operating results with those planned is the bridge connecting profit planning and budgetary control.

SIGNIFICANCE CRITERION

When variations from planned performance occur, the significance of the variation must be determined. This determination must disclose whether the variation is large enough to warrant management attention. Since this decision must be made for each variation, a standard criterion should be established for determining the significance of each variation.

Absolute or percentage variation may be employed in determining significance. Absolute variations between actual and planned may be either in dollars or units. The decision rule for determining significance may include both absolute and percentage variation criteria as each is a separate measurement of significance. Should either the absolute or percentage criterion be exceeded, the variation will be identified for analysis and disposition. The use of only one criterion could result in a failure to identify a significant variation. For example, if a 10 percent variation criterion were employed, an absolute variation of $9,500 would not be identified if the planned level were $100,000. Similarly, a 100 percent variance would not be identified if the absolute criterion was $1,000, the planned level was $900, and the actual result was $1,800.

The absolute and percentage criteria cannot be used without exception as they may identify variations that are not significant. For example, a variation of $15 for an expense planned to be $100 would be noted if the percentage criterion was 15 percent or more, and a $110 variation on a planned expense of $10,000 would be identified if the absolute variation criteria were $100, even though the percentage variation was only 1.1 percent.

A generally accepted method for the use of both absolute and percentage variation criteria is to rank the attention priority of the variance. Under this method the most important variations or those with the highest priority would be those that exceeded both the absolute and percentage limits. Next in priority would be those which exceeded only the absolute limit, and the lowest priority would be those which exceeded only the percentage limit.

The same criterion should not be applied to all revenue, expense and profit variations. For example, some revenues are less susceptible to accurate forecasting than are expenses, so the revenue criterion might be broader than that employed for expenses. Similarly, some expenses may be more accurately forecast than others and thus employ a different variation criterion.

VARIANCE ANALYSIS

Having determined that a significant variation exists, the reason for this variance must then be determined. Variance analysis assists in this determination by isolating the causes in terms of price, volume, usage and mix variances, and may be applied to both revenues and expenses.

REVENUE VARIANCE ANALYSIS

Continuing with the profit planning example of Big Ski, Inc., the budgeted and actual rooms revenues for the month of January are as presented in Exhibit 18.1. Total actual rooms revenue exceeded budgeting revenue by $3,385 or 4.3 percent. Within the types of rooms sold revenues were higher than projected for

EXHIBIT 18.1

Budgeted and Actual Rooms Revenue

Rooms	Budgeted	Actual	Variance Dollars	Variance Percentage
Type I	$ 32,000	$ 34,740	$ 2,740	8.6%
Type II	36,000	38,448	2,448	6.8
Type III	9,000	7,210	(1,790)	(19.9)
Two-room Suites	2,000	1,987	(13)	0.6
Total Rooms Revenue	$ 79,000	$ 82,385	$ 3,385	4.3%

some and lower for others. However, from this brief comparison it is not possible to determine if the variations were caused by variance from the expected average room rates or the projected number of room nights sold. To isolate the total variations caused by volume and price changes, it is necessary to review the original basis for the rooms revenue forecast. Exhibit 18.2 shows the calculation of the budgeted rooms revenue for January. This budget information provides the basis for price and volume analysis.

EXHIBIT 18.2

Rooms Revenue Forecast

Room Type	Room Night Sales	Average Room Rate	Revenue
Type I	2,000	$ 16.00	$ 32,000
Type II	2,000	18.00	36,000
Type III	450	20.00	9,000
Two-room Suites	50	40.00	2,000
Total	4,500	$ 17.55	$ 79,000

Exhibit 18.3 is the actual room night sales and average room rate for January.

EXHIBIT 18.3

Actual Room Nights Sales and Average Room Rates

Room Type	Room Nights Sales	Average Room Rate	Revenue
Type I	2,000	$ 17.37	$ 34,740
Type II	2,136	18.00	38,448
Type III	350	20.60	7,210
Two-room Suites	49	40.55	1,987
Total	4,535	$ 18.16	$ 82,385

Type I rooms revenues and average room rates variance analysis shows a favorable (F) variance.

	Room Nights	Average Room Rate	Revenue
Planned	2,000	$ 16.00	$ 32,000
Actual	2,000	17.37	$ 34,740
Variance	0	$ 1.37(F)	$ 2,740(F)

The actual number of Type I room nights sold was the same as the number forecast, so there was no volume variance. However, the average rate per occupied room was $1.37 more than planned, resulting in room revenue of $2,740 more than planned. This $2,740 favorable (F) variation is accounted for by the 2,000 room nights sold times the additional $1.37 (2,000 × $1.37 = $2,740). This favorable price variance of $1.37 per room night was the complete explanation for the favorable revenue variance of $2,740.

Type II rooms provide an example of no price variance but a favorable volume variance of 136 room nights resulting in a favorable revenue variance as follows:

	Room Nights	Average Room Rate	Revenue
Planned	2,000	$ 18.00	$ 36,000
Actual	2,136	18.00	38,448
Variance	136(F)	$ -	$ 2,448(F)

The complete explanation for the favorable revenue variance is the sale of 136 more rooms than planned at the planned average room rate of $18.00 (136 × $18.00 = $2,448).

Type III rooms provide an example of an unfavorable (U) variance of $1,790 caused by both volume and price variances.

	Room Nights	Average Room Rate	Revenue
Planned	450	$ 20.00	$ 9,000
Actual	350	20.60	7,210
Variance	100(U)	$ .60(F)	$ 1,790(U)

The unfavorable volume variance of 100 room nights resulted in an unfavorable revenue variance of $2,000 (100 × $20.00 = $2,000), and the favorable price variance of $.60 provided a $270 favorable revenue variance (450 × $0.60 = $270). However, $2,000 unfavorable volume variance and the $270 favorable price variance ($2,000 - $270 = $1,730) does not totally account for the $1,790 unfavorable revenue variance. The additional factor to be considered is the compound variance, the volume-price variance. As the volume variance was calculated using the planned price, and the price variance was calculated using the planned volume, a calculation must be made to include the combined impact of the 100-room night unfavorable volume variance and $0.60 favorable price variance. Thus, 100 room nights that were not sold at the $0.60 increased average room rate must be deducted. This unfavorable volume-price variance is $60 (100 × $0.60).

The total variance analysis for Type III rooms revenue is as follows:

Variance	Volume	Price	Dollar Variance
Volume	100(U)	$ 20.00	$ 2,000(U)
Price	450	0.60(F)	270(F)
Volume-Price	100(U)	0.60(F)	60(U)
Total			$ 1,790(U)

The two-room suite revenues remain to be analyzed in order to complete the example. In this case the absolute variance is $13 and the percentage variance is 1.6 percent. The significance criterion would probably indicate that a significant variance did not exist for two-room suites.

	Room Nights	Average Room Rate	Revenue
Planned	50	$ 40.00	$ 2,000
Actual	49	40.55	1,987
Variance	1(U)	$ 0.55(F)	$ 13(U)

Here the unfavorable volume variance results in revenue loss of $40 (1 × $40.00 = $40), the favorable price variance of $0.55 results in a revenue gain of $27.50 (50 × $0.55 = $27.50), and the unfavorable volume-price variance of $0.55 (1 × $0.55 = $.55) results in an unfavorable revenue of $13.05.

Following is the computation of the three variances for the two-room suites.

Variance	Volume	Price	Dollar Variance
Volume	1(U)	$40.00	$ 40.00(U)
Price	50	.55(F)	27.50(F)
Volume-Price	1(U)	.55(F)	.55(U)
Total			$ 13.05(U)

A summation of the individual variances by types of rooms follows.

Type I	$ 2,740 (F)
Type II	2,448 (F)
Type III	(1,790) (U)
Two-room Suites	(13) (U)
Total Dollar Variance	$ 3,385 (F)

The favorable variance can be analyzed for total rooms revenue resulting in the following volume and price composite variations.

	Room Nights	Average Room Rate	Revenue
Planned	4,500	$ 17.55	$ 78,975
Actual	4,535	18.16	82,355
Variance	35(F)	$ 0.61(F)	$ 3,380(F)

For total rooms revenue the favorable volume variance was the result of selling 35 more rooms than planned and was $614.25 (35 × $17.55 = $614.25). The favorable price variance of $2,745 was the result of selling 4,500 rooms at an additional $0.61 (4,500 × $0.61 = $2,745). And the volume-price variance was $21.35 (35 × $0.61 = $21.35), resulting in a total favorable revenue variance of $3,380 as shown.

Volume	$ 614
Price	2,745
Volume-Price	21
	$ 3,380

COMPOUND VARIANCES

Where a variation from planned performance is the result of two variances, analysis of this variation will result in a compound variance such as the volume-price variances which occurred in Type III rooms and two-room suites. The explanation for the existence of such variances is best presented graphically. Exhibit 18.4 is a graph showing the variances for Type III rooms.

The area of the rectangle ABCD is the planned room revenue. The area of the rectangle AEFG is the actual room revenue ($7,210). The rectangle GICD represents the effect of the volume variance (GD). This volume variance is calculated by multiplying the volume variance (GD) by the planned price (AB). The effect of the price variance is computed by multiplying the price variance (BE) by the planned volume (AD). This price variance is represented by the rectangle BEHC. However, the rectangle IFHC is *not* included in either the planned revenue ABCD, or the actual revenue AEFG. Therefore, the difference between the planned and actual, the revenue variance, should not include IFHC. This additional variance is the compound volume-price variance (IFHC) and must be deducted. This example of a compound variance shows one variance as favorable and the other variance as unfavorable.

Compound variances also occur where both variances are either favorable or unfavorable. For example, a catering company planned on orders for 4,000 meals

EXHIBIT 18.4

January Type III Room Revenues

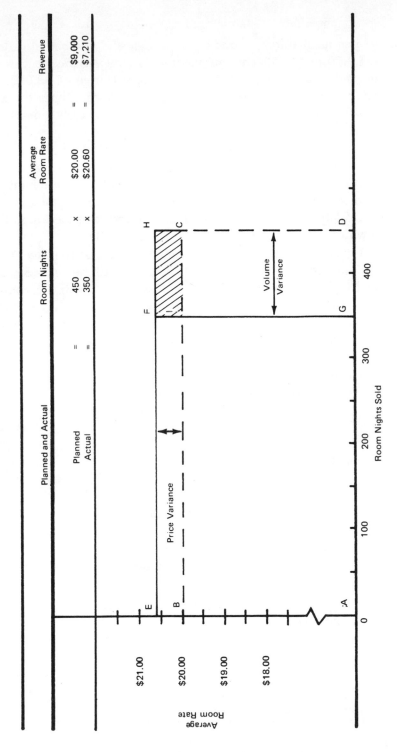

Planned and Actual		Room Nights		Average Room Rate		Revenue
Planned	=	450	×	$20.00	=	$9,000
Actual	=	350	×	$20.60	=	$7,210

437

at $3.00 per meal during a one-week period, and the actual orders were 3,000 meals at $2.50 per meal. The unfavorable volume variance in this example is the 1,000 meals less than planned times the planned price of $3.00, or $3,000. The unfavorable price variance is the 4,000 planned meals times the $.50 price variance, or $2,000. And the volume-price variance is 1,000 meals times $.50, or $500, for a total revenue variance of $4,500.

In this example (Exhibit 18.5) the volume variance (GD) results in a revenue of GHCD and the price variance (EB) results in a revenue variance of EBCI. However, the rectangle FHCI has been included in both these individual variances. Since both the volume and the price variances are unfavorable, the volume-price variance must be considered as favorable to effect a reduction in the unfavorable variance which has been overstated by the area FHCI.

If the example were to reverse planned and actual to reflect planned revenue of AEFG and actual revenue of ABCD it would still be necessary to consider the rectangle FHCI as a favorable variance. This results from the computing volume variance as GFID, and the price variance as EBHF, excluding FHCI from both calculations. When the price and volume variances are favorable, the compound variance is added to properly reflect the total favorable variance. A price and quantity in excess of that planned is favorable for a revenue variance and unfavorable for expense variance. The following chart can be used in the determination of whether a compound variance is favorable or unfavorable.

	Compound Revenue Variance	Compound Expense Variance
Individual Variances Same	Favorable (F)	Unfavorable (U)
Individual Variances Opposite	Unfavorable (U)	Favorable (F)

With knowledge of the variances which caused the outcome, steps may be taken to determine the reasons for the variances. For example, if the estimate of the Type I average room rate was based on a $14.00 single occupancy rate, a $18.00 double occupancy rate, and a 1.5 double occupancy factor,[1] a $16.00 average room rate would result.

$14.00 × .5	=	$ 7.00
$18.00 × .5	=	$ 9.00
		$16.00 Average Room Rate

---

1. A 1.5 double occupancy or multiple occupancy factor indicates that the average occupied room contained 1.5 people, or that if only single or double occupancy is possible, one-half of the rooms were single occupancy and the other half double occupancy.

EXHIBIT 18.5

Weekly Catering Company Meals, Planned and Actual

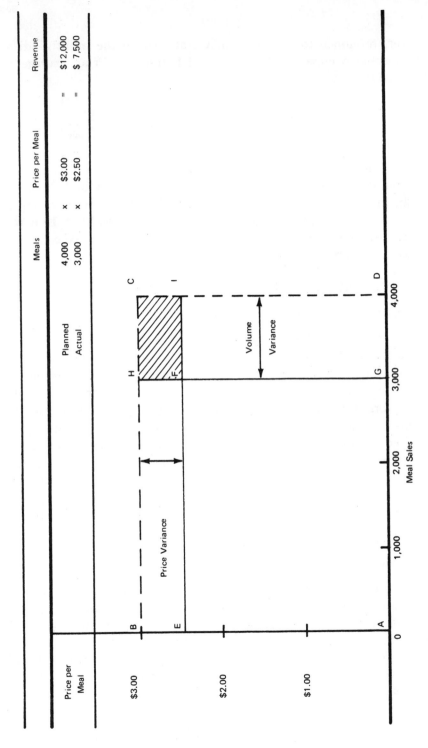

However, reference to the occupancy statistics for the month indicates that the actual double occupancy factor was 1.84, resulting in an average room rate of $17.36, as follows.

$$
\begin{array}{lcl}
\$14.00 \times .16 & = & \$ \ 2.24 \\
\$18.00 \times .84 & = & \underline{\$15.12} \\
& & \underline{\$17.36}
\end{array}
$$

This revenue variance analysis has dealt exclusively with rooms revenue. The same techniques may be applied to all revenue variances. Exhibit 18.6 provides the actual departmental sales for the month of January and the year to date for Big Ski, Inc., the planned sales for the month and year to date, and the variances stated in dollars and percentages. For Big Ski, Inc., Exhibit 18.6 represents the primary revenue control tool, and all variances which exceed the significance criterion should result in management action.

VARIANCES RESULTING FROM SALES-MIX

Food and Beverage Revenues

The Big Ski dining room had sales of $52,100, or $9,100 more than the planned $43,000. Total food revenue is the result of the number of covers served and the average check price. The average check price is the result of the mix of menu items sold. Where there are a substantial number of menu items, the expected average check price is calculated using the expected sales-mix. This use of an expected sales-mix adds an additional variance in the analysis of food sales.

Since a menu analysis to determine the sales-mix is not normally maintained by most restaurants, comparison of the actual to expected sales-mix may take place only where a special or periodic menu analysis is made. In the absence of a current menu analysis, the expected average check price serves primarily to indicate a need for a menu analysis where a significant variance exists between the expected and the actual average check price.

Food and Beverage Costs

Variances occurring as the result of a mix variance are common for both revenues and expenses in the hospitality service industries. Examples include food cost where a mix will result from the various menu items, and beverage cost where the mix might be caused by beer, wine and liquor sales.

The following example shows the isolation of cost and mix variances for a food service operation offering a choice of four dinners: prime rib, fried chicken, filet of sole and spaghetti. Planned food cost percentages for each of the four are

EXHIBIT 18.6

Big Ski, Inc.
Departmental Sales Forecast and Actual
January 31, 197X (C)

	Month		Variance		Year to Date		Variance	
	Budgeted	Actual*	Dollars	Percent	Budgeted	Actual*	Dollars	Percent
Rooms								
Type I	$ 32,000	$ 34,700	$ 2,700	8.4%	$106,000	$111,300	$5,300	.5%
Type II	36,000	38,400	2,400	6.7	127,000	128,200	1,200	.9
Type III	9,000	7,200	(1,800)	(20.0)	28,000	24,700	(3,300)	(11.8)
Two-room Suite	2,000	2,000	-	-	6,000	5,100	(900)	(15.0)
Total	$ 79,000	$ 82,300	$ 3,300	4.2%	$267,000	$269,300	$ 2,300	.9%
Food								
Big Ski Dining Room	$ 43,000	$ 52,100	$ 9,100	21.2%	$147,000	$161,100	$14,100	9.6%
Schuss Snack Bar	27,000	23,500	(3,500)	(13.0)	62,000	54,500	(7,500)	(12.1)
Yodeler Warming Hut	14,000	15,500	1,500	10.7	23,000	24,100	1,100	4.8
Vending Machines	8,000	7,800	(200)	(2.5)	18,000	17,100	(900)	(5.0)
Total	$ 92,000	$ 98,900	$ 6,900	7.5%	$250,000	$256,800	$ 6,800	2.7%
Beverage								
Cave Cocktail Lounge	$ 27,000	$ 29,700	$ 2,700	10.0%	$ 74,000	$ 74,300	$ 300	.4%
Big Ski Dining Room	14,000	19,500	5,500	39.2	46,000	56,800	10,800	23.5
Yodeler Warming Hut	4,000	4,100	100	2.5	7,000	7,300	300	4.3
Total	$ 45,000	$ 53,300	$ 8,300	18.4%	$127,000	$138,400	$11,400	9.0%
Mountain (Lift Tickets)								
Full Day	$ 64,000	$ 69,700	$ 5,700	8.9%	$109,000	$117,500	$ 8,500	7.8%
Half-day	12,000	11,100	(900)	(7.5)	21,000	20,000	(1,000)	(4.8)
Junior	8,000	9,300	1,300	16.3	14,000	15,900	1,900	13.6
Total	$ 84,000	$ 90,100	$ 6,100	7.3%	$144,000	$153,400	$ 9,400	6.5%
Ski School and Rentals								
Group Lessons	$ 10,000	$ 10,900	$ 900	9.0%	$ 17,000	$ 17,600	$ 600	3.5%
Private Lessons	2,000	2,200	200	10.0	4,000	4,200	200	5.0
Rentals	10,000	12,000	2,000	20.0	18,000	19,800	1,800	10.0
Totals	$ 22,000	$ 25,100	$ 3,100	14.1%	$ 39,000	$ 41,600	$ 2,600	6.7%
Other	$ 1,000	$ 1,300	$ 300	30.0%	$ 4,000	$ 4,300	$ 300	7.5%
Total Revenue	$323,000	$351,000	$ 28,000	8.7%	$831,000	$863,800	$32,800	4.0%

*Actual performance figures are reported to the nearest hundred dollars.

441

Item	Planned Food Cost Percentage
Prime Rib	40%
Fried Chicken	32
Filet of Sole	25
Spaghetti	20

Based on the past sales patterns, revealed through menu analysis, the projected sales-mix among these four items is as follows.

Item	Projected Percentage of Food Revenue
Prime Rib	40%
Fried Chicken	25
Filet of Sole	20
Spaghetti	15
	100%

As a result of the planned food cost percentage and projected sales-mix, an overall food cost of 32.0 percent is expected, calculated as follows.

Item	Sales-Mix		Food Cost		
Prime Rib	40%	x	40%	=	16.0%
Fried Chicken	25	x	32	=	8.0
Filet of Sole	20	x	25	=	5.0
Spaghetti	15	x	20	=	3.0
Weighted Average Food Cost					32.0%

Actual food cost for the period was 34.7 percent, and management wishes to know what portion of that revenue is caused by the deviation from the expected sales-mix pattern, and what portion is caused by food cost variances. The actual sales-mix and food cost percentages were:

Item	Actual Sales-Mix	Actual Food Cost Percentage
Prime Rib	38%	45%
Fried Chicken	20	36
Filet of Sole	25	28
Spaghetti	17	20
	100%	34.7%

In order to calculate the mix and cost variances it is necessary to calculate each variance for each menu item. Following are the mix, cost and mix-cost variance computations.

Mix Variance

Item	Mix Variance		Planned Cost		
Prime Rib	2.0% (F)	x	40.0	=	.80% (F)
Fried Chicken	5.0 (F)	x	32.0	=	1.60 (F)
Filet of Sole	5.0 (U)	x	25.0	=	1.25 (U)
Spaghetti	2.0 (U)	x	20.0	=	.40 (U)
Mix Variance					.75% (F)

Cost Variance

Item	Planned Mix		Cost Variance		
Prime Rib	40.0%	x	5.0% (U)	=	2.00% (U)
Fried Chicken	25.0	x	4.0 (U)	=	1.00 (U)
Filet of Sole	20.0	x	3.0 (U)	=	.60 (U)
Spaghetti	15.0	x	-	=	-
Cost Variance					3.60% (U)

Mix-Cost Variance

Item	Mix Variance		Cost Variance		
Prime Rib	2.0% (F)	x	5.0% (U)	=	.10% (F)
Fried Chicken	5.0 (F)	x	4.0 (U)	=	.20 (F)
Filet of Sole	5.0 (U)	x	3.0 (U)	=	.15 (U)
Spaghetti	2.0 (U)	x	-	=	-
Mix-Cost Variance					.15% (F)

The 2.70 percent (34.7% – 32.0%) unfavorable total cost percentage is accounted for as follows.

Mix Variance	.75% (F)
Cost Variance	3.60 (U)
Mix-Cost Variance	.15 (F)
Total Food Cost Percentage Variance	2.70% (U)

Thus, a 3.60 percent increase in the food cost percentage resulted from actual cost percentages exceeding planned cost percentages. However, this was partially offset (0.75 percent) by a shift in the sales-mix to items with lower food cost percentages. The combined cost-mix variance accounted for an additional 0.15 percent favorable variance resulting in an overall unfavorable food cost percentage variance of 2.70 percent.

Although the examples apply variance analysis only to revenue and variable expenses, the technique has wider application. Wherever there is a variation, be it in dollars, units, percentages or whatever, and the results are dependent upon the internal relationships between two or more factors, variance analysis may be employed to determine the effect that each individual variation had upon the outcome, thus pinpointing the specific areas requiring attention.

EXPENSE VARIANCE ANALYSIS

Since variable expenses by definition should change proportionately with changes in volume, an additional variance must be dealt with. Traditionally, this expense variance component is known as a *volume variance*. The quantity variance in expense analysis is referred to as the *usage variance*. Thus, the variances that must be dealt with in expense analysis are the volume, usage and price variances. Additionally, an expense mix variance, similar to a revenue mix variance, occurs where composite expenses are encountered.

In estimating the rooms department housekeeping payroll of $5,500 for January, maid expenses were calculated as follows:

Expected number of room night sales (Includes two-room suites as two rooms)		4,550
Number of rooms cleaned per hour per maid		2
Number of maid hours required (4,550 ÷ 2)	=	2,275
Expected hourly maid wage rate		$1.80
Planned maid payroll expense (2,275 x $1.80)	=	$4,095

For the month of January, in which 4,584 room nights were sold, (two-room suites equal two rooms), maid payroll expense was $4,584, an unfavorable variance of $489. This was a result of 2,692 maid hours and an average hourly rate of approximately $1.70.

	Room Nights	Hours/Room	Wage Rate	Maid Expense
Planned	4,550	0.50	$ 1.80	$ 4,095
Actual	4,584	0.59	1.70	4,584
	34 (U)	0.09 (U)	$ 0.10 (F)	$ 489 (U)

Since only two variances can be dealt with simultaneously, the usage variance and the wage variance are combined as the budget variance and expressed in terms of maid cost per room. Planned maid cost per room was $0.90 (0.50 × $1.80). Actual maid cost per room was $1.00 (0.59 × $1.70), an unfavorable variance of $0.10 per room. This $0.10 per room variance would have amounted to a $455 unfavorable budget variance accounted for as follows.

Type of Variance							Dollar Variance
Price	4,500	x	0.50	x	$0.10	=	$ 228 (F)
Usage	4,500	x	0.09	x	1.80	=	723 (U)
Price-Usage	4,500	x	0.09	x	0.10	=	40 (F)
							$ 455 (U)

With the budget variance now determined, the overall maid expense variance may be calculated. This expense variance will be composed of the volume variances and the budget variance.

	Room Nights	Cost per Room	Maid Expense
Planned	4,550	$ .90	$ 4,095
Actual	4,584	1.00	4,584
Variance	34 (U)	$ .10(F)	$ 489 (U)

Variance			
Volume	34 x $0.90		$ 31 (U)
Budget	4,550 x 0.10		455 (U)
Volume-Budget	34 x 0.10		3 (U)
			$ 489 (U)

As a result of these computations, the $489 unfavorable maid expense variance is composed of:

Price	⎫	$228 (F)	⎫
Usage	⎬ Budget	723 (U)	⎬ $455 (U)
Price-Usage	⎭	40 (F)	⎭
Volume		31 (U)	
Volume-Budget		3 (U)	
Total		$489 (U)	

This variance analysis technique is applicable wherever three or more variances are encountered. The approach is to consolidate and work with only two variances at a time.

FLEXIBLE BUDGETS

If revenues for an operating period occur as projected with the same mix, the same number of units of each revenue category sold and at the projected selling price, the proforma income statement and departmental profit statement are ideal cost control tools for comparing actual with planned cost. However, if revenues do not occur as projected, perhaps with a different mix, number of units of each sold, and selling price, then the projected statements are not useful as cost control tools since the utility of the static or fixed activitiy level profit plan diminishes as the actual activity level varies from the projected level. This is because costs which are effected by volume and are planned for a particular level and mix of activity should not be used as control standards at a different level of mix and activity. What is needed is a means of establishing cost standards for all cost activity levels other than those projected, based upon the operating plan.

The flexible, or dynamic, budget provides expected or planned revenues, expenses and profits for alternative levels of activity. The budget is flexible because it responds to various levels of activity by setting forth the particular revenues, expenses and profits that are planned for that particular level. Exhibit 18.7 is an example of a flexible budget for a one-year period for a motor hotel.

Not only are percentages provided in the flexible budget, but also shown are revenues and expenses related to rooms available, a frequently employed industry technique for comparing lodging facility operations. Because operating management is to be held responsible for gross operating profit this flexible operating plan does not project below this caption in the income statement.

In the planning phase of the profit-planning process operations must be examined and plans prepared for alternative levels of activity. This may be done by preparing a forecast at the most likely activity level and then preparing a forecast above and below this at optimistic and pessimistic activity levels. For instance, the 70 percent occupancy level in Exhibit 18.7 might be the most likely activity level, with the 65 percent level the pessimistic forecast and the 75 percent level the optimistic forecast.

The flexible budget appearing in Exhibit 18.7 is an example of a tabular presentation of revenues and expenses at three selected volume (occupancy) levels. This multiple-level tabular presentation is the usual method of preparing the flexible budget in many categories of the hospitality service industries.

STATIC BUDGETS

In contrast to the flexible or dynamic budget which provides for various levels of volume, the static budget is prepared at a fixed level of volume. Its usefulness is limited where revenues and expenses are sensitive to volume, and as a control tool for such items, it is useful only where the planned volume is realized.

However, many expenses in the hospitality service industries are not volume-related. This would include most capital expenses, such as real estate taxes, interest, depreciation, and the fixed portion of any rent expense. The deductions from income (administration and general, advertising and sales promotion, heat, light and power, and repairs and maintenance) generally have little direct relationship to volume within a relevant range. These types of expense can be budgeted and any variations from this static budget in excess of the specified limit identified for management attention.

REPORTING

A reporting framework must be designed to facilitate the comparison of actual with planned. It must provide for immediate comparisons and quickly isolate significant variations because these variations are the focal point around

EXHIBIT 18.7

Estimated Annual Operating Results
200 Available Rooms
$15.00 Average Daily Rate per Occupied Room

| | Occupancy | | | | | | | | |
| | 65 Percent | | | 70 Percent | | | 75 Percent | | |
	Amount	Percent	Per Available Room	Amount	Percent	Per Available Room	Amount	Percent	Per Available Room
Total Sales and Income									
Rooms	$ 711,800	46.4%	$ 3,559	$ 766,500	47.5%	$ 3,832	$ 821,300	48.5%	$ 4,107
Food	530,100	34.6	2,651	545,800	33.8	2,729	561,500	33.1	2,808
Beverage	238,500	15.5	1,192	245,600	15.2	1,228	252,700	14.9	1,263
Telephone	42,700	2.8	214	46,000	2.9	230	49,300	2.9	246
Other Income	10,000	.7	50	10,000	.6	50	10,000	.6	50
Total	$1,533,100	100.0%	$ 7,666	$1,613,900	100.0%	$ 8,069	$1,694,800	100.0%	$ 8,474
Cost of Foods Sold and Departmental Wages and Expenses									
Rooms	$ 213,800	13.9%	$ 1,069	$ 221,800	13.8%	$ 1,109	$ 229,900	13.6%	$ 1,150
Food and Beverage	590,100	38.5	2,951	602,000	37.3	3,010	611,500	36.1	3,057
Telephone	44,800	2.9	224	47,400	2.9	237	49,500	2.9	248
Total	$ 848,700	55.3%	$ 4,244	$ 871,200	54.0%	$ 4,356	$ 890,900	52.6%	$ 4,455
Gross Operating Income	$ 684,400	44.7%	$ 3,422	$ 742,700	46.0%	$ 3,713	$ 803,900	47.4%	$ 4,019
Deductions from Income									
Administrative and General	$ 128,200	8.3%	$ 641	$ 129,400	8.0%	$ 647	$ 130,600	7.6%	$ 653
Advertising and Sales Promotion	35,000	2.2	175	35,000	2.1	175	35,000	2.1	175
Heat, Light and Power	43,000	2.8	215	43,400	2.7	217	43,800	2.6	219
Repairs and Maintenance	50,000	3.3	250	51,200	3.2	256	52,200	3.1	261
Total	$ 256,200	16.6%	$ 1,281	$ 259,000	16.0%	$ 1,295	$ 261,600	15.4%	$ 1,308
House Profit	$ 428,200	28.1%	$ 2,141	$ 483,700	30.0%	$ 2,418	$ 542,300	32.0%	$ 2,711
Store Rentals	15,000	1.0	75	15,000	.9	75	15,000	.9	75
Gross Operating Profit	$ 443,200	29.1%	$ 2,216	$ 498,700	30.9%	$ 2,493	$ 557,300	32.9%	$ 2,786

which the entire budgetary control system revolves. Reports must be in the same format as the profit plan. Similarly, the profit plan and the reported actual results must be in a form which isolates performance by responsibility centers. Without the properly designed format and timely reports, no budgetary control system can function.

PAYROLL MONITORING

Because salary and wage expenses represent a substantial portion of the operating expenses of any hospitality service industries operation, a control tool by which this major expense can be readily monitored by the responsibility center is necessary. An example of this payroll monitoring control is presented in Exhibit 18.8. Columns seven and eight provide a ratio of payroll expense to related revenues, or productivity per payroll dollar. For example, in the monthly budgeted productivity column (column seven) for the front desk payroll, budgeted room sales per payroll dollar are $17.50. Actual room sales per payroll dollar are $17.20, indicating that either payroll costs were high or sales low. Variance analysis could be used to determine the effect of revenue and payroll costs variances upon this relationship.

An underlying assumption in using this ratio for payroll cost monitoring is that payroll expenses should change proportionately with volume. For many payroll expense classifications this is not the case, but within the relevant range this ratio or productivity approach can be useful for monitoring payroll expenses.

If desired, columns may be added for yearly productivity to date.

SUMMARY

Using the profit plan as a standard of comparison, budgetary control provides the means of isolating and analyzing variances. The results of this analysis can be the basis for actions to prevent the reoccurrence of the variation.

The first consideration in the control process is to determine the significances of individual variations. This may be most efficiently carried out through the utilization of established significance criterion using absolute and/or percentage variations.

The second phase in budgetary control is the analysis of variances between actual and planned to disclose the underlying causes. This frequently results in a compound variance as a result of the combined effect of two individual variances.

The full effectiveness of a profit-planning and control system can only result from the feedback obtained by comparing the planned and actual operations, and the actions taken.

EXHIBIT 18.8

Big Ski, Inc.
Departmental Payroll Budget and Actual
January 197X

	Month				Year to Date				Monthly Productivity (Dollar Sales/Dollar Payroll)			
	Budgeted	Actual[3]	Variance $	%	Budgeted	Actual[3]	Variance $	%	Budgeted	Actual	Variance $	%
Rooms												
Front Desk	$ 4,500	$ 4,800	300 /	6.7%	$ 15,800	$ 16,700	900 /	5.7%	$ 17.50	$ 17.20	$(.30)/	(1.7%)
Housekeeping	5,500	5,900	400	7.2	17,000	17,200	200	1.2	14.40	14.00	(.40)	(2.8)
Total	$ 10,000	$ 10,700	$ 700	7.0%	$ 32,800	$ 33,900	$ 1,100	3.4%	7.90	7.70	(.20)	(2.5)
Food												
Big Ski Dining Room												
Service	$ 6,000	$ 6,400	400	6.7%	$ 19,300	$ 19,900	600	3.1%	$ 9.50[1]	$ 11.20[1]	1.70	17.9%
Preparation	7,000	7,200	200	2.9	21,100	21,200	100	.5	6.15	7.20	1.05	17.0
Dishwashing	4,000	4,800	800	20.0	13,000	15,600	2,600	20.0	10.70	10.80	.10	.9
Total, Big Ski	$ 17,000	$ 18,400	$ 1,400	8.2%	$ 53,400	$ 56,700	$ 3,300	6.2%	3.30[1]	3.90[1]	.60	18.2
Schuss Snack Bar	7,000	7,300	300	4.3	16,000	14,400	(1,600)	(10.0)	3.90	3.20	(.70)	(17.9)
Yodeler Warming Hut	5,000	3,700	(1,300)	(26.0)	8,800	8,800	-	-	3.60	5.30	1.70	47.2
Total	$ 29,000	$ 29,400	$ 400	1.4%	$ 78,200	$ 79,900	$ 1,700	2.2%	3.80[1]	4.20[1]	.40	10.5
Beverage												
Cave Cocktail Lounge	$ 9,000	$ 11,600	$ 2,600	28.9	$ 28,700	$ 31,300	$ 2,600	9.1%	3.00	2.00	(1.00)	(33.3)
Mountain												
Lifts and Grooming	$ 11,000	$ 14,800	$ 3,800	34.5	$ 28,600	$ 29,100	$ 500	1.7%	7.65	6.10	(1.55)	(20.3)
Snowmaking	9,000	9,200	200	2.2	19,300	19,900	600	3.1	9.35	9.80	.45	4.8
Total	$ 20,000	$ 24,000	$ 4,000	20.0%	$ 47,900	$ 49,000	$ 1,100	2.3%	4.20	3.75	(.45)	(10.7)
Ski School and Rentals												
Ski Instructors	$ 6,000	$ 6,800	$ 800	13.3	$ 10,000	$ 10,800	$ 800	8.0%	2.00	1.90	(.10)	(5.0)
Rental Clerks	4,000	4,600	600	15.0	7,200	7,300	100	1.4	2.50	2.85	.35	14.0
Total	$ 10,000	$ 11,400	$ 1,400	14.0%	$ 17,200	$ 18,100	$ 900	5.2%	2.20	2.20	-	-
Administrative and General	$ 12,000	$ 15,100	$ 3,100	25.8	$ 74,000	$ 81,500	$ 7,500	10.1%	27.00[2]	23.00[2]	(4.00)	(14.8)
Repairs and Maintenance	$ 5,000	$ 6,000	$ 1,000	20.0	$ 40,000	$ 42,600	$ 2,600	6.5%	65.00[2]	59.00[2]	(6.00)	(9.2)
Total Payroll	$ 95,000	$108,200	$13,200	13.9%	$318,800	$336,300	$17,500	54.9%	3.40	3.20	(.20)	(5.9)

1. Includes both food and beverage sales.
2. Ratio to total revenue.
3. Actual performance figures are reported to the nearest hundred dollars.

Discussion Questions

1. Discuss the three steps in budgetary control.
2. What are the problems of using absolute variances alone for significance criterion? Percentage variance alone?
3. What are the benefits of variance analysis?
4. How is variance analysis carried out when there are more than two variances?
5. What is a compound variance?
6. What is a flexible budget and under what circumstances is it better than a static budget?

Problem 1

The following information refers to the maid expense for the month of December at the Fair Oaks Hotel.

	Number Room Nights Sold	Number of Hours Required to Clean One Room	Maid's Average Hourly Wage	Total Maid Expense
Planned	5,000	.6	$1.80	$5,400
Actual	5,500	.5	$2.00	$5,500

Using this information analyze the $100 variance in total maid expense. Your answer should include the following variances: volume, volume-budget, price, usage and price-usage.

Problem 2

The planned and actual amounts for ten revenue expense and profit items which have been extracted from the records of the Pullman Hotel are shown. In addition, significance criteria in terms of both absolute and percentage limits are presented. Using the method presented in this chapter, rank the significant unfavorable variances according to their priority for managerial attention.

Problem 2 (continued)

The percentage variance limits are as follows:

Revenues   20%
Expenses   10%
Profit Items   15%

Item	Planned	Actual	Absolute Limit
Room Sales	$ 65,000	$ 67,000	$ 10,000
Food Sales	52,000	47,000	7,000
Beverage Sales	17,000	13,500	2,500
Food Cost	20,000	21,800	1,500
Beverage Cost	5,000	4,000	300
Advertising	3,600	4,000	500
Total Wages	51,000	58,000	3,000
Repairs and Maintenance	6,300	5,800	500
House Profit	31,800	30,800	4,000
Net Profit	7,800	6,750	1,000

Problem 3

Mr. H.O. Joe operates a restaurant in Middle America. He prepares a monthly achievement plan and always compares the actual results with the achievement plan to determine variances. Segments of the planned and actual results for November have been included. You have been asked to analyze the following variances.

1. The variance in food and beverage sales. (Use price and volume.)
2. The variance in dollar food and beverage cost. (Use cost/cover and volume.)
3. The variance in the food and beverage cost percentage. (Use planned cost percentage and mix percentage.)

Planned and Actual Food and Beverage Sales and Costs for the Month of November

Item	Sales-Mix*	Number of Covers	Average Check	Total Sales	Food and Beverage Cost Percentage	Food and Beverage Cost/Cover	Total Food and Beverage Cost
PLANNED							
Chicken	15%	900	$4.00	$ 3,600	30%	$1.20	$ 1,080
Clams	25%	1,500	$5.00	7,500	32%	$1.60	$ 2,400
Ham	20%	1,200	$5.50	6,600	36%	$1.98	$ 2,376
Steak	40%	2,400	$6.00	14,400	40%	$2.40	$ 5,760
	100%	6,000	$5.35	$32,100	36.2%	$1.94	$11,616
ACTUAL							
Chicken	15.0%	960	$4.25	$ 4,080	28%	$1.19	$ 1,142
Clams	29.5	1,888	$4.75	$ 8,968	35%	$1.66	$ 3,134
Ham	18.0	1,152	$5.50	$ 6,336	36%	$1.98	$ 2,281
Steak	37.5	2,400	$5.75	$13,800	45%	$2.59	$ 6,216
Total	100%	6,400	$5.19	$33,184	38.5%	$1.99	$12,773

*As a percentage of total covers.

CHAPTER 19

Sources and Uses of Funds

The analysis of the sources and uses of funds is used to complement the information provided by the core financial statements: the balance sheet, the income statement, and the statement of retained earnings. Accounting statements and reports have different significance for different users, and the analysis of the sources and uses of funds in an accounting statement is useful for both internal and external users.

For the investor and lender the statement of sources and uses of funds gives information to assess the expected risk and return of existing or prospective loans or investments in the firm. The sources and uses of funds statement is particularly useful to management and owners, for it gives information about the net changes in the composition of the balance sheet over the past period or for a projected period in the planning process. The liability and equity side of the balance sheet sets down the net sources of funds, and the asset side shows their net uses. A knowledge of the major transactions affecting the balance sheet and the changing make-up of the balance sheet can be of importance in management's analysis of operations or groups of operations within a firm.

The sources and uses of funds statement is a report on the main capital transactions and events that have been recorded over a period of time in the respective balance sheet accounts. The balance sheet shows the financial condition of the firm, but of major interest to management, owners and creditors is the firm's ability to earn profits. The income statement supplements the balance sheet in this connection as it states the business earnings or income for the reporting time period. Like the income statement and statement of retained earnings, the statement of sources and uses of funds (the funds statement) summarizes events that have taken place over the specified time period. The income statement concentrates specifically on one pattern of change in owners' equity. The funds statement, in contrast, is much wider in scope and extends beyond the analysis of the net income reported for the period.

WHAT ARE FUNDS?

The concept of funds has varied in practice. For example, "funds" is sometimes considered to mean cash or its equivalent, and the resulting funds statement is a summary of cash provided and used. This is a natural concept of funds, as cash is the most liquid asset. In accounting, this definition of funds as cash does not suffice, as the term *funds* has a wider and more general meaning.

In accounting, the most common concept of funds is that of the difference between current assets and current liabilities, and a funds statement prepared under this concept is a summary of working capital provided and used. Current assets are those assets that are expected to be sold or consumed during the normal operating cycle of the firm. Current liabilities are those liabilities which are expected to be paid within the same operating cycle. The concept of the operating or working capital cycle was designed for the industrial or commercial product firm and is considered to be the time interval that covers the current operations, shown as follows.

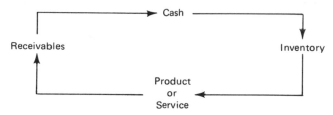

In most areas of the hospitality service industries this complete cycle does not exist or may cover a shorter time interval than that of the manufacturer's cycle time. Where the complete cycle does not exist, a shorter cycle takes its place in which either or both inventory or receivables do not occur in the cycle.

The identification of funds with working capital brings focus upon only the noncurrent part of the total assets and liabilities that change form over the period. Under this definition, funds include net cash, receivables, inventory and other current assets. Not only the net current assets but the composition and change of all assets have to be considered in the sources and uses of funds. This definition of funds as working capital is associated with the usual construction of the funds statement.

Such a definition of funds and the concept of the funds statement eliminates the intra-working capital transactions that can be numerous and may be of importance in the total analysis of the firm's financial progress. This deficiency can be corrected by presenting a supplementary report of the changes in working capital accounts during the same period as the primary statement of sources and uses of funds.

SOURCES AND USES OF FUNDS

Before considering the analysis of sources and uses of funds, it is necessary to consider what the main sources and uses of funds are.

Funds are working capital and represent purchasing power. The liability and equity side of the balance sheet lists the net sources of funds and the asset side indicates their net uses. It is the net sources and uses of funds for the period that are reported in the funds statement.

A simple example of the source and use of funds would be to raise money to build a new hotel by obtaining 50 percent of the amount from a bank loan and 50 percent by issuing common stock. The source of funds to build the hotel is obtained by sale of the common stock, which appears as a credit in the equity section, and receipt of cash from the mortgage, which appears as a credit under long-term liabilities of the balance sheet. The use of the funds is shown on the asset side of the balance sheet by an equal increase in the building and property assets. (It has been assumed the money raised by the mortgage and stock sale is exactly equal to the cost of the new property.)

The first step in locating the sources and uses of funds is to examine the components of the balance sheet.

EXHIBIT 19.1

Grouped Balance Sheet Accounts

Assets	Liabilities and Shareholders' Equity
Current Assets	**Current Liabilities**
Cash	Accounts Payable
Marketable Securities	Taxes Payable
Accounts Receivable	Dividends Payable
Less: Allowance for Bad Debts	Accrued Expenses
Inventory	Current Portion of Long-term Debt
Prepaid Expenses	
Long-term Assets	**Long-term Liabilities**
Land	Loan Payable
Buildings and Equipment	Mortgage Payable
Less: Accumulated Depreciation	
Other Assets	**Shareholders' Equity**
Investment in Affiliates	Common Stock at Par
Cash Surrender Value of Life	Capital in Excess of Par
Insurance	Retained Earnings

Using the main headings and combining current assets and current liabilities into a single figure of net working capital, the balance sheet format in Exhibit 19.1 can be reduced to:

Assets	Liabilities and Shareholders' Equity
Net Working Capital	Long-term Liabilities
Long-term Assets	Shareholders' Equity
Other Assets	

The combination of current assets and current liabilities under one heading has been used to simplify the breakdown of the balance sheet. Many published fund statements present the single line net working capital. However, this combining to a net working capital figure should not be taken as a fixed rule, as the funds statement should be flexible in form.

Long-term assets are land, buildings, equipment and other assets of a permanent nature. The accumulated depreciation, representing the estimated expired cost utility of the asset, is deducted from the respective items resulting in a net value of the long-term asset. Liabilities are creditor's claims against the firm, and consist of short-term debts and long-term debts. With this simplified classification of the balance sheet, sources and uses of funds can more easily be located, as follows.

Assets

Sources of Funds	Uses of Funds
Decrease in Long-term Assets	Increase in Long-term Assets
Decrease in Other Assets	Increase in Other Assets

Liabilities and Shareholders' Equity

Sources of Funds	Uses of Funds
Increase in Long-term Liabilities	Decrease in Long-term Liabilities
Increase in Stockholders' Equity	Decrease in Shareholders' Equity

A simple breakdown of balance sheet changes is shown in Exhibit 19.2. These changes during the year can be summarized into the sources and uses of funds.

The funds statement process so far has confined the source and application of funds to the simple consideration of balance sheet changes. Additional sources of information other than the balance sheet are available to help analyze these changes in more detail.

Of particular interest are the detailed balance sheet accounts as listed in Exhibit 19.1. In addition to these listed accounts the income statement summarizes the changes in the shareholders' equity over the same period covered by the balance sheets and the statement of retained earnings. Brief examples of these additional statements are set forth in Exhibit 19.3 for the Blue Grass Motel Corporation owning and operating a fifty-unit motel.

EXHIBIT 19.2

**Blue Grass Motel Corporation
Summary of Balance Sheet Changes
for Year Ended December 31, 197X**

	January 1	December 31	Increase or (Decrease)
Assets			
Net Working Capital	$120,000	$150,000	$ 30,000
Long-term Assets (Less Depreciation)	250,000	290,000	40,000
Other Assets	25,000	20,000	(5,000)
Total	$395,000	$460,000	$ 65,000
Liabilities and Stockholders' Equity			
Long-term Liabilities	$115,000	$105,000	$ (10,000)
Stockholders' Equity	280,000	355,000	75,000
Total	$395,000	$460,000	$ 65,000

MAJOR SOURCES OF FUNDS

Internal Sources

Operations of the Firm

The most important single source of funds is the current profitable operations of the business. Many entities in the hospitality service industries depend on funds from current operations to meet a large portion of their long-term mortgage debts, to pay for the continuing replacement of furnishings and equipment, and to help finance the expansion of the unit.

An understanding of how funds are generated by current operations requires an understanding of the operating cycle of a hospitality service business. The cycle is as follows:

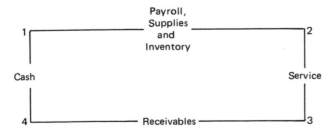

There are basically four stages to this operating cycle.

EXHIBIT 19.3

Blue Grass Motel Corporation
Income Statement
for Year Ended December 31, 197X

Total Sales and Income	
Rooms	$160,000
Food	150,000
Beverages	70,000
Other Income	11,000
Total	$391,000
Cost of Goods Sold and Departmental Wages and Expenses	
Rooms	$ 50,000
Food and Beverages	170,000
Total	$220,000
Gross Operating Income	$171,000
Deductions from Income	
Administrative and General	$ 45,000
Advertising and Sales Promotion	8,000
Heat, Light and Power	15,000
Repairs and Maintenance	17,000
Total	$ 85,000
House Profit	$ 86,000
Real Estate Taxes	22,000
Profit After Real Estate Taxes but Before Other Capital Expenses	$ 64,000
Depreciation Expense	31,000
Income Before Federal and State Income Taxes	$ 33,000
Provision for Federal and State Income Taxes	$ 8,000
Net Income After Income Taxes	$ 25,000
Retained Earnings — January 1, 197X	150,000
Retained Earnings — December 31, 197X	$175,000

Purchase of Materials, Payroll and Supplies. Cash is used to purchase materials, labor, supplies, goods, etc. to be placed into the operating cycle; these purchases of goods and services are inventoried until they are used as part of the final service.

Production. The use of inventory in producing the final product depends upon the type of industry. Hospitality service industries such as hotels, motels, clubs, and restaurants use the inventory as part of the service provided to the guest. In manufacturing, inventory is processed using labor and machines to produce the finished tangible product to be shipped to the distribution outlets. The time span for the manufactured inventory could be as long as three to six months, whereas the time span in the hospitality service industries is as short as a few days.

Credit Sales. The guest may receive the service but may not immediately pay cash for it. This is a receivable, indicating that the payment for this service by the servicee (guest) is outstanding. The credit time span in the hospitality service industries is generally much shorter than the product sold on credit.

Collections. In the final step, outstanding payments are received from the guest or their credit agencies.

Funds are generated in the form of income produced by the cycle of operations, provided, of course, that the cost of producing the services does not exceed the money received. The relationship between net income and the amount of funds provided by operations is illustrated in the following condensed simplified form of the Blue Grass Motel Corporation's income statement (Exhibit 19.4).

EXHIBIT 19.4

Blue Grass Motel Corporation
Single Step Income Statement
for the Year Ended December 31, 197X

Sales Revenue and Income	$391,000
Cost of Goods Sold, Departmental and Capital Expenses	327,000
Gross Funds Produced by Operations	$ 64,000
Less Income Taxes	8,000
Net Funds Produced by Operations	$ 56,000
Less Depreciation	31,000
Net Income	$ 25,000

The total amount that will appear in the funds statement representing a source of funds is $56,000. To obtain this figure the depreciation is added to the net income, as depreciation does not represent an outflow of funds. It is an expense charged to operations for the expired cost of plant and equipment and other depreciable assets, but requires no use of funds (working capital) at the time the depreciation expense is recorded in the accounts.

Sale of Long-term Assets. Furnishings, furniture or equipment are the more common noncurrent assets that may be sold. Their sale will result in a decrease in long-term assets and the proceeds from the sale are a source of funds.

In Exhibit 19.2, the long-term assets of the Blue Grass Motel Corporation increased by $40,000 from $250,000 to $290,000 for the year ended December 31, 197X. From the income statement (Exhibit 19.3) the total depreciation charge was $31,000. If depreciation was the only charge affecting the long-term assets they would have declined by $31,000. To achieve a net increase of $40,000 the increase in long-term assets before depreciation must have been $71,000. Thus, it would seem that $71,000 of new long-term assets were purchased during the period. A review of the information relating to the financial statements will complete the analysis of additions and retirements of long-term assets.

From the combined information available in the balance sheet, the income statement and the information relating to the financial statements, a statement of long-term asset changes can be prepared (Exhibit 19.5).

EXHIBIT 19.5

Blue Grass Motel Corporation
Statement of Long-term Asset Changes
for the Year Ended December 31, 197X

	Asset Cost	Accumulated Depreciation	Net Book Value
Balance as of January 1, 197X	$408,000	$158,000	$250,000
Additions	76,000	31,000	45,000
	$484,000	$189,000	$295,000
Retirements and Sales	20,000	15,000	5,000
Balance as of December 31, 197X	$464,000	$174,000	$290,000

Long-term assets purchased amounted to $76,000. From the income statement it is seen that the total depreciation for the year amounted to $31,000. Assets originally costing $20,000 with a net value of $5,000 were retired during the same period, so the total additions are $76,000 rather than the $71,000 that originally appeared as purchases for the period.

Suppose that the proceeds from the sale of the retired assets were $4,000 instead of $5,000. The income statement would show a loss on sale of equipment of $1,000. The funds statement would show a source of funds from the sale of assets of $4,000. In a similar treatment for depreciation, the $1,000 loss is added back to net income as a part of funds provided by operations as the $1,000 loss did not use funds. It is important to note that all operating expenses that do not represent an outflow of funds (working capital) are added back to net income in order to determine the total funds provided by operations of the firm.

Gains from the sale of long-term assets are treated in an opposite manner to losses and are not an inflow of funds from operations. For example, instead of being sold for $5,000 the kitchen equipment might have been sold for $8,000, a net gain of $3,000. This $3,000 gain would be in the net income for the period and the $3,000 must be deducted from net income to report the correct funds generated from operations for the period. The gain is not an inflow of funds from operations, but rather the $3,000 is a portion of the $8,000 of funds provided from the sale of kitchen equipment.

External Sources

Short-term Debt

Short-term debt amounts provided by creditors are recognized when the funds concept is considered to be the flow of cash. When the more common concept of working capital is used the variation in short-term debt is part of the net change in working capital. All of the following current liabilities are forms of short-term debt provided by the bank, vendors, employees, the government and others.

1. Bank Loans
2. Accounts Payable
3. Accrued Taxes Payable, Including Income Taxes
4. Accrued Wages, Salaries and Other Expenses

Long-term Debt

Long-term debt consists of loans made with maturity periods of longer than one year. This form of debt includes promissory notes, debenture bonds, convertibles, and mortgages maturing after one year. Generally the promissory note or bond in the hospitality service industries is secured by a mortgage on the personal property and real estate.

Increases in long-term debt during the period indicates an increase in credit financing and thus an increase in the source of working capital (funds provided). A decrease in long-term debt during the period is the repayment of a portion of the debt which reduces the firm's working capital (use of funds).

Stockholders' Equity

The main sources of funds in this category are from present or new investors who purchase shares of stock and from the earnings retained from the operations of the business. The funds provided from stock sold is the amount that the investor has paid for the stock irrespective of the par value of the shares. In the profitable corporation, retained earnings may be a continuous major source of funds for the entity because cash dividends paid to stockholders are taxable income to the shareholders, subject to steeply graduated state and federal income tax rates. In contrast to paying dividends, a continuous policy of retaining earnings will increase the resources of the corporation and the value of the stock. Hence, the stockholder should be able to sell his shares at a price higher than his cost and this gain is subject to the lower capital gains tax rates. Because of this difference in tax rates between ordinary income and capital gains, some corporations may not pay any of its earnings to stockholders as dividends but retain these earnings to strengthen and increase the value of the stockholders' common stock interest.

SOME MAJOR USES OF FUNDS

Unprofitable Operations

When the operations of a firm are unprofitable, there will be a shrinkage of resources. For example, the Blue Grass Motel in Exhibit 19.4 might have had a serious fire during the year and there was no revenue for almost a month. The Blue Grass Motel had no business interruption insurance and operating expenses continued during the renovations. In these circumstances the annual condensed income statement of the Blue Grass Motel Corporation might be as follows:

Sales Revenue and Income	$332,000
Expenses (Outflow of Funds)	300,000
Gross Funds Generated by Operations	$ 12,000
Less Real Estate Taxes and Interest	22,000
Net Funds Produced by Operations	$ (10,000)
Add Depreciation	31,000
Net (Loss)	$ (41,000)

This shows that the operations failed to produce funds and sustained a loss before income tax credits of $41,000. A continued annual reduction in resources through operating losses would result in insolvency and bankruptcy.

Capital Expenditures

The main capital expenditures in the hospitality service industries are in land and buildings, with lesser amounts in furnishings and equipment. Except for land, their economic utility is used and worn out over a period of years. In most categories of the hospitality service industries this loss of economic utility is a fairly rapid process. With the rapid rate of change in the desires and tastes of the guests (users) of the hospitality firm, coupled with the recognition of this inherent obsolesence in the annual income tax allowances for depreciation, there should be continuous major expenditures for renovation and replacements of furnishings, equipment and other capital improvements that would be visible to the guest for his comfort, taste and convenience.

Dividend Payments and Retirement of Long-term Debt

Owners of a firm may receive a current cash return on their stock investment or capital account. These dividends or withdrawals result in an outflow of cash and thus the use of working capital. The retirement or refinancing of long-term debts and the occasional purchasing of the firm's stock or of a partner's interest may be a major use of funds. These major financing events are infrequent and should be planned well ahead of time to ensure that sufficient funds in excess of normal requirements are available.

Depreciation: A Non-Source of Funds

Depreciation expense is not a source of funds. It does not generate funds; rather, it is a bookkeeping reduction of both net income and long-term assets. The depreciation expense in the income statement does not result in the use of funds (working capital) as other expenses do. As depreciation is not a use of funds it can not make funds available to the firm. Depreciation and other accruals that do not represent an outflow of funds (working capital) are added back to net income to obtain the total funds produced by operations. The accounting recognition of depreciation does not provide funds and the same can be said of all other cost accruals.

However, depreciation has the effect of reducing corporation income taxes. The Internal Revenue code allows depreciation and obsolesence to be charged as an annual expense. This reduces the reported net income on which income taxes are computed, and has the effect of making more funds available to the firm as it reduces working capital needed for taxes. This is illustrated in Exhibit 19.6. By including $200,000 in annual depreciation to be charged as an expense for federal and state income tax purposes funds are increased by $100,000, the decrease in federal and state income tax liability.

THE ANALYSIS OF FUNDS

The objective of the analysis of funds is to prepare a statement that shows the sources and uses of funds (funds statement). The objectives of the funds statement are to summarize the flow of the financing and investment activities including the amount of funds generated internally and to provide information to supplement the income statement and the balance sheet. Some of the information for the analysis of funds is available from the income statement and the balance sheet,

EXHIBIT 19.6

Depreciation Effects on the Net Funds
Produced by Operations

	Without Depreciation		With Depreciation	
	Income Statement	Sources and Uses of Funds	Income Statement	Sources and Uses of Funds
Sales	$2,000,000	$2,000,000	$2,000,000	$2,000,000
Expenses	1,200,000	1,200,000	1,200,000	1,200,000
Depreciation	-	-	200,000	-
Net Income Before Taxes	$ 800,000	$ 800,000	$ 600,000	$ 800,000
State and Federal Income Taxes (Estimated 50%)	400,000	400,000	300,000	300,000
Net Income	$ 400,000		$ 300,000	
Funds Provided by Operations		$ 400,000		$ 500,000

but some is not. The funds statement is intended to provide information that is not completely available in the other statements. Further, the funds statement requires that the information for its preparation be analyzed and classified in a meaningful form, so as to provide the financial statement users with a complete picture of the flow of funds and the resulting change in financial position for the period. The funds statement should provide useful information to a variety of users for a variety of economic decisions. Hence, the funds statement must be sufficiently comprehensive to insure a full disclosure to these various interested users.

The analysis of funds for the preparation of the funds statement requires information from various sources; they are:

1. Balance sheets for the beginning and end of the period with full details of the accounts.
2. The income statement for the period.
3. A statement of changes in owner's equity.
4. Other information relating to the financial statements to explain transactions during the period not explained by the three basic or core financial statements.

The analysis and preparation of funds flow during a period must use all of the listed sources of information. The following case illustrates the complete process of analysis and preparation of the source and use of funds statement.

EXHIBIT 19.7

Tahoe Motel Corporation
Comparative Balance Sheet

Assets	December 31, 197X	January 1, 197X	Increase or (Decrease)
Current Assets			
Cash	$ 31,200	$ 11,000	$ 20,200
Accounts Receivable	19,000	18,000	1,000
Less: Allowance for Bad Debts	(1,400)	(1,000)	(400)
Inventory	6,000	4,000	2,000
Prepaid Expenses	2,200	1,800	400
Total Current Assets	$ 57,000	$ 33,800	$ 23,200
Long-term Assets			
Land	$ 2,200	$ 2,200	$ -
Buildings and Equipment	214,150	180,000	34,150
Less: Accumulated Depreciation	(49,000)	(38,000)	(11,000)
Total Long-term Assets	$167,350	$144,200	$ 25,180
Total Assets	$224,350	$178,000	$ 46,350
Liabilities and Shareholders' Equity			
Current Liabilities			
Accounts Payable	$ 4,000	$ 3,300	$ 700
Accrued Expenses	6,000	5,200	800
Income Taxes Payable	4,000	3,500	500
Current Portion of Long-term Liabilities	5,800	5,200	600
Deposits on Advance Reservations	2,100	2,200	(100)
Total Current Liabilities	$ 21,900	$ 19,400	$ 2,500
Long-term Liabilities — Mortgage Payable	53,700	48,100	5,600
Total Liabilities	$ 75,600	$ 67,500	$ 8,100
Shareholders' Equity			
Capital Stock at Par	15,500	15,000	500
Capital in Excess of Par	45,000	38,000	7,000
Retained Earnings	88,250	57,500	30,750
Total Shareholders' Equity	$148,750	$110,500	$ 38,250
Total Liabilities and Shareholders' Equity	$224,350	$178,000	$ 46,350

The analysis of funds for preparing the funds statement would include the following steps to obtain selected information.

1. Comparative dollar analysis of the balance sheet changes.
2. A detailed breakdown or explanation of the balance sheet changes from the other given sources of information.

EXHIBIT 19.8

Tahoe Motel Corporation
Income Statement
for Year Ended December 31, 197X

Total Sales and Income	
Rooms	$160,000
Food	80,000
Beverage	50,000
Telephone	4,000
Other Income	6,000
Total	$300,000
Cost of Goods Sold and Departmental	
Wages and Expenses	
Rooms	$ 40,000
Food and Beverages	94,000
Telephone	6,000
Total	$140,000
Gross Operating Income	$160,000
Deductions from Income	60,000
House Profit	$100,000
Interest Expense	$ 5,000
Real Estate Taxes	7,000
Loss on Sale of Equipment	2,000
Depreciation Expense	12,000
	$ 26,000
Profit Before Income Taxes	$ 74,000
Income Taxes (State and Federal)	32,000
Net Income	$ 42,000

EXHIBIT 19.9

Tahoe Motel Corporation
Changes in Stockholders' Equity
for Year Ended December 31, 197X

	Capital Stock	Capital In Excess of Par	Retained Earnings
Balance—January 1, 197X	$ 15,000	$ 38,000	$ 57,500
Net Income for Year			42,000
Cash Dividends			(11,250)
Sale of an Additional 500 Shares of Stock at $15 per Share	500	7,000	
Balance—December 31, 197X	$ 15,500	$ 45,000	$ 88,250

Other Information

1. Equipment at the cost of $5,000 and accrued depreciation of $1,000 was sold for $2,000.

2. The current installment of $5,200 on the mortgage payable at January 1, 197X, was paid during the year.

COMPARATIVE ANALYSIS OF BALANCE SHEET CHANGES

The initial step in the analysis of funds is to list the changes in the various balance sheet accounts that have taken place during the period. From the balance sheets in Exhibit 19.7 the balance sheet changes are computed in Exhibit 19.10.

EXHIBIT 19.10

Tahoe Motel Corporation
Changes in Account Balances
for the Year Ended December 31, 197X

	Changes In Account Balances Increase or (Decrease)	Source of Funds	Use of Funds
Current Assets			
Cash	$ 20,200		$ 20,200
Accounts Receivable	1,000		1,000
Less: Allowance for Bad Debts	(400)	$ 400	1,000
Inventory	2,000		2,000
Prepaid Expenses	400		400
Total Current Assets	$ 23,200		
Land	$ -		
Buildings and Equipment	34,150		34,150
Less: Accumulated Depreciation	(11,000)	11,000	
Total Assets	$ 46,350		
Current Liabilities			
Accounts Payable	$ 700	700	
Accrued Expenses	800	800	
Income Taxes Payable	500	500	
Current Portions of Long-term Debt	600	600	
Revenue Collected in Advance	(100)		100
Total Current Liabilities	$ 2,500		
Mortgage Payable	5,600	5,600	
Total Liabilities	$ 8,100		
Stockholders' Equity			
Capital Stock at Par	500	500	
Capital in Excess of Par	7,000	7,000	
Retained Earnings	30,750	30,750	
Total Stockholders' Equity	$ 38,250		
Total Liabilities and Stockholders' Equity	$ 46,350	$ 57,850	$ 57,850

Two columns are headed, respectively, sources of funds and uses of funds, and each change in the account balance is classified depending on its effect on working capital. This first step in the analysis of funds has produced the following information from the balance sheet.

1. It has associated each change in the account balances with either a source or a use of funds.

2. It has insured that major sources of funds and uses of funds have been accounted for.

A review of Exhibit 19.10 indicates that the main source of funds was from current operations and the main use of funds was for expansion of its building and equipment. Exhibit 19.11 can now be prepared to classify and summarize the changes in the balance sheet during the period.

EXHIBIT 19.11

Tahoe Motel Corporation
Summary of Balance Sheet Changes
for the Year Ended December 31, 197X

Source of Funds

Increase in Current Liabilities	$	2,500
Increase in Long-Term Liabilities		5,600
Increase in Shareholders' Equity		38,250
Total	$	46,350

Uses of Funds

Increase in Current Assets	$	23,200
Increase in Long-Term Assets		23,150
Total	$	46,350

DETAILED BREAKDOWN OF BALANCE SHEET CHANGES

The next step in the analysis is to make use of all the sources of information available. The balance sheet, the income statement, the statement of the changes in shareholders' equity, and other information supplements are studied to produce a more detailed analysis of the sources and uses of funds.

Funds Generated by Current Operations

The income statement shows the provision for depreciation and a loss on sales of equipment, both of which are added back to the net income.

Net Income	$ 42,000
Loss of Sale of Equipment	2,000
Depreciation	12,000
Net Sources of Funds from Operations	$ 56,000

The depreciation charge of $12,000 for the year is in excess of the net change in accumulated depreciation by $1,000. Other information shows that $1,000 of accumulated depreciation was removed from the accounts when the equipment was sold.

Accumulated Depreciation December 31, 197X		$ 49,000
Accumulated Depreciation January 1, 197X	$ 38,000	
Depreciation Removed in Sale of Equipment	1,000	
		37,000
Depreciation During Year		$ 12,000

Changes in Shareholders' Equity

There is a net change in shareholders' equity of $38,250. Exhibit 19.9 reports that cash dividends of $11,250 were declared, so changes in shareholders' equity can be stated as follows.

Sources of Funds		
Net Income		$ 42,000
Sale of Stock at Par	$ 500	
Capital in Excess of Par	7,000	
		7,500
Total		$ 49,500
Uses of Funds		
Cash Dividends Declared		11,250
Net Increase in Stockholders' Equity		$ 38,250

Purchase and Sale of Long-term Assets

During the year there was a net increase of $34,150 in long-term assets. Other information shows that $5,000 of equipment was sold. The following activity schedule for the buildings and equipment account can be prepared from this information.

Balance, December 31, 197X	$214,150
Balance, January 1, 197X	180,000
Net Increase During Year	34,150
Equipment Sold	5,000
Equipment Purchased During Year	$ 39,150

Long-term Liabilities

Other information shows a $5,200 payment on the mortgage during the year. This results in net mortgage proceeds of $10,800, computed as follows:

Mortgage Payable December 31, 197X		$ 53,700
Mortgage Payable January 1, 197X	$ 48,100	
Paid During the Year	5,200	
		42,900
Source of Funds from Additional Borrowings		$ 10,800

All of the information has now been accumulated and analyzed so that the source and use of funds statement in Exhibit 19.12 can be prepared.

EXHIBIT 19.12
Tahoe Motel Corporation
Source and Use of Funds Statement
for the Year Ended December 31, 197X

Sources of Funds		
Operations		
Net Income	$ 42,000	
Depreciation	12,000	
Loss of Sale of Equipment	2,000	
		$ 56,000
Sale of Capital Stock		
At Par	$ 500	
Premium in Excess of Par	7,000	
		7,500
Proceeds of Mortgage Borrowing		10,800
Sale of Equipment		2,000
Total Funds Provided		$ 76,300
Uses of Funds		
Purchase of Building and Equipment	$ 39,150	
Dividends on Capital Stock	11,250	
Payments on Mortgage	5,200	
		$ 55,600
Increase in Working Capital		20,700
Total Funds Applied		$ 76,300

The information obtained in the funds analysis process may be recorded on a work sheet to assist in the preparation of the funds statement. The work sheet is designed to be self-balancing and can serve as a check on accuracy in the process of preparing the funds statement. Exhibit 19.13 is the work sheet for the preparation of the Tahoe Motel Corporation's statement of sources and uses of funds for the year ended December 31, 197X.

SUMMARY

The most common concept of funds is working capital, the excess of current assets over current liabilities. Funds may be used for the purchase of long-term assets, the retirement of debt, the payment of dividends or the purchase of treasury stock. Major sources of funds include operations, sale of long-term assets, long-term borrowing and the sale of additional stock.

The sources and uses of funds statement can provide important information for many varied users. When combined with the analysis of the prime financial statements, the sources and uses of funds gives additional information concerning the ability of the organization to pay dividends, meet commitments and undertake new capital investment projects. Used as a supplementary planning tool, projections of funds statements can estimate an organization's future fund excesses and deficiencies.

Depreciation must be added back to net income after taxes to arrive at the total funds flow from operations. This reporting of depreciation in the funds

EXHIBIT 19.13
Tahoe Motel Corporation, Work Sheet for Source and Use of Funds Statement

	January 1, 197X 12/31/69	December 31, 197X 12/31/70	Net Change Debit	Net Change Credit	Adjustments Debit	Adjustments Credit	Funds Used	Funds Sources	Working Capital Increase	Working Capital Decrease
Current Assets	33800	57000	23200						23200	
Long-Term Assets										
Land	7200	7200								
Building and Equipment	138000	214750	34750		(1) 5000	(A) 39750				
Less: Accumulated Depreciation	(31000)	(44000)		11000	(B) 12000	(2) 1000				2500
Total Assets	175000	224450								
Current Liabilities										
Notes Long-Term Debt	5200	5300		2500	(3) 10800	(3) 5200				
Other	14200	16100		5300						
Long-Term Debt	19400	21700		500	(E) 500					
Capital Stock at Par	38000	45000		7000	(E) 7000					
Capital in Excess of Par	5750	89350		30750	(2) 42000	(2) 11250				
Retained Earnings	110500	149750								
	175000	224350	57350	57350						
Sources of Funds										
Operations:										
Net Income						(E) 42000	39750	42000		
Depreciation						(B) 12000	11250	12000		
Loss on Sale of Equipment					2000	(1) 5000	5700	3000		
Sale of Capital Stock					1000	(E) 7500		7500		
Proceeds of Mortgage Borrowing						(2) 10800		10800		
Sale of Equipment						(2) 3000		3000		
Uses of Funds										
Purchase of Buildings and Equipment					(K) 39750		55100		21200	2500
Retirement of Capital Stock					(1) 11250		30700	78300	23200	20700
Payment on Mortgage					(3) 6300		74600	74300		23200
Increase in Working Capital						135900	135900			

statement has sometimes resulted in an incorrect conclusion that depreciation is a source of funds. However, the add-back of depreciation is merely to reverse the non-cash expense of depreciation, as this expense did not use working capital.

Discussion Questions

1. Define funds.
2. How does the balance sheet reflect the effect of sources and uses of funds?
3. What are the major sources of funds?
4. Describe the four stages of the operating cycle.
5. What are the major uses of funds?
6. Describe the objective of a funds statement.
7. What information is required for the preparation of a sources and uses of funds statement?

Problem 1

Big Bear Lodge Co., Inc.
Comparative Balance Sheet
December 31

Assets

	1971	1970
Current Assets		
Cash	$ 325,774	$ 577,973
Treasury Bills	-	149,608
Trade Accounts Receivable	1,086,074	966,146
Other Receivables	150,179	150,478
Inventories	601,329	64,810
Prepaid Expenses	152,756	108,142
Total Current Assets	$2,316,112	$2,017,157
Plant Assets		
Land	$ 281,322	$ 143,910
Buildings and Equipment (at Cost)[1]	1,831,719	1,714,393
	$2,113,041	$1,858,303
Less: Accumulated Depreciation	402,752	330,431
Total Plant Assets	$1,710,289	$1,527,872
Other Assets	$ 45,727	$ 20,034
Total Assets	$4,072,128	$3,565,063

Liabilities and Stockholders' Equity

	1971	1970
Accounts Payable	$ 802,433	$ 754,243
Accrued Expenses	508,912	487,461
Total Current Liabilities	$1,311,345	$1,241,704
Long-term Debt—Convertible Debentures	$1,390,682	$1,111,682
Total Liabilities	$2,702,027	$2,353,386
Total Stockholders' Equity	$1,370,101	$1,211,677
Total Liabilities and Stockholders' Equity	$4,072,128	$3,565,063

Problem 1 (continued)

Big Bear Lodge Co., Inc.
Comparative Income Statement and Retained Earnings
Years Ended December 31

	1971	*1970*
Sales	$10,913,664	$10,735,154
Other Income	12,736	11,661
Total Income	$10,926,400	$10,746,815
Cost and Expenses [2]	$10,264,091	$10,029,565
Income Before Federal Taxes	$ 662,309	$ 717,250
Estimated Taxes on Income		
Federal	$ 354,500	$ 383,500
State	1,157	1,727
	$ 355,657	$ 385,227
Net Income for Year	$ 306,652	$ 332,023
Retained Earnings		
January 1	1,211,677	1,027,873
	$ 1,518,329	$ 1,359,896
Cash Dividends Paid	148,228	148,219
Retained Earnings		
December 31	$ 1,370,101	$ 1,211,677

1. Note that the $28,093 of depreciated equipment written off is the difference between the $100,414 of depreciation expense for the year and the $72,321 which is the net change in accumulated depreciation for the year. This total is added to the net change in buildings and equipment to determine the total purchase price of buildings and equipment.

2. Includes depreciation expense of $100,414 in 1971 and $77,596 in 1970.

Required

1. Prepare a source and uses of funds statement.

Problem 2

Bogey Hill Country Club
Comparative Balance Sheet
December 31

Assets

	1971	1970
Cash	$ 76,957	$ 74,548
Accounts Receivable	53,249	52,670
Inventories	4,544	5,462
Prepaid Expenses	19,803	19,192
Total Current Assets	$ 154,553	$ 151,872
Land	$ 466,287	$ 464,446
Building	816,764	762,401
Machinery	214,901	209,724
Furniture and Fixtures	267,862	253,141
Less: Accumulated Depreciation	(612,661)	(584,530)
Total Property and Equipment	$1,153,153	$1,105,182
Total Assets	$1,307,706	$1,257,054

Liabilities and Members' Equity

	1971	1970
Accounts Payable	$ 122,990	$ 139,016
Accrued Expenses	63,742	56,439
Total Current Liabilities	$ 186,732	$ 195,455
Long-term Debt	$ 54,370	$ 80,777
Total Liabilities	$ 241,102	$ 276,232
Total Members' Equity	$1,066,604	$ 980,822
Total Liabilities and Members' Equity	$1,307,706	$1,257,054

Additional Information

1. In the members' equity account, new additions consisted of dues restricted for improvements, $31,935; special assessments, $45,000; transfer fees, $35,700; and equity released by senior members, $2,800.
2. There was an interest payment of $4,151.
3. There was a reduction of fixed assets of $25,000 worth of fully depreciated assets.

Problem 2 (continued)

Bogey Hill Country Club
Comparative Statement of Income and Expense
Years Ended December 31

	1971	*1970*
Club General		
Membership Dues and Green Fees	$376,919	$373,044
Direct Expenses (Committee		
Expenses Net of Revenue)		
Course Maintenance	$ 66,814	$ 60,937
Golf Activity Committee	16,887	14,505
Caddy Committee	2,667	2,867
Swimming Pool Committee	7,022	4,636
Tennis Committee	8,333	8,375
Winter Sports Committee	7,870	6,521
Entertainment Committee	8,589	4,191
	$118,182	$102,032
Net Club General Revenue	$258,737	$271,012
Operating Departments Profit or (Loss)		
Restaurant	$ (3,941)	$ (31,401)
Buffet	27,674	7,478
Locker Rooms	(4,363)	(9,303)
Clubhouse Rentals	8,662	8,496
Other Income	-	498
	$ 28,032	$ (24,232)
Gross Operating Income	$286,769	$246,780
Undistributed Operating Expenses		
Clubhouse	$ 38,600	$ 37,749
Administrative and General	75,721	63,666
Payroll Taxes and Employee Benefits	22,464	19,367
Heat, Light and Power	15,776	13,629
Maintenance and Repairs	12,075	16,425
Ground Maintenance	9,839	9,489
	$174,475	$160,325
Net Operating Income Before		
Insurance and Property Taxes	$112,294	$ 86,455
Insurance and Property Taxes		
Insurance	$ 12,115	$ 11,539
Property Taxes	72,550	69,525
	$ 84,665	$ 81,064
Net Operating Income Before Depreciation	$ 27,629	$ 5,391

Required

1. Prepare a statement of source and application of funds.
2. Compute the change in working capital.

Problem 3

Hotel Trouble
Comparative Balance Sheets
December 31

Assets

	1971		*1970*
Current Assets			
Cash	$ 56,690		$ 60,356
Marketable Securities	58,000		75,000
Accounts Receivable	18,870		19,575
Inventories	37,755		38,024
Prepaid Expenses	14,650		13,675
Total Current Assets	$ 185,965		$206,630
Fixed Assets			
Land	127,815		127,815
Building	$1,504,775		$1,204,775
Less: Accumulated Depreciation	964,469		917,194
	540,306		287,581
Furniture and Equipment	$ 574,853		$ 597,853
Less: Accumulated Depreciation	261,964		300,664
	312,889		297,189
Operating Equipment	$ 26,924		$ 15,924
Less: Accumulated Depreciation	8,850		6,250
	18,074		9,674
Total Assets	$1,185,049		$928,889

Liabilities and Stockholders' Equity

	1971		1970
Current Liabilities			
Accounts Payable	$ 18,430		17,370
Notes Payable	23,750		24,315
Accrued Expenses	23,355		23,705
Income Taxes Payable	6,554		5,864
Current Portion — L.T.D.	15,400		13,500
Total Current Liabilities	$ 87,489		$ 84,754
Long-term Debt	342,140		207,540
Total Liabilities	$ 429,629		$ 292,294
Stockholders' Equity			
Common Stock, $10 Par	260,000		200,000
Capital Surplus	135,800		100,000
Retained Earnings	359,620		336,595
Total Liabilities and Stockholders' Equity	$1,185,049		$ 928,889

Problem 3 (continued)

Hotel Trouble
Summary Income Statement
for the Year Ended December 31, 1971

Total Revenues	$798,166
Less: Departmental Expenses	512,191
Gross Operating Income	$285,975
Less: Undistributed Operating Expense	158,524
House Profit	$127,451
Add: Store Rentals	7,741
Gross Operating Profit	$135,192
Municipal Taxes and Insurance	22,288
Profit before Depreciation	$112,904
Depreciation Expense	73,975
Net Operating Profit	$ 38,929
Gain on Sale of Equipment	550
Net Profit before Income Taxes	$ 39,479
Provision for Income Taxes	12,454
Net Profit to Retained Earnings	$ 27,025

Additional Information

1. Fully depreciated furniture which originally cost $60,000 was written off during 1971.
2. Operating equipment costing $3,000 which had accumulated depreciation of $2,800 was sold for $750.
3. A $4,000 cash dividend was declared and paid during 1971.
4. Six thousand shares of common stock were sold for $95,800 during 1970.
5. The current portion of long-term debt as of 12/31/70 ($13,500) was paid during the year.

Required

1. Develop a statement of sources and applications of funds for the year 1971. (Include a supporting columnar work sheet used to assist you in preparation of the funds statement.)

CHAPTER 20

Nature and Importance of Working Capital

Every day hospitality service industries managers are required to make decisions involving working capital and its components. Inventory levels, credit and collection, cash management, and purchasing, are examples of working capital areas requiring continuous revision by the manager.

Net working capital is the excess of current assets over current liabilities. The net working capital of a business and its components are illustrated in Exhibit 20.1. Not all current assets or current liabilities are shown; only those account categories which most frequently appear in the financial statements of hospitality service industries are included.

EXHIBIT 20.1

Statement of Net Working Capital

Current Assets		
Cash	$10,000	
Accounts Receivable	30,000	
Inventories, Food and		
Beverages	10,000	
Prepaid Expenses	10,000	
Total Current Assets		$60,000
Deduct: Current Liabilities		
Accounts Payable	$30,000	
Wages Payable	10,000	
Taxes and Other Accounts	10,000	
Total Current Liabilities		50,000
Net Working Capital		$10,000

THE MANAGER'S ROLE

Because most hospitality service businesses are not large, usually the person who is responsible for the overall management of the company also manages its working capital. He must control and supervise all liquid resources, locate depositories for cash and securities, design systems of control over receivables and inventories, decide how funds are to be appropriated or spent, and determine when excess funds exist so they may be used to the fullest advantage.

LEVELS OF WORKING CAPITAL

A company's working capital consists of the liquid funds it has available to operate the business in its normal cash-to-cash cycle. Working capital assets would include all cash, accounts receivable, inventories and other current assets.

In the hospitality service industries, this cash-to-cash cycle begins when inventory is purchased and/or employees are hired for cash, and ends when cash is received in payment for goods furnished or services rendered. The cycle in the hospitality service industries typically runs from one to four weeks in length. Product companies must operate under a longer cash-to-cash cycle and will require a greater amount of working capital than the company in the hospitality service industries.

No established levels of required working capital have been set down for the hospitality service firm. The primary reason for this lack is the wide variety of sizes, locations, and types of services offered within the hospitality service industries. At present the most acceptable method to determine guidelines is to compare individual operations with successful businesses that are similar in size and nature.

APPROACH TO WORKING CAPITAL MANAGEMENT

The successful management of working capital requires a complete knowledge of the relationship of the components of working capital and the mechanics of cash forecasting and planning. In addition, the successful manager must have knowledge of the seasonal or cyclical flow of business volume and the effect on the cash needs of the business, and the complete debt structure and amortization schedule for his hospitality service industries entity.

CASH MANAGEMENT

Cash is the most liquid component of working capital. The relationship between cash and the other major working capital components is important and must be fully understood. Exhibit 20.2 illustrates the effect the major working capital components have on cash.

As sales are made on account rather than for cash, the balance of accounts receivable will grow, while cash decreases as it is expended for various daily operating expenses. But as collections are made accounts receivable will decrease and the cash balance increase.

EXHIBIT 20.2

The Effect of Working Capital on Cash

```
Cash normally increases as
    —accounts receivable decrease,
    —inventory decreases,
    —borrowings increase, and
    —accounts payable and accrued expenses increase.

Cash normally decreases as
    —accounts receivable increase,
    —inventory increases,
    —borrowings decrease, and
    —accounts payable and accrued expenses decrease.
```

As management increases its inventory, cash will be disbursed to pay for the goods, thereby resulting in a decrease of cash. But if management postpones payment of its liabilities, accounts payable will increase while cash is allowed to accumulate. Conversely, if payments on payables are accelerated, cash will be reduced.

Capital Cash vs. Working Cash

Many managers fail to recognize the differences between capital cash and working cash. Capital cash represents cash to be spent for buildings, furniture, and equipment; that is, it represents items that become fixed assets on the balance sheet. Sources of capital cash are equity investment funds, earned and retained profits from operations, and mortgage or other term borrowings.

Working cash represents cash to be spent for inventory, labor, and overhead—all expense items incidental to the normal day-to-day operation of the business. The principal source of working cash must be from a sound original financial structure plus continued income produced from operations. In the seasonal resort this cash can be provided by short-term bank loans. Working cash, as the term implies, is that portion of the working capital on deposit and not moving from cash through the cycle and returning to cash. During the normal course of operations, cash "flows" as it changes into inventory and labor and overhead, then into receivables and finally back into cash. This is the complete cash-to-cash cycle.

In preparing a cash budget, receipts and disbursements for both capital and working cash requirements must be considered.

CASH PLANNING

Cash planning is the process of estimating, for a specific period of time in the future, all sources and uses of cash available to a business, and providing for cash deficits or excesses.

The cash budget is a forecast, or estimate, of cash receipts and disbursements against which actual cash experience may be measured. This forecast is extremely important to the hospitality manager because a primary reason for failure in some hospitality service industries enterprises, such as restaurants, is often the lack of cash planning. The prime requirement of continuing business existence is to have cash available with which to meet obligations as they fall due. A firm can earn handsome profits but if those profits are tied up in inventory, or receivables, or other non-cash assets, the firm will encounter financial trouble. Current debts due cannot be paid with inventory, receivables, or fixed equipment.

Cash budgets can guide management in determining current cash requirements as well as in estimating long-term financial needs for improvements, replacements and renovation programs. Normally, a cash projection is made for no longer than one year. Long-term cash planning (that is, planning for cash requirements for periods longer than one year) is less effective because of the time lapse between current expectations and actual results. The short-term cash plan, or budget, is usually prepared on an annual basis, broken down by quarters and months.

EXAMPLES OF CASH PLANNING

Cash budgets may be simple statements, or they may be detailed and complex. The simple cash budget, as shown in Exhibit 20.3, can be prepared with limited knowledge of accounting techniques or forecasting methods. This budget simply sets out a projected estimate of receipts and disbursements for several months in the future. The quarterly projection example in Exhibit 20.3 could be accumulated for the first quarter and extended monthly and quarterly over the year.

Although the cash forecast may be made on a month-to-month basis at the beginning of each month, it is more useful when projected monthly over a longer period such as a year. If the income statement forecast indicates a normal continuing profit, and if inventory balances and accounts receivable are maintained at normal levels, the cash balance will increase from month to month, unless there are unusual non-operating drains on the bank account such as payments for dividends, fixed assets, or repayment of borrowed money.

In the cash budget shown in Exhibit 20.3 the planner anticipated no fluctuations in sales levels during the three-month period. However, he anticipated that collections on receivables would be slow in February; this would make it necessary for the company to borrow $10,000 for thirty days to meet obligations to vendors (accounts payable), employees (payroll), and an increased amount for a real estate tax payment due in February.

EXHIBIT 20.3

Tahoe Motel Corporation
Cash Budget
for the Three Months Ended March 31

	January	February	March
Cash Balance at Beginning of Month	$ 5,000	$ 2,000	$ 4,000
Receipts			
Cash Sales	20,000	25,000	28,000
Accounts Receivable Collection	30,000	20,000	30,000
Loan Proceeds	-	10,000	-
Other Receipts	1,000	-	2,000
Total Cash Available	$56,000	$57,000	$64,000
Disbursements			
Accounts Payable	$40,000	$35,000	$36,000
Payroll	13,000	12,000	14,000
Taxes	1,000	6,000	1,000
Loan Repayment	-	-	10,000
Total Disbursements	$54,000	$53,000	$61,000
Cash Balance at End of Month	$ 2,000	$ 4,000	$ 3,000

Further analysis indicates that cash is projected to decrease by $2,000 over the three-month period. Assuming no change in the other current assets and current liabilities, this indicates the firm is operating at a loss, since the cash balance has decreased and funds have not been expended to reduce debt, purchase new investment assets, or paid out to owners as dividends or distributions.

Exhibit 20.4 outlines the steps necessary to prepare a simple cash budget. They are as follows:

1. Enter the cash balance at the beginning of the period.
2. Add the cash receipts expected from any and all sources during the month or period. (In Exhibit 20.3, cash sales, collection on accounts receivable, loan proceeds, and other miscellaneous receipts are listed.)
3. The resulting total is an estimate of cash that will become available to the firm during the month or period.
4. From this total, subtract the total of all disbursements.
5. The results of this estimate of total receipts and disbursements is a projected cash position at the end of the period.

EXHIBIT 20.4

Preparation of Cash Budget

Procedure	Description
1. Determine cash balance at beginning of the budget period.	a. Savings accounts. b. Checking accounts. c. Other unrestricted cash available, such as certificates of deposit.
2. Add expected cash receipts during the period.	a. Cash sales. b. Collections on accounts receivable. c. Proceeds from any loans.
3. Subtract expected cash disbursements during the period.	a. Payment of accounts payable. b. Payroll expense. c. Payment of accrued taxes and expenses. d. Repayment of any loans.
4. The resulting balance is the projected cash balance at the end of the budget period (and is the beginning cash balance for the following period).	

INVESTING EXCESS CASH

An important advantage of the cash forecast is that it will show existence of excess cash in the future. Management must be alert to these possible future cash excesses, and use these available opportunities to invest those cash excesses to produce maximum income. If excess cash is allowed to remain idle in a company's bank account, management is not fulfilling their responsibility to the owners. Excess cash can be available for the short run only. Any excess cash created by operations that is not needed for replacement or expansion of the assets must be returned to the owners. Therefore, excess cash will exist for a temporary period and the investment decision must consider the period of time that the cash will be available for investment.

In all segments of the hospitality service industries depreciation is a major expense in the determination of periodic income or loss from operations. Depreciation is a non-cash cost of operations so that excess cash provided from profitable operations may be far greater than the reported net after tax profits. To the extent that cash provided by operations is not used to repay debts or pay dividends, it will be available for investment pending its disbursement for replacements of capital assets. In the lodging and food service segments of the hospitality service industries, the guests expect continued renewals and replacements of capital assets. In these circumstances where guest preferences require newness, the replacement cycle is short and there should be a periodic temporary cash excess pending the purchase of the renewal or replacement assets.

The following factors must be considered and evaluated in the decision to invest idle cash:

1. *Rate of Return.* What interest rate can be expected from the investment and how much income is this cash capable of earning over the estimated time period?
2. *Liquidity.* How fast can the investment be converted into cash and at what cost in lost interest income? For example, a company's forecast may show that the extra cash will be available for only 180 days. An investment must be located which will allow conversion into cash within that time limit and there should be a minimum loss of earnings should an unexpected need for the cash arise prior to the 180 days.
3. *Safety.* What is the measured risk involved when idle company funds are invested on a temporary basis?
4. *Size.* How much cash is required to make the investment? Certain investments are available only in large minimum amounts (such as selected government securities and various types of bank certificates of deposits).
5. *Cost.* What is the direct cost of brokerage fees or finders fees in obtaining the investment and the indirect costs of increased bank service charges due to the smaller balance in the company's checking account?

Several types of short-term investments for excess cash are bank and savings and loan interest-bearing accounts; bank certificates of deposit; U.S. Governmental Agency Bonds; and U.S. Treasury notes and bills. The rate of return and risk on these are about the same because they are all guaranteed by the Federal government up to a stated amount. Certain Treasury bills must be purchased in specific amounts, and usually earn a lesser rate or no interest if cashed prior to their maturity date. Regular savings accounts, which compound interest daily, are convenient and widely used as a means of earning interest on idle cash.

PLANNING FOR CASH DEFICITS

The estimated cash position will be a negative amount (deficit) if estimated disbursements exceed estimated cash available. This is a signal for management to prepare in advance to meet the shortage of cash. This function of the cash forecast makes it a particularly valuable tool for efficiently controlling a firm's financial resources. The alternatives available for meeting a cash shortage include obtaining a loan, deferring the payment of amounts due or obtaining the amounts from additional investments of the owners.

Short-term Financing

At some time in its life almost every business organization can find itself "cash poor" and in need of short-term bank borrowing. Also, seasonal cash deficiences may appear in a cash budget for a resort because of the flow of its business. This would require the resort to borrow cash to meet its obligations as they become due at the beginning of the season. A copy of the resort's cash budget, along with other required financial data, is submitted with the loan application at the lending institution. This cash budget will not only indicate the estimated shortage, but will show that subsequent excess cash will be available after the season for loan repayment.

When they have the advance warning from the budget estimates, managers have time to study and analyze the lending markets to find the lowest interest rate and consider the security required. Various sources and types of short-term financing are available as follows:

1. *Loans from Partners or Stockholders.* When cash is needed for only a short period, and repayment is certain within a few days or is contingent upon some event within control of the officers, the owners of the business may finance the deficiency. In the smaller, closely held entity these loans may be informal and non-interest-bearing.

2. *Commercial Bank Loans.* When a company has a periodic need for short-term funds as would be the case of a combination summer and ski resort where expenses must be paid prior to the opening of each season, a "line of credit" may be established at a bank. This enables the company to borrow up to a stipulated amount whenever it needs cash. A lending institution may require a pledge of the company's accounts receivables as security for the loan. Essentially, the company sells its receivables at a discounted rate, as a means of raising cash. In the hospitality service industries this method of borrowing through pledging of receivables is not prevalent, as there is no transfer of title to a product to support the accounts receivable but rather an intangible service which has been consumed immediately by the guest. Therefore, this source of short-term cash in the hospitality service industries takes a different form such as credit cards or direct bank borrowing with seasonal receivables plus other assets as direct security.

An important part of successful working capital management is knowing when and where to borrow funds. The "when" may be seen in the cash forecast. The "where" must be determined only after investigating all possibilities available to the particular hospitality service industries entity.

CASH MANAGEMENT FOR THE FUTURE

Inventories are defined as "raw materials and supplies, goods finished and in process of manufacture, and merchandise on hand, in transit, in storage, or consigned to others at the end of an accounting period."[1] Though inventory usually is associated with salable product merchandise, it also applies to food, beverage and supplies in the hospitality service industries. Cash is also an inventory and it must be managed with sound inventory controls. To obtain the maximum use of cash, a manager must know at any given moment the exact amount of cash on hand, in bank accounts, between bank accounts, and on deposit in interest-bearing savings accounts. The cash budget is of no use unless it is frequently compared with actual cash balances and adjusted.

It is good practice for a hospitality service industries manager to make daily reports showing the actual balance of cash in bank accounts. These reports show deposits added to and disbursements deducted from the previous day's balance, resulting in the current balance. This procedure is a simple method of maintaining a daily inventory of cash.

CREDIT MANAGEMENT

The cash budgeting and cash flow analysis outlined showed that accounts receivable directly affected the level and flow of cash. As accounts receivable increased, cash decreased; and as accounts receivable decreased, cash increased.

A company would have fewer operational cash problems if none of its sales were made on credit. For example, in fast food drive-in restaurant, sales are all cash; as sales increase, cash increases, and as sales decrease, cash decreases. But in most hospitality service industries, management must follow the pattern of to-day's hospitality business, and extend credit to guests.

In hotels and motor hotels, guests are automatically extended credit at check-in, and normally are expected to pay at check-out. Thus, all room sales, which usually account for over 50 percent of a hotel's business, and a good percentage of food and beverage sales, become accounts receivable (guest ledger accounts) which will not become cash until the guest departs. More often this flow to cash upon guest departure is broken as management accepts more city ledger charges and credit cards. Now the more usual sale-to-cash cycle in the hotel, motel, club or restaurant is not completed until thirty to forty-five days after the date of sale.

Credit management is necessary today to handle the hospitality service industries' accounts receivable. Credit management involves not only the decision of when to grant credit, but also how to effect prompt collection of the account receivable. Credit management and credit levels established must take into

1. Eric L. Kohler, *A Dictionary for Accountants*, 2nd ed. (Englewood Cliffs, N.J.: Prentice-Hall, Inc., 1957), p. 271.

account the company's working capital needs. If cash is needed to meet obligations, and money is owed to the company in accounts receivable, the usual procedure in a product sale is either to press for collection, or withdraw credit privileges to present customers in order to accelerate incoming cash. These methods of collecting accounts for the usual commercial product sale are possible because they can be effective. For example, a retail sale of home furnishings can be repossessed if the account remains unpaid. The failure of the shoe factory to ship shoes to a delinquent retail outlet will put the retailer out of business. In the hospitality service industries the product is a service which is consumed immediately so there is no security for repossession, and no guest will "go out of business" if the hospitality firm refuses further credit. Therefore, when commercial credit and collection policies are used in the hospitality service industries, they must be adjusted for these basic differences in the sale, customer and terms.

Several types of credits are available in the accommodations industry. In the most common type the account is established for the guest at check-in. These accounts are known as house accounts, and typically include a guest room, telephone, restaurant and cocktail lounge charges, in addition to any paid-outs (postage, etc.) made by the "front desk" for the guest. House accounts become due at the time the guest checks out. If a guest leaves without paying his account or making arrangements to do so, he is known as a "skipper" and for the most part there is no way to obtain collection of his account.

City ledger accounts are a privilege extended to certain guests upon departure and to local residents. Originally, the city ledger represented charges (usually banquet or restaurant) incurred by non-house guests who were known to the management. Today, the city ledger is the collection point for all accounts receivable for a hotel or motor hotel, other than house accounts. To encourage sales, hotel management has extended the privilege of establishing a city ledger account to commercial clients and others with good credit references. Typically, city ledger local accounts become due at the end of the month in which they were charged. Unpaid accounts are billed at the end of each subsequent month until they are paid or determined to be uncollectible and written off the books.

Credit cards are a third type of accounts receivable. A hospitality service business may offer its own credit card, or may accept specified local, regional or national credit cards. In-house credit cards are handled according to the policies and terms agreed upon when the card is issued. Usually, billing is made once a month and handled similarly to city ledger accounts. The main advantage to in-house credit cards is that they provide a current centralized list of active customers for sales promotional purposes.

Regional and national credit cards are usually accepted in lieu of cash, charging the house amount to the city ledger at check-out. Credit cards also are frequently used instead of cash by non-guests in the restaurant and cocktail lounge. Each of the national credit card companies has its own policies, but most require that the signed vouchers be submitted for reimbursement on a fixed schedule. The credit card companies deduct their service charge (3 to 7 percent of the dollar total) before remitting. The credit card companies then accept responsibility for collection from the customer, assuming, of course, that only valid credit cards have been accepted by the hospitality firm. If all conditions are met and all procedures followed, the typical credit card charge will be paid between twenty to thirty days. However, with several bank credit cards, vouchers can be deposited in the bank and credit received immediately (net of the service charge) as if cash has been deposited.

Another form of accounts receivable represents amounts due from officers and employees. Although these accounts are not operational in nature, the manager should be aware of their existence. Occasionally it is necessary to advance money to an employee and usually these accounts are repaid by payroll deductions. Goods and services may be received by a company officer, for which an account receivable is established on the books, or these amounts will be reported as regular operating costs of the hospitality firm.

Once cash needs and levels are apparent, credit policy may be used to manage the flow of cash and to maximize sales. In a restaurant, charge sales and accounts may increase during the winter holiday months due to a shortage of cash by local guests, or credit card sales and accounts may increase during the summer tourist months. All patterns should be determined before credit management techniques are implemented. Effective credit management recognizes that sales may be increased by granting credit, and cash balance levels may be increased by stepping up collection of accounts receivable.

The cash budget shown in Exhibit 20.5 indicates that tax payments are due in April. In this illustration, management should probably attempt to reduce the accounts receivable and increase the amount of cash available for the tax payment during March and April. Several other methods are available to the manager. Assuming the cash budget shown in Exhibit 20.5 is for a hotel, the manager might take the following steps.

House Accounts. A policy could be established such that when accounts at the "front desk" rise above a certain dollar amount, they are collected immediately instead of at the time the guest checks out. Another method of controlling collection of house accounts is to submit bills to house guests every three to seven days.

City Ledger Accounts. It is the practice in most hotels and motels to mail a bill to city ledger debtors immediately following the guests' departures rather

EXHIBIT 20.5

Tahoe Motel Corporation
Six-Month Cash Budget
January — June

	January	February	March	April	May	June
Balance at Beginning of Month	$ 5,000	$ 5,000	$15,000	$35,000	$35,000	$25,000
Cash/Receipts on						
Cash Sales	25,000	25,000	25,000	35,000	25,000	25,000
Accounts Receivable	30,000	40,000	40,000	35,000	30,000	30,000
Subtotal	$60,000	$70,000	$80,000	$105,000	$90,000	$80,000
Cash/Disbursements for						
Accounts Payable	$50,000	$50,000	$40,000	$50,000	$60,000	$50,000
Taxes	-	-	-	15,000	-	-
Long-term Debt	5,000	5,000	5,000	5,000	5,000	5,000
Subtotal	$55,000	$55,000	$45,000	$70,000	$65,000	$55,000
Balance at End of Month	$ 5,000	$15,000	$35,000	$35,000	$25,000	$25,000

than waiting until the end of the month. This procedure is easy to follow, and often results in payment before the end of the month.

Another procedure used in manufacturing and rental industries is to offer a discount for early payment, or assess a penalty (service charge) for late payment. These procedures are not used in the hospitality service industries generally, but could be helpful in stepping up collection of both current and past due accounts. Other methods used in the hospitality service industries are a series of collection letters, telephone calls and the use of collection agencies.

Credit Card Accounts. The manager must be certain that all charge vouchers are submitted for collection to the credit card company on schedule. This is his only means of keeping the level of credit card accounts at the minimum.

INVENTORY MANAGEMENT

Although inventories are not a major asset in the hospitality service industries the inventory policy and inventory levels can affect the cash balances. If management permits inventory levels above ordinary business requirements, cash balances will be reduced. As inventory levels increase, cash balances decrease, and as inventory is reduced, more cash is available for other purposes.

In most of the hospitality service industries, inventories are food and beverages and supplies for the restaurant and housekeeping departments. Many of the food items are highly perishable, subject to variations in price, and require special storage space. Purchasing practices for beverages, and in some cases for foods, allow for discounts on quantity purchases, which can result in high inventory levels and a low inventory turnover.

Management's major inventory problem is to determine optimum levels for the various inventories. When inventories are too high, cash which otherwise could be used in the business is tied up in the storeroom, and when inventories are too low, guests may be disappointed and quantity discounts may be lost. The opportunity cost of carrying excess inventory should be calculated to indicate the expense involved in high inventories.

A step in determining the excess inventory problem is to monitor the rate of inventory turnover. If possible a comparison of inventory turnover rates should be made to other similar operations, and to the industry as a whole.

Many situations arise in day-to-day operations which may cause the manager to maintain his inventories at other than the determined levels. Cash discounts, free merchandise for quantity purchases, and lack of delivery dates all tend to encourage purchasing more than is required for immediate needs. In each instance, the manager must weigh the cost savings generated with the need for cash and the opportunity cost of carrying the higher level of inventory.

CURRENT LIABILITIES AND WORKING CAPITAL

Current liabilities are primarily trade accounts payable, accrued expenses, and current maturities on debt. All purchases in the hospitality service industries during a period are recorded as accounts payable until paid. The majority of these purchases incurred during a month become due within ten to fifteen days after the bill is rendered. Accounts payable and other current liabilities may be paid before they are due, on the due date or at a later time. In the flow of cash, when accounts payable balances and accrued expenses increase, cash balances should also increase.

Early payment

Early payment of liabilities results in a good credit rating, but also reduces the level of cash that might have been invested and earning interest until the bill comes due. For example, a company receives a large shipment of food on April 20, and is billed by May 1. The bill states that the balance is due within ten days. The company has enough cash on May 1 to meet this bill and other liabilities currently due. Management decides to establish a good payment record with the vendor, so it pays the invoice on May 1, or ten days early. If the excess cash had been invested for the ten days instead of being transferred to the food company the company would have earned interest income for the period. If this early payment example was the continuous policy of the company, the lost interest income could be significant.

Timely Payment

Timely payment of liabilities is sound business and one major advantage of cash budgeting is that it helps management to manage cash so that funds are available when bills become due. There is a penalty for early payment and a penalty for late payment. A hospitality service industries business should make timely payment on all liabilities, for there is a general recognition in the hospitality service industries that late payment of liabilities is one of the first signs of a failing business. If projections indicate that cash will not be available to pay liabilities on time, arrangements should be made to borrow cash on a short-term basis, or the vendor should be contacted and requested to extend the due date. The company will incur a cost for interest on a short-term loan, but this interest cost is usually less than the late payment charge assessed by the vendor. In the hospitality service industries, it is good practice to select the short-term borrowing alternative to cover cash deficiencies, rather than to pay creditors late. The vendors know the short cycle in the hospitality service industries and their only alternative is to stop supplying the late-paying customer, or place them on a cash (C.O.D.) basis. Either alternative could have a significant impact on the overall financial structure of the business and its ability to continue operations.

SUMMARY

Net working capital is the excess of current assets over current liabilities. The major assets in working capital are cash, accounts receivable and inventory.

The relationship between cash and the other components of working capital must be recognized as well as the flow or cycle of assets in the daily operation. Briefly, cash balances increase as accounts receivable and inventory decrease. As accounts payable increase, cash balances increase.

The cash budget is a management technique of planning for the future cash needs of the business. As cash excesses appear in the periodic budgeting process, provision should be made to transfer this excess to an income-producing investment. Similarly, as cash deficiencies are budgeted, steps should be taken to cover this estimated deficiency by borrowing.

Proper management of credit, inventories, banking and vendors are all important for a coordinated and complete program of effective total cash management.

Discussion Questions

1. Define net working capital.
2. Describe the knowledge required to successfully manage working capital.

3. Describe the circumstances when cash normally increases and decreases.
4. What is cash planning?
5. What is a cash budget?
6. List the steps necessary to prepare a cash budget.
7. Why is it undesirable to have "excess" cash on hand?
8. What are some of the methods one can use to obtain short-term cash?
9. What factors should management evaluate before making a decision to invest idle cash?
10. List and describe types of credit available in the lodging category of the hospitality service industries.
11. What is the major problem of effective inventory management?
12. What are the results or effects of the timing policy for the payment of liabilities?

Problem 1

The following account balances are listed in random order and represent only a portion of the ledger balances of the American Motel as of December 31, 197X.

Cash on Hand	4,000
Unearned Income	7,062
Rental Agent's Commission	572
Investment	97,000
Deposits on Long-term Lease	3,670
Funds in Hands of Trustees	600
Due to Affiliated Companies	4,035
Taxes Payble	4,085
Notes Payable	10,000
Accounts Receivable	36,000
Inventory	7,432
Accrued Salaries and Wages	5,670
Accrued Interest	432
Trade Advertising Due-bills Outstanding	800
Credit Balances in Accounts Receivable	100
Accounts Payable	22,000
Trade Advertising Contracts	3,672
Prepaid Expense	870
Marketable Securities	48,765
Cash Surrender Value of Life Insurance	4,000

Required

1. Prepare in good form the working capital position by arranging the appropriate items in the usual balance sheet sequence.

Problem 2

The following account balances are listed in random order and represent only a portion of the ledger balances of the Hale Catering Company at December 31, 197X.

Problem 2 (continued)

Delivery Equipment	$11,860
Allowance for Uncollectible Accounts	900
Cash	7,200
Accrued Interest on Notes Payable	200
Advance Deposits on Convention (Deferred Revenue)	1,700
Notes Payable	19,000
U.S. Government Bonds	9,400
Accrued Salaries	700
Accounts Receivable	32,800
Accounts Payable	18,400
Accrued Interest Receivable	550
Food and Beverage Inventory	20,950
Accumulated Depreciation: Delivery Equipment	1,860
Owner's Equity	40,000

Required

1. Compute working capital by arranging the appropriate items in the usual balance sheet sequence.
2. Prepare a formal balance sheet as of December 31, 197X.

Problem 3

Big Resort Corporation
Balance Sheet
December 31, 197X

Assets

Current Assets		
Cash and Cash Investments		$ 408,000
Accounts Receivable, Trade—Net of		
Allowance, $10,000		437,000
Insurance Claims Receivable		602,000
Income Taxes Refundable		96,000
Inventories—at Cost		688,000
Prepaid Expenses		234,000
Deferred Income Tax Charges		38,000
Total Current Assets		$ 2,503,000
Fixed Assets—at Cost		
Buildings and Improvements		$14,334,000
Equipment		4,777,000
Improvements in Progress		25,000
		$19,136,000
Less Accumulated Depreciation		9,558,000
Total Fixed Assets—Net		$ 9,578,000
Franchises and Licenses—at Cost		48,000
Deferred Charges		29,000
Total Assets		$12,158,000

Problem 3 (continued)

Big Resort Corporation
Balance Sheet
December 31, 197X

Liabilities and Stockholders' Equity

Current Liabilities	
Accounts Payable	$ 520,000
Accrued Salaries and Wages	125,000
Other Taxes Payable and Accrued	204,000
Other Current Liabilities	333,000
Long-term Debt Due Within One Year	157,000
Total Current Liabilities	$ 1,339,000
Long-term Debt	
Notes Payable	$ 2,700,000
Other Note Payable	95,000
	$ 2,795,000
Less Portion Due Within One Year	157,000
Total Long-term Debt — Net	$ 2,638,000
Deferred Income Tax Credits	$ 252,000
Stockholders' Equity	
Common Stock — Authorized 1,500,000	
Shares; Par Value $5.00 Per Share; Issued	
and Outstanding 1,048,000 Shares	5,240,000
Additional Paid-In Capital	304,000
Retained Earnings	2,385,000
Total Stockholders' Equity	$ 7,929,000
Total Liabilities and Stockholders' Equity	$12,158,000

Required

1. Prepare a statement of financial position which will clearly indicate the net
    working capital position of the Big Resort Corporation as of December 31,
    197X.

CHAPTER 21

Capital Budgeting

THE CAPITAL BUDGETING DECISION

Capital budgeting decisions involve the long-range commitment of large amounts of a firm's resources, or capital. The fact that capital budgeting decisions involve large amounts of capital alone makes the decision process important. Typical capital budgeting decisions include whether to lease or to buy land or equipment; the profitability of renovating an existing restaurant; whether to replace manual elevators with automatic equipment, to add new rooms, to build another motel, dormitory or nursing home.

The effects of these decisions are spread over a long period. For example, a commitment to build a new dormitory involves a payment now or in the future, with a payback over the life of the facility. A dishwashing machine replaces higher manual operating costs with (lower) machine operating costs over the future life of the machine against an immediate outlay for the machine. This realization of benefits over many future periods is the distinguishing characteristic of capital budgeting decisions. Capital budgeting is a problem of planning, and of measuring the estimated profitability of alternative use of a firm's resources.

CAPITAL PLANNING AND THE TIME VALUE OF MONEY

The Exemplary Holiday Resort has an offer by an outside firm to process all of its laundry. The relevant factors were listed as:

Cash from selling EHR's laundry equipment if outside processing is adopted	$ 75,000
Cost of laundering outside	$ .12 per pound
Cost savings from outside laundering, representing wages, power and supplies saved	$ .10 per pound
Estimated annual laundry	500,000 pounds

The continuation of EHR laundering for itself would involve the sacrifice of the $75,000 cash sale value of the equipment (an opportunity foregone by the decision to continue laundering for itself), but it would also involve the savings of $.02 per pound in laundry expenses (12¢ outside less 10¢ inside), which would be $10,000 annually (500,000 pounds at 2¢ per pound).

In planning whether or not to continue operating its own laundry, EHR must compare the $75,000 available cash from the sale with the $10,000 per year operating savings from continuing. Suppose the EHR's laundry equipment is expected to last for ten years, after which its salvage value is expected to be negligible. If EHR continued to launder for itself over the entire ten-year period, it would save a total of $100,000 in operating expenses, while it would sacrifice the cash from the sale of the equipment for $75,000 today. While the amount of the savings is $100,000 and the cost is $75,000, the savings are spread over a period of ten years into the future, while the $75,000 would be received immediately. At the heart of this decision is the fact that money has a time value, and money today commands a premium over money which is to be received in the future.

The amount of this premium for money to be received in the future will be dependent on three basic considerations: money rates, risk, and the anticipated rate of inflation. First, money received today can be invested and will increase by an amount equal to the going rate of interest. For example, if you receive $100 today and are able to invest it at 10 percent, you would have $110 in one year ($100 + 10 percent of $100 or $10 = $110). Therefore, the present value of $110 to be received in one year with a discount rate of 10 percent is $100.

Second, money received today is certain while a promise to receive money in the future has some degree of risk. The degree of risk associated with a particular investment may vary from practically no risk (such as a savings account insured by an agency of the Federal Government), to a high degree of risk usually associated with a convertible loan to a new small corporation. Of course, interest earned on the savings account, while certain, is substantially less than the potential earnings from the higher risk convertible loan. This difference in earnings is to compensate the investor for the much greater risk associated with a loan to a new small corporation.

The third factor in the time value of money is the possible erosion of the purchasing power of the dollar through inflation. If the inflation rate is 5 percent annually, then $100 received one year from now has the same purchasing power as $95 dollars today. An investor must not only be compensated for the opportunity cost of his money and the degree of risk, but also he must receive an additional increment to provide for the decline in the purchasing power of his original investment over the period of the investment.

In the Exemplary Holiday Resort example, it can now be seen that the opportunity to receive $75,000 today must be compared not with the cumulative $100,000 future savings, but rather with the $100,000 adjusted for the time value of money.

CAPITAL BUDGETING METHODS

Various methods for evaluating capital expenditure proposals are available. The assumed facts in Exhibit 21.1 will be used to illustrate these methods.

EXHIBIT 21.1

Proposal to Invest in Automatic Dishwashing Machine

Estimated Total Cost

Cost of Machine	$ 11,250
Installation of Machine	1,435
Total Cost	$ 12,685

Estimated Salvage Value of Machine   Zero

Estimated Useful Life   8 Years

Estimated Costs and Cost Savings

Future Years	1	2	3	4	5	6	7	8	Total
Machine Operating Costs									
Wages	$ 7,000	$ 7,250	$ 7,500	$ 7,750	$ 8,000	$ 8,250	$ 8,500	$ 8,750	
Power	400	400	400	400	400	400	400	400	
Supplies	510	520	530	540	550	560	570	580	
Repairs				300	300	300	500	500	
Total	$ 7,910	$ 8,170	$ 8,430	$ 8,990	$ 9,250	$ 9,510	$ 9,970	$10,230	$72,460
Cost of Manual Washing									
Wages	$10,000	$10,300	$10,600	$10,900	$11,200	$11,500	$11,800	$12,100	
Supplies	315	325	335	345	355	365	375	385	
Total	$10,315	$10,625	$10,935	$11,245	$11,555	$11,865	$12,175	$12,485	$91,200
Net Difference (Savings)	$ 2,405	$ 2,455	$ 2,505	$ 2,255	$ 2,305	$ 2,355	$ 2,205	$ 2,255	$18,740

ACCOUNTING RATE OF RETURN ON INVESTMENT

The accounting rate of return method (ARR) is a simple, quick measurement equating the expected profit from a project against the amount of investment which the project requires. It is calculated by dividing the expected income by the average investment base.

$$ARR = \frac{\text{Average Annual Income over Project Life}}{\text{Average Investment}}$$

The average annual accounting income for the dishwasher project is $757, calculated as follows.

Average Cost Savings per Year ($18,740 ÷ 8)	= $2,342
Less Annual Straight-Line Depreciation on New Machine ($12,685 ÷ 8)	= 1,585
Average Annual Net Income	= $ 757

The accounting rate of return is 11.94 percent before income taxes and is computed as follows, assuming straight-line depreciation.

$$ARR = \frac{\$757}{\$12,685 \div 2} = \frac{\$757}{\$6,342} = \underline{11.94\%}$$

A minimum rate of return is normally used as a cutoff to decide whether to go ahead with the project. If the cutoff rate was 15 percent before income taxes, the dishwasher would not be purchased, since the expected rate of return of approximately 12 percent before taxes falls below the required minimum. This minimum rate will depend upon the risk of a project, the cost of money, alternative available projects, business or competitive needs and other variables.

The accounting rate of return method is widely used. As a quick review of the possible economic feasibility of the capital outlay, it is familiar and simple in both its conceptual and mechanical aspects. The accounting rate of return, because of its comparability with accounting reports, permits follow-up of capital expenditure projects. The claimed effects on accounting income can be compared with the effects that actually occur. In the example given, the firm could look for a decrease of about $750 per year in expenses.

The disadvantage of the ARR is that it averages income over the life of the proposed project, and therefore, ignores differences in time patterns of income or cost reductions which might occur over the project life. For example, the projects shown in Exhibit 21.2 have the same accounting rate of return, assuming identical initial costs.

Considering the time value of money, alternative three would be preferable over the other two alternatives because it presents the largest total cost savings in the early periods. Alternative two is the least preferable of the three. It should be

EXHIBIT 21.2

Income Flows from Alternative Projects

	1	2	3	4	5	6	7	8	Total
Alternative 1	$2,405	$2,455	$2,505	$2,255	$2,305	$2,355	$2,205	$2,255	$18,740
Alternative 2	1,605	1,855	2,105	2,055	2,505	2,755	2,805	3,055	18,740
Alternative 3	3,205	3,055	2,905	2,455	2,105	1,955	1,605	1,455	18,740

remembered, however, that since the ARR method ignores the time value of money, it treats the three alternatives equally because they have the same average savings. Therefore, other factors must also be considered when using ARR analysis.

PAYBACK METHOD

The payback method of evaluating the economic feasibility of a project estimates the number of years it will require to return the total investment. It is calculated as the original investment divided by the estimated average annual cash inflow or estimated annual cash cost savings from the project. The method ignores depreciation and the impact of depreciation on the calculation of annual Federal and state income taxes.

$$\text{Payback Period} = \frac{\text{Investment}}{\text{Average Annual Cash Flow}}$$

In the earlier example of the dishwasher, the payback period is 5.42 years, calculated as follows:

$$\text{Payback Period} = \frac{\$12,685}{\$2,342}$$

$$= \quad 5.42 \text{ Years}$$

That is, at an average cash inflow before depreciation and income taxes of $2,342 per year, it would take almost 5 1/2 years to recover the cash outlay of $12,685. The minimum cutoff for this firm's projects might be a full cash payback within five years and in this case, the estimated payback of 5 1/2 years would not meet that standard.

The payback method may be expressed as the payback reciprocal. This is the ratio of average cash inflow to initial investment, which is nothing more than the reciprocal of the payback period. That is, the initial cash outlay of $12,685 is recaptured at a rate of 18.46 percent per year.

$$\text{Payback Reciprocal} = \frac{\text{Average Annual Cash Flow}}{\text{Investment}}$$

$$= \frac{\$2,342}{\$12,685}$$

$$= 18.46\%$$

The payback method is perhaps the easiest and quickest method of evaluation available, and since its computation ignores depreciation and income taxes, it is not tied to any particular accounting depreciation policy or to any assumed income tax impact. Average cash inflow is used in the payback method and the payback reciprocal method, which ignores the true timing of the cash flows. In addition, neither the payback method or the payback reciprocal will evaluate longevity and amount of the cash flow beyond the payback period and hence will not provide the full answer to the evaluation of the alternatives. Exhibit 21.3 illustrates alternatives that have different cash flows beyond the payback period.

EXHIBIT 21.3

Cash Flows from Alternative Projects

Periods	1	2	3	4	5	6	7	8	Total
Alternative 1	$2,405	$2,455	$2,505	$2,255	$2,305	$2,355	$2,205	$2,255	$18,740
Alternative 2	2,405	2,455	2,505	2,255	2,305	2,355	0	0	14,280
Alternative 3	2,405	2,455	2,505	2,255	2,305	2,355	5,000	5,000	24,280

Alternative three is the most desirable since for the first six years the alternatives are the same, but the returns in years seven and eight are greater for the third alternative.

PRESENT VALUE METHODS

Since neither the ARR nor the payback methods take into account the time value of money, a technique is required to measure the inflows in terms of their value at the time of the investment decision. The investment cost must be in comparable dollars to the expected future benefits. The question then is how much greater must the time adjusted value be than investment cost in order to accept a particular investment opportunity. Because all capital investment decisions involve inflows that occur over a period of time rather than at one time, this present value method is used to discount the inflows to the date of the investment.

The present value of $110 one year from now at 10 percent is $100, but what is the present value of $121 two years from now, $133 three years from now and

$146 four years from now? The present value of each of those future receipts is $100.

Initial Investment	$100
First Year's Interest	10
Investment at End of Year One	$110
Second Year's Interest	11
Investment at End of Year Two	$121
Third Year's Interest	12
Investment at End of Year Three	$133
Fourth Year's Interest	13
Investment at End of Year Four	$146

Thus, if the expected rate of return were 10 percent, the opportunity to receive $108 one year from now for the investment of $100 would be declined, because at least $110 would be required as an acceptable return. However, if the expected rate of return is adjusted downward to six percent, the opportunity would be accepted.

NET PRESENT VALUE METHOD

The net present value method of measuring the economic acceptability of a proposed project assumes a rate of return, and discounts the expected future receipts back to their present value using this assumed desired acceptable rate. The present value of the future receipts is then compared to the project cost to arrive at a *net present value*. The net present value is calculated by subtracting the project cost from the present value (PV) of the receipts. If the net present value (NPV) is positive or zero then the project is acceptable, and if it is negative then it is unacceptable. If the NPV is positive, that is, if the PV of the receipts exceeds the project cost, then the rate of return on the project exceeds the desired or acceptable rate of return. If the NPV equals zero, the rate of return just equals the desired rate of return, and, if the NPV is negative, the rate of return is less than the expected rate of return and is thus unacceptable.

Present Value Tables

In order to simplify the calculation of present values, pre-calculated PV tables are available using PV factors for various rates and numbers of periods. These tables are referred to as "present value tables" of "discount tables." Portions of the two most commonly used versions of these tables appear in Exhibit 21.4.

The tables are constructed using $1.00 as the amount of the receipt(s). For amounts other than $1.00 a simple conversion must be made. Table I, entitled "Present Value of $1.00 Received in the Future," shows the PV of a one-time receipt of $1.00. In the 10 percent column the PV of $1.00 received five years from now is $.62. Similarly the PV of $1.00 received thirteen years hence with a

EXHIBIT 21.4

TABLE I. PRESENT VALUE OF $1.00 RECEIVED IN THE FUTURE

Periods Hence	1%	2%	4%	6%	8%	10%	12%	14%	15%	16%	18%	20%	22%	24%	25%	26%	28%	30%	35%	40%
1	0.990	0.980	0.962	0.943	0.926	0.909	0.893	0.877	0.870	0.862	0.847	0.833	0.820	0.806	0.800	0.794	0.781	0.769	0.741	0.714
2	0.980	0.961	0.925	0.890	0.857	0.826	0.797	0.769	0.756	0.743	0.718	0.694	0.672	0.650	0.640	0.630	0.610	0.592	0.549	0.510
3	0.971	0.942	0.889	0.840	0.794	0.751	0.712	0.675	0.658	0.641	0.609	0.579	0.551	0.524	0.512	0.500	0.477	0.455	0.406	0.364
4	0.961	0.924	0.855	0.792	0.735	0.683	0.636	0.592	0.572	0.552	0.516	0.482	0.451	0.423	0.410	0.397	0.373	0.350	0.301	0.260
5	0.951	0.906	0.822	0.747	0.681	0.621	0.567	0.519	0.497	0.476	0.437	0.402	0.370	0.341	0.328	0.315	0.291	0.269	0.223	0.186
6	0.942	0.888	0.790	0.705	0.630	0.564	0.507	0.456	0.432	0.410	0.370	0.335	0.303	0.275	0.262	0.250	0.227	0.207	0.165	0.133
7	0.933	0.871	0.760	0.665	0.583	0.513	0.452	0.400	0.376	0.354	0.314	0.279	0.249	0.222	0.210	0.198	0.178	0.159	0.122	0.095
8	0.923	0.853	0.731	0.627	0.540	0.467	0.404	0.351	0.327	0.305	0.266	0.233	0.204	0.179	0.168	0.157	0.139	0.123	0.091	0.068
9	0.914	0.837	0.703	0.592	0.500	0.424	0.361	0.308	0.284	0.263	0.225	0.194	0.167	0.144	0.134	0.125	0.108	0.094	0.067	0.048
10	0.905	0.820	0.676	0.558	0.463	0.386	0.322	0.270	0.247	0.227	0.191	0.162	0.137	0.116	0.107	0.099	0.085	0.073	0.050	0.035
11	0.890	0.801	0.650	0.527	0.429	0.350	0.287	0.237	0.215	0.195	0.162	0.135	0.112	0.094	0.086	0.079	0.066	0.056	0.037	0.025
12	0.857	0.788	0.625	0.497	0.397	0.319	0.257	0.208	0.187	0.168	0.137	0.112	0.092	0.076	0.069	0.062	0.052	0.043	0.027	0.018
13	0.879	0.778	0.601	0.469	0.368	0.290	0.229	0.182	0.163	0.145	0.116	0.093	0.075	0.061	0.055	0.050	0.040	0.033	0.020	0.013
14	0.870	0.758	0.577	0.442	0.340	0.263	0.205	0.160	0.141	0.125	0.099	0.078	0.062	0.049	0.044	0.089	0.032	0.025	0.015	0.009
15	0.861	0.748	0.555	0.417	0.315	0.239	0.183	0.140	0.123	0.108	0.084	0.067	0.051	0.040	0.035	0.031	0.025	0.020	0.011	0.006

TABLE II. PRESENT VALUE OF $1.00 RECEIVED AT THE END OF EACH OF N YEARS

Periods (N)	1%	2%	4%	6%	8%	10%	12%	14%	15%	16%	18%	20%	22%	24%	25%	26%	28%	30%	35%	40%
1	0.990	0.980	0.962	0.943	0.926	0.909	0.893	0.877	0.870	0.862	0.874	0.833	0.820	0.806	0.800	0.794	0.781	0.769	0.741	0.714
2	1.970	1.942	1.886	1.833	1.783	1.736	1.690	1.647	1.626	1.605	1.566	1.528	1.492	1.457	1.440	1.424	1.392	1.361	1.289	1.224
3	2.941	2.884	2.775	2.673	2.577	2.487	2.402	2.322	2.283	2.246	2.174	2.106	2.042	1.981	1.952	1.923	1.868	1.816	1.696	1.589
4	3.902	3.808	3.630	3.465	3.312	3.170	3.037	2.914	2.855	2.798	2.690	2.589	2.494	2.404	2.362	2.320	2.241	2.166	1.997	1.849
5	4.853	4.713	4.452	4.212	3.993	3.791	3.605	3.433	3.352	3.274	3.127	2.991	2.864	2.745	2.689	2.635	2.532	2.436	2.220	2.035
6	5.795	5.601	5.242	4.917	4.623	4.355	4.111	3.889	3.784	3.685	3.498	3.326	3.167	3.020	2.951	2.885	2.759	2.643	2.385	2.168
7	6.728	6.472	6.002	5.582	5.206	4.868	4.564	4.288	4.160	4.039	3.812	3.605	3.416	3.242	3.161	3.083	2.937	2.802	2.508	2.263
8	7.652	7.325	6.733	6.210	5.747	5.335	4.968	4.639	4.487	4.344	4.078	3.837	3.619	3.421	3.329	3.241	3.076	2.925	2.598	2.331
9	8.566	8.162	7.435	6.802	6.247	5.759	5.328	4.946	4.772	4.607	4.303	4.031	3.786	3.566	3.463	3.366	3.184	3.019	2.665	2.379
10	9.471	8.983	8.111	7.360	6.710	6.145	5.650	5.216	5.019	4.833	4.494	4.192	3.923	3.682	3.571	3.465	3.269	3.092	2.715	2.414
11	10.368	9.787	8.760	7.887	7.139	6.495	5.988	5.453	5.234	5.029	4.656	4.327	4.035	3.776	3.656	3.544	3.335	3.147	2.752	2.438
12	11.255	10.575	9.385	8.884	7.536	6.814	6.194	5.660	5.421	5.197	4.798	4.439	4.127	3.851	3.725	3.606	3.387	3.190	2.779	2.456
13	12.434	11.848	9.986	8.873	7.904	7.103	6.424	5.842	5.583	5.342	4.910	4.533	4.203	3.912	3.780	3.656	3.427	3.223	2.799	2.468
14	13.004	12.106	10.568	9.295	8.244	7.367	6.628	6.002	5.724	5.468	5.008	4.611	4.265	3.962	3.824	3.695	3.459	3.249	2.814	2.477
15	13.865	12.849	11.118	9.712	8.559	7.606	6.811	6.142	5.847	5.575	5.092	4.675	4.315	4.001	3.859	3.726	3.483	3.268	2.825	2.484

rate of 16 percent is approximately $.14. If, for example, $250.00 instead of $1.00 is to be received thirteen years hence using a rate of 16 percent, the conversion would be made by multiplying $250 × .145 (the factor for thirteen years at 16 percent from Table I), or $36.25.

Table II of Exhibit 21.4, entitled "Present Value of $1.00 Received at the End of Each of N Years," shows the PV of the constant flow of income for multiple periods over a range of rates and a number of periods. It is constructed by adding individual factors from Table I. For example, from Table I at a rate of 12 percent the PV of a $1.00 receipt one period hence is $.89, two periods hence, $.80 ($.797 rounded), and three periods hence, $.71. This is the same as receiving $1.00 each period for three periods. Adding the three factors together,

$$\begin{array}{r} .893 \\ .797 \\ \underline{.712} \\ 2.402 \end{array}$$

results in a factor of 2.402. In Table II the PV of $1.00 received at the end of three periods at 12 percent the factor is 2.402.

Table II is a cumulative tabulation of Table I and is available to discount constant reoccuring inflows. For example, what is the PV of $750 received for eight years using a discount rate of 15 percent? In Table II where the 15 percent column intersects the eight-period row is the factor 4.487, which results in a PV of $3,365 (4.487 × $750 = $3,365).

Returning to the example of the restaurant contemplating replacing hand dishwashing with machine washing, we can calculate the net present value of the decision by multiplying each year's net cash flow by the appropriate PV factor, as in Exhibit 21.5.

EXHIBIT 21.5
Present Value of Dishwashing Project

Future Years	(1) Net Cash Flow	(2) PV Factor at 14%	(3) = (2) × (1) PV of Cash Flow
Immediately	$ − 12,685	1.000	$ − 12,685
1	+ 2,405	0.877	+ 2,109
2	+ 2,455	0.769	+ 1,888
3	+ 2,505	0.675	+ 1,691
4	+ 2,255	0.592	+ 1,335
5	+ 2,305	0.519	+ 1,196
6	+ 2,355	0.456	+ 1,074
7	+ 2,205	0.400	+ 882
8	+ 2,255	0.351	+ 792
Net Present Value			$ − 1,718

The before-income-tax rate of return which management requires is 14 percent. At this desired rate, the project is not acceptable, as its net present value is negative.

The primary advantage of the net present value method is that it recognizes the time value of money. It evaluates the differences in the timing of cash inflows in addition to the amount and it is not affected by the accounting method of depreciation. For instance, in Exhibit 21.2 three alternative projects are shown and the timing of the receipts is quite different among the three. Using a 10 percent discount rate results in the present values and net present value as shown in Exhibit 21.6.

EXHIBIT 21.6
Income Flows from Alternative Projects

	Present Value (10% Rate)	Net Present Value (Equated to $12,685)
Alternative 1	$ 12,578	($107)
Alternative 2	11,954	(731)
Alternative 3	13,207	522

Thus, while the ARR computation results in equal ranking of all three alternatives, the NPV results in a difference and, using an estimated 10 percent discount rate, only alternative three is positive.

The net present value method is one of the most complicated, both conceptually and mechanically. However, it does not provide a means of comparing alternative investments of different magnitudes (for example, a $10,000 project with a NPV of $400 as compared to a $1,000 project with a NPV of $200). NPV alone would suggest that $10,000 project was better, but in relation to the size of the investment the $1,000 project is more attractive. This may be corrected by ranking acceptable projects by their NPV as a percentage of the required investment. In the example the percentage for the $10,000 investment is 4 percent, while the percentage for the $1,000 investment is 20 percent.

INTERNAL RATE OF RETURN

The net present value method is occasionally determined by equating the discount rate to the obtainable known internal rate of return. The net present value method uses a selected discount rate, whereas with the internal rate of return (IRR) method, the discount rate is equal to the alternative earnings rate available to the firm.

The net present value method employed a selected rate of return to compute a plus or minus dollar figure to evaluate a project. In the internal rate of return method a rate of return is computed that results in a NPV of zero. Hence the IRR method computes what the rate of return is for the estimated cash flow from any given project. Thus, the cash flow from alternative projects may be measured and compared by the various calculated rates of return.

The calculation of the internal rate of return is not as convenient as the net present value. To determine the IRR it is necessary to use trial and error. For example, in the dishwashing problem on page 503, if the NPV of $ −1,718 had worked out to zero, 14 percent would be our internal rate of return. But as it did not work out to zero, trial and error with different percentages must be employed. If the dishwashing problem is worked out using 10 percent (from page 502) and 9 1/2 percent (not on page 502), zero is approached:

Future Years	(1) Net Cash Flow	(2) at PV Factor	(3) = (2) × (1) 9 1/2 % PV of Cash Flow	(4) at PV Factor	(5) = (4) × (1) at 10% PV of Cash Flow
Immediately	$ −12,685	1.000	$ −12,685	1.000	$ −12,685
1	+ 2,405	.913	+ 2,196	.909	+ 2,186
2	+ 2,455	.834	+ 2,047	.826	+ 2,028
3	+ 2,505	.762	+ 1,909	.751	+ 1,881
4	+ 2,255	.696	+ 1,569	.683	+ 1,540
5	+ 2,305	.635	+ 1,464	.621	+ 1,431
6	+ 2,355	.580	+ 1,366	.564	+ 1,328
7	+ 2,205	.530	+ 1,169	.513	+ 1,131
8	+ 2,255	.484	+ 1,091	.467	+ 1,053
			$ + 126		$ − 107

By use of interpolation it can be seen that the IRR approaches 9 3/4 percent. (Note: Simple interpolation is not an accurate method where actuarial tables are concerned, but is satisfactory in this instance.)

While the IRR takes longer to calculate, it is a useful variation on the NPV technique for evaluating the economic feasibility of a proposed project.

SELECTING THE BEST METHOD

Project evaluation methods should not be used to make the capital budgeting decision, but to assist the managers in making the investment decision. Therefore, a method which is useful, in that it leads to profitable decisions, should be employed without regard to other considerations.

Frequently payback is used as an initial screening device for all projects and another method or combination of methods used on all cases that pass the screening test. For example, the payback cutoffs might be expressed as below three and above seven years, instead of a single cutoff of five years. All projects with a payback of below three years would be accepted, those above seven years would be automatically rejected, and those lying between three and seven years would be subjected to a closer analysis using a method that recognizes the time value of the entire expected cash flow.

The choice between project evaluation methods is made easier by the fact that they possess some distinct similarities, and tend to give similar rankings to proposed capital expenditures.

CONTROL OF CAPITAL PROJECTS

Control over capital outlay decisions usually involves three phases:

1. Control over the original decision.
2. Control over implementing the decisions.
3. Follow-up information on the decision.

These phases differ in relative importance among hospitality service industries segments and firms.

Since large amounts are involved, the original decision usually requires strict control. Most firms adopt the following procedures to assist in the control over the original capital budgeting decisions:

1. The adoption of a standard procedure for evaluating all proposals which have been made. This involves a standard method (or a series of methods) which is used to decide whether or not the project should be undertaken.
2. A responsibility-allocating procedure whereby higher levels of management are required to authorize larger expenditure requests.

For example, the manager of a hotel restaurant could be permitted to authorize only expenditures up to $500; the hotel manager could be given responsibility up to $5,000; and the vice-president of finance, a special committee of the board or the entire board of directors might be required to decide upon cases where larger amounts are involved.

Implementation of the capital outlay decision is the second control point. It is not enough to decide to undertake a project; care must be taken to ensure that it becomes fully operational as planned. For example, a decision to develop a network of nursing homes in a given area must be implemented so that all phases of the plan are carried out successfully, including location, construction, advertising, staffing and management.

Follow-up information about the capital decision is difficult to collect. Its importance lies in the check which it provides on the entire capital budgeting process. First, the knowledge that the increase in profitability from a proposed project is going to be measured is an incentive to avoid exaggerating the estimated profitability when the project is submitted for approval. Second, and perhaps more important, follow-up information tells the decision-maker how accurate his original estimates were. This is one of the reasons for the general acceptance in practice of a number of capital-planning methods which permit easy follow-up or control.

SUMMARY

Capital budgeting decisions involve a large commitment of funds to specific projects for long periods. The life of the project presents the problem of dealing with the time value of money. There are a number of methods and variations for evaluating the investment proposals. These methods all attempt to quantify the elements of the capital budgeting decisions, to put the relevant factors into figures. Not all factors can always be put into figures, but many of the uncertainties surrounding a project can be accommodated in the capital budgeting methods by altering the cutoff rate or the discount rate. The various methods which have been outlined in this chapter are guides in managerial capital budgeting decision-making, and will not replace the managerial judgment needed in arriving at the final capital expenditure decision.

Discussion Questions

1. What are the three considerations inherent in the time value of money? Explain each.
2. Contrast the accounting rate of return (ARR) method with the payback method.
3. What is the advantage of using discounted cash flow methods in evaluating potential capital investments?
4. Contrast the net present value (NPV) and internal rate of return (IRR) methods and explain how each is computed.
5. Why are capital budgeting decisions important?
6. What is the difference between the "present value of $1.00 in the future" table and the "present value of $1.00 received at the end of each of N periods" table?

7. What are the three phases of controlling capital projects and the purpose of each?

Problem 1

The Quandry Hotel is contemplating the purchase of assorted mechanical equipment for the front office, equipment which costs a total of $12,000. These machines would be depreciated over five years (straight-line) and would have no salvage value at the end of that time. The Hotel's front office cost structure with and without this equipment for the five-year period is given.

Future Years	Total	1	2	3	4	5
Machine Operating Costs						
Wages	$107,990	$20,000	$20,800	$21,530	$22,380	$23,280
Power	500	100	100	100	100	100
Supplies	4,100	800	810	820	830	840
Maintenance	1,300	200	200	300	300	300
Total	$113,890	$21,100	$21,910	$22,750	$23,610	$24,520
Manual Operating Costs						
Wages	$127,470	$23,500	$24,460	$25,450	$26,490	$27,570
Supplies	3,100	600	610	620	630	640
Total	$130,570	$24,100	$25,070	$26,070	$27,120	$28,210
Net Difference	$ 16,680	$ 3,000	$ 3,160	$ 3,320	$ 3,510	$ 3,690

Note: Ignore income taxes for the purpose of the following calculations.

Required

1. Using the accounting rate of return (ARR), determine whether the hotel should buy the front office machines. The desired rate of return is 15 percent annually.
2. Using the payback method, determine whether the hotel should buy the equipment. The owners want to recapture their investment in three years.
3. Determine the internal rate of return (IRR) on the proposal. If the required rate of return is 15 percent, should the hotel purchase the equipment?
4. Would your decision in number two change if they could sell the machines at the end of the fifth year for $2,000?

Problem 2

The Sierra Tahoe Resort is considering the purchase of a new automatic filtration system for their swimming pool. The present filtration system originally cost $9,000 eight years ago and had an estimated useful life of fifteen years at that time. If the present system is kept it will require a $2,500 major overhaul next year which should keep it operating for the remainder of its useful life. Its present disposal value is $1,250 and it will have no salvage value at the end of fifteen years.

The new automatic filtration system under consideration would cost $22,000 installed and have an estimated life of seven years, at which time its salvage value would be $2,500. Tests performed by an independent laboratory have shown that the new system filters water twice as fast as the old system. Additionally, the new automatic system will save $4,250 in annual labor expense.

Maintenance on the new system is expected to be $500 annually, in contrast to the $600 annual expense for the present system. The new system is expected to require a $3,500 overhaul during the fourth year.

The Sierra Tahoe Resort uses the net present value method (NPV) for evaluating projects and desires a 10 percent return.

Should the resort purchase the new equipment? Disregard any income tax considerations.

CHAPTER 22

Income Tax—
Planning and Decisions

More than 50 percent of a corporation's pre-tax business earnings are consumed by Federal, state, and city income taxes. For non-incorporated businesses the graduated Federal and state income tax rates for individuals apply and the combined tax impact on earnings can be greater than the corporate rate. With such a substantial portion of pre-tax business earnings required for income taxes, it is important that every effort be made to defer or reduce the impact of income taxes on business profits. Tax planning influences the timing and the amount of the income tax liability by choosing alternatives which would result in either the reduction of the tax or the deferring of the payment of tax. Planning is accomplished by the careful selection of the accounting methods and the timing of reporting income and expense items, as well as the selection of organizational form of the business and the proper casting of the more important business transactions.

The income tax laws, regulations and rulings provide a number of alternative methods for reporting income and expenses. The selection of the most advantageous alternatives can favorably affect the long-range profitability of the hospitality service industries firm. An understanding of the important choices available under the income tax laws to the hospitality service industries should be made a part of all planning activities. The payment of taxes on income is not an automatic procedure over which the taxpayer has no control; in many circumstances the timing of the tax payment and the effective rate of tax can be controlled.

HISTORY OF INCOME TAXATION

The largest and most important tax on business income is the Federal income tax. The need of the Federal government for revenue has existed since the founding of the United States. Economic, political and social policies have dictated the type of tax used to generate revenue for the Federal government. Protected tariffs were used as the principal source of revenue up to the beginning of the Civil War. At that time the first progressive income tax and death tax law was enacted. The constitutionality of such taxes was questioned and after the Civil War tariffs were once again used as the principal source of governmental income.

The continuing need for revenue by the Federal government resulted in the passing of the Sixteenth Amendment to the Constitution in 1913, which permitted a tax on income from whatever source derived. The two World Wars and the large debts from these wars have resulted in an almost permanently high income tax rate, the principal source of governmental revenue. The Exhibit 22.1 charts the Federal government revenue by source for 1969.

EXHIBIT 22.1
Source of Federal Government Revenue

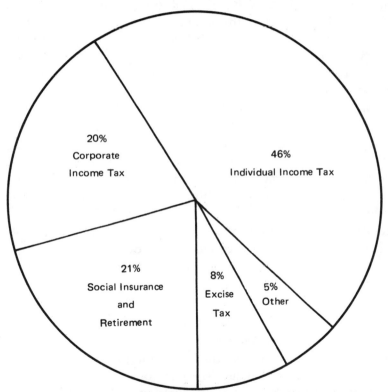

Source: Publication 21, Department of Treasury, Internal Revenue Service (Washington, D.C.: Government Printing Office).

Since 1913 the income tax law has been codified twice and amended many times. It has been altered and adjusted often to prevent revenue loss, and to ease the pressures on special groups. The cumulative effect of these amendments and changes has resulted in a patchwork that is almost impossible to understand.

Further adjustments and changes have occurred over the years as income taxes have been used by the Federal government to implement social and economic change. Two examples of the Federal government's use of the tax as an important fiscal policy tool are the investment tax credit and the surtax charge.

The investment tax credit has been used at different times in the past to stimulate the purchase of capital equipment in periods of slower economic activity. In concept, the investment tax credit is a reduction in the income tax liability computed as a percentage of the cost of certain capital equipment purchases. If the equipment had a reasonably long, useful life, a maximum percentage of the cost of the equipment was allowed as the tax credit and this credit was used to reduce the tax payment in the year the equipment was put into use. Equipment with depreciable shorter lives had a smaller effective tax credit, and there have been various limits imposed on the amount of investment tax credits.

The surtax is a fiscal policy tool device that has been used in periods when the economy was undergoing inflationary trends. The surtax is an added tax calculated after the income tax was developed using the existing rates. The 1968-70 surtax ranged from 5 to 10 percent of the income tax before the surtax.

Since World War II the cost of the expansion of services by state governments has resulted in all but a few states enacting income tax laws. Most states used a method of calculating taxable income similar to the Federal income tax. State income tax rates are generally a fraction of the Federal tax rates but are usually graduated and increasing rates. When companies operate in more than one state a number of different allocation methods have been used to prorate income for state and local income taxation.

In addition to Federal and state income tax an increasing number of municipal and county governments have enacted income tax laws. This development, which is currently in existence in six states, is an indication of a possible trend in increased income taxation.

TAX AVOIDANCE

Tax avoidance can be defined as choosing methods under the existing Internal Revenue Code and Regulations which prevent the incurring of a tax liability, delay the tax liability, or subject income to a lower tax rate. The principal methods of tax avoidance include accelerating expense deductions, postponing the recognition of income, dividing income among a number of taxpayers or taxable years, and converting ordinary income to capital gains income. The prime advantage of these methods to avoid taxation is that monies not used to make current or future tax payments can be used to provide working capital. Thus, avoidance provides an interest-free method of obtaining working capital. Tax avoidance in this sense does not mean that the tax will never have to be paid, but that no current obligation to pay the tax exists.

One of the techniques used to avoid taxes is the recognition of expense at the earliest possible time. The deduction resulting from the early recognition of expense is used to offset taxable income, thereby reducing the amount of tax which must be paid currently. For example, earlier recognition of expense can be accomplished by the use of an accelerated depreciation method and the use of reserve methods for bad debts and vacation pay. Income may also be postponed for tax purposes through the use of the installment method of recognition of income. The selection of the last-in-first-out method of inventory valuation in periods of rising prices would be another example of maximizing deductions. Similarly, the postponement of taxable income through the selection of the cash basis or the installment method of recognition of income is an equally effective technique to avoid current tax payment.

The method chosen for recognizing most income and expense items for income tax reporting need not be the same as that used for financial accounting and reports. The financial and operating accounts are based on accounting methods which provide the information for both internal and external users and the control needed to manage the business. For example, a doughnut machine may provide an even stream of usefulness over its economic life span. In these circumstances, straight-line depreciation would be appropriate for the financial accounts and for the financial statements. The advantages of lower taxable income in the early years of the asset use would dictate using an accelerated depreciation method for tax purposes.

The basic idea of tax planning should be to choose a method that avoids the payment of tax. The initial action taken or selection made is frequently binding for tax purposes, for it will determine the tax method to be used in all future years.

One of the most important of the methods of accelerating expenses for the hospitality service industries is the selection of a depreciation method which provides a larger amount of depreciation expense in the early years and lesser expense as the asset gets older, as opposed to the straight-line depreciation which results in a uniform depreciation expense over the estimated useful life of the asset. The accelerated depreciation method which results in a larger depreciation deduction from taxable income in earlier years results in working capital being made available to the extent of the tax payment which is deferred. The taxpayer may choose the depreciation method and estimate the economic life to be used for determining the depreciation deduction at the time the asset is placed in service.

There are two commonly used accelerated depreciation methods. One is a declining balance method. Under this method, depreciation can be taken in an amount as high as 200 percent of the straight-line method based on asset life. The 200 percent rate is computed on the undepreciated balance and is limited to new tangible fixed assets other than buildings. A rate of 150 percent of the straight-line depreciation can be used for buildings. No salvage value is used in computing the annual depreciation under the declining balance method. However, the asset cannot be depreciated below a reasonable salvage value.

The other accelerated depreciation method is the sum-of-the-years-digits method. The depreciation under this method is based on the ratio of the remaining years' life of the asset to the sum of the digits representing each of the years of the estimated life. Under sum-of-the-years-digits depreciation, for example, an asset with a four-year life would take 4/10 of the asset cost less salvage as depreciation in the first year, 3/10 in the second year, 2/10 in the third year and in the final year, 1/10.

The economic life of certain fixed assets used in the hospitality service industries is often very short. An example of these short-lived assets is furniture and decorations used by restaurants. The need to provide attractive surroundings often requires that these items be replaced before their physical usefulness is exhausted. In these circumstances, the use of an accelerated depreciation method for financial reporting purposes as well as for tax purposes would closely reflect the matching of income with expense.

An illustration of how accelerated depreciation methods provide expense deductions in the early years, as compared with depreciation computed under the straight-line method, is presented in Exhibit 22.2 (assuming an asset costing $100,000 with an economic life of 10 years).

By depreciating fixed assets using the double-declining balance method, the depreciation deduction would be $19,040 greater than straight-line depreciation in the first four years. At an estimated 50 percent income tax rate the larger deduction in the early years would reduce the tax payment by approximately $9,500. The sum-of-the-years-digits depreciation would provide an even greater deduction in the first four years. The depreciation under this method would exceed straight-line depreciation by $21,818 and reduce the tax payment by about $10,900. In the latter four to five years of the asset life the depreciation deduction would be less than the straight-line depreciation allowed. When a business is expanding with continuous purchases of new assets or assets are being constantly replaced, it is possible to offset the lower depreciation amounts of the latter years by the higher depreciation on the more recent purchases. The replacement cycle is short in many divisions of the hospitality service industries and in

EXHIBIT 22.2
Comparison of Straight-Line and Accelerated Methods of Depreciation

Year	Double-Declining Depreciation			Sum-of-Years-Digits Depreciation	
	Straight-line	Expense Deduction	Amount Over or (Under) Straight-line Depreciation	Expense Deduction	Amount Over or (Under) Straight-line Depreciation
1	$ 10,000	$ 20,000	$ 10,000	$ 18,182	$ 8,182
2	10,000	16,000	6,000	16,364	6,364
3	10,000	12,800	2,800	14,545	4,545
4	10,000	10,240	240	12,727	2,727
5	10,000	8,192	(1,808)	10,909	909
6	10,000	6,554	(3,446)	9,091	(909)
7	10,000	5,243	(4,757)	7,273	(2,727)
8	10,000	4,194	(5,806)	5,455	(4,545)
9	10,000	3,355	(6,645)	3,636	(6,364)
10	10,000	2,684	(7,316)	1,818	(8,182)
	$100,000	$ 89,262	$ (10,738)	$100,000	$ 0

these circumstances it is possible to continuously defer payment of the income taxes and provide working capital for the business on an indefinite basis through the use of accelerated depreciation.

In addition the Internal Revenue Code allows a taxpayer to elect and take additional depreciation of 20 percent of the cost of personal property in the first year. This deduction of additional depreciation is limited in amount to $2,000 for each taxpayer, and a further requirement is that the asset must have at least a six-year life.

The election as to the time of recognition of bad debts for tax purposes is another example of how early recognition of expense can lower income tax payments. Bad debts occur after the related transactions have been included in income. The Internal Revenue Code allows either a deduction for a specific worthless debt or a deduction for an addition to a reserve for bad debts based on the bad debt experience of the firm. By choosing the reserve method for bad debts, the expense deduction is obtained earlier than for the alternative method of taking the deduction when the debts become worthless. The reserve method estimates the current taxable year's bad debt expense in an amount equal to the firm's historical experience for bad debts. For example, if history has shown that a reserve is needed of 5 percent of the accounts receivable balance, a bad debt expense deduction would be taken to bring the reserve balance up to 5 percent of the year-end accounts receivable balance. During any year, accounts which become uncollectible reduce the reserve and recoveries of accounts previously written-off increase the reserve. The net result of the reserve method is that an earlier expense deduction is obtained than by taking the bad debt deduction when the account finally proves to be worthless.

A similar option is available in the timing of the deduction for vacation pay expense. Employees generally earn their vacation pay in the year prior to receiving it. A recognition of the liability and the recording of the related deduction for expense is allowed when it can be definitely established that the employee has an uncontested right to the vacation pay amount and will not lose this payment if he terminates his employment. The alternative to this method is to take the deduction for vacation pay in the year that it is paid. The accrual method is advantageous to the company because it obtains an indefinite deferral of the tax through the earlier reporting of the expense and in this manner permanent working capital is provided for the use of the firm.

The two accounting methods used in reporting of taxable income are the cash basis and the accrual basis. The cash basis can be elected where inventories are not material in the measurement of periodic income. Under the cash method, income is recognized when cash (or its equivalent value) is actually or constructively received. In contrast, the accrual method recognizes income in the period when the right to receive the income is earned. Similar rules apply to deductions. Under the cash method, expenses are deducted in the period paid unless they must be taken in another period to provide a clearer computation of periodic income. For example, a deduction cannot be taken for an item of equipment when purchased, but must be taken as depreciation over its useful life.

Many small hospitality service industries and other small service businesses are on the cash basis and can to some extent regulate the amount of tax paid for a particular year. Frequently, expenses are incurred prior to the collection of income cash. When this happens the expenses can be paid in cash and deducted prior to the recording of income. When the income cash is received in the next tax year a deferment of tax occurs.

THE TAX CONSEQUENCES OF ORGANIZATIONAL FORM

When a new business is organized, it may choose the organizational form that is the most advantageous taxwise. The income tax considerations that are relevant to this choice include the tax rates that apply to the different organizational forms, treatment of capital gains and losses, the tax impact on earning distributions, and the tax treatment of compensation and other employee benefits.

The organizational form determines what tax rate applies to the taxable income of the business. When it is a sole proprietorship or partnership, the business income from these forms of organizations is combined with the other income of the individual owners and then the income tax is computed based on the applicable graduated tax rates for individuals. The tax rates for individuals are progressive in nature and rates vary for the family status of the taxpayer.

When the business organization form is a corporation, a different tax rate applies. The tax on corporate business income consists of a normal tax on all taxable income and a surtax on income over $25,000. Historically the normal tax rate has been approximately 25 percent and the surtax rate approximately the same, so the effective corporate rate has been approximately 50 percent. At the lower income levels, business income of a sole proprietorship or partnership is taxed at rates lower than the corporation rate. At higher levels of income, the reverse may be true. Each decision as to the form of organization must be examined in light of the expected business income and the other personal income of the individual owners to determine the organizational form that will have the lowest effective rates on expected future taxable income.

For sole proprietorships and partnerships the annual earnings of the business are included in the taxable income of the owners in the year earned regardless of whether or not an actual cash distribution of earnings has been made. The corporation is a taxpayer and after the corporation pays its income taxes the earning distributions (dividends) are included in taxable income of the owners. Hence, one of the disadvantages to the corporate form is that earnings are taxed when earned and when distributed. Because the corporate form of organization is a taxable entity there are a number of other applicable portions of the Income Tax Code and Regulations that should be considered in tax planning. They include early year loss treatment, accumulation of undistributed earnings and the reasonableness of compensation.

In all segments of the hospitality service industries, there is an extraordinary long period of time from inception of a project to the full production of revenue. During this time considerable expenses are incurred for advertising, selection and training of employees and promotion. These pre-opening expenses are substantial and may cause operating losses for the first taxable years. In addition to these pre-opening expenses the lodging and food service segments of the hospitality service industries usually require a few years for full public acceptance and hence full profit performance. Early year losses are characteristic of the hospitality service industries.

If the individual owners have other income subject to income tax, the sole proprietorship or partnership form allows the individual owners to offset the opening business losses against other income and therefore reduce their total tax payment. For these reasons, it is frequently advantageous to use this type of organizational form in the early years of the business life, and to form a corporation later when full earnings potential is reached. If the corporate form is desired for other business reasons, it may be possible for the stockholders to elect to be treated as a tax option (Sub-Chapter S) corporation, provided they meet certain requirements. Under the tax option corporation, the stockholders elect to include in their income their proportionate share of the corporation's taxable income or loss, and in this way the stockholders are treated as if they were a partner in a partnership. The requirements under this section of the Internal Revenue Code include less than ten individual stockholders, only one class of stock and a domestic corporation that is not a member of an affiliated group. The advantage to this election is the early year losses used as offsets against the owners' other taxable income. When this advantage is no longer present, the corporation may revoke its election and be taxed as a regular corporation.

Annual net operating losses can be carried back three years and carried forward five years and used to offset taxable income in any of these eight years. When the taxable entity has had income in the past three years this carryback rule enables the taxpayer to obtain a refund of prior years' taxes. Lacking an opportunity to carry the loss backwards, the business can carry it forward for five years and offset it against income earned in future periods.

One tax advantage that the corporate form has over other business forms is that it can exercise some discretionary power in the timing of earnings distribution. When there is a single stockholder or a small group of friendly stockholders, it is possible to declare dividends at a time when it is advantageous for the stockholders to include dividends in their taxable income. This ability to select the time for taxation to the owners is not available for sole proprietorships and partnerships. To prevent abuse of this option, the Internal Revenue Code provides an additional tax on the unreasonable accumulation of earnings for corporations. Corporate earnings of up to $100,000 can be accumulated without any danger of this undistributed earnings tax being assessed. Retained earnings accumulated above $100,000 are not subject to the extra accumulated earnings tax if the corporation can establish a business need for the additional retained earnings.

In order to prevent the closely held corporation from paying large salaries which are deductible corporate expenses instead of dividends, which are not deductible expenses, the regulations provide that salaries paid employees are deductible expenses only to the extent that they represent reasonable compensation. The measurement of reasonableness is based on the amount of compensation that would be paid to individuals performing similar tasks in other businesses. The amount of salaries and bonuses paid large stockholders and members of their families are always subject to review for reasonableness. When the compensation is considered unreasonable, the excessive portion is denied as an expense deduction to the corporation, but it is still taxable income to the recipient as a dividend. Proper tax planning for the small closely held corporation should include careful considerations of the amount of compensation paid to avoid the loss of the full expense deduction because of unreasonableness.

The corporate form provides the greatest flexibility in choice of employee fringe benefits and of deferred methods of compensation. Deferred compensation provides retirement income and also subjects income to lower tax rates by spreading compensation over a greater number of tax years. The typical employee will have greater overall after-tax income if he receives some of his salary after he retires and has less taxable income as the progressive income tax rates on individual incomes will take a smaller portion of income when income is spread out over a longer period of time. Corporations may provide deferred employment contracts, profit-sharing and pension plans for their employees.

As profit-sharing plans and pension plans may be discriminatory, they are subject to special rules. These plans and the related trust agreements must be reviewed by the Internal Revenue Service to determine that they do not discriminate in favor of officers or other highly compensated stockholder-employees. The annual contributions by the corporation to a trust are deductible expenses, yet are not taxable compensation to the employee at the time the contribution is made, and the income on trust investments is not taxable to the trust. The maximum employer's contribution is limited to a percentage of the employee's salary.

Noncorporate employers can also establish retirement plans which, when qualified, allow the proprietorship or partnership a deduction from taxable income for the contribution made to a retirement plan. The amount of the deduction, and hence the ultimate benefits, may be much smaller for the self-employed owners than for the corporate stockholder executives. The maximum deduction for a noncorporate owner is limited to a percent of the earned income from the business up to a flat maximum amount. In addition, all employees who have been employed by the self-employed person for three or more years must be included in the plan, and the contribution made for these employees must be deducted from earned income before computing the contribution allowed the self-employed individual.

Corporations sometimes distribute stock dividends rather than cash. If the stockholder cannot elect to receive cash, a stock dividend does not result in taxable income. A nontaxable stock dividend is taxed when the new shares of stock are sold. The cost basis of the stock obtained is an allocated proportion of the total cost basis.

INCOME TAX IMPACT ON THE CAPITAL
EXPENDITURE DECISION

One of management's most difficult decisions is in the allocation of funds to the many possible alternative investments in new projects or replacements of plant equipment, fixtures and furnishings. There are two parts to this decision. The first is to decide whether or not to acquire an asset for use by the business and the second is how to finance the transaction. The latter can be a choice between the use of existing funds, borrowing to purchase the asset, or leasing the asset. The potential income tax effect on both of these parts of the capital expenditure decision should be included in the decision-making process.

The first part of the capital expenditure decision is to decide whether or not to acquire the asset. The usual reasons for purchasing fixed assets are either for the income its use will generate or for the savings it will obtain in expense outlays. Capital expenditures involve the immediate outlay of resources to receive some future benefit and therefore the cash flow is a better measure of the value of the expenditure when it is adjusted for the time value of money. Further, this cash flow must be adjusted for the tax consequences, since the income tax impact is a reduction in the cash flow.

To illustrate, let us consider the purchase of a piece of equipment costing $10,000 which will have an economic life of four years and have no salvage value. The use of this equipment will result in income or cost savings of $4,000 a year. If, for example, the required rate of return is 6 percent after taxes the analysis in Exhibit 22.3 would determine if the equipment should be purchased.

EXHIBIT 22.3
Use of Present Value of After-Tax Cash
Flow for Capital Expenditures Decisions

Year	Earning	Sum-of-Years-Digits Depreciation	Net Income Subject to Tax	Tax at 50%	After-tax Cash Inflow or (Outflow)	Present Value of Cash Flow (Discounted at 6%)
0	–	–	–	–	$(10,000)	$(10,000)
1	$4,000	$4,000	$ –	$ –	4,000	3,774
2	4,000	3,000	1,000	500	3,500	3,115
3	4,000	2,000	2,000	1,000	3,000	2,519
4	4,000	1,000	3,000	1,500	2,500	1,980
Net						$ 1,388

The present value of the after-tax cash flow exceeds the cost by $1,388 and the equipment purchase meets the predetermined standard of at least a return of 6 percent net after taxes.

The second part of the capital investment decision involves what method should be used to finance the acquisition of the asset. Two possible alternatives are to borrow the funds or to lease the equipment. When the funds are borrowed the nature of the repayment agreement will determine the net cash flow and the interest expense will be a deductible item in determining taxable income. If the equipment is leased the full rental is deductible for tax purposes in lieu of depreciation because the asset is not owned. The decision to borrow or lease should be made after determining the present values of the after-tax cash flow under each alternative.

It is not unusual for capital assets to have some disposal value at the end of the useful life. This salvage value is estimated as part of determining the estimated annual depreciation. If the asset is sold for an amount in excess of the depreciated book cost, a gain results. This gain may be subject to capital gains treatment and therefore taxed at a lower rate than ordinary income. For fixtures and equipment held for at least six months, gains are treated as capital gains to the extent the gain exceeds the amount of depreciation taken since 1961 on the particular fixture or equipment. To the extent the gain does not exceed the depreciation since 1961, the gain is considered as "recaptured depreciation" and is treated as ordinary income for tax purposes. Gains on the sale of buildings, leaseholds and similar types of real property can also be treated as capital gains subject to similar recapture rules related to accelerated depreciation.

FINANCIAL STATEMENT PRESENTATION OF INCOME TAX

When determining the financial statement net income for the year, it is appropriate to provide an estimated income tax expense equal to the current rate in effect on the financial accounting income before income taxes. With the various elections available to the taxpayer, it is advantageous to elect to report certain income and expense items on a different basis for tax purposes than that used for financial accounting. These differences result in an amount of income tax payable in a given year, different from the amount recognized as income tax expense for that year on the current financial statements. These differences can be substantial and must be recorded on the balance sheet as a liability for deferred income tax. The deferred tax liability recognizes the tax on those items which because of timing differences will be reported as taxable income in future periods. The balance sheet should disclose the amount of taxes currently payable and the amount of deferred tax which may be due at some time in the future, and the income statement should also report the estimated current and deferred portion of the income tax provision.

SOURCES OF TAX ASSISTANCE AND TAX LAW INFORMATION

The legislation and statutes comprising Federal income tax law are enacted by Congress and known as the Internal Revenue Code. The current Code is the 1954 Code, and it has been amended by legislative act almost annually since 1954. The recent Tax Reform Act of 1969 made substantial changes in the Internal Revenue Code. While Congress enacts the law, an important source of interpretation and application of that law is from the administration of the law by the Internal Revenue Service, which operates as a branch of the Treasury Department and administers the decisions of various courts involving tax cases. The Internal Revenue Service issues regulations (treasury decisions, or TD's) and revenue rulings. The regulations, which are finally adopted in the form of TD's, furnish explanations and interpretations of various sections of the Internal Revenue Code. The revenue rulings may be unpublished responses to questions from taxpayers on specific issues concerning the Internal Revenue Code and the regulations, or they may be public rulings published in the Internal Revenue Bulletins. From time to time the IRS will publish an announcement of its acquiescence or nonacquiescence to a tax court decision. A nonacquiescence of a tax court decision is an indication that the Internal Revenue Service will not follow the tax court decision but will continue to enforce the particular issue as before.

In addition to the IRS publications and the judicial decisions from the tax court, district courts, Court of Claims, Court of Appeals or the U.S. Supreme Court, there are a number of unofficial sources of interpretations of the tax law. Included in this group are tax periodicals and published proceedings of tax institutes and conferences. There are also a number of tax services whose publications are helpful in presenting current and historical tax information in a highly organized manner. The complexity of the current tax law makes it necessary for many taxpayers to obtain professional counsel from Certified Public Accountants and from attorneys who engage in tax practice.

MEETING THE REPORTING REQUIREMENTS
OF THE FEDERAL TAX LAW

Individuals and business entities of all types and sizes are faced with a multitude of tax reporting requirements from all levels of government. The Federal tax reporting requirements are common to all taxpayers, and the income tax reporting requirements are different for each type of taxpayer.

The sole proprietorship business entity will report its annual income statement on Schedule C of the individual tax return and file its income tax by April 15 of each year. The business income or loss is included with all other personal income and deductions. Individuals are required to estimate and prepay their income tax when they have an annual income not subject to withholding tax or have an expected annual income above a stipulated amount. The estimated payments are due by the fifteenth of April, June, September, and January of the following year.

Corporate income tax returns are due two and one-half months after the close of the tax year, but an automatic extension for filing the return can be obtained for a period of three months by filing a prepared request form. The corporation is required to estimate its income tax and to make four payments during the year the income is earned. The payments are due the fifteenth day of the fourth, sixth, ninth, and twelfth months of the tax year. Any balance of the tax not paid under the estimating process is due on the fifteenth day of the third and sixth months of the following year.

A partnership is not a taxable entity and no tax is paid by the partnership. Its tax return is an information return that must be filed by the fifteenth day of the fourth month after the close of the tax year. This information return reports the income and expenses of the partnership as well as the distribution of net taxable income or loss and other items which will be reported on the individual partner's income tax returns.

Federal payroll tax returns must also be filed by all business entities (employers) to report amounts withheld from employees for income taxes and Federal Insurance Compensation Act (FICA) taxes. Amounts withheld from employees' salaries for these taxes must be deposited promptly in designated banks for the credit of the Federal government. A tax return must be filed quarterly with the Internal Revenue Service which lists the amounts of FICA tax wages paid to each individual employee and in total the amount of withholding of income tax. The due date for filing this quarterly payroll tax return is the last day of the month following the end of each quarter. With the fourth and final return due in January, the annual wages, withholding taxes and FICA tax must be itemized for each employee on a W-2 form. A reconciliation of the tax amounts shown on the four quarterly returns for the year must be prepared and filed. The final Federal payroll tax return covers the payment due under the Federal Unemployment Tax Act for businesses employing four or more individuals. This return is due on January 31 each year and covers the previous calendar year.

Many organizations within the hospitality service industries are exempt from income taxes under the provisions of the Internal Revenue Code. Social clubs operating for the pleasure, recreation, and other non-profit purposes of the membership qualify for tax-exempt status. Also hospitals, nursing homes, educational auxiliary services and other not-for-profit hospitality service industries have tax-exempt status. However, if such organizations have any unrelated business income it is subject to tax, and in social clubs only membership-originating income and income that is used for tax-exempt purposes is not subject to the income tax. An annual information return which reports gross income, receipts, and disbursements is required from each exempt organization, as well as a tax return reporting the amount of unrelated business income (or loss) which is subject to the income tax.

SUMMARY

The opportunity to manage income taxes by planning and analyzing the tax effect of alternatives is available to all managers. In the case of the most profitable corporations, income taxes take about fifty cents of every dollar earned.

A brief selection of alternative means of reporting income and reducing income taxes temporarily or permanently would include the business organizational form used, the choice of depreciation methods, the treatment of bad debts and vacation pay, and other alternative accounting methods. In the hospitality service industries the selections from among these alternatives may result in a substantial tax liability deferral or reduction.

Discussion Questions

1. What is the objective of tax planning and how is it accomplished?
2. Define tax avoidance and give several principal methods of tax avoidance.
3. What is the advantage of accelerating expenses?
4. What are the two methods of reporting bad debt expense for tax purposes?
5. How may temporary tax avoidance from accelerated depreciation become almost permanent?
6. When is it beneficial from an income tax viewpoint to incorporate?
7. What are the benefits of a tax option (Sub-Chapter S) corporation?
8. How does the income tax enter into capital budgeting decisions?
9. What are some of the methods or techniques available to defer compensation?

CHAPTER 23

Electronic Data Processing in
the Hospitality Service Industries

Electronic data processing (EDP) is a well-established fact of life in business today. Nonetheless, the hospitality service industries have been relatively slow in adopting EDP techniques on a widespread basis. The notable exception is the airline sector, which has embraced EDP as a necessary technique to an extent paralleled in few if any other industries.

Though few managers will find it necessary or desirable to develop a substantial technical knowledge of the workings of computers, many will be required to intelligently discuss the feasibility of using a computer or to guide a team of technicians in applying computer techniques to an organization. Furthermore, most managers in the future will be encountering even greater amounts of output from a computer. Therefore, managers should have a general idea of what a computer is, the functions performed by its various parts, the significance of programming, and the tasks it can accomplish. The purpose of this chapter is to provide this background and introduction to the fundamentals of computer systems; the major application areas currently operational in the hospitality service industries; current trends in applications development; the financial implications of EDP; and management's relation to the EDP function.

DATA AND INFORMATION

Management must have information as the basis on which decisions can be made and actions taken. Validity, completeness, understandability, and timeliness of the information presented to managers are vital ingredients in sound management.

Data processing involves the transformation of data into information. To be useful to management, data must be collected, manipulated and communicated to the user. These functions are commonly described as input, processing and output. The effectiveness of data processing depends on the adequacy of these functions plus the definition of management's information requirements, and the availability of necessary data.

Data in this connection is taken to mean an unregimented collection of facts: John Doe worked eight hours; Richard Roe remitted $100 on account; and so forth. By themselves, these facts are of little use to management. Properly marshalled into information, they become meaningful in that they describe the past and present activities of the organization, and permit projections into the future.

The importance of a complete knowledge of management's information requirements cannot be overstressed. The precise nature of management's need for information must be known in order for systems to be designed and implemented effectively. Many "management information systems" have been implemented which were collections of inadequately designed applications, and therefore have cost heavily in terms of inefficient computer operations and inadequate basis for management decisions.

EVOLUTION OF DATA PROCESSING EQUIPMENT AND TECHNIQUES

Data processing is a general term used to refer to the accumulation, classification, analysis and reporting of large volumes of information. It is applicable to any of the three levels of record keeping: manual, mechanical, and electronic. The basic concept is the same whether personnel or equipment are used to accomplish the results.

Automated data processing (ADP) refers to a data processing system that captures in one recording all of the information that will be required in subsequent reports, thus eliminating human copying. The familiar punch card represents the heart of many ADP systems.

PUNCHED CARD TABULATING EQUIPMENT

The punched card represents the origin of modern EDP technology and is still in wide use as a computer input medium. The punched card is simply a means for holding encoded information in machine-readable form, with each card containing up to eighty alphabetic, numeric, or special symbols.[1]

Machines were developed to read, reproduce, sort and collate these cards and to enable the data content of cards to be printed as reports. These machines are termed "unit record" equipment. The instructions or program under which unit record machines operate are embodied in wiring interconnections made in a patch

---

1. Although the eighty-column card developed by IBM is the industry standard, ninety-column Univac cards are still in occasional use, and IBM in 1970 announced a new small computer which uses a smaller format ninety-six column card.

panel by the programmer. Thus every operation requires the creation of a patch panel wired for that purpose. This requirement imposes limitations on the number of instruction steps which can be handled. These limitations, and the speed limitations imposed by the physical passing of cards through the equipment, were ultimately overcome by general-purpose computers. As a result unit record tabulating systems are becoming extinct in the hospitality service industries as well as in other industries.

ELECTRONIC ACCOUNTING MACHINES

Accounting machines, which first mechanized accounting systems with their typing capabilities and mechanical accumulators for collecting totals, have undergone a series of improvements with the advent of magnetic storage techniques. These have ranged from storage using magnetic strips on ledger cards to the inclusion of programmable memories in the accounting machines and automatic print-out characteristics. Thus, electronic accounting machines are oriented to the maintenance of data in ledger cards or similar media. This has been a logical extension of the unit record concept originally developed in punched card-oriented machines.

Because electronic accounting machines can handle all of the necessary accounting they have a valid area of applicability in the hospitality service industries, particularly in connection with small operations. Even in large organizations that can justify the use of general-purpose computers for the bulk of their data processing, specific areas may now be served most efficiently by electronic accounting machines.

GENERAL-PURPOSE COMPUTERS

As electronic and magnetic memories came into use, stored-program computers were developed as a logical outgrowth of the wired-program machines. The stored-program computer uses its memory rather than a patch panel to hold the program of instructions. It is often called a general-purpose computer.

In the stored-program computer, the memory is used to hold encoded processing instructions as well as the data being processed. Because memories are readily altered, the instructions can be easily changed, and the rigid limitation of the wired-program machine thus overcome.

Computer memories are simply vast arrays of switches capable of being set to an "off" or "on" position. Each switch corresponds to a bit of data. The bits comprising a memory are conventionally treated as groups of six, eight, or more bits to comprise characters, bytes, or words. These are then used to represent alphabetic, numeric, or other symbols. Memory capacities are described in terms of thousands of bytes, usually referred to as "K" (from "kilo," one thousand).

The internal memory of a computer is part of the central processing unit. The functions of a central processing unit (CPU) include performing calculations, manipulating data according to the programmed instructions, and controlling the operation of the system.

In addition to the CPU, a computer system must also have input/output devices and other peripheral equipment. One type of peripheral equipment is external memory storage devices for storing data for processing which is too large to be stored in the central processing unit. Exhibit 23.1 is a block diagram of a computer or electronic data processing (EDP) system.

COMPUTER AND PERIPHERAL EQUIPMENT

A wide variety of computer peripheral equipment is being produced and marketed by the major computer manufacturers and by innumerable smaller firms specializing in this market.

Computer peripheral equipment may be classified in several ways, as follows.

Input/Output Equipment

This category includes:

1. Card readers and punches capable of reading and/or punching standard punched cards.
2. Paper tape perforators and readers that serve the same basic purpose as punched cards but use punched paper tape as the medium.
3. Optical character recognition (OCR) equipment that can read typewritten and in some instances, handwritten characters.
4. Magnetic ink character recognition (MICR) equipment that can read stylized characters imprinted with special magnetic inks.
5. Printers capable of speeds up to 3,000 lines per minute.
6. Communication terminals, such as typewriter and cathode ray tube (CRT) terminals.

While these are the most common types of input/output equipment, many special purpose devices have been developed as well.

All of the input/output devices cited are very slow by comparison to the central processing unit (CPU), which is geared to microsecond (millionths of a second) timing. Accordingly, the action of the input/output devices can be overlapped so that the computer serves a number of them concurrently.

EXHIBIT 23.1

Block Diagram of an Electronic Data Processing System

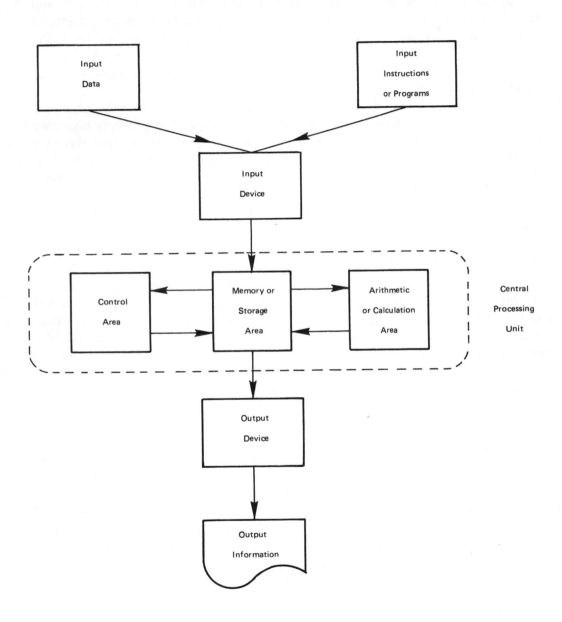

Auxiliary Storage

The effective use of the capabilities of the stored program computer demands the availability of a more efficient medium than punched cards to hold and transfer data held in long-term or interim storage. Early development efforts concentrated on magnetically coated tapes for this purpose, and they are today the most widely used storage medium. The computer manufacturers offer a wide variety of tape units capable of transferring data to a computer at rates as high as 320,000 bytes per second.

The use of tapes requires that data be passed to the computer sequentially. If it is desired to find a record in the middle of a tape reel, it is generally necessary to read the records from the beginning of the tape before the desired record is located. The shortcomings of this sequential access method led to the development of direct access (often called random access) equipment. This equipment involves the use of drums or disc platters spinning constantly under the read/write mechanism. Under these circumstances, it takes no longer than a single revolution time to gain access to any desired record.

Communications Equipment

Auxiliary terminals that can be used to communicate with computers include remotely located teletypewriters, card readers and punches, paper tape readers and punches, magnetic tapes, printers, and of course, other computers. A wide variety of devices is offered by many manufacturers specializing in this area. The equipment interconnection problem has been simplified by the development of equipment which permits the use of an ordinary telephone as the transmitter/ receiver for digital communication at limited speeds.

Of particular interest is the cathode ray tube (CRT) terminal, which consists of a TV-like screen with an accompanying typewriter keyboard. This permits the computer to display messages on the screen, and the operator to compose messages, review them, and make alterations, prior to transmitting to the computer. The CRT terminal has speed, flexibility, and convenience capabilities that far transcend the teletypewriter.

The various types of communication equipment and their application would depend on whether the specific system was off-line or on-line. Off-line systems process requests and other input to storage devices before they go to the computer, thus delaying responses. On-line systems, the input/output devices, are directly connected with the computer, bypassing storage. On-line systems may provide for immediate responses and are therefore said to operate in "real-time."

Minicomputers

The late 1960's saw the development of a number of small, relatively inexpensive general-purpose computers. The original definition of a minicomputer focused on the price of the Central Processing Unit (CPU), and those priced under $20,000 were defined as minicomputers. They typically were reasonably fast word-oriented machines. The instruction sets were limited and the language capabilities generally included only relatively simple programming languages. Nonetheless, these machines rapidly became powerful tools in the hands of expert systems analysts and programmers who had the skill to make do without the sophisticated hardware and software aids provided by the larger machines.

Minicomputers have been extensively used as an adjunct to large "conventional" machines in communication networks, in which they are often used as concentrators—in effect, funnels to concentrate data from many disparate points and feed the central computer using efficient high-capacity communications lines. This approach has been used by one large chain-wide hotel reservations system.

Software

In its usual connotation, software is taken to include:

1. Programs that are involved with the control of data processing hardware equipment and its communications adjuncts;
2. Compiler programs that are used to convert the programmer's work into actual machine usable language;
3. Various operating system programs that are used to manage the flow of data into, through, and out of the programs that do the actual processing work;
4. Utility programs that perform standard functions such as data sorting.

OPERATING SYSTEMS

The term *operating systems* is used to denote a class of master control programs, which are capable of managing the work of a computer. The functions include hardware control, communications control, program control, the use of compilers, the generation and maintenance of program libraries, and many other data management functions, some of which are extremely complex.

Operating systems are not a single program, but consist rather of a master control program (often called "executive" or "supervisor") which, in turn, calls on the specialized programs applicable to the various control or data management functions.

Multiprogramming

Modern operating systems have been able to enhance the classical "batch" method of data processing (in which one batch or job is processed after another) by resorting to such techniques as the automatic initiation of a second job when the first is finished, without operator intervention, and by multiprogramming. The computer can execute several jobs concurrently because the CPU is much faster than the peripheral units. While a transfer to or from a peripheral device is taking place in connection with job A, the computer suspends further processing on job A and starts to process job B until there is an occasion for an input or output action in connection with B. At that time, the processor, under control of the operating system, may move on to job C, or alternately revert to further work on job A.

Multiprocessing

Not to be confused with multiprogramming is multiprocessing. This is a technique in which a computer system consisting of two or more CPU's linked together and under the control of a single master control program uses these CPU's to execute the jobs that are brought from the queue or waiting line. In most instances, multiprocessor systems fall into the very large or super-computer categories.

Communications-Oriented Systems

Communications-oriented systems present special problems because the systems are subject to loads on a completely unscheduled basis. A reservations system is a good example: the requesters of reservations information do not call on any predetermined schedule, but at random. The computer system must be able to satisfy many different kinds of transactions coming from many different sources or terminals on a completely unscheduled basis.

In this type of situation, the techniques are in some ways similar to the techniques used in batch multiprogramming. The processing of one transaction is carried on until an input/output transfer is necessary. At that time, the system devotes its attention to the processing of a different transaction.

Time-Sharing Systems

A different type of communications-oriented system is called *time-sharing*. The concept of true time-sharing systems is that each user equipped with a terminal (usually a teletype or CRT) may create any program that he wishes; input any data that he wants to enter for processing using programs that he has created or general programs available in the system; and in general process as though he had sole use of the computer. In some time-sharing systems, there are no limitations as to the size of the program that the user may write or, where there are limitations, they are sometimes so high as to be practically non-existent. Users may have access to their own files, which are not accessible to other users.

The important difference between this type of system and the communications system described previously as a single-purpose system is that in time-sharing the system designer has no prior knowledge of the requirements and limitations of the user programs, whereas in the reservation example cited, these factors are under his control.

SERVICE BUREAUS

Because smaller organizations generally do not have sufficient data processing requirements to warrant the acquisition of a computer, organizations with computers and other EDP equipment will provide data processing services on a fee basis. These organizations have computer systems and service many clients' data processing needs. These processing services are known as "service bureaus."

Service bureaus are in existence in almost any location. Additionally, it is possible to air-ship data to a service bureau located hundreds of miles away and have it processed and returned within a few days.

With the availability of time-sharing computers, a new type of service bureau has come into existence. A time-sharing service bureau may have clients located all over the country and connected to the computer by regular telephone lines used only when data transmission is desired, or by leased lines.

PROGRAMMING LANGUAGES AND THEIR PROCESSING

Operating systems control the means by which the work of human programmers is converted to machine code. The programs that do this are called *compilers*, *assemblers*, or *report generators*; as a group they are called *language processors*. A number of programming languages have been developed and standardized to some degree; some of the programming languages are supported by the software of many computer manufacturers. Among the higher-level languages that have attained wide acceptance are Cobol, Fortran, PL-1 and Algol. These are designated as "higher-level" languages because they seek to approximate the natural language of the programmer—either English or mathematical notation.

Cobol is a pseudo-English language more widely used than any other in business applications because of its similarity to English. Fortran and Algol are languages expressly designed for mathematical and algebraic formula translation. A simplified offshoot of Fortran, called Basic, is widely used in time-sharing applications because it is simple and easily learned by time-sharing users who are not professional programmers. The PL-1 language seeks to combine some of the more advantageous features of Cobol and Fortran to achieve a more universally acceptable language.

Unlike the higher-level languages, assembly language is machine-oriented in that its program statements correspond directly to machine instructions. Accordingly, assembly languages are a direct function of the machine instruction set and often exhibit wide dissimilarities from machine to machine.

Report generators are the final language processor categories. These languages are primarily concerned with the development and formatting of reports from files that are in the computer system. These languages are easy to use, but have limited manipulative and calculative power. The most commonly used language is called "RPG."

APPLICATION OF EDP TO PROBLEMS

The successful application of EDP techniques can yield benefits in terms of improved flow of information to management, internal control, service to customers, cash flow control, and sometimes net reduction in operating expenses. The unsuccessful application of EDP can wreak havoc.

The solution to a problem must start with the definition of the problem. It is crucial that management's information needs be accurately defined, for all levels of management, in terms of *what* information is needed, *by whom* and *when*. Priorities, possible areas of standardization, and organizational interrelationships all enter into this definition of requirements. Once management's need for information has been defined, the alternative techniques of fulfilling the need can be evaluated. Conventional EDP batch processing techniques; electronic accounting machines; bookkeeping machines; a variety of computer-communications techniques; and conventional and time-sharing service bureau facilities must all be considered.

The criteria of cost, internal control, cash flow, capacity for growth, system integrity, impact on the customer, and ease of implementation must all be considered. The net result of this effort is the conceptual design of a system. This design must then be translated into specifications considering the capabilities offered by the various vendors, including major computer manufacturers, minicomputer manufacturers, peripheral equipment and terminal vendors, independent software houses and service bureaus. In each case, cost, performance, support by the vendor, and other factors must be considered and evaluated.

The required computer programs must then be designed, coded, tested and debugged individually and on an integrated systems basis. EDP operations personnel and user department personnel must be trained and user procedures defined and documented.

All of these activities must be planned, scheduled, and estimated in detail in order for the project to succeed. Finally, the involvement of top management must be continuing to assure that the design effort does not lose sight of management's real needs. Otherwise, management is prone to expect too much or to settle for too little.

The development of an EDP system may be summarized in seven phases:

1. Feasibility study: objectives, preliminary cost versus benefit analysis studied.
2. Systems analysis: business objectives, system objectives, input, processing and output analysis; development of system specifications.
3. Systems design: a system layout consistent with the specifications.
4. System selection: supplier hardware and software proposals evaluated.
5. System construction: installation plan developed; selected and trained staff; the system programmed.
6. Systems operation: the programming tested, productive operations commenced.
7. Systems review: resulting benefits reexamined, performance evaluated, deviations from specifications and changes in requirements modified.

EDP IN THE HOSPITALITY SERVICE INDUSTRIES

Recently, an in-depth nationwide survey was conducted to probe the status of EDP in the hotel/motel and health care segments of the hospitality service industries.[2] It was found that the use of in-house EDP equipment in the hotel-motel field was limited to less than 10 percent of the properties, including almost no small independent properties. Computer use in hospitals was somewhat more widespread, with 19 percent of all hospitals surveyed reporting the use of in-house equipment.

These industry figures are quite low, compared with many other industries. However, 25 percent of the hotels and 42 percent of the hospitals indicated that they used external EDP facilities provided by banks, service bureaus, and others to process some of their applications. The surveys also indicated a nearly unanimous response from organizations using EDP that the effectiveness of their operations had been enhanced by the use of EDP.

---

2. *Processing in the Health Care Industry*, Hospital Financial Management Association, 1970 and *The State of Information Processing in the Hotel-Motel Industry—A Survey Report*, Harris, Kerr, Chervenak & Co., 1970.

ACCOUNTING APPLICATIONS

"PACKAGE" APPLICATIONS

Many "package" applications (also commonly referred to as "off-the-shelf" programs because they are designed, i.e., "packaged" for widespread application) have been written by equipment manufacturers, independent software firms and service bureaus, particularly in accounting areas common to all business organizations. These packaged programs include applications for payroll, inventory, accounts receivable, accounts payable and general ledger functions.

By the nature of the requirement that these packages appeal to a large number of potential users, they are generally written to include many features and capabilities. Most users generally do not require all of these features, but often need features not provided in the package. As a result, packages can rarely if ever be installed "as written," without compromising either management needs or operating efficiency, or both. Despite these shortcomings, packages can be a practical approach, particularly for the small EDP user. However, they should not be considered a panacea requiring little effort on the user's part. The various package approaches, and the modifications that may be required, should be carefully examined.

Some of the most frequent EDP accounting applications in the hospitality service industries are payroll, accounts receivable billing, accounts payable, general ledgers and to a lesser extent, inventory records.

PAYROLL AND PERSONNEL

In the hospitality service industries, preparation of payrolls is more highly computerized than any other single accounting application. While payroll preparation is not intrinsically a difficult EDP application, its implementation in the hotel, hospital, and food service industries has been complicated by the high personnel turnover that characterizes many organizations in the hospitality service industries, and by the special requirements imposed on hotel and food service organizations relative to accounting for gratuities and free or low cost employee meals.

Literally hundreds of organizations, including banks and commercial service bureaus, are processing payrolls. There has generally been, however, a lack of "standard" or "packaged" payroll systems sufficiently flexible to accommodate the special hospitality service industry requirements on a broad basis. For example, many clubs, restaurants and hotels have had to resort to individualistic variations of the basics of payroll processing in order to meet their minimum needs.

The basic scheme of an EDP payroll processing system involves processing input data against an employee master file. Such a file includes all information about an employee that is relatively invariable. Common items include employee name and address, pay rate, deductions, taxing information and other personnel data. To make a payroll system work, the input data need only contain employee identification, hours worked and data as to the departmental distribution of labor. The computations involved in developing net pay from gross, and taking into account the various deductions, are handled by the program.

One concept which has particular advantages to hotel chain operators is that of incorporating personnel master file information into the basic payroll-oriented employee master file. Doing so enables management to determine rather easily which employees meet certain criteria. Criteria such as job history and language skills may be encoded into such a file to facilitate the personnel management of the larger organization.

ACCOUNTS RECEIVABLE

The requirements imposed by the accounts receivable function vary enormously within the hospitality service industries. They range from the member accounts billed by clubs, which are quite static in nature, to the city ledger operations of commercial hotels, which typically feature a high percentage of one-time accounts as well as house or chain credit card accounts, third-party credit card accounts, and convention accounts. The health care segment bills most of its receivables to third parties, including insurance carriers and governmental agencies.

The application of early punched card data processing resulted in the "country club" style of billing, in which copies or stubs of guest checks accompany the statement to describe the goods or services billed. The alternative approach, called *descriptive billing*, identifies the goods or services directly on the statement rather than via enclosed copies of chits. Descriptive billing is much more amenable to modern computer system techniques than country club billing, since it involves the manipulation of only magnetic records. It makes possible the elimination of punched cards, except for data entry. Alternative methods of data entry are also available and often economically preferable. With the exception of clubs and the larger third-party credit card organizations, the hospitality service industries have largely adopted descriptive billing techniques.

It is paradoxical that the large credit card firms, who have some of the largest and most sophisticated computer equipment and staffs in the industry, have retained country club billing. The reasons are a combination of sheer volume of paperwork and the problems of encoding an almost limitless variety of goods sold for subsequent manipulation and identification to the customer, and finally, customer acceptance. In actuality, some of the systems in use by these firms are now hybrid systems incorporating statements with some items billed descriptively as well as some supported by individual charge records.

A major impetus to the automation of the accounts receivable function is the need for improved cash flow in many organizations, due in part to slow billing and inefficient collection procedures. However, as in other applications, the use of the most modern processing techniques is not of itself a guarantee of successful operations. Inappropriate credit policies, or inadequate guest identification can result in excessive write-offs despite the use of a computer.

Hospital billing procedures became increasingly complex as the incidence of third-party billing increased. The complexity is brought about by governmental regulations; by the need to prorate gross bills to a multitude of third-party payment plans; by the authority of the third-party payer to reject bills in whole or part; and by the accounts which depend on prior authorizations by the third-party payer. Billing has also been complicated by changing eligibility criteria for the various governmental support programs, and difficulties encountered by many hospitals with the capture of valid data.

INVENTORY

Computerized inventory systems have found some limited acceptance in the hospitality service industries. In the lodging and food segments the situation has been complicated by the fact that it is not always feasible or desirable to maintain full requisition-oriented inventory systems for all classes of stock. Most hotels and restaurants do not use requisition-oriented systems for perishables, dairy products, etc., so that industrial-type inventory systems must be modified or used only for perpetual-inventory stocks. There is direct applicability to liquor stocks, for which perpetual inventories are commonly used. In this connection, the system can be adapted to accommodate inventory valuation on a retail basis as well as on purchase cost. Although hospital supply situations lend themselves to computerized inventory management techniques, few hospitals have actually implemented such systems. However, there is a trend toward inventory computerization in the management of medical supplies, particularly narcotics and controlled drugs.

Inventory records lend themselves readily to computerization. The basic approach is to maintain a master file of stock items, with appropriate item numbers, descriptions, quantities on hand, etc. The record for each item is changed when requisitions against inventory are drawn, or when inventory is replenished. In addition to maintaining a count of quantities on hand, the record pertaining to each stock item can contain data as to the vendor, quantity, price, date of last order, low and high stock limits, delivery lag and economic order quantity.

ACCOUNTS PAYABLE

The accounts payable application is an area in which manufacturing and distribution-oriented industries led the way in computerization. However, the application is becoming increasingly automated in the hospitality service industries. When properly defined and implemented, the accounts payable application interacts closely with the purchasing and inventory functions.

In no way does the philosophy of processing invoices on an electronic computer differ from that of a well-designed manual system. However, the computerized application can automatically maintain a vendor master file, reflecting all transactions with a vendor. A cross-file by product is also readily maintained. These files can be used to optimize purchasing power by making vendor performance and price histories readily available to the purchasing agent.

The well-designed accounts payable system incorporates a number of internal checks to preclude the processing of unauthorized invoices, dummy vendors, and similar techniques for fraud. The internal checks will result in the generation of exception reports—for example, a listing of invoices which do not match purchase orders, vendors not listed in the master file, etc. The system can provide safeguards, but these must be backed up by sound management review procedures.

GENERAL LEDGER MAINTENANCE

The use of computer techniques to maintain general ledger and operating ledger accounts has spread widely. A number of general ledger "packages" designed for broad applicability have been written and implemented, and these are used in the hospitality service industries as well as elsewhere. General ledger maintenance systems merely update the status of ledger accounts by accepting data derived from transactions which affect the various ledger accounts. Thus the "master file" simply consists of ledger account records.

In many businesses, the bulk of the ledger transactions come from other accounting applications which are readily computerized: payroll, accounts payable, and accounts receivable. Accordingly, the general ledger application should be integrated to minimize undesirable reentry of data which is already available directly from another application. When the account balances are available, the production of the balance sheet, operating statements and operating ratios merely becomes a matter of arithmetically manipulating account balances. The fact that many sectors of the hospitality industries use Uniform Systems of Accounts has facilitated the processing of general ledger work by service bureaus.

In addition to deriving figures for the current period from the ledger balances, the system can, and should, provide cumulative totals for the year to date. By the same token, computerization of financial report preparation facilitates the use of detailed budget figures for comparison. By using an account-oriented budget as one of the inputs, detailed comparisons, including percentage variances, are readily derived for both the current period and the cumulative year-to-date.

EXCEPTION REPORTING

The use of exception reporting in connection with management-oriented financial statements is attractive in that attention is focused on those accounts that vary significantly from the budget. Exception reporting is easily implemented in computerized applications. The result of this technique is to highlight for management attention those areas that are in variance from the budget. These areas can be presented in detail. Its advantages lie in the elimination of unnecessary detail, and in the focusing of attention on those details which are meaningful. Although budgetary comparisons have been used to illustrate the point, other comparisons can be used.

By and large, the hospitality service industries have not embraced this concept to a great extent in actual practice. However, the utility of the technique deserves consideration as the capability for its easy implementation is available through computerized preparation of reports. Since computers have the capability to spew out large quantities of data (all too frequently not all needed by management), exception reporting can greatly minimize the time spent reading the computer-generated reports.

SPECIAL HOSPITALITY SERVICE INDUSTRY APPLICATIONS

AIRLINE RESERVATION SYSTEM

Airlines are among the largest and most sophisticated users of communication-oriented computer systems. Without exception, the major carriers, domestic as well as foreign, have implemented complex reservation systems, and have in some cases extended them to serve the needs of the smaller feeder airlines. These systems are characterized by large-scale central computers and peripherals, sizeable quantities of random access storage, vast communications networks, and hundreds, even thousands, of remote terminals.

Unlike the older airline reservation systems which kept track only of the number of available seats, the newer systems are complete passenger name record (PNR) systems. Complete itinerary as well as the name, address and any special requirements associated with the passenger are kept in storage until the flight is completed.

In most of the newer systems, the airline keeps track of the total number of its own seats as well as the availability of seats on other airlines. One major carrier, for instance, maintains the seat availability for forty-three other carriers in its system. Thus, a passenger can call airline A, book space on that airline and continuing space on airline B, all in the same call. Airline A then forwards reservation information to airline B through a complex network of communications lines and computers. Conversely, airline B must keep airline A, as well as all other airlines, constantly up-to-date regarding its seat availability.

In addition to reservations, airlines also use computers for several other non-accounting applications, the most common of which are:

> Flight schedule planning
> Crew scheduling
> Aircraft scheduling
> Maintenance scheduling
> Cargo reservations
> Seat selection

Having proved the value of data processing, the airlines are hard at work designing systems for the future. The most talked-about advanced applications are automatic ticket writing and automatic passenger check-in. While some forms of both of these applications are already in existence, neither has been worked out to the complete satisfaction of the airlines.

HOTEL/MOTEL RESERVATION SYSTEM

In the period covered in the hotel/motel EDP survey, about one half of the American hotels and motels made use of computerized reservation systems. For the most part, these were in-chain systems such as Sheraton's Reservatron and Holiday Inn's Holidex, or external systems offered by firms such as American Express, Telemax, International Reservations Corporation, and National Data Corporation. These major systems are alike in that they do not operate as "inventory" systems, actually controlling the inventory of available rooms in a property. Only a few properties are exceptions, in that they do use the external systems for full rooms inventory management.

In all cases, the primary function of the computer is to switch messages concerning reservations to the property affected; but the responsibility for room management is in the hands of the individual property, not under the control of the computer system. Thus it is the hotel's front office manager who must keep track of room inventories and reservation commitments in the traditional manual fashion. He then advises the system, through a coded message from his terminal, as to the availability of various types of rooms for various days. This information is retained by the computer system in direct access storage, and appropriate responses are generated to reservation inquiries.

When a reservation is booked, the computer generates a message to the property involved, sending the reservation information to the terminal at that property, using the dial telephone network (or leased lines, in some systems). Except for certain traffic logging records which are created in the computer system, this ends the transaction. Cancellations and changes are handled in a similar fashion. If the hotel's reservation manager does not "close out" a day when fully booked, the computer system continues to accept reservations for that day, and sends the messages to the property. The computer system does not protect the property from inadvertent overbooking. By the same token the computer system denies reservation requests for days for which the property has closed out, whether or not there are in fact unsold rooms. Some of the external reservations systems allow the property to specify a number of rooms which the system can sell for a given day; the computer then closes out automatically when that limit is reached. A few properties have used this capability, which is built into some of these systems, to do complete rooms inventory management. This practice has not spread, largely because of the service charges levied by the firms operating the services.

The reservation systems described here are not designed to maintain a guest-oriented reservation record created at reservation time. Some of the systems do not maintain such a record at all after the output message has been acknowledged by the receiving property. Those which do maintain one do so only to facilitate its retrieval for changes and cancellations. In this regard, the hotel reservation systems are significantly less powerful than the airline reservation systems' incorporating a passenger name record (PNR) capability.

Accommodations reservation systems are no less critical to hospitals than to hotels, but the problems of room management differ significantly. Although hospitals usually have little advance knowledge of bed availability, elective admissions can be used to maintain the desirable occupancy rate. Given a high rate of elective admissions, as is common in high-occupancy hospitals, the demand for space usually exceeds the supply, and patients acquiesce to elective admission on short notice. The use of computers in hospital admission systems has not spread widely. Those systems which have been developed rely extensively on manual decisions prior to processing the data. Generally, they function more as retrieval and message systems rather than as true control systems; in this sense they are similar to the "external" hotel reservation systems discussed previously.

"INTEGRATED" HOTEL SYSTEMS

The concept of a fully "integrated" inventory-oriented system has received wide attention from both the outside service organizations providing the existing external reservation systems, and from several computer manufacturers. The term "integrated" is used here to connote interaction between two or more areas, specifically the reservation and registration functions, as well as the guest accounting functions, and ultimately the systematic maintenance of a guest history file. A few pioneer in-house installations have incorporated at least some of these functions, using minicomputers in one instance, and a conventional general-purpose computer in another.

The advent of the minicomputer appears to hold significant promise in making integrated systems feasible, particularly where the collection and maintenance of in-house guest accounting files is involved. The implementation of an integrated system involving access to the computer system from CRT or other terminals for all transactions including reservations, registrations, charges to guest ledger, payments, transfers, and check-outs, generates a sizeable volume of message traffic. Accordingly, the options must be examined between larger systems capable of serving multiple hotels via telecommunications from a remote location, and smaller in-house systems. For this reason, minicomputer manufacturers have become actively involved in the integrated hotel systems market.

Detailed studies of a number of commercial hotels have indicated that a significant amount of rooms department revenue is lost because of weak reservations and room management techniques. Empty rooms on nights when reservation requests were denied, and inadequately managed "special" rates, appear to be prime factors in these instances. The problem appears to be not managerial inadequacy but an insufficiency of valid room management information on which managers can base decisions.

These are areas in which integrated hotel systems can provide assistance to the hotel manager. They thus represent design targets for these new systems. Other important design targets include the automation of the night audit function; improved marketing-oriented data derived from guest history files; and improved credit management and cash flow.

SPECIAL HOSPITAL SYSTEMS

The major computer manufacturers have generally taken the "package" approach to integrated hospital systems. Many of these concentrated on accounting applications, and were geared to use by several institutions sharing a computer system. The packages available were so lacking in flexibility and applicability that not a single hospital in the United States had successfully implemented a full package system, although a number of institutions were using partial packages, generally with modifications. Most hospitals using in-house computer systems are operating with a patchwork of several applications separately developed.

A number of approaches have been under development, generally under sponsorship of individual institutions, to attack the problems of admissions office automation, medical records retrieval, communications-oriented nursing station automation, outpatient demand billing, etc. In general, these approaches have not yet resulted in highly visible improvements applicable to the industry as a whole, although some benefits have undoubtedly accrued to individual institutions. The cost justifications for some of the approaches are open to question.

A variety of medical applications are also maturing, some with promising results. Among these are systems in support of cardiology, clinical pathology, pulmonary function laboratories, and poison control. Quite a few of these systems are basically search-and-retrieval systems using direct access and communications terminal techniques. Systems of this type are largely dependent on the successful formulation of a suitable protocol, with indexing of the data base in accordance with the protocol.

FINANCING EDP

EQUIPMENT ACQUISITION

The EDP equipment user generally has a number of options available as to the contractual basis for equipment acquisition: rental from the manufacturer, outright purchase, and third-party leasing.

Rental. All the major computer manufacturers make their equipment available on a rental basis at published, non-negotiable rates. The usual minimum lease term is one year; some manufacturers offer lower rentals on longer-term leases. In most instances, the manufacturer provides routine equipment maintenance service as part of the rental contracts. Non-routine maintenance service is generally billed to the user at a stipulated hourly rate.

Purchase. Equipment purchased from the manufacturer is at published, non-negotiable prices. The manufacturers will provide maintenance service for their equipment, under a maintenance contract which provides the purchaser the same maintenance as is provided to rental customers.

Most computer manufacturers extend a purchase option to the rental customer, under which some fraction of rentals paid are applied to the purchase price if the user decides to purchase the rented equipment within a specified time period.

A user wishing to upgrade purchased equipment by exchanging it for larger equipment of the same manufacture can usually obtain significant trade-in credits; there is often some leeway for price negotiation on the trade-in.

Third-party Leases. A number of financial firms offer third-party leases of EDP systems and equipment at rentals well below those of the manufacturers. These leases may be long-term leases which are simply time-purchase plans, or they may be nonpayout arrangements in which the lessor assumes a risk position in the equipment. Equipment maintenance under third-party leases is usually provided by the manufacturer under contract with the lessee.

The advantageous rates offered by third-party leases, which can be as much as 25 percent below manufacturers' rentals, must be weighed against several disadvantages:

1. Some third-party lessors have turned out to be financially unstable.
2. Most third-party lessors are reluctant, if not completely unwilling, to accept equipment traded-in for larger equipment.
3. Although manufacturers theoretically extend the same services and support to original users of purchased equipment, which third-party lessees are as to users of rented equipment, the user's relationship to the manufacturer is reduced in a third-party lease situation. This can lead to difficult situations in the event of substandard equipment performance, for instance.

MANAGEMENT'S RELATION TO THE EDP FUNCTION

Planning is vital to the successful implementation of EDP. In order to make planning and implementation of plans effective, management must provide an appropriate organizational framework for the EDP function. Further, a mechanism for feedback or monitoring of progress must exist in the organization. These management considerations are not unique to data processing. The details of organizational, planning, and monitoring arrangements should be tailored to the needs of each organization, but they must be provided.

The success of any computer project, no matter how large or small, depends upon the people that operate and direct it. Management's attitude toward the computer is a key factor in its success or failure regardless of how well the system is designed and operates. It is the responsibility of management to become involved in the EDP system so as to assure that its operation can be managed with sufficient knowledge and expertise. A technical knowledge of the EDP system is not a requisite, but a broad general knowledge is a necessity.

The topic of a new computer application within an organization should be approached by management with care and understanding. Many people are afraid of computers, suspecting that their jobs may be eliminated. These facts must be recognized by the management who must inform employees of prospective computerization. The possibility of having a computer should be presented to employees before the feasibility study begins. At this time and at frequent intervals thereafter, management must be actively involved and interested in the EDP application.

PERIODIC EVALUATION

It is desirable for management to have the data processing function audited periodically, from the viewpoint of overall effectiveness rather than accounting verification. An effectiveness audit examines all the aspects of the data processing organization, including technical, personnel and managerial considerations. Its purpose is to determine the deficiencies of the EDP function and to develop corrective measures.

SUMMARY

The utilization of electronic data processing is certain to continue to expand in the hospitality service industries until computerized record-keeping and information processing will be commonplace. It is therefore incumbent on management to understand the nature of EDP, its capabilities and limitations. Such initial steps as the processing of payroll and accounts receivable billing could lead to a completely computer-based accounting system. At the same time, computerized reservations and personnel management systems will be developing, along with a marketing data base. Finally, this will all be integrated to allow management the most timely, accurate and complete information possible.

Discussion Questions

1. Describe "unit record" equipment.
2. What are the major limitations of tabulating equipment?
3. Distinguish between mechanical and electronic accounting machines.
4. What is the principal capability of general-purpose computers?
5. Describe some of the available input/output peripheral equipment.
6. Describe the different functions of "software."
7. What criteria must be considered in investigating the feasibility of a proposed EDP installation?

8. Describe briefly the most widely used accounting application of EDP in the hospitality service industries.
9. What is a service bureau and how does the existence of service bureaus offer EDP to smaller organizations?
10. Contrast off-line and on-line data processing.
11. List and describe three methods of EDP equipment acquisition.

CHAPTER 24

Mathematical and Statistical Methods in Business

The past two decades have witnessed an acceleration in the variety and complexity of analytical decision-making methods. Decision-making in most spheres has been changed by these new methods. Many of the methods were prompted by the increased availability and capability of computers, which greatly decreased their cost per calculation and made their use economically feasible. Regardless of the source of these methods, many have been adapted to business applications.

The development and application of these quantitative analytical techniques are referred to as *operations research*. Frequently, these techniques have resulted from the combined efforts of engineers, mathematicians, statisticians and accountants. In most cases, the techniques are designed around the capability of the computer, and though they may be used without a computer, all are facilitated and broadened where computer access is available.

This chapter is an introduction to a representative and pertinent sample of quantitative decision-making tools.

MODELS AND MODEL-BUILDING

A model is an attempt to represent the real world, or some portion of it. Generally, models are simplifications either out of necessity (the real world is too complex to duplicate exactly) or desire (the user wishes to facilitate his understanding of the real world).

In operations research (OR) the models are mathematical representations of the interrelationships of factors, or variables, whose outcome is of interest to the user. By design its components are the most pertinent variables affecting the working of its real world counterpart.

Models are assembled to explain the outcome of past events, or to predict future events. For example, a very simple mathematical model of rooms revenue is the formula: number of rooms sold times average room rate equals rooms revenue. As an explanation of a past outcome, historical rooms revenue for a period of time is a result of the number of rooms sold and the average room rate.

To predict future rooms revenue for a particular period of time, the model indicates that a projection of room night sales and the average room rate will provide a projection of rooms revenue.

Such a model is useful as a predictor of the future only to the extent that its components may be more accurately predicated than the outcome itself. Otherwise, the model serves only to indicate the effects of variations in the components upon the outcome.

This rooms revenue model is of limited value without considering the factors underlying the number of rooms sold and average room rate. A more comprehensive and useful model would take into account those underlying variables such as economic climate, competitive conditions, marketing efforts, and others.

Since there are many different models of the world, why do they differ, and how do we choose from among them? The second question is more relevant here, and fortunately it is easier to answer. We choose to employ a model if, and only if, it assists us in making decisions—if it is *useful*. (This perhaps explains why models differ: because different people, or groups of people, ordinarily have different problems to solve, or different uses to which the model is put.) Most of the models to be described in the following pages have long ago passed the usefulness test.

DETERMINISTIC AND PROBABILISTIC MODELS

Deterministic models are familiar: They set forth exact relationships between variables. For example, a cost-volume-profit relationship such as the following is a deterministic model.

$$NI = (S \times X) - (V \times X) - FC$$

(NI = Net Income, S = sales price, X = unit sales, V = variable costs per unit, and FC = fixed costs.) The values of S, X, V and FC are given, and they *determine* the (one) exact value of NI. *Probabilistic* models are less familiar but no less important. They recognize the uncertainty of the future and, hence, are suitable for business decision-making. For example, we might decide that the volume of sales (X) in the equation cannot be estimated for sure. We might assign it many possible values, which would result in net income (NI) taking on many possible outcomes.

We shall consider one example of each of the two types of models. The example of a deterministic model will be a mathematical program, in particular, *linear programming*. The example of a probabilistic model will be *simulation techniques*, which have recently become useful.

LINEAR PROGRAMMING—DETERMINISTIC MODEL

A *mathematical program* is one where there exists, due to the nature of the particular problem, the following three elements.

1. Variables of choice; for example, various goods and services available.
2. Constraints which restrict the number of possible choices; for example, an income constraint which does not permit a consumer to buy as much of every good and service as he would like.
3. An objective function, or mathematical representation of a preference for alternative combinations of the variables of choice; for example, a consumer's preference for a trip to Europe versus a summer home.

In general, element one provides the set of all logically conceivable choices, or solutions; the addition of element two, the constraints, reduces this set to the subset of *feasible* solutions. Finally, element three, the objective function, allows us to narrow the subset of feasible solutions down to the *optimum* solution.

A *linear program* is a special type of mathematical program, in which both the constraints and the objective function are expressed as linear relationships among variables. (Geometrically, the relationships are drawn as straight, not curved, lines.) An example of a simple linear program follows.

A restaurant, for example, has heavy demand for steak and potatoes. However, due to a railroad strike only 25 steaks and 30 potatoes are available per week, these being flown in. The customers are very particular; they will only eat steak and potatoes together, one potato with one steak. The problem faced by the restaurant may be stated in the following manner, letting X stand for steak, and Y for potatoes.[1]

1. Variables of Choice: X, Y
2. Constraints: $X \leq (1)$ 25 (Steaks)
   $\qquad\qquad\quad Y \leq (1)$ 30 (Potatoes)
   $\qquad\qquad\quad X = Y$ (desired ratio)
3. Objective Function: Maximize $X + Y$

The solution of course, is to serve the 25 steaks with 25 potatoes. This is an easy solution, but the non-quantitative reader will be surprised to learn that he has just solved a linear programming problem.

Most linear programs are more difficult to express and to solve than our restaurant's supply problem. Fortunately for the users of linear programming techniques, the *simplex algorithm* for solving more complicated problems is

---

1. The symbol $\geq$ means equal to or greater than and $\leq$ means equal to or less than. These are inequality signs since they do not specify equality.

available. This simple method provides answers to general form linear programming problems. Standard computer routines are available to make the solving of linear programming problems more manageable. Before proceeding to the general form of linear programming problems, their underlying structure is illustrated through some simple problems.

Linear Programs and Scarce Resources

The previous illustrations of the cost-volume-profit relationships bypassed one rather crucial problem because they did not consider why a firm would ever restrict its volume. For a single-product firm, if the product's selling price (S) exceeds its variable cost (V), the optimum strategy would be to produce and sell as many units as possible. Every additional unit produces an additional amount of profit of (S-V).

However, the addition of a *capacity constraint* would limit this particular strategy. Nevertheless, the solution to a single-product cost-volume-profit problem with an added capacity constraint is still a single one: if S exceeds V, then production should be up to the limit of the capacity constraint.

The addition of a possible alternative use of the productive capacity is what creates the need for linear programming.[2] The production of multiple products from common facilities introduces a problem of choice in allocating the given amount of facilities ("scarce resources") to the production of the individual products. The existence of more than one possible use of the limited production facilities introduces *opportunity costs*. The one-product firm expands output up to capacity and only checks that S exceeds V. The multiple product firm, however, must take into account the opportunity cost in producing one product, that is, of not using its facilities to produce another, or other products.

Two Products, One Constraint

Let us assume that our illustrative company, the Exemplary Holiday Resort, produces only two products. They are rooms and meals, and denoted by X and Y respectively. A room sells for $20.00 per day and incurs variable costs per occupied day of $8.00 and a meal sells for $5.00 and incurs variable expenses of $2.60. Both rooms and meals share the one common facility of space. The total restaurant, kitchen and guest room space is assumed to be given (constrained) at fifty thousand square feet. One room takes up four hundred square feet including access spaces. Facilities to provide one meal take up twenty-five square feet,

---

2. Note that cost-volume-profit relationships are linear, and are therefore easily adapted to linear programming.

everything included. The problem is one of allocating the scarce resource of space so as to maximize the profit of EHR.

Fixed costs are ignored because they are not affected by the allocation of space. Hence, the problem of maximizing the profit of EHR can be restated as one of maximizing the total contribution margin. The linear program is therefore:

1. Variables of Choice: X, Y

2. Constraints: 50,000 square feet of space
    or: $400\,X + 25\,Y \leqslant 50,000$
    and: $X, Y \geqslant O$

3. Objective Function: Max CM = $\$12.00\,X + \$2.40\,Y$

That is, we need to choose the values of X and Y, the number of rooms and meals, that maximize the total contribution margin. The contribution of one room is $12.00 ($20.00 - $8.00); the contribution of one meal is $2.40 ($5.00 - $2.60). We have also added the constraint that the number of rooms (X) and the number of meals (Y) must both be positive.

This simple problem can be solved by comparing the profit contribution that each activity earns per square foot of space that it takes up.

Product	Contribution	Square Feet	Contribution/ Square Feet
X	$12.00	400	$ .030
Y	2.40	25	.096

It appears that, in this example, EHR should only serve meals. Every square foot of space devoted to rooms would better be utilized in meal facilities. This result follows directly from the fact that we are dealing, by assumption, with linear relationships. A graphical representation of the result (that only one product is produced) is instructive.

The solid line in Exhibit 24.1 represents the constraint of floor space. Only points in the hatched area including points on the outer boundary of the hatched area (i.e., on the solid line) are feasible because any solution to the right of this constraint requires more floor space than is available.

The broken lines represent various levels of total contribution margin. The greater the number of rooms and/or meals, the greater is the contribution. Hence, the contribution increases as we move to the northeast (NE).

The maximum contribution is at that feasible point which falls on the highest broken line (contribution margin). Since the slope of the constraint line is different than that of the contribution lines, the combined criteria of (a) feasibility and

EXHIBIT 24.1

Two Products, One Constraint

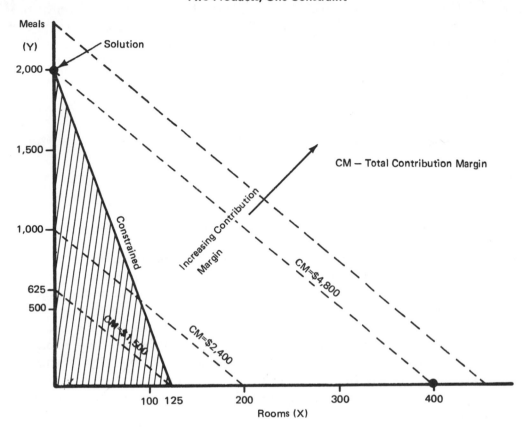

(b) maximum contribution ensures a corner-point solution.[3] In this case, the corner point (Y = 2,000, X = O) is our solution. This point can be shown as the maximum by noting that solutions, contribution lines, with contributions other than $4,800 will be either:

    1. to the NE of the corner point, and therefore *infeasible* because they require more than the available 50,000 square feet of space; or

    2. to the SW of the corner point, involving the production of both rooms and meals, and therefore *undesirable* because they give rise to a profit contribution of less than $4,800.

---

3. If the slopes were identical, the solution would degenerate; the contributions per square foot would be the same.

Two Products, Two Constraints

Few (if any) hospitality service industries operations are characterized by the two product, one constraint model. A more realistic example is one which produces an optimum solution involving both rooms and food. Let us assume that EHR has a manpower constraint as well as a space constraint and its available manpower is 6000 man-hours per week. Further, a room requires two hours of total labor per day and a meal consumes one-half of one hour of available staff time. The linear program is now:

1. Variables of Choice: X, Y

2. Constraints: $400 \ X + 25 \ Y \leqslant 50{,}000$
$$2 \ X + 0.5 \ Y \leqslant 600$$
$$X, Y \geqslant O$$

3. Objective Function: Maximum CM = \$12.00 X + \$2.40 Y

For illustrative purposes, labor has been assumed to be a fixed cost, as if it were under contract for the season.

The change which the second constraint adds to the graphical analysis is of one more constraint line. The change to the optimum solution is that both X and Y are now produced. In graphical terms, the solution is no longer on the axis, but is still at a "corner point."

The solid lines still represent constraints. The hatched feasible area is no longer bounded by only one constraint line. The contribution lines remain as before. The optimum feasible solution is once again obtained by moving the contribution line to the NE until it is maximized, while still observing the constraints. In this case, the maximum contribution is reached when the contribution line touches the point of intersection of the manpower and space constraint lines. This solution turns out to be:

$$X \ = \ 66.67$$
$$Y \ = \ 933.33$$
$$C \ = 12(66.67) \ + \ 2.4 \ (933.33)$$
$$= \ \$3{,}040$$

Note that the solution involves points *on* (and not to the SW of) both of the constraint lines. Thus, there is *no idle capacity* in the utilization of either space or manpower. From this fact, it follows that the *inequalities:*

$$400 \ X + \ 25 \ Y \leqslant 50{,}000$$
$$2 \ X + 0.5 \ Y \leqslant \quad 600$$

EXHIBIT 24.2

Two Products, Two Constraints

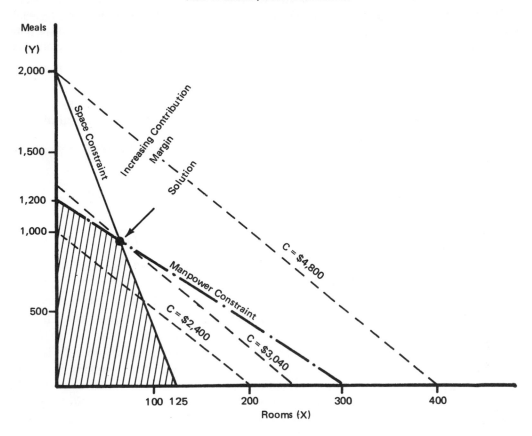

can be written as equalities, since all of the 50,000 square feet and 600 man-hours are utilized. Further, the solution can be derived by solving the two equalities, or equations, because we have exactly as many activities as we have constraints.

$$400\ X\ +\ 25\ Y\ =\ 50{,}000$$
$$\text{and}\quad 2\ X\ +\ 0.5\ Y\ =\ 600$$

This is a case of two equations and two unknowns (X, Y), and is therefore capable of solution.[4] The values of 66.67 for X and 933.33 for Y satisfy the two equations.

---

4. Any system of M equations and N ⩾ M unknowns allows us to solve for all but N-M of the unknowns.

The Simplex Algorithm

Not all linear programming solutions involve no idle capacity. It is unlikely that a firm with a large number of constraints (for example, financial, managerial and legal constraints) and a large number of possible product combinations will utilize all of its facilities completely. Hence, the linear programming problem is usually one of solving a system of inequalities. It is not usually as simple as solving a system of simultaneous equations, such as the one last mentioned.

However, a system of inequalities is very easily converted into a system of equalities by adding what are known as *slack variables*. That is, we can always write the problem in these terms:

1. Variables of Choice: X, Y, U_1, U_2
2. Constraints: $400 \text{ X} + 25 \text{ Y} + U_1 = 50{,}000$

$$2 \text{ X} + 0.5 \text{ Y} + U_2 = \geqslant 600$$

$$X, Y \ U_1 \ U_2 \geqslant O$$

3. Objective Function: CM = $12.00 \times $2.40 Y + $0.00 U_1 + $0.00 U_2

Note that the slack variables are assigned zero value in the objective function, since they contribute nothing.

The addition of the possibility of non-zero slack variables has introduced the possibility of more unknown variables (X, Y, U_1, U_2) than equations. Thus, a different method than the familiar method of solving simultaneous equations must be found. Such a method is provided by the simplex algorithm referred to earlier.[5] The essence of the simplex method is its restriction to considering only corner-point, or extreme, solutions until the optimum feasible solution is found. The reader will recall that the solutions in Exhibits 24.1 and 24.2 were both corner points; the simplex method relies on a proof that all optimum solutions are corner points.

In our second example, with two constraints, the simplex method would have entailed an analysis of the few corner points.

1. X = O,   Y = O
2. X = O,   Y = 2,000
3. X = 125,   Y = O
4. X = 66.67, Y = 933.33

The reader could attempt to prove for himself that all other points will be dominated by one of the four, since such points must (by definition) fall on one line segment only.

---

5. An algorithm is merely a method which involves repeating a procedure until an optimum solution is found.

The next problem is that of choosing between these points. One method would be that of numerically evaluating the contribution from each point (each of the four X, Y combinations) and choosing the combination with the largest contribution. When the number of corner points is large, this is a prohibitively time consuming method. The simplex method is designed to cut down on the computational expense of arriving at the optimum solution. It virtually ensures that each new corner-point solution is more optimal than its predecessor. For example, the point (X = O, Y = 1,200) in Exhibit 24.2 is better than the preceding point (X = O, Y = O) because it provides $2,880 contribution rather than none at all. The simplex method assures that the next point to be tried would be (X = 66.67, Y = 933.33) and *not* the fourth corner point (X = 125, Y = O). Note that the guaranteed point has a higher total contribution of $3,040, yet the unconsidered point has a lower contribution of $1,500. The desirable aspect of the simplex method is that it does not need to directly compute the contribution of the fourth point in order to reject it from consideration. Further, it always knows the optimum solution when it reaches it, without directly computing the contributions of other feasible solutions.

The General Form Linear Program

We shall not delve into the mechanics of the simplex method, for that would require a lengthy introduction to matrix algebra.[6] We shall, however, state the general form of a linear programming problem. The preceding examples, and many business problems may be cast in this general form.

$$\text{Maximize:} \quad Z = C_1 X_1 + C_2 X_2 + C_3 X_3 + \ldots + C_m X_m$$

$$\text{Subject to:} \quad a_{11} X_1 + a_{12} X_2 + a_{13} X_3 + \ldots + a_{1m} X_m = b_1$$

$$a_{21} X_1 + a_{22} X_2 + a_{23} X_3 + \ldots + a_{2m} X_m = b_2$$

$$a_{n1} X_1 + a_{n2} X_2 + a_{n3} X_3 + \ldots + A_{nm} X_m = b_n$$

$$X_1, X_2, X_3, \ldots, X_m \geqslant 0$$

Where: $\quad M > N$

and:
- C = the alternative activities
- X = the amount of each activity
- a = the amount of each limited resource (constraint) required for each activity
- b = constraints
- m = a notation for each activity
- n = a notation for each constraint

---

6. See George Hadley, *Linear Programming* (Reading, Mass.: Addison-Wesley Publishing Co., Inc., 1962) for one exposition.

In our rooms-meals example, m = 4, since there were two activities (rooms and meals) and two slack activities which were introduced to make the model a system of equalities, rather than inequalities.

Of course, we could not graph a problem of more than two activities because of the limitations on the number of axes available[7] (though we could add as many constraints as we desired). The computer routines which solve linear programs allow as many activities and constraints as one is likely to encounter. The development of these computer routines is one of the reasons why linear programming is a popular mathematical method in business application.

In the hospitality service industries, the potential applications of linear programming are many and varied. Examples include capital investment decisions, where not only financial resources, but also manpower and management capacity are limited; and decisions to enter into management contracts.

SIMULATION—A PROBABILISTIC TECHNIQUE

Most of us are familiar with vagaries of our uncertain future. We cannot predict, with absolute confidence, the outcome of a toss of a two-sided coin. Hence, the outcome is uncertain. Similarly, the weather is uncertain, as are the outcomes of personal investments. Business decisions also relate to the future and hence their outcomes are uncertain. It is not surprising that quantitative decision-making techniques are sometimes constructed in a manner which allows for the existence of uncertain outcomes.

Most decision-making techniques ignore the problem of uncertainty completely. That is, they act as if the future were known with complete certainty. For example, traditional capital expenditure decision-models compute the net present value of an investment as the present value of the discounted cash flow less the investment cost. This present value method assumes that the useful life, the cash flows for each year over that life, the discount rate(s), and the initial investment outlay are known for sure—that they can take on only one outcome. When the future is assumed to be uncertain, as it most certainly is, the present value method is limited as it fails to take into account this uncertainty.

Some attempts have been made to develop decision-making methods for uncertainty using basic probability concepts, which are the prime tools for dealing analytically with uncertainty.

---

7. With two variables the horizontal and vertical axes are sufficient. With three variables it is necessary to use a three-dimensional graph. Beyond three the problem is obvious.

Probability Distributions

Suppose we were interested in determining the average number of days that a room is occupied in a year. One approach might be to look at the past record, assuming (for illustration only) that past occupancy rates are a good guide for the future. Due to problems in determining each room's occupancy with great accuracy, it has been established to the nearest twenty-five days.

Number of Rooms	Days per Year
3	100-124
2	175-199
8	200-224
9	225-249
4	250-274
2	325-349
Total Rooms 28	

We could graph these data on what is known as a *histogram*. A histogram represents each occurrence (here, each room) by any equal area in a graph which relates the number of days per year to the number of rooms which were occupied that many days. This is illustrated in Exhibit 24.3.

EXHIBIT 24.3

Histogram with Course Grid

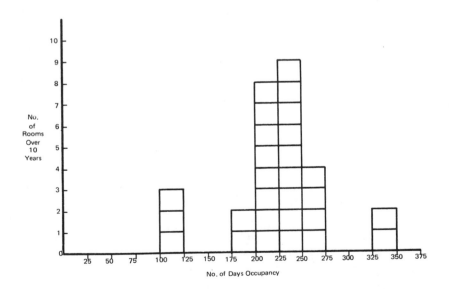

If the records of this company were sufficiently accurate, we could make the grid a little finer. For example, we could make our estimates count to the nearest five days, instead of twenty-five. Furthermore, we might have more than one year of data. We could have data for 30 rooms for 10 years, or a total of 300 room-years of data. Treating each room-year as a separate observation, our histogram would now look similar to the one in Exhibit 24.4.

EXHIBIT 24.4

Histogram with Fine Grid

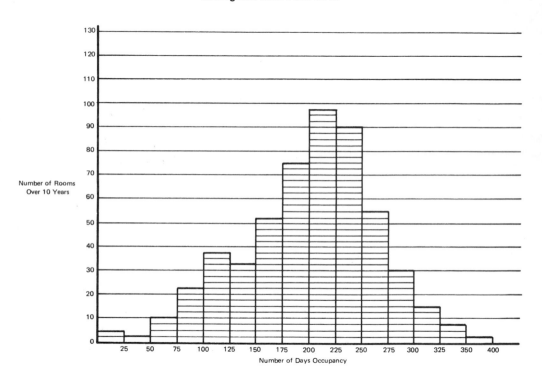

It is clear that we could further increase both (a) the degree of fineness with which the occupancy rate of the rooms is measured; and (b) the number of observations which are being considered. As we increased the fineness and the number of observations, the same sort of changes that occurred between Exhibit 24.3 and 24.4 would continue to occur. In particular, the relationship between the number of rooms (measured by the height of the histogram) and the number of days of occupancy would become gradually smoother.

If we increased the number of observations and the fineness of recording much more the histogram would begin to look like Exhibit 24.5, which is a graphical representation of a *frequency distribution*. Remember that these are 30

EXHIBIT 24.5

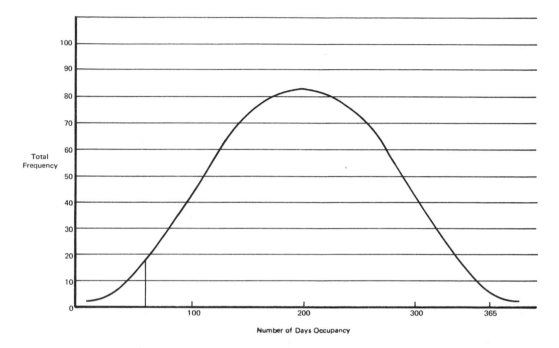

Frequency Distribution

Number of Days Occupancy

rooms times 10 years or 300 room-years being investigated. Hence, Exhibit 24.5 shows frequencies which add to 300. A rather simple but useful modification of Exhibit 24.5 is to record relative, not total, frequency. Relative frequency is calculated by dividing the total frequency through by the total number of observations, in this case, three hundred. Since the area under the total frequency distribution is 300 (remember, equal area was given to each of the 300 observations), the area under the relative frequency distribution is 300 divided by 300, or 1.0.

One interpretation of a relative frequency distribution is that relative frequencies of occurrence denote *probabilities*, and that Exhibit 24.6 is therefore a *probability distribution*. Other concepts of probability exist, but we shall pass them aside for our purposes.

Exhibit 24.6 says, in effect, that the occupancy rate of a room may take on many values, from zero to 365 days a year, with differing probabilities. It also says that the extremes (near zero and total occupancy) occur less frequently than intermediate values such as 200.

EXHIBIT 24.6
Number of Days Occupancy
Probability Distribution

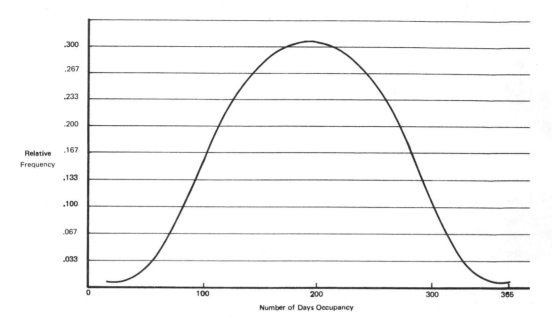

Fortunately, statisticians have developed more concise and more powerful ways of describing probabilities. Two of the ways that have been developed are of immediate interest. They are:

1. The development of types, or categories, of probability distributions, designed to describe the more typical types of probability distributions which occur in practice; and

2. The use of characteristics to describe differences within a class of probability distributions.

Two frequently-encountered types, or classes, of probability distributions are the normal and binomial distributions. They are frequently encountered in the sense that they, and particularly the normal, appear to describe well certain occurrences. The normal distribution is typical of many situations in which a large number of observations is involved.

The two characteristics which describe the normal distribution are the mean and the standard deviation. As we have seen earlier, the mean is the sum of the individual observations in a frequency distribution divided by the number of observations.

The standard deviation is an indicator of the variability or dispersion of the observations. In other words, the standard deviation indicates how far the typical observation is from the mean. The standard deviation is calculated by squaring the difference between each observation and the mean, summing the total of the squared deviations, dividing by the number of observations, and taking the square root of the result. Together, the mean and the standard deviation completely describe any normal distribution. For example, we could describe Exhibit 24.5 entirely by saying that it is a normal probability distribution with a mean of 207.3 and a standard deviation of 222.1.

SIMULATION

One of the earliest applications of simulation was to test the nuclear defense systems which were devised to provide an umbrella without holes against nuclear attack. Simulation was used to test whether the model on which the system was to be based did, in fact, have no holes. Since it was too risky to wait until an attack to test the system, a very large number of attacks were simulated via a technique which was called "Monte Carlo analysis." Our present aim is to show how probability theory combined with Monte Carlo analysis can be used as a valuable tool in managerial decision-making. Turning back once again to the cost-volume-profit models, we wish to focus upon their failure to recognize that variables such as volume and selling price are not known for certain.

Let us focus upon two components of cost-volume-profit models, volume and selling price. We have seen that the occupancy rate of rooms might more realistically be said to have several possible outcomes, from zero to 365 days, and that these expected relative frequencies of occurrence (probabilities) can be described by probability distributions. A decision-maker might not be interested in an estimate of net income of $750,000, if he knows that he is not sure that it will be $750,000. For example, he might be interested in the probability that net income will be less than zero (a loss). Since the occupancy rate affects volume, and volume is assumed to relate to net income according to the equation:

$$NI = (S \times X) - (V \times X) - FC$$

then it must be true that uncertainty as to the occupancy rate makes net income uncertain. The key question is how uncertain?

This is the first advantage of simulation studies. They allow us to attach uncertain outcomes to variables such as S, X, V and FC and, by using probability distributions, estimate the uncertainty of variables such as NI. Since it is highly unlikely that a decision-maker is indifferent to uncertainty, this is an important improvement. For example, the following two normal frequency distributions have the same mean net income, but the second has greater uncertainty, as reflected in the higher standard deviation of net income. If the decision-maker had only been given a best guess at net income, he would have rated the two cases equally, since the best guess would have been $750,000 for each. Knowledge of

	Case A	Case B
Mean	$750,000	$750,000
Standard Deviation	25,000	100,000

the possible outcomes which lie behind the mean of $750,000 would lead a risk-averter to choose case A, with its lower degree of uncertainty, because he would be more sure of being close to the average of $750,000. Case B deviates more from the average than does case A.

However, this is by no means the only advantage of simulation techniques. Best guesses cannot be combined except under the rarest of circumstances. An example will illustrate this point. Suppose that sales price and volume each take upon two possible outcomes. But the outcomes for sales price and volume are *not independent*. In fact, higher price might be expected to be associated with lower volume, and vice versa.

	Sales Price	Volume	Total Revenue
Possibility A	$ 10	100,000	$1,000,000
Possibility B	5	140,000	700,000
Average	$7.50	120,000	$ 850,000

In the example, the best guess or price is $7.50 and of volume is 120,000. But the product of $900,000 is not equal to the best guess of total revenue. The general rule that total revenue equals price times volume has to be examined more closely when price and volume are uncertain.

The techniques of simulating total revenue by Monte Carlo analysis can be described in the following way.

For each of the uncertain variables (in the examples, S and X), a probability distribution must be estimated. The assumption of normal distributions reduces this to estimating (a) the mean and (b) the standard deviation of each of the variables. This stage of estimation is up to the decision-makers, with assistance from a technical advisor.

The decision-maker must specify relationships between the variables. For example, he must relate selling price to volume. In doing so, he must specify both (a) the form, and (b) the strength of the relationship. Thus he might say that:

(a) X = 150,000 - 5,000 S and

(b) the correlation co-efficient between X and S is 0.35.[8] This is a measure of how closely X varies with S and, therefore, of the relative importance of other factors in affecting X.

The next step is up to the simulation program. Simulation programs may be written in any one of a number of specifically-designed computer languages. The computer is used by the program to, in essence, draw from a hat. Since, in our example, S and X can take on many possible values, we could simulate the real world with two hats. If we put pieces of paper with values of $10, $11.25, etc., into a hat in proportion to the relative frequency that we expect them to occur in the real world ($10.00, 150; $11.25, 115; $40.00, 2; etc.), then by drawing from the hat we would simulate the real world. If we were very careful at specifying the relationship between the price "hat" and the volume "hat," as in the preceding figure, we could draw from each hat simultaneously. On each draw we could multiply S by X, and have the total revenue for that draw. By repeating this process many times, we could build up a probability distribution for total revenue, by drawing from the probability distributions (hats) of price and value.

Finally, the *derived* probability distribution of total revenue is printed out by the computer in summary form. Such a summary might look like the following.

Total Revenue — Summary of Possible Outcomes

Average expected revenue	$ 846,000
Revenue expected to be exceeded 90 percent of the time	641,000
Revenue expected to be exceeded 10 percent of the time	1,147,000
Probability of being at or below break-even volume	.07

The feasibility of simulation as a technique depends heavily upon the economies of taking a large number of drawings from the probability distributions of variables such as S and V. The advent of computers and simulation computer languages has made simulation an inexpensive and powerful decision-making tool.

---

8. We shall not enter into a discussion of correlation. See almost any introductory statistics book.

SENSITIVITY ANALYSIS

Sensitivity analysis is a method which lies mid-way between the deterministic and the probabilistic models which have been illustrated. Like the probabilistic models, sensitivity analysis admits that variables can take on more than one outcome in an uncertain world. But unlike the probabilistic models, sensitivity analysis, in its general form, does not rely upon probability theory, although it may be used occasionally. Sensitivity analysis asks "if-then" questions. It primarily addresses itself to two types of problems:

1. If the value of an input to a decision model is changed, how is the decision changed?

2. If the structure of the decision model itself is changed, how is the decision changed?

For example, the decision-maker in our cost-volume-profit analysis of chapter eleven might have estimated only one value of fixed costs, $100,000. He might ask: "How sensitive is the break-even point calculation to my estimate for the fixed costs?" His answer might be of the form: "Break-even drops 100 units for every $1,000 drop in fixed costs." We could take a probabilistic example: a decision-maker might be concerned with the effect of re-estimating the correlation between sales and volume, in the previous simulation example, at - 0.40 instead of - 0.35. His answer would be in the form of a new, printed-out summary, similar to the one shown. The effect of the change in estimation would be highlighted.

Sensitivity analysis has the rather important advantage of allowing a decision-maker to "experiment" with a model, instead of with the real world (which can be expensive). It allows him to explore the relationships within his quantitative model, and allows him to develop an intuitive "feel" for it. It is, therefore, a powerful extension of all decision-making techniques.

SUMMARY

With the ever increasing sophistication of business techniques have come many new quantitative methods. Such techniques as linear programming, simulation, and sensitivity analysis are in common usage with larger companies. In future years it may be expected that the hospitality service industries will make even greater use of these techniques and more that have yet to be developed.

Discussion Questions

1.   What is a model and how does model building relate to business?

2. Contrast deterministic and probabilistic models.
3. In terms of linear programming applications, what are common constraints in the hospitality service industries?
4. What is simulation and how does it differ from sensitivity analysis?
5. What does a normal frequency distribution represent?

Bibliography

Anthony, Robert N. *Cost Control.* Homewood, Ill.: Richard D. Irwin, Inc., 1965.

———. *Management Accounting.* 3rd ed. Homewood, Ill.: Richard D. Irwin, Inc., 1964.

Anthony, Robert N.; Dearden, John; and Vancil, Richard F. *Management Control Systems.* Homewood, Ill.: Richard D. Irwin, Inc., 1965.

A.P.B. Accounting Principles. Vol. 1 and 2. American Institute of Certified Public Accountants, 1969.

Backer, Morton and Jacobson, Lyle E. "Use of Costs in Pricing Decisions," in *Cost Accounting—A Managerial Approach*, pp. 506-542. New York: McGraw-Hill Book Co., 1964.

Barbour, Henry O. *Private Club Administration.* Washington, D.C.: Club Managers Association of America, 1968.

Berg, Ralph L. "Payroll Pre-Control Systems," *Food and Lodging Hospitality* 2 (January, 1963): 54-56.

Blomstrom, Robert L. *The Commercial Lodging Market.* East Lansing, Mich.: School of Hotel, Restaurant and Institutional Management, Michigan State University Press, 1967.

Blumenthal, Sherman C. *Management Information Systems.* Englewood Cliffs, N.J.: Prentice-Hall, Inc., 1969.

Bonham, D.H. "Is Historical Cost Obsolete?" *Canadian Chartered Accountant* 84 (January, 1964): 57-59.

Borsenik, Frank D. *Literature of the Lodging Market.* East Lansing, Mich.: Bureau of Business and Economical Research, Graduate School of Business Administration, Michigan State University Press, 1966.

Brennan, Charles W. *Wages Administration: Plans, Practices and Principles.* Homewood, Ill.: Richard D. Irwin, Inc., 1963.

Brodner, Joseph; Maschal, Henry T.; and Carlson, Howard M. *Profitable Food and Beverage Operation.* New York: Ahrens Book Co., Inc., 1962.

Brown, Robert G. *Smoothing, Forecasting and Prediction of Discrete Time Series.* Englewood Cliffs, N.J.: Prentice-Hall, Inc., 1963.

Cadmus, Bradford. *Internal Control against Fraud and Waste.* Englewood Cliffs, N.J.: Prentice-Hall, Inc., 1963.

Carter, J.H., Jr. "Management Cost Control System for Industry," *NAA Bulletin* 45 (January, 1964): 3-9.

Cash Flow Analysis for Managerial Control. National Association of Accountants, Research Study No. 38, 1961.

Cash Flow Analysis and the Funds Statement. Mason, Perry, Accounting Research Study No. 2, American Institute of Certified Public Accountants, 1961.

Cost Reduction and Cost Control in the Small Business. American Institute of Certified Public Accountants, 1960.

Clubs in Town and Country. Chicago, Ill.: Harris, Kerr, Forster & Company, published annually.

Davidson, Sidney. *Handbook of Modern Accounting.* New York: McGraw-Hill Book Co., Inc., 1970.

Dean, Joel. "Profit Performance Measurement of Division Managers," *The Controller* 35 (September, 1957): 423-424.

Dearden, John. *Cost Accounting.* Englewood Cliffs, N.J.: Prentice-Hall, Inc., 1962.

———. *Cost and Budget Analysis.* Englewood Cliffs, N.J.: Prentice-Hall, Inc., 1962.

Diggory, T.J. "Role of Standards for Cost Control and Pricing," *Cost and Management* 38 (January, 1964): 25-33.

Dukas, Peter and Lundberg, Donald E. *How to Operate a Restaurant.* New York: Ahrens Book Co., Inc., 1960.

Eckert, Fred W. *The Hotel Lease.* The Hotel Monthly Press, John Willis, Inc., 1947.

Enger, Norman L. *Management Information Systems.* American Management Association, 1969.

Expense and Payroll Dictionary. American Hotel Association, 1962.

Expense and Payroll Dictionary for Clubs. The Club Managers Association of America, 1967.

Financial Statements Restated for General Price-Level Changes. American Institute of Certified Public Accountants, APB No. 3, 1969.

Finney, H.A., and Miller, Herbert E. *Principles of Accounting Intermediate.* Englewood Cliffs, N.J.: Prentice-Hall, Inc., 1965.

Foulks, Roy A. *Practical Financial Statement Analysis.* New York: McGraw-Hill Book Co., Inc., 1968.

Gonzalez, Richard F., and McMillan, Claude. *Systems Analysis.* Homewood, Ill.: Richard D. Irwin, Inc., 1965.

Heckert, J. Brooks and Willson, James D. *Business Budgeting and Control.* New York: The Ronald Press Co., 1967.

Hekimian, James S. *Introduction to Management Control in Life Insurance Branch Offices.* Cambridge, Mass.: Harvard Business School Division of Research, Harvard University Press, 1965.

Helfert, Erich A. *Techniques of Financial Analysis.* Homewood, Ill.: Richard D. Irwin, Inc., 1957.

Henderson, Ernest. *The World of Mr. Sheraton.* New York: Popular Library, Inc., 1962.

Hilton, Conrad. *Be My Guest.* Englewood Cliffs, N.J.: Prentice-Hall, Inc., 1957.

Horngrenn, Charles T. *Accounting for Management Control: An Introduction.* Englewood Cliffs, N.J.: Prentice-Hall, Inc., 1965.

———. *Cost Accounting, A Managerial Emphasis.* Englewood Cliffs, N.J.: Prentice-Hall, Inc., 1967.

Horwath, Ernest B.; Toth, Louis; and Lesure, John P. *Hotel Accounting.* New York: The Ronald Press Co., 1963.

Internal Auditing Management Acceptance. Institute of Internal Auditors, 1951.

Internal Control. Committee on Auditing Procedure, American Institute of Certified Public Accountants, 1949.

James, Marjorie D., ed. *Portfolio of Accounting Systems for Small and Medium-Sized Businesses.* Englewood Cliffs, N.J.: Prentice-Hall, Inc., 1970.

Kemp, Patrick S. *Accounting for the Manager.* Homewood, Ill.: Dow Jones-Irwin, Inc., 1970.

Knight, W.D., and Weinwurm, E.H. *Managerial Budgeting.* New York: The MacMillan Co., 1964.

Lattin, Gerald W. *Modern Hotel and Motel Management.* 2nd ed. San Francisco, Calif.: W.H. Freeman and Co. Publishers, 1968.

Lewis, Ralph F. *Planning and Control for Profit.* New York: Harper & Row, Publishers, 1961.

Lodging Industry. Annual Report on Hotel and Motor Hotel Operations. Laventhol, Krekstein, Horwath & Horwath, published annually.

Lundberg, Donald E. *The Hotel and Restaurant Business.* Boston, Mass.: Cohners Publishing Co., 1970.

———, and Armatas, James P. *The Management of People in Hotels, Restaurants and Clubs.* Dubuque, Iowa: Wm. C. Brown Company Publishers, 1964.

McCarthy, Clarence F., et al. *The Federal Income Tax: It's Sources and Applications.* Englewood Cliffs, N.J.: Prentice-Hall, Inc., 1968.

Meigs, Walter B., and Larsen, E. John. *Principles of Auditing.* Homewood, Ill.: Richard D. Irwin, Inc., 1969.

Miller, Edmund. *Profitable Cafeteria Operation.* New York: Ahrens Book Co., Inc., 1966.

Moore, Carl L., and Jaedicke, Robert K. *Managerial Accounting.* Cincinnati, Ohio: South-Western Publishing Co., 1967.

Neter, John and Wasserman, William. *Fundamental Statistics for Business and Economics.* Boston, Mass.: Allyn & Bacon, Inc., 1961.

Prescott, Samuel C. *Food Technology.* New York: McGraw-Hill Book Co., Inc., 1937.

Price Level Changes and Financial Statements: Basic Concepts and Methods. American Accounting Association, 1956.

Reporting the Effects of Price-Level Changes. American Institute of Certified Public Accountants, ARS No. 6, 1963.

Spurr, William A., and Bonini, Charles P. *Statistics for Business Decisions.* Homewood, Ill.: Richard D. Irwin, Inc., 1967.

The Statement of Source and Application of Funds. Accounting Principles Board Opinion No. 3, American Institute of Certified Public Accountants, 1963.

Stokes, John W. *How to Manage a Restaurant or Institutional Food Service.* Dubuque, Iowa: Wm. C. Brown Company Publishers, 1967.

Taylor, Philip and Nelson, Benjamin O. *Management Accounting for Hospitals.* Philadelphia, Penn.: W.B. Saunders Co., 1964.

Trends in the Hotel-Motel Business 1970. Chicago, Ill.: Harris, Kerr, Forster & Company, 1970.

Uniform System of Accounts and Expense Dictionary for Motels-Motor Hotels, Small Hotels. New York: American Hotel and Motel Association, 1968.

Uniform System of Accounts for Clubs. Washington, D.C.: The Club Managers Association of America, 1967.

Uniform System of Accounts for Hotels. New York: Hotel Association of New York City, Inc., 1969.

Uniform System of Accounts for Restaurants. Chicago, Ill.: National Restaurant Association, 1968.

United States Master Tax Guide. Chicago, Ill.: Commerce Clearing House, Inc., published annually.

Vallen, Jerome J. *The Art and Science of Modern Innkeeping.* New York: Ahrens Book Co., Inc., 1968.

Walsh, Francis J., Jr. *Internal Control.* National Industrial Conference Board, 1963.

Welsch, Glenn A. *Budgeting—Profit Planning and Control.* Englewood Cliffs, N.J.: Prentice-Hall, Inc., 1964.

Weston, J. Fred and Brigham, Eugene F. *Essentials of Managerial Finance.* New York: Holt, Rhinehart & Winston, Inc., 1968.

Index